DATABASE MANAGEMENT

DATABASE MANAGEMENT

THIRD EDITION

Fred R. McFadden

Department of Business Information Systems
University of Colorado
Colorado Springs, Colorado

Jeffrey A. Hoffer

School of Business
Indiana University
Bloomington, Indiana

The Benjamin/Cummings Publishing Company, Inc.
Redwood City, California • Menlo Park, California •
Reading, Massachusetts • New York •
Don Mills, Ontario • Wokingham, U.K. • Amsterdam •
Bonn • Sydney • Singapore • Tokyo • Madrid • San Juan

To our families and students, for their guidance and inspiration

Sponsoring Editor: Michelle Baxter
Production Editor: Mary Shields
Copy Editor: Rene Lynch
Part Opener Design: Dick Kharibian
Cover Design: Mark Ong
Composition: Graphic Typesetting Service

Library of Congress Cataloging-in-Publication Data

McFadden, Fred R., 1933–
    Data base management / Fred R. McFadden, Jeffrey A. Hoffer.
      Third Edition
    Includes bibliographies and index.
    1. Data base management.   I. Hoffer, Jeffrey A.   II. Title.
    QA76.9.D3M395   1991   90-15524
    005.74--dc20   CIP

ISBN 0-8053-6040-9
ABCDEFGHIJ-DO-9543210

The Benjamin/Cummings Publishing Company, Inc.
390 Bridge Parkway
Redwood City, California 94065

PREFACE

This text is designed for an introductory course in database management. Such a course is usually required as part of an information systems curriculum in business schools, computer technology programs, and applied computer science departments. The Data Processing Management Association (DPMA), Association for Computing Machinery (ACM), and International Federation of Information Processing Societies (IFIPS) curriculum guidelines all outline this type of database management course. This third edition is an extensive update of the second edition, which has been used successfully at both undergraduate and graduate levels, as well as in management and professional development programs.

The third edition updates and expands material in areas undergoing rapid change due to improved managerial practices, systems design methods and tools, and technology. Sections of the text that have been considerably enhanced because of these changes include those on

- Relational database technology (including SQL, embedded SQL, and programming with relational systems)
- Personal computer database systems (including dBASE IV, R:BASE for DOS, and PARADOX)
- Strategic data modeling and the relationship between business planning and data planning
- The entity-relationship data model and the integration of ER modeling with relational database design
- The object-oriented data model
- Distributed databases

In addition, the third edition includes many pedagogical improvements to make the book easier and more interesting. A major enhancement is an extensively illustrated introductory chapter devoted to a realistic and complete example for the design and operation of a database. Chapter 2 shows the development of this database and integrates data modeling, database design, and database processing in query languages, forms/screen design tools, and report generators. This unique chapter gives an understandable yet comprehensive picture early in the text of what the student will be able to do after completing the database course. This expanded example also makes clearer later short illustrations, taken from the same situation.

Also new in this edition is a complete chapter on database programming with relational database systems. Chapter 14 thoroughly covers the dBASE IV programming language and the use of the standard SQL relational language within COBOL programs. Also introduced in this chapter is the dBASE Application Generator, which is very useful for prototyping new applications. This chapter follows two extensively updated chapters on the SQL interactive programming language and on personal computer relational systems (dBASE, R:BASE, and PARADOX). The third edition now has four chapters on relational database systems, plus additional chapters that cover database design (including normalization).

Many chapters from the second edition have been totally rewritten to improve clarity and to update the material. One chapter now concentrates on understanding data and on notations for modeling organizational data. The technology background needed to understand database implementation design and programming with database management systems is consolidated into one chapter. Finally, the design of databases is now presented in a logical sequence of chapters, beginning with three on database planning and conceptual design and ending with two on the physical design of databases. These five chapters are then followed by one on data and database administration, which ties these concepts and methods to the management of data resources in an organization.

These chapters now put greater emphasis on relating databases to business needs than to technology. This evolution in focus supports two important trends in business: (1) the decentralization of information professionals into business units and (2) the associated greater concern for solving business problems (rather than technical ones) that is expected from business school IS graduates.

As in previous editions, the third edition of *Database Management* provides sound, clear, and current coverage of concepts, skills, and issues needed for coping with the expanding organizational data resource. Since industry is populated with a wide variety of both mainframe and personal computer database technologies, the text still presents a balanced coverage of these (from the ever present IBM IMS to such emerging object technologies as GemStone from Servio Logic). Although all approaches are included, greater emphasis is now placed on the dominant technology of today—relational.

ORGANIZATION OF THE BOOK

We encourage instructors to customize their use of the book to meet the needs of both the curriculum and student career plans. The modular nature of the text (five logically sequenced sections), its broad coverage, extensive illustrations of both personal computer and mainframe technologies, and the inclusion of advanced topics and emerging issues make customization easy. Further, the many references make it possible to develop supplemental reading lists or to expand lecture discussion beyond the material in the text.

Because of the reordering of material from the second edition, we believe the sequence of topics better represents a logical progression of concepts and skills. Depending on the focus of your course, however, alternative sequences are possible. Chapter 2 (an extensive database application example) can be read just before or after Chapters 12 or 13 in SQL and personal computer technologies, respectively. Chapters 12 and 13 each now stands on its own, so either can be skipped, or they can be read in reverse order. The coverage of the hierarchical and network data models has been greatly reduced in the early sections of the book, so instructors who wish to skip these technologies now can simply drop Chapter 10 (IMS) or Chapter 11 (network). It is strongly recommended that Chapter 1 be read first, since it provides a background and overview for the whole text.

SCOPE OF THE BOOK

Database Management was originally developed, and has been enhanced, to meet an unfilled need. Many excellent database texts and reference books are available today; however, most of these books emphasize issues relevant in a computer science curriculum (basically, the design of database management system software and operating system file access methods) or concentrate on one particular technology (like IMS or SQL). More than in prior editions, the goal of this text is to provide adequate technical detail while emphasizing the management and implementation issues relevant in a business information systems curriculum. Thus, the book stresses design and use of databases and the role of technology in meeting business information needs.

The expanded third edition includes

- Emphasis on the concept of information as a corporate resource and on managers as stewards of this resource

- A separate chapter on strategic database planning (Chapter 4), with clear linkage to the process of database design and development

- Emphasis on data administration, with extensive discussion of its role and organizational placement

- Integrated coverage throughout the book on concepts and notations for modeling organizational data, with reference to the now widely used entity-relationship notation

- Significantly updated material on the data repository as a tool in planning and controlling the information resource

- Complete discussion of database design, including normalization and view integration

- Coverage of a wide range of database technologies, with emphasis on understanding factors to be considered when selecting such packages. Particular database systems covered include SQL/DS and DB2, INGRES, Query-By-Example, IDMS, IMS, dBASE IV, R:BASE for DOS, PARA-DOX, and ORACLE.

- Coverage of *both* mainframe and personal computer database development environments, including screen formatters, report writers, application generators, menu systems, and PC-mainframe data transfer

- Thorough coverage of integrity and security issues of multiple-user databases, including rules for data validation, restrictions on data access, concurrent update control, local area network issues, and distributed databases

- Coverage of third- and fourth-generation programming languages for database processing

- Discussion of the design and performance of distributed database technologies, database computers and client/server architectures, and databases in expert systems

LEARNING AIDS AND SUPPLEMENTS

To assist the student and instructor, *Database Management* includes the following learning aids:

- Realistic **Case Examples** illustrate important concepts throughout the text. Two running case examples highlight concerns from industry: Pine Valley Furniture Company for the manufacturing sector and Mountain View Community Hospital for the service sector. Illustrations from these situations address production, marketing, accounting, and human resource management information needs. Three additional situations, Lakewood College, Vacation Property Rentals, and Hy-Tek Corporation, appear to a lesser degree for some variety and to illustrate points not inherent in the two primary example situations. Case examples are identified by symbols in the margins.

- A **Summary** at the end of each chapter capsulizes the main concepts of the chapter and links it to other chapters.

- The **Chapter Review** tests students' knowledge. The **Review Questions** check their grasp of new terms, important concepts, and significant issues. **Problems and Exercises** require the students to apply their knowledge to realistic situations and, in some cases, to extend this knowledge to new situations. Matching questions help the students to distinguish critical terms.

- A **Glossary of Acronyms** (about 100 entries) and a **Glossary of Terms** (about 300 terms) are included.

The text is part of a complete educational package designed to provide a high level of support to the instructor:

- The *Instructor's Guide* is a comprehensive guide containing numerous instructional resources. First, for each chapter there are 6 to 10 **Teaching Suggestions:** lecture outlines, teaching hints, and student projects that make use of the chapter content. Second, there are complete solutions to both the Review Questions and the Problems and Exercises in the text. Third, there are 350 multiple-choice questions (approximately 25 per chapter) with answers, completely revised for the third edition. Fourth, new to the third edition is a set of 100 examination problems, similar to the Problems and Exercises from the text, with solutions. The multiple-choice questions and examination problems form a test bank that can be used for in-class or take-home examinations or assignments. Fifth, the *Instructor's Guide* includes a set of masters for overhead transparencies of enlarged illustrations and tables from the text. Finally, two diskettes are included. One diskette contains an ASCII file with all the test bank questions as well as data, screen format, and report layout files from Chapter 2. The test bank questions can be imported into a variety of word processors; the data, screen definition, and report layout files can be used for class demonstrations and projects. The second diskette contains graphic files for selected figures and tables from the text, which can be used with a popular electronic slideshow program to enhance class lectures.

- Many of the figures and tables from the text are also provided on diskette in a variety of formats suitable for projection in a computer-based classroom. These diskettes permit the instructor to develop an electronic slide show as part of the lecture. Instructors should contact their local sales and marketing representative or call toll free (see below) for more information on the exact format and use of these diskettes.

- The third edition of the *Case Book for Database Management* contains 10 realistic cases for course projects, including three that emphasize managerial issues. Most of these cases are taken from actual company situations. The solutions and implementations can be worked out using either mainframe computers, minicomputers, or personal computers. Solutions for these cases, including implementations in several popular packages, are available from the publisher.

- *The Student Edition of dBASE IV* by James Senn provides a comprehensive introduction to this popular microcomputer database tool, emphasizing the menu user interface to dBASE. For more advanced programming coverage of dBASE, *The Student Edition of dBASE IV, Programmer's Version* by Rob Krumm is recommended. These student versions of dBASE IV are fully functional and limited only by the size of the databases that can be created. Although dBASE is extensively illustrated in *Database Management*, our text does not attempt to provide the reference material a student needs for major course projects.

- The use of Hands-On dBASE IV by Larry Metzelaar and Marianne Fox, provides a brief introduction to this software package. (This optional guide is appropriate for business programs not requiring a version of the software.)

For more information about the text and to request any of the supplements, please contact your local sales and marketing representative or call toll free (800) 227-1936, or, in California, (800) 982-6140.

ACKNOWLEDGMENTS

We are very grateful to numerous individuals who contributed to the preparation of the third edition of this textbook. First, we wish to thank our reviewers for their detailed reviews and many suggestions, characteristic of their thoughtful teaching styles. Those who reviewed the third edition and who provided guidance for the redesign from the second edition were Doug Bock, Southern Illinois University at Edwardsville; Joe Davis, Indiana University; Daniel Dolk, Naval Postgraduate School; Jim Fry, University of Michigan; Helmut Jain, University of Wisconsin-Milwaukee; Bill Korn, University of Wisconsin-Eau Claire; Randy Marak, Hill College; Scott McIntyre, University of Colorado-Colorado Springs; Sunder Rao Mendu, St. Cloud State University; Gladys Norman, Linn-Benton Community College; Roger Pick, University of Cincinnati, Anthony Verstraete, The Pennsylvania State University; Margaret Wu, University of Iowa; and Marilyn Zimmerman, Roosevelt University.

Those who reviewed the second edition were George Diehr, University of Washington; Alan Duchan, Canisius College; Ralph Duffy, North Seattle Community College; Dean James, Embry-Riddle Aeronautical University; Bill Korn, University of Wisconsin-Eau Claire; and Charles J. Wertz, Buffalo State College.

Next we wish to thank our typists, Patty Hoffer, Kathy Abeyta, and Kathy Claybaugh-Norgaard, who were tireless and meticulous in capturing the manuscript on word processing systems so that the inevitable revisions could be accomplished with relative ease. We also benefited from discussions with our colleagues, especially Joe Davis (Indiana University) and Scott McIntyre (University of Colorado-Colorado Springs). Of special significance are the contributions of material for the text and *Instructor's Guide* by Doug Bock (Southern Illinois University at Edwardsville), Tom Finneran (independent consultant, Princeton, New Jersey, Gary Kern (University of Notre Dame), and Steve Michaele (S. J. Michaele and Associates, Trenton, New Jersey. We also recognize and sincerely appreciate the unique contributions of two of our students who provided the comprehensive examples of dBASE and SQL/DS with COBOL programming examples in two of the appendices: Peter Dowd (Indiana University) and William Bunney (University of Colorado-Colorado Springs).

Doug Bock (Southern Illinois University at Edwardsville) made an extraordinary contribution to the third edition. His thorough review of all art work and manuscript has been instrumental in coordinating the many changes made from the second edition. He provided significant input to the *Instructor's Guide.* His rigor and intense attention to clarity has been highly valued.

We are very grateful to the staff of Benjamin/Cummings for their support and guidance throughout the project. In particular, we wish to thank Michelle Baxter (editor), Sally Elliot (general manager), Lisa Weber (editorial assistant), and Mary Shields (production supervisor) for their encouragement and care. Our thanks also go to our many students who helped test the manuscript in its various stages.

To all of these individuals, and to our families, we give our thanks. Much of the value of this text is due to their assistance, but we alone bear responsibility for any errors or omissions that remain between the covers.

Fred R. McFadden
Jeffrey A. Hoffer

BRIEF CONTENTS

DETAILED CONTENTS

PART II   Database Planning and Conceptual Design   133
DATABASE PLANNING IN AN ENTERPRISE-WIDE DISTRIBUTED
ENVIRONMENT

Federal Express

CHAPTER 4   **Strategic Data and Systems Planning   135**

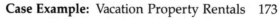

PART III   Physical Design and Data Administration   252

DATABASE CONCURRENCY CONTROL

Apple Computer, Inc.

CHAPTER 7   Data Structure and Storage Techniques   255

CHAPTER 8   Implementation and Physical Design   303

CHAPTER 9   Data Administration   337

PART IV   Classical Systems   392

MANUFACTURING SUPPORT WITH IMS

McDonnell Douglas

PART V   Relational and Distributed Systems   484

IMAGE STORAGE AND RETRIEVAL IN A DISTRIBUTED RELATIONAL ENVIRONMENT

AT&T

CHAPTER 12   SQL and Relational Implementations on Mainframes   487

PART I

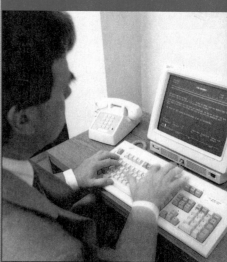

Database Concepts for Management

LEVERAGING THE VALUE OF DATA

Sears, Roebuck and Co.

In this first part of the text, you are introduced to the hypothetical Pine Valley Furniture Company and to the concept of data as a resource to be managed by the firm. As you read Part I, compare the data management methods available to Pine Valley Furniture with those of Sears, Roebuck and Co. Sears has developed numerous computer-based applications that support retail stores. These systems provide a very sophisticated degree of application integration that enables Sears to "leverage" the value of data to management.

The integrated systems include price look-up, credit, inventory replenishment and control, merchandise receiving, point-of-sale (POS) reservation, error correction, and financial reporting and management reporting by using a common set of databases. These systems provide managers with the information needed to support decision-making and to provide timely answers to a variety of possible customers inquiries. Managers are supported by an electronic mail facility. Data capture is through the latest technology available for barcode scanning at POS terminals.

As customers of Sears, many of you have seen these systems in action although you might not be aware of the activities taking place behind the scenes. The price look-up system enables accurate price determination through the use of barcode scanning technology. The credit system can be used to answer queries on active customer accounts. Positive credit approval is available through POS terminals for instant approval on merchandise sales. The system accesses customer credit limit information stored in mainframe databases.

As sales are processed, the inventory replenishment system automatically updates product inventory databases. This system also supports queries about products. By entering a product item number, a salesperson can determine the quantity of items stocked in the retail store warehouse. For special orders or items not stocked at local retail stores, a POS reservation system automatically reserves merchandise for customers and processes customer orders for merchandise that is stored at central warehouse locations and sources throughout the country. This system insures that accurate delivery date information is provided to customers. If an item is out-of-stock at the central warehouse, the reservation system can even let managers know when the item is expected back in stock!

The error correction system is a back-office operation that enables personnel to correct data entry mistakes that are automatically flagged by the computer. This cleans up entry errors before they can affect "downstream" inventory management application systems. When goods are received, a receiving system is used to automatically update the databases that are accessed by the inventory system. In the near future, Sears willl have barcode reading devices to speed up processing at the loading dock by scanning the purchase order data for incoming shipments of products. Sears also uses EDI to transmit ordering information to its source.

These integrated systems support approximately 850 stores with 29 central inventory facilities primarily through use of the DB2 database management system. Literally thousands of transactions are processed in each store on a daily basis. By providing instant up-to-date information at the touch of a finger, customers are provided services not previously available, products are delivered in less time than was previously required, and inventory management is optimized.

CHAPTER 1

The Database Environment

INTRODUCTION

This book is about the data resource of organizations and about the management of that resource. Many observers of trends in business believe that the organizations that will excel in the 1990s will be those that manage information as a major resource and structure it as efficiently as they do other resources. Of course, information can be an asset only if it is accurate and available when needed, which can occur only if an organization purposely organizes and manages its data. The database has become the standard technique for structuring and managing data in most organizations today.

Data (and information derived from data) are used for a variety of purposes in organizations. Data are used to represent and track the status of business entities such as customers, products, orders, and employees. For example, to determine whether a particular sofa is in stock, a salesperson in a furniture store would probably display an inventory record for the item rather than physically searching for it in the warehouse. Also, data are used to measure performance and report on the financial health of the enterprise; the furniture store manager would rely on monthly accounting reports to determine whether the store was profitable during each period and to determine patterns and trends.

One of the most important uses of information in an organization is to support managerial decision making. In planning new furniture purchases, for example, a buyer in the furniture store would examine summary information showing trends by furniture type and style. The success of an organization generally depends on the quality of such management decisions; this quality in turn depends heavily on the quality and timeliness of information available to support decision making.

A course in database management has emerged as one of the most important courses in the information systems curriculum today. As an information systems professional, you must be prepared to design and implement databases within the overall context of information systems development. Also, you must be prepared to consult with end users who are increasingly using database technology to design and implement their own information systems. Managers and other end users in organizations must understand the potential competitive advantages available through the creative use of technology, including databases.

INFORMATION RESOURCE MANAGEMENT

Databases should be understood within the larger context of information resource management. Information resource management (IRM) is the concept that information is a major corporate resource and must be managed using the same basic principles that are used to manage other assets, such as employees, materials, equipment, and financial resources. McLeod and Brittain-White (1988) suggest the following basic principles of IRM:

1. A business organization is composed of resources that flow into the organization from its environment and then return to the environment.

2. There are two basic types of resources: (a) physical resources, such as personnel, materials, machines, facilities, and money and (b) conceptual resources, consisting of data and information.

3. As the scale of operations grows, it becomes more difficult to manage the physical resources by observation, which forces the manager to rely on the conceptual resources.

4. The same basic principles can be applied in the management of conceptual resources as have been developed for the management of physical resources.

5. Management of data and information includes acquisition prior to the time they are needed, security measures designed to protect the resources from destruction and misuse, quality assurance, and removal procedures that discharge the resources from the organization when they are no longer needed.

6. Management of data and information can be achieved only through organizational, not individual, commitment.

Data Versus Information

In this text we distinguish between data and information. The word *data* refers to raw facts concerning people, objects, events, or other entities; for example, a collection of individual responses from a marketing research study would qualify as data.

An organization collects and stores vast quantities of data from both internal and external sources, an amount that would generally be overwhelming if it were left in its original state. *Information* is data that have been processed and presented in a form suitable for human interpretation, often with the purpose of revealing trends or patterns. The marketing research data, for example, would be analyzed and summarized through the use of statistical measures such as means and ranges.

Databases

As we have seen, data provide the raw material that is used to produce information (the finished product). The following steps are required in converting data into information: acquisition, storage, manipulation, retrieval, and distribution. To perform these steps efficiently and effectively, organizations must often organize their data in the form of databases. A **database** is an integrated collection of data, organized to meet the needs of multiple users in an organization. Later in this chapter we will expand on this definition, compare databases with conventional files, and discuss the objectives and advantages of databases.

Since this definition is very general, it would apply to manual databases as well as to those organized for computer processing—for example, a manual card catalog in a library would certainly qualify as a database. However, in this text we restrict our discussion to computer databases.

Types of Databases   Although a business captures and retains a vast amount of data, they can be classified into a few basic categories. As shown in Figure 1-1, the organizational data pyramid consists of operational, managerial, and strategic databases. Although new data can enter this pyramid at any level, the vast majority is captured at the base of the pyramid in operational databases. **Operational databases** contain the business transaction history of daily business activities such as customer orders, shipments, purchases, and payments and are thus used to support the ongoing daily activities of the organization.

Managerial and strategic databases are typically subsets, summaries, or aggregations of operational databases, with external data as supplements. **Managerial databases** are used primarily by middle-level managers for planning and control; for example, summaries of sales by product and type of customer are used to allocate sales efforts. **Strategic databases** are used by senior managers to develop corporate strategies and seek competitive

Figure 1-1
Types of databases
(Source: DeHays
1990)

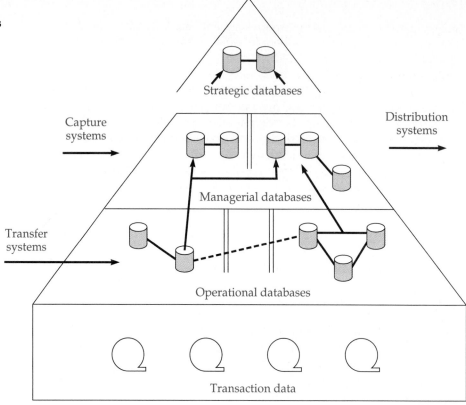

advantage; they often contain information on competitors and economic factors, as well as corporate information.

Figure 1-1 also illustrates three generic types of database applications. **Data capture** applications capture transaction data, populate databases, and maintain the currency of data. **Data transfer** applications move data from one database to another (for example, from operational to managerial). These applications also extract, summarize, and aggregate data. **Data distribution** applications resulting from data analysis, essentially convert data into useful information and present them to the manager (or other users) in a readily understandable form.

Implementing IRM

Information resource management is essentially a mindset or concept designed to elevate the importance of managing data and information in organizations. Successful implementation of IRM is the responsibility of an organization's senior management. But from a practical point of view, how does an organization go about implementing IRM? Students of information

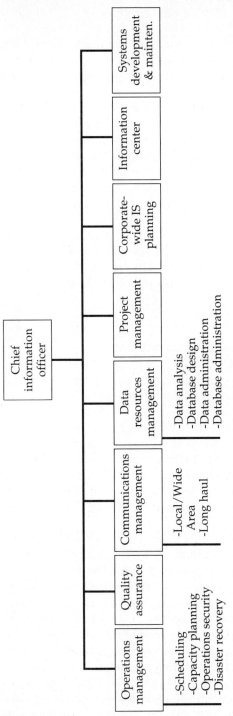

Source: Reprinted with permission of Idea Group Publishing. From Information Resources Management Journal, Vol. 1, No. 1. Copyright 1988.

Figure 1-2
Functions of information resources management (Source: Reprinted with permission of Idea Group Publishing. From Information Resources Management Journal, Vol. 1, No. 1. Copyright 1988).

resource management suggest that there are eight functions of IRM that are absolutely necessary. These major functions (shown in Figure 1-2) are Operations Management, Quality Assurance, Communications Management, Data Resources Management, Project Management, Corporate-wide IS Planning, Information Center (or user-computing support), and Systems Development and Maintenance.

Among the IRM functions shown in Figure 1-2, the one most closely aligned with the IRM concept is Data Resources Management, which is the principal topic of this textbook. The subfunctions of data resources management shown in Figure 1-2 are the following: data analysis, database design, data administration, and database administration. All of these topics are covered in depth in this text. In addition, we include a chapter (Chapter 4) on database planning, since it is an integral part of Corporate-wide IS Planning.

We describe the database approach and its advantages and disadvantages by means of a realistic case example. In this example, a small company progresses from manual information systems to a minicomputer, using traditional files, and finally to a contemporary relational database system.

Case Example: Pine Valley Furniture

Pine Valley Furniture Company manufactures high-quality, all-wood furniture and distributes it to stores in a metropolitan area. There are several product lines, including dinette sets, stereo cabinets, wall units, living room furniture, and bedroom furniture. Pine Valley Furniture employs about 50 persons at the present time and is experiencing rapid growth.

Pine Valley Furniture was founded about 15 years ago by Donald Knotts, its general manager and majority owner. Mr. Knotts had made custom furniture as a hobby and started the business in his own garage. Pine Valley Furniture operated out of a rented warehouse until five years ago, when it moved to its present location.

Managing the data resources at Pine Valley Furniture was relatively simple during the first years of its operation. At first, Mr. Knotts kept most of the information needed to run the business in his head, although a few records were kept, mostly for tax purposes. When the business expanded into the rented warehouse, there were about ten employees. It was then that Mr. Knotts hired a part-time bookkeeper to keep a small set of books, including a general ledger and accounts receivable and payable ledgers. The books, in effect, contributed a small, centralized database that provided most of the information needed to run the company at that time.

When Pine Valley Furniture moved into its present location, its product line had expanded and its sales volume had doubled in two years. Its work force had grown to over 30 employees. With this organizational growth and complexity, Mr. Knotts found that he could no longer manage the operation

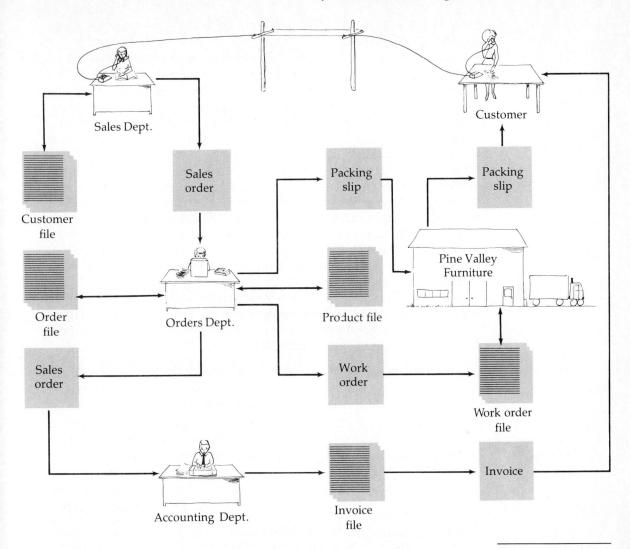

Figure 1-3
Manual information systems at Pine Valley Furniture Company

by himself. He therefore organized the company into functional areas of responsibility. He organized manufacturing operations into three main sections: Fabrication, Assembling, and Finishing, each of which had a manager. Separate departments were also established for several business functions: a Sales Department, an Orders Department, an Accounting Department, and a Purchasing Department. Pine Valley Furniture thus emerged from the entrepreneurial mode of operation to a formal organization with functional departments and managers.

When Pine Valley Furniture organized into functional departments, it also changed its approach to managing its data resources. The single set of books that it had used previously was no longer adequate to run the business. Instead, each department now had its own books—files, ledgers, and so on—and informal lines of communication were established to transfer data between departments.

Figure 1-3 shows the manual information system at Pine Valley Furniture. This diagram depicts the flow of data for the mainstream functions—order processing, billing, shipping, and processing work orders. Most customer orders are received in Sales by telephone. The Sales Department refers to a customer file to check the customer's credit and then prepares a sales order. The sales order is then sent to the Orders Department, which checks a product file to determine whether the requested item is in stock. If the item is in stock, the clerk prepares a packing slip. If the item is not in stock (or if the stock level has dropped below a predetermined level), the clerk prepares a work order to send to the Manufacturing Department to prepare a lot of the item. One copy of the sales order is sent to the Accounting Department, and another copy is filed in the Orders Department. The Accounting Department prices the sales order and prepares an invoice for items shipped to the customer. A packing slip is also included with each customer shipment.

Notice in Figure 1-3 that each department has a separate file (or files) to support its operations and answer its questions. The files shown in Figure 1-3, and typical user questions that might be answered by referring to these files, are shown in the following table:

Department	File	Typical Questions
Sales	Customer	What is customer ABC's address and credit limit?
Orders	Product	How many tables (product no. 123) do we have in stock?
Accounting	Invoice	How much does customer ABC owe us on invoice no. 567?
Manufacturing	Work Order	How many units of product no. 123 are we scheduled to build today?

Other departments also have files to support their operations. For example, the Purchasing Department has a file of purchase orders to indicate what materials are currently on order from vendors.

The information system portrayed in Figure 1-3 is a manual system, in which the data files are decentralized, and each department works with a subset of the organization's data. Although the system works, it has a number of deficiencies or disadvantages:

1. A constant stream of paperwork (in the form of memos, reports, transactions, and so on) and telephone calls is required to communicate changes and keep the files synchronized.

2. The system cannot easily provide answers to more complex operational questions. For example, to answer the question "What invoices are outstanding for order no. 123 from customer ABC?" will probably require some research on the part of the Orders Department.

3. Managers cannot easily obtain summary information required for decision making.

4. Duplicate data exist throughout the organization, resulting in lack of consistency and miscommunication. For example, information concerning customer orders is maintained in the Sales, Orders, Accounting, *and* Shipping departments at Pine Valley Furniture.

It is tempting to assume that a computer would help eliminate many of these typical shortcomings of a manual information system, and it is true; a computer will often permit data to be processed faster and more accurately. However, considering the traditional file processing environment that has prevailed for decades, many of the preceding problems would remain or might even be amplified. This is because in the traditional approach the designer essentially seeks to automate existing manual systems, as we will explain in the following section.

FILE PROCESSING SYSTEMS

Traditional File Processing Systems

The traditional approach to information systems design focuses on the data processing needs of individual departments in the organization. The information systems (IS) group responds to user requests by developing (or acquiring) new computer programs, often one at a time, for individual applications such as accounts receivable, payroll, and inventory control. Each application program or system that is developed is designed to meet the needs of the particular department or user group. That is, there is no overall map, plan, or model to guide the growth of applications.

Each new computer application is typically designed with its own set of data files. Much of the data in these new files may already be present in existing files for other applications. However, to meet the needs of the new application, the existing files would have to be restructured, which, in turn, would require that existing programs that use these same files be revised or completely rewritten. For this reason, it is often far simpler (and also less risky) to design new files for each application.

File Processing Systems at Pine Valley Furniture

Pine Valley Furniture Company had experienced numerous operating problems, including declining customer service and increasing inventory levels. Although the company had grown rapidly, profits had failed to keep pace. Mr. Knotts decided that the manual information system that existed at that time was no longer sufficient to manage a fast-growing business, and, after some evaluation, a minicomputer was selected and installed at Pine Valley Furniture in the early 1980s.

Most of the applications that have subsequently been installed on the computer are in the accounting and financial areas, such as order filling, invoicing, accounts receivable, inventory control, accounts payable, payroll, and general ledger. Most of these application programs were purchased from a software vendor who modified the programs to meet the requirements of the Pine Valley Furniture Company.

Three of the computer applications at Pine Valley Furniture are depicted in Figure 1-4. The systems illustrated are order filling, invoicing, and payroll, and the figure shows the major data files associated with each application system.

Notice that each application system in Figure 1-4 has its own data files, which is typical of traditional applications. For example, the Inventory Master File used in the Order Filling System and the Inventory Pricing File used in the Invoicing System both contain data describing products sold by Pine Valley Furniture. Also, these application systems both use a Customer Master File. Is this master file actually one file or two distinct files with duplicate information? In this case, the two applications happen to share a single Customer Master File; however, there is a large amount of duplicated data in the files used in the various applications at Pine Valley Furniture.

Notice, too, the similarity in design between the computer systems at Pine Valley Furniture and the earlier manual systems they replaced (compare Figures 1-3 and 1-4). In each case, the approach was to develop procedures and associated data files to solve data processing problems for individual functional departments. With the computer systems, the data files are no longer physically located within the individual departments, as in the manual system. However, since they are tailored to the needs of each application or department, they are generally regarded as "belonging" to that department or application, rather than as a resource to be shared by all departments or users.

The computer applications at Pine Valley Furniture have generally been successful. They have allowed the company to reduce its paperwork burden and improve its response to customer orders. They have also provided management with better information concerning costs, sales, and profits. Nevertheless, managers at Pine Valley are dissatisfied with several aspects of the new computer system. While the applications have helped improve the operations management function, they have had little impact on middle management and still less on top management. Mr. Knotts and the other managers at Pine Valley Furniture have come to realize that there are basic limitations to traditional file processing systems. Some of these limitations are described next.

Disadvantages of File Processing Systems

The basic disadvantages of file processing systems are uncontrolled redundancy, inconsistent data, inflexibility, limited data sharing, poor enforce-

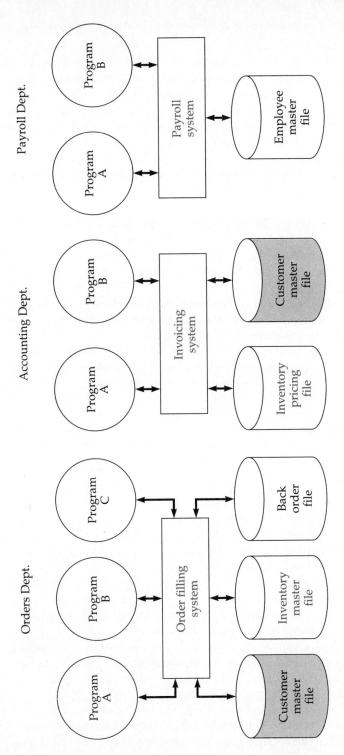

Figure 1-4
Three application
systems at Pine Valley
Furniture

ment of standards, low programmer productivity, and excessive program maintenance.

Uncontrolled Redundancy   In file processing systems, each application has its own files, an approach that inevitably leads to a high level of data redundancy. There are several disadvantages to recording the same data item in multiple files: first, valuable storage space is wasted, second, the same data may have to be input several times to update all occurrences of a data item, and third, inconsistencies (or various versions) often result, which require time to resolve and correct. As we shall see, some replication of data can be useful but careful control is required.

Inconsistent Data   When the same data are stored in multiple locations, inconsistencies in the data are inevitable. For example, several of the files at Pine Valley Furniture contain customer data. Suppose that there is an address change for one of the customers. If the files are to be consistent, this change must be made simultaneously (and correctly) to each of the files containing the customer address data item. Since the files are controlled by different users, however, it is very likely that some files will reflect the old address while others reflect the new address.

Inconsistencies in stored data are one of the most common sources of errors in computer applications. They lead to inconsistent documents and reports and undermine the confidence of users in the integrity of the information system. The outdated customer address just described, for example, may lead to the customer invoice being mailed to the wrong location, and, as a result, the invoice may be returned and the customer payment delayed or lost.

Inflexibility   A file processing system resembles a mass production facility. It produces numerous documents and reports routinely and efficiently, provided that these outputs were anticipated in the original design of the system. Such systems, however, are often quite inflexible and cannot easily respond to requests for a new or redesigned "product." In other words, an application system cannot readily satisfy demands for information in a new format that was not anticipated in the original design. This often leads to considerable frustration on the part of the users, who cannot understand why the computer system cannot give them information in a new format when they know it exists in the application files.

For example, the Order Filling System at Pine Valley Furniture contains three files: Customer Master, Inventory Master, and Back Orders (see Figure 1-4). Suppose that the Orders Department manager wants to obtain a list of back-ordered items for a given customer. Unless this request was anticipated when the system was designed, it will be difficult to satisfy. If the request represents a new requirement, a new application program may be required to extract the required records from each file and produce the desired report. Depending on the backlog in the information systems department, it may take months to complete the request.

Limited Data Sharing With the traditional applications approach, each application has its own private files and there is little opportunity for users to share data outside of their own applications. Referring to Figure 1-4, you will notice that users in the Accounting Department have access to the Invoicing System and its files but they may not have access to the Order Filling System files, which are used primarily by the Orders Department.

One consequence of limited data sharing is that the same data may have to be entered several times in order to update files with duplicate data. For example, at Pine Valley Furniture, a change in the description for an inventory item would have to be entered separately into the Order Filling and Invoicing systems, since each contains its own version of an inventory file.

Another consequence of limited data sharing is that in developing new applications, the designer often cannot (or does not) exploit data contained in existing files. Instead, new files are designed that duplicate much of the existing data. Suppose that the manufacturing manager at Pine Valley Furniture requests a new system for scheduling production orders. Such a system would undoubtedly require an inventory file in order to provide economical order quantities, status of existing orders, and related inventory information. Of course, an Inventory Master File already is being used in the Order Filling System; a redesign of this file would be required, however, to meet the requirements of the scheduling application. This, in turn, would probably require a complete rewrite of Programs A, B, and C in the Order Filling System (see Figure 1-4). Instead the designer would specify a new Inventory File for the Production Scheduling System. In file processing systems, the cycle of limited data sharing and redundancy is perpetuated in this manner.

Poor Enforcement of Standards Every organization requires standard procedures so that it may operate effectively. Within information systems, standards are required for data names, formats, and access restrictions. Unfortunately, data standards are difficult to make known and enforce in a traditional file processing environment, mainly because the responsibility for system design and operation has been decentralized. Two types of inconsistencies may result from poor enforcement of standards: synonyms and homonyms. A **synonym** results when two different names are used for the same data item—for example, student number and matriculation number. A **homonym** is a single name that is used for two different data items—for example, in a bank the term *balance* might be used to designate a checking account balance in one department and a savings account balance in a different department.

Enforcement of standards is particularly difficult in larger organizations with decentralized responsibility and decision making. Without centralized control or coordination, users in various departments may purchase their own computers and develop their own private applications without regard for compatibility or sharing of data. However, even in a small company, the achievement of standards is often difficult in an applications environment. At Pine Valley Furniture, the individual applications purchased from the software vendor were of a stand-alone variety and were not really compatible with one another (although all the applications were integrated with the Accounting General Ledger System). The various application programs often used different names and formats for the same data items, which made modifications more difficult and precluded data sharing.

Low Programmer Productivity   In traditional file processing systems, the programmer must often design each record and file used by a new application program and then code the data definitions into the program (this process can sometimes be simplified—by using standard data division descriptions together with copy libraries, for example). The programmer must also select the file access method and write procedural input/output statements in the program. The programmer repeats this burden of designing files and records, describing data, and writing procedural input/output statements for each application program, which constitutes a major portion of the system development effort. As such, it is a major contributor to low programmer productivity—a problem that continues to plague the data processing industry and, in turn, increases software costs, such as those for the packaged software products purchased by Pine Valley Furniture.

Excessive Program Maintenance   In file processing systems, descriptions of files, records, and data items are embedded within individual application programs. Therefore, any modification to a data file (such as a change of data name, format, or method of access) requires that the program (or programs) also be modified. To illustrate, suppose that the data item CUSTOMER NAME had to be expanded from a 20-character field to a 25-character field in the Customer Master File at Pine Valley Furniture. As a result of this simple change, several programs in the Order Filling System and Invoicing System would have to be modified. The process of modifying existing programs is referred to as **program maintenance**. In many organizations today, 80% or more of the programming effort is devoted to this activity. Much of the shortage of computer programmers and the large backlog of new applications can be attributed to the burden of maintaining programs in file processing systems.

The disadvantages discussed here were especially pronounced in first- and second-generation application systems. In third-generation systems, a number of powerful support packages and tools have been introduced to help overcome (or at least minimize) some of the disadvantages. These software support packages include access methods for secondary keys, generalized file management and report writers, on-line query processing, transaction processing systems, data dictionaries, and high-level programming languages. However, even with these facilities, the fundamental deficiencies of file processing systems remain: redundant data, low sharing of data, lack of standards and control, and low productivity.

DATABASE APPROACH

Richard Nolan (1984) postulated that organizations experience six stages of growth in their information systems (see Figure 1-5):

1. *Stage I: Initiation.* Computer data processing is first introduced to the organization.
2. *Stage II: Contagion.* Computer usage spreads rapidly through the organization as users automate basic applications.
3. *Stage III: Control.* Management becomes alarmed at the rapid escalation of data processing costs and institutes budgeting and procedural controls.
4. *Stage IV: Integration.* The organization seeks to integrate stand-alone applications so that the resulting applications can cross functional boundaries.
5. *Stage V: Architecture.* The organization develops an enterprise-wide data model (or information architecture) to support present and future applications.
6. *Stage VI: Distribution.* The enterprise distributes its data and computer processing throughout the organization.

Figure 1-5
Stages in the growth of information systems
(Source: Nolan 1984)

As shown in Figure 1-5, these six stages can be divided into two eras: the Data Processing era (stages I to III) and the Information Technology era

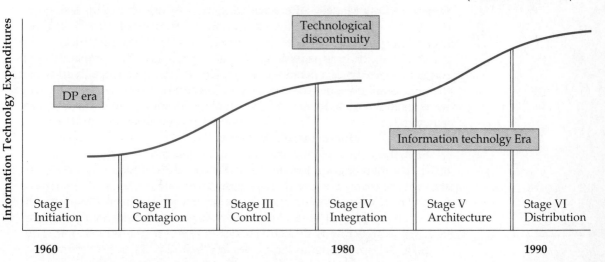

Source: Nolan, R. 1984. "Managing the Advanced Stages of Computer Technology: Key Research Issues".

(stages IV to VI). The Data Processing (DP) era emphasizes the automation of individual functions and uses the file processing approach we have just described. The Information Technology era emphasizes the integration and sharing of data and uses the database approach, which will be described next. Notice that there is a "technological discontinuity" between the two eras, which implies that the entire organization (starting with top management) must reorient its thinking to embrace information resource management (described at the beginning of the chapter). A major reorientation in thought process (sometimes referred to as a "paradigm shift") is difficult for most organizations; however, many are making this shift today and in the process are learning that information can be used as a competitive weapon.

Database Approach for Pine Valley Furniture

By the late 1980s, competition in furniture manufacturing had intensified, and competitors seemed to respond more rapidly than Pine Valley Furniture to new business opportunities. While there were numerous reasons for this trend, the managers felt constrained by their data processing systems, for reasons described earlier. At the suggestion of their data processing manager, Sharon Larson, the company formed a task group to investigate the potential of the database approach at Pine Valley Furniture Company. The task group (chaired by Ms. Larson) consisted of a mix of end-user managers and information specialists, plus a consultant who was hired to assist with the preliminary study.

Enterprise Data Model   After evaluating the existing system, the task group decided to develop a preliminary enterprise data model for Pine Valley Furniture Company. This step corresponds to stage V, Architecture, in Figure 1-5. First, the group identified the major entities in the company's environment. An *entity* is a person, place, object, event, or concept about which the organization wishes to record data. The entities identified by the group were customers, customer orders, invoices, products, work orders, raw materials, and vendors. The task group recognized that many more entities would be added to the model over time.

Next, the group developed an enterprise data model. An **enterprise data model** is a map or graphical model that shows the entities and the relationship among them. The preliminary enterprise data model for the company is shown in Figure 1-6. In this diagram, arrows are used to specify the relationship among entities. An arrow with no head indicates a "one" relation, while an arrow with a crow's foot indicates a "many" relation. Thus the relationships shown in Figure 1-6 are the following:

1. For each Customer, there may be no orders or many (that is, zero, one, or more). However, each Order is for exactly one Customer.

2. Each order may be for more than one Product; each Product may appear on more than one Customer Order.

3. Each Product may require several Raw Materials (wood, screws, and so on); each Raw Material may be used in many Products.

4. Each Raw Material may be purchased from more than one Vendor; each Vendor may supply many Raw Materials.

5. Each Product may have several Work Orders; however, a Work Order pertains to only one Product.

6. Each Customer Order may result in more than one Invoice (corresponding to multiple shipments); each Invoice is for exactly one Customer Order.

7. Each Product may be billed on many Invoices; each Invoice often includes multiple Products.

8. Each Customer may be sent multiple Invoices; however, a given Invoice is sent to exactly one Customer.

Notice the following characteristics of the enterprise model:

1. The data model is a model of the organization, telling us a great deal about how the organization functions and about the important constraints.

2. The data model stresses the *integration* of data and processes by focusing on relationships as well as entities.

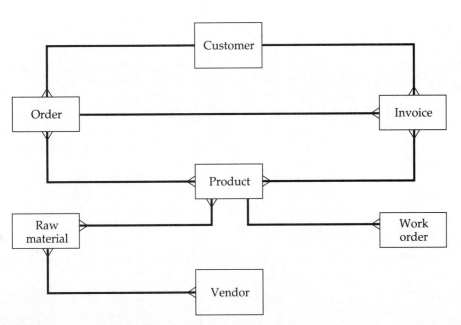

Figure 1.6
Enterprise model (preliminary) for Pine Valley Furniture Company

Relational Database   After the preliminary study was completed, management was convinced of the advantages of the database approach at Pine Valley Furniture Company. The company decided to upgrade their minicomputer and to implement a modern relational database management system. In the relational data model, all data are viewed in the form of tables. Figure 1-7 shows relations (or tables) describing three entities from the conceptual data model (Product, Customer, and Order) at Pine Valley Furniture Company. Each column of a table represents an attribute (or characteristic) of the entity, while each row is an instance (or occurrence) of that entity. In this chapter we introduce the relational model only briefly; it is defined in detail in subsequent chapters.

An important property of the relational model is that relationships between entities are represented by values stored in the columns of the corresponding tables. For example, referring to Figure 1-6, you recall that each Customer may have several Orders. Now refer to the Order table in Figure 1-7; customer number is one of its attributes. As a result, we can easily link

Figure 1-7
Three relations at
Pine Valley Furniture

PRODUCT

Product #	Description	Finish	Room	Unit-Price
0100	Table	Oak	DR	500
0350	Table	Maple	DR	625
0625	Chair	Oak	DR	100
0975	Wall Unit	Pine	FR	750
1000	Dresser	Cherry	BR	800
1250	Chair	Maple	LR	400
1425	Bookcase	Birch	LR	250

CUSTOMER

Customer #	Name	Address
C100	Contemporary Casuals	100 Oak Pala Alto CA
C150	Value Furniture	200 Walnut Cupertino CA
C325	Home Furnishings	300 Maple San Jose CA
C468	Western Furniture	400 Locust San Francisco CA
C500	Impressions	500 Pine Redwood City CA

ORDER

Order #	Date	Customer #
A1000	9/16/9X	C325
B2500	10/15/9X	C468
C3000	8/20/9X	C325
D1500	11/1/9X	C500

Orders to Customers: For example, there are two orders (order A1000 and C3000) for customer C325. There is one order each for customer C468 and C500, and no orders for customer C100 or C150. These linkages allow users to easily retrieve data from the various tables using a powerful query language, as we will see in the next chapter.

Benefits of the Database Approach

The database approach offers a number of potential advantages compared to traditional file approaches. These benefits include minimal data redundancy; consistency of data; integration of data; sharing of data; enforcement of standards; ease of application development; uniform security, privacy, and integrity controls; data accessibility and responsiveness; data independence; and reduced program maintenance.

Minimal Data Redundancy   With the database approach, previously separate (and redundant) data files are integrated into a single, logical structure. In addition, each occurrence of a data item is recorded ideally in only one place in the database. For example, the fact that the address for a specific customer of Pine Valley Furniture is 300 Maple Street might be recorded in two separate files in a file processing system (see Figure 1-4). In a database system, however, this fact will normally be recorded only once (as shown in Figure 1-7).

We are not suggesting that *all* redundancy can or should be eliminated. Sometimes there are valid reasons for storing multiple copies of the same data (for example, data access efficiency and data validation checks). In a database system, however, redundancy is *controlled*. It is designed into the system to improve performance (or provide some other benefit), and the system is (or should be) aware of the redundancy.

Consistency of Data   By eliminating (or controlling) data redundancy, we greatly reduce the opportunities for inconsistency. For example, if each address is stored only once, we cannot have disagreement on the stored values. When controlled redundancy is permitted in the database, the database system itself should enforce consistency by updating each occurrence of a data item when a change occurs. If the data item address is stored in two separate records in the database, then the database system should update this data value in both records whenever a change occurs. Unfortunately, many systems today do not enforce data consistency in this manner.

Integration of Data   In a database, data are organized into a single, logical structure, with logical relationships defined between associated data entities. In this way, the user can easily relate one item of data to another. For example, take another look at Figure 1-6. Suppose the user identifies a particular Product. Since this entity is logically related to the Raw Material entity, the user can easily determine what raw materials are required to build the product. Also, the user can check to see what raw materials are on order from a vendor, since the Raw Material entity is logically related to the Vendor entity. Data management software (described later) performs the function of associating logically related data items, regardless of the physical organization or location of the items in the database.

Sharing of Data   A database is intended to be shared by all authorized users in the organization. For example, the database at Pine Valley Furniture will be designed to satisfy the information needs of Accounting, Sales, Manufacturing, Purchasing, and other departments. The company will thus essentially return to the single set of books that it had when it was first founded. Most database systems today permit multiple users to share a database concurrently, although certain restrictions are necessary, as described in later chapters.

In a database system, each functional department is provided with its own view (or views) of the database. Each such departmental view (or **user view**) is a subset of the conceptual database model. Figure 1-8, for example, shows three possible user views for Pine Valley Furniture. The first user view is for the Sales Department and shows the relationship between the Customer and Order entities. The second is for the Accounting Department and shows the relationships among the Customer, Order, and Invoice entities. The third is for the Purchasing Department and shows the relationships among the Product, Vendor, and Raw Material entities. These user views simplify the sharing of data since they provide each user with the precise view of data required to make a decision or perform some function without making the user aware of the overall complexity of the database.

Enforcement of Standards   Establishing the data administration function is an important part of the database approach. This organizational function has the authority to define and enforce data standards. When the data administration function is established at Pine Valley Furniture, this office will approve all data names and formats and grant access rights throughout the company. Moreover, data administration will have to approve all changes to data standards. Data administration is discussed in Chapter 9.

Figure 1-8
Three possible user views (Pine Valley Furniture)

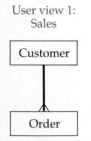

User view 1:
Sales

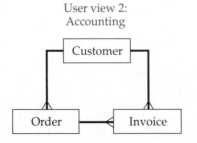

User view 2:
Accounting

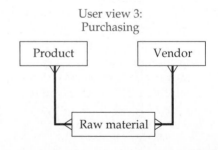

User view 3:
Purchasing

Ease of Application Development   A major advantage of the database approach is that it greatly reduces the cost and time for developing new business applications. Studies show that once the database has been designed and implemented, a programmer can code and debug a new application at least two to four times faster than with conventional data files (even greater improvements are possible with very high level languages). The reason for this improvement is that the programmer is no longer saddled with the burden of designing, building, and maintaining master files; thus, the cost of software development is reduced, and new applications are available to the user in a much shorter time span.

Uniform Security, Privacy, and Integrity Controls   The data administration function has complete jurisdiction over the database and is responsible for establishing controls for accessing, updating, and protecting data. Centralized control and standard procedures can improve data protection, compared to that provided by a dispersed data file system. However, if proper controls are not applied, a database probably will be *more* vulnerable than conventional files, since a larger user community is sharing a common resource. We describe measures for database security, privacy, and integrity in Chapter 9.

Data Accessibility and Responsiveness   A database system provides multiple retrieval paths to each item of data, giving a user much greater flexibility in locating and retrieving data than with data files. Retrieval of data can cross traditional departmental boundaries. To illustrate, refer to the conceptual model for Pine Valley Furniture (Figure 1-6). Suppose that a customer calls requesting information about several items that have been back-ordered. While on the phone, the salesperson can look up the Customer record, display the particular Order in question, and then display the Product record for each item on that order. Finally, the salesperson can display the Work Order status for each back-ordered item to determine its completion date.

This example represents a routine, planned sequence of retrievals. But a database system (especially a relational database) allows end users to satisfy many ad hoc (one-time) requests for data through the use of a query language or report writer. For example, the manager of the Product Department at Pine Valley Furniture wanted a listing of all wall units that sold for more than $500. He was able to quickly obtain such a listing by entering the following command at a terminal:

```
SELECT PRODUCT#, DESCRIPTION, UNIT-PRICE
FROM PRODUCT
WHERE DESCRIPTION = 'Wall Unit'
              AND UNIT-PRICE > 500
```

The language for this command is called *structured query language* (or SQL), which is a standard fourth-generation query language for relational database systems. It specifies the columns or attributes to be listed (PROD-UCT#, DESCRIPTION, and UNIT-PRICE), the table from which the data is to be extracted (PRODUCT#), and the conditions for selecting rows from the table. You will study how SQL can be used to build and manipulate databases in Chapter 2 and in subsequent chapters.

Data Independence   The separation of data descriptions from the application programs that use the data is called **data independence**. As a result of this, an organization's data can change and evolve (within limits) without necessitating a change in the application programs that process the data. Data independence is one of the major objectives of the database approach.

In traditional systems, the descriptions of the data and the logic for accessing those data are built into each individual application program; thus, the program is *dependent* on the data files. Any change to the data file requires modifying or rewriting the application program. In contrast, in the database approach all data descriptions are stored separately from application programs, in a central location called the repository. The contents of the repository are under the control of the database administration group (we describe the properties of the repository in Chapter 9).

Reduced Program Maintenance   Stored data must be changed frequently for a variety of reasons. New data item types are added, data formats are changed, new storage devices or access methods are introduced, and so on. In a data file environment, these changes require modifying the application programs that access the data. The term *maintenance* refers to modifying or rewriting old programs to make them conform to new data formats, access methods, and so forth.

In a database system, data are independent of the application programs that use them. Within limits, either the data or the application programs that use the data can be changed without necessitating a change in the other factor. As a result, program maintenance can be significantly reduced in a modern database environment.

In this section, we have identified ten major potential benefits of the database approach. However, we must caution the reader that many organizations have been frustrated in attempting to realize some of these benefits. For example, the goal of data independence (and therefore reduced program maintenance) has proven elusive due to the limitations of older data models and database management software. Fortunately, the relational model provides a significantly better environment for achieving these benefits. Another reason for failure to achieve the intended benefits is poor organizational planning and database implementation—even the best data management software cannot overcome such deficiencies. For this reason, we stress database planning and implementation in this text.

Costs of the Database Approach

As with any business decision, the database approach entails some additional costs and risks that must be recognized and compared with the potential benefits.

New, Specialized Personnel Frequently, organizations that adopt the database approach or purchase a database management system (DBMS) need to hire or train individuals to maintain the new database software, develop and enforce new programming standards, design databases to achieve the highest possible performance, and manage the staff of new people. Although this personnel increase may be more than offset by other productivity gains, an organization should not minimize the need for these specialized skills, which are needed to obtain the most from the potential benefits. We will discuss these staff requirements for database management in Chapter 9.

Need for Explicit Backup Minimal data redundancy, with all its associated benefits, may also fail to provide backup copies of data. Such backup or independently produced copies are helpful in restoring damaged data files and in providing validity checks on crucial data. To ensure that data are accurate and available whenever needed, either database management software or additional procedures have to provide these essential capabilities. A database management system usually automates many more of the backup and recovery tasks than a file system. This book covers database security, integrity, and recovery throughout.

Interference with Shared Data The concurrent access to shared data via several application programs can lead to some problems. First, when two concurrent users both want to change the same or related data, inaccurate results can occur if access to the data is not properly synchronized. Second, when data are used exclusively for updating, different users can obtain control of different segments of the database and lock up any use of the data (so-called deadlock). Database management software must be designed to prevent or detect such interferences in a way that is transparent to the user.

Organizational Conflict A shared database requires a consensus on data definitions and ownership as well as responsibilities for accurate data maintenance. Experience has shown that conflicts on how to define data, data length and coding, rights to update shared data, and associated issues are frequent and difficult managerial issues to resolve. Handling these organizational issues requires organizational commitment to the benefits of the database approach, organizationally astute database administrators, and a sound evolutionary schedule for database development.

COMPONENTS OF THE DATABASE ENVIRONMENT

The major components of a typical database environment and their relationships are shown in Figure 1-9. You have already been introduced to some (but not all) of these components in previous sections. Following is a brief description of the nine components shown in Figure 1-9.

1. Computer-Aided Software Engineering (CASE) Tools: automated tools used to design databases and application programs. We describe the use of CASE tools for database design and development in Chapter 9.

2. Repository: centralized knowledge base containing all data definitions, screen and report formats, and definitions of other organizations and system components. We describe the repository in Chapter 9.

3. Database Management System (DBMS): commercial software (and occasionally, hardware and firmware) system used to provide access to the database and also to the repository. We describe the functions of a DBMS in Chapter 9.

4. Database: an integrated collection of data, organized to meet the information needs of multiple users in an organization. It is important to distinguish between the database and the repository: The repository contains *definitions* of data, while the database contains *occurrences* of data.

5. Application Programs: computer programs that are used to create and maintain the database and provide information to users.

6. User Interface: languages, menus, and other facilities by which users interact with various system components such as CASE tools, application programs, the DBMS, and the repository.

7. Data Administrators: persons who are responsible for designing databases and for developing policies regarding database security and integrity. Data administrators use CASE tools to improve the productivity of database planning and design. We describe the functions of data administration in detail in Chapter 9.

8. System Developers: persons such as systems analysts and programmers who design new application programs. System developers often use CASE tools for system requirements analysis and program design.

9. End Users: persons through the organization who add, delete, and modify data in the database and who request or receive information from the database. All user interactions with the database must be routed through the DBMS.

With advances in software, the user interface is becoming increasingly user-friendly. Examples of such advances are menu-driven systems, use of a "mouse," and voice-recognition systems. These systems promote *end-user*

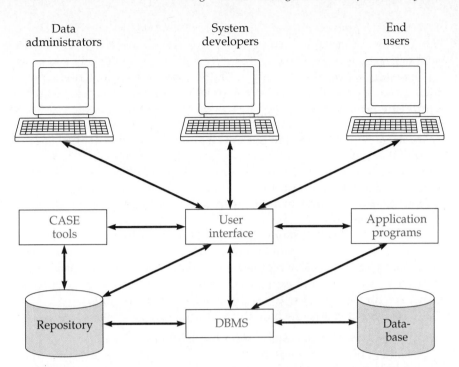

Figure 1-9
Components of the
database
environment

computing—that is, users who are not computer experts can define their own reports, displays, and simple applications. In fact, some organizations are creating *information centers*—organizational units that can be consulted to assist users in this endeavor. Of course, in such an environment, database administration must ensure the enforcement of adequate security measures to protect the database.

To simplify the presentation in this first chapter, numerous other components of a typical database environment are not shown in Figure 1-9. These components (including the operating system and teleprocessing monitor) are described in Chapter 9.

In summary, the DBMS operational environment shown in Figure 1-9 is an integrated system of hardware, software, and people that is designed to facilitate the storage, retrieval, and control of the information resource and to improve the productivity of the organization.

USING DATABASES IN ORGANIZATIONAL INFORMATION SYSTEMS

We conclude this chapter by describing how databases support organizational information systems. Earlier in this chapter we defined three types (or levels) of databases: operational, managerial, and strategic (see Figure

1-1). We may similarly define three levels of information systems: transaction processing systems, management information systems, and decision support systems (see Figure 1-10).

Transaction Processing Systems (TPS) support everyday operations of the business, providing detailed information such as status reports, action documents, and displays. The primary objectives in the transaction processing systems are accuracy, rapid response, and ease of use.

Management Information Systems (MIS) provide information required by middle- and upper-level managers for planning and control. Much of this information is provided in the form of periodic reports—income statements, budget reports, and so on—however, an MIS should also support ad hoc requests for information. In an MIS, the emphasis is on flexibility and ease of use.

Decision Support Systems (DSS) support managerial decision making in complex situations, by providing both information and tools for analysis. A DSS is typically used by high-level managers for relatively unstructured decisions such as capital expansion, mergers, and new product introductions. A DSS must be easy to use, flexible, and easy to modify.

A DSS will normally include the following components:

1. A terminal (or personal computer) located in a manager's office or other convenient location.

2. A DBMS for building, accessing, and manipulating local files or databases.

3. A powerful, high-level language for retrieving and manipulating data.

4. Modeling tools (such as forecasting and simulation) for evaluating various alternative decisions.

A simple (but very common) example of a DSS is shown in Figure 1-11. In this example, a personal computer (used by a manager) is linked to the organization's mainframe computer. The mainframe computer uses a DBMS to maintain the organization's databases, which contain transaction data.

Figure 1-10
Three levels of
information systems

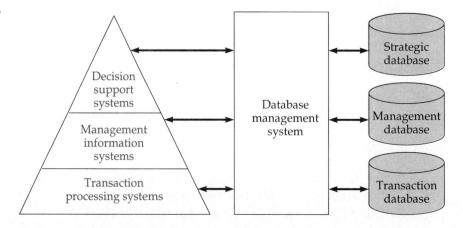

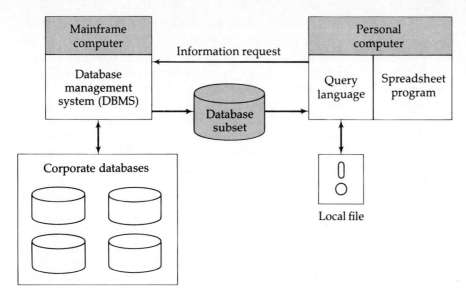

Figure 1-11
Example of a simple decison support system (DSS)

The manager uses the personal computer with a high-level query language to formulate English-language requests for data relevant to a particular decision-making situation. These requests are passed to the mainframe computer, which uses the DBMS to extract the requested data from the database. This data is passed to the personal computer, where it may then be displayed or summarized and stored as a local file or database. Also, the manager may use the data in a model (in this case, a financial spreadsheet program) to evaluate various alternatives. In this way the transaction databases can be used as a source of data for a DSS.

SUMMARY

Information is a major corporate resource and must be managed using the same basic principles used to manage other assets, such as employees, materials, equipment, and financial resources. Information is an asset only if it is accurate and available when needed; this can occur only if an organization purposely organizes and manages its data. Databases have become the standard technique for structuring and managing data in most organizations today.

A database is an integrated collection of data, organized to meet the information needs of multiple users in an organization. Data consist of raw facts concerning people, objects, events, or other entities; information is data that have been processed and presented in a form suitable for human interpretation. Although some organizations have manual databases, in this text we restrict our attention to computer databases. There are three levels of information systems in many organizations. Transaction processing systems capture transaction data and build and maintain operational databases. These systems are used by clerical personnel and first-level managers. Management information systems are used by middle-level managers for planning and control, using managerial databases that are extracted or summarized from operational databases. Decision support systems are used mostly by upper-level managers for less structured decisions, employing both a strategic database and modeling tools to allow managers to evaluate decision alternatives.

The traditional approach to information systems focuses on the data processing needs of individual departments or work groups. Each computer application is designed with its own set of files, which often duplicate data already stored in other files. This duplication (or redundancy) often results in inconsistent data in the various files, and also, the files cannot be easily shared among the various users. Another disadvantage of file processing systems is that they are inflexible—users cannot request data in a new format without waiting for new application programs.

The database approach is designed to overcome many of the disadvantages of file processing systems. With this approach, databases are designed from an organization-wide viewpoint to minimize data redundancy. All data definitions are stored in a central location called a repository. Databases are managed by a commercial software system called the database management system (DBMS), and all user requests for data must be routed through the DBMS. Objectives of the database approach include improved data consistency, better sharing of data, easier access to data, and improved productivity for both end users and information system specialists.

To implement the database approach, organizations must establish a data administration function. The data administration group is responsible for developing an overall database plan, for designing and implementing databases, and for establishing policies concerning database security and quality assurance.

Chapter Review

REVIEW QUESTIONS

1. Define each of the following terms:
   a. data
   b. information
   c. database
   d. information resource management (IRM)
   e. application program
   f. repository

g. synonym
h. enterprise data model
i. data independence
j. database management system (DBMS)

2. Contrast the following terms:
   a. data dependence; data independence
   b. database management system; decision support system
   c. database; repository
   d. operational information system; management information system
   e. data; information
   f. synonym; homonym

3. List and briefly describe seven disadvantages of many traditional application systems.

4. Explain why data redundancy is so common in traditional application systems.

5. List and briefly describe ten benefits that can often be achieved with the database approach, compared to traditional application systems.

6. Briefly describe nine components in a database environment.

7. Describe three types of databases in a typical organization.

8. Where are data definitions maintained in each of the following environments:
   a. traditional file processing system
   b. database system

9. List eight functions of information resource management. In what courses are these functions covered in your information systems programs?

10. What is a decision support system? List four components of a typical DSS.

PROBLEMS AND EXERCISES

1. Match the following terms and definitions:

_____ IRM

_____ entity

_____ CASE

_____ relationship

_____ DBMS

_____ repository

_____ data

_____ information

_____ database

_____ enterprise data model

a) data processed for human interpretation

b) graphical model of entities and relationships

c) raw facts

d) integrated collection of data

e) information considered as a resource

f) person, object, or concept

g) commercial software system

h) automated design tools

i) central collection of data definitions

j) logical association between entities

2. Draw an enterprise data model for the following situation:
   - Student takes several Courses; each Course has many Students
   - An Instructor teaches several Courses, but each Course is taught by one Instructor
   - Course has several Sections; each Section pertains to one Course
   - Course may have several Textbooks; a given Textbook is used in only one Course

3. Draw an enterprise data model for each of the following situations (state any assumptions you make):
   a. Football team: entities are Team, Coach, Player, Agent, Game
   b. Family: entities are Mother, Father, Home, Children, Car, Clothes
   c. Bank: entities are Branch, Customer, Teller, Account, Deposit, Withdrawal

4. Add the entity Employee to the enterprise data model for Pine Valley Furniture Company (Figure 1-6). Assume that a given Work Order may require one or more Employees. Also, assume an Employee may work on zero, one, or more than one Work Order.

5. Draw a user view (similar to those in Figure 1-8) for a production scheduling system at Pine Valley Furniture Company. This new application requires information about the following entities: Product, Work Order, Raw Material, Order (*hint:* see Figure 1-6 for the relationships among these entities).

6. Write a SQL command to produce a listing of the following data from Figure 1-7:
   a. List the product number and description for all dining room furniture (ROOM = 'DR').
   b. List the order number, customer number, and total amount for all orders whose date is 10/15/9X.
   c. List the name and address for customer number C325.

7. Draw an enterprise data model for an organization you are familiar with (Girl Scouts, fast-food restaurant, and so on). First, list about six major entities for the organization. Then draw the relationships between the entities.

8. Visit an organization that has installed a database system. Talk to a person in data administration and determine each of the following:
   a. Which of the benefits of the database approach have been realized by the organization? Which have not been realized?
   b. What major components of a database system (Figure 1-9) are present in the organization?
   c. Does the organization have a conceptual data model? If so, in what form is it represented?

REFERENCES

Auerbach Publishers, eds. 1981. *Practical Data Base Management.* Princeton, N.J.: Auerbach.

DeHayes, D. W., J. A. Hoffer, E. W. Martin, and W. C. Perkins. 1991. *MIS for Managers.* New York, N.Y.: MacMillan.

Guimaraes, T. 1988. "Information Resources Management: Improving the Focus." *Information Resources Management Journal* 1 (1) (Fall): 10-21.

Martin, E. W., D. W. DeHayes, J. A. Hoffer, and W. C. Perkins. 1991. *Managing Information Technology: What Managers Need to Know.* New York, N.Y.: MacMillan.

Martin, J. 1981. *An End-User's Guide to Data Base.* Englewood Cliffs, N.J.: Prentice-Hall.

Martin, J. 1983. *Managing the Data-Base Environment.* Englewood Cliffs, N.J.: Prentice-Hall.

McLeod, Raymond, Jr., and Kathy Brittain-White. 1988. "Incorporation of IRM Concepts in Undergraduate Business Curricula." *Information Resources Management Journal* 1 (1) (Fall): 28-38.

Nolan, R. 1984. "Managing the Advanced Stages of Computer Technology: Key Research Issues." In F. Warren McFarlan, ed., *The Information Systems Research Challenge.* Boston, Mass.: Harvard Business School Press.

Vetter, M. 1987. *Strategy for Data Modeling.* New York: Wiley.

CHAPTER 2

A Database Application for Pine Valley Furniture

INTRODUCTION

Chapter 1 introduced the operations of Pine Valley Furniture Company, a manufacturer of all-wood furniture. Figures 1-3, 1-4, 1-6, 1-7, and 1-8, along with associated text, described the basics of the organization and activities in this business. Chapter 2 illustrates a database application to meet some of the transaction processing and management information system needs of this company. There are several purposes for this chapter at this point in the book.

First, it is likely that you have not developed or used an information processing application based upon database technology, nor are you familiar with how one is developed. In general, the goal of this book is to provide the concepts and many of the skills that will allow you to design and build database applications. This chapter therefore briefly illustrates some of what you will be able to do after you complete a database course using this text.

Second, many students learn best from a text full of concrete examples. Although all the chapters of this book contain many examples, illustrations, and actual database diagrams and code, each chapter concentrates on specific aspects of database management. This chapter is thus designed to provide an overview and to show how the various aspects of database management are related. This chapter is the closest we can come to a demonstration of a working system in the format of the printed page.

Finally, many instructors want you to begin now, early in your database course, the initial steps of a database development group or individual course project. Due to the logical progression of topics in this book (database planning, data analysis, logical database design, physical design, and implementation), you will study many pages before you will see your target for the project. This chapter gives you an idea of where you are headed and, by illustration, some basic skills you can begin to employ now, until a more rigorous treatment of topics is presented later in the book. Thus, this chapter can provide the information you need to get a "jump start" on developing a database application in your course. Obviously, since this is only Chapter 2 of the book, many of the examples we will use will be much simpler than you would encounter in a real company or than you will have to deal with in your project or other course assignments.

This chapter illustrates the development and operation of a working database application system; that is, all the sample screens and reports shown here are generated from a system that has actually been implemented. The chapter also illustrates the use of automated tools to assist in the development of a database. A **database application system** includes the data definitions, stored data, transactions, inquiries, and reports needed to capture, maintain, and present data from a database. Like any other application system you might have encountered in practice or analyzed and designed in a systems analysis and design course, a database application is developed in steps. These steps involve analysis of business needs, functional design of a system that meets these requirements, physical design of a working system that efficiently meets time and space expectations, and programming (using a combination of programming and database processing languages). In addition, testing, documentation, installation, and training must occur. We will not attempt in this chapter to provide illustrations of all of these activities; rather, we will give the essence of this process, so you can put the more detailed coverage of these topics later in the book into perspective.

The example database application of this chapter includes both transaction processing and management information and decision support requirements. These types of systems were defined in Chapter 1. A **business transaction** is the data about some important business event, such as receipt of a customer order, notice of an employee address change, or the issuance of a customer sales invoice. Such transactions change the contents of a database (add, delete, or change data), so we usually associate transaction processing with populating and maintaining a database. Some simple inquiries (such as displaying the status of a customer order, determining the on-hand balance of a product, or checking the credit status of a customer) are also considered transactions. An important feature of a transaction is its integrity; that is, only correct and consistent data should be permitted in the database. For example, if we discover some error during the input of a new customer order or are unable to complete the input, the whole order should probably be rejected. The careful control of business transactions is central to transaction processing applications. We will illustrate some simple controls in this chapter.

Both business transactions and management information and decision support processing needs tell us what type of data must be stored in a database and the necessary space and response time to meet business expectations. Thus, we begin this chapter with an illustration of the data analysis of these processing requirements for Pine Valley Furniture, followed by an illustration of the needed database and associated computer programs for transaction and information processing. First, however, we provide an overview of the database development process and of the Pine Valley Furniture enterprise.

The Development of a Database Application

Table 2-1 provides a simple outline of a typical database development project. We will illustrate most, but not all, of these steps in this chapter. Also, we will study only a very small portion of the database requirements at Pine Valley Furniture.

Table 2.1.   Database Development Project Outline

ENTERPRISE MODELING
— Analyze current data processing
— Analyze the general business database needs
— Plan database development project
— Develop preliminary conceptual data model

LOGICAL DATABASE DESIGN
— Normalize transactions and reports
— Integrate views into conceptual data model
— Design screens, reports, and applications
— Identify data integrity and security requirements

PHYSICAL DATABASE DESIGN AND CREATION
— Define database to DBMS
— Decide on physical organization of data
— Design programs

PROGRAMMING
— Code and test programs
— Complete database documentation
— Install database and convert from prior systems

A database development project begins with **enterprise modeling**, which is where the scope and the general contents of the database are sketched. This step involves reviewing current systems, analyzing the nature of the business area to be supported, describing the data needed at a very high level of abstraction, and planning the rest of the project. Database planning, the topic of Chapter 4, is conducted in this phase. Figure 1-6 from Chapter 1, which shows a preliminary enterprise model for part of Pine Valley Furniture, is typical of one result of enterprise modeling. It is important to note that since such a chart is really preliminary, transactions, reports, screens, and inquiries have not been detailed. However, it helps for subsequent analysis to define the scope involved.

Logical design performs the detailed review of individual reports, transactions, screens, and so on to determine exactly what data (and their nature) are to be maintained in the database. In illustrating this phase, we will introduce data normalization, which will help us to logically structure data that should have long-term meaning to Pine Valley Furniture. With this structure in place, we can also begin to identify the needs for particular computer programs and queries to maintain and report the database contents.

In **physical design and creation,** the database developer decides on the organization of the database on computer storage (usually disk) and defines the physical structures to the database software (the database management system). Programs to process transactions and to generate anticipated management information and decision support reports are mapped out. The final step that we will illustrate is **programming,** in which the programs are written, tested, and implemented. Programming may occur in standard programming languages (like COBOL or C), in special database processing languages (like SQL or the dBASE IV query language), or via special purpose fourth-generation languages to produce stylized reports and screens, possibly including graphs. We will illustrate several of these options.

The components of the database environment were introduced in Figure 1-9, and we will illustrate several of them in this chapter. Obviously, the database itself as well as a database management system (DBMS) and application programs are essential for a database application and will be illustrated here. A very simple repository, associated with the DBMS we will use, will be shown and several forms of user interfaces will be used. Specifically, we will illustrate the

- **Menu system** module of the DBMS that will help us to define the database and to write queries and programs to maintain and report data

- **Report writer** module of the DBMS that will provide special commands for summarizing and aggregating data, and for producing custom-designed column headings and other report layout features

- **Screen painter** module of the DBMS that assists in creating readable and easy-to-use CRT screens for data entry, maintenance, and simple queries

The DBMS used in this chapter to illustrate a database application for Pine Valley Furniture is dBASE IV, from Ashton-Tate Corporation (1988). dBASE has been one of the most popular personal computer database systems, starting with the original dBASE II package. We will actually use the student version of dBASE IV (see Senn, 1990 and Krumm, 1990), which provides all the functionality of the full package but places a few restrictions on the size of the database that can be created. Chapters 13 and 14 will cover dBASE IV and other personal computer products in detail. Whenever possible, we will use the SQL subsystem within dBASE IV (although we will need to use features of the dBASE menu system and proprietary dBASE languages sometimes). SQL is a standard for database programming languages that has been adopted by many of the mainframe and personal computer DBMS vendors. This chapter thus not only illustrates a database application but also serves as a case study introduction to what is becoming the most prevalent standard database processing language, SQL. SQL will be covered in depth in Chapter 12.

We use dBASE IV here for several reasons. First, one of the versions of dBASE is used in many database courses, so you may be asked to use this product in your class, and dBASE IV is the latest version and the most advanced. If you use dBASE III Plus, for example, the commands you enter and the menu interface will not be exactly the same as shown here. However, the examples in this chapter will serve as analogies for you to develop queries, reports, and so on in course assignments. Second, dBASE IV contains an SQL sublanguage, which makes much of what you will see in this chapter transferable to other DBMSs with an SQL sublanguage. Finally, dBASE is a very popular personal computer product, which means that it has relevance for small organizations as well as departmental or end-user databases in larger organizations. Our market analysis for this book clearly shows that, for this reason, personal computer products are more frequently covered in a database course than are mainframe computer DBMSs. In later chapters this text covers both, but some students may skip the mainframe chapters, so this chapter will still have relevance to those who study only PC databases.

The Enterprise Database for Pine Valley Furniture

Pine Valley Furniture, like any organization, has a wide variety of data and information processing requirements, some of which were described in Chapter 1. Figure 1-6 depicts a preliminary enterprise database for just some of these requirements, and we will limit ourselves in this chapter to an even smaller subset. Figure 2-1 shows the scope of the database to be covered in our sample application of this chapter. This chart would be developed from the enterprise modeling phase of a database development project, and hence it is called an enterprise data model.

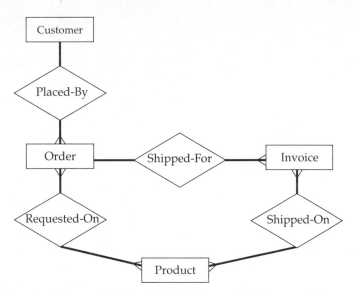

Figure 2-1
Pine Valley Furniture
sample enterprise
data model

In comparison to Figure 1-6, the Raw Material, Work Order, and Vendor data entities have been dropped, as have any processing requirements associated with this type of data. This has been done simply to create a more manageable example. In addition, Figure 2-1 uses the basic entity-relationship (E-R) diagramming notation. In this form, a diamond symbol is used to highlight each relationship, which is also assigned a name. Such charts can be generated from a variety of Computer-Assisted Software Engineering (CASE) tools, such as E-R Designer (Chen and Associates, 1988), which is a personal computer-based tool for developing such database descriptions.

TRANSACTION PROCESSING REQUIREMENTS FOR PINE VALLEY FURNITURE

We will concentrate our attention on the order entry, invoicing, customer service, and product management areas at Pine Valley Furniture (PVF). The basic business transactions include entry and maintenance of customer and product data (such as changing a customer's address or entering data about a new product), as well as entry of new customer orders and invoices. A customer is invoiced for each shipment. As stated in Chapter 1, partial shipments on an order are made, so there may be multiple invoices for a given customer order. The identification of all the business transactions would happen during the logical design phase of the database development project, as a detailed understanding of the business is developed.

Pine Valley Furniture has decided that all transaction processing will be done on-line, so data entry and maintenance will be via CRT screen displays. Because of this decision, database designers must be concerned with various issues of concurrent on-line access to the database and security in a full system implementation. For example, if two people enter data about separate shipments for the same product at the same time, the new balance of inventory on hand should accurately represent both transactions, not just one. We will highlight later some examples of how such data integrity controls can be included. A data analyst would identify the need for such controls during the logical design step of developing the database.

Product and Customer Data Entry

Figure 2-2a shows a sample product display screen that is used for data entry, maintenance, and simple status checks on the products Pine Valley Furniture manufactures. Each product is uniquely identified by a number (Product No), called a primary key, and is defined in the Description data element. The product's standard price (Unit Price), type of wood finish (Finish), and intended application (Room) are also shown. In addition, the quantity of the product in stock (Quantity on Hand) is shown.

The product display is summarized in E-R notation in Figure 2-2b. The bubbles attached to the Product entity rectangle indicate facts about each Pine Valley product. One requirement for the product display screen (as well as for the customer, to be shown next) is that during data entry, duplicate products (or customers) may not be entered. Similarly, the typical process for deleting or modifying product (or customer) data is to first display a

Figure 2-2
Sample product display:
(a) product display screen
(b) E-R diagram for product display screen

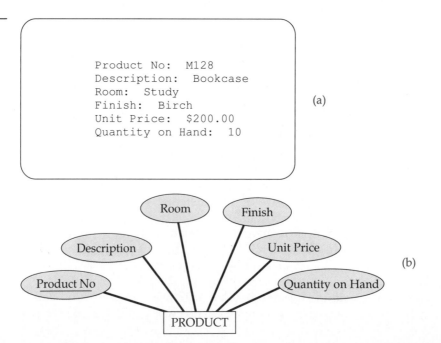

```
Product No:  M128
Description:  Bookcase
Room:  Study
Finish:  Birch
Unit Price:  $200.00
Quantity on Hand:  10
```
(a)

(b)

formatted screen that shows all the data names for product (or customer) data. Then the clerk enters the primary key (for example, Product No for product data). The remainder of the data for that record would then be displayed for visual verification that the correct key was entered. Only when it is verified that the correct record has been retrieved would it be deleted or changed, thus avoiding errors in maintaining the database.

Figure 2-3a shows a sample customer display screen that Pine Valley wants to use for entry and maintenance of customer data. Each customer is assigned a unique number (Customer No). Other customer data included are the customer's full name (Name), street address (Address), city information (City-State-Zip), and agreed-upon price discount (Discount%). The price discount is applied across the board on all purchases by the customer.

This customer display is summarized using E-R notation in Figure 2-3b. Customer No is underlined because it is the primary key. Note that the city information has been combined into one data element; this is done only after verifying that these are not three separate pieces of data. We will assume for simplicity that there will be no use for city, state, or zip code separately (although this would not be true in most circumstances).

Customer Order Entry

A sample Pine Valley Furniture customer order entry screen appears in Figure 2-4a. Orders are entered on-line from paper documents (either official Pine Valley order forms or, more typically, orders printed by customers

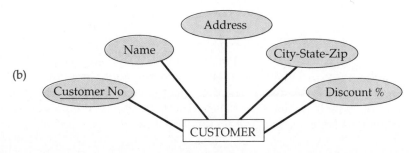

(a)
```
Customer No: 1273
Name: Contemporary Designs
Address: 123 Oak St.
City-State-Zip:   Austin, TX 28384
Discount %:   5%
```

(b)

Figure 2-3
Sample customer display:
(a) customer display screen
(b) E-R diagram for customer display screen

Figure 2-4
Sample customer order:
(a) order entry screen
(b) E-R diagram for order entry

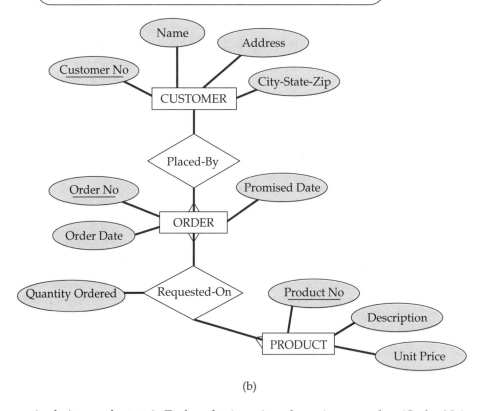

```
Order No: 61384              Customer No: 1273

        Name:  Contemporary Designs
        Address:   123 Oak St.
        City-State-Zip: Austin, TX 28384

Order Date: 11/04/90   Promised Date: 11/21/90     (a)
```

Product No.	Description	Quantity Ordered	Unit Price
M128	Bookcase	4	200.00
B381	Cabinet	2	150.00
R220	Table	1	500.00

(b)

in their own formats). Each order is assigned a unique number (Order No) to track each individual customer request (this is an internal Pine Valley number; any order number that a customer might provide is not to be included in the database). The date that the order is received (Order Date) and the date by which Pine Valley expects to ship all the products ordered (Promised Date) also appear on this screen. Obviously, each order is from some customer, indicated by Customer No on the screen. The other customer data (Name, Address, and City-State-Zip) are not actually entered for each order. Rather, they are automatically displayed on this screen once the Customer No is entered, by referencing the previously entered customer data. Thus, an order can only be entered if the data for the associated customer has already been entered. Also, there is no distinction between the sold-to, bill-to, and ship-to customers; for the way Pine Valley does business, they are all the same customer. Similarly, product data (Description and Unit Price) are displayed from the associated product record as each line on the order is entered by Product No. The Quantity Ordered must, of course, be entered for each line item.

The customer order contains more complex data than the customer or product display transaction screens. This is because some of the data potentially occur a multiple number of times, when there is more than one product on an order. Further, a customer order actually refers to existing customer and product data, as well as new order and order line item data. Figure 2-4b depicts this set of data associated with the different data entities. For example, an order is placed by one customer, so the customer data is shown as being attached to the related customer, not to the order directly. In Chapter 6 we will describe a process called data normalization that can help us to organize data to achieve desirable properties that will make data maintenance easy. Associated customer data with only the customer entity and product data with only the product entity is the result of normalization.

An order may include many line items (and a given product can appear on many orders). The quantity ordered is a characteristic of neither the order (which is really order heading type of data) nor the product individually but rather relates jointly to a product on an order, which is the meaning of the Requested On relationship. The type of relationship, like Requested On, that occurs a multiple number of times for each of the entities it relates to is called a many-to-many relationship. Another way to state this is that one or many products are associated with each order, and zero, one, or many orders are associated with each product. So, Quantity Ordered is attached to the Requested On diamond. We will see later how to store the data in a many-to-many relationship, but Figure 2-4b clearly shows that Quantity Ordered is neither order nor product data per se.

Invoice Entry

The final transaction activity we will consider is invoicing for the shipment of goods to a customer. As explained in Chapter 1, Pine Valley Furniture invoices each shipment separately and will partial ship an order, so many invoices may occur for an order. Figure 2-5a displays a copy of a sample invoice screen. A billing clerk enters a unique Invoice No for each invoice, the Order No, and the date the invoice is issued (Invoice Date). The Customer No, Name, Address, and City-State-Zip fields are retrieved from the

Figure 2-5
Sample invoice display:
(a) invoice screen
(b) E-R diagram for invoice screen

```
Invoice No: 16389                    Order No: 61384
Invoice Date: 11/22/90               Paid? (Y/N)   Y


    Customer No:  1273
    Name:  Contemporary Designs
    Address:   123 Oak St.
    City-State-Zip: Austin, TX 28384
```

Product No.	Description	Qty. Ord.	Prev. Ship.	Qty. Ship.	Unit Price	Total Price
M128	Bookcase	4	0	2	200.00	400.00
B381	Cabinet	2	0	1	150.00	150.00
R210	Table	1	0	1	500.00	500.00

```
                              Total Amount   1050.00
                               5% Discount     52.50
                                Amount Due    997.50
```

(a)

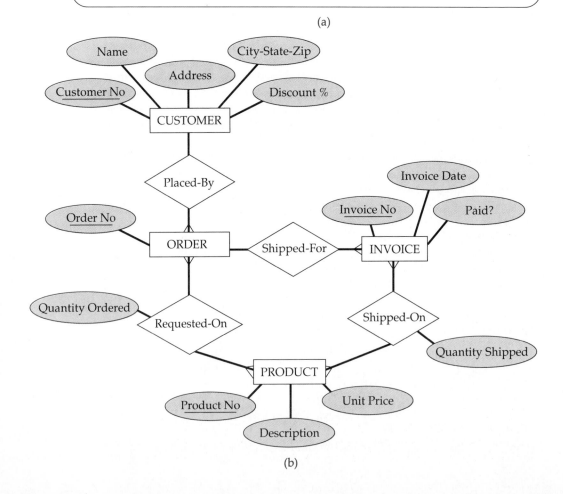

(b)

order and customer records for the identified order. The detailed bottom portion of the screen is then displayed, using data from the Requested On and Product records for the referenced order, as well as past invoices on this order. Prev Shipments is the total of quantity shipped from previous invoices on this order. The clerk then enters for each line item the new data of Quantity Shipped. Then total price per line item (Total Price) as well as the total invoiced amount (Total Amount), calculated Discount amount, and Amount Due are displayed. A printed invoice is then prepared with this information.

Pine Valley requires that customers pay for each invoice separately; the Paid field is used when this same screen is displayed upon receipt of a customer check. In this case, the Invoice No is entered, and all the rest of the invoice data is displayed. The clerk can then indicate if the invoice is paid (this same procedure also is used to check on the payment status of an invoice).

Several validity checks have to occur in processing an invoice. First, only assigned Order Nos may be entered. Second, the Quantity Shipped plus Prev Shipments cannot exceed the Quantity Ordered for any line item. Finally, some form of financial controls have to be instituted to match the actual payments with the entry of paid status on this screen (such controls will not be discussed in the illustration here).

The invoice display is the most complex of the transactions we have encountered since, as we will see, it involves the whole database. Figure 2-5b shows the E-R diagram for the data of this display. Once the Order No for the invoice is entered, the order and customer data can be found using the Shipped For relationship and then the Placed By relationship. Then the line item data can be retrieved from the Requested On relationship and the product data associated with Requested On for this order. The only new data is the Quantity Shipped, which is associated with the Shipped On relationship diamond. Previous shipment quantities can be calculated from Invoice, Shipped On, and Product data associated with prior invoices for this order.

Now that all the transaction processing requirements have been analyzed, the consolidated database must be formed by combining the requirements of each of the transactions. Figure 2-6 contains the E-R diagram for the database, which includes all of the data referenced so far. Each of the previous E-R diagrams is a subset of this figure. At least until we analyze additional reporting requirements that support management information and decision support, Figure 2-6 represents a logical model of the database needed by Pine Valley Furniture. At this point a data analyst would also collect all of the integrity statements mentioned above (for example, no two customers can have the same Customer No, or the sum of Quantity Shipped and Prev Shipped cannot exceed Quantity Ordered for each line item on an invoice) so that later stages of database development can ensure that these rules are met. The next step, before implementation, is to analyze the management reporting requirements, to see if additional data are needed.

MANAGEMENT INFORMATION REQUIREMENTS FOR PINE VALLEY FURNITURE

Management information requirements include information to check the status of business activities as well as that needed to make informed business decisions. Some information is simply data retained in the database; other information is produced by summarizing, aggregating, comparing, or combining various pieces of data stored in the database.

An example of a simple management need for information in Pine Valley Furniture is to review an individual customer's discount rate. The business question would be "What discount are we giving customer X?" Figure 2-7a shows a sample CRT screen for this inquiry. For this query, the manager enters the appropriate Customer No, and then the application system retrieves the corresponding customer record and displays the Name and Discount% data. In this situation, only one database record, from the Customer data

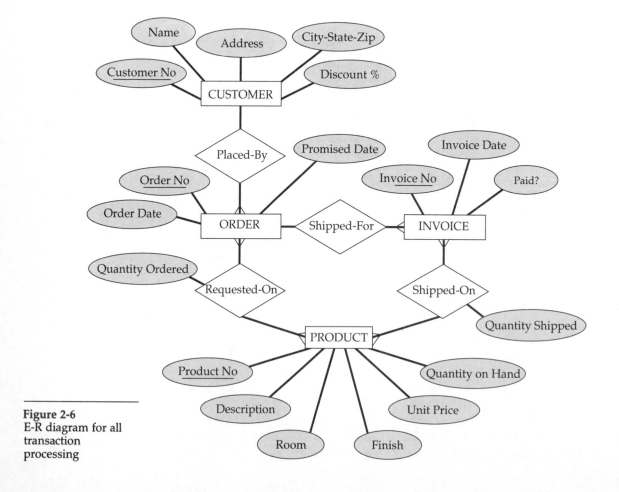

Figure 2-6
E-R diagram for all transaction processing

entity of Figure 2-6, is required. Figure 2-7b shows the data required for this query using E-R notation.

Another rather simple management information requirement in PVF is the daily customer order log. This report, depicted in Figure 2-8a, lists all the orders submitted to PVF on a specified date, in sequence by Customer

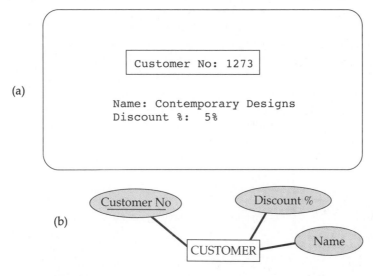

Figure 2-7
Discount rate query:
(a) discount rate inquiry screen
(b) E-R diagram for discount rate inquiry

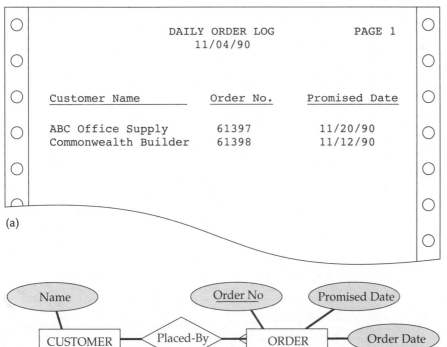

Figure 2-8
Daily order log report:
(a) sample daily order log
(b) E-R diagram for daily order log

Name. The head of the Customer Service Department scans this report and the report is used as a printed copy of daily order activity. Each row of the report is an extract of data from one customer order; however, as shown in Figure 2-6, the Customer Name is not stored with the order but in the customer record related to it. Thus, this report requires access to data in the Order and Customer entities. This is depicted in E-R notation in Figure 2-8b.

Each sales manager in PVF has responsibility for a set of major customers. As part of this job, each manager occasionally checks on the order activity of a given customer assigned to him or her. This information is used to identify low- and high-activity customers and to obtain a general understanding of the buying pattern of a customer. Figure 2-9a shows a typical customer order history report, which is displayed on the sales manager's CRT. For this report, a sales manager specifies the desired customer and the period of time (start and end order dates) over which orders are to be reviewed. Data from Customer, Placed By, Order, Requested On, and Prod-

Figure 2-9
Customer order
history query:
(a) sample customer
    order history
(b) E-R diagram for
    customer order
    history

```
              CUSTOMER ORDER HISTORY

     Customer No: 1273
     Start Date: 11/01/90     End Date: 11/30/90


                                        Quantity
     Order Date  Order No.  Product No.  Ordered        (a)

      11/04/90     61384        M128        4
                                B381        2
                                R210        1
      11/06/90     61390        T100        2
                                T160        1
```

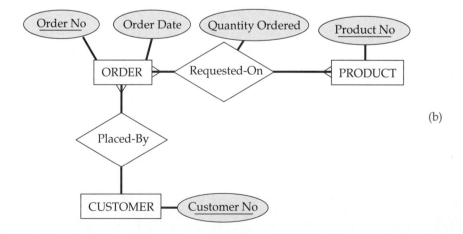

(b)

uct entities and relationships are needed to produce this report, as shown in the E-R diagram of Figure 2-9b.

PVF also has product line managers who are responsible for groups of related products (such as office furniture or the budget line). Among the many queries that the product line managers ask is: "What customer is the largest total purchaser of a given product during a specified period?" Large customers frequently receive special attention and can provide highly informed insights into product quality and end customer acceptance. Figure 2-10a shows a typical large customer query. For this report, a product line manager specifies the desired product and the period of time (start and end order dates) over which to review orders to find the purchaser (customer) who has bought the largest total quantity of the product. Data from Customer, Order, Requested On, and Product entities and relationships from Figure 2-6 will be needed to answer this query, as shown in Figure 2-10b.

The last report we will mention here is the backlog summary. PVF keeps track of the quantity of orders for each product that have been received but

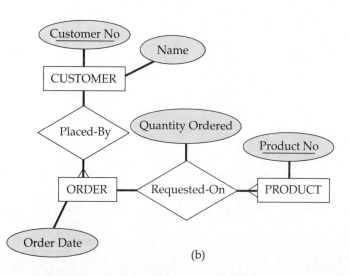

```
        Large Customer Query
           Product No: M128
       11/01/90   thru   12/31/90


       Customer No:  1256
       Name:   Commonwealth Builder
       Volume:  30
```

(a)

(b)

Figure 2-10
Large customer query:
(a) sample large customer query
(b) E-R diagram for large customer query

not yet shipped, the so called backlog. Backlog is a measure of load on the assembly operation. A week-by-week backlog for several weeks into the future would be helpful (this could be calculated by assuming an order will be shipped on the promised delivery date). However, PVF simply wants to see an aggregate figure for total outstanding orders by product. Figure 2-11a illustrates this report, which requires data from Product, Requested On (from which to determine total ordered), and Shipped On (from which to determine total shipped so far) entities and relationships. No data from Order and Invoice entities are needed, but these are shown since they match with Product on the two relationships that are needed. See the E-R diagram of Figure 2-11b.

Since the E-R diagrams for the management information requirements did not introduce any new data, the E-R diagram of Figure 2-6 still represents a comprehensive conceptual description of the database required in Pine Valley Furniture (to support the requirements outlined here).

Figure 2-11
Backlog summary report:
(a) sample backlog summary report
(b) E-R diagram for backlog summary report

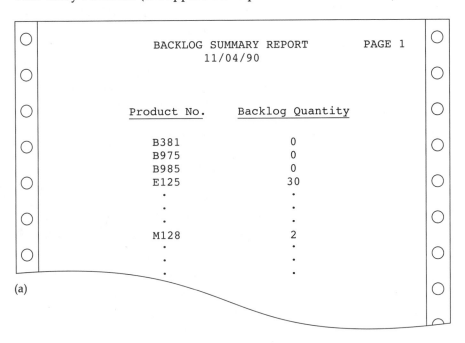

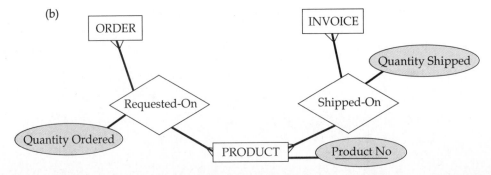

DATABASE DEFINITION IN dBASE IV

Defining a database involves giving a database management system (DBMS) commands (in a special data definition language or prompted by menus) that specify

- The tables or files (corresponding to the entities and some of the relationships from the conceptual data model) that should be created
- The structural elements that should be included in the database to implement the relationships between entities from the conceptual data model
- The data elements (including their formats) that should be included in each table
- The physical characteristics the database should have to make it operate efficiently
- The rules that should be used during data entry and maintenance to ensure that only data of high integrity are entered and only those authorized to see or manipulate data are permitted to do so

dBASE IV is an example of a relational database management system (RDBMS), which means that the above specifications will follow a certain style. The relational database approach is more formally introduced in Chapter 3 and is extensively covered in Chapters 12, 13, and 14. You should at this point simply realize that the approach illustrated in this chapter is not used by all DBMSs (since relational is only one type of DBMS).

In the relational approach, each entity and each many-to-many relationship from the conceptual model becomes a table (or file, in dBASE terminology) in the database. Further, in dBASE, a database is defined along with all the screens, reports, and other elements into a catalog. One-to-many relationships are implemented by a cross-referencing method. In this method, the primary key value for the entity occurrence from the one-side is placed in each of the associated entity occurrences on the many-side. For example, to represent the Placed By relationship of Figure 2-6, each Order record will contain the Customer No for the customer who submitted that order. This is implicitly done, even though Customer No was not shown as directly attached to the Order entity in Figure 2-6.

Decisions must be made during database definition concerning the name (limited to ten characters and only certain special symbols in dBASE), type, length, format, and other physical characteristics of each piece of data. In dBASE, each data element, called a field, has a field type, width (including sign, decimal point, and decimal places, if needed), and number of decimal digits (if relevant to the type chosen). The field types permitted are:

- **Character** (any alphanumeric string)
- **Numeric** (digits 0-9 plus decimal point and sign)
- **Floating point** (used to represent very small or large numbers in scientific notation base 10)

- **Logical** (true or false)
- **Memo** (very long and highly variable length character data that is stored separately from the main file)
- **Date** (month/day/year format)

dBASE can also be told to create an index (a kind of card catalog to quickly locate records based upon their contents) on any field or combination of fields.

Table Definitions

Given the conceptual database for Pine Valley Furniture shown in Figure 2-6, six tables need to be defined for our example database, four for the entities Product, Customer, Order, and Invoice and two for the many-to-many relationships Requested On and Shipped On. dBASE provides three mechanisms for defining tables: direct entry of the proper dBASE table definition commands, direct entry of the proper SQL commands, and prompting through the dBASE menu system called the Control Center. We will use this last approach since it is simpler and more appropriate for our novice understanding of dBASE at this point.

Figure 2-12 shows the completed menu screen in the Control Center after defining the Product file to dBASE. Each line represents a different field, so there are six actual fields (the seventh line is where dBASE is waiting in case we need to continue defining fields for this file). Field names are limited to ten characters, so some of the data element names from the conceptual database description had to be abbreviated. Further, a field name may not have embedded blanks, so an underscore character was used where possible to make the field name readable.

The field types were chosen after carefully considering all the possible

Figure 2-12
Product table definition

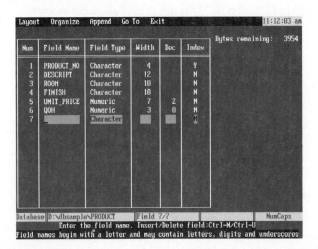

values each field could have. Character is the most general type and provides little integrity control. Character was used for Product No even though the format is actually one character followed by three digits; a more refined template for this field will be handled later during data entry since it cannot be controlled here. Unit Price and Quantity on Hand were naturally chosen as numeric. Since dBASE does not support a dollar data type, numeric with two decimal places was the best choice for Unit Price. Decimal places for Unit Price would not be needed if all prices were in whole dollars, but we will assume that not all Pine Valley prices are integers.

Since Product No is the primary key for this file, Figure 2-12 shows that we have chosen to create an index on this field. Usually, applications will require rapid access to a table based upon primary key value, so this is a safe choice. We can drop this index later if we observe that it is not used frequently enough to warrant the storage space and maintenance costs it consumes. Figure 2-13 shows another menu screen where this index is defined in more detail. Here it is specified through the YES choice on the menu item "Display first duplicate key only" that no two Product records may have the same value for Product No. Given this statement, dBASE will not allow duplicate product numbers to be entered; not all index fields are unique, which is why this must be an option.

Figure 2-14 similarly shows the definition screen for the Customer table. Here, Customer No (CUST_NO in dBASE) is strictly numeric. We have also chosen to represent the Discount% in integer form, rather than to have the user enter a decimal point (calculations will simply divide by 100). Not shown here is that the Customer No index for this file was, as above, defined to be unique.

The definition of the Order entity table appears in Figure 2-15. (*Note:* the Order table is called CUORDER. The word ORDER is a key word in SQL for specifying that data are to be displayed in sorted sequence. Hence, the word cannot be used as a database file name.) As stated earlier, the

Figure 2-13
Product number
index organization

Figure 2-14
Customer table
definition

Figure 2-15
Order table definition

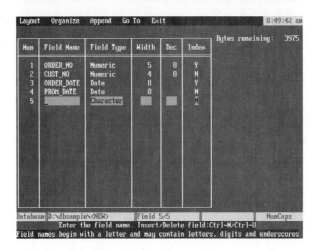

Customer No field has been included to provide the linkage between the
Order and Customer tables. Note that the same data element name (as well
as type, width, and so on) has been used here as was used in the Customer
table. Using the same data element name is not necessary, but it does make
it clear that the Order table is referring to the same field that is in the
Customer table. The two dates were assigned the date data type (dBASE
automatically filled in the length for these since this is a predefined format).
We have chosen to index this table on both the primary key, Order No
(which was defined as unique as done above) and Order Date (for which
we left the default as nonunique, which is appropriate). The second index
was chosen after analyzing the transaction and management information
processing. It was determined that this field is frequently used to qualify
which orders are to be retrieved.

Figure 2-16 shows the definition of the Invoice table. As in the other
cases, field lengths were chosen after a thorough analysis of the meaning

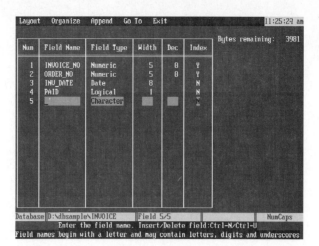

Figure 2-16
Invoice table
definition

of each data element. Specifically, in this case it was determined that a Paid field could take only one of two values—fully paid and not paid; so, a logical field type is sufficient. Since the field definition can be changed later, this is not permanently restrictive, in case Pine Valley's method of doing business changes.

It might be desirable to impose other integrity rules on the data. For example, the Invoice Date should not be earlier than the Order Date. dBASE does not have a facility to define this integrity rule with the table definition; rather, such rules can be included later when we define data entry screens for this file. Cross-reference key control is another restriction that would be desirable to specify here; that is, the Order No field in each row of the Invoice table should match some existing value in the Order table. Again, this so-called referential integrity cannot be placed with the table definition in dBASE, but it can be handled via data entry application programming. Some other relational systems support including such restrictions with the table definition. In this way, any user of the database, not just those using a particular screen definition or program, will have to abide by such rules. This would be a more desirable integrity feature.

Figures 2-17 and 2-18 show the definition of the tables for the Requested On and Shipped On relationships, the Request and Shipment tables, respectively. In each, the primary keys of the two related tables are included, along with the data element associated with the relationship, as shown in Figure 2-6. A rather subtle integrity rule that could be applied to the Shipment table is: The sum of the Ship_Qty for a given product across all the Shipment rows in all the Invoices associated with a particular order should not exceed the Order_Qty for that product on that order. As above, however, dBASE cannot handle this rule.

We will not take the space here to include security controls on this database definition, but when multiple individuals will use the database, such controls are desirable. We might want to limit update of the database to

Figure 2-17
Request table
definition

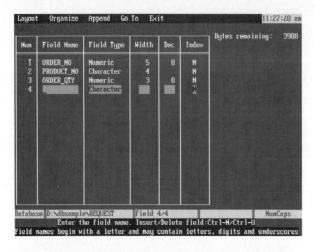

Figure 2-18
Shipment table
definition

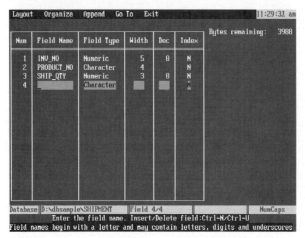

only authorized users (for example, only order entry clerks can update an order and only accounts receivables personnel can update invoices). Later chapters of the text will illustrate such security features, which would be implemented at this point in the database development.

PROCESSING TRANSACTIONS IN dBASE IV

You will recall that we identified four transactions for our example database: entry and maintenance of (1) product data, (2) customer data, (3) customer orders, and (4) invoices. All transactions will be processed on-line, so a major responsibility to implement this transaction processing is the design of screen displays that match the desired input format. Fortunately, dBASE provides a screen design and processing module in the Control Center as

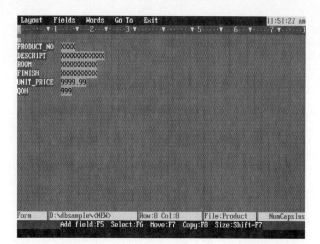

Figure 2-19
Default product form

well as other commands to handle the entry, editing, and display of data from stylized screen formats. In fact, dBASE provides a default screen display for each file that is defined in a database.

Product and Customer Transactions

Figure 2-19 is the default screen (or, in dBASE terms, a form) for the Product file. This form shows one record or row from the Product table on the screen at a time. Each field appears on a separate line and a default menu appears at the top for controlling data entry and display. This is obviously a rather plain format, and the computer field names, not user-meaningful prompts, are used for each field. Using the custom screen design editor, we can move the fields around and add headings and more meaningful field labels.

We will not outline the step-by-step process involved in using the forms designer to produce a more readable screen layout. Rather, only the final result showing the screen layout work surface appears in Figure 2-20. In this figure, a screen title has been added, each field has been labeled with a clear phrase, and a template indicating the valid format of each field has been included. Although the Product No field is a character field, its input template has been redefined for this screen as A999, meaning the first position is an alphabetic and the next three must be digits. A dollar sign was added in front of the Unit Price field to clarify the unit of measure. A fence character was added to make clear the length of the character fields (since dBASE will shade the screen space for data entry up to the length of the field, the fence is redundant, but it is used in case the user's screen cannot show shading for some reason).

Figures 2-21 through 2-23 show how some of these and other data editing and validation rules are defined for a form. In Figure 2-21 the PRODUCT_ NO field space on the form is changed to a new template. The

Figure 2-20
Final product form

Figure 2-21
Template for
PRODUCT_NO
field

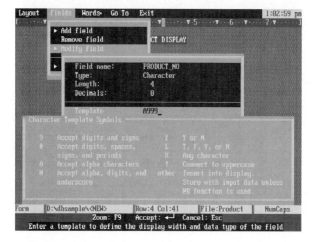

menu window shows the possible codes that can be used, and the A999 format is chosen since this represents the coding scheme for product numbers.

Figure 2-22 illustrates other editing criteria for the UNIT_PRICE field. For this field we have added a message to be displayed on a screen status line that gives a more descriptive explanation of the field; this will be shown when the user is on the Unit Price line. Further, the field has been defined to have 0 as its smallest allowed value, to restrict erroneous entry of a negative number. If a user tried (by mistake) to enter a negative quantity, dBASE would forbid this, generate a standard error message, and request a new value. Figure 2-23 illustrates editing for not only a minimum value for the QOH (Quantity on Hand) field but also use of a default value that will be automatically stored if the user fails to enter any value. Some database operations may be sensitive to missing data, so entry of a default may be both natural—a new product is likely to have zero on hand to begin with—and helpful for subsequent processing. Zero is not the only possible

Figure 2-22
Editing rules for
UNIT_PRICE
field

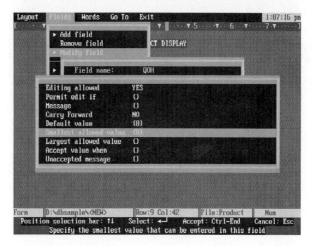

Figure 2-23
Editing rules for
QOH field

default in all circumstances, so care should be taken in selecting a default value. We will discuss the handling of missing data in Chapter 9.

A sample data entry screen using this form for the Product file appears in Figure 2-24. This same screen format can be used to enter new records, to update existing records, to delete records, and to display records, all one record at a time. Much more complex screen formats with multiple pages, automatic display of date and time, and other editing rules can be devised.

We decided to design the customer data entry transaction screen similarly. The resultant screen with sample data appears in Figure 2-25. In this screen, the cursor is currently sitting on the DISCOUNT field, for which a special display message was defined to appear on the bottom status line, as is shown. For the integrity of customer data, it is important to ensure valid entry of the price discount percentage field. This was accomplished by using the field editing screen in the form design module to limit this field to values between and including 0 and 15%. The editing window for

Figure 2-24
Sample product entry
transaction

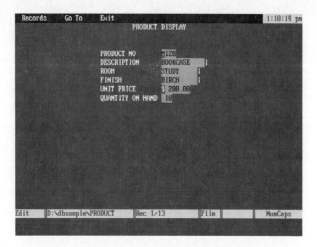

Figure 2-25
Sample customer
entry transaction

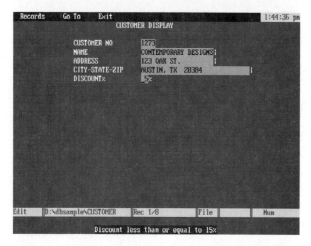

this rule, which also shows the status message for this field, is shown in Figure 2-26. Finally, Figure 2-27 illustrates what might happen if a user tried to enter an inadmissable value of 22%. dBASE generates a standard error message on the status line, indicating the proper range. Obviously, this value range editing capability is very helpful. It only works, however, for continuous ranges of values and not, for example, for a discrete list of possible character field codes.

Order and Invoice Transactions

The product and customer transactions were relatively straightforward to implement; each involved the maintenance of one record in only one file. The order and invoice transactions are, however, more complicated. Upon review of Figure 2-4, the customer order transaction, you will see that four

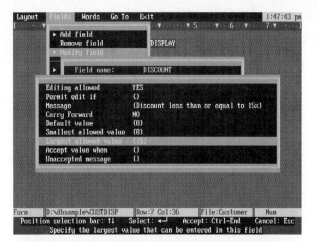

Figure 2-26
Editing rules for
DISCOUNT field

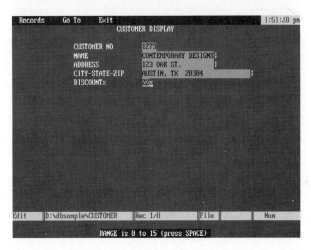

Figure 2-27
Sample entry of
invalid discount

of the dBASE files have to be accessed: Order, Customer, Product, and Request. Further, two of these, Order and Request, have to be changed when a new order is added or an order is changed. The dBASE forms subsystem permits only one file to be used per form, so we will not be able to use just one form for this transaction in a dBASE implementation.

We must also ensure the data integrity of each transaction. Suppose that during order entry or update the user decides to abort the transaction (or the computer system malfunctions). The application program must ensure that none of that transaction's data are stored in the database, even those that may have already been accepted and confirmed as accurate. All of these circumstances suggest a much more complex transaction processing approach than we have seen above.

Figure 2-28 outlines in a pseudolanguage a minimal sequence of steps needed to properly process an order transaction. This is truly minimal, and an experienced database programmer would suggest many other features,

Figure 2-28
Order transaction
processing

```
CLEAR SCREEN
BEGIN TRANSACTION
Accept Order No entry from keyboard
Do While Order No already exists
     Display duplicate order error message
     Accept Order No entry from keyboard
End While
CUST: Accept Customer No from keyboard
     Do While Customer does not exist
          Display Customer does not exist message
          Accept Customer No from keyboard
     End While
     Display Customer record for verification of correct customer
          record
     If incorrect customer, GOTO CUST:
     Accept Order Date and Promised Date
     Store Order record
     Do While more lines to add to order
PROD:     Accept Product No from keyboard
          Do While Product does not exist
               Display product does not exist message
               Accept Product No from keyboard
          End While
          Display Description and Unit Price for verification of
               correct Product record
          If incorrect product, GOTO PROD:
          Accept Quantity Ordered
          Store Request record
     End While
     END TRANSACTION
```

but we will stick with the basics here. The BEGIN TRANSACTION and END TRANSACTION commands are used to control transaction and database integrity. Suppose a fatal error occurs or the user aborts the transaction after a BEGIN TRANSACTION but before an END TRANSACTION command is executed. In this case, a ROLLBACK command can be given to restore the database to its contents just before the BEGIN TRANSACTION was executed. This ensures that the whole transaction or none of the transaction impacts the database.

The main logic of the process is as follows:

- First, the Order No is entered and the program verifies that an order with this Order No does not exist. The While loop keeps requesting an Order No until a new one is entered.

- Second, the Customer No for the order is entered and a While loop is used again to continue to request entry of a Customer No until one is entered for an existing customer record. Optionally, the procedure might allow the user to add a new customer record at this point, using the format presented earlier for this purpose.

- Third, the customer record for the entered Customer No is displayed and the user confirms that this is the customer who actually placed the order; if not, the Customer No entry sequence is restarted.

- Fourth, the remainder of the data for the Order record is entered and the Order record is stored (it is stored in a kind of suspense file until the END TRANSACTION makes the addition permanent).

- Fifth, each line item on the order is entered in turn. Within this part of the program, the Product No being ordered is entered and the While loop continues to prompt the user for an existing Product No. As with the customer cross reference, a visual verification for correct product is made by displaying the Description and Unit Price fields and looping back to the entry of a Product No if an incorrect Product No is entered. Then the order quantity is entered and the Request record is stored. This process repeats until all lines (Request records) for this order have been entered, then the END TRANSACTION commits the changes to the database and the full integrity of the transaction is guaranteed.

At this point in the text, the full programming of this transaction is beyond our scope. (The logic for the invoice transaction is very similar to that above, involving the data outlined in Figure 2-5.) Implementation would require that we use the proprietary dBASE programming language, a structured language, examples of which will be shown in Chapter 14. Thus, we will assume for now that the order and invoice transactions have been implemented and the associated data entered in the Order, Request, Invoice, and Shipment files.

This completes an explanation of the four transactions for our sample application. Our attention now turns to the management reporting requirements.

PROCESSING INFORMATION REQUESTS IN dBASE IV

In this section we use the SQL and report writer modules of dBASE IV to illustrate how a database and database management system can be used to meet the management information retrieval and analysis needs of Pine Valley Furniture. The dBASE SQL and report writer features are much like similar features in many personal computer database management systems. SQL also contains commands for transaction processing, but within dBASE, this would have meant that we could not control the input screen format; that is, the dBASE implementation of SQL does not support custom forms input.

We will see in this section that SQL is a concise language for data access. The output from an SQL command is in the form of a single table, where the columns are the requested data elements and the rows are composed from records that we select via qualification statements. When we want to customize the layout of reports (add subtotals and page numbers, change column headings, add titles, and so on), the dBASE report writer is useful.

Introduction to SQL

SQL, or Structured Query Language, is a language in which the programmer (or manager writing ad hoc queries) specifies which data she wants, not how to retrieve data record by record. SQL is a fourth-generation, nonprocedural language that was designed for database processing. There are many different commands in SQL to perform input, data retrieval, and modification, as well as other commands to control data accuracy and security, but the command used most frequently for information processing is SELECT.

The general structure of SELECT is

SELECT <list of desired data elements>
    FROM <list of tables or views in which data is stored>
        WHERE <qualification on what records to include>;

As we will see, other parts of the SELECT command can sort the result, group and subtotal data, and store the result in a temporary table to avoid cost of repeatedly recalculating the same intermediate results. At this point, since our goal is to illustrate a database application, we will use the following examples to illustrate this command.

Simple Queries in Pine Valley Furniture

Figure 2-7, the discount rate inquiry, presented earlier, is an example of a very simple management information requirement. For this request, the data elements requested are Name and Discount%, the single table involved is the Customer table, and only one record is needed, that identified by a specific Customer No. Thus, the SQL command for this inquiry would be

SELECT NAME, DISCOUNT
    FROM CUSTOMER
        WHERE CUST_NO = 1273;

NAME	DISCOUNT
CONTEMPORARY DESIGNS	5

To emphasize the power of such database access, imagine the programming necessary to produce this result in COBOL, BASIC, FORTRAN, or some other third-generation programming language with which you are familiar. Your program would have specified HOW to retrieve this data (which record to retrieve first, in what sequence to search for the desired record, and so on). Although it is certainly not natural English, the SQL style of language requires less special training and less technical understanding of computer data processing than do third-generation languages.

The daily order log of Figure 2-8 is a slightly more complex inquiry example for Pine Valley Furniture since this inquiry requires qualified data from two database tables, Customer and Order. In this case we will use SQL not only to specify what data we want but also to indicate on what basis to associate an Order with its Customer. At this point, we will not concern ourselves with the precise display format outlined in Figure 2-8a for this information request.

This request specifies three data elements for display: the Name from the Customer table and the Order No and Promised Date from the Order table. Thus, two tables, Customer and Order, must be referenced in the command. Qualification involves two parts: first, selecting orders placed on a certain Order Date, and second, specifying on what basis to match an order with a customer. The results are to be sorted by Name. Thus, the SQL command becomes

```
SELECT CUSTOMER.NAME, ORDER_NO, PROM_DATE
   FROM CUORDER, CUSTOMER
      WHERE ORDER_DATE = CTOD("11/10/90") AND
         CUORDER.CUST_NO = CUSTOMER.CUST_NO
         ORDER BY CUSTOMER.NAME;
```

Since the FROM clause involves two tables, it needs to be clear to the SQL language processor in which table to find each data element. SQL assumes the first table listed, and data from other tables need to be clarified by prefixing the field name with the table name (for example, CUS-TOMER.NAME). CTOD is a built-in function that translates a character date into the internal date format used to store date type fields so the date qualification can be processed. Thus, the first part of this WHERE clause specifies the day (Order Date) for which the daily order log is to be gen-erated. The second part of the WHERE clause specifies the means for asso-ciating the two tables in the query. This association is via the cross-reference provided by the CUST_NO fields that are in both tables. For each order, there is one customer number, so the cross-reference from the CUORDER table to the CUSTOMER table is unambiguous. The ORDER BY clause indi-cates the desired sequence for data. The result, for the sample data we have entered, is

CUSTOMER→NAME	CUORDER→ORDER_NO	CUORDER→PROM_DATE
ABC OFFICE SUPPLY	61397	11/20/90
COMMONWEALTH BUILDER	61398	11/12/90

Obviously, this format is somewhat awkward (cryptic column labels, lack of blank lines and spaces to make the result more readable, and so on), but the results were obtained rather directly by stating what data were desired and under what conditions.

The last of the simpler queries we will cover is the customer order history query of Figure 2-9. The E-R diagram of Figure 2-9b implies that this query will involve three tables: Customer, Order, and Product. However, you will recall from the database definitions discussed earlier that each Order record contains the CUST_NO as a cross-reference from Order to Customer. Thus, since it is only the Customer No that is needed for this query (because we only want to select orders for a given customer), the Customer file will not be needed. Similarly, since the Request file, which represents the Requested On relationship, has the relevant PRODUCT_NO in it, the Product file will not be needed. Thus, this query also involves only two tables, Order and Request.

We will illustrate two ways this query could be written. The first approach, as in the previous information processing examples, is to write a specific and complete query for the desired CUST_NO. So, for the example of Figure 2-9a, the query would be

SELECT ORDER_DATE, CUORDER.ORDER_NO,
    REQUEST.PRODUCT_NO,
    REQUEST.ORDER_QTY
  FROM CUORDER, REQUEST
    WHERE CUST_NO = 1273 AND
      ORDER_DATE BETWEEN CTOD("11/01/90") AND
        CTOD("11/30/90") AND
      CUORDER.ORDER_NO = REQUEST.ORDER_NO;

As before, each field name must be prefixed with the table name, unless the field comes from the first table listed. In this case, since ORDER_NO is in both tables, it must always have a table name prefix to clarify which ORDER_NO is to be used. The first part of the WHERE clause says that orders for only one particular customer are sought. The second part states the relevant date range, using the BETWEEN key word to define the smallest and largest values, and the third part specifies on what basis to relate rows from the two tables. The answer to this query, given the sample data in our database, would be:

CUORDER→ORDER_DATE	CUORDER→ORDER_NO	REQUEST→PRODUCT_NO	REQUEST→ORDER_QTY
11/04/90	61384	M128	4
11/04/90	61384	B381	2
11/04/90	61384	R210	1
11/06/90	61390	T100	2
11/06/90	61390	T160	1

The amount of query writing to produce this query result for any customer and for any date range can be reduced by use of a view. A **view** is a virtual, or imaginary, table. The other tables that we have defined so far are real, or so-called **base tables**. A view is constructed by forming a table from fields in one or more related base tables. Thus, the user can query or report data from a view without having to select and append the desired data each time the query or report is submitted. A view gives a current, but restricted, "window" into the database, that is, a view is not a temporary table that has to be rebuilt when changes are made to the original data. Because the contents of a view are derived (by the DBMS) as needed from base tables, a view is always up to date with the latest changes made in any of the base tables used to compose it.

For the customer order history query, as in Figure 2-9, a view table would contain not only the four fields displayed above but also the fields used for selecting which rows from the view to display; thus, the CUST_NO field would also be needed. All of these five fields are in either the Order or Request table. The appropriate view table would be defined by:

```
CREATE VIEW HISTORY AS
      SELECT CUST_NO, ORDER_DATE, CUORDER.ORDER_NO,
          REQUEST.PRODUCT_NO, REQUEST.ORDER_QTY
      FROM CUORDER, REQUEST
          WHERE CUORDER.ORDER_NO = REQUEST.ORDER_NO;
```

The customer order history query based upon this view then becomes:

```
SELECT ORDER_DATE, ORDER_NO, PRODUCT_NO, ORDER_QTY
      FROM HISTORY
          WHERE CUST_NO = 1273 AND
              ORDER_DATE BETWEEN CTOD("11/01/90") AND
              CTOD("11/20/90");
```

and the result would be, similar to the above:

ORDER_DATE	ORDER_NO	PRODUCT_NO	ORDER_QTY
11/04/90	61384	M128	4
11/04/90	61384	B381	2
11/04/90	61384	R210	1
11/06/90	61390	T100	2
11/06/90	61390	T160	1

This query based upon the history view is simpler than the original customer order history query for two reasons:

- Since all the data appear to come from one table, field names do not need prefixes.
- The more technical cross-reference fields are not needed in the WHERE clause.

Further, the view provides additional convenience and security, especially for those involved in end-user computing who are not programmers. For example, we could restrict end users from accessing base tables and give them access only to the views pertinent to their information rights and needs.

Report Writer Features for Database Processing

The customer order history query result above does not resemble the format of Figure 2-9a. To produce a report that is more readable and closer to the desired format, the dBASE report writer module can be used. The dBASE report writer helps the report designer to develop a stylized report like the screen painter (or forms) module we used earlier for transactions. A form lays out *one* row of a table on a screen. In contrast, a report includes *all* the rows of the table or view, with the appropriate summary figures, using as many pages as is necessary to print all the data.

One restriction of the report writer is, however, that all the data must be in one table or view. Thus, since the data for this report come from two tables (Request and Order), we must first construct a dBASE view (which is built differently than the SQL view we have just seen). Further, since a dBASE report prints *all* the data in a view, in the desired format with control breaks, headings, and so on, a separate view has to be developed for each time period and customer. That is, we cannot produce a dBASE report for qualified rows in a view. To illustrate the general features of a report writer, we have chosen to include all customers in the report, so the view will only limit Order and Request data to the desired Order Date range.

Whereas in SQL a view is defined as the result of a standard SQL query, a dBASE view created in the Control Center is defined via an approach called Query by Example, or QBE. QBE will be covered in more detail in Chapters 12 and 13, since it is now quite a common database query language available with many different relational database systems.

As with the forms module, we will not outline every step in the construction of a dBASE view. Figure 2-29 shows the view definition screen after the view has been composed. The two templates on the top of the screen show the layout of each of the base tables from which the view is derived. Only part of the CUORDER table is shown since not all the fields can fit on the screen at once. The bottom template lists the fields that have

Figure 2-29
dBASE view for
customer order
history query

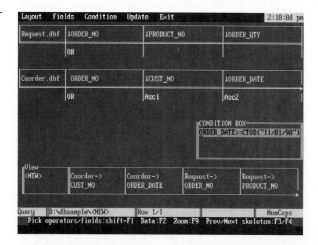

been placed into the view; again, one additional field, ORDER_QTY, does not fit on the screen.

The ORDER_NO fields in the two base tables are used to match rows from the tables—the example value 'OR' is included under each to show this linkage. Also, we decided that the view data should be sorted (in ascending sequence) first on CUST_NO and second on ORDER_DATE (as specified by the 'Asc' codes under these fields in the templates). Finally, the Condition Box includes a qualification on which rows of the CUORDER table to include in the view (that is, those for orders that fall within the desired date range). Figure 2-30 "zooms" in on this box to show its complete contents. Thus, the view table, HISTORY, contains all the fields we need for the report and just those rows for orders during the desired period.

dBASE can generate a standard default report format for a table or view; this default format for the HISTORY view appears in Figure 2-31. Each report format is arranged into *bands*. The **page header band** specifies what

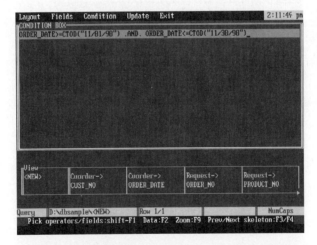

Figure 2-30
Condition box for customer order history view

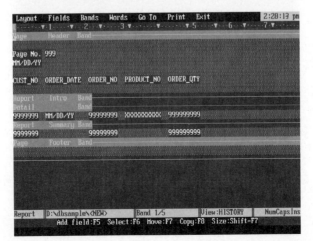

Figure 2-31
Default customer order history report format

is to appear on the top of each page. The **report intro band** lays out text that usually describes and provides an explanation of the contents of the report. The **detail band** represents the fields that will be printed for each row in the view. The **summary band** specifies the fields for which subtotals, averages, counts, or other summary data are to appear at the end of the report. The **page footer band** specifies text or data that are to appear at the bottom of each printed page. Each field is identified by a template format just as we saw with forms.

Figure 2-32 shows the final report layout we have designed for this application, which includes more descriptive column headings, and only the necessary fields appear in the detail band. Further, since rows in the detail band are grouped by customer, we have created a **group intro band**, with associated **group summary band.** This will help us to highlight each

Figure 2-32
Final customer order history report format

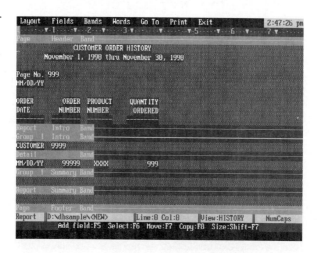

Figure 2-33
Suppress repeated values menu window

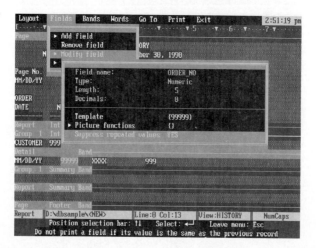

time the customer changes on the report; we have pulled the CUST_NO out onto a separate line in the group intro band. Since we are not interested in any group subtotals, and so on, the group summary band is empty.

One final feature of this report format that we decided to include was to suppress the printing of the ORDER_DATE and ORDER_NO fields since they repeat for the different products on an order. This is specified through the Modify Field menu and the Suppress repeated values option. The window menu on which this is specified for the ORDER_NO field appears in Figure 2-33. The final report for all customers with orders during November, 1990 appears in Figure 2-34.

```
                    CUSTOMER ORDER HISTORY
         November 1, 1990 thru November 30,1990

    Page No.    1
    12/15/90

    ORDER                ORDER      PRODUCT     QUANTITY
    DATE                 NUMBER     NUMBER      ORDERED
    CUSTOMER    1069
    11/10/90             61397      0800           2
                                    0625           3
    11/22/90             61396      0100           2

    CUSTOMER    1256
    11/10/90             91398      0100          10
                                    M128          10
    11/11/90             61399      M128          20

    CUSTOMER    1273
    11/04/90             61384      M128           4
                                    R210           1
                                    B381           2
    11/06/90             61390      T160           1
                                    T100           2

    CUSTOMER    2345
    11/20/90             61395      B975           3
                                    B985           4
                                    B381           6

    CUSTOMER    3434
    11/02/90             61401      E350           4
    11/24/90             61402      E125          12
```

Figure 2-34
Customer order history report

More Complex Queries in Pine Valley Furniture

The large customer query of Figure 2-10, as depicted in part (b) of this figure, requires more complex data associations than any of the queries we have illustrated so far. As in the previous example, the Product table is not really needed since the Request table also contains the Product No. for cross-reference purposes (the only Product data included in the query). The Placed By relationship in Figure 2-10b is represented by a cross-reference key of CUST_NO stored in the Order table, but the Customer table is still needed to retrieve the Name.

This is another situation where a view would be very helpful in simplifying the query, but we will use a different approach for this query to illustrate additional capabilities of a database application. In this case we will assume that when a product line manager needs this query he will usually enter a series of such queries, each for different products or date ranges. Thus, to save computational time for these queries, instead of a view table we will create a temporary intermediate real table. This will be more efficient since a view must be physically reconstructed for each query that references it, whereas we will build the temporary table once (per session or series of queries).

The dBASE SQL implementation, as do many others, supports an additional optional clause to specify that, instead of being displayed, the results of a query are to be stored in a table that is automatically defined and created by the query result. We will follow a similar logic as with the view above. That is, the temporary table will be used to append together the fields from several tables that are in the output of this general query, plus those fields needed for the WHERE clause. Thus, for this query (see Figure 2-10), the fields CUST_NO (from either the Customer or Order table), NAME from the Customer table, ORDER_DATE from Order, and PRODUCT_NO and ORDER_QTY from Request are the fields that would appear. Actually, the ORDER_QTY field is used to derive the data that appears in the SELECT and WHERE clauses of the query.

Thus, the query to create the temporary table from which we can produce several large customer queries for different products and different date ranges is:

```
SELECT CUSTOMER.CUST_NO, NAME, CUORDER.ORDER_DATE,
    REQUEST.PRODUCT_NO, REQUEST.ORDER_QTY
        FROM CUSTOMER, CUORDER, REQUEST
            WHERE REQUEST.ORDER_NO = CUORDER.ORDER_NO AND
                CUORDER.CUST_NO = CUSTOMER.CUST_NO
                    SAVE TO TEMP DETAIL (CUST_NO,NAME,
                        ORDER_DATE, PRODUCT_NO, ORDER_QTY);
```

In this query, the fields are the ones needed for display and qualification of any large customer query. The WHERE clause contains the field match specifications for relating a Request record with an Order record, and then an Order record with a Customer record. The SAVE TO TEMP clause provides the column names for the temporary table, called DETAIL, that is created. The contents of the table Detail for our sample application and data appear in Figure 2-35.

The particular query of Figure 2-10 for Product No M128 and the period from November 1, 1990 through December 31, 1990, which is derived from the Detail temporary table, then is:

```
SELECT CUST_NO, NAME, SUM(ORDER_QTY)
        FROM DETAIL
            WHERE PRODUCT_NO = "M128" AND
                ORDER_DATE BETWEEN CTOD("11/01/90") AND
                            CTOD("12/31/90")
            GROUP BY CUST_NO, NAME
            ORDER BY 3;
```

This query introduces several additional SQL clauses and typical requirements for database processing: creating subtotaled data for groups of data and sorting data by ascending or descending value. In this case, a product line manager wants total sales volume by customer; SQL requires grouping by all fields that are not to be subtotaled (so both CUST_NO and NAME

Figure 2-35
Sample detail table

CUST_NO	NAME	ORDER_DATE	PRODUCT_NO	ORDER_QTY
1273	CONTEMPORARY DESIGNS	11/04/90	M128	4
1273	CONTEMPORARY DESIGNS	11/04/90	B381	2
1273	CONTEMPORARY DESIGNS	11/04/90	R210	1
1273	CONTEMPORARY DESIGNS	11/06/90	T100	2
1273	CONTEMPORARY DESIGNS	11/06/90	T160	1
1273	CONTEMPORARY DESIGNS	12/01/90	B975	5
1273	CONTEMPORARY DESIGNS	12/01/90	B985	5
1273	CONTEMPORARY DESIGNS	12/01/90	M128	10
1278	FURNITURE WAREHOUSE	10/10/90	M128	30
1278	FURNITURE WAREHOUSE	10/10/90	O100	3
1278	FURNITURE WAREHOUSE	10/10/90	T160	3
1278	FURNITURE WAREHOUSE	01/03/90	E350	6
2345	FRED'S FURNITURE	11/20/90	B975	3
2345	FRED'S FURNITURE	11/20/90	B985	4
2345	FRED'S FURNITURE	11/20/90	B381	6
1069	ABC OFFICE SUPPLY	11/22/90	O100	2
1069	ABC OFFICE SUPPLY	11/10/90	O625	3
1069	ABC OFFICE SUPPLY	11/10/90	O800	2
1256	COMMONWEALTH BUILDERS	11/10/90	M128	10
1256	COMMONWEALTH BUILDERS	11/10/90	O100	10
1256	COMMONWEALTH BUILDERS	11/11/90	M128	20
3211	L. L. FISH	12/01/90	E125	3
3211	L. L. FISH	12/01/90	E177	8
3211	L. L. FISH	12/01/90	E350	2
3434	KENNEBUNKPORT TRADER	11/02/90	E350	4
3434	KENNEBUNKPORT TRADER	11/24/90	E125	12
3434	KENNEBUNKPORT TRADER	12/15/90	E177	20
3434	KENNEBUNKPORT TRADER	12/15/90	E125	24

are listed, although this is redundant). To pick quickly the largest volume customer, the resultant subtotals are sorted by the subtotal column, the third column in the result (so ORDER BY 3, meaning column three). The result of this query for our sample Detail file would be

CUST_NO	NAME	SUM1
1273	CONTEMPORARY DESIGNS	14
1256	COMMONWEALTH BUILDER	30

Thus, the answer to the query is in the last row and is as displayed in Figure 2-10a.

The backlog summary report of Figure 2-11 presents an even more complex computational problem in handling data. In this case, the Backlog Quantity column is not only group level data but is also the difference between two group level sums, the total Quantity Ordered and the total Quantity Shipped by Product No. There are many ways this report could be generated; we will illustrate one rather straightforward, multiple-step approach. Although one very complex query could be written, it is often easier to break a query into more easily understood pieces, ones that the DBMS is less likely to misinterpret.

The sequence we will follow will be to build two intermediate temporary tables that contain the Product No and group sum by Product No of the quantity ordered and quantity shipped so far, respectively. The first table, for total ordered, is derived from the Product and Request tables; the second table, for total shipped, is derived from the Product and Shipment tables. You might wonder why the Product table is needed here, since Product No is in the Request and Shipment tables, which would be sufficient for computing the group totals. The reason is that if the generation of the temporary tables did not include the Product table, products that had never been ordered or shipped would not be placed in the temporary tables, thus causing interesting data to be missing in the result. This is a subtle trait of many query situations that always needs to be considered when formulating a query.

Thus, the SQL command to generate the total ordered temporary table would be:

```
SELECT PRODUCT.PRODUCT_NO, SUM(REQUEST.ORDER_QTY)
    FROM PRODUCT, REQUEST
        WHERE PRODUCT.PRODUCT_NO = REQUEST.PRODUCT_NO
            GROUP BY PRODUCT.PRODUCT_NO
                SAVE TO TEMP TOTALO (PRODUCT_NO, SUMORDERS);
```

and the contents of this table for our sample database would be:

```
SELECT * FROM TOTALO;
```

PRODUCT_NO	SUMORDERS
B381	8.00
B975	8.00

B985	9.00
E125	39.00
E177	28.00
E350	12.00
M128	74.00
O100	15.00
O625	3.00
O800	2.00
R210	1.00
T100	2.00
T160	4.00

The SQL command for the total shipped table would be:

SELECT PRODUCT.PRODUCT_NO, SUM(SHIPMENT.SHIP_QTY)
    FROM PRODUCT, SHIPMENT
        WHERE PRODUCT.PRODUCT_NO = SHIPMENT.PRODUCT_NO
        GROUP BY PRODUCT.PRODUCT_NO
            SAVE TO TEMP TOTALS (PRODUCT_NO, SUMSHIPS);

with the following results:

SELECT * FROM TOTALS;

PRODUCT_NO	SUMSHIPS
B381	8.00
B975	8.00
B985	9.00
E125	9.00
E177	6.00
E350	6.00
M128	72.00
O100	10.00
O625	3.00
O800	2.00
R210	1.00
T100	2.00
T160	4.00

The final answer to the query then is rather simply computed as the difference in matching rows in these tables, as:

SELECT TOTALO.PRODUCT_NO, TOTALO.SUMORDERS_TOTALS.SUMSHIPS
    FROM TOTALO, TOTALS
        WHERE TOTALO.PRODUCT_NO = TOTALS.PRODUCT_NO
        ORDER BY 1;

TOTALO→PRODUCT_NO	EXP1
B381	0.00
B975	0.00
B985	0.00
E125	30.00
E177	22.00
E350	6.00
M128	2.00
O100	5.00
O625	0.00
O800	0.00
R210	0.00
T100	0.00
T160	0.00

SUMMARY

This chapter has illustrated the development of a database application. You will be able to develop even more complex applications using a variety of database systems after completing a course using this text. You can see from this example that the development of a database application is a multiple-step process with considerable discretion on the design of the database, data entry screens, and reports. The many choices possible at each step allow considerable customization but also require careful consideration to avoid poor choices (for both computer system performance as well as human ease of use).

Chapter 3 begins the discussion of the concepts and tools needed to organize organizational data for computer efficiency and understandable use of the organizational data resource. This chapter introduced many of these concepts and tools through the example application. By now you should have a general understanding of data entities, elements, relationships, a database, an application, a transaction, integrity constraints, query, report, and database programming. We also briefly introduced (through the order transaction processing illustration) the control of concurrent access to data and the recovery of a contaminated or destroyed database. All of these topics will be considered more fully later in the text.

This chapter also introduced one particular type of database management system, relational, which is today the most popular style for developing new database applications. Although dBASE IV, the specific program product we used, is very popular, it does not provide all the features we might like. In fact, no one package is superior to all others in every respect.

But this early application and illustration of some of the features of dBASE can make you more alert for comparative advantages and disadvantages as you see other systems demonstrated in class or illustrated in this text.

Chapter Review

REVIEW QUESTIONS

1. Define each of the following terms:
   a. database
   b. database application
   c. database management system
   d. business transaction
   e. database transaction
   f. enterprise data model
   g. report writer
   h. entity
   i. relationship
   j. data integrity
   k. many-to-many relationship
   l. SQL

2. Contrast each of the following terms:
   a. table; file
   b. database; file
   c. file; index
   d. primary key; index
   e. form; report
   f. base table; view
   g. view; temporary table

3. What purpose do the commands START TRANSACTION and END TRANSACTION achieve in a database program?

4. What are the four major steps in the development of a database application?

5. What is the purpose of data normalization?

6. What characteristics of data and a database are defined when a database is created in dBASE IV?

PROBLEMS AND EXERCISES

1. In this chapter we illustrated one method for handling missing data during data entry, using a default value. What other methods can you think of and why would you want to use each method?

2. What purpose does a field template serve in defining a data entry form/screen?

3. The claim was made in this chapter that although controlling data integrity during data entry via edit and range rules stored with a form is helpful, this is not the most desirable place to store these rules. What would be a better place to store the data editing rules, and why?

4. Using the same type of pseudoprogramming as in Figure 2-28, write the logic for processing the invoice entry transaction of Figure 2-5.

5. Why were so many of the queries for the sample application of this chapter written in the SQL language? Why was this the best instructional choice, as opposed to using the proprietary dBASE language, in which we could have done everything?

6. Write an SQL query to display the complete contents of the PRODUCT table.

7. Write an SQL query to display the Promised Date for each Request involving Product B975.

8. Construct a view in SQL that would allow the question of Problem 7 to be answered for any Product No.

REFERENCES

Ashton-Tate Corporation. 1988. *Using the Menu System, Advanced Topics,* and *dBASE IV Language Reference*. Torrance, Calif.: Ashton-Tate.

Chen and Associates. 1988. *E-R Designer Reference Manual*. Baton Rouge, La.

Krumm, R. 1990. *The Student Edition of dBASE IV, Programmer's Version*. Reading, Mass.: Addison-Wesley.

Senn, J. A. 1990. *The Student Edition of dBASE IV*. Reading, Mass.: Addison-Wesley.

CHAPTER 3

Data Concepts and Modeling

INTRODUCTION

Organizations maintain many different databases, such as the one depicted in Chapter 2. Frequently, we are not exactly sure of the meaning of data in such a database or of the information produced from it. This uncertainty may be because we were not the source for those data or we did not develop the database. What we need are basic concepts and notations that will allow systems professionals and managers alike to unambiguously and accurately communicate their understanding of this vast quantity of organizational data. We need ways to explain the growing organizational data resource.

In this chapter, we describe the nature of data and develop many of the basic concepts and structures used in describing databases. These notations and techniques are necessary in the process of planning and designing databases, which will be the topics of the next few chapters. We emphasize here the understanding of data, not their representation in computer systems. Such understanding must precede the building of database systems. We also describe the views of data required by their various users and lay the foundation for an important concept in data management: data independence.

NATURE OF DATA

In this section, we provide the basic definitions of data. As shown in Figure 3-1, three realms, or levels of abstraction, must be considered in describing data: reality (the real world), metadata (information about data), and the actual data.

Figure 3-1
Three realms used to describe data

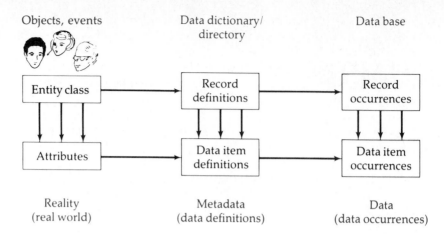

Reality

Reality consists of the organization itself, the various parts of the organization, and the environment in which the organization operates. Any organization is a collection of people, facilities, and artifacts (or objects) that are organized to satisfy certain goals. Each organization interacts with its environment and both influences and is influenced by that environment.

Figure 3-2 depicts the relationship between various data terms about reality that are introduced in this section. An **entity** is an individual object (a person, place, or thing), concept, or event about which the organization chooses to collect and store data. An entity may be a specific tangible object, such as a particular employee, product, computer, or customer, or an entity

Figure 3-2
Reality data terminology

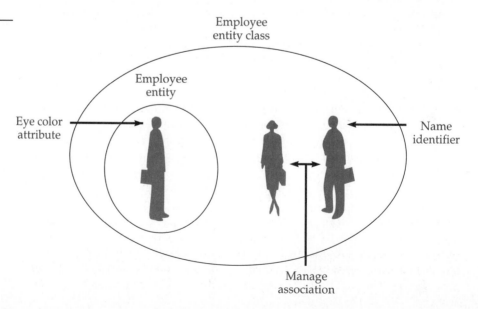

may be an intangible concept or event, such as a particular bank account, cost center, part failure event, airline flight, or the sale of goods to a customer. Frequently, especially in the case of an event, a business document exists that is an abstraction of the event. Examples of entities at Pine Valley Furniture Company include customer, product, customer sales order, work center, and employee.

An **entity class** is a collection of entities that have similar characteristics, such as Customers, Students, and Patients. Entity classes are sometimes called entity sets or entity types.

In general, each entity is assigned to one, and only one, entity class. However, the definition of a specific entity class, as well as the assignment of an entity to an entity class, may be somewhat arbitrary. For example, consider the Employee entity class. Does this consist of persons who are full-time employees only, or does it also include part-time employees? And what entities constitute the entity class Work Center: individual machines, machine groups, or entire departments? Questions such as these must be resolved before accurate models of organizational data can be developed. Further, precise notations are needed to represent such subtleties clearly so that everyone can have a common understanding.

The number of entity classes for an organization depends on the size and complexity of that organization. For example, a medium-sized corporation typically has several hundred entity classes, whereas a small company such as Pine Valley Furniture would probably have less than a hundred.

For each entity class, there are many characteristics or attributes of interest to an organization. An **attribute** is a property of an entity that we choose to record. For example, two entity classes at Pine Valley Furniture Company are Customers and Products. Here are some of the possible attributes for these entities:

Customers	Products
customer number	product number
name	description
address	finish
telephone number	price
credit limit	weight
balance	quantity on hand

An organization with several hundred entity classes may have several thousand attributes.

Each entity in an entity class must have at least one attribute (or several in combination) that distinguishes it from other entities in that class. This unique property of an entity is called an **identifier.** For example, a Social Security number is an identifier for an employee, and a product number is an identifier for a product. In some situations, the identifier will be a combination of two or more attributes—for example, invoice number and product number.

An entity identifier is said to *functionally determine* other attributes about that entity. For example, once we know in which employee we are interested, by stating her Social Security number, then we unambiguously know which current age, gender, and last name are affiliated with that employee.

Attributes are properties of individual entities. Another essential type of property is the **association,** which is a relationship between two (or more) entities. Associations may exist between entities of the same entity class or between entities from two (or more) entity classes. Here is an example of each type of association at Pine Valley Furniture:

1. In the Employee entity class, some employees are managers while the remainder are workers. An association called Manages allows us to determine the workers reporting to a given manager (or the manager of a given worker).

2. There is an entity class called Customers and another called Orders. By defining an association called Open Orders between entities from these two entity classes, we can determine all outstanding orders for a given customer.

The direct representation of associations between entities is one of the main features that distinguishes the database approach from conventional file applications, as was discussed in Chapter 1.

It is usually impractical for a manager (or other employee) to decide or act based on direct observation of entities. Imagine a manager having to walk to a warehouse to count the items in a bin whenever an inventory action is required, or having to call a customer to obtain the shipping address before dispatching each shipment. Instead of direct observation, the organization relies on a *model* of the entities that describes their properties. This brings us to the second realm of data: metadata. Table 3-1 summarizes many of the terms introduced in this section along with their equivalent terms from the metadata and data levels, which will be detailed in the following two sections.

Metadata

Metadata are information about the data in an organization. Database administrators and others use metadata to develop logical models of an organization's entities and the associations between those entities. Metadata are stored and maintained in the organization's data dictionary/directory or repository (which was introduced in Chapter 1) or are stored with actual data to make those data more accessible.

Corresponding to each entity class in the real world, there is normally one record type defined in the metadata realm. Also, corresponding to each attribute, there is a data item type defined in the metadata realm (see Figure 3-1).

Table 3-1   Approximate Equivalence of Terminology in the Three
Realms of Data

Reality	Metadata	Data
Entity class	Record type	File
Entity	Record	Record occurrence
Attribute	Data item	Field
Identifier	Primary key	N/A
Association	Association or relationship	N/A

A **data item** is a unit fact. It is the smallest named unit of data in a database and therefore the smallest unit of data that has meaning to a user. Examples of data items are Employee-Name, Student#, and Order-Date (recall that we often use # as an abbreviation for number).

Various information needed to clearly describe each data item is normally cataloged in the data repository. This information includes the data item name, alias names (synonyms) used in different parts of the organization, length, type (or representation), a brief narrative description, range of valid values, display format, and source.

Data items are sometimes called data elements, fields, or attributes, but we prefer to use the term *data item* when referring to a unit of data. *Field* is a physical rather than logical (that is, abstract) term that refers to the column positions within a record where a data item is located. We have already defined *attribute* as a property of a real-world entity rather than as a data-oriented term; however, attribute, data item, and data element are often used interchangeably.

A **data aggregate** is a collection of data items that is named and referenced together. For example, a data aggregate called Name might include the data items Last-Name, First-Name, and Middle-Initial. Also, a data aggregate called Sales might consist of four data items: Sales-First-Quarter, Sales-Second-Quarter, Sales-Third-Quarter, and Sales-Fourth-Quarter. Data aggregates must be defined in the data repository. Metadata that are recorded for each data aggregate type include the data aggregate name, description, and names of the included data items. In COBOL, data aggregates are referred to as group items.

A **record** is a named collection of data items and/or data aggregates. Most organizations define one record *type* for each entity class. Thus, if there is an entity class called Sales Order, we might choose to define a record type called SALES-ORDER-RECORD. Metadata defining each record type are also cataloged in the data repository. These metadata include the record name, description, size (or length), component data items and aggregates, and identification of primary and secondary keys (which will be described shortly).

In addition to describing entities, some records describe associations (relationships) between entities. Often this type of record (called an **intersection record**) arises when some event has occurred involving the associated entities.

A **key** is a data item used to select one or more records. There are two basic types: primary keys and secondary keys.

A **primary key** is a data item that uniquely identifies a record. The primary key of a record corresponds to the identifier of a real-world entity. For example, Product# would normally be the primary key for PRODUCT records. As with identifiers, there may be several possible (or candidate) primary keys for the same record. Also, two or more data items may be required in combination to identify a record. Most data systems do not permit a primary key field to have a missing value.

A **secondary key** is a data item that normally does not uniquely identify a record but identifies several records that share the same property. For example, the data item Finish might be a secondary key for PRODUCT records to distinguish the subset of products that are maple from those that are oak, and so on. Secondary keys are useful when data are referenced and managed by groups, such as all the customers in the same zip code or all the orders to be shipped today.

Data

The third (and last) realm in Figure 3-1 consists of data **occurrences.** For each entity in the real world, there is normally a record occurrence that contains data item values describing that entity. For example, at Pine Valley Furniture, there are 50 employees in the Employee entity class—thus, there are 50 EMPLOYEE record occurrences in the database. However, there is only one definition of this record type in the metadata.

A **file** is a named collection of all occurrences of a given record type. For example, the EMPLOYEE file at Pine Valley Furniture Company consists of 50 EMPLOYEE records.

Notice the important distinction between metadata (data definitions) and data (data occurrences). Metadata (such as data item definitions) are not stored in the database. Conversely, occurrences of user data are not stored in the data repository. Both metadata and data must be managed; this is why many modern data management systems permit a user to query the data repository with the same language used for database processing.

We may visualize a file as a two-dimensional array, called a **flat file.** An example of a flat file arrangement of data is shown in Figure 3-3. The table, or two-dimensional array, shown in this figure contains sample data from the Product entity class in Pine Valley Furniture Company. Each column of the table contains values for a particular data item. The data item names at the top of the table correspond to product attributes. Each row of the table represents a record occurrence and corresponds to one product entity. Notice

Data items

Figure 3-3
Flat file
representation of data
(Pine Valley
Furniture)

PRODUCT#	DESCRIPTION	FINISH	ROOM	PRICE
0100	TABLE	OAK	DR	500
0350	TABLE	MAPLE	DR	625
0625	CHAIR	OAK	DR	100
0975	WALL UNIT	PINE	FR	750
1000	DRESSER	CHERRY	BR	800
1250	CHAIR	MAPLE	LR	400
1425	BOOKCASE	PINE	LR	250
1600	STAND	BIRCH	BR	200
1775	DRESSER	PINE	BR	500
2000	WALL UNIT	OAK	LR	1200

Data item names → (at left)

Records (at left)

Primary key — Secondary keys

there is only one value at the intersection of each row and column, which is an important property of flat files.

The primary key for the records in the PRODUCT file is PRODUCT#. A particular value of PRODUCT# (such as 1250) uniquely identifies a record occurrence. The data items DESCRIPTION, FINISH, and ROOM have been designated as secondary keys. A particular value for one of these keys designates a subset of records (rather than a particular record). It is conceivable that managers in Pine Valley Furniture may want to retrieve data based upon qualifications on these data items. For example, the description "wall unit" identifies two records (product numbers 0975 and 2000).

To complete the description of the three realms in Figure 3-1, we may simply define a **database** as a named collection of interrelated files. Thus, a database contains data occurrences that describe one or more entity classes *and* the associations between those entity classes. We will elaborate and refine this definition later in the text after more concepts are developed.

ASSOCIATIONS BETWEEN DATA ITEMS

A key element of all the notations presented later in this chapter for modeling data is the ability to describe three basic components of organizational data: data elements, data entities, and the associations between them. Thus, before formally presenting data models, this and the next section review the basics of representing these three basic components. In this section, we show simple graphical techniques for representing data items and the associations between them. Our goal here is to begin to build notation that will allow us to describe unambiguously organizational data. Then in the following section we will expand this notation to be able to show associations *between* entities and records, and we will illustrate a variety of ways to represent such relationships. In this section, each type of data item is represented by an ellipse (or "bubble") with the data item name enclosed, as follows:

Similar to the definition earlier for association between entities, an association between data items is a logical, meaningful connection. An association implies that values for the associated data items are in some way dependent on each other. This dependency is not mathematical (that is, we cannot somehow calculate the Customer-Address from the Customer#). Rather, a value for Customer # allows us to distinguish what value for Customer-Address to associate with it.

A database contains hundreds (or even thousands) of data items, and there are many possible associations among these. Fortunately, many of these are meaningless and of no interest to the organization. For example, there probably is no meaningful association between the following two data items:

However, there is an important association between these two data items:

The association exists because each employee has an address. We will represent data item associations by arrows connecting the data item bubbles, as in this illustration.

Types of Associations

Suppose that we have two data items, A and B. From data item A to data item B there are two possible associations, or mappings: a one-association and a many-association. We will represent these two possible associations with the following notation:

One-association

Many-association

A **one-association** from data item A to data item B means that at any point in time, *a given value* of A has one and only one value of B associated with it: That is, if we know the value of A, then the value of B is implicitly known. This is what we referred to earlier as one data item functionally determining another data item. We represent a one-association with a single-headed arrow. Assuming that at a given point of time each employee has exactly one address, the following mapping, discussed above, is a one-association:

Note the importance of time in understanding these data. Clearly, employees can move, so an employee may have a history of several addresses. However, this diagram states that only one address is needed, which might be the current one, the one to which we sent the last W-4 tax statement, or some other one specific address. We will discuss in depth later in this chapter the role of time in modeling organizational data.

A **many-association** from data item A to data item B means that at any point in time, a given value of A has one or many values of B associated with it. We represent a many-mapping with a double-headed arrow. Assuming that for a specified period of time each employee may be taking one or more than one training course, the following mapping is a many-association:

In this example, Course # is called a **multivalued attribute** since it occurs potentially multiple times for each Employee #.

There is an important extension to the associations between data items outlined above, called a **conditional association.** With this, for a given value of data item A there are two possibilities: Either there is no value of data item B or there is one (or many, in the case of a many-association) value(s) of data item B. We diagram a conditional association with a zero recorded on the arrow near the conditional item:

Here is an example of a conditional association in a hospital environment:

That is, each hospital bed either will be assigned to one patient or, at some instant in time, may be unassigned.

The term used by data analysts that is represented by the arrow heads and zeros on the arrows is *cardinality*: That is, a one-association and a many-association are statements of cardinality. To incorporate conditional associations, cardinality can be thought of as having minimum and maximum values. For example, for the association from Bed # to Patient # above, the minimum value is 0 and the maximum value is 1. For the Employee # to Course # association, the minimum was 0 and the maximum was N, where N stands for any positive integer.

Reverse Associations

If there is an association from data item A to data item B, there is also a reverse association from B to A. This leads to three possible associations between data items: one-to-one, one-to-many, and many-to-many, with conditionalities possible in either direction. Figure 3-4 shows the notation used for these three types of associations and a conceptual diagram of the differences among them.

A **one-to-one association** means that for any point in time, each value of data item A is associated with zero (if so specified) or exactly one value

Figure 3-4
Data associations:
(a) association
    notation
(b) conceptual
    diagrams of
    associations

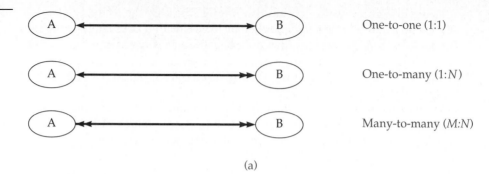

(a)

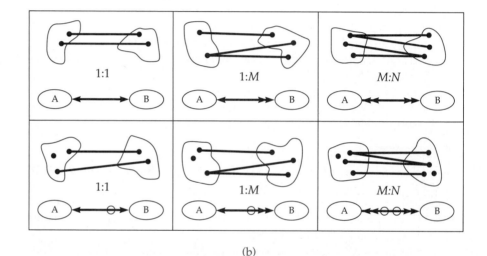

(b)

of data item B. Conversely, each value of B is associated with one value of A.

A **one-to-many association** means that for any point in time, each value of data item A is associated with zero (if so specified), one, or many values of data item B. However, each value of B is associated with exactly one value of A. The mapping from B to A is said to be many-to-one, since there may be many values of B associated with one value of A.

A **many-to-many association** means that for any point in time, each value of data item A is associated with zero (if so specified), one, or many values of data item B. Also, each value of B is associated with zero, one, or many values of A.

Examples of these three associations are shown in Figure 3-5. If we assume that no two students have the same name, then the association between Student# and Student-Name is 1:1 (in reality, duplicate student names are possible). The association between Student# and Medical-Exam# is a conditional 1:N (each student may take zero or several medical exams, but each exam pertains to a particular student). Finally, the association

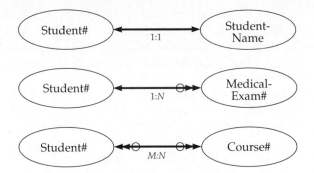

Figure 3-5
Examples of
associations between
data items

between Student # and Course # is *M:N*, with conditionality in both directions (each student registers in zero or many courses, and each course has
zero or many students registered).

In modeling an organization's data, we are not always interested in a
given reverse association. If a particular reverse association is not of interest, the arrowheads are simply omitted in the link from data item B to data
item A.

Importance of Associations

You may wonder why we are so careful in defining data and the associations
between data items. The reason is that data are a corporate asset. We must
represent data associations accurately in order to control data, yet allow a
database to evolve over time. According to Percy (1986):

> The data a company owns differentiates it from its competitors. What uniquely
> defines data entities, what information can be determined by individual occur-
> rences of those entities, and what rules are associated with attributes and rela-
> tionships, are largely what makes an enterprise unique and what drives its
> idiosyncratic success.

The association between two data items is defined for a given instant of
time or for a specified period of time. For example, in defining the association between Bed and Patient as 1:1, we are clearly referring to the *current*
occupant. If the patient's history is kept, then we must either change this
relationship or else define an additional relationship representing the relationship between Bed and Patient over time.

Bubble Charts

The notation we have introduced for representing data items and associations can be used to develop complex data models. We will use the term
bubble charts to refer to such data models. Bubble charts are useful for
grouping data items into records and for deriving more complex data models.

For example, consider the PRODUCT record type for Pine Valley Furniture Company (see Figure 3-3). A bubble chart showing the structure of this record appears in Figure 3-6. The data item PRODUCT# is underlined to show that it is the primary key for this record type. Note that reverse associations have been ignored for now.

We represent record types by rectangles containing the names of the data items included in the record. A representation of the PRODUCT record type is shown in Figure 3-7a, while Figure 3-7b shows one occurrence of this record type.

Bubble charts also provide insight into the nature of secondary keys. Assume that a secondary key does not uniquely identify a record (this is

Figure 3-6
Bubble chart of
PRODCT record type
(Pine Valley
Furniture)

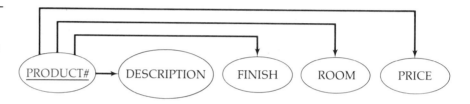

Figure 3-7
Representing record
types and
occurrences (Pine
Valley Furniture):
(a) PRODUCT record
     type
(b) PRODUCT record
     occurrence

PRODUCT#	DESCRIPTION	FINISH	ROOM	PRICE

(a)

0975	WALL UNIT	PINE	FR	750

(b)

Figure 3-8
Representing
secondary keys (Pine
Valley Furniture):
(a) bubble chart with
     secondary key
     (FINISH)
(b) occurrences for a
     particular
     secondary key
     value (OAK)

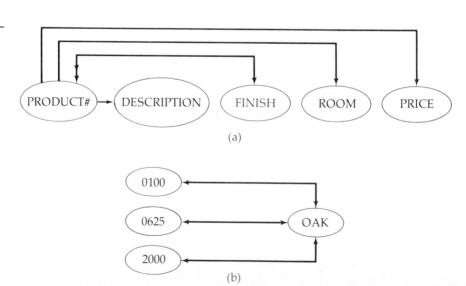

the usual case). Therefore, there is a one-to-many association from that secondary key to the primary key of the record, since there may be many primary key values associated with a given value of the secondary key. For example, FINISH is a secondary key for the PRODUCT record type. Therefore, there is a one-to-many association from FINISH to PRODUCT# (see Figure 3-8a). Figure 3-8b shows one occurrence, where the secondary key value is OAK. There are three hypothetical associated product numbers shown: 0100, 0625, and 2000.

Secondary keys provide a powerful technique for retrieving selected data records without searching an entire file. In the PRODUCT file, we can list all products whose DESCRIPTION is WALL UNIT or whose FINISH is OAK (or a combination of these two factors).

ASSOCIATIONS BETWEEN RECORDS

When we represent data in the form of a bubble chart, the next step is to group the data items into records (as is illustrated in Figure 3-7). When this is done, the result is a set of record types with associations between them. Recall that record types correspond to entity classes from the reality level of data. For example, Figure 3-9 shows the result of grouping typical data items about customers and orders into records. There are two resulting record types: CUSTOMER and ORDER.

In Figure 3-9 we also introduce the "crow's foot" notation that is now commonly used to distinguish one and many associations between entities and records. We will continue to use bubble charts to indicate associations between data items. In the crow's foot notation, a one-association between two record types is shown using a line with no "feet"; a many-association is represented by a crow's foot. Since the association between the primary keys (CUSTOMER# and ORDER#) is conditional 1:N, the association between the record types is the same. This reflects that in the real world, at a given instant in time, a customer may have zero, one, or more than one outstanding order, and an order must be associated with exactly one customer.

Types of Associations

Between any two record types there are three possible associations: one-to-one, one-to-many, and many-to-many, with conditionality possible on

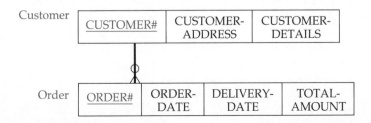

Figure 3-9
Association between two record types (Pine Valley Furniture)

Figure 3-10
Types of associations
between records

HUSBAND	EMPLOYEE	STUDENT

WIFE	DEPENDENT	COURSE

Figure 3-11
Data structure
diagram (Pine Valley
Furniture)

CUSTOMER

CUSTOMER#	CUSTOMER-ADDRESS	CUSTOMER-DETAILS

Open orders
ORDER

ORDER#	ORDER-DATE	DELIVERY-DATE	TOTAL-AMOUNT

Items ordered
ORDER LINE

ORDER #	PRODUCT#	QUANTITY-ORDERED	EXTENDED-PRICE

Products on order
PRODUCT

PRODUCT#	DESCRIPTION	PRODUCT-DETAILS	PRICE	QUANTITY-ON-HAND

either or both sides. Examples of these associations are shown in Figure 3-10. The associations between record types have the same meanings as the associations between data items. In Figures 3-9 and 3-10 (and other similar figures), the lines represent associations between *records*—they do not connect or represent associations between individual data items in those records. That is, the lines connect the whole boxes, not just the data items near where the lines meet the boxes.

A diagram like Figure 3-9 can grow to show dozens of record types. A more comprehensive portion of a database for Pine Valley Furniture Company is shown in Figure 3-11.

The particular notation used in Figures 3-9 and 3-11 is called a **data structure diagram** (the term *Bachman diagram* is also used, named after the person who first proposed this notation). Later in this chapter we will switch to the more common but very similar entity-relationship notation. Notice that in Figure 3-11 we have chosen to place relationship names alongside the arrows that represent associations. These names help to explain the nature of data and improve our understanding of the metadata being described.

Having developed this initial appreciation for representing organizational data, we now turn to a more general discussion of modeling the meaning of organizational data. The basic data concepts and notations introduced so far are the building blocks for comprehensive notations used to model, or represent, organizational data. Before we introduce two popular notations, entity-relationship and relational, we will outline in the next section the different contexts in which data modeling is done and the different types of data models that are developed.

DATA MODELS

A **model** is a representation of real-world objects and events and their associations. It is an abstraction from reality (that is, in a different form) and, as such, often is simplified for ease of understanding and manipulation. Model airplanes that allow aeronautical engineers to design better airplanes, mathematical models that allow business analysts to improve the operation of an enterprise, and model people (dolls) that allow children to practice the responsibilities of parenthood all suitably represent some real-world situation. Models are developed using a notation or basic building blocks, but because it is an abstraction, a model does not necessarily imply what materials are used in the composition of the reality it represents.

A **data model** is an abstract representation (a description) of the data about entities, events, activities, and their associations within an organization. More liberally, a data model represents (describes) an organization itself, since, for example, it is the association between customers and the orders they submit that leads to associations between Customer records and Order records.

The purpose of a data model is twofold: first, to represent data and second, to make the data understandable. The various data models presented in Chapter 2 for different transactions and reports in Pine Valley Furniture can be checked for these two properties. A data model should imply the meaning of data. If a data model accurately and completely represents required data and is understandable, then it can be easily used to design and access a database.

Careful thought on the model airplane analogy will suggest there are three types of airplane models for different applications:

1. Models (or submodels) that each "user" of an airplane conceives. For example, the pilot sees the airplane as a set of instruments and equipment for maneuvering the plane; the aeronautical engineer sees the plane as shapes, lines, and aerodynamics. These are called **external models** or **user views**.

2. Models that consolidate the aerodynamics, the internal cockpit physical layout, and other views to check for inconsistencies (for example, there may be fine aerodynamic features but not enough passenger capacity to be economical). These models are used by a general design

engineer responsible for the overall architecture and objectives of the project. (The design engineer in the database realm is called a data administrator.) These are **conceptual models.**

3. Fabrication models that put every part in its place in some abstract form (often a blueprint) so that the airplane can actually be constructed and used. These models are useful to an assembly foreman, construction project manager, and workers responsible for production and daily operations. (The blueprint in the database realm is developed by a database designer or administrator and is used by programmers and others who build application programs.) These are **internal models.**

Figure 3-12 shows the correspondence between the levels of data models in Pine Valley Furniture and the levels of airplane models just presented. There is no direct relationship between examples in the same box other than that they are at the same level of modeling.

Figure 3-12
Levels of data models compared to airplane models

Systems analysts and line personnel use **external data models** or **user views** to understand data requirements (see Chapter 2, in which the entity-relationship notation was used to represent various transaction and report

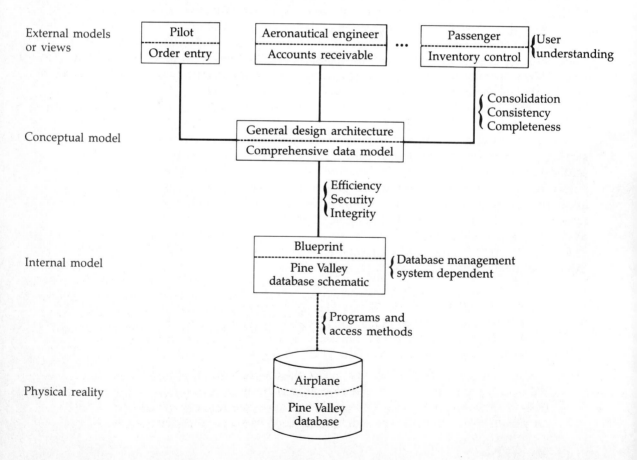

user views). User views are used in training to explain to new employees how an information system is used. Here, user understanding is very important, so the model clearly conveys only what a given user wants from a database. Data flow diagrams (see DeMarco, 1978), bubble charts, and the variety of notations presented in this chapter can be used to depict user views. End users may directly interact with a database by using a query language or problem-oriented language to formulate ad hoc inquiries. Thus, external data models also depict, for a specific data processing technology, the data used. This latter type of external model is often called a **subschema**.

For a **conceptual data model**, we need to be able to combine user views, check for consistency (for example, do all users refer to the same data item by the same name?), and confirm that all data and relationships have been identified. This was done in Chapter 2 when the user views for the various transactions and reports were combined into one conceptual data model in Figure 2-6.

It is important at the conceptual level to capture a consistent and comprehensive semantic definition of data. For example, one user may mean *all* customer orders when she says "orders," but another may use this term only to refer to orders that still have products to be delivered. Further, information about who can do what with data must be captured and represented for later use in developing the database. Finally, the conceptual model, since it is the basis for design of the internal database, should be supplemented with information about database usage and maintenance so an efficient internal structure can be devised.

The final model of data, the **internal model** (often called a **schema**), provides the interface with computer technologies: database management systems, operating system access methods, and other programs. In Chapter 2, the table and index definitions for the Pine Valley Furniture database define the internal data model. This model type uses structures to build complex architectures for organizing data in secondary memory (disks). The internal data model relates data from different files (for example, Customer to Order). Because this data model type deals with specific technologies, we will see that each DBMS can have its own unique internal data model or schema architecture.

We have thus outlined three classes of data models:

1. **External data models**, of which there are two subclasses:
   (a) **logical external data models** or **views** used to elicit and describe data requirements in a technology-independent manner
   (b) **subschema data models**, which describe only the data required for a given data processing task but which are defined using a technology-dependent style (such as a COBOL Data Division, FORTRAN dimension statements, data definition language [DDL] of a DBMS, and so on)
2. **Conceptual data models**, used to define comprehensively all the database requirements of all users into a consistent and singular database description

3. **Internal data models**, used to comprehensively define the whole database using a technology-dependent style—that is, models that are limited by the capabilities of the technology and that explicitly state how the technology will be used to manage data

This so-called **three-schema architecture** (also called the ANSI/SPARC architecture, after the standards group that popularized it) provides an integrated view of the data resource for the entire organization. The various data models evolve over time—that is, new data definitions are added as the firm's data needs expand.

The advantage of this three-schema architecture is that it provides **logical and physical data independence.** With logical data independence, the conceptual schema can evolve without affecting the external schemas; as a result, existing application programs need not be changed as the database evolves. With physical data independence, the internal schema can change without affecting the external schemas and application programs.

A summary of this very important concept of logical and physical data independence appears in Table 3-2. The table lists the typical changes that can be made for each type of independence without altering application programs. Although database management systems differ in the amount and level of data independence they provide, only the relational data model (to be introduced later in this chapter) provides most of the types of data independence shown in the table.

The purpose of the remainder of this chapter is to review various data model styles that have proved to be appropriate at the external and con-

Table 3-2   Important Types of Data Independence

Level of data independence	Examples of changes
	Logical
Data item format	Data item type, length, representation, or unit of measure
Data item usage	How a data item is derived, used, edited, or protected
Logical record structure	How data items are grouped into logical records
Logical data structure	Overall logical structure or conceptual model
	Physical
Physical data organization	How the data are organized into stored records
Access method	What search techniques and access strategies are used
Physical data location	Where data are located on storage devices
Storage device	Characteristics of the physical storage devices used

ceptual levels of this three-schema architecture for a database. Thus, we delay coverage of the hierarchical and network models until later chapters that will deal with these models and systems in detail.

CAPTURING THE MEANING OF DATA IN DATA MODELS

Because data models are abstractions (and, hence, simplifications) of real data, it is difficult, as well as often impractical or unnecessary, to capture in them all the nuances of data. Further, arguably the most difficult part of analyzing organizational data is recognizing and capturing the meaning of data and data relationships for all situations. Each type of data model represents certain aspects of the complete meaning of data fairly well, but it may not recognize other aspects at all. The meaning of data is frequently referred to as **data semantics.**

Many types of semantics deal with relationships between different kinds of data. These types of semantics are, in essence, rules about the integrity of the database. We have already seen one very important semantic in this chapter: the cardinality (sometimes called **connectivity**) of a relationship (1:1, 1:*M*, and *M:N*), including conditionality. Some of the other most important data semantics that need to be captured when modeling data are degree, existence dependency, time, uniqueness, class, and aggregation. In general, the more clearly a data model notation can represent these semantics, the better that data model is. We will return to this point at the end of the chapter in the section on "Factors in Selecting a Data Model."

Degree

Degree is the number of entities that participate in a relationship. So far in this chapter we have seen only the binary relationship, but this is only one of the possibilities. The three most typical degrees for relationships are unary, binary, and ternary. Examples for these three degrees of relationships are shown in Figure 3-13.

A **unary relationship,** also called a recursive relationship, is a relationship between instances of the same entity class. For example, Marriage is a 1:1 (in most societies) relationship between instances of, say, an Employee entity. Unary relationships, as all others, may be 1:1, 1:*M*, or *M:N*. Parent, for example, would be a *M:N* unary relationship between Person entities.

A **binary relationship** is a relationship between instances of two entity classes. For example, Products on Order is a 1:*M* binary relationship between an instance of the Product entity and instances of the Order entity.

A **ternary relationship** is a (simultaneous) relationship among instances of three entity classes. For example, Shipment is a ternary relationship among Product, Vendor, and Warehouse entity classes. That is, a shipment

Figure 3-13
Example relationships of different degrees

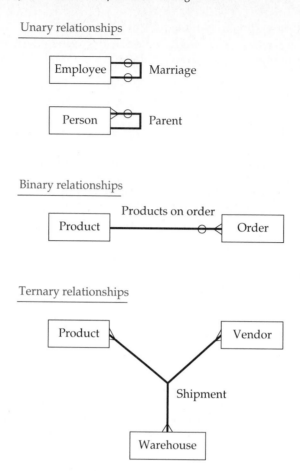

Unary relationships

Binary relationships

Ternary relationships

is about some product that is sent from some vendor and delivered to some warehouse. Each entity may be a 1 or a *M*(any) participant in a ternary relationship (that is, a ternary relationship may be 1:1:1, 1:1:*M*, and so on).

You may be surprised to know that a ternary relationship is not the same as three binary relationships. For example, the Quantity-Shipped, an attribute of the Shipment relationship in Figure 3-13, is the amount of a given product, shipped from a specific vendor to a particular warehouse. The Quantity-Shipped cannot be properly associated with any of the three possible binary relationships among these three entities. For example, the quantity shipped of a particular product to a particular warehouse is not the data item Quantity-Shipped mentioned above. Rather, this quantity shipped is an aggregation of the more detailed Quantity-Shipped values for all the vendors who have shipped that product to that warehouse.

There is an alternative and equally correct way to represent the shipment data outlined above. Shipment could be considered an entity, which would then participate in three relationships with the other entities. A relationship that can be considered an entity is called a **gerund.** The Shipment entity and its relationships are depicted in Figure 3-14. In this figure, we depict

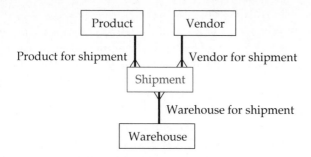

Figure 3-14
Shipment entity and
relationships

the same semantics as in the ternary relationship Shipment; each of the Product, Vendor, and Warehouse entity classes is a nonconditional (mandatory) participant in the three relationships (that is, there is no small circle near these entities on the relationship arrows). Higher-degree relationships are possible but are rare.

Existence Dependency

Sometimes an instance of one entity cannot exist without the existence of an instance of some other entity. For example, a customer order cannot exist without the associated customer (that is, an order has to be from somebody about whom we already know some characteristics). Such an existence dependency was also true above for the Shipment entity in Figure 3-14. (The opposite of an existence dependency is conditional association, as defined previously.) One ramification of an existence dependency is that, for example, a Customer entity instance cannot be dropped without first deleting all associated Customer Order instances.

A special case of an existence dependency occurs when part of the primary key of one entity is the primary key of some other entity. For example, if we do not assign unique order numbers to each customer order, then we may choose to use as the Customer Order entity identifier a combination of Customer# and Date. Here, not only must a Customer entity exist for each Customer Order entity, but also each Customer# for a Customer Order must match the Customer# for some Customer. This type of semantic is called **referential integrity** in those data models that place the primary key of one record in associated records. Chen (1977) reviews existence dependency semantics in considerable detail.

Time

Time is a multifaceted and subtle component of data. In this section we review various ways in which time affects the meaning and structure of a database.

In the most simple case, database contents vary over time. If only the current value is required, then only that value needs to be represented; however, when history is required, a series of data must be represented.

For example, the price Pine Valley Furniture charges for a given product will likely change as material and labor costs fluctuate. For accounting, billing, and manufacturing control purposes, it will be necessary to record the prices and the time periods over which each was in effect. This can be conceptualized simply as a series of prices and effective dates associated with the product entity. In many traditional programming languages, like COBOL, a data aggregate that includes fields for effective date and price would repeat a variable number of times within the PRODUCT record. However, in some data model notations, these prices would be represented separately from the product data, with a cross-reference between them to tie each date and price to some product.

In addition, how time is represented depends on what data processing is to be supported. A simple approach, suggested above, is to time stamp or tag each data value to show the time the value was entered (transaction time), the time the value becomes valid or stops being valid, or the time critical actions were performed on the data (for example, updates, corrections, or audits). Such an approach implies a series of time-dependent values for a data element. If we view data as two-dimensional (as in Figure 3-3), conceptually time simply adds a third dimension, which is shown in Figure 3-15a. Figure 3-15b, in which rows are added and deleted over time, is a more realistic picture of the effects of time. But Figure 3-15b oversimplifies many situations in which individual data elements, such as price, will vary at times independent from when product records are added or deleted, or when other data elements change value. At least with such time stamps, queries such as "display the contents of a specific shipment record AS-OF a particular time" can be handled.

At a conceptual level, simply representing that a history of price values is required is sufficient to capture the database requirements. At the internal data model level, however, studies have shown that reasonably volatile data quickly become unmanageable with a similar simple storage approach. In particular, consider the example of Figure 3-15b if the prices of *all* products do not change at the same time, in which case, a considerable portion of these data is redundant across time. Sometimes, it is simpler to store the original data and then, in a separate file (a so-called **differential file**) store the changes or difference for just those values that change. This saves considerable storage over retaining the complete contents of the whole shipment record or file when only one data element in one record changes at each time stamp.

One aspect of time is the conditions that must exist over time for data to be legitimate or even allowed to exist. For example, when a customer shipment of products is formed, data about it may exist even before it is assigned to some carrier, whereas data about the shipment cannot be stored unless there is one or more associated customer orders. The type of restriction illustrated here—creating a shipment without an order—is called an **insertion restriction** and relates to the time at which data are first stored in a database.

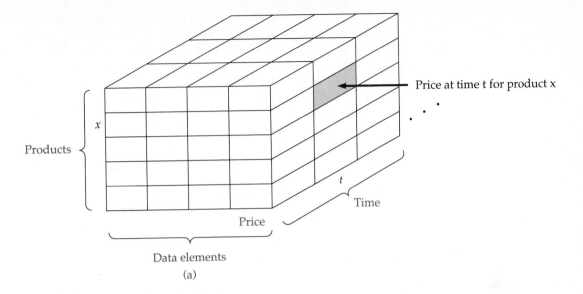

Price at time t for product x

Data elements

(a)

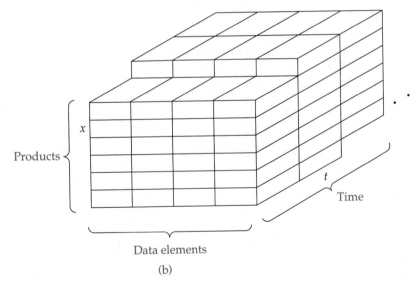

Data elements

(b)

Figure 3-15
Conceptualizing time
with data:
(a) simple view of
time effects on
data
(b) more realistic
view of time
effects on data

Once the shipment leaves the warehouse (that is, becomes active), it must always be assigned to some shipper but, because of transshipment, the carrier may change. When the shipment is received, it (and any associated data, such as customer orders being filled by the shipment) must be disassociated from any carrier. Thus, the meaning of the relationship between shipper and shipment relates to the time period covered by the relationship. This restriction (the so-called **retention restriction**) on relationships involves, in general, the following choices: (1) fixed—the original association must be maintained; (2) mandatory—some association must always be maintained; and (3) optional—from time to time, no association may occur.

This shipment situation example involves a *current shipper* relationship in which a shipment may exist without an associated carrier and may change associated carrier over time; the association from shipment to carrier is many-to-one. A totally different relationship would maintain the complete history of carriers handling a shipment. Although the shipment may exist without a carrier when it is created, once associated with a shipper it will always be associated with that shipper (and possibly others). When a history is maintained, explicit reference to time may be required to be able to retrieve the actual description of the business situation at any current or past point (or even future if forecasts are included). Now the relationship from shipment to carrier becomes many-to-many.

Time is not used like other pieces of data (as demonstrated in the interpretation of the shipment versus shipment history relationship). Time series data, past versus current versus pending data, and the temporal nature of user data requests make time a special dimension of organizational data. Time also plays a role in database recovery, which will be addressed in Chapter 9.

The following example illustrates how data maintenance can effect subtle changes to time-dependent information. Suppose one characteristic of a product in Pine Valley Furniture is the product line or group of products to which it is assigned. Customer orders are processed throughout the year and monthly summaries and trends (which involve comparing current sales to the prior month's sales) are reported by product line. Figure 3-16a illustrates the Product Line, Product, and Order data and some typical relationships. In the middle of the year, due to a reorganization of the sales function, products may be reassigned to new product lines. The Pine Valley Furniture database in Figure 3-16a is not designed to show that products may have different product lines over different periods of time. Thus, all sales reports will show historical sales for a product based on a product's *current* product line, not the one at the time of the sale. We have discussed this problem of time-dependent data with several organizations that are considered leaders in the use of database technologies and data modeling. We have discovered that current data models (and database management systems based on these data models) are so inadequate in handling time that organizations ignore this problem and hope that such inaccuracies balance each other out.

Figure 3-16
Pine Valley product database:
(a) database not recognizing product reassignment
(b) database recognizing product reassignment

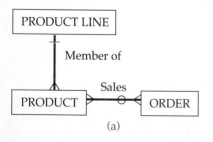

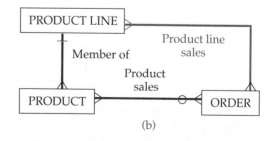

Figure 3-16b shows a simple database design change that accommodates this time-dependent relationship.

It can safely be said that no data model adequately handles time. Clifford and Warren (1983) suggest extensions to the relational model to deal with the time semantic. Time frequently is masked from view when looking at a data model, so auxiliary data and relationship definitions may be necessary to communicate the time dimension.

Uniqueness

We have already encountered one uniqueness restriction, called a primary key, but uniqueness arises in other contexts, as well. For example, each student who is enrolled in a course section (a particular time and place offering of a course) will receive a grade and no single student may receive more than one grade in each section. That is, although multiple grade entity instances will exist for the same section (for multiple students), those associated with the same student will be unique by course section. Uniqueness of primary keys is handled in most data models. However, uniqueness among entity instances related to some other entity instance is really only explicitly recognized in some versions of the network data model.

Another form of uniqueness is called **exclusivity.** Exclusivity means that one of several kinds of data or relationships may be present, but not all. For example, a particular type of task in the production of a product in Pine Valley Furniture may be performed by an hourly worker or a salaried employee, but not both; or two Pine Valley Furniture employees may be related as supervisor/subordinate, husband/wife, or parent/child, but no two of these relationships may hold for the same pair of employees.

Class-Subclass or Generalization

The term *customer* may not have the same meaning to all people in the organization. For Pine Valley Furniture there may be several subclasses of customers: Some customers are national account furniture store (chain-type store) business customers, some are single-site furniture stores, some are individual persons, and some are interior designers. A subclass of entities not only inherits the properties (data elements) of its superclass but may have some properties pertinent to only that subclass. For example, although all customers have some of the same type of characteristics (name, address, telephone number, and so on), each type of customer may have data elements not ascribed to other subclasses (national account furniture store customers, for example, have a credit limit and number of outlets that other types of customers do not have).

Some reports deal with only specific types of customers; other reports summarize data from all customers independent of type. One frequently used way to identify subclasses of an entity is to associate a categorical data element (for example, type of customer for the above situation) with the entity. But this may not be an acceptable method when the set of data elements varies across subclasses (since data models do not allow variable content definitions for different instances in the same class). The Customer entity above is frequently referred to as an **abstraction** of more specialized entities (such as National Customer, Interior Designer, and so on). One sales manager may refer to the term *customer* and mean a different type of entity from another sales manager who uses the same term. Hence, the Pine Valley Furniture data model may need to represent different but related types of customers and customer classes.

Although most data models can represent generalized entity types, only the entity-relationship and semantic data models reviewed later in the chapter explicitly recognize this type of data semantic. Smith and Smith (1977) describe the generalization semantic in more detail.

Aggregation

An **aggregation** is a collection of entities. An instance of a Work Order entity for Pine Valley Furniture, for example, would actually be the collection of all Raw Material, Tool, Work Center, and Factory Worker entity instances needed to produce a certain piece of furniture. A Work Order aggregate entity will be associated with a particular Customer entity when products are made to order, but changing customer requests may mean that a work order is reassigned to different customers while it is active. In addition to inheriting the data elements about component entities, an aggregate entity can have data elements not found in its component entities. For example, a work order might have a promised completion date, as well as material descriptions, tool codes, and so on from the component entities.

Some Pine Valley Furniture database users will simply want to refer to the Work Order (aggregate) entity as if it were a basic entity. The relational data model (using a concept called a view) and the Semantic Data Model (using an explicit definition of an aggregate entity) are best among the data models reviewed here in dealing with this type of data semantics. Smith and Smith (1977) also discuss the need for this type of data semantic.

Summary of Data Semantics

Other semantics have been identified and will be considered in more detail as we review, in the following sections of this chapter and in later chapters, other data models that handle such semantics.

The remainder of this chapter surveys two specific notations or architectures for data models. Since our focus is on a conceptual understanding and representing the meaning of data (not their representation in technology), we will survey the data model notation predominantly used today to conceptually model data, the entity-relationship data model. We then turn our attention to the relational data model since today it is used the most often in implementing databases and is used in some steps of data analysis, namely normalization (described in Chapter 6). Then we will review other so-called semantic data models and the emerging object-oriented data model, which some believe will replace relational as the basis for the next generation of database management systems.

We have chosen to delay our discussion of two other important data models, hierarchical and network, until Chapters 10 and 11, respectively. These models have historical and practical significance in the evolution of data management; today they are most relevant, however, for implementing databases, not for understanding organizational data, which is our focus at this point in the text.

THE ENTITY-RELATIONSHIP DATA MODEL

The data models used in modern database management systems—hierarchical, network, and relational—have proved to be effective schemes for organizing data for convenient and efficient processing. With a few limitations (especially for hierarchical), data and a wide variety of relationships can be easily modeled using these architectures. This means that at the internal data model level, we can build databases to support data processing efficiently for a wide range of data, as well as to support query and maintenance processing. The implementation of databases using systems based on these three data models are the topics of Chapters 10-14.

Some people in the database field, however, have argued that for enterprise, external, and conceptual data models, it is better to use description notations and conventions that are independent of the particular DBMS. In this way, a database designer can specify comprehensive database requirements without a bias (albeit subtle) toward use of a particular DBMS. Also, for a truly distributed, multiple data model (and DBMS) database, a central data model is needed to encompass all distributed components and to be able to translate among all data models used.

By far, the data model that is most commonly used for enterprise, external, and logical data analysis is the entity-relationship data model. Many Computer-Assisted Software Engineering (CASE) tools and database analysis aids include this modeling convention, and much attention has been given it, with many extensions proposed since the original version (Chen 1976, 1977).

Entity-Relationship Data Model Basics

The entity-relationship (E-R) data model is a simple extension of the type of graphical notations we have used so far in this chapter. E-R uses a few

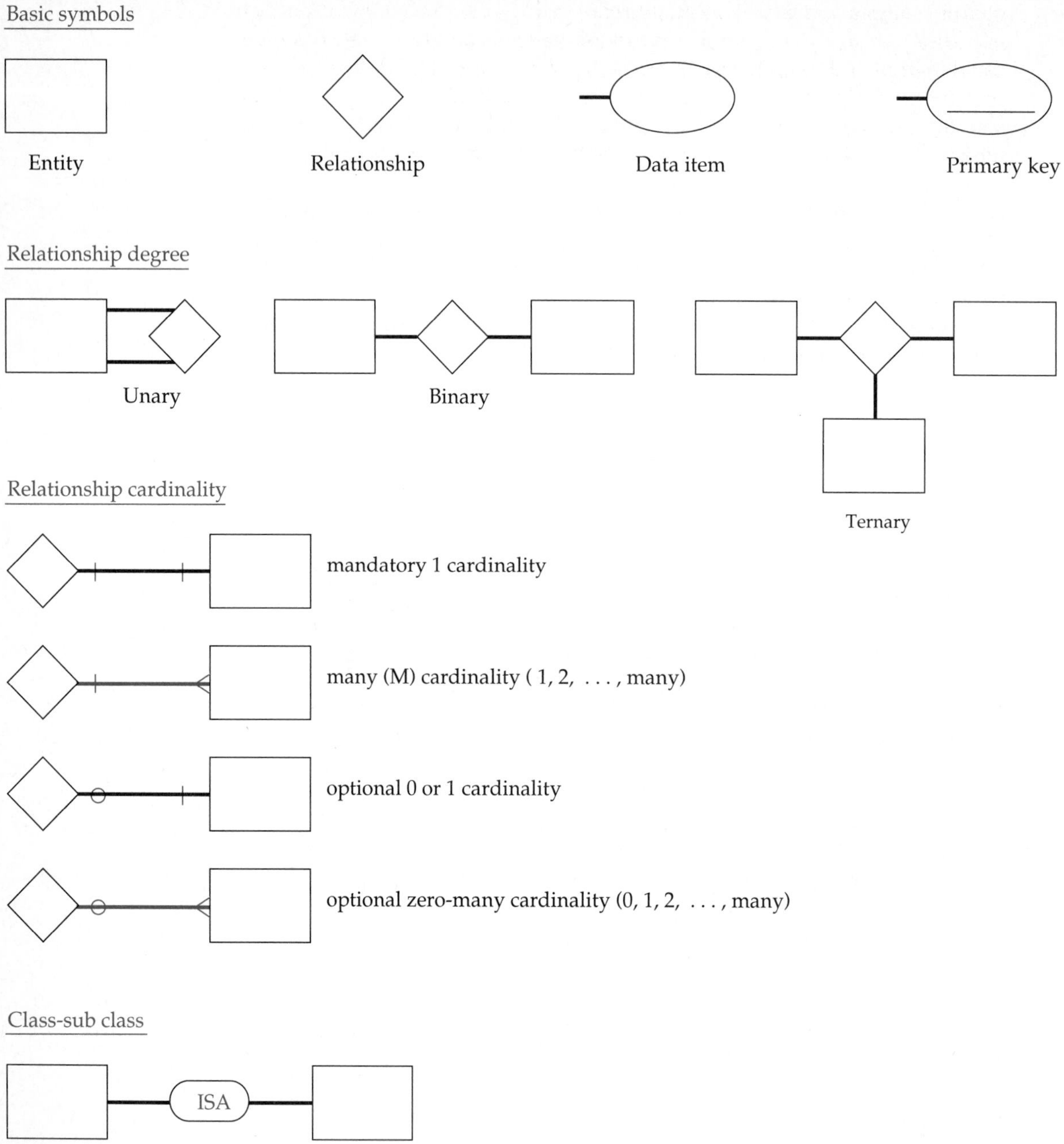

Basic symbols

Entity	Relationship	Data item	Primary key

Relationship degree

Unary   Binary

Ternary

Relationship cardinality

mandatory 1 cardinality

many (M) cardinality (1, 2, . . . , many)

optional 0 or 1 cardinality

optional zero-many cardinality (0, 1, 2, . . . , many)

Class-sub class

ISA

Figure 3-17
Entity-relationship
notation

special symbols, such as the diamond, to indicate a relationship. We used the E-R notation extensively in Chapter 2 to depict database requirements in Pine Valley Furniture.

Figure 3-17 shows the E-R symbols we will use in this text. (Since there have been several independent extensions to the original E-R notation, there is no universal standard E-R notation; we do not attempt here to include every capability ever conceived for E-R modeling.) The symbols we use here are very similar to those found in an E-R drawing tool called E-R Designer (Chen and Associates, 1988). Even within the E-R Designer tool, there are alternatives for representing certain data model aspects. These symbols are not explained here but rather, examples used in Chapter 2 and in the remainder of this section serve to illustrate these notations.

Figure 3-18 illustrates this notation (excluding attributes) by depicting some typical entities and relationships. Each diamond represents a different relationship. The so-called crow's foot notation specifies the cardinality on each side of the relationship (for example, for the Orders-for-Customer relationship, there is exactly one Customer instance and zero, one, or many Order instances). Further, a diamond (for example, Sources-of-Goods) exists whether or not intersection data are present. This means that an E-R diagram does not have to be redrawn if such intersection data (for example, the vendor's price for a product) are recognized later.

An E-R data model can also include data elements, as shown in Figure 3-19 (although some E-R diagramming tools record attribute information only in the data repository, to minimize the "clutter" on a diagram). Note in this case that both entities and (some) relationships may have data element bubbles associated with them. Data element bubbles for a relationship are intersection data; both 1:1 and $M{:}N$ relationships may have data, but not 1:M. For example, Marriage (a 1:1 relationship between Employees) could have a Date, and the Sources-of-Goods relationship in Figure 3-19 could have a Price; but any data we might try to associate with, say, the Orders-for-Customer relationship in Figure 3-19 would have to be either Customer or Order data.

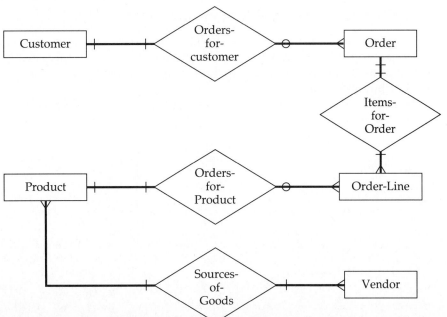

Figure 3-18
Example of an entity-relationship diagram

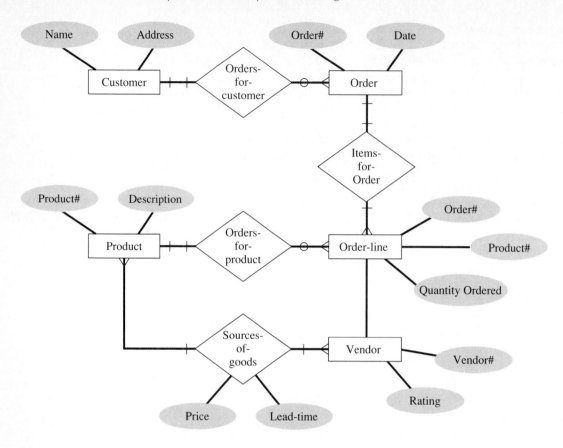

Figure 3-19
Example of an E-R
diagram with data
elements

Advanced Semantics in E-R Modeling

Figure 3-20 illustrates the way the E-R data model depicts nonbinary relationships. Figure 3-20a shows the E-R version of the ternary relationship of Figure 3-13, and Figure 3-20b is the E-R representation for the unary relationship of Figure 3-13.

Because relationships can have associated data, the E-R data model poses an interesting dilemma: Is a relationship (diamond) an entity "in sheep's

Figure 3-20
Examples of E-R data
model:
(a) ternary
    relationship
(b) unary relationship

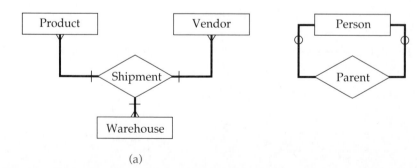

(a)

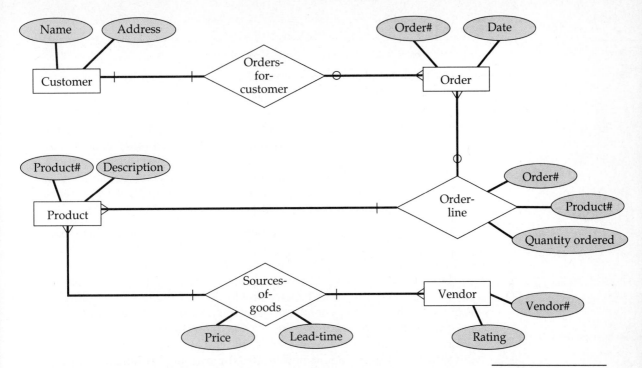

clothing"? Consider Figure 3-21, which also depicts the database of Figure 3-19. Compare Figures 3-19 and 3-21: Note that in Figure 3-19, Order-Line is depicted as an entity, but in Figure 3-21 it is a relationship. Because there is associated data with Order-Line, a relation or record type would appear in an internal implementation, so in this case the distinction between entity and relationship is simply a matter of how one views the data.

The E-R model can represent more than only simple attributes, for example; consider the situation depicted in Figure 3-22. Here, each Department may be housed in many locations. All we know about each location is its name, so there is no reason to create an entity for location. The double oval indicates the repeating attribute.

This situation highlights one of two important rules for determining whether a concept is an attribute or an entity. These rules are:

- An entity must have both a primary key and at least one nonkey (descriptor) attribute.

- There must be more than one instance of an entity.

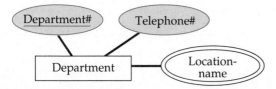

Figure 3-21
E-R diagram with an Order-Line relationship

Figure 3-22
Example of a multi-valued attribute

E-R modeling includes a special notation for showing a class-subclass relationship, or what E-R calls an **ISA** relationship. Subclasses are needed under either or both of two circumstances:

1. Different attributes are used to describe each entity subclass; for example, a business customer has a credit limit, but a retail customer does not.

2. Each entity subclass participates in different relationships; for example, an out-patient is not assigned a bed, but all other patients are. (*Note:* A conditional relationship may be eliminated when entity subclasses are included in a data model, since an ISA relationship makes conditional participation of a superclass more explicit by showing which subclasses participate.)

Figure 3-23 shows an example of an ISA relationship. In this case, both reasons outlined above for using subclasses are shown. All Patients (of both subclasses) have a responsible Physician assigned and have an Admit-Date attribute. Only Resident-Patients are assigned a Bed (and a Bed may be currently empty). Both Out-Patients and Resident-Patients are identified by Patient#, although, in general, special attribute names may be used locally for each subclass. Out-Patients have a Check-Back-Date when they are to return for further testing, and a Resident-Patient has a Discharge-Date. In this situation, every Patient now under the care of this hospital must be either an Out-Patient or a Resident-Patient, but not both. This property is called **generalization.** The case where an entity instance may be in zero or exactly one subclass is called **specialization.** Since this database depicts only current hospital status, the actual real-world patient may fall into either subclass at different times, which is not shown in this data model.

Figure 3-23
Example of an ISA relationship

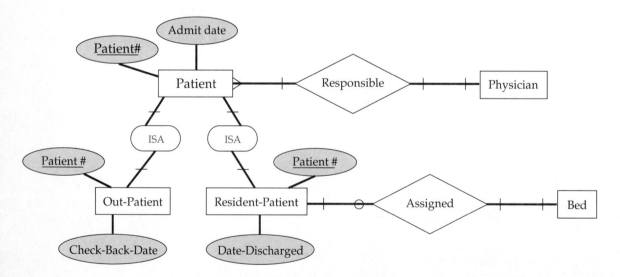

Extension to the E-R Data Model

The exact form and notation for the E-R model is still evolving since, unlike the technology-based data models, the E-R model has not been standardized. Newer, more recent versions of the E-R model have been developed specifically to include more semantics.

Figure 3-24 shows an example of the use of some recent variations to the E-R model to represent a portion of a database for Mountain View Community Hospital. In this example, the Patient, Staff, and Hourly-Staff entities are classes with subclasses of entities, and the Hourly-Staff subclass is itself a subclass of the Staff entity. The identifier of the Service entity includes keys from the Patient entity and the Nurse or Nonprofessional entities (called an **ID dependency**), as shown by the Performed-On and Performed-By identifying relationships. A Service is performed on a Patient

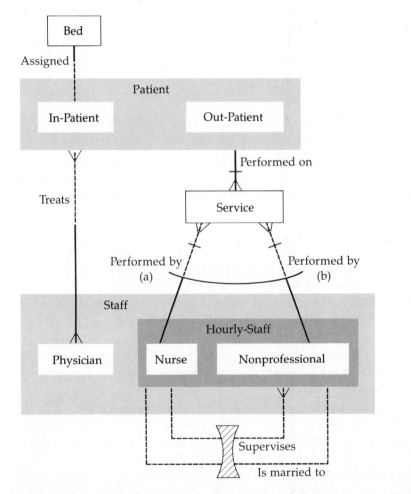

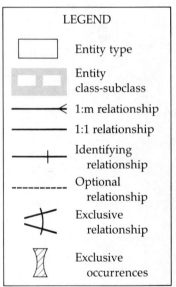

Figure 3-24
E-R model for variation on Mountain View Community Hospital database

by either a Nurse or a Nonprofessional employee, but not both, as shown by the exclusive arc across the Performed-By relationships. Each Patient must have at least one Service provided to him or her, but an individual Hourly-Staff member may never perform a Service attributable to any particular Patient since the Performed-By relationships indicate optional Service. An Hourly-Staff member may supervise zero, one, or many other Hourly-Staff members and Hourly-Staff may be married to each other, but Staff married to each other may not supervise each other, as shown by the exclusive occurrences notation on the Supervises and Is-Married-To relationships; such relationships or restrictions involving Physicians are of no concern. Each In-Patient is assigned to one Bed, but a Bed may be unoccupied; Out-Patients are not assigned to a Bed. A Patient must be treated by at least one Physician to be a true Patient, but a Patient may be treated by many Physicians.

The E-R data model is used almost exclusively for describing data in conceptual terms; it must then be converted to another model for database implementation. Since today the most prevalent implementation model is relational, we will review this model next. Also, the relational model is sometimes used instead of the E-R model to represent organizational data.

THE RELATIONAL DATA MODEL

The choice of many database builders and users (as we illustrated in Chapter 2) is the relational data model. As we will see, the relational model is different from other models not only in architecture but also in the following ways:

1. **Implementation independence.** The relational model logically represents all relationships implicitly, and hence, one does not know what associations are or are not *physically* represented by an efficient method. Relational shares this property with E-R.

2. **Terminology.** The relational model uses its own terminology, most of which has equivalent terms in other data models.

3. **Logical key pointers.** The relational data model uses primary (and secondary) keys in records to represent the association between two records, whereas E-R (and network and hierarchical) use arcs between entity boxes.

4. **Normalization theory.** Properties of a database that make it free of certain maintenance problems have been developed within the context of the relational model (although these properties can also be designed into an E-R or a network data model).

5. **High-level programming languages.** Programming languages have been developed specifically to access databases defined via the rela-

tional data model; these languages permit data to be manipulated as groups or files rather than procedurally one record at a time.

Definitions

The relational data model uses the concept of a relation to represent what we have previously called a file; that is, a relation represents an entity class. A **relation** is viewed as a two-dimensional table. Three examples of relations for Pine Valley Furniture are shown in Figure 3-25. A relation has the following properties:

1. Each column contains values about the same attribute, and each table cell value must be simple (a single value).
2. Each column has a distinct name (attribute name), and the order of columns is immaterial.
3. Each row is distinct; that is, one row cannot duplicate another row for selected key attribute columns.
4. The sequence of the rows is immaterial.

As shown in Figure 3-25, a **tuple** is the collection of values that compose one row of a relation. A tuple is equivalent to a record instance. An *n-tuple* is a tuple composed of *n* attribute values, where *n* is called the **degree** of the relation (not to be confused with our previous definition of the degree of a relationship, meaning the number of entities participating in the relationship). PRODUCT is an example of a four-tuple. The number of tuples in a relation is its **cardinality** (again, not to be confused with the cardinality of a relationship defined earlier).

A **domain** is the set of possible values for an attribute. For example, the domain for QUANTITY-ON-HAND in the PRODUCT relation is all integers greater than or equal to zero. The domain for CITY in the VENDOR relation is a set of alphabetic character strings restricted to the names of U.S. cities.

We can use a shorthand notation to abstractly represent relations (or tables). The three relations in Figure 3-25 can be written in this notation as

PRODUCT(<u>PRODUCT#</u>,DESCRIPTION,PRICE,QUANTITY-ON-HAND)
VENDOR(<u>VENDOR#</u>,VENDOR-NAME,VENDOR-CITY)
SUPPLIES(<u>VENDOR#</u>,<u>PRODUCT#</u>,VENDOR-PRICE)

The primary key, which may involve a combination of values, of each relation is underlined. The relational data model requires that a primary key of a tuple (or any component attribute if a combined key) may not contain a null value. Although several different attributes (called **candidate keys**) might serve as the primary key, only one (or one combination) is chosen. The other keys are then called **alternate keys.**

The SUPPLIES relation above requires two attributes in combination to identify each tuple uniquely. A composite or **concatenated key** is a key that consists of two or more attributes appended together. Concatenated keys

PRODUCT relation   Attributes

PRODUCT#	DESCRIPTION	PRICE	QUANTITY-ON-HAND	Relative record#
0100	TABLE	500.00	42	1
0975	WALL UNIT	750.00	0	2
1250	CHAIR	400.00	13	3
1775	DRESSER	500.00	8	4

Tuples

Primary key

VENDOR relation

VENDOR#	VENDOR-NAME	VENDOR-CITY
26	MAPLE HILL	DENVER
13	CEDAR CREST	BOULDER
16	OAK PEAK	FRANKLIN
12	CHERRY MTN	LONDON

SUPPLIES relation

VENDOR#	PRODUCT#	VENDOR-PRICE
13	1775	250.00
16	0100	150.00
16	1250	200.00
26	1250	200.00
26	1775	275.00

Figure 3-25
Example of a
relational data model

appear frequently in a relational database, since many-to-many relationships are represented by relations, usually with such a concatenation of keys from the related relations (PRODUCT and VENDOR in this case). Intersection data, like VENDOR-PRICE, may be included. Each part of a concatenated key can be used to identify tuples in another relation. In fact, values for all component keys of a concatenated key must be present, although nonkey attribute values may be missing.

We can relate tuples in the relational model only when there are common attributes in the relations involved. Thus, relationships are implicit in the relational model, whereas the arcs between entities in the E-R make relationships explicit.

Codd (1970) popularized the use of relations and tables as a way to model data. At first glance, this view of data may appear to be only a different perspective on the E-R data model (all we have done is replace graphical symbols with logical references, or **cross-reference keys,** to show relationships). Several debates have essentially argued this point (see "The Data Base Debate," 1982, and Olle, 1975). Codd and many others have shown that relations are actually formal operations on mathematical sets. Further, most data processing operations (for example, printing of selected records and finding related records) can also be represented by mathematical operators on relations. The result of mathematical operations can be proved to have certain properties. A collection of operations, called normalization, has been shown to result in databases with desirable maintenance and logical properties. This mathematical elegance and visual simplicity have made the relational data model one of the driving forces in the information systems field.

Relationships in the Relational Data Model

The basic construct for representing a relationship in the relational data model is to place a common attribute in each related relation. To see how this works for Pine Valley Furniture, consider the following set of relations that defines a relational database for the E-R diagram of Figure 3-18:

CUSTOMER(CUSTOMER#,CUSTOMER-ADDRESS,CUSTOMER-
    DETAILS)
ORDER(ORDER#,CUSTOMER#,ORDER-DATE,
    DELIVERY-DATE,TOTAL-AMOUNT)
PRODUCT(PRODUCT#,DESCRIPTION,PRICE,QUANTITY-ON-HAND)
ORDER-LINE(ORDER#,PRODUCT#,
    QUANTITY-ORDERED,EXTENDED-PRICE)
VENDOR(VENDOR#,VENDOR-NAME,VENDOR-CITY)
SUPPLIES(VENDOR#,PRODUCT#)

In this example, CUSTOMER, PRODUCT, and VENDOR are basic relations that exist independently of all other data. The ORDER relation, too, can exist independently, but one of its attributes, CUSTOMER#, called a **cross-reference key,** implements the Orders-for-Customer relationship from Figure 3-18. The attribute CUSTOMER# in the ORDER relation could have any name (say, ACCOUNT#). As long as the domain of values and the meaning of CUSTOMER# and ACCOUNT# are the same, then proper linking of related tuples can occur. We will use a dashed underline to denote a cross-reference key. The problem with using different names in different relations for the same attribute is that a reader of a relational database definition may not readily understand that these two attributes can be used to link related data. Use of a cross-reference key in the relational data model means that, for example, any value of CUSTOMER# found in an ORDER tuple logically should exist as a CUSTOMER# in some unique existing CUSTOMER tuple.

The ORDER relation has its own unique key, ORDER#. An alternate key might be the combination of CUSTOMER# and ORDER-DATE (if customers do not submit two or more orders in a day). If ORDER# was not an essential piece of data for applications of this database, then the following SALE relation would be sufficient:

SALE(CUSTOMER#,ORDER-DATE,DELIVERY-DATE,
    TOTAL-AMOUNT)

Here the CUSTOMER# key appears as (part of) the primary key in each related record (tuple). In this case, CUSTOMER# is referred to as a **foreign key.** The term **referential integrity** applies to both cross-reference and foreign keys and means that the key value must exist in the associated relation for database integrity. Thus, a SALE cannot be created unless a CUSTOMER row exists for the referenced customer *and* a CUSTOMER row may not be deleted if this will leave any SALE row without a referenced CUSTOMER. Foreign keys are common in relational databases due to the way they are designed, as was demonstrated in Chapter 2.

The ORDER-LINE and SUPPLIES relations exist because of *M:N* relationships. ORDER-LINE is called an intersection record in some data models, where QUANTITY-ORDERED and EXTENDED-PRICE are the intersection data. The concatenated key is composed of the keys of the related relations. The SUPPLIES relation, being void of meaningful contents, simply links related VENDOR and PRODUCT data. In this database, we do not care to know anything about this *M:N* relationship other than the PRODUCT and VENDOR associations themselves.

Ternary and higher-degree relationships can also be represented. The relational version of Figure 3-20a is

PRODUCT(PRODUCT#,DESCRIPTION,PRICE,QUANTITY-ON-HAND)
VENDOR(VENDOR#,VENDOR-NAME,VENDOR-CITY)
WAREHOUSE(WAREHOUSE#,W-CITY,W-CAPACITY)
P-W-V(PRODUCT#,WAREHOUSE#,VENDOR#,LEAD-TIME)

LEAD-TIME is included to show how intersection data would appear in this case. It is important to note that the relational data model here includes only four relations, whereas the equivalent E-R model includes three entities and one relationship. The difference, as always, is that relationships are implicit from attributes in different relations that have common domains. Although necessary for relating two relations, having common domains is not a sufficient condition for sensible relating (called joining). For example, QUANTITY-ON-HAND and W-CAPACITY may have the same domain (any positive integer with a specified upper limit), but we would find it difficult to describe a meaningful relationship that relates PRODUCT and VENDOR using this domain and these attributes.

A unary relationship is represented in the relational model by including as an additional attribute the relation's primary key. For example, a relationship that groups customers from a common parent organization would be shown with the following modification of the CUSTOMER relation previously given:

CLIENT(<u>CUSTOMER#</u>,CUSTOMER-ADDRESS,
      PARENT-CUSTOMER#)

Here both CUSTOMER# and PARENT-CUSTOMER# have the same domain of values. PARENT-CUSTOMER is dashed underlined since it is a cross-reference key. In this case, this cross-reference key does not have referential integrity, since not all customers will have a parent (for example, the parent customers themselves, or customers not part of a parent company).

A class-subclass (ISA) relationship can also be depicted in a relational database. Consider the following relational data model for the class relationship example of Figure 3-23:

PHYSICIAN(<u>PHYSICIAN#</u>,...)
BED(<u>BED#</u>,...)
PATIENT(<u>PATIENT#</u>,PHYSICIAN#,ADMIT-DATE)
OUT-PATIENT(<u>OPATIENT#</u>,CHECK-BACK-DATE)
RES-PATIENT(<u>RPATIENT#</u>,DATE-DISCHARGED,<u>BED#</u>)

The common domain for PATIENT#, OPATIENT#, and RPATIENT# allows PATIENT data elements to be combined with OUT-PATIENT or RES-PATIENT data elements and for these subclass entities to be related to PHYSICIAN. However, since only the RES-PATIENT relation contains the BED#, only this subclass of patient can be related to beds. Some relational database management systems support definition of a **view** that could be used to define such a class relation as a merger of attribute values from each of the subclass relations.

Any table that satisfies the four properties presented in the previous section can be a relation. In fact, a table with these properties is said to be in **first normal form.** Experience has shown that although sufficient for data processing, first normal form (1NF) relations can still have some undesirable data maintenance properties. In general, these problems are inconsistencies that can occur in a database after records are inserted, deleted, or modified. The process of ridding a database definition of these problems or anomalies is called **normalization** and because it is a process of database design, it will be covered in Chapter 6. The result is the addition of two properties to the four enumerated on page 113 for relational databases. These two properties are:

5. *All* nonkey attributes should be *fully dependent* on the *whole* key; that is, in the case of a concatenated key, the whole key should functionally determine the nonkeys.

6. Each nonkey attribute should be dependent only on the relation's key, not on any other nonkey. Violation of this property is called a **transitive dependency** and implies that the relation combines data from several entities.

Summary of the Relational Data Model

We have described in this section the basics of the relational data model. Chapter 2 provided an extensive illustration of the operation of one relational DBMS, dBASE IV. Thus, Chapters 2 and 3 present a rather complete introduction to this important data model and approach to database processing.

Because of its independence from the physical database, the relational model has become an effective tool not only for managing data via a DBMS but also for external data modeling. Normal forms, easily checked within the relational model, are often used as rules of database design. Data manipulation languages based on relational algebra (shown in Chapter 2 and later in Chapters 13 and 14) and calculus (illustrated in Chapter 12) are often called "user-friendly" and are the model for fourth-generation programming languages (also discussed in later chapters).

The relational data model does have some caveats, which are outlined in more detail in Chapter 6:

- The relational model redundantly stores keys as cross-references between related entities, which can lead to considerable extra space and vulnerability to erroneous updates.

- Relational database management systems, at least until very recently, have been less efficient for transaction processing than have other DBMSs. This has caused some organizations to create both production and information retrieval databases to separate transaction processing from the less structured query processing.

- The relational data model has a lack of semantic quality control compared to the E-R and object-oriented data models; many relational systems have included an INTEGRITY clause on relations to overcome this shortfall.

This concludes our discussion of the primary notations (relational and E-R) used today for external and conceptual data models. The following section briefly outlines the salient features of a relatively new data model architecture that some claim is semantically richer and more general than those we have studied so far. This approach is called the object-oriented data model (OODM), which is an evolution from the Semantic Data Model (due originally to Hammer and McLeod, 1978, based upon Smith and Smith, 1977 and discussed in Teorey and Fry, 1982). The OODM incorporates all of the various semantics we have introduced and more and also represents a significant departure from the structured entity approaches of the E-R and relational data models. After covering the OODM, this chapter will then conclude with a review of data models, including consideration of human factors of various models (error proneness, understandability, and user satisfaction).

OBJECT-ORIENTED DATA MODELS

The origin of the object-oriented data model (OODM) is, as mentioned above, in the work of Hammer and McLeod (1978) and Smith and Smith (1977) (along with the work of many others in the area of object-oriented programming languages), who introduced many of the semantics we have discussed in this chapter. We will begin this section with a brief review of their Semantic Data Model. See Hull and King (1987) for a thorough review and history of semantic data models.

The Semantic Data Model

The Semantic Data Model (SDM), like the relational model, is not a diagrammatic model but a definitional one. An example of an SDM for part of the database of Figure 3-19, with some enhancements to illustrate the extensive descriptive clauses of the SDM, appears in Figure 3-26. The SDM is extensive, and not all definitional clauses are shown here; only some are included to suggest the richness of this data model. The purpose of the Semantic Data Model is to capture all meaning of data and to embed this as integrity and structural clauses in the database definitions. Such concepts as class-subclass, aggregation, dynamic properties and structure, and handling objects of different types (images, voice prints, as well as text and data) are included in the SDM and other semantically rich data models.

The figure shows that each entity class can be defined by a name (for example, CUSTOMER), a description, an interclass connection (in the case of entity class CUST-ORDER), and a set of member attributes. The interclass connection for CUST-ORDER specifies that instances of this entity are a specialization of ORDER entities, specifically those that are Build-to-Stock Orders. The member attributes of an entity class are described by a name and a set of clauses that indicate the domain of permissible values (for example, Name of CUSTOMER must come from a set of values called NAMES, defined elsewhere). In addition, attributes can be given a more precise meaning by indicating if values may change, if they may be missing/null, whether they are related to values in other entities (the inverse clause), and if they are nonsimple fields of multiple values (for example, Contact attribute of CUSTOMER, which is a list of CUST-ORDER references). An entity class itself, as well as instances of the entity class, may have attributes. For example, the CUST-ORDER class as a whole (that is, as an aggregate entity) is characterized by Total-$-Value, which is a sum of the Value attributes

CUSTOMER
    Description: all people and organizations that have purchased
                 products from Pine Valley Furniture
    Member attributes:
        Name
            Value class: NAMES
            Not changeable
            May not be null
        Address
            Value class: ADDRESSES
        Contact
            Value class: CUST-ORDER
            Inverse: Client
            Multivalued
ORDER
    Description: all orders for products by customers and orders
                 written to build inventory
    Member attributes:
        Order#
            Value class: ORDER-NUMBERS
            Not changeable
            May not be null
        Date
            Value class: DATES
        Type
            Value class: ORDER-TYPES
        Value
            Value class: MONEY
        Status
            Value class: STATUS-VALUES
CUST-ORDER
    Description: all orders for products by customers
    Interclass connection: subclass of ORDER where Type=CUST
    Member attributes:
        Client
            Value class: NAMES
            Inverse: Contact
            Not changeable
    Class attributes:
        Total-$-Value
            Value class: MONEY
            Derivation: Sum of all Values across all members
        Number-of-Orders-Active
            Value class: INTEGERS
            Derivation: number-of-members of this entity class
                        where Status=Active

Figure 3-26
Example of the
Semantic Data Model

across all instances of this set, and the Number-of-Orders-Active, which is a count of the number of active CUST-ORDERs.

As can be seen from this example, the SDM is capable of representing almost any of the semantics we have mentioned and can be extended to include others. Although the SDM has itself not become popular for data modeling, it has encouraged the comprehensive study of describing the meaning of data. One of the most significant of its features is the ability to represent arbitrary and compound objects, thus going beyond the rather structured and uniform models discussed so far. The object-oriented data model has been developed with this same goal.

Object-Oriented Data Model

Suppose you are an engineer designing new automobiles. During the design of a new automobile, you might:

- Create a body for a car composed of a custom-tailored collection of fenders, a roof, doors, and windows other engineers created earlier; you want your body (including its weight or other physical characteristics) to be automatically updated whenever the other design engineers modify components of your car body

- Modify an earlier version of an engine you designed and want to be sure that you distinguish this new engine from prior versions so that you can selectively use whichever version you want in subsequent automobiles on which you work

- Redesign a power lock system and want to incorporate this into all models of a certain automobile

In these situations, the object being manipulated is of arbitrary and dynamic structure not known in advance of use, is kept in several versions, and frequently inherits properties of other objects with which it is related. The structured, record-oriented data models discussed in this chapter are cumbersome in dealing with such free form and ad hoc circumstances. This is because the data needed for a particular task is usually scattered across multiple record types, which must be drawn together by original programming.

More formally, an **object** is an inseparable *package* or capsule of data definitions and values and the procedures (sometimes called methods) that act upon the data. Because each object has its definition as part of itself, each object can be unique from other objects. An object may contain any type of data: text, numbers, voice, or pictures. Further, an object may contain other objects, which may contain other objects, and so forth. Finally, an object may be a superclass or a subclass of other objects, as discussed before under the generalization semantic.

For our automobile example above, Figure 3-27 depicts a simple object database with typical classes, subclasses, and attributes. Note that both entities and attributes are objects. There are two types of relationships shown:

Figure 3-27
Example OODM for a
vehicle database

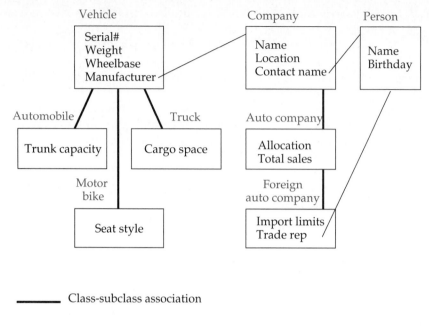

_____ Class-subclass association

_____ Attribute / aggretion association

class-subclass and aggregation. A subclass inherits the attributes of its superclasses. For example, the superclass of Vehicle might have attributes of Serial#, Manufacturer, and Wheelbase, which would be inherited by the subclasses of Automobile and Truck. Although this example shows a hierarchy of classes, a lattice or network, in which an object may be a subclass of several superclasses, is permitted in some OODMs. Because of class-subclass associations, query processing is slightly different in OODM systems than in the relational systems illustrated in Chapter 2. For example, a query asking for Vehicles where Manufacturer-Name is "Ford" is inherently different from one asking for Vehicles where Type is "Truck." Thus, an OODBMS requires a more intelligent query processing capability than does a structured record system.

A major goal of OODM is to model the behavior, not just the structure of data. Objects interact by understanding certain messages, which are passed between objects. A message, together with any arguments in the message, activates a procedure. The object reacts to the message by executing the appropriate procedure and returning an object in response. This scenario is depicted in Figure 3-28.

We distinguish between object classes and instances, much as we did entity classes and instances. An **object class** is a logical grouping of object instances that share the same attributes and operations. An **object instance** is one member (or materialization) of an object class. All of the attributes and procedures for the class are described in one place (the class object). For example, the operation LENGTH would be defined with the string object class to calculate the number of characters in a character string. Fur-

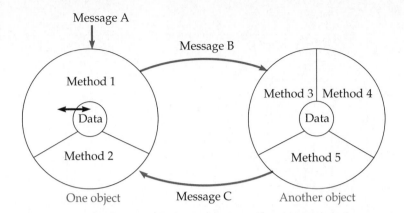

Figure 3-28
The object-oriented
environment of
objects, methods,
and data

ther, object instances may contain attributes or procedures that are just for that instance and, hence, not shared with the other instances of the same class. Table 3-3 shows the approximate equivalences of various object-oriented and conventional data modeling terms.

The combination of values of all the attributes of an object instance represent the **state** of that object instance. Attributes are themselves objects, with subattributes such as type and value. A primitive object, such as an integer or a character string, has no subattributes. Because each object is built up in a custom fashion from primitive objects, objects are not constrained as are relations or record types. As long as new primitive objects can be defined, the capabilities for data modeling can be extended in the OODM.

Objects cut across the boundaries of entities and relations. A property of an object need not be a simple data value object but can be other complex objects. An object can include a set of values. For example, consider Figure 3-29, which depicts a customer object. This object includes data from both Customer and Order entities and is a mixture of simple and complex attribute objects. Compared to the relational data model, the Customer object will be linked to its related Order objects without the need for cross-reference data. Thus, this is no concern with referential integrity: An Order is or is not part of a specific Customer object.

Table 3-3 Approximate Equivalences of Object-oriented and Conventional Data Modeling Terms

Object-oriented	Conventional
Object	Record instance, row
Object class	Record type, table
Instance attribute	Field
Instance attribute constraint	Field type, coming in
Message	Procedure call
Method	Procedure

Figure 3-29
Example of a complex customer object

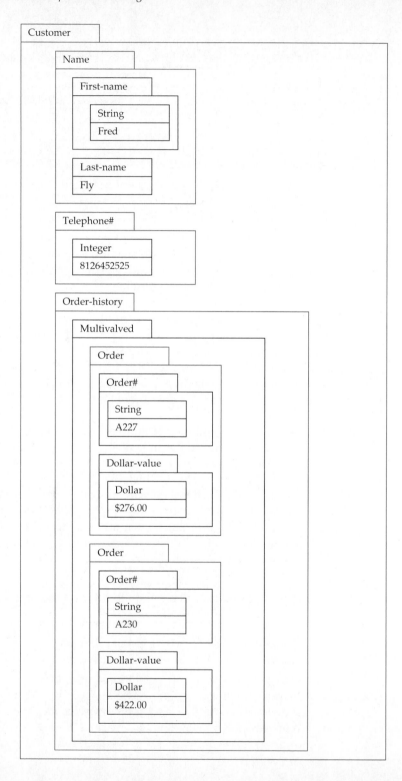

A wide variety of procedures can be associated with an object, and as such, any program that uses an object automatically has available the procedures associated with the object. Thus, the object-oriented data model possesses a high degree of reusability and ease of maintenance. For instance, the object class Product in Pine Valley Furniture may be associated with the method "Print stockout," which would display the products with zero quantity on hand when properly activated. If there were several subclasses of Products (for example, Custom Product, Stock Product, and Purchased Product), each would inherit this procedure. Further, if Purchased Product were also a subclass of the Purchased Materials object (since subclasses may form a lattice structure, not just a tree), it would inherit the attributes and procedures of that superclass as well. If we wish to change a procedure, we need only change it in one place.

The kind of object discussed above is called a **passive object,** since it performs a given operation only when it is asked to do so (sent a message indicating what procedure to invoke with what inputs). An **active object,** sometimes called an actor, performs operations even in the absence of an external stimulus. Active objects are independent tasks that can operate concurrently with interaction.

Data, data definitions, and procedures are uniformly modeled in the object-oriented approach. For example, a Product object may have an attribute of Volume, which is another object which activates a procedure for calculating the value of this attribute. Equally important is that in the object-oriented approach, object classes and instances may be dynamically created, so the database is not bound by any initial structure. The concepts of object, method, attribute, class-subclass, inheritance, and so on are the structural elements of the database, which can be dynamically combined as needed.

In a pure object environment, each operation is associated with some object, so operations (including programs) do not exist in isolation. Thus, the design of database applications under an object orientation concentrates on the identification of objects rather than on procedures. Procedures may have either or both input and output.

The object-oriented approach is not just for data modeling, but it is also the basis for database management systems. Two products, Gemstone by Servio Logic Corp and Vbase by Ontologic, Inc. are now operational on a variety of hardware platforms.

FACTORS IN SELECTING A DATA MODEL

The diversity of data models presented in this chapter would suggest that the developer of a database has a difficult choice in selecting an appropriate data model. No single choice is best in all situations; in fact, the evidence suggests that the best choice is to use several data models, each for different purposes.

The choice of an appropriate internal data model should not be made until the conceptual database is described, since the nature of the database (types of relationships present, data processing requirements, and so on) will dictate the best internal data model. Basically, this choice is coupled with the selection of a DBMS and will be based primarily on the adequacy of implementing the conceptual database, the efficiency of the DBMS product, vendor support, price, and various other technical and managerial factors. Chapter 9 will review this choice in more detail. For our purposes here, however, it will be useful to concentrate on one multifaceted factor that can be called "ease of use" as a perspective on evaluating any data model.

For an internal data model and associated DBMS, ease of use primarily relates to the programming interface of the database software. Reisner (1981) has reviewed a wide range of research on database query languages. These studies have defined ease of use via such precise, quantitative variables as number and severity of errors made during programming, correctness of interpreting the true meaning of a query statement, correctness of specifying the result of a query against a sample database, training time to reach a specific level of expertise, time to write queries, and confidence that queries written are correct. Most of these studies have been conducted over short time periods, so long-term retention and the effects of prolonged use of query languages or the data models they use are still unknown.

Although these studies reported by Reisner have done much to structure an approach to evaluating query languages and data models, the results have been inconclusive. Some studies have recognized that inexperienced computer users are able to perform better with relational query languages both before and after minimal exposure to such languages than with query languages associated with hierarchical or network database management systems. More seasoned computer users—those with training in procedural languages—are able to deal with all languages equally well after minimal exposure. Studies have concluded that it is difficult to separate the effects of the query language from the underlying data model; thus, we are not certain whether problems are in the syntax and grammar of query languages or in the internal data models themselves.

One specific study by Brosey and Shneiderman (1978) tried to isolate the effects of the data model by measuring the results of manually using a sample database. Their results indicated that a hierarchical model was easier for beginners to use, but there was no difference in ease of use for more experienced subjects. However, these researchers readily admitted that the database used in the study had a "natural tree structure," which parallels the hierarchical data model structure. Related, basic research in psychology on human information organization has shown similar results. People are able to use a variety of data organizations effectively, as long as they are not forced to use a structure incapable of capturing the true meaning of data. Thus, it would appear that the "natural" structure of data, more than individual, personal preferences, is what matters.

Another study (Hoffer, 1982) confirms this observation in an environment more akin to conceptual data modeling than programming. In an experiment in which subjects were asked to represent a database for a situation described in narrative form, a wide variety of data models were used, and often hybrids were developed. Although relational-like architectures were used frequently, the most popular was flow diagrams! Again, more questions were raised than were answered, but several conclusions from this and other work are apparent. First, no one data model dominates others in understandability or any sense of ease of use. Second, since different people with different skills and experience are able to use different data models with various abilities, a database practitioner must be able to use a variety of data models appropriate for the database and the user. Finally, data modeling is closely tied to information systems modeling (flowcharts), and the true meaning of data comes from understanding the whole data processing environment. That is, data modeling is part of information systems modeling, and database design is part of information systems design.

Finally, a recent study by Batra, Hoffer, and Bostrom (1990) directly compared a form of E-R modeling to relational. Here subjects were given a narrative description of a business and asked to develop a data model that described that organization. One group used E-R notation and the other used relational. The results suggest that in most dimensions of data modeling, E-R was superior for inexperienced data analysts. This is an important result for end-user development of systems since most end-user managers are not experienced in data analysis or processing. Thus, there is growing evidence that E-R (and potentially other semantically rich data modeling styles), due to its explicit, graphical notation and ability to incorporate many semantics, is today the best choice for conceptual data modeling.

SUMMARY

This chapter has reviewed the basic concepts of data, data modeling, and the major data models that influence the data management field. The fundamental concepts such as attribute, entity, and association, on which all data models are based, were systematically developed. These concepts and models have been reviewed apart from their technological implementations. It is important to recognize that data models are distinct from database management systems and that data must first be understood before it can be accurately represented in databases.

The entity-relationship data model was reviewed as the primary tool used today by professional data and systems analysts for external and conceptual data modeling. Various data semantics (cardinality, degree, uniqueness, time, class-subclass, aggregation, and existence) were introduced and it was illustrated if and how different data modeling styles deal with such characteristics of data.

The challenge to database and data processing professionals is to learn various data models in order to be able to use each as the situation dictates. This chapter addressed the ability of the E-R, relational, and object-oriented data models and the data concepts on which they are based to represent data and relationships. Further, this chapter addressed these data models independently of particular database management systems (to be covered in Chapters 10 to 14)—thus, these principles can be applied in the use of any DBMS.

Chapter Review

REVIEW QUESTIONS

1. Define each of the following terms:
   - a. entity
   - b. entity class
   - c. association
   - d. metadata
   - e. attribute
   - f. data item
   - g. data aggregate
   - h. record
   - i. file
   - j. primary key
   - k. secondary key
   - l. data model
   - m. external data model
   - n. conceptual data model
   - o. internal data model
   - p. unary relationship
   - q. class-subclass relationship
   - r. aggregation relationship
   - s. relation
   - t. functional dependency
   - u. object
   - v. method
   - w. relational data model
   - x. entity-relationship data model

2. Contrast the following items:
   - a. physical data independence; logical data independence
   - b. primary key; secondary key
   - c. conceptual model; external model
   - d. attribute; data item
   - e. entity; entity class
   - f. entity class; object

3. Briefly describe each of the following:
   - a. conceptual model
   - b. external model
   - c. internal model

4. Briefly describe the three realms used in describing data.

5. Many people have trouble distinguishing an entity from a relationship. For example, do you regard marriage as a relationship or an entity? Why?

6. Explain why it is desirable to use a technology-independent data model for external or conceptual data modeling.

7. Explain the purpose of the inverse clause in the Semantic Data Model.

PROBLEMS AND EXERCISES

1. Match each term with the appropriate definition.

_____ metadata	**a)** performs operation only when asked
_____ attribute	**b)** object or event
_____ data item	**c)** adopting properties of a superclass
_____ data aggregate	**d)** named collection of data items
_____ secondary key	**e)** information about data
_____ entity	**f)** one row of a relation
_____ entity class	**g)** data elements must have common values
_____ primary key	**h)** the number of entities that participate in a relationship
_____ data model	**i)** uniquely identifies a record
_____ referential integrity	**j)** collection of related entities
_____ aggregation	**k)** set of possible values for an attribute
_____ passive object	**l)** number of tuples in a relation
_____ intersection record	**m)** property of an entity
_____ inheritance	**n)** collection of similar entities
_____ tuple	**o)** identifies records that share a common property
_____ domain	**p)** unit fact
_____ cardinality of relation	**q)** contains meaningful data
_____ functional dependency	**r)** not chosen as primary key
_____ degree of relationship	**s)** relationship between attributes
_____ alternate keys	**t)** an abstract representation of data in an organization

2. Consider each of the following changes to a database. Assuming that an application program is unaffected by the change, indicate whether it is an example of logical or physical data independence.
   a. Move the data to newer, faster storage devices.
   b. Change a data item called ZIP-CODE from a five-digit field to a nine-digit field.
   c. Change from indexed sequential access method (ISAM) to virtual sequential access method (VSAM).
   d. Add a new data item called CARPOOL to an existing EMPLOYEE record type.
   e. Add a new record type called TEXTBOOK to an instructional database.

3. Give two examples (other than those in the text) of each of the following associations between two entities:
   a. one-to-one
   b. one-to-many
   c. many-to-many
   d. unary one-to-many
   e. unary many-to-many

4. Examine the PRODUCT data in Figure 3-3 and answer the following questions:
   a. What items are designated bedroom (BR) furniture? (Give the item numbers.)
   b. What items have PINE finish?
   c. What items have a PRICE that is $500 or less?
   d. What items of PINE bedroom furniture sell for $500 or less?

5. Draw a bubble chart (similar to Figure 3-8b) for the secondary key value ROOM'LR' in Figure 3-3.

6. Draw a bubble chart showing the associations between the following data items (make any assumptions that are necessary): STUDENT#, STUDENT-NAME, TELEPHONE#, COURSE#, COURSE-NAME, UNITS, INSTRUCTOR-NAME, INSTRUCTOR-OFFICE#.

7. Combine the following user views into a single view:

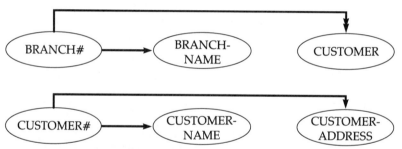

   Show your answer first in one bubble chart and second in one E-R diagram.

8. Draw a data structure diagram for each of the following associations:
   a. A given course can have several prerequisite courses, and a given course can be a prerequisite for several other courses.
   b. A student can register in several courses, and a course can have many students registered.
   c. A computer can run a number of software packages, and each software package can run on zero, one, or many computers.
   d. A student can have zero, one, or many roommates (who are also students).

9. Consider the entities of Vehicle, Buyer, Owner, Sales Invoice, and Service Visit for an automobile dealership. Design a relational and an entity-relationship data model for this situation. Assume any data items you need to give this situation meaning to you.

10. Consider the entities of Project, General Task, and Employee in a project management or job shop organization. Specify relations with typical attributes to represent these entities and the relationships between them.

11. The Bureau of Motor Vehicles can issue an individual several types of driver's licenses: passenger car, chauffeur, farm vehicle, motor bicycle, and so on. Show how to represent this class-subclass relationship using E-R notation.

REFERENCES

Batra, D., J. A. Hoffer, and R. P. Bostrom. 1990. "A Comparison of the Representations Developed Using the Relational and Entity-Relationship Data Models." *Communications of the ACM* (Dec.), 126–140.

Brosey, M., and B. Shneiderman. 1978. "Two Experimental Comparisons of Relational and Hierarchical Database Models." *International Journal of Man-Machine Studies* 10, 625–637.

Chen and Associates. 1988. *E-R Designer Reference Manual.* Baton Rouge, La.: Chen and Associates.

Chen, P. P-S. 1976. "The Entity-Relationship Model—Toward a Unified View of Data." *ACM-TODS* 1 (Mar.), 9-36.

Chen, P. P-S. 1977. *The Entity-Relationship Approach to Logical Data Base Design.* Wellesley, Mass.: Q.E.D. Information Sciences, Data Base Monograph Series no. 6.

Clifford, J., and D. S. Warren. 1983. "Formal Semantics for Time in Databases." *ACM-TODS* 8 (June), 214–245.

Codd, E. F. 1970. "A Relational Model of Data for Large Shared Data Bases." *Communications of the ACM* 13 (June), 77-387.

"The Data Base Debate." 1982. In *Computerworld,* a transcript of part of Data Base '82, a portion of the Wang Institute of Graduate Studies' short summer course.

Date, C. J. 1981. *An Introduction to Data Base Systems.* 3d ed. Reading, Mass.: Addison-Wesley.

DeMarco, T. 1978. *Structured Analysis and System Specification.* New York: Yourdon Press.

Hammer, M., and D. McLeod. 1978. "The Semantic Data Model: A Modelling Mechanism for Data Base Applications." *Proceedings of ACM-SIGMOD Conference 1978,* Austin, Tex., 26-36.

Hoffer, J. A. 1982. "An Empirical Investigation into Individual Differences in Database Models." *Proceedings of Third International Information Systems Conference,* Ann Arbor, Mich. (Dec.), 153–168.

Hull, R. and R. King. 1987. "Semantic Database Modeling: Survey, Applications, and Research Issues." *Computing Surveys* 3 (Sept.), 201–260.

Olle, T. W. 1975. "A Practitioner's View of Relational Data Base Theory." *ACM-SIGMOD FDT-Bulletin* 7 (3-4), 29-43.

Percy, T. 1986. "My Data, Right or Wrong." *Datamation* (June 1), 123.

Reisner, P. 1981. "Human Factor Studies of Database Query Languages: A Survey and Assessment." *Computing Surveys* 13 (March), 13-31.

Smith, J. M., and D. C. P. Smith. 1977. "Database Abstractions: Aggregation and Generalization." *ACM-TODS* 2 (June), 105–133.

Teorey, T. J., and J. P. Fry. 1982. *Design of Database Structures.* Englewood Cliffs, N.J.: Prentice-Hall.

PART II

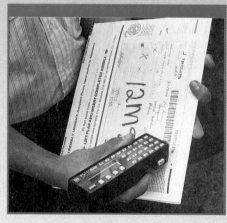

Database Planning and Conceptual Design

DATABASE PLANNING IN AN ENTERPRISE-WIDE DISTRIBUTED ENVIRONMENT

Federal Express

In Part 2 we examine the topics of database planning and conceptual design. The chapters introduce a methodology for database planning. Research has proven the importance of a solid methodological approach to the planning and design process. Keep in mind, however, that successful large information systems are those that blend technology with people, sound management practices, and management vision. A company which has proven this time and again is Federal Express, the leading international firm in the overnight shipping industry.

The technological backbone of Federal Express service is COSMOS (Customer, Operations, Service, Master On-line System). This state-of-the-art package tracking system services Federal Express customers worldwide. Other industry package tracking systems rely on paperwork associated with a shipment and usually track individual pack-

ages only where problems have occurred. Only Federal Express physically tracks each package from the point of origin to final destination. This system enables customer service agents to provide information on the actual location of any package shipped with the firm at any point in time.

Federal Express couriers carry a hand-held device called a SuperTracker while making package pickups and deliveries. The Super-Tracker is a microprocessor with 392k memory. It stores routing codes and data processing tables and is used to scan barcoded airbills on packages and envelopes. Each Federal Express delivery vehicle is equipped with a Digitally Assisted Dispatch System (DADS) terminal. While a courier is driving between destinations, the SuperTracker is placed into a receptacle in the DADS terminal. DADS interrogates the SuperTracker and uploads data into Federal Express's central COSMOS system (19 call centers in a distributed network). Within three to five minutes of pickup, a customer can call the toll-free 800 service center number to check the status of a shipment.

Further, the telephone will never be busy because COSMOS senses when a particular call center is approaching capacity and automatically switches the customer to an alternative center in the network. Theoretically, a customer normally serviced by the Sacramento, California center could be serviced by a representative at the Columbia, Maryland center with no loss of quality of service.

COSMOS presents a seamless image to customer contact employees or anybody else in Federal Express with a computer terminal, even though the data are stored in multiple databases in a distributed environment. Yet this system did not develop overnight. The need for a positive tracking system was recognized as early as 1976. The Federal Express airbill containing an 11-digit barcode was introduced in 1980. COSMOS was activated in January 1979. The SuperTracker as a portable microprocessor was tested in 1984 and implemented in 1986. This evolution and the underlying database planning was accomplished effectively and efficiently even though the firm was experiencing tremendous growth rates (1989 annual revenue exceeded $5 billion). While the planning and evolution of COSMOS proves the importance of database planning, it also proves the importance of other factors which you will study in this part of the book. These include management vision and the necessity for management commitment to the long-term development of database application systems.

CHAPTER 4

Strategic Data and Systems Planning

INTRODUCTION

Database systems were first installed in business enterprises during the late 1960s. Since that time, thousands of organizations have converted to this approach, yet the promise of database remains largely unrealized in many companies. According to Voell (1980):

> Database and data administration have, by and large, not lived up to the expectations and promises made in most writings. The corporate database integrated to reduce redundancy, accessible to multiple applications, protected from the unauthorized, and controlled so that it contains only valid information is a myth. Today, database is largely just an access method. Similarly, the data administration function is not controlling a global view of information. The real promise and benefits of a corporate database are valid, but are yet to be realized.

Although much progress has been made since 1980, many organizations today are still not realizing the benefits of the database approach. According to a recent survey of Fortune 500 companies, only 40% of the companies are using database technology for a majority of their applications. Many of these companies have discovered that their present information systems are inadequate to cope with today's competitive pressures. For example, Sony Corporation of America wanted to consolidate and track information on over 16,000 different products and on its customers. The company discovered they had 24 different profit centers, each with its own separate

135

information systems. As a result, the company could not share information across functional boundaries. Sony is now in the middle of a long-term program to integrate its information systems using database technology that will allow it to share data and processes across functional areas in the company (Moad, 1989).

In some ways, rapid advances in technology have hindered (rather than supported) a true database approach. The explosion in personal computers, inexpensive data management software, and end-user computing have often resulted in a proliferation of redundant databases and the erosion of data quality throughout the organization. Only by careful planning can an organization harness these trends and move toward the goal of information resource management.

Strategic data and systems planning is an orderly means of assessing the information needs of an organization and defining the systems and databases that will best satisfy those needs. Strategic data and systems planning (hereafter called strategic IS planning) is a top-down process that takes into account the outside forces that drive the business and the factors critical to the success of the firm. It looks at data and systems in terms of how they help business achieve its objectives (Index Technology, 1988).

IMPORTANCE OF STRATEGIC IS PLANNING

Traditionally, information systems have not really been planned at all but have evolved in a "bottom-up" fashion as stand-alone systems to solve isolated organizational problems. In effect, traditional information systems ask the question: What procedure (application program) is required to solve this particular problem as it exists today? The problem with this approach is that the required organizational procedures are likely to change over time as the environment changes. For example, a company may decide to change its method of billing customers, or a university may change its procedures for registering students. When such changes occur, it is usually necessary to modify existing application programs.

In contrast, data resource management essentially asks the question: What database requirements will satisfy the information needs of the enterprise today and well into the future? A major advantage of this approach is that an organization's data is less likely to change (or will change more slowly) than its procedures. For example, unless an organization changes its business fundamentally, its underlying data structures will remain reasonably stable over a ten-year period. However, the procedures used to access and process the data will change many times during that period. Thus, the challenge of data resource management is to design stable databases that are relatively independent of the languages and programs used to update them.

To benefit from this database approach, the organization must analyze its information needs and plan its databases carefully. If a database approach is attempted without such planning, the results may well be disastrous.

The resulting databases may support individual applications but will not provide a resource that can be shared by users throughout the organization.

The need for improved information systems planning in organizations today is readily apparent, when we consider factors such as the following:

1. The cost of information systems has risen steadily and approaches 40% of total expenses in some organizations.

2. Systems cannot handle applications that cross organizational boundaries.

3. Systems often do not address the critical problems of the business as a whole, or support strategic applications.

4. Data redundancy is often out of control, and users may have little confidence in the quality of data.

5. Systems maintenance costs are out of control as old, poorly planned systems must constantly be revised.

6. Application backlogs often extend three years or more, and frustrated end users rush to create (or purchase) their own systems, often creating redundant databases in the process.

Strategic information systems planning will certainly not solve all of these problems in itself. However, we believe that this type of planning, driven by top management commitment, is a prerequisite if the benefits of information resource management are to be realized. According to Holland (1980): "A very few organizations are superimposing a data model over their business systems plan. These are the electronic organizations of the future that will significantly reduce their maintenance costs, provide program and data independence, add new applications with ease and enjoy an effective user environment."

PHILOSOPHY OF IS PLANNING

Before describing the steps in modern strategic information systems planning, we discuss two important planning premises:

1. Strategic information systems planning must be closely integrated (or linked) with strategic business planning.

2. A major goal of IS planning is to achieve "application independence," so that data is stored in subject databases completely independent of user applications.

Integration with Business Planning

Strategic information systems planning must be an integral part of strategic business planning, if information systems are to support the business directions. For example, if a hospital is planning to merge with another hospital, or to launch a series of community treatment centers, its information sys-

Figure 4-1
Linking strategic
business and IS
planning

tems plans must be sufficiently comprehensive to support these new business directions.

Figure 4-1 shows this close linkage between business planning and information systems planning. The downward-pointing arrow in this figure indicates that the information systems plan is determined directly from the business plan (or better yet, is an integral part of that plan). Of course, to achieve this integration, the chief information officer must be a member of the senior management planning team.

Notice that there is also an upward-pointing arrow in Figure 4-1. This indicates that a comprehensive strategic information systems plan can also be used to shape the business plan. That is, the organization should use the information systems plan in its search for strategic business opportunities.

Application Independence

As we stated in Chapter 1, database management systems support data independence—that is, data definitions are separated from application programs. The purpose of this approach is to allow various users to easily share data and to allow certain kinds of changes to occur to the data without massive program maintenance. Unfortunately, these goals are often subverted because organizations often design and implement databases for individual applications. Thus there is a database for order processing, another for inventory control, still another for shipping and billing, and so on (this is especially likely to occur where end users develop their own applications without coordination). As a result there is extensive data duplication, and it is difficult to share data across applications and functions.

A major goal of IS planning is to correct this problem through application independence, so that the source of data is transparent to the user-manager. A set of "subject databases" are created independent of organizational applications. Typical subject databases in corporations are the following (Martin, 1982): products, customers, parts, vendors, orders, and personnel. These databases may have redundancy, but the redundancy is carefully planned and controlled. Consistent data definitions are used throughout all the subject databases.

As shown in Figure 4-2, there are three types of databases in this new architecture: operational, managerial, and strategic (these types were introduced in Chapter 1). Three types of data systems are also recognized: data capture, data transfer, and distribution.

Data capture systems are used to acquire and edit data and then maintain the databases in which these data are stored. These might be data found in business transactions or from external sources. **Data transfer systems** extract, summarize, and aggregate data and transfer it to other databases (for example, from operational to managerial or strategic databases). **Distribution systems** provide printed reports, analysis, and inquiry responses to user-managers.

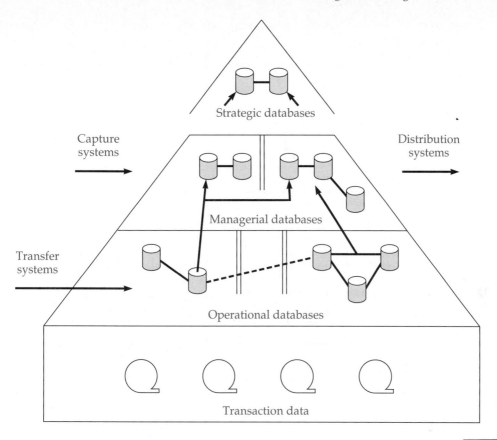

Figure 4-2
Subject databases

Subject databases are designed and implemented entirely independently of applications (this requires strong coordination from the data administration function). When a new application is developed, the existing databases are first checked to determine whether the necessary data to support the application already exist. If not, data administration authorizes new subjects to be added to the database to support this application.

STRATEGIC IS PLANNING PROCESS

In this section we describe a methodology (or process) for strategic information systems planning (see Figure 4-3). Although there is no standard methodology for IS planning, most methodologies have certain techniques in common (Index Technologies, 1988):

1. **A top-down approach.** Planning begins with the business and the data it uses and leads to ideas for specific projects.

Figure 4-3
IS planning process

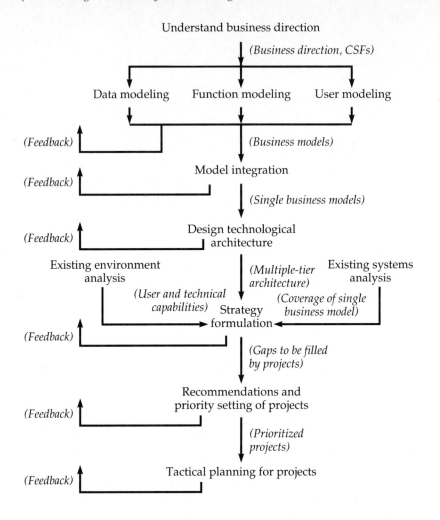

2. **Modeling.** Planners define models of business functions, data use, and related factors, often in matrix form.

3. **Involvement and accountability.** A planning team is established, and planning involves all levels of management.

4. **Time limits.** Because information technology (and business conditions) change so rapidly, planning should be completed quickly—in three to six months, if possible.

Planning Prerequisites

Before the planning process shown in Figure 4-3 commences, three important preliminary steps must be accomplished.

1. **Top management commitment.** Top management must be fully committed and prepared to become actively involved in the planning process.

2. **Project team.** A project team comprised of user-managers and information systems specialists should be appointed to perform strategic information systems planning. The team should have a strong leader (preferably a user-manager) and should act under the guidance of top management.

3. **Planning methodology.** The team should select a planning methodology that is consistent with corporate needs and that is supported by comprehensive CASE tools (we discuss CASE tools later in this chapter).

Planning Steps

Following is a brief discussion of the steps in the planning process shown in Figure 4-3. Most of these steps (which are illustrated throughout the chapter) require extensive interviews with all managers in organization.

1. **Understanding business direction.** Define and/or understand business goals, strategies, and critical success factors.

2. **Business modeling.** Develop formal models for data, functions, and users.
   a. **User modeling.** Develop models of the organization showing the organizational components, decisions made at each level, the flow of information, and the need for information by each manager.
   b. **Function modeling.** Define business functions, processes, and activities.
   c. **Data modeling.** Define business entities and model the relationships among entities.

3. **Model integration.** Combine the models from the previous step through a series of matrices into an integrated business model.

4. **Design technological architecture.** Design an architecture (hardware, data communications, database, organization, systems software) to support the strategic direction of the organization over the planning horizon (at least three to five years).

5. **Strategy formulation.** Combine the results of the previous steps with an analysis of existing systems to identify gaps to be filled with new systems projects.

6. **Recommendations and priority setting of projects.** Identify new systems projects to fill the gaps identified in the previous step, and establish priorities for the projects.

7. **Tactical planning for projects.** Develop project schedules and resource allocations for new projects.

There are two major outputs (or deliverables) from the strategic planning process just described:

1. An evolving information systems architecture for the organization over the planning horizon
2. A prioritized set of projects (systems and databases) over the planning horizon

CASE Support for Planning

The planning process we have described requires collecting, organizing, and analyzing vast amounts of data. Realistically, this process can only be accomplished with the support of CASE (Computer-Assisted Software Engineering) tools. Some of the important benefits of using CASE tools in strategic IS planning are the following:

- CASE tools provide a structural environment with a common database, a common approach, a standard vocabulary, and a standard user interface.
- Various users can work on different parts of the study at the same time, with the CASE tools providing the necessary integration.
- CASE tools provide a repository for storing vast quantities of information.
- CASE tools provide a decision support environment for analyzing complex relationships and asking "what-if" questions.
- Very importantly, CASE tools simplify the process of updating the strategic plan over time as business conditions change.
- The database developed during strategic planning can become the basis for the following stages of system analysis and project management.

In this section we briefly describe some of the features of the PRISM software product. PRISM stands for people, resources, information, and strategic management (Index Technology, 1988).

Planning Database   The first step in the planning process is to decide what data to collect and how to organize it. The planning data will be stored in the CASE tool repository, and the project team must define the objects (or entities), and the relationships among those objects. The CASE tool provides a database management system (DBMS) for defining, storing, and retrieving the data in the planning database.

If you examine the IS planning process that we are describing (see Figure 4-3), you will notice that the planning team will be collecting data about the following entities: data, functions, users, critical success factors, projects, and information systems. A database structure showing these objects and their relationships is shown in Figure 4-4. The distinction between Figures

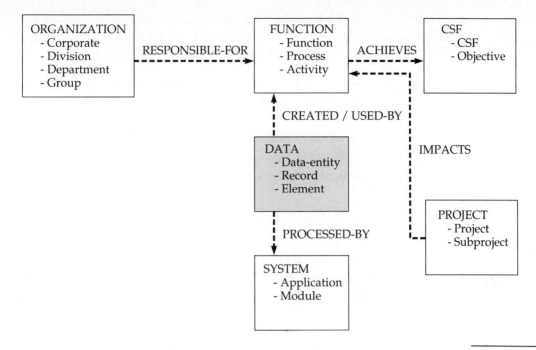

Figure 4-4
Planning database

4-3 and 4-4 is the following: Figure 4-3 defines a process (or series of steps) for strategic planning, while Figure 4-4 defines a database structure that will be used to organize information collected during the planning process.

There are six entities shown in Figure 4-4. Each entity in turn is broken down into several levels, as appropriate. The entities shown in this figure are the following:

1. **Organization:** information on organizational positions at the corporate, division, department, and group level

2. **Function:** information on organizational functions, processes, and activities (we define these terms in the next section)

3. **Critical success factors (CSFs):** information on those areas where things must go right for the company to succeed

4. **Data:** information on data requirements throughout the organization (subcategories are entities, records, and elements)

5. **System:** information on the organization's automated information systems (present and proposed)

6. **Project:** information about candidate projects that will be considered by the organization

A CASE tool such as PRISM is completely flexible and allows the users to define new objects or relationships (or modify or delete existing objects or relationships). For example, the project team could add a new entity called Location (with subdivisions such as Region, State, and City) to record information about the geographical distribution of systems and/or data.

Planning Matrices   We have already noted that the planning database (Figure 4-4) shows the relationships among the planning entities. Each of these relationships is represented as a matrix; for example, one matrix shows the impact of projects on functions. The five matrices that correspond to the relationships in Figure 4-4 are shown in Figure 4-5. They are the following:

1. **Organization Versus Process.** This shows the involvement of managers in the organization with business processes (D = manager directs the process; S = manager supports the process).

2. **Process Versus CSF.** This shows the impact of business processes on CSFs (E = process is essential to the CSF; D = process is desirable or supportive but not essential).

3. **Process Versus Entity.** This shows the creation and use of entities by business processes (C = process creates an entity; U = process uses an entity).

4. **System Versus Entity.** This shows the use of entities by application systems (I = input; P = process; O = output).

5. **Project Versus Process.** This shows the impact of projects (actual or candidate) on business processes.

The CASE tool is used by the project team to construct the planning matrices and analyze the relationships (this corresponds to the Model Integration step shown in Figure 4-3). A typical sequence for analyzing the matrices is the following:

1. Prioritize the organizational CSFs, and use the Process versus CSF matrix (Figure 4-5b) to prioritize business processes.

2. Use the Organization versus Process matrix (Figure 4-5a) to identify management responsibility for high-priority processes.

3. Use the Process versus Entity matrix (Figure 4-5c) to identify data entities created and used by high-priority processes (this step in essence allows the organization to prioritize database development projects).

4. Use the Entity versus System matrix (Figure 4-5d) to identify system applications that input, process, and output high-priority data entities.

5. Use the Project versus Process matrix (Figure 4-5e) to develop candidate projects and prioritize these projects (this corresponds to the "Recommendations and Priority Setting of Projects" step in Figure 4-3).

Although this is a typical sequence, in reality the project team will use the CASE tool iteratively to perform a series of "what-if" analyses. The

Figure 4-5
Systems planning
matrices

Process

Manager				
D				
	D	S	S	
	D			
S	S	D		
		S	D	

(a)

This matrix shows the
involvement of managers
with business processes
(D = directs; S = supports)

CSF

Process				
E		D	D	
	E	E		
D		D	E	
		E		
	D			

(b)

This matrix shows the impact
of business processes on CSFs
(E = essential; D = desirable)

Entity

Process				
C	U		U	
U		U		
	C		U	
C			U	
	U	C		

(c)

This matrix shows the
creation and use of entities
by business processes
(C = creates, U = uses)

Entity

System				
	P		I	
O		P	I	
	I		P	
P	O	O	I	
O	P	I		

(d)

This matrix shows the
use of entities by
application systems
(I = input; P = process;
O = output)

Process

Project				
X		X		
	X		X	
		X		
X			X	
	X	X		

(e)

This matrix shows the
impact of projects
(present and proposed)
on business processes

CASE tool does not automate the planning process but provides the team
with a powerful tool for structuring and analyzing planning data. The objective is to translate organizational goals, objectives, and critical success factors into a series of prioritized projects for databases and information systems.

TOP-DOWN PLANNING AND BOTTOM-UP DESIGN

As shown in Figure 4-6, developing corporate databases requires both top-down planning and bottom-up design. Top-down planning, which is the topic of this chapter, starts with basic organizational goals and objectives. Using CASE tools, we analyze organizational functions, processes, activities, and entities. We then develop an information model in the form of an entity-relationship diagram that portrays the major entities of the organization and the associations between those entities.

Detailed database design is a bottom-up process (see Figure 4-6). Analysts begin with user views of data and apply normalization techniques to develop detailed data models (database design is described in Part 3). In database design, the data models are cross-checked against the information model to ensure that they are complete and accurate. Thus, the top-down information model plays three important roles:

1. It provides an overall, integrative view of corporate entities and data.

2. It provides a basis for segmenting the overall corporate data model into a number of manageable database projects.

3. During detailed database design, it provides a cross-check and means of integrating the individual database into the overall corporate framework.

According to Goodhue, Quillard, and Rockart (1986), organizations frequently modify or abbreviate this complete database planning process. Drastic reduction of this process, however, can lead to failure of the database planning effort. The following cautions need to be observed:

- Although commitment from key business managers is often difficult to obtain and the process is very time consuming, sufficient commitment of time and people is essential.

- Expectations need to be well managed so that all involved realize that this is a long-range planning effort and not one geared to the detailed design of specific applications systems. In fact, a good planning effort designs for business functions, not specific applications.

- Strong reliance on purchased applications systems, designed for narrow applications, can force compromises in the coverage of the database plan. Since organizations are increasingly choosing to purchase application software, those based on database concepts and technology are more desirable since they can more easily be fit into the overall database architecture.

- The bottom-up design is especially vulnerable to business changes. Since a typical database plan can take from 6 to 12 months, the process must be at a high level (as well as base level) of analysis so that these business changes can be incorporated and their effects clearly seen.

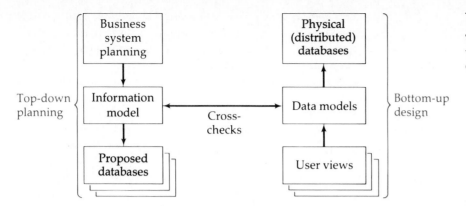

Figure 4-6
Top-down planning
versus bottom-up
design

Reducing the effort of database planning is most effectively done by reducing the *scope* of the database plan. Goodhue, Quillard, and Rockart (1986) have found that this is accomplished by:

1. Targeting each database planning effort on one part (function) of the business (for example, marketing) or division (for example, consumer products). As long as common standards are used for naming and describing data, later cross-database integration is easier.

2. Applying an 80/20 rule to guide database planning. For example, the firm may focus on Customer, Product/Service, and Facility entities as being the most crucial to the business and, hence, providing 80% of the value of database process for 20% of the effort (by eliminating most planning for other subjects of the business, such as Employee, Vendor, Inventory, and other entities).

Database planning is not a trivial effort. The need for professional database planners or administrators is very strong, especially in medium-to-large organizations. User-managers must also be involved especially in information modeling since it is driven from a model of the business. Effective database design not only follows a logical process, as outlined in this chapter, but also requires a team approach involving business experts, database specialists, and application system experts. This team should always be guided by the fact that the objective of database planning is not to better manage data (for its own sake), but rather to solve business problems and exploit opportunities to take advantage of database concepts and technologies.

BUSINESS FUNCTION MODELING

One of the major steps in the IS planning process is modeling business functions (see Figure 4-3). The goal of this process is to analyze the basic business functions and subfunctions of the organization, identifying present and future information needs to support these functions. This analysis of business functions (sometimes called functional decomposition) is independent of existing organizational lines. A top-down graphic approach is used to identify organizational functions. First, the major functions of the organization are identified, each of these functions is then divided into a group of subfunctions, called processes; each process, in turn, is divided (where appropriate) into a set of elementary subfunctions called activities. The business entities required by each of the processes are also identified during the analysis. An example of such an analysis in a manufacturing firm is shown in Figure 4-7 in the form of a simple chart called an **enterprise chart**. In this chart (for example), Materials Management is a business function, Purchasing is a Process within Materials Management, and Select Vendor is an activity within Purchasing.

Business functions are broad groups of closely related activities and decisions that contribute to a product or service life cycle. In Figure 4-7, the functions for the manufacturing firm are identified as follows: planning, materials management, production planning, production operations, and quality assurance. Several additional functions would normally be identified (see Chapter Review exercises). A small company such as Pine Valley Furniture Company may have from 5 to 10 functions, while a large corporation such as IBM or AT&T might have 20 or more functions.

A business function may correspond to an existing organizational unit, or it may cut across several existing units. For example, the quality assurance business function in Figure 4-7 may actually be spread across several organizational units, such as engineering, purchasing, and quality control. It is far better to relate database design to basic organizational functions and processes than to organizational units, since the latter are subject to frequent change.

Business processes are decision-related activities that occur within a function and often serve to manage people, money, material, or information. In Figure 4-7, the materials management function has been subdivided into the following processes: requirements planning, purchasing, receiving, inventory accounting, and warehousing. Business processes should again reflect related activity groupings rather than existing departmental functions. Each business function within an organization can normally be modeled with some three to ten processes.

Business activities are specific operations or transactions that are required to carry out a process. When you ask an employee what he or she is doing at a particular time, his (or her) response is likely to be an activity, for example: "I am admitting a patient." If an activity is automated, it will be as a single module or procedure.

Martin (1982) lists the following guidelines to identify well-formed activities:

1. An activity produces some clearly identifiable results (product, idea, decision, and so on). It should be possible to identify the purpose and result of the activity in a single sentence.

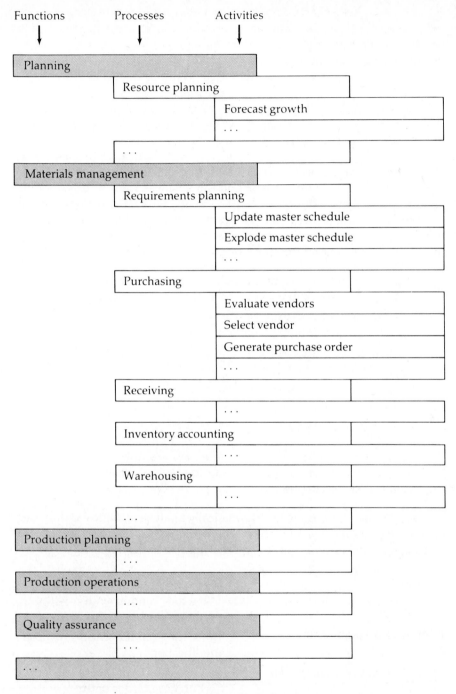

Figure 4-7
Business chart for a manufacturing company

Functions   Processes   Activities

Planning

Resource planning

Forecast growth

. . .

. . .

Materials management

Requirements planning

Update master schedule

Explode master schedule

. . .

Purchasing

Evaluate vendors

Select vendor

Generate purchase order

. . .

Receiving

. . .

Inventory accounting

. . .

Warehousing

. . .

. . .

Production planning

. . .

Production operations

. . .

Quality assurance

. . .

. . .

2. An activity has clear boundaries—there is a clear beginning and ending. Activities do not overlap with each other.

3. An activity is carried out as a unit, by a single person or a team.

4. Once initiated, an activity proceeds largely independently of other activities (thus there is more interaction between team members than between separate teams).

5. Business entities are persons, objects, or events about which information is recorded in the database. Many of the entities associated with a business process can be identified by reviewing the activities for that process. For example, by reviewing the activities for the purchasing process, we identify the following entities: Vendor, Purchase Orders, and Invoices.

To identify all important entities and their relationships, we must fully understand each business process and the business rules or practices that govern each activity within the company. To gain this depth of understanding, the database analyst must work closely with the end users who perform each activity. It is helpful to realize that each activity normally affects one (or more) entities in one (or more) of the following ways:

1. **Creates a new entity occurrence.** For example, the activity "admit student" creates a new occurrence of the Student entity.

2. **Deletes an entity occurrence.** For example, the activity "fire employee" deletes an occurrence of the Employee entity.

3. **Modifies an entity.** For example, the activity "promote employee" modifies an occurrence of the Employee entity.

4. **Establishes a relationship between two (or more) entities.** For example, the activity "enroll student" establishes a relationship between a Student entity occurrence and a Course entity occurrence (other activities may modify or delete relationships between entities).

5. **Uses an entity without modification.** For example, the activity "evaluate vendors" uses occurrences of the Vendor entity without modifying those occurrences.

We may use these rules to systematically analyze activities and to identify entities and their relationships. Following is the result of applying this technique to the activities in the purchasing process of Figure 4-7:

Activity	Result
1. Evaluate Vendors	1. Uses the Vendor entity without modification
2. Select Vendor	2. Uses the Vendor entity without modification
3. Generate purchase order	3. a. Creates a new occurrence of the Purchase Order entity b. Creates an association between the entities Vendor, Purchase Order, Buyer, and Parts

Case Example: Mountain View Community Hospital

The strategic IS planning process we have described is illustrated in this section with the case example of a hospital, an organization familiar to most people. Although the example is hypothetical, it does contain many of the elements of a real hospital environment. The same case is used in later chapters to illustrate detailed database design and implementation.

Identifying the Business Environment

Mountain View Community Hospital is a not-for-profit, short-term, acute-care general hospital. It is a small to medium-size hospital, with 100 beds at the present time. Mountain View Community is the only hospital in the city of Mountain View, a rapidly growing city in the heart of the Rocky Mountains with a population of about 25,000 people.

An organizational chart for Mountain View Community Hospital is shown in Figure 4-8. Like most hospitals, Mountain View Community is divided into two organizational groups. The physicians, headed by Dr. Browne (chief of staff), are responsible for the quality of medical care provided to their patients. The group headed by Ms. Baker (administrator) provides the nursing, clinical, and administrative support the physicians need to serve their patients.

Understanding the Business Direction

Mountain View Community Hospital has a long-range plan that was prepared two years ago with the assistance of a management consulting firm. The plan, which covers a ten-year period, defines the hospital's service area and its forecasted growth, identifies basic goals and objectives, and identifies the capacity and resources that will be required to meet future needs.

Although most admissions to Mountain View Community Hospital are from the city of Mountain View, some patients are also admitted from the surrounding rural areas. As a result, the entire county in which Mountain View is located (Mesa County) was defined as the hospital's service area. The population of Mesa County is about 40,000 at present and has been growing at an annual rate of 8%, a trend that is expected to continue for several years.

The basic goal of Mountain View Community Hospital is to continue to meet the needs of Mountain View and Mesa County for high-quality health care, while containing costs that have been rising in accordance with national trends in recent years.

To support the expected demand for services, the long-range plan calls for the expansion and modernization of facilities, including the addition of a new wing in five years, allowing expansion from the present 100 to 150 beds. Adequate land already exists for this expansion, as well as for addi-

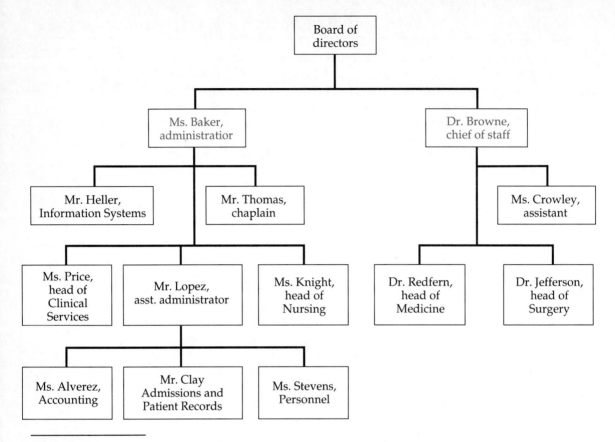

Figure 4-8
Organization chart
for Mountain View
Community Hospital

tional parking facilities. Also, several existing facilities are to be renovated, including the Admitting and Outpatient registration areas. Two new service facilities are planned over a five-year period: Ultrasound and Occupational Therapy.

Existing Information Systems

Mountain View Community has a minicomputer that was leased several years ago. The system has 4 MB central memory and 300 MB on-line disk storage capacity. Plans call for adding a faster processor and additional memory and disk storage capacity during the coming year; the extent of these additions, however, has yet to be determined.

Present information systems are batch oriented and include application programs for patient accounting, billing and accounts receivable, and financial accounting. These application packages were obtained from a software vendor specializing in hospital applications.

Mr. Heller, who was recently appointed manager of Information Systems, identified the following deficiencies with the present systems:

1. The systems do not support the medical staff by recording or reporting the results of laboratory tests and procedures.

2. Since the systems are batch oriented, they do not support on-line procedures such as patient registration or inquiries regarding billing.

3. The systems do not accumulate costs by department or cost centers.

4. The systems are inflexible and do not respond well to changing management needs or to the frequent changes in reporting requirements of external health agencies.

Management at Mountain View Community had for some time recognized that the present information systems were not responsive to their needs. Mr. Lopez (assistant administrator), who had previous experience with database in a large city hospital, had advocated that Mountain View Community investigate this approach. Mr. Heller was hired as manager of Information Systems partly because of his experience with database systems. A new systems analyst (Mr. Helms) also was recently hired. Mr. Helms had experience in database design, and it was expected that he would be a candidate for the data administrator position if and when it was approved by the board of directors.

At a meeting of the board of directors, Mr. Heller explained the concept of data resource management. Ms. Baker (hospital administrator) proposed that Mountain View Community adopt this approach and that Mr. Helms be appointed data administrator. The board of directors agreed with the concept but insisted on a study to estimate costs and benefits as well as develop an overall strategic information systems plan. Ms. Baker formed a study team with the following members: Mr. Lopez, assistant administrator (leader); Ms. Knight, head of nursing; Mr. Crowley, assistant chief of staff; Mr. Heller, manager of Information Systems; and Mr. Helms, systems analyst. An outside consultant was hired to assist them, who spent several days helping the team outline the study approach and establish schedules. At the suggestion of the consultant, the hospital acquired the PRISM CASE tool to support the planning effort.

Critical Success Factors

The study team interviewed Ms. Baker (hospital administrator) and other top managers to determine critical success factors (CSFs) for the hospital. CSFs are those key factors (usually between three and six in number) that must be done well if an organization is to succeed. For example, in a microelectronics company, critical success factors might include product innovation, high quality, and strict cost controls.

The study team identified three critical success factors for Mountain View Community Hospital: excellence in care, cost control, and recruitment and retention of skilled personnel (especially nurses). Each CSF can be broken down into several lower-level objectives. For example, three objectives were identified for the cost control CSF:

1. Improved inventory control
2. Improved staff scheduling
3. Improved vendor selection

At this point the study team had completed the first step in the IS planning process: Understand Business Direction (Figure 4-3). The team entered information describing the organization, existing information systems, and CSFs into the PRISM database (Figure 4-4).

Business Function Modeling

The study team reviewed Mountain View Community Hospital's long-range plan and proceeded to model the business functions, processes, and activities. First, the team identified the basic functions of a small general hospital, which, illustrated in Figure 4-9, consist of the following:

- **Patient Care Administration,** to manage the logistical and record-keeping aspects of patient care
- **Clinical Services,** to provide laboratory testing and procedures and patient monitoring and screening
- **Patient Care Service,** to provide patients with medical care and support services
- **Financial Management,** to manage the financial resources and operations of the hospital
- **Administrative Services,** to provide general management and support services

Figure 4-9
Hospital business functions (Mountain View Community Hospital)

Having identified the basic functions, the study team's next step was to define the processes for each function. The project team spent considerable time interviewing managers and other key staff members throughout the

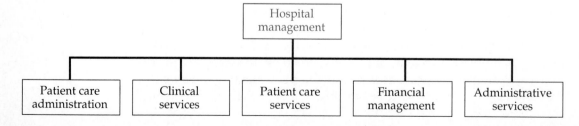

hospital to clarify the process definitions. In total, 22 processes were identified for Mountain View Community Hospital (see Figure 4-10). As the functions and processes were defined, their descriptions were entered into the PRISM database, and also the team members entered data defining relationships among the organization components, processes, entities, and critical success factors (see Figure 4-5).

As each process was defined, the team members also defined key activities within each process: For example, one of the activities within Rehabilitation is "Perform Physical Therapy." (A few of these activities are shown in the enterprise chart (Figure 4-10).) The activity descriptions were also added to the PRISM database.

As the processes and activities were defined, the study team also identified ten entity classes for the hospital that are directly related to the processes and activities in Figure 4-10: Hospital, Physician, Patient, Ward, Staff, Laboratory, Test, Medical/Surgical Item, Supply-Item, and Vendor. These are broad classes of data (or subject databases) that will be further refined during logical database design. Descriptions of these entity classes were entered into the PRISM database, together with process-versus-entity and system-versus-entity data (Figure 4-5c and 4-5d).

Model Integration

When all of the planning data had been entered into the CASE database, the planning team proceeded to analyze the data and integrate the various models. This step included constructing an entity-relationship diagram for the hospital and analyzing the planning matrices.

Entity-Relationship Diagram   The team analyzed the relationship among the ten entity classes and constructed an entity-relationship diagram (see Figure 4-11). Following is a brief description of the relationships shown in the figure.

- A Hospital maintains a number of Laboratories (radiology, electrodiagnosis, hematology, and so on).
- A Hospital contains a number of Wards (obstetrics, emergency, rehabilitation, and so on).
- Each Ward is assigned a certain number of staff members (nurses, secretaries, and so on).
- A Hospital has a number of physicians on its medical staff. In general, a Physician may be on the staff of more than one Hospital.
- There are two associations between Physician and Patient: Diagnoses and Treats (that is, prescribes treatments). Each patient may be diagnosed and/or treated by more than one physician.

Figure 4-10
Business chart
(Mountain View
Community Hospital)

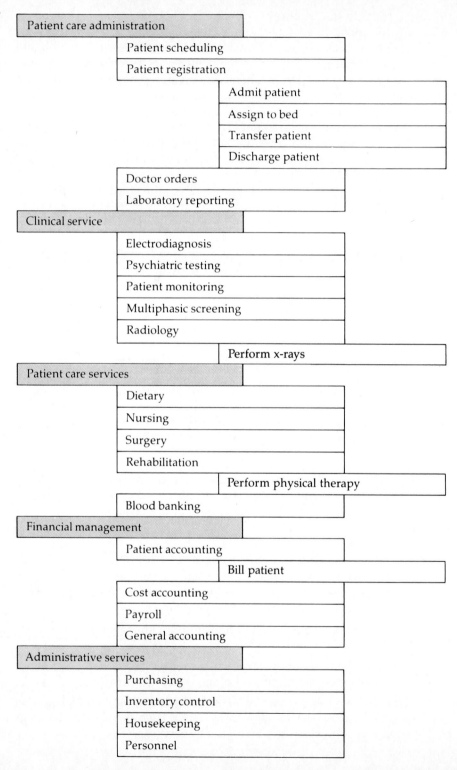

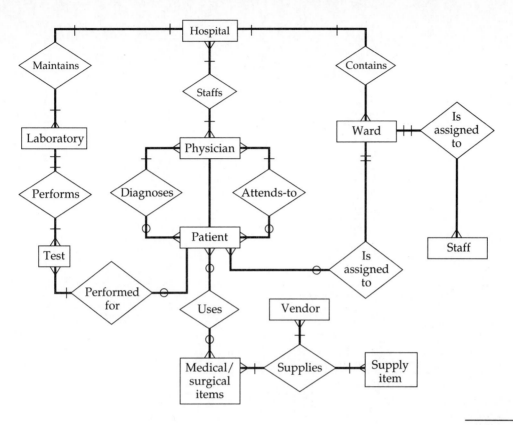

Figure 4-11
Entity-relationship
diagram (Mountain
View Community
Hospital)

- Patients use Medical/Surgical Items, which are supplied by the Vendors. Vendors also provide items called Supply Items that are used for housekeeping and maintenance.

- Laboratories are used to perform Tests for Patients.

The study team recognized that the E-R diagram shown in Figure 4-11 is preliminary in nature. Some additional entity classes that will have to be added to the model in the future include the following: Equipment, Blood Donor, Volunteer, and Benefactor. However, the present model represents an important subset of the information resources for a small hospital.

Process-Versus-Entity Matrix   The study team used PRISM to print a first version of the process-versus-entity class matrix (see Figure 4-12). This matrix maps the 22 processes in Figure 4-10 versus the 10 entity classes shown in Figure 4-11. A "C" indicates that a process creates an entity, while a "U" indicates that a process uses an entity. For example, in Figure 4-12 we see that the Patient Registration process creates a Patient entity and uses the Ward entity. By *create* we mean that the process creates an instance of the entity (a creating process may also update and delete an instance). A process

Figure 4-12
Process versus entity class matrix (preliminary)

Process \ Entity class	Hospital	Physician	Patient	Ward	Staff	Laboratory	Test	Medical/ surgical item	Supply item	Vendor
Patient registration			C	U						
Patient scheduling		U	U			U				
Physician orders		U	U				U			
Laboratory reporting			U			U	U			
Electrodiagnosis							C			
Psychiatric testing							C			
Patient monitoring			U							
Multiphasic screening			U			U	C			
Radiology						U	C			
Dietary			U							
Nursing			U							
Surgery		U	U							
Rehabilitation			U							
Blood banking			U			U				
General Accounting	C			C		C				
Cost accounting	U		U	U		U				
Patient accounting			U	U		U	U			
Payroll		U			U	U				
Purchasing								C	C	C
Inventory control								U	U	
Personnel		C			C				U	
Housekeeping									U	

that uses an entity may read an instance of an entity but may not create, update, or delete that instance.

Each row in Figure 4-12 indicates the entity classes that are created or used by a particular process, and each column of the figure shows all of the processes that create or use a particular entity. However, the matrix can be made more useful by rearranging the columns in Figure 4-12 (the result is shown in Figure 4-13). This rearrangement is accomplished as follows: Select the first process in Figure 4-12 that *creates* an entity (Patient Registration, which creates the Patient entity). Move that entity (Patient) to the first column, as shown in Figure 4-13. Now select the next process that creates an entity (Electrodiagnosis, which creates a Test entity) and move that entity

Process \ Entity class	Patient	Test	Hospital	Ward	Laboratory	Vendor	Medical surgical item	Supply item	Physician	Staff
Patient registration	C			U						
Patient scheduling	U				U				U	
Physician orders	U	U							U	
Laboratory reporting	U	U			U					
Electrodiagnosis		C								
Psychiatric testing		C								
Patient monitoring	U									
Multiphasic screening	U	C			U					
Radiology		C			U					
Dietary	U									
Nursing	U									
Surgery	U								U	
Rehabilitation	U									
Blood banking	U				U					
General Accounting			C	C	C					
Cost accounting	U		U	U	U					
Patient accounting	U	U		U	U					
Payroll				U					U	U
Purchasing						C	C	C		
Inventory control							U	U		
Personnel								U	C	C
Housekeeping								U		

Figure 4-13
Process versus entity class matrix (final)

to the second column. Proceed in this manner, moving entity classes to the left as you proceed downward through the processes.

The purpose of rearranging the matrix is to group the processes and data into major subsystems, which are shown as boxes along or near the main diagonal in Figure 4-13. For example, the first box in the figure indicates a patient administration subsystem that includes four processes: Patient Registration, Patient Scheduling, Physician Orders, and Laboratory Reporting. This subsystem creates and uses the Patient entity (the four processes also use entities in other subsystems). The second subsystem consists of a package of clinical services (Electrodiagnosis, Psychiatric Testing, Patient Monitoring, Multiphasic Screening, and Radiology) that creates instances of the Test entity. Examine Figure 4-13 and identify three additional subsystems. These subsystems provide the basis for subdividing the overall development into manageable projects.

Strategy Formulation

The project team decided to use critical success factors (CSFs) for Mountain View Community Hospital as a basis for planning IS projects (Shank, Boynton, and Zmud, 1985). They listed the process-versus-CSF matrix using PRISM (see Figure 4-14), showing the processes that are essential (E) and desirable (D) to achieve each CSF. For example, five processes were considered essential to achieve the Excellent Care CSF: Patient Monitoring, Multiphasic Screening, Dietary, Nursing, and Rehabilitation. Eight other processes (shown in the figure) were considered desirable but not essential for this CSF.

The project team listed the five processes that are *essential* for the Excellent Care CSF (see Figure 4-15). They then examined the process-versus-entity matrix (Figure 4-13) and listed those entities that are created and used by these processes: Patient, Test, and Laboratory (Figure 4-15). Thus Figure 4-15 is a submatrix of Figure 4-13 for one CSF. However, the Patient and Laboratory entities are used (but not created) by any of the five essential processes; thus it was necessary to add two essential processes (Patient Registration and General Accounting), which are the processes that create (C) Patient and Laboratory, respectively.

If Excellent Care is the most important CSF, then Figure 4-15 shows the highest-priority processes and entity classes for development, needs that can also be stated in terms of the subsystems shown in Figure 4-13. The processes in Figure 4-15 require the first subsystem (Patient Care Administration), the second subsystem (Clinical Service), and General Accounting from the third subsystem. Since our greatest interest is in database planning, we conclude from Figure 4-15 that for Excellent Care the following three entity classes are essential: Patient, Test, and Laboratory.

Final Report

The study team completed their IS strategic plan in approximately three months. They then prepared a final report summarizing the plan for Mountain View Community Hospital (much of the documentation for the plan was prepared using the CASE tool). The report included a statement of business direction, critical success factors, an enterprise model (functions, processes, and activities), an entity-relationship diagram, several planning matrices, and a prioritized list of IS projects. The entity-relationship diagram provided an overall map for database design and implementation, and the prioritized list of projects included a set of priorities for database design. The report concluded with a timetable for data and information systems design and implementation over the next three years.

CSF / Process	Excellent care	Cost control	Staff retention
Patient scheduling	D		
Patient registration			
Physician orders	D		
Laboratory reporting	D		
Electrodiagnosis			
Psychiatric testing	D		
Patient monitoring	E		
Multiphasic screening	E		
Radiology	D		
Dietary	E		
Nursing	E	E	E
Surgery	D	D	
Rehabilitation	E		
Blood banking	D		
Patient Accounting	D	E	
Cost accounting		E	
General accounting			
Purchasing			
Inventory control		E	
Housekeeping		D	
Personnel			E

Figure 4-14
Three critical success factors (E = essential, D = desirable)

Process	Entity class Patient	Test	Laboratory
Patient monitoring	U		
Multiphasic screening	U	C	U
Dietary	U		
Nursing	U		
Rehabilitation	U		
Patient registration	C		
General accounting			C

Figure 4-15
Processes and entity classes essential for excellent care CSF

The study team presented the strategic IS plan to the board of directors at their regular meeting the following month. The board endorsed the plan and shortly thereafter approved the creation of the data administration position. Ms. Baker appointed Mr. Helms to this position, to report initially to Mr. Heller.

PITFALLS IN STRATEGIC IS PLANNING

There are numerous risks and pitfalls in strategic IS planning; if planning is to be successful, these risks must be managed and the pitfalls must be overcome. We describe some of these hazards briefly. For an extended discussion, see Hoffer, Michaele, and Carroll, 1989 and Lederer and Sethi, 1989.

1. Top management is not committed to strategic IS planning or to implementing the plan. In the former case, the plan will be inadequate or incomplete; in the latter case, it will collect dust and never be implemented.

2. There is lack of clarity on organizational direction, or the direction shifts abruptly. Thus strategic IS plans cannot be integrated with business plans.

3. Planning is decentralized among business units and lack of coordination may result in inconsistent or incomplete plans.

4. Tools to assist in the transition from planning to development may not exist. Tools are needed to provide a continued linkage between IS planning and ongoing development.

5. System and user-managers who feel ownership of current applications frequently resist a new system architecture. Involvement of key personnel throughout the planning process is essential to overcome this resistance.

6. The strategic IS plan is not kept up to date as business conditions change, so that the plans become obsolete.

SUMMARY

Strategic data and systems planning (or strategic IS planning) is an orderly means for assessing the information needs of an organization and defining the systems and databases that will best satisfy those needs. Strategic IS planning is a top-down process that takes into account the outside forces that drive the business and the factors critical to the success of the firm.

Strategic IS planning is essential if organizations are to realize the benefits of information resource management. The need for improved IS planning is apparent for reasons such as the following: The cost of information systems is rising rapidly, systems cannot handle applications that cross organizational boundaries, systems often do not address critical success factors, data redundancy is often out of control, and system maintenance costs continue to rise. Strategic IS planning is itself a critical success factor in addressing these problems.

Strategic IS planning must be closely integrated with strategic business planning. A major goal of IS planning is to achieve application independence, so that the source of data is transparent to the user-manager. This is accomplished through the development of subject databases that are independent of applications. Typical subject databases are products, customers, parts, vendors, orders, and personnel. Consistent data definitions must be used throughout the subject databases.

There is no single standard methodology for strategic IS planning. In this chapter we describe a methodology that is typical of the one used in many organizations today. It is a top-down approach that begins with identifying the business direction and organizational CSFs and then identifies and summarizes the business functions, processes, and activities in the form of an enterprise chart. Entity classes (corresponding to subject databases) are also identified, and an entity-relationship diagram is prepared. All of this organizational metadata is captured and stored in a repository using a suitable CASE tool. A series of planning matrices is also developed to integrate the models and analyze the data. The end result of the methodology is a series of prioritized projects for data and information systems design and implementation.

We have illustrated many of the steps in the planning process with a case example for a small hospital. We emphasized the necessity of using a CASE tool to organize the vast amount of information collected during the planning process. The CASE tool used should provide a linkage between IS planning and implementation.

There are numerous risks and potential pitfalls in strategic IS planning. These hazards include lack of top-management commitment, fragmentation of responsibility for planning, inadequate methodologies and CASE tools, resistance to change, and failure to update the IS plan as business conditions change. Those responsible for strategic IS planning must anticipate these problems and ensure that they do not undermine the planning process.

Chapter Review

REVIEW QUESTIONS

1. Define each of the following terms:
   a. application independence
   b. subject database
   c. data capture system
   d. data transfer system

    e. critical success factor

    f. business function

    g. business process

    h. business activity

    i. business entity

2. Contrast the following terms:
   a. top-down planning; bottom-up design
   b. strategic business plan; strategic IS plan
   c. business process; business activity
   d. CSF; CASE
   e. subject database; application database

3. List six factors that provide evidence for the need for improved information systems planning today.

4. How should strategic IS planning be integrated with business planning?

5. Describe four techniques or characteristics that most planning methodologies have in common.

6. Describe three important prerequisites for strategic IS planning.

7. Describe seven steps in the strategic IS planning process described in this chapter.

8. What are critical success factors and how do they relate to the strategic IS planning process?

9. What are the two major outputs of the strategic IS planning process?

10. Describe six benefits of using CASE tools in strategic IS planning.

11. The planning database used in PRISM in this chapter contains information about what organizational entities?

12. Briefly describe five planning matrices used in the PRISM database.

13. Why is the process-versus-entity matrix (Figure 4-12) rearranged as shown in Figure 4-13?

14. Briefly describe six risks or pitfalls in strategic IS planning.

15. Describe four guidelines that identify well-formed activities.

PROBLEMS AND EXERCISES

1. Match the following terms and their definitions:

_____ business function	a) persons, objects, events, etc.
_____ business process	b) decision-related activities
_____ business activity	c) source of data is transparent to user
_____ data modeling	
_____ business entity	d) redundancy is carefully controlled
_____ subject database	e) identify system gaps to be filled
_____ application independence	f) specific operations or transactions
_____ strategic formulation	g) define entities and relationships
_____ enterprise chart	h) broad groups of related activities

_____ critical success factor

i) key areas where things must go right

j) shows functions, processes, activities

2. A family can be regarded as a small business organization.
   a. Define several major functions, processes, and activities of a family and draw an enterprise chart.
   b. Define the family entities and draw an E-R diagram.
   c. Define three critical success factors (CSFs) for a family.

3. Examine the enterprise chart for a manufacturing firm (Figure 4-7).
   a. List three additional functions that would be included in the business chart for a typical manufacturing firm.
   b. List three processes that would be included in the Quality Assurance function. (*Hint:* Consider various points in a manufacturing firm where quality must be planned or measured.)
   c. List three activities that would be included in the receiving process.

4. Examine the enterprise chart for Mountain View Community Hospital (Figure 4-10). List three activities for each of the following processes:
   a. nursing
   b. payroll
   c. housekeeping

5. List three additional entities that might appear in the entity-relationship diagram for Mountain View Community Hospital (Figure 4-11).

6. Complete the following table, showing the effect of each business activity at Mountain View Community Hospital on the relevant entities:

Activity	Result
Admit patient	Creates a new Patient occurrence
Assign to bed	
Perform a treatment	
Discharge patient	

7. A professional football team is a business organization.
   a. Define several functions, processes, and activities of a football team and draw a preliminary enterprise chart.
   b. Define several entity classes and draw a preliminary E-R diagram.
   c. Draw a matrix mapping the processes versus the entity classes (see Figure 4-12).
   d. Define three critical success factors (CSFs) for a professional football team.

8. Consider a high school as a business enterprise.
   a. Define several functions, processes, and activities and draw a preliminary enterprise chart.
   b. Define several major entity classes and draw a preliminary E-R diagram.
   c. Map the processes versus the entity classes (see Figure 4-12).
   d. Define four critical success factors (CSFs) for a high school.

9. Examine the enterprise chart for Mountain View Community Hospital (Figure 4-10). List three activities for each of the following processes:
   a. patient accounting
   b. blood banking
   c. rehabilitation

10. Expand the E-R diagram for Mountain View Community Hospital (Figure 4-11) by adding the following entities (and associated relationships): Equipment, Volunteers, Blood Donors.

11. Figure 4-15 shows the processes and entity classes that are *essential* for the Excellent Care CSF. Expand this table by including the processes and entity classes that are both essential (E) and desirable (D) for this CSF (refer to Figure 4-14).

12. Develop a table (similar to Figure 4-15) of processes and entity classes that are essential (E) for the Cost Control CSF (refer to Figure 4-14).

13. Develop a table (similar to Figure 4-15) of processes and entity classes that are essential (E) for the Staff Retention CSF (refer to Figure 4-14).

14. Develop a composite table (similar to Figure 4-15) of processes and entity classes that are essential (E) to all three CSFs: Excellent Care, Cost Control, and Staff Retention. (*Note:* This problem combines Figure 4-15 with the results of Problems 12 and 13.)

REFERENCES

Business Systems Planning: Information Systems Planning Guide. 1975. White Plains, N.Y.: IBM Corporation.

Goodhue, D. L., J. A. Quillard, and J. F. Rockart. 1986. "The Management of Data: Preliminary Research Results." Center for Information Systems Research, Sloan School of Management, MIT. Working Paper No. 140 (May).

Hoffer, J. A., S. J. Michaele, and J. C. Carroll. 1989. Kona, Hawaii: "The Pitfalls of Strategic Data and Systems Planning: A Research Agenda." *Proceedings of the Twenty-Second Annual Hawaii International Conference on System Sciences.* Vol. IV: *Emerging Technologies and Applications*, 348–356.

Holland, R. H. 1980. "Data Base Planning Entails Return to Basics." Computerworld (October 27).

Introduction to PC Prism. 1988. Cambridge, Mass.: Index Technology.

Lederer, A. L., and V. Sethi. 1989. "Pitfalls in Planning." *Datamation* 35 (11) (June 1), 59-63.

Martin, J. 1982. *Strategic Data Planning Methodologies.* Englewood Cliffs, N.J.: Prentice-Hall.

Moad, J. 1989. "Navigating Cross-Functional Waters." *Datamation* 35 (5) (Mar. 1), 38–43.

Shank, M. E., A. C. Boynton, and R. W. Zmud. 1985. "Critical Success Factor Analysis as a Methodology for IS Planning." *MIS Quarterly* 9 (2) (June), 121–129.

Voell, R. F. 1980. "Data Base Planning." In T. A. Rullo, ed., *Advances in Data Base Management*, Vol. 1. Philadelphia: Heyden.

CHAPTER 5

Database Requirements Definition

INTRODUCTION

This is the first of three chapters devoted to the important topic of database design. In this chapter, we introduce the basic steps in database design and describe requirements definition, which is the important first step in the design process. Database design is guided by the database planning process described in Chapter 4.

Database design is the process of developing database structures from user requirements for data. It starts with requirements definition, which identifies user needs (present and future) for data. It then proceeds by translating these user requirements first into a logical, then a physical database design. The resulting design must satisfy user needs in terms of completeness, integrity, performance constraints, and other factors.

Database design is a complex and demanding process that requires the commitment and participation of the entire organization. Also, it requires the use of an organized approach or methodology. Until recently, such a methodology did not exist, and database design was often a haphazard process. However, a number of tools and techniques (including computer-assisted design) are now available to facilitate database design. We describe a number of such techniques in these chapters.

167

DATABASE DESIGN PROCESS

The database design process is closely related to the three-schema architecture introduced in Chapter 3 (see Figure 3-12). A simplified version of the three-schema architecture is shown in Figure 5-1. The three levels in this architecture are the following:

1. **External level.** At this level we identify user views such as reports, displays, and transactions. These views represent user requirements in a technology-independent manner.
2. **Conceptual level.** At this level all user requirements are merged into a single logical database description that is technology-independent.
3. **Internal level.** At this level we develop one or more internal data models (or schemas) that define the database in a technology-dependent manner.

In the following sections we describe the steps in the database design process and indicate how each step relates to the three-schema architecture in Figure 5-1.

Steps in Database Design

The major steps in database design are shown in Figure 5-2. The four steps shown in this figure are: requirements definition, conceptual design, implementation design, and physical design. The interconnections (or inputs and outputs) for each of the design steps are also shown in the figure.

Requirements Definition   The purpose of requirements definition is to identify and describe the data that are required by users in the organization. This step is related to the external level (Figure 5-1) since we identify and model user views. The inputs to requirements definition are user infor-

Figure 5-1
Three-schema
architecture

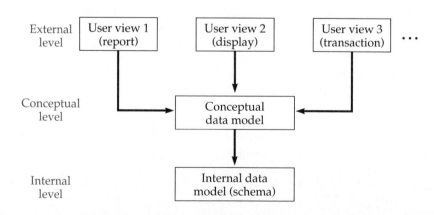

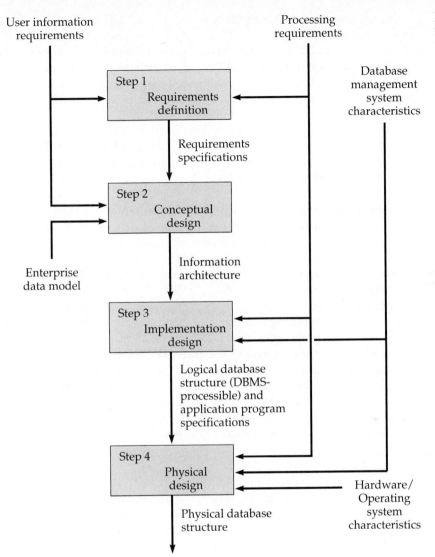

Figure 5-2
Major steps in
database design

mation requirements and user processing requirements (such as required response times and security constraints). The output of requirements definition is a formal set of requirements specifications that describe both the data required by users and the constraints on that data.

Conceptual Design The purpose of conceptual design is to develop a conceptual data model (or information architecture) that will support the diverse information needs of users throughout the organization. Conceptual database design is a data-driven process—that is, it is completely independent of hardware and software implementation details.

Conceptual design corresponds to the conceptual level of the three-schema architecture (Figure 5-1). The inputs to logical design are the requirements specifications derived during requirements definition and the enterprise data model developed during the database planning process (see Chapter 4). The output of conceptual design is an overall information architecture for the organization. This architecture may be expressed in the form of entity-relationship diagrams, normalized relations, and so on.

As the conceptual data model is developed, it is cross-checked against the enterprise data model as described in Chapter 4 (see Figure 4-11). The enterprise data model is used as an overall map to guide the design process. CASE tools are often used to support the conceptual design process.

Implementation Design   The purpose of implementation design is to map the logical data model into a schema that can be processed by a particular DBMS. First, the conceptual data model is mapped into a hierarchical, network, or relational data model. Then DBMS-processable schemas and subschemas are developed using the data description language for the DBMS to be used.

Implementation design is considered an intermediate step between conceptual and physical design. In terms of the three-schema architecture (Figure 5-1), implementation design is concerned with mapping the conceptual data model (conceptual level) to the internal data model (internal level). The input of implementation design is the information architecture developed during conceptual design. The output of implementation design is a logical database structure that can be processed by a DBMS. Generally, this logical database structure is in the form of a hierarchical, network, or relational data model (relational is most common today).

Physical Design   Physical design is the last stage of database design. In this stage the logical database structures (normalized relations, trees, networks, and so on) are mapped to physical storage structures such as files and tables. Indexes are specified, as well as access methods, record blocking, and other physical factors. A major objective of physical design is to provide adequate performance for user applications in terms of response times, throughput rates, and so on. Also, physical database design is concerned with database security, integrity, backup, and recovery. Physical design is related to the internal level of the three-schema architecture (Figure 5-1).

The four steps of database design are summarized in Figure 5-3, which shows the relationship of each design step to the three-schema architecture.

Stepwise Refinement

The steps in database design are pictured in Figure 5-2 as proceeding in sequential fashion. In reality, however, there is iteration between the steps. For example, during conceptual design, it may be discovered that there are gaps in the data definitions, thus pointing out the need for additional

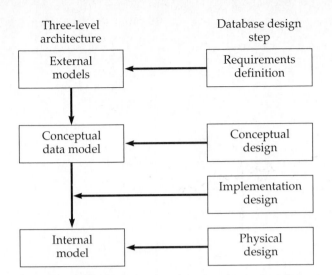

Three-level architecture | Database design step

External models

Conceptual data model

Internal model

Requirements definition

Conceptual design

Implementation design

Physical design

Figure 5-3
Summary of database design steps

requirements definition. As the design proceeds, analysts may suggest new data or information that can be made available to users. The entire design process is best viewed as one of stepwise refinement, where the design at each state is progressively refined through this type of iteration. Design reviews should be performed at the end of each stage before proceeding to the next stage.

REQUIREMENTS DEFINITION

Requirements definition is the process of identifying and documenting what data users require in the database to satisfy present and future needs for information. During requirements definition, we are concerned with two types of information:

1. Information describing data *structure,* such as entities, attributes, and relationships. This information is often expressed in graphical form such as entity-relationship diagrams.
2. Information depicting rules or constraints that preserve data *integrity.* Often called business rules, these constraints should be captured in the data dictionary/directory (or repository) of the organization.

Information Collected During Requirements Definition

To understand the information that must be collected during requirements definition, we need to anticipate the components of the conceptual data model. The components of this model are outlined in Figure 5-4.

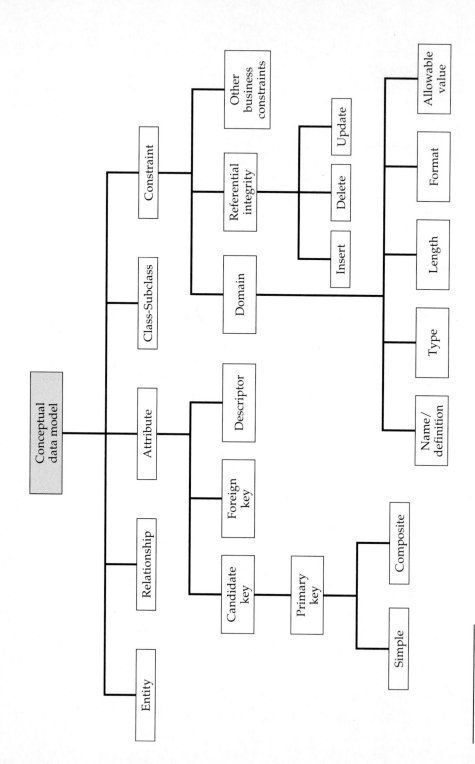

Figure 5-4
**Components of the
conceptual data
model**

The first four components of the conceptual data model (entity, relationship, attribute, and class-subclass) are primarily concerned with data structure. You encountered all of these components in previous chapters (especially Chapters 2 and 3). The last component (constraint) is primarily concerned with data integrity. There are three major types of constraints, as shown in Figure 5-4:

1. **Domain constraints.** These constraints define the type, length, format, and allowable values for individual data item.

2. **Referential integrity constraints.** These constraints ensure the integrity of references between the rows of one table and the rows of another table (or several tables).

3. **Other business constraints.** These constraints ensure the integrity of a data item value in one table, given one or more data item values in the same table or in other tables.

An Example: Vacation Property Rentals

To illustrate each of the various types of information collected during requirements definition, let us consider a simple example. Vacation Property Rentals (VPR) is a company that rents desirable vacation units throughout the United States. There are two basic types of properties: mountain properties and beach properties. Most rentals are made on a weekly basis.*

There are four user views at Vacation Property Rentals that will be used to illustrate some of the key steps of requirements definition: Renter, Beach Property, Mountain Property, and Rental Agreement.

Renter   The Renter view is shown in Figure 5-5a. This view is simply a list of persons who have rented properties from VPR in the past, are renting properties at the present time, or are prospective customers. The view shows the Renter name, address, phone number, and maximum weekly rental the person indicates he or she is willing to pay.

An E-R diagram for the Renter view is shown in Figure 5-5b. This view is composed of a single entity (Renter). The primary key is Name. The remaining attributes (Address, Phone-Number, and Max-Rent) are descriptors.

Beach Property and Mountain Property   These two views are shown in Figure 5-6a, respectively representing Beach and Mountain Property listings for VPR. The Beach Property listing includes an attribute that records the number of blocks to the closest beach, while the Mountain Property listing shows what type of skiing is available at nearby resorts (alpine, nordic, or both). At first glance, it might appear that Beach Property and Mountain Property represent separate entities. However, on closer inspec-

*This example is adapted from Fleming and von Halle (1990), pp. 5–15, with permission.

Renter

Name	Address	Phone-Number	Max-Rent
Margaret Simpson	15 Ridge St., Dallas, TX 75083	219-473-4928	200
Arnold Thomas	50 Main St., Cupertino, CA 95014	409-123-0195	350
Phyllis Martinez	114 Maple Ave., Denver, CO 80328	303-111-4891	400

(a)

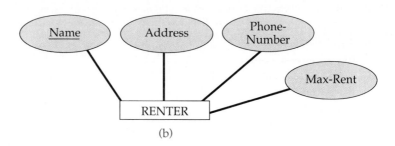

(b)

Figure 5-5
Renter view and E-R diagram. Adapted from Data Resource Management (New York: Auerbach Publishers). © 1990 Warren Gorham & Lamont, Inc.

tion we see that these entities share several attributes; in fact, only the last attribute (Blocks-to-Beach, Skiing) is different. We conclude that Beach Property and Mountain Property are subclasses of Property (which is a superclass). We represent this as two ISA relationships, so the E-R diagram appears as shown in Figure 5-6b.

In the E-R diagram (Figure 5-6b), the primary key for Property (the class) is a composite key consisting of Street-Address and City-State-Zip. This is also the primary key for each subclass (Beach Property and Mountain Property). The Property entity also contains the descriptors No-Rooms and Typical-Rent. Notice that the subclasses do not contain these descriptors. We say that Beach Property and Mountain Property inherit these characteristics (or descriptors) from Property. However, Beach Property does contain the descriptor Blocks-to-Beach and Mountain Property contains Skiing. Each of these descriptors is unique to its subclass.

Rental Agreement   The Rental Agreement view is shown in Figure 5-7a. This view associates a Renter with a rental property during a specific interval of time (specified by a Begin-Date and an End-Date).

The corresponding E-R diagram for Rental Agreement is shown in Figure 5-7b. Notice that the primary key for this entity is a composite key consisting of the attributes Street-Address, City-State-Zip, and Begin-Date. This combination of attributes uniquely identifies a property and a rental Begin-Date and therefore must be unique. That is, no two rental agreements for the same property may have the same Begin-Date (unless a mistake has been made)! In Chapter 6 we discuss formal tools for analyzing functional

BEACH PROPERTY

Street-Address	City-State-Zip	No-Rooms	Typical-Rent	Blocks-to-Beach
120 Surf Dr.	Honolulu, HI 99987	3	500	2
360 Sail St.	Orlando, FL 10389	4	400	1/2

MOUNTAIN PROPERTY

Street-Address	City-State-Zip	No-Rooms	Typical-Rent	Skiing
400 Hill Rd.	Aspen, CO 87394	3	300	A, N
100 Mogul Dr.	Jackson, WY 89204	3	250	N

(a)

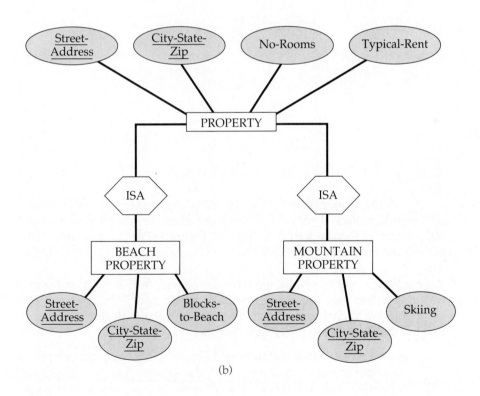

(b)

Figure 5-6
Property views and E-R diagram

Figure 5-7
Rental agreement
view and E-R
diagram

RENTAL AGREEMENT

> Name: Arnold Thomas   Date: 12/3/9X
> Street-Address: 360 Sail St.
> City-State-Zip: Orlando, FL 10389
> Begin-Date: 1/15/9X
> End-Date: 1/29/9X
> Rental-Amount: 350

(a)

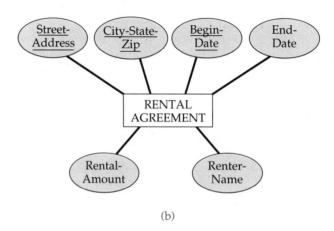

(b)

dependencies between attributes, which is necessary in identifying candidate keys.

One of the remaining attributes in Rental Agreement (Renter-Name) is a foreign key, since it represents the same attribute (called Name) that is the primary key in the Renter entity (see Figure 5-5b). The remaining attributes in Rental Agreement (End-Date and Rental–Amount) are descriptors.

Relationships   At this point we have developed an E-R diagram for each of the separate user views (Figures 5-5b, 5-6b, and 5-7b). We may next analyze the relationships between the entities in these diagrams. There are two relationships (shown in Figure 5-8):

1. Since Property.Street-Address and Property.City-State-Zip are part of the composite primary key of Rental Agreement, there is a relationship (which we call "Is Rented By") between Property and Rental Agreement. This is a 1:M conditional association, as shown in Figure 5-8.

2. Since Renter-Name is a foreign key in Rental Agreement, there is a relationship (which we call "Signs") between Renter and Rental

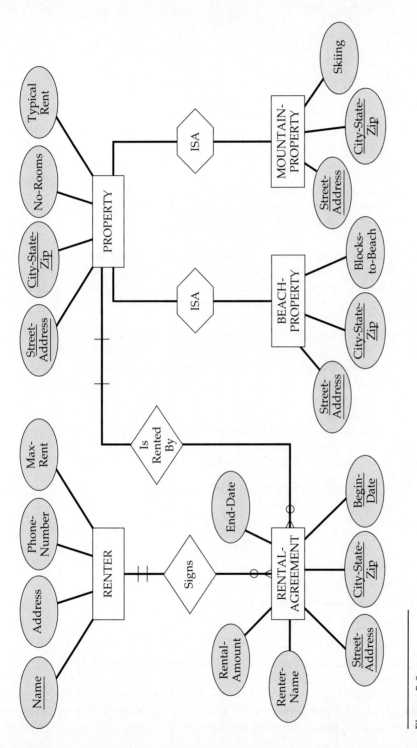

Figure 5-8
Relationships between entities

Agreement. This is a 1:M conditional association, also shown in Figure 5-8.

Figure 5-8 is a *portion* (or segment) of a conceptual data model for Vacation Property Rentals. In Chapter 6 we discuss additional considerations and constraints in forming a conceptual data model from E-R diagram segments.

Constraints

The E-R diagram in Figure 5-8 shows the *structure* of the data for Vacation Property Rentals, but it does not capture the constraints that serve to maintain the integrity of the data. These constraints result from additional business rules that have not yet been considered.

Domain Constraints   These constraints are rules that define allowable data types, lengths, formats, and values for each data item (or attribute) that was defined earlier. These domain definitions serve as editing criteria when the database is used; for example, a data value that is in the wrong format or exceeds an allowable value will be rejected.

Several domain definitions for Vacation Property Rentals are shown in Figure 5-9 (not all domains are defined). Notice that the domain name may or may not have the same name as the corresponding attribute. For example, for the attribute Name (that is, Renter-Name) the corresponding domain name is Names. During requirements analysis, the database analyst must define each domain (as in Figure 5-9) and also associate attribute names with domain names (all of this information is stored in the data dictionary/ directory or repository). Following is the assignment of several attribute names to the domains described in Figure 5-9:

Attribute Name	Domain Name
Name	Names
Max-Rent	Rental Amounts
Typical-Rent	Rental Amounts
Rental-Amount	Rental Amounts
Skiing	Skiing Codes
Phone-Number	Phone Numbers
Renter-Name	Names

Notice that in the above table, the following three attributes are defined over the same domain (Rental Amounts): Max-Rent, Typical-Rent, and Rental-Amount. Each of these different names is referred to as a *role name*; that is, the name describes the role that attribute plays in describing the entity. For example, Max-Rent indicates the maximum weekly rental a Renter is willing to pay, while Typical-Rent indicates the usual rent for a property. Despite

Domain Name: Names
    Definition: Names of renters (past, present, or prospective) for VPR
    Type/Length: Character 35
    Format:
        Last-Name Character 18
        Middle-Initial Character 2
        First-Name Character 15
    Allowable Values: May not be null

Domain Name: Rental Amounts
    Definition: Weekly rental for VPR property
    Type/Length: Decimal 9
    Format: XXXXXX.XX
    Allowable Values: May not be negative

Domain Name: Skiing Codes
    Definition: Codes indicating type of skiing available
    Type/Length: Character 5
    Allowable Values: A (= alpine), N (= Nordic), or both

Domain Name: Phone Numbers
    Definition: Phone numbers of renters
    Type/Length: Character 12
    Format: AAA-NNN-NNNN
        AAA = 3-digit area code
        NNN-NNNN = local telephone number

Figure 5-9
Selected domain definitions

these different role names, each attribute is defined over the same domain. One of the advantages of domains is conservation of effort; instead of creating a separate definition for each attribute, we create a separate definition for each domain and several attributes can share that domain.

Another important role that is performed by domains is assuring that foreign key values in one entity are compatible with the corresponding key values in a related entity. For example, in Figure 5-8, Name (in Renter) and Renter-Name (in Rental-Agreement) are defined over the same domain (called Names). Since these two attributes are defined over the same domain, we are assured that corresponding entities can be properly matched (for example, we can find all Rental Agreements "signed" by a particular renter).

The ability to define domains directly and associate every attribute with a domain is an essential feature of contemporary database management (especially relational DBMS). Unfortunately, many current relational DBMS's have not yet implemented domains. In fact, domains are not yet a standard feature of the SQL language, which is the de facto standard relational database language (Wood, 1990). A few relational DBMS products, however, do provide domain support and this facility is likely to become standard (or at least common) in the future.

Figure 5-10
Referential integrity
constraints (VPR)

Referential Integrity Rules

1. Insertion
   a. Do not insert a new Rental-Agreement unless the following conditions are true.
      i. There exists a valid Renter, so that:
         Rental-Agreement.Renter-Name = Renter.Name
      ii. There exists a valid Property, so that:
         Property.Street-Address = Rental-Agreement. Street-Address and Property.City-State-Zip = Rental-Agreement.City-State-Zip
   b. Do not insert a new Beach-Property unless there exists a valid Property, so that: Beach-Property.Street-Address = Property. Street-Address and Beach-Property.City-State-Zip = Property. City-State-Zip
   c. Mountain-Property constraint (same as Beach-Property)
2. Deletion
   a. Do not delete a Renter occurence if there exists one or more Rental-Agreements, so that: Renter.Name = Rental-Agreement. Renter-Name
   b. Property constraint (similar to Renter constraint)

Referential Integrity   This type of constraint is concerned with the validity of references for an occurrence of one entity to the occurrence (or occurrences) of another entity. To illustrate, consider Vacation Property Rentals (Figure 5-8). Would VPR want to insert a new Rental Agreement (an occurrence) into the database if no valid Renter already existed for that agreement? Most likely they would not. Also, VPR would not want to delete an occurrence of a Renter (or of a Property) if there existed one (or more) valid Rental Agreements for those entities.

Referential integrity constraints for insertion and deletion are shown in Figure 5-10 (these are the constraints of greatest interest). You should study these constraints and make sure you understand their meaning (we ask you to complete two of them in the chapter exercises).

As with domain constraints, referential integrity is not supported by all contemporary relational DBMS. However, some systems do support at least basic referential integrity features (we discuss referential integrity in greater detail in Chapter 9).

Other Business Rules   Domains and referential integrity constraints provide a solid foundation for protecting the integrity of a database. However, in most situations there are additional business rules or constraints that

Other Business Rules

Figure 5-11
Other business rules

1. IF Rental-Agreement.Begin-Date >= Rental-Agreement.End-Date
    THEN Reject Transaction, Print Error Message

2. IF Rental-Agreement.Begin-Date (for a new Rental-Agreement)
    = Rental-Agreement.Begin-Date (for an existing Rental Agreement)
    THEN Reject Transaction, Print Error Message

3. IF Rental-Agreement.Begin-Date (for a new Rental-Agreement)
    > Rental Agreement.Begin-Date (for an existing Rental-Agreement)
    THEN
    IF Rental-Agreement.Begin-Date (for the new Rental-Agreement)
    <= Rental-Agreement.End-Date (for same existing Rental-Agreement)
    THEN Reject Transaction, Print Error Message

4. IF Rental-Agreement.Begin-Date (for a new Rental-Agreement)
    < Rental-Agreement.Begin-Date (for an existing Rental-Agreement)
    THEN
    IF Rental-Agreement.End-Date (for the new Rental-Agreement)
    >= Rental-Agreement.Begin-Date (for same existing Rental-Agreement)
    THEN Reject Transaction, Print Error Message

should be included to protect data integrity. We refer to these as "other business rules." In most environments today, these rules are formalized as logic in application programs that manipulate the database, rather than as part of the database description. As we will soon see, however, there are important advantages to incorporating these rules as part of the database description.

To illustrate one such type of business rule, consider the E-R diagram for Vacation Property Rentals (Figure 5-8). Notice that each Rental-Agreement has a Begin-Date and an End-Date. It is important to assure that Begin-Date and End-Date are consistent for each Rental-Agreement and that no two agreements have overlapping dates. A set of four business rules to enforce these constraints is shown in Figure 5-11:

1. For any Rental-Agreement, the Begin-Date must be earlier than the End-Date (internal consistency).

2. The Begin-Date for a *new* Rental-Agreement must not be equal to the Begin-Date for *any existing* Rental-Agreement (prevents overlap).

3. If the Begin-Date for a *new* Rental-Agreement is later than the Begin-Date for *any existing* Rental-Agreement, then the Begin-Date for the new Rental-Agreement must be later than the End-Date for that existing Rental-Agreement (prevents overlap).

4. If the Begin-Date for a *new* Rental-Agreement is earlier than the Begin-Date for *any existing* Rental-Agreement, then the End-Date for the

new Rental-Agreement must also be earlier than the Begin-Date for that existing Rental-Agreement (prevents overlap).

The above rules are stated informally. In Figure 5-11 each of these rules is stated more formally as an IF-THEN (or IF-THEN-ELSE) statement. Statements of this form are sometimes referred to as "production rules" and are often incorporated in expert systems (we discuss expert systems in Chapter 15).

Few contemporary database management systems provide support for the type of rules shown in Figure 5-11. However, emerging technology is making it feasible to incorporate these rules within a database environment. Two such technologies are the following:

1. **Object-oriented database systems.** These systems store objects (introduced in Chapter 3), which may include rules as methods. We illustrate object-oriented representation in the next section.

2. **Intelligent database systems.** These systems link expert systems that contain rules (such as those in Figure 5-11) with a contemporary DBMS (often relational). (See Chapter 15.)

In the preceding sections we have described three types of constraints: domain, referential integrity, and other business rules. Where possible, these constraints should be incorporated into the database description and controlled by the DBMS, rather than by application programs. According to Wood (1990), removing this work from application programs provides several important advantages:

1. Provides faster application development with fewer errors
2. Reduces maintenance effort and expenditures
3. Provides faster response to business changes
4. Facilitates end-user involvement in developing new systems and manipulating data
5. Provides for consistent application of integrity constraints
6. Reduces time and effort to train application programmers
7. Promotes ease of use of a database

Association Entities: Another View

Often in requirements definition there are alternate ways to model a user view (or views). For example, recall that in the E-R diagram (Figure 5-8) the Rental-Agreement view has a composite primary key consisting of the following attributes: Property.Street-Address, Property.City-State-Zip, and Rental-Agreement.Begin-Date. To retrieve an occurrence of this entity, a user would have to supply a value for each of these three attributes. The management at Vacation Property Rentals may decide that Rental-Agreement is such an important entity that it should have a simple primary key to facilitate retrieval. Suppose they add a new attribute called Agreement-Number to uniquely identify this entity. The E-R diagram for Rental-Agreement would now appear as follows:

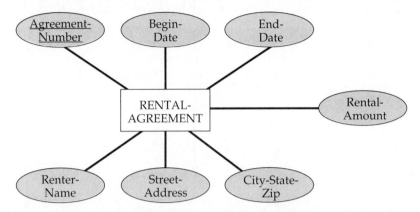

In this diagram, Agreement-Number is the new primary key for Rental-Agreement. Street-Address and City-State-Zip (previously components of the primary key) instead become part of a composite foreign key. Which of these two representations is better? They are both equally correct—the answer depends on how managers want to view the Rental-Agreement entity.

STEPS IN REQUIREMENTS DEFINITION

In the preceding section, we described informally the process of requirements definition, focusing on the metadata (or data structure) and on database constraints. In this section we define the requirements definition process more formally. Figure 5-12 shows the major steps in requirements definition. Notice that CASE tools may be used to support several steps in this process.

Historically, requirements definition has been a relatively unstructured and intuitive process. However, the need to improve the requirements definition process, together with the emergence of new methodologies and CASE tools, now requires a much more structured approach. The six steps that are shown in Figure 5-12 are described below. As with the overall design process, the steps in requirements definition are performed iteratively, with stepwise refinement at each stage.

Define Scope of the Database

Ideally, an organization would design and implement a single, global database that would support all of its functions. However, in most organizations, such a database would be prohibitively large, complex, and costly to

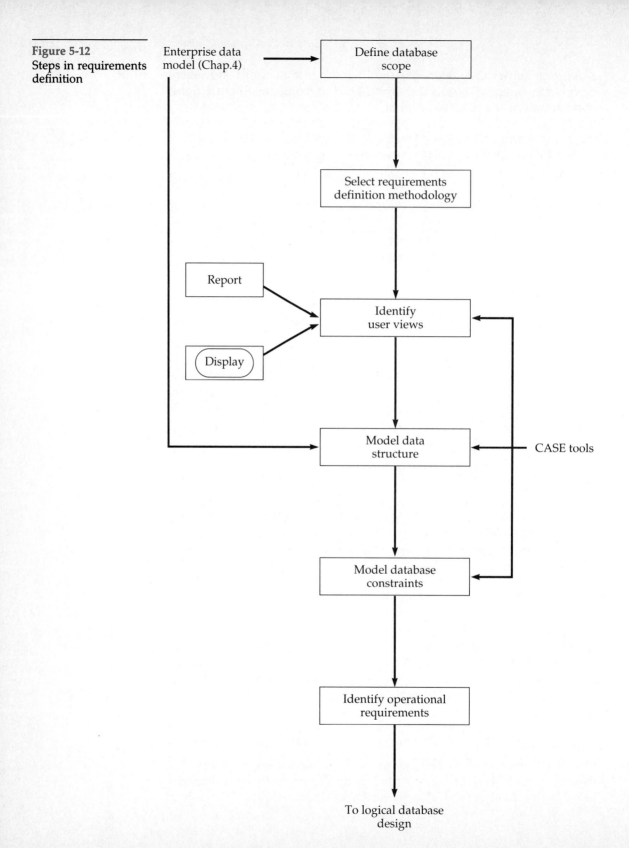

Figure 5-12
Steps in requirements definition

Enterprise data model (Chap.4)

Define database scope

Select requirements definition methodology

Report

Display

Identify user views

Model data structure

CASE tools

Model database constraints

Identify operational requirements

To logical database design

develop. As a result, a better strategy is to design and implement several smaller databases, all within the context of an overall plan, as described in Chapter 4. This "divide and conquer" strategy must be carefully orchestrated to achieve a confederation of databases that are reasonably integrated and can be shared.

A strategy for partitioning the database design effort should be part of the overall strategic database plan. The study team should review the organization's information systems plan before proceeding with the requirements definition. This plan should include business charts, an enterprise information model, and database priorities and implementation plans as described in Chapter 4. These plans should be used as an overall framework for database design.

Select Requirements Definition Methodology

During requirements definition, database analysts interview users and identify the various views of data and information that they use for decision making and other activities. User views of data appear in a large variety of formats—reports, displays, queries, forms, ledgers, and so on. The analysts must interview all managers and key operating personnel in the areas within the scope of the database design effort, using structured interview techniques, including standard data collection forms and interview procedures.

It is essential that the requirements definition team select an appropriate methodology and set of CASE tools to support this effort. The methodology provides the standardized procedures and data collection formats that are required to manage the collection of metadata in a disciplined way. The CASE tools provide computer-based support for building a repository of metadata and developing structured views of that metadata. The CASE tools used during requirements definition should be linked to those used during database planning (Chapter 4) as well as those used in subsequent design stages. We use E-R diagrams as the principal tool for modeling user views, since they are by far the most common CASE tools for requirements definition today.

Identify User Views

Data collection initially focuses on user views of data. A **user view** is a subset of data required by a particular user to make a decision or carry out an action. We identify user views by reviewing tasks that are performed or decisions that are made by users and by reviewing the data required for these tasks and decisions. Existing reports, files, forms, documents, and displays (both input and output) are important sources of information about user views, and the analysts should collect sample copies of all such documents and formal information sources, as well as formats of summary data used for decision support. In addition to formal information sources, informal sources should be identified, such as telephone calls and personal contacts. Also, it is important to anticipate future requirements for data where possible.

In addition to the actual format and content of data, database analysts must also determine how people in the organization use these views in their decision-making processes. Typical questions are: Who uses the data? How often is it used? What are the requirements for accuracy and response times? How can the data format and/or content be improved for better decision making?

In attempting to evaluate future information needs, the analysts must allow for proposed business or organizational changes. When they can be anticipated, it is generally simpler to incorporate future data needs into the database design. However, not all needs can be anticipated, and so the database system must be sufficiently flexible to handle growth and change without undermining existing applications.

Model Data Structure

This step imposes a consistent structure on each user view that was identified during the previous step. In the previous section (and throughout most of this chapter), we use E-R diagrams to model data structure. Referring to Figure 5-4, modeling user views in the form of E-R diagrams requires that for each view we identify the relevant entities, relationships, attributes, and class-subclass hierarchies. This of course also requires that we define candidate keys, primary keys, foreign keys, and descriptors.

During requirements definition we choose not to integrate the individual E-R diagrams (each representing a user view) into an overall conceptual data model. Rather, we defer this step to Chapter 6 (Conceptual Database Design), since there are some additional issues (such as data normalization) that need to be addressed at that time. However, requirements definition and conceptual database design are logically very closely linked activities.

Model Database Constraints

During requirements definition the database analysts must also identify the basic constraints that preserve database integrity. In the previous section we identified three basic classes of constraints: domains, referential integrity, and other business rules (see Figure 5-4). As these rules and constraints are identified, they should be recorded in the data dictionary (or repository), using available CASE tools.

Identify Operational Requirements

The analysts must also collect information concerning user operational requirements for data. This includes requirements for each of the following areas:

1. **Security.** Who is authorized to access and modify the data?
2. **Response times.** What are reasonable limits for response times in accessing data?
3. **Backup and recovery.** What are the parameters for backing up and recovering the database in the event of loss?
4. **Archiving.** How long must data be retained, and in what form?
5. **Growth projections.** How will databases grow in volume and complexity in the future?

These topics are largely the concern of database administration, and a person familiar with these areas should be part of the requirements definition team. We discuss most of these topics in detail in Chapter 9 (Data Administration).

MODELING COMPLEX USER VIEWS

Modeling the data structure for Vacation Property Rentals was relatively simple since each user view generally corresponded to a single entity (although there was a class-subclass relationship involved). Often, however, a single user view will involve multiple entities. For example, consider the Customer Order for Pine Valley Furniture Company. An Order Entry Screen that displays a sample Customer Order is shown in Figure 5-13a, while the E-R diagram for the Customer Order is shown in Figure 5-13b (the Customer Order was first introduced in Chapter 2; see Figure 2-4).

Following is an analysis of the Customer Order view.

1. Each Customer Order view involves one Customer entity. As shown in Figure 5-13b, Customer-No is the primary key of this entity, while Name, Address, and City-State-Zip are descriptors.

2. Each Customer Order view also involves one Order entity. As shown in Figure 5-13b, the primary key of Order is Order-No. Descriptors are Order-Date and Promised-Date. Customer-No is also included in the Order entity and so is a foreign key.

3. Since Customer-No is a foreign key in Order, there is a relationship (which we call "Placed By") between Customer and Order (as shown in Figure 5-13b). Since a Customer may place more than one Order, Placed-By is a 1:M relationship.

4. Each Customer Order view may specify several Products, as shown in Figure 5-13a. The primary key of Product is Product-No (see Figure 5-13b). Descriptors are Description and Unit Price.

5. There is an M:N relationship between Order and Product. That is, each Order may specify several Products (such as in Figure 5-13a); on the other hand, a given Product may appear on several Orders. In Figure 5-13b we name this relationship "Requested-On." Notice

Figure 5-13
Sample customer
order and E-R
diagram

ORDER NO: 61384   CUSTOMER NO: 1273

                    NAME: CONTEMPORARY DESIGNS
                    ADDRESS: 123 OAK ST.
                    CITY-STATE-ZIP: AUSTIN, TX 28384

ORDER DATE: 11/04/9X   PROMISED DATE: 11/21/9X

PRODUCT NO	DESCRIPTION	QUANTITY ORDERED	UNIT PRICE
M128	BOOKCASE	4	200.00
B381	CABINET	2	150.00
R210	TABLE	1	500.00

(a)

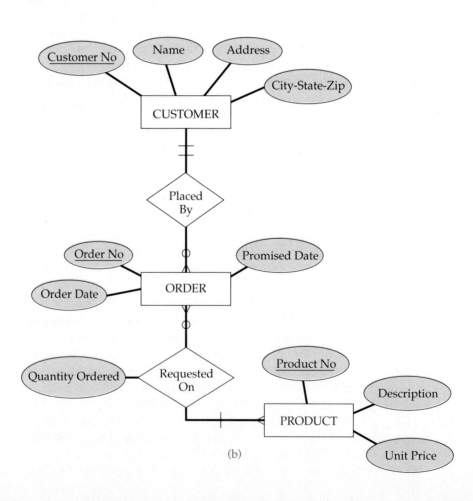

(b)

that the attribute Quantity-Ordered is a descriptor that is associated with the relationship Requested-On. In other words, Quantity-Ordered is not associated with either Order or Product but with a particular product on a particular order.

During requirements definition, a data analyst typically analyzes user views using a rather intuitive process such as that described above and produces E-R diagrams such as the one shown in Figure 5-13b. In Chapter 6 we describe normalization, which provides more formal tools for analyzing primary keys, foreign keys, and relationships between entities.

OBJECT-ORIENTED REPRESENTATION

In the examples throughout this chapter, we have used entity-relationship (E-R) diagrams as the principal modeling tool. As we have seen, E-R diagrams are powerful tools for modeling data structure. They allow us to model some semantic constructs such as cardinality of relationships (1:M, M:N, and so on) and class-subclass hierarchies. However, E-R diagrams do not provide a direct means for representing integrity constraints such as domains, referential integrity constraints, and other business rules. For example, in discussing Vacation Property Rentals, these constraints were stated outside the context of E-R diagrams (see Figures 5-9, 5-10, and 5-11).

Object-oriented representation is an emerging tool that helps overcome some of these limitations of E-R models. The advantage of object-oriented techniques is that they allow us to incorporate integrity rules (as well as other database operations) directly in the database model or description, in the form of methods or procedures. In this section we illustrate the use of object-oriented representation for some of the examples considered earlier in the chapter.

Objects

We introduced objects in Chapter 3; a brief review is presented here in the context of representing user views. An **object** is a named representation of a real-world entity. Objects are equivalent to nouns in English-language statements. For example, the following are objects: customers, products, accounts, students, and courses. Notice that some objects are physical (customers, products, students) while others are intangible (courses, accounts).

There are two types of characteristics that are naturally associated with objects: attributes and operations (see Figure 5-14). **Attributes** are properties of objects that are of interest to the organization. Attributes are equivalent to adjectives in English-language statements. For example, some attributes associated with the object Bicycle are Make, Model, Serial Number,

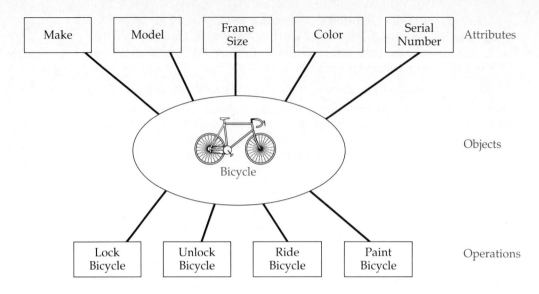

Figure 5-14
Characteristics of
objects

Frame Size, and Color (Figure 5-14). **Operations** (also called **methods**) are actions that may be performed on objects and that may change the values of attributes of the object. Operations correspond to verbs in English-language statements. For example, some operations that are performed on the Bicycle objects are Lock Bicycle, Unlock Bicycle, Ride Bicycle, and Paint Bicycle. The Paint Bicycle operation may change the value of the attribute Color (say from blue to red).

The combination of all the values of the attributes of a given object represents the **state** of that object. For example, the values of Make, Model, Serial Number, Frame Size, and Color determine the state of a Bicycle object at a given point in time. Some operations (such as Paint Bicycle) may change the state of the object. In a larger sense, a database represents the state of an organization; the state changes constantly through time as operations (such as transactions) occur.

Classes and Instances

We distinguish between object classes and instances. A **class** is a logical grouping of objects that share the same attributes and operations. An **instance** is one member (or materialization) of that class. For example, Bicycle is a class object; Mary's bicycle is an instance of that class. All of the attributes and operations for the class are described in one place (the class object). Object instances may contain attributes or operations that are peculiar to that instance but are not shared by other instances of the class.

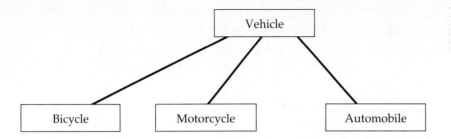

Figure 5-15
Generalization
hierarchy

Inheritance

An important characteristic of the object-oriented methodology is generalization, the ability to define class hierarchies. That is, we recognize that an object class we have already defined is really a subclass of a more general class (called a superclass). For example, Bicycles, Motorcycles, and Automobiles are subclasses of a superclass called Vehicles (see Figure 5-15).

Inheritance is an important property of a generalization hierarchy. By **inheritance** we mean that each subclass inherits the attributes and operations of the superclass to which it belongs. For example, the attributes Make, Model, Serial Number, and Color would apply to the superclass Vehicle in Figure 5-15. These attributes would be defined once for Vehicle and would automatically be inherited by the Bicycle, Motorcycle, and Automobile subclasses. However, each subclass often possesses additional attributes and operations that do not apply to the superclass. For example, the attribute Frame Size would apply to the Bicycle subclass only, while the attribute Engine Displacement would apply to Motorcycle and Automobile (but not to Bicycle).

Modeling User Views

In this section we illustrate how we can use object-oriented representation to model both data structure and integrity constraints. For an example we use the Rental Agreement for Vacation Property Rentals (see Figure 5-7).

Rental Agreement is an object (actually a class) that is of interest to Vacation Property Rentals. If the database analyst is using an object-oriented representation, she or he might define this object using an object schema such as that shown in Figure 5-16. An object schema is a description of an object using a concise language to define the object name, a brief description, object attributes, contained objects (if any), and allowable operations.

Notice first that the attributes of Rental Agreement are defined in the schema. Each attribute is associated with a domain name (domains are generally supported by object-oriented models). For example, Agreement-Date, Begin-Date, and End-Date are all associated with a domain named

Figure 5-16
Object schema for
rental agreement

Object Name: RENTAL AGREEMENT

Description: Formal Agreement between Vacation Property Rentals
and Customer to rent stated property during specified rental period

Attributes:
Agreement-Date: Dates
Begin-Date: Dates
May not be null
End-Date: Dates
May not be null
Rental-Amount: Rental Amounts

Contained Objects:
RENTER (single-valued)
PROPERTY (single-valued)

Operations:
1. Create Instance
    a. VPR Salesperson only
    b. Valid RENTER instance must exist
    c. Valid PROPERTY instance must exist
    d. Begin-Date < End-Date only
    e. May not overlap another Rental Agreement
        (see rules 3 and 4, Figure 5-11)
2. Delete Instance
    a. Authorized VPR accountant only
    b. Retention period is six months

Dates. Each domain that is named in an object schema is defined as another object elsewhere in the model.

In Figure 5-16 we see an example of how an object may contain other objects. In this example, we say that Rental Agreement "contains" both the Renter and Property objects. By this we mean that when people use Rental Agreement, they logically associate this object with both a Renter object and a Property object. Both of these objects are shown as single valued, since a Rental Agreement instance is associated with exactly one Renter object and one Property object.

The object schema also shows the allowable operations for this object. In Figure 5-16 we show only two operations—Create Instance and Delete Instance—but other operations (such as Change End-Date or Change Rental Amount) could also be included here.

Notice that the definition of each operation includes the integrity constraints that are to be enforced when performing that operation. For example, the Create Instance operation includes both referential integrity constraints (valid Renter instance must exist) and other business rules (Begin-Date < End-Date). Unlike E-R diagrams, these types of rules can (and should) be incorporated in the object schema.

Object-oriented database management systems are beginning to emerge for commercial applications. As this technology becomes readily available, it will become feasible not only to capture database descriptions in object-oriented representation but to implement those databases without the necessity of translating the descriptions to another model.

Case Example: Mountain View Community Hospital

The requirements definition process described in this chapter will now be illustrated for Mountain View Community Hospital (this case was introduced in Chapter 4). Requirements definition was performed under the direction of Mr. Helms, the data administrator. Mr. Helms was assisted in this effort by Mrs. Green, whose title was data analyst. Mrs. Green was previously a systems analyst with Mountain View Community Hospital and had attended a college class on database analysis and design. A database consultant assisted in organizing the overall design approach as well as the approach to be used for requirements definition. However, requirements definition was performed almost entirely by the design team of Mr. Helms and Mrs. Green over a period of approximately three months.

The design team initiated this effort by reviewing the enterprise data model that was developed during the data and systems planning process (see Figure 4-11). This figure is shown again in Figure 5-17 for ease of reference.

The entities shown in Figure 5-17 provide a starting point for requirements definition. By interviewing users and examining detailed user views, the design team developed a detailed definition of data requirements for the hospital.

Define Database Scope

The first step of requirements definition is to define the scope of the database (see Figure 5-12). The enterprise data model (Figure 5-17) and other documents developed during the planning process proved helpful during this step. In particular, Figures 4-14 and 4-15 show the hospital processes and entity classes that are important to achieve Excellent Care, an important critical success factor for the hospital. Since Excellent Care was a priority CSF, the project team decided to focus its initial effort on the Patient entity and other entities related to Patient, such as Physician, Test, and Medical/ Surgical Items. However, the project team also planned to broaden the requirements definition to other areas as time permitted.

Select Requirements Definition Methodology

The design team decided to use E-R diagrams as the basic tool for modeling data structure during requirements definition. A PC-based CASE tool was

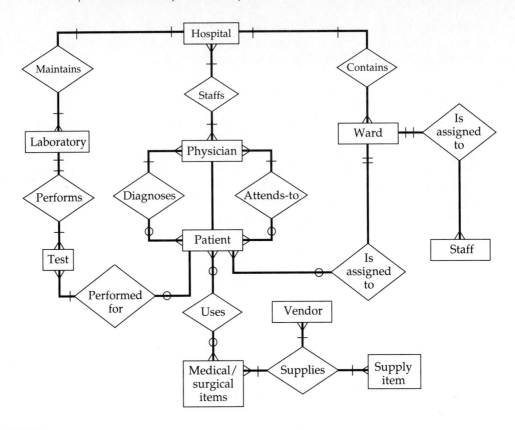

Figure 5-17

used to draw E-R diagrams and record descriptive data in a data dictionary. The team also decided to document integrity constraints as they were identified. Many of these constraints could not be recorded directly as part of the E-R diagrams but were instead entered in the data dictionary.

Identify User Views

The design team interviewed users throughout Mountain View Community Hospital, including nurses, doctors, administrators, technicians, and clerks. It obtained samples of existing reports and other operating documents, as well as the formats of forms and displays, and drew an overview diagram identifying the various user views to be analyzed during requirements definition. A portion of this overview diagram is shown in Figure 5-18. It identifies four significant user views of data for the hospital: Patient Bill, Room Utilization Report, Patient Display, and Physician Report.

When the overview diagram was completed, with a total of 20 views, the design team reviewed it with users to ensure that they had identified all significant views within the present scope of the requirements definition.

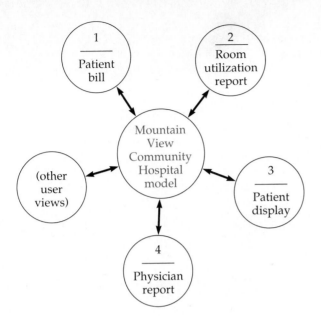

Figure 5-18
User views for
Mountain View
Community Hospital

Model Data Structure and Constraints

We select the four user views shown in Figure 5-18 to further illustrate the view modeling process.

USER VIEW 1: PATIENT BILL

The first user view is that of the Patient Bill (see Figure 5-19a). Charges incurred by each patient are accumulated during the patient's stay at the hospital. After the patient is discharged, a statement is mailed to the patient. The Patient Bill shown in Figure 5-19a is a simplified version of this statement.

An E-R diagram representing the structure of the Patient Bill is shown in Figure 5-19b. The Patient Bill represents the combination of two entities: Patient and Item (those items for which a Patient is billed). The primary key of Patient is Patient#, while the primary key of Item is Item-Code. As shown in Figure 5-19b, the association between Patient and Item is *M:N*. This association, which is named "Is Billed For" in the figure, has an attribute called Charge that represents the amount the patient is billed for this particular item. If every patient were billed exactly the same amount for a given item, then Charge would be an attribute of Item. However, since we assume that two different patients may be billed different amounts for the same item, the attribute Charge is an attribute of the "is billed for" relationship.

Domains   Several domain definitions for Mountain View Community Hospital are shown in Figure 5-20. Some of these domains are for attributes

Figure 5-19
Patient Bill and E-R Diagram

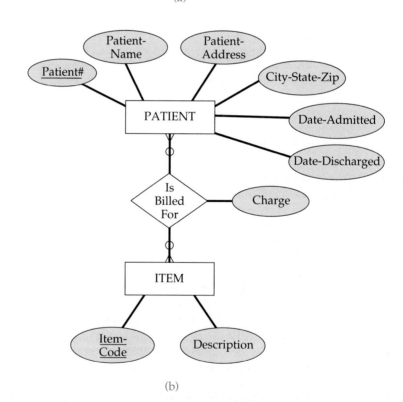

| Mountain View Community Hospital |
| 200 Forest Dr. Mountain View, Co. |

Statement of account for:

Patient name: Baker, Mary   Patient#: 3249
Patient address: 300 Oak St.   Date admitted: 09-10-9X
City-State-Zip: Date discharged: 09-14-9X
   Mountain View, Co. 80638

Item Code	Description	Charge
200	Room semi-pr	150.00
205	Television	10.00
307	X-ray	25.00
413	Lab tests	35.00
	Balance Due	220.00

(a)

(b)

Figure 5-20
Selected Domain
Definitions

Domain Name: Patient Names
    Definition: Names of Mountain View Community Hospital patients
    Type/Length: Character 32
    Format:
        Last-Name Character 18
        First-Name Character 12
        Middle-Initial Character 2
    Allowable Values: May not be null

Domain Name: Item Codes
    Definition: Unique identifier for a hospital supply item
    Type/Length: Character 6
    Allowable Values: May not be null

Domain Name: Charges
    Definition: Amount billed to a patient for a supply item
    Type/Length: Decimal 8
    Format: $DDDDD.DD

Domain Name: Locations
    Definition: Unique identifier for a hospital bed location
    Type/Length: Character 5
    Format: RRR-B
      RRR = room number
        B = bed location in room
    Allowable Values: May not be null

Domain Name: Accommodations
    Definition: Designator for type of room accomodation
    Type/Length: Character 2
    Allowable Values: PR (= private), SP (= semiprivate)

from the Patient Bill, while others are for other user views described later in this chapter.

Referential Integrity Following are some referential integrity rules that apply to the "is billed for" relationship shown in Figure 5-19b.

1. **Insertion rule.** An occurrence of "is billed for" cannot be created unless there exists a valid Patient entity and a valid Item entity.

2. **Deletion rules.**
   a. A Patient item cannot be deleted if it is a member of one or more "is billed for" instances.
   b. An Item entity cannot be deleted if it is a member of one or more "is billed for" instances.

Other Business Rules The project team identified the following business rule, to be included in the database description: Date-Admitted may not be later than Date-Discharged.

Figure 5-21
Room utilization report and E-R diagram

Room Utilization Report Date: 10-15-9X				
Location	Accom	Patient#	Patient Name	Exp Discharge Date
100-1	PR	6213	Rose, David	10-17-9X
101-1	PR	1379	Cribbs, John	10-15-9X
102-1	SP			
102-2	SP	1239	Miller, Ruth	10-16-9X
103-1	PR	7040	Ortega, Juan	10-19-9X

(a)

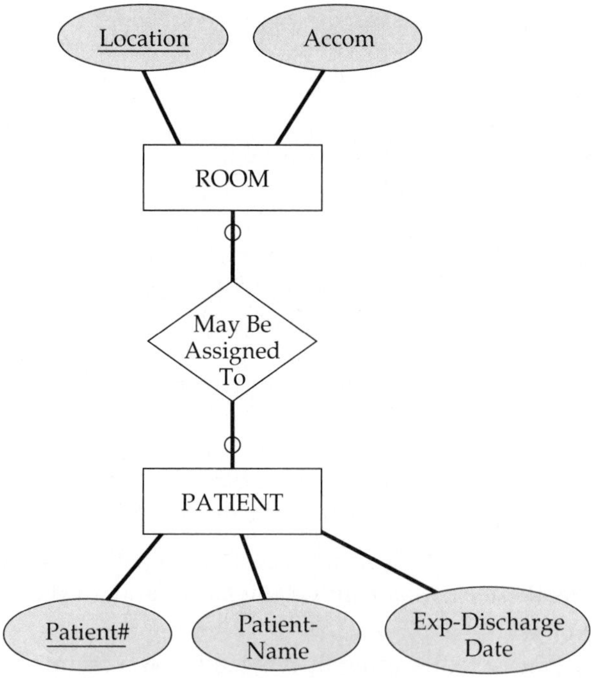

(b)

USER VIEW 2: ROOM UTILIZATION REPORT

The Room Utilization Report (Figure 5-21a) is a daily report that shows the status of each room and bed location at Mountain View Community Hospital. This report is used primarily for bed scheduling and to track room and bed utilization.

The Location column in this report indicates the room number and bed number: For example, location 102-2 means room number 102, bed number 2. The ACCOM column indicates type of accommodations (PR = private, SP = semiprivate). The remaining columns contain information about the patient (if any) assigned to the bed location at the time the report was prepared.

An E-R diagram for the Room Utilization Report is shown in Figure 5-21b. There are two entities: Room and Patient. The relationship is 1:1 and is conditional in both directions. That is, a room/bed location may or may not be assigned a patient at a given point in time. On the other hand, a patient may or may not be assigned to a bed (for example, an out-patient). The primary key of Room is Location, while Patient is the primary key of Patient. The relationship between these entities is named "May Be Assigned To," as shown in the figure.

The project team identified the following referential integrity rules:

1. **Insertion rule.** an occurrence of "May Be Assigned To" cannot be created unless there is a valid and unassigned Room location occurrence and a valid Patient occurrence.

2. **Deletion rule.** an occurrence of Room cannot be deleted if it is a member of "May Be Assigned To."

USER VIEW 3: PATIENT DISPLAY

The Patient Display (Figure 5-22a) is presented on demand to any doctor, nurse, or other qualified member who uses a visual display. We will assume that the user must enter the patient number to display data for a particular patient (in practice, the system would probably support look-up based on patient name as well).

An E-R diagram for Patient Display is shown in Figure 5-22b. Since Patient is the only entity in this diagram, there are no new referential integrity rules. A business rule enforcing the integrity of Date-Admitted and Date-Discharged was stated previously (see description under Patient Bill).

USER VIEW 4: PHYSICIAN REPORT

The Physician Report is prepared daily for each physician on the staff of Mountain View Community Hospital (see Figure 5-23a), showing the patients who have been treated and the name of the treatment (or procedure). To simplify the analysis, we assume that each patient may receive only one treatment from a given physician each day.

An E-R diagram representing the Physician Report is shown in Figure 5-23b. There are two entities: Physician and Patient. The relationship (named "attends to") is *M:N* and is conditional in both directions. Notice that Procedure is an attribute of "attends to," since it is not an attribute of either the Physician entity or the Patient entity.

We ask you to state referential integrity rules for "attends to" in the chapter exercises.

Figure 5-22
Patient display and
E-R diagram

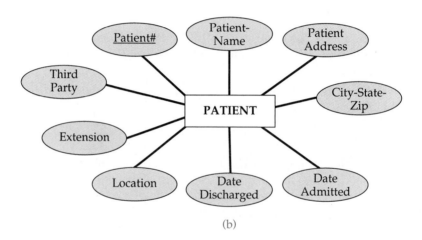

```
Patient#:  3249
Patient Name:  Baker, Mary
Patient Address:  300 Oak St.
City-State-Zip:  Mountain View, Co. 80638
Date Admitted:  09-12-9X
Date Discharged:  XX-XX-XX
Location:  437-2
Extension:  529
Third Party:  Blue Cross
```

(a)

(b)

SUMMARY

This is the first of three chapters devoted to the important topic of database design. Database design is the process of creating database structures from user requirements for data. The resulting design must satisfy user requirements in terms of completeness, integrity, and performance, among other factors. Database design is a complex and demanding process that requires the commitment and participation of the entire organization.

There are four steps in database design: requirements definition, conceptual design, implementation design, and physical design. The purpose of requirements definition is to identify and describe the data required by users throughout the organization. The purpose of conceptual design is to develop a conceptual data model (or information architecture) that is independent of implementation considerations. Implementation design is concerned with mapping the conceptual design to a technology-dependent

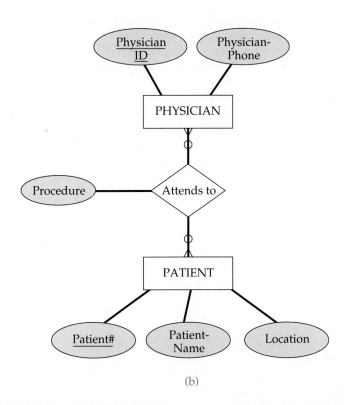

Mountain View Community Hospital
Physician Report

Date: 10-17-9X   Physician ID: Wilcox
                                  Physician Phone: 329-1848

Patient	Patient Name	Location	Procudure
6083	Brown, May	184-2	Tonsillectomy
3157	Miller, Ruth	216-1	Observation
4139	Majors, Carl	107-3	Chemotherapy

(a)

(b)

Figure 5-23
Physician report and
E-R diagram

model such as hierarchical, network, or relational. Physical design is concerned with factors such as stored record design and the selection of indexes—important factors, since they affect database performance and ease of use.

Database design is closely related to the three-level architecture. Requirements definition is concerned with the external level of that architecture, while conceptual design is concerned with the conceptual level. Implementation design is concerned with mapping from the conceptual level, while physical design is concerned with the internal level. Thus the database design process that we describe in Chapters 5, 6, and 8 supports the three-level (or three-schema) architecture that is commonly used today.

Requirements definition is concerned both with the structure of data and with integrity constraints related to the use of those data. The steps in requirements definition are the following: define database scope, select requirements definition methodology, identify user views, model data structure, model database constraints, and identify operational requirements. The outputs of requirements definition are a formal set of requirements specifications that are used as inputs to conceptual design.

During requirements definition, it is important to identify constraints that are used to maintain database integrity. We described three types of integrity constraints: domains, referential integrity constraints, and other business rules. Domains (or domain constraints) are rules that define allowable data types, lengths, formats, and values for each attribute. Referential integrity constraints are rules that ensure the validity of references for an occurrence of one entity to the occurrence (or occurrences) of another entity. Other business rules are constraints that are required to protect data integrity in a database.

There are several important advantages to incorporating integrity constraints into the database description, rather than in application programs. Some of these advantages are faster application development, reduced maintenance effort, faster response to business changes, and greater end-user involvement in application development. Unfortunately, many commercial database management systems today provide only limited facilities for database integrity constraints.

Chapter Review

REVIEW QUESTIONS

1. Define each of the following terms:
   a. database design
   b. requirements definition
   c. conceptual design
   d. user view
   e. object
   f. attribute
   g. domain
   h. operation
   i. class
   j. instance
   k. inheritance
   l. physical design
   m. identifier

2. Contrast the following terms:
   a. class; instance
   b. conceptual design; physical design
   c. attribute; domain
   d. user view; object
   e. subclass; superclass

3. What is the major output of each of the following stages of database design?
   a. requirements definition
   b. conceptual design
   c. implementation design
   d. physical design

4. List and briefly describe six steps in requirements definition.

5. Describe six advantages in incorporating integrity rules into the database definition (instead of within applications).

6. What are database operational requirements? List five categories of operational requirements.

7. What are other business rules? Give an example of this type of rule for Vacation Property Rentals.

8. What is inheritance? Give an example of inheritance (other than those discussed in the text).

9. What is a role name? Give an example of a role name for Vacation Property Rentals.

10. Why is a structured methodology required to support requirements definition?

PROBLEMS AND EXERCISES

1. Match the following terms and definitions.

_____ requirements definition	**a)** preserves integrity of references
_____ object	**b)** role an attribute plays
_____ class	**c)** properties of objects or entities
_____ instance	**d)** reflects organizational policy
_____ inheritance	**e)** logical grouping of objects
_____ referential integrity	**f)** process of identifying and documenting data
_____ identifier	**g)** subset of data required by a user
_____ domain	**h)** uniquely identifies an entity
_____ attribute	**i)** named representation of a real-world entity
_____ business rule	**j)** applies to subclasses and superclasses
_____ user view	**k)** defines allowable data types and values
_____ role name	**l)** member of class

2. Draw a generalization hierarchy (similar to Figure 5-15) for the following object classes: Vehicle, Land Vehicle, Air Vehicle, Water Vehicle, Ocean Vessel, River Raft, Helicopter, Rail Vehicle, Coastal Vessel, Plane, Road Vehicle.

3. Draw a chart showing the characteristics (attributes and operations) of the following objects (similar to Figure 5-14):
   a. airplane
   b. college class
   c. library

4. Develop an object schema for the Physician Report at Mountain View Community Hospital (Figure 5-23).

5. Figure 5-24 shows a Grade Report that is mailed to students at Lakewood College at the end of each semester.
   a. Prepare an E-R Diagram for Grade Report. Assume that each course is taught by one instructor (your solution should involve three entities).
   b. Prepare domain descriptions for the attributes in Figure 5-24.
   c. State referential integrity rules for the entities in your E-R diagram.

6. State referential integrity rules for the entities in the Physician's Report at Mountain View Community Hospital (Figure 5-23).

7. Review the Invoice Screen for Pine Valley Furniture Company and the E-R diagram for this screen (see Figure 2-5).
   a. Why is the attribute Quantity-Shipped associated with the "Shipped-On" relationship diamond?
   b. State referential integrity rules for the E-R diagram (Figure 2-5b).
   c. Can you think of any "other business rules" or constraints that would apply to this model? (*Hint:* Consider the attributes Quantity-Ordered and Quantity-Shipped.)

8. Figure 5-25 is a Salesperson Annual Summary Report prepared by Pine Valley Furniture Company. Prepare an E-R diagram for this user view.

Figure 5-24
Grade report

LAKEWOOD COLLEGE GRADE REPORT FALL SEMESTER 199X				
NAME: Emily Williams ID: 268300458 CAMPUS-ADDRESS: 208 Brooks Hall MAJOR: Information Systems				
COURSE-ID	TITLE	INSTRUCTORS NAME	INSTRUCTORS LOCATION	GRADE
IS 350	Database Mgt.	Codd	B104	A
IS 465	System Analysis	Parsons	B317	B

SALESPERSON ANNUAL SUMMARY REPORT, 199X

REGION	SALESPERSON	QUARTERLY ACTUAL SALES			
		FIRST	SECOND	THIRD	FOURTH
NORTHWEST & MOUNTAIN	HAWTHORNE	22000	17500	21300	19800
	BAKER	19500	14600	13300	12000
	HODGES	11000	9500	17000	12000
MIDWEST & MID-ATLANTIC	STEPHENSON	7500	6600	8000	8000
	SWENSON	11000	9800	10000	9000
	FRANKLIN	11000	12000	17000	9000
NEW ENGLAND	BRIGHTMAN	25000	28000	26000	33000
	KENNEDY	31000	19000	27000	28000

Figure 5-25
Salesperson annual summary report

8. Figure 5-25 is a Salesperson Annual Summary Report prepared by Pine Valley Furniture Company. Prepare an E-R diagram for this user view.

9. Obtain a common user view such as a credit card statement of account, a phone bill, or some other common document. Prepare an E-R diagram for this document.

10. Prepare an object schema for the document in Problem 9.

11. Draw an E-R diagram for the following situation (Batra, Hoffer, and Bostrom, 1988).

Projects Inc. is an engineering firm with approximately 500 employees. A database is required to keep track of all employees, their skills and projects assigned and departments worked in. Every employee has a unique number assigned by the firm, required to store his or her name and date-of-birth. If an employee is currently married to another employee of Projects Inc., then it is required to store the date of marriage and who is married to whom. However, no record of marriage need be maintained if the spouse of an employee is not an employee of the firm. Each employee is given a job title (for example, engineer, secretary, foreman, and so on). We are interested in collecting more data specific to the following types: engineer and secretary. The relevant data to be recorded for engineers is the type of degree (e.g., electrical, mechanical, civil, etc.) and for secretaries is their typing speeds. An employee does only one type of job at any given time, and we need to retain information material for only the current job for an employee.

There are eleven different departments, each with a unique name. An employee can report to only one department. Each department has a phone number.

To procure various kinds of equipment, each department deals with many vendors. A vendor typically supplies equipment to many departments. It is required to store the name and address of each vendor and the date of the last meeting between a department and a vendor.

Many employees can work on a project. An employee can work in many projects (for example, Southwest Refinery, California Petrochemicals, and so on) but can only be assigned to at most one project in a given city. For each city, we are interested in its state and population. An employee can have many skills (preparing material requisitions, checking drawings, and so on), but she or he may use only a given set of skills on a particular project. (For example, an employee MURPHY may prepare requisitions for Southwest Refinery project and prepare requisitions as well as check drawings for California Petrochemicals.) An employee uses each skill that she or he possesses in at least one project. Each skill is assigned a number. A short description is required to be stored for each skill. Projects are distinguished by project numbers. It is required to store the estimated cost of each project.

REFERENCES

Batra, D., J. A. Hoffer, and R. B. Bostrom. 1988. "A Comparison of User Performance Between the Relational and Extended Entity Relationship Model in the Discovery Phase of Database Design." *Proceedings of the Ninth International Conference on Information Systems*, Minneapolis, Minn.: Nov. 30-Dec. 3. 295–306.

Fleming, C. C., and B. von Halle. 1990. "An Overview of Logical Data Modeling." *Data Resource Management* 1 (1) (Winter), 5-15.

Gorman, K., and J. Choobineh. 1990. Kona, Hawaii: "An Overview of the Object-Oriented Entity Relationship Model (OOERM)." *Proceedings of the Twenty-Third Annual Hawaii International Conference on Information Systems*, (Vol 3), 336–345.

Storey, V. C., and R. C. Goldstein. 1988. "A Methodology for Creating User Views in Database Design." *ACM Transactions on Database Systems*, 13 (3) (Sept.), 305–338.

Teorey, T. J., and J. P. Fry. 1982. *Design of Database Structures*. Englewood Cliffs, N.J.: Prentice-Hall.

Wood, D. 1990. "A Primer of Features and Performance Issues of Relational DBMSs." *Data Resource Management*, 1 (1) Winter.

CHAPTER 6

Conceptual Database Design

INTRODUCTION

Conceptual database design is the second major phase of the database design process, following requirements definition (see Figure 5-1). Conceptual database design is the process of constructing a detailed architecture for a database that is independent of implementation details such as the target database management system, application programs or programming languages, or any other physical considerations. Conceptual design is also referred to as logical design by some authors.

The primary inputs to conceptual database design are the structured requirements defined during requirements definition, as described in Chapter 5. Structured requirements may be stated using entity-relationship diagrams, objects, or other forms of representation (in Chapter 5 we emphasized the use of E-R diagrams). Other inputs to logical database design are the enterprise data model (which is used as a guide to conceptual design) and CASE tools (which are used to support this stage of database design).

The conceptual data model that is developed in this chapter consolidates all of the individual E-R diagrams (or other logical data models) that were developed during requirements definition. Thus, the conceptual data model (also called the conceptual schema) is an integrated view of business data throughout the organization. According to Fleming and von Halle, 1990, the conceptual data model should meet the following criteria:

1. **Structural validity:** consistency with the way the business defines and organizes data

2. **Simplicity:** ease of understanding by both IS professionals and non-technical users

3. **Nonredundancy:** each piece of information represented exactly once in the model

4. **Shareability:** all qualified users sharing the data in the conceptual model

5. **Extensibility:** ability to evolve to support new requirements with minimal impact on existing users

6. **Integrity:** consistency with the way the business uses and manages data

STEPS IN CONCEPTUAL DATABASE DESIGN

In this section, we describe a five-step process for conceptual database design, as shown in Figure 6-1:

1. **Develop conceptual data model.** During this step, the E-R diagrams that were developed for each user view during requirements definition are combined to form a single, integrated conceptual data model. Database analysts must perform this step carefully to ensure that the resulting model (called the conceptual schema) is nonredundant and logically consistent.

2. **Transform data model to relations.** During this step, E-R diagrams (or other logical data models) are converted to relations. This step might also be considered part of implementation design (rather than conceptual design). However, we include this step here since it is preliminary to normalization, which we consider part of conceptual design.

3. **Normalize the relations.** During this step, the relations that were derived in the previous step are normalized (that is, converted to logically simple data structures). We describe normalization in detail later in this chapter.

4. **Integrate the relations. View integration** is the process of merging individual user views (in the form of E-R diagrams or 3NF relations) into an integrated data structure (or conceptual schema).

5. **Develop action diagrams.** Action diagrams are high-level definitions of data operations that maintain a database in a current and consis-

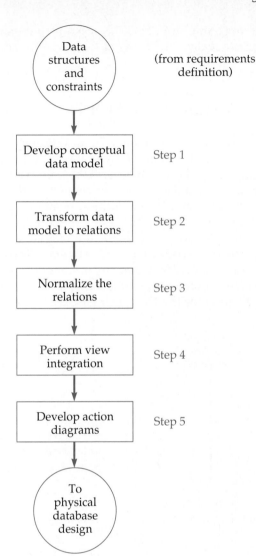

Figure 6-1
Steps in conceptual
database design

tent state. Typical database operations add and delete records, modify records, and produce output in the form of reports and displays.

The steps shown in Figure 6-1 are typical of those performed during
conceptual database design. Important variations on this process would be
to normalize the data during requirements definition (as the E-R diagrams
for each user view are being developed) or during conceptual data model
development (step 1 in Figure 6-1). With either of these variations, normalizing the relations (step 3 in Figure 6-1) would be eliminated, and transforming the data model to relations (step 2 in Figure 6-1) could become part

of implementation design (described in Chapter 8). The description of normalization in this chapter applies equally well to any of these approaches.

DEVELOPING THE CONCEPTUAL DATA MODEL

During requirements definition (described in Chapter 5), an E-R diagram is developed for each user view within the scope of the analysis. In developing the conceptual data model, we need to combine all of these individual E-R diagrams to form a single, integrated data model. In combining these views, we include all of the relevant components (entities, relationships, attributes) but eliminate redundant components. As a result, the conceptual data model is a nonredundant superset of the individual E-R diagrams.

To illustrate this process, consider the user views and corresponding E-R diagrams developed for Pine Valley Furniture Company in Chapter 2 (see Figures 2-2 through 2-5). The E-R diagram for the Product Display is shown in Figure 6-2a, while the E-R diagram for the Customer Display is shown

Figure 6-2
E-R diagrams for product and customer displays

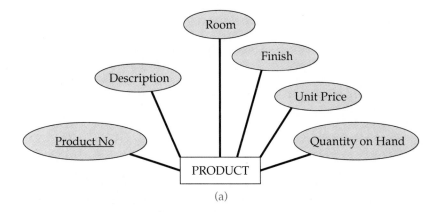

(a)

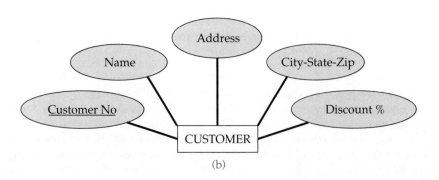

(b)

in Figure 6-2b. These E-R diagrams are for different entities, and there is no redundancy between the two views

The E-R diagrams for the Order Entry and Invoice screens are considerably more complex (see Figure 6-3), with extensive redundancy. In fact, the E-R diagram for the Order Entry screen (Figure 6-3a) is basically a subset of that for the Invoice screen (Figure 6-3b). However, the Order entity in Figure 6-3a contains two attributes (Order-Date and Promised-Date) that do not appear in Figure 6-3b, so that Order Entry is not truly a subset of Invoice.

The conceptual data model for Pine Valley Furniture Company is developed by combining these four E-R diagrams. The result is shown in Figure 6-4. Notice that this diagram has the following two properties:

1. There is no redundancy (each entity, relationship, and attribute appears exactly once).
2. Each of the individual E-R diagrams (Figures 6-2 and 6-3) is a subset of this model. Thus no components of the individual E-R diagrams have been omitted in developing the conceptual data model.

The composite E-R diagram in Figure 6-4, together with the constraints for the model, is called a conceptual data model (or conceptual schema). As new entities, relationships, attributes, and constraints are discovered, they are added to this model. Thus the conceptual data model is an evolving model that presents an integrated view of the data for an entire organization or for a subset of that organization.

TRANSFORMING E-R DIAGRAMS TO RELATIONS

By expressing the conceptual data model as an E-R diagram (such as Figure 6-4) we provide a highly visible view of the organization's data, which is readily understandable to end users. However, few (if any) DBMS products implement the E-R model today. As a result, the E-R diagram must be transformed to a DBMS-processable model (such as hierarchical, network, or relational) before it can be implemented. Since the relational model is most commonly used in new implementations, we describe transforming the E-R diagrams to relations in this section. This in turn sets the stage for a discussion of normalization in the next section.

Each entity in an E-R diagram is transformed to a relation. The primary key (or identifier) of the entity becomes the primary key of the corresponding relation, and descriptors (nonkey attributes) of the entity become nonkey attributes of the relation. Figure 6-5 shows the Customer entity for Pine Valley Furniture Company (taken from Figure 6-4) and the corresponding relation. Customer-No is the primary key for the entity, as well as for the CUSTOMER relation.

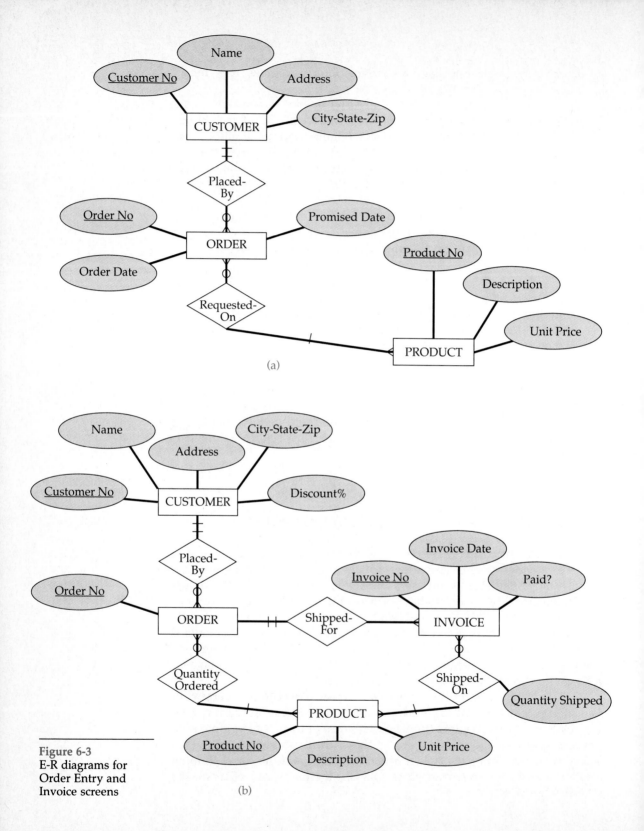

Figure 6-3
E-R diagrams for
Order Entry and
Invoice screens

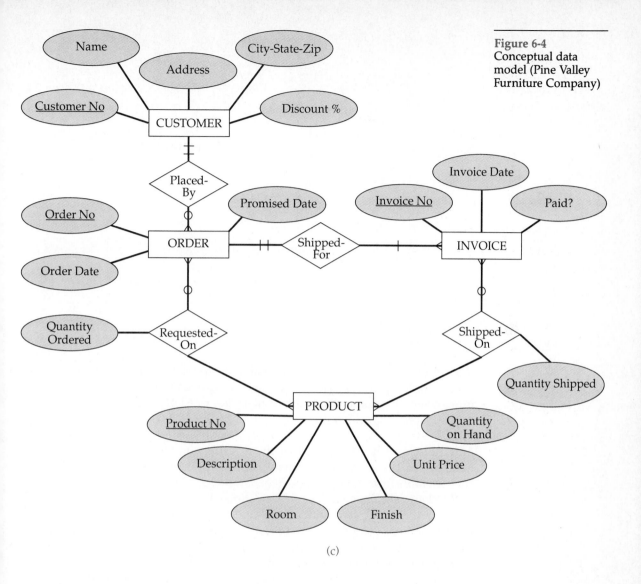

Figure 6-4
Conceptual data
model (Pine Valley
Furniture Company)

(c)

Relationships

1:N Relationship   A one-to-many (1:N) relationship in an E-R diagram is
represented by placing a foreign key in the relation that represents the entity
on the many-side of the relationship. This foreign key is the primary key
of the entity on the one-side of the relationship.

An example of this rule is shown in Figure 6-6. Figure 6-6a shows the
"Placed-By" relationship linking CUSTOMER and ORDER at Pine Valley
Furniture Company (see Figure 6-4). Figure 6-6b shows how this relation-
ship was transformed into two relations: CUSTOMER and ORDER. Notice

Figure 6-5
Transforming an
entity to a relation

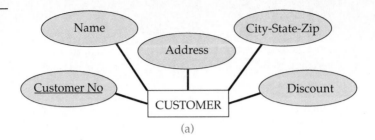

(a)

CUSTOMER

Customer-No	Name	Address	City-State-Zip	Discount
1273	Contemporary Designs	123 Oak St.	Austin, TX 38405	5%
6390	Casual Corner	18 Hoosier Dr.	Bloomington, IN 45821	3%
• • •				

(b)

that ORDER (which is on the many-side of the 1:*N* relationship) contains Customer-No as a foreign key (we use a dashed underline to indicate a foreign key). Customer-No is the primary key of CUSTOMER (the one-side of the Placed-By relationship).

***M:N* Relationship**   Suppose that the E-R diagram has a binary *M:N* relationship (that is, an *M:N* relationship between two entities). There are two such relationships in Figure 6-4: Requested-On, and Shipped-On. For each such relationship, we create a new relation (thus, there are three relations: one for each of the two entities and one for the relationship). The key of this relation is a composite key consisting of the primary key for each of the two entities in the relationship.

    Figure 6-7 shows the result of transforming the Requested-On relationship from Figure 6-4. First, a relation is created for each of the two entities in the relationship (Order and Customer), if they have not been created previously. Then a relation (called ORDER-LINE in Figure 6-7) is created for the Requested-On relationship. The primary key of ORDER-LINE is the combination (Order-No, Product-No), which are the respective primary keys of ORDER and PRODUCT.

    In some cases, there may be an n-ary relationship among three or more entities. In such cases, we create a relation that has as a primary key the composite of the primary keys of each of the participating entities. This rule is a simple generalization of the rule for an *M:N* relationship.

ISA Relationships (Class-Subclass)   The relational data model does not directly support class-subclass (or ISA) relationships. However, there are various strategies that database designers can use to represent ISA relation-

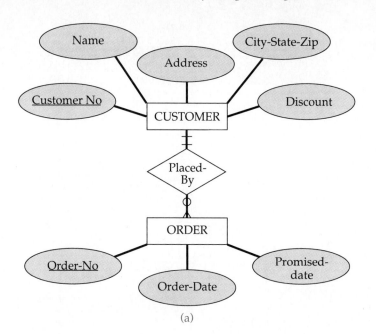

Figure 6-6
Representing a 1:*N*
Relationship

(a)

CUSTOMER

Customer-No	Name	Address	City-State-Zip	Discount
1273	Contemporary Designs	123 Oak St.	Austin, TX 38405	5%
6390	Casual Corner	18 Hoosier Dr.	Bloomington, IN 45821	3%
• • •				

ORDER

Order-No	Order-Date	Promised-Date	Customer-No
57194	3/15/9X	3/28/9X	6390
63725	3/17/9X	4/01/9X	1273
80149	3/14/9X	3/24/9X	6390

(b)

ships using relations (Chouinard, 1989). For our purposes we use the following strategy:

1. Create a separate relation for the class and for each of the subclasses.

2. The table (relation) for the class consists only of the columns that are common to all of the subclasses, plus a subtype identification column.

3. The table for each subclass contains only its primary key and the columns unique to that subclass.

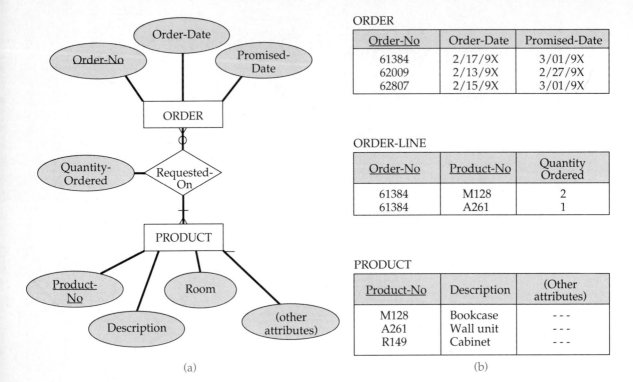

ORDER

Order-No	Order-Date	Promised-Date
61384	2/17/9X	3/01/9X
62009	2/13/9X	2/27/9X
62807	2/15/9X	3/01/9X

ORDER-LINE

Order-No	Product-No	Quantity Ordered
61384	M128	2
61384	A261	1

PRODUCT

Product-No	Description	(Other attributes)
M128	Bookcase	- - -
A261	Wall unit	- - -
R149	Cabinet	- - -

(a)   (b)

Figure 6-7
Representing *M:N*
relationship

4. The primary keys of the class and each of the subclasses are from the same domain.

An ISA relationship (with two subclasses) appears in the E-R diagram for Vacation Property Rentals (see Figure 5-7b). This relationship is again shown in Figure 6-8a, and the relations that are derived by applying the above rules are shown in Figure 6-8b. Notice that there are three relations: PROPERTY, BEACH, and MOUNTAIN. The primary key of each of these relations is the composite key (Street-Address, City-State-Zip). Although the primary key of a subclass does not have to have the same name as the primary key of the class (as in this example), they must be from the same domain.

The PROPERTY relation contains those descriptors that are common to both subclasses: No-Rooms, and Typical-Rent. In addition, it contains the subtype identifier (Subtype). The relations BEACH and MOUNTAIN (representing the subclasses) have the same primary key as PROPERTY. Each contains an attribute, however, that is unique to the subclass (Blocks-to-Beach for BEACH, Skiing for MOUNTAIN). A complete subclass with its

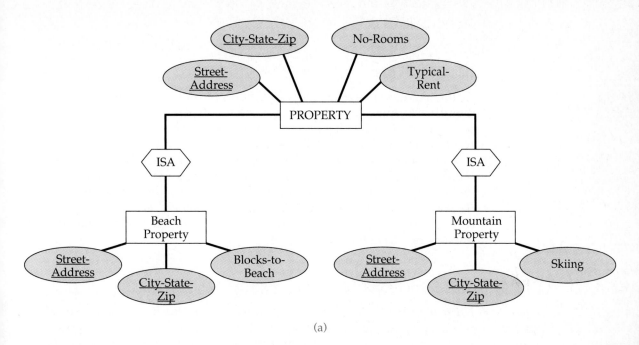

(a)

PROPERTY

Street-Address	City-State-Zip	No-Rooms	Typical Rent	Subtype
120 Surf Dr.	Honolulu, HI 99987	3	500	Beach
100 Mogul Dr.	Jackson, WY 89204	3	250	Mountain

BEACH

Street-Address	City-State-Zip	Blocks-to Beach
120 Surf Dr.	Honolulu, HI 99987	2

MOUNTAIN

Street-Address	City-State-Zip	Skiing
100 Mogul Dr.	Jackson, WY 89204	N

(b)

Figure 6-8
Representing ISA relationships

inherited attributes can be obtained by joining the subclass relation with the class relation.

Several other strategies are available for representing ISA relationships with the relational model. Each strategy offers advantages and disadvantages in terms of performance, referential integrity, ease of retrieval, and other factors. For an extended discussion, see Chouinard, 1989.

NORMALIZING THE RELATIONS

Basic concepts

At this point, we have described a process of constructing E-R diagrams, then transforming those diagrams to relations. Unless normalization has been included during these early steps in the design process, however, the resulting relations may not have an optimal structure and therefore may contain some redundancy. **Normalization** is the process of grouping attributes into well-structured relations. The principles of normalization were defined by E. F. Codd, who is considered the founder of the relational database model. Although normalization is generally associated with the relational model, it is a technique for logical design that is independent of the type of DBMS that will be used.

Well-Structured Relations

Normalization is the process of grouping attributes into well-structured relations. What is a well-structured relation? Intuitively, it is one that contains a minimum amount of redundancy and allows users to insert, delete, and modify rows in the table (or relation) without errors or inconsistencies resulting from those operations. To illustrate, consider the relation shown in Figure 6-9. This relation (called COURSE) shows training courses in which employees have enrolled this year. Assume that the following rules apply to the COURSE relation:

1. Each employee can enroll in only one course at a given time.
2. Each course has a standard fee (independent of the employee who has enrolled for the course).

The COURSE relation is certainly simple—it consists of only three columns—but is it a well-structured relation? If you examine the table, you

Figure 6-9
COURSE relation

COURSE

Employee-ID	Course-ID	Fee
E130	C200	75
E200	C300	100
E250	C200	75
E425	C400	150
E500	C300	100
E575	C500	50
• • •	• • •	• • •

COURSE

will note that there is redundancy in the data; each course fee is repeated for each employee. As a result, there may be errors or inconsistencies (called *anomalies*) when a user attempts to update the data in the table. Three types of anomalies are possible: insertion, deletion, and modification.

1. **Insertion anomaly.** Suppose a new course (C600) is offered by the company. This course cannot be added to the table until at least one employee has enrolled for the course (since each row of the table must contain an Employee-ID).

2. **Deletion anomaly.** Suppose that employee E425 decided to withdraw from course C400. Since that employee is the only one enrolled for this course, if this row is deleted from the table we lose the information that the fee for course C400 is $150 (see Figure 6-9).

3. **Update anomaly.** Suppose that the fee for course C200 is to be increased from $75 to $100. This modification must be made in each of the rows in which course C200 appears (two occurrences are shown in Figure 6-9), else the data will be inconsistent.

Because of these anomalies, we conclude that COURSE is not a well-structured relation. We therefore use normalization theory (described below) to divide COURSE into two relations, EMPLOYEE-COURSE and COURSE-FEE (see Figure 6-10). Each of these new relations is well structured, since it is free of the anomalies described earlier (you should examine the relations in Figure 6-10 and verify that they do not suffer from the three types of anomalies).

Problems with Normalized Relations

While normalization eliminates (or helps eliminate) update anomalies, you should be aware that it is not free and may introduce other types of problems. In particular, normalization may contribute to two additional issues: performance problems and referential integrity problems. We illustrate these problems for the COURSE example described earlier.

Employee-ID	Course-ID
E130	C200
E200	C300
E250	C200
E425	C400
E500	C300
E575	C500
• • •	• • •

EMPLOYEE-COURSE

Course-ID	Fee
C200	75
C300	100
C400	150
C500	50
• • •	• • •

COURSE-FEE

Figure 6-10
Structuring COURSE into two relations

Suppose that we wish to produce a listing of the data shown in the COURSE table (Figure 6-9). Before normalization, this can be accomplished with a simple SQL command such as the following:

```
SELECT *
FROM COURSE
```

After normalization (Figure 6-10), the data in EMPLOYEE-COURSE and COURSE-FEE will have to be joined (or recombined) before it can be listed. The SQL command to accomplish this appears as follows:

```
SELECT Employee-ID, Course-ID, Fee
FROM EMPLOYEE-COURSE, COURSE-FEE
WHERE EMPLOYEE-COURSE.Course-ID
= COURSE-FEE.Course-ID
```

This command will produce the same result as the simpler command for the COURSE table but will require longer to execute (how much longer depends on the implementation and on physical design factors that we discuss in the next chapter).

Referential integrity (described in Chapter 5) means maintaining consistency of references between two related tables. For example, referring to the EMPLOYEE-COURSE and COURSE-FEE tables in Figure 6-10, we note that:

1. A new row should not be added to the EMPLOYEE-COURSE table unless the Course-ID for that row already appears in the COURSE-FEE table. That is, we should not add a course for an employee unless the fee for that course has already been established.

2. A row in the COURSE-FEE table should not be deleted if there are one or more rows in the EMPLOYEE-COURSE table with the same Course-ID. That is, a course should not be dropped if one or more employees are enrolled for that course.

Despite these problems, the advantages of normalization outweigh the disadvantages. The reason for this is that the problems can be addressed through improved physical design and implementation. For example, performance can be improved through the judicious use of indexes (we discuss indexes in Chapter 8). Referential integrity can be enforced through features built into the DBMS (however, these referential integrity features also tend to degrade performance). Progressive organizations today are experiencing the benefits of normalization.

Functional Dependencies and Keys

Normalization is based on an analysis of functional dependencies. A **functional dependency** is a relationship between two attributes. Attribute B is functionally dependent on attribute A if, at a given point in time, the value of A determines the value of B. In other words, given the value of A, we know the value of B. This functional dependency is diagrammed as follows:

A → B

Consider the following example: ISBN → Book-Title. Thus, given a book's ISBN, we know its title. We say the Book-Title is functionally dependent on the ISBN. Notice that the opposite is not true: ISBN is not functionally dependent on Book-Title. The reason is that there may be two (or more) books with the same title. This might appear as follows:

ISBN 0-8061-1342

ISBN 0-6439-2006 → Calculus with Analytic Geometry

ISBN 0-1748-3429

Notice that the association from ISBN to Book-Title is N:1 (there are several books or ISBNs with the same title). In general, if attribute B is functionally dependent on attribute A, the association from A to B is N:1.

The attribute on the left-hand side of the arrow in a functional dependency is called a **determinant.** Thus, in the previous example, ISBN is a determinant.

Now let's look at the three functional dependencies in the COURSE relation (Figure 6-9).

Employee-ID → Course-ID
Employee-ID → Fee
Course-ID → Fee

Notice that, although there are three functional dependencies, there are only two determinants: Employee-ID and Course-ID (you should make sure you understand the definitions of functional dependencies and determinants by applying them to the data in Figure 6-9).

A **primary key** (or simply **key**) is an attribute (or a group of attributes) that uniquely identifies a row in a relation. All of the nonkey attributes in the relation are functionally dependent on the key. The key in COURSE (Figure 6-9) is Employee-ID since the other two attributes (Course-ID and Fee) are functionally dependent on Employee-ID). Although Course-ID is a determinant, it is not a key (Employee-ID is not functionally dependent on Course-ID).

Every relation must have a key; also, the values of the key must be unique (for example, in Figure 6-9 each Employee-ID appears exactly once in the COURSE table). It follows that each row in a table must be distinct (that is, no two rows are exactly alike).

Functional dependencies may be permanent or temporal. For example, the following functional dependency is permanent (since the title of a book does not change over time):

ISBN → Book-Title

On the other hand, the following functional dependency is temporal:

Employee-ID → Course-ID

That is, a given employee may be enrolled in different courses over time. However, *at a given point in time* each employee is enrolled in only one course (by assumption).

It frequently happens that two (or more) attributes must be grouped to form a key for a relation. For example, consider the relation EMPLOYEE-SCHEDULE in Figure 6-11, which shows the starting dates for courses in which employees are enrolled. None of the three attributes is individually a determinant (you should verify this statement), but the combination of Employee-ID and Course-ID is a determinant.

Employee-ID, Course-ID → Starting-Date

That is, if we know the identity of *both* the employee and the course, we know the starting date. The following is also a functional dependency:

Employee-ID, Starting-Date → Course-ID

In other words, if we know the identity of the employee and the starting date for the course, we also know the Course-ID.

Since the combination (Employee-ID, Course-ID) determines the remaining attribute (Starting-Date) for EMPLOYEE-SCHEDULE, it is a candidate key for that relation. For the same reason, the combination (Employee-ID, Starting-Date) is also a candidate key. A **candidate key** is a determinant that can be used as a key for a relation. In some relations there is only one candidate key, while in other relations there may be more than one.

Suppose that the combination (Employee-ID, Course-ID) is chosen as the key for EMPLOYEE-SCHEDULE. Since this key consists of more than one attribute, it is called a composite key. A **composite key** is a key that consists of the concatenation of two or more attributes.

Figure 6-11
EMPLOYEE-
SCHEDULE relation

Employee-ID	Course-ID	Starting-Date
E130	C200	10/18
E130	C300	12/10
E200	C200	11/04
E200	C400	10/18
E425	C400	3/03
E130	C400	3/03
• • •	• • •	• • •

EMPLOYEE = SCHEDULE

In a functional dependency, each value of A determines exactly one value of B:

$$A \rightarrow B$$

It sometimes happens that there is a relationship between two attributes A and B, but A does not uniquely determine B. That is, for each value of A there is a well-defined set of values for B. This is illustrated as follows:

$$A \rightarrow\!\!\!\rightarrow B$$

For example, consider the EMPLOYEE-SCHEDULE relation (Figure 6-11). The association from Course-ID to Starting-Date is multivalued:

$$\text{Course-ID} \rightarrow\!\!\!\rightarrow \text{Starting-Date}$$

That is, a given course does not have a single starting date but a well-defined set or list of starting dates (in Figure 6-11, course C200 has two starting dates shown in the sample data: 10/18 and 11/4). This type of dependency is called a **multivalued dependency.** We will return to this topic later in this chapter.

Steps in Normalization

We have described normalization as the process of grouping attributes into well-structured relations. Normalization is often accomplished in stages (see Figure 6-12). Each stage corresponds to a normal form. A **normal form** is a state of a relation that corresponds to the type of dependencies that remain in the relation. We describe these states briefly in this section, then illustrate them in the next section.

1. **First normal form (1NF).** Any repeating groups have been removed, so that there is a single value at the intersection of each row and column of the table.

2. **Second normal form (2NF).** Any partial functional dependencies have been removed.

3. **Third normal form (3NF).** Any transitive dependencies have been removed.

4. **Boyce-Codd normal form (BCNF).** Any remaining anomalies that result from functional dependencies have been removed.

5. **Fourth normal form (4NF).** Any multivalued dependencies have been removed.

6. **Fifth normal form (5NF).** Any remaining anomalies have been removed.

There is one additional normal form, called Domain/Key normal form (DK/NF), not shown in Figure 6-12. DK/NF assures that all of the other normal forms have been attained and that a relation can have no remaining anomalies. We discuss DK/NF briefly later in this chapter.

Figure 6-12
Steps in
normalization

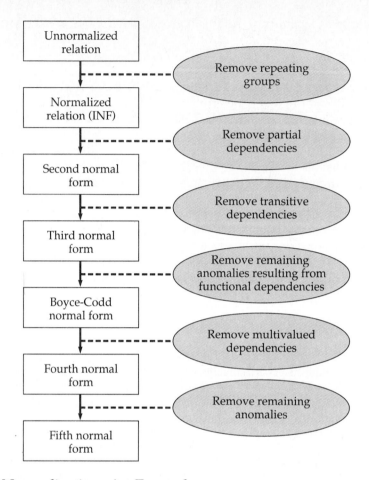

Normalization: An Example

We illustrate the steps in normalization by means of an example. Consider the Grade Report introduced in Chapter 5 (Figure 5-24); we show this same view in Figure 6-13 for ease of reference.

The first step in normalizing the data in Grade Report is to construct a table and enter sample data from the report into this table (see Figure 6-14). Notice that the attributes in the header (or top) of Grade Report are entered in the left-most columns of Figure 6-14, while the attributes in the body of the report are entered in the right-most columns. Although the order of columns in the table is actually unimportant, we find that this approach is more understandable to most persons. To clarify the structure of the table, data for a second student have also been entered into the table.

First Normal Form   The table in Figure 6-14 is an example of an unnormalized relation. An **unnormalized relation** is one that contains one or more repeating groups, and in Figure 6-14, the course data (starting with Course-ID and extending to the remaining columns) repeat for each student. As a result, there are multiple values at the intersection of certain rows and

LAKEWOOD COLLEGE					Figure 6-13
GRADE REPORT					User view: GRADE-
FALL SEMESTER 199X					REPORT

NAME: Emily Williams ID: 268300458
CAMPUS-ADDRESS: 208 Brooks Hall
MAJOR: Information Systems

COURSE-ID	TITLE	INSTRUCTOR-NAME	INSTRUCTOR-LOCATION	GRADE
IS 350	Database Mgt	Codd	B 104	A
IS 465	Systems Analysis	Parsons	B 317	B

columns. For example, there are two values for Course-ID (IS350 and IS465) for the student Williams.

To convert the table in Figure 6-14 to first normal form, we must remove the repeating groups, which we accomplish easily by extending downward the data in columns 1-4 for each student to fill the remaining rows. The result is shown in Figure 6-15.

The relation in Figure 6-15 is in first normal form since there is a single data value at the intersection of each row and column. However, if you examine the table you will notice that there is much redundancy. The table actually contains data describing each of three separate entities, student, course, and instructor, which are repeated several times in the table.

The table shown in Figure 6-15 could be implemented and used to store the data required to produce Grade Report. This relation, however, would be subject to all of the anomalies discussed in the previous section, for example:

1. **Insertion anomaly.** A new course cannot be inserted into the table until a student has registered for that course.

2. **Modification anomaly.** If the student Baker changes her major from accounting to finance, this fact will have to be recorded in several rows in the table.

The relation also suffers from deletion anomalies; examine the table and identify at least one example of this type of anomaly.

Second Normal Form To further normalize this relation, we must analyze the functional dependencies and select a key for the relation. After discussing the report with users, we discover that the following functional dependencies hold:

Student-ID → Student-Name, Campus-Address, Major
Course-ID → Course-Title, Instructor-Name, Instructor-Location
Student-ID, Course-ID → Grade
Instructor-Name → Instructor-Location

Student-ID	Student-Name	Campus-Address	Major	Course-ID	Course-Title	Instructor-Name	Instructor-Location	Grade
268300458	Williams	208 Brooks	IS	IS350 IS465	Database Mgt Systems Analysis	Codd Parsons	B 104 B 317	A B
543291073	Baker	104 Phillips	Acctg	IS 350 Acctg 201 Mktg 300	Database Mgt Fund Acctg Intro Mktg	Codd Miller Bennett	B 104 H 310 B 212	C B A

Figure 6-14
Unnormalized relation: GRADE REPORT

Student-ID	Student-Name	Campus-Address	Major	Course-ID	Course-Title	Instructor-Name	Instructor-Location	Grade
268300458	Williams	208 Brooks	IS	IS350	Database Mgt	Codd	B 104	A
268300458	Williams	208 Brooks	IS	IS465	Systems Analysis	Parsons	B 317	B
543291073	Baker	104 Phillips	Acctg	IS 350	Database Mgt	Codd	B 104	C
543291073	Baker	104 Phillips	Acctg	Acctg 201	Fund Acctg	Miller	H 310	B
543291073	Baker	104 Phillips	Acctg	Mktg 300	Intro Mktg	Bennett	B 212	A

Figure 6-15
First normal form: GRADE-REPORT

Figure 6-16

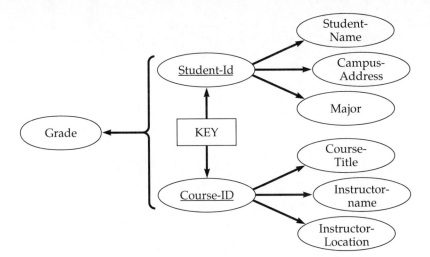

A candidate key for the relation consists of the minimum set of determinants (attributes on the left-hand side) that uniquely determines the right-hand-side attributes. Inspecting the above functional dependencies shows that there is one candidate key for this relation and that it consists of the attributes Student-ID and Course-ID. Notice that although Instructor-Name is a determinant, it is not required as part of the key since Instructor-Location is functionally dependent on Course-ID. The attributes Student-ID and Course-ID are underlined in Figure 6-15, since they constitute the key for this relation.

Now that we have selected (Student-ID, Course-ID) as a composite key, let us examine the functional dependencies on this key (see Figure 6-16). Three attributes (Student-Name, Campus-Address, and Major) are functionally dependent on part of the key (Student-ID). Similarly, the three attributes, Course-Title, Instructor-Name, and Instructor-Location, are functionally dependent on part of the key (Course-ID). These six attributes are said to be *partially dependent* on the key; only the attribute Grade is functionally dependent on both Student-ID and Course-ID (that is, we must know both the student and the course taken to identify the grade). This attribute is said to be *fully dependent* on the key.

To transform the relation in Figure 6-15 to second normal form, we must remove the partial dependencies. Examining Figure 6-16, we notice that we can remove the partial dependencies by creating *three* new relations from the one shown in Figure 6-15:

1. The first relation (called STUDENT) with the attributes Student-ID (key), Student-Name, Campus-Address, and Major

2. The second relation (called COURSE-INSTRUCTOR) with the attributes Course-ID (key), Course-Title, Instructor-Name, and Instructor-Location

Figure 6-17
Second normal form:
GRADE-REPORT

STUDENT

(a)

Student-ID	Student-Name	Campus-Address	Major
268300458	Williams	208 Brooks	IS
548291073	Baker	104 Phillips	Acctg
• • •			

(3NF)

COURSE-INSTRUCTOR

(b)

Course-ID	Course-Title	Instructor-Name	Instructor-Location
IS350	Database Mgt	Codd	B104
IS465	Systems Analysis	Parsons	B317
IS350	Database Mgt	Codd	B104
Acctg 201	Fund Acctg	Miller	H310
Mktg 300	Intro Mktg	Bennett	B212
• • •			

(2NF)

REGISTRATION

(c)

Student-ID	Course-ID	Grade
268300458	IS 350	A
268300458	IS 465	B
548291073	IS 350	C
548291073	Acctg 201	B
548291073	Mktg 300	A
• • •		

(3NF)

3. The third relation (called REGISTRATION) with the composite key (Student-ID, Course-ID) and the attribute Grade, which is fully dependent on this key.

The resulting relations are shown in Figure 6-17. These relations are in second normal form, since each nonkey attribute in a relation is fully dependent on the key for that relation (examine each of the three relations and verify that this statement is true).

Third Normal Form   As we will soon see, two of the relations in Figure 6-17 (STUDENT and REGISTRATION) are already in third normal form. However, the other relation (COURSE-INSTRUCTOR), in second normal form, is not yet in third normal form and, as a result, is subject to the same anomalies we discussed earlier.

1. **Update anomaly.** Suppose we wish to change the location for the instructor Codd from B104 to C300. This change must be made in multiple rows in the table.

2. **Deletion anomaly.** Suppose we decide to delete the course Acct 201 from the table. If this is the only row for Acct 201, we may lose the information that the instructor Miller is located in H310.

Identify at least one example of an insertion anomaly in COURSE-INSTRUCTOR.

The reason for the anomalies in the COURSE-INSTRUCTOR relation is that data concerning the entity Instructor are "hidden" within COURSE-INSTRUCTOR. A diagram of the dependencies within this relation appears as follows:

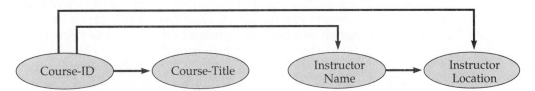

Notice that each of the nonkey attributes is functionally dependent on Course-ID. However, Instructor-Location is also dependent on Instructor-Name—that is, there is a unique location (or office number) for each instructor. This is an example of a **transitive dependency,** which occurs when one nonkey attribute (such as Instructor-Location) is dependent on one or more nonkey attributes (such as Instructor-Name). A simple transitive dependency appears as follows:

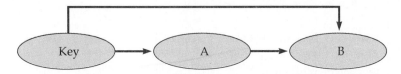

In this case, there is a transitive dependency between the key and attributes A and B. Transitive dependencies result in insertion, deletion, and update anomalies, similar to those for partial dependencies. To eliminate these anomalies, it is necessary to remove transitive dependencies from the relation with a further normalization step, which converts a relation to third normal form. A relation is in **third normal form** (3NF) if it is in second normal form and contains no transitive dependencies. A relation in third normal form has the following simple dependency relationships:

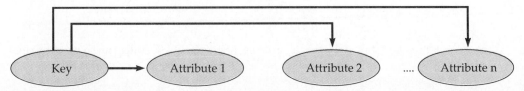

That is, each nonkey attribute is fully dependent on the key, and there are no transitive ("hidden") dependencies.

To remove the transitive dependency from COURSE-INSTRUCTOR, we divide it into the two relations shown in Figure 6-18: COURSE and INSTRUCTOR. COURSE contains the following attributes: Course-ID (key), Course Title, and Instructor-Name. INSTRUCTOR contains two attributes: Instructor-Name (key), and Instructor-Location.

Although the attribute Instructor-Name becomes the key in the new INSTRUCTOR relation, it is also a nonkey attribute in the new COURSE relation (see Figure 6-18). Instructor-Name is said to be a foreign key in the COURSE relation. A **foreign key** is a nonkey attribute in one relation (such as COURSE) that also appears as a primary key in another relation (such as INSTRUCTOR). In this example, the foreign key allows us to associate a particular course with the instructor who teaches that course. We indicate a foreign key by underlining it with a dashed line, as in Figure 6-18.

The normalization process is now completed. The Grade Report user view (Figure 6-13) has been transformed through a series of simple steps to a set of four relations in third normal form. The 3NF relations are summarized in Figure 6-19, both in tabular form and in shorthand notation. These 3NF relations are free of the anomalies described earlier. Since each entity is described in a separate relation, data concerning that entity can easily be inserted or deleted without reference to other entities. Also, updates to the data for a particular entity are easily accomplished, since they are confined to a single row within a relation.

Figure 6-18
Relations in third
normal form

COURSE

(a)

Course-ID	Course-Title	Instructor-Name
IS350	Database Mgt	Codd
IS465	Systems Analysis	Parsons
Acctg 201	Fund Acctg	Miller
Mktg 300	Intro Mktg	Bennett
• • •		

(3NF)

INSTRUCTOR

(b)

Instructor-Name	Instructor-Location
Codd	B 104
Parsons	B 317
Miller	H 310
Bennett	B 212
• • •	

(3NF)

In the process of normalizing Grade Report, no information is lost from the original user view. In fact, the Grade Report in Figure 6-13 can be recreated by combining the data from the 3NF relations in Figure 6-19.

Normalizing Summary Data

Databases to support management control and strategic levels of an organization often contain subsets and summarizations of data from operational databases. These "information bases" to support higher levels of management also need to be normalized to avoid all the same anomalies found in operational databases.

Consider the Grade Report database of Figure 6-19. Deans, degree program heads, and department chairs may be concerned only with grade

Student-ID	Student-Name	Campus-Address	Major
268300458	Williams	208 Brooks	IS
548291073	Baker	104 Phillips	Acctg
• • •			

STUDENT (Student ID, Student-Name, Campus-Address, Major)

Figure 6-19
Summary of 3NF relations for GRADE-REPORT

Course-ID	Course-Title	Instructor-Name
IS350	Database Mgt	Codd
IS465	Systems Analysis	Parsons
Acctg 201	Fund Acctg	Miller
Mktg 300	Intro Mktg	Bennett
• • •		

COURSE (Course ID, Course-Title, Instructor-Name)

Instructor-Name	Instructor-Location
Codd	B 104
Parsons	B 317
Miller	H 310
Bennett	B 212
• • •	

INSTRUCTOR (Instructor-Name, Instructor-Location)

Student-ID	Course-ID	Grade
268300458	IS 350	A
268300458	IS 465	B
548291073	IS 350	C
548291073	Acctg 201	B
548291073	Mktg 300	A
• • •		

REGISTRATION (Student-ID Course-ID, Grade)

(c)

summaries by department or major. For example, one report view for summarized data of grades by major would be represented by:

MAJOR-GRADES (<u>Major</u>, No-Students, Avg-GPA)

Here, No-Students is the number of students in a given major and Avg-GPA is the average grade point for students in a given major. This relation is in 3NF; note that Avg-GPA, although *mathematically* related to No-Students, is *functionally dependent* only on Major.

The MAJOR-GRADES table is derivable from the STUDENT and REGISTRATION tables of Figure 6-19. Whether MAJOR-GRADES is a view on an operational database or an independent table for an information base is a decision to be made later during physical design. This decision will be based on such factors as time to derive MAJOR-GRADES and response time required when MAJOR-GRADES is requested, cost of data storage for this table, and costs to keep MAJOR-GRADES contents consistent with operational data from which it is derived (for integrity).

At the requirements definition and logical design stages, a database designer should determine normalized relations for user views where possible, even of summarized data. Thus, MAJOR-GRADES would be added as another table to the Grade Report database, and the database analyst should note how No-Students and Avg-GPA are derived from data in other tables.

It is also possible that new data elements will be used in summary tables. For example, MAJOR-GRADES might also include data on the home department and its head or chairperson for each major, which would be represented by:

MAJ-GRADES (<u>Major</u>, Dept, Head, No-Students, Avg-GPA)

Since it is very likely that each department has only one head (Head functionally dependent on Dept), MAJ-GRADES is not in 3NF (but is in 2NF). It can be put into 3NF as:

MAJ-GRADES (<u>Major</u>, Dept, No-Students, Avg-GPA)
DEPARTMENT (<u>Dept</u>, Head)

Since information bases are frequently designed after operational databases are implemented (especially if databases are *not* planned as described in Chapter 4), a database analyst must be careful to clearly identify derived data and recognize the associated operational data source. If this is not done, the result can be unplanned redundancy and inconsistency within the database.

Beyond Third Normal Form

Relations in third normal form are sufficient for most practical database applications. However, 3NF does not guarantee that all anomalies have been removed. As shown in Figure 6-12, there are several additional normal forms that are designed to remove these anomalies: Boyce-Codd normal form, fourth normal form, and fifth normal form. We describe each of these normal forms (as well as domain–key normal form) in this section.

Boyce-Codd Normal Form When a relation has more than one candidate key, anomalies may result even though the relation is in 3NF. For example, consider the ST-MAJ-ADV relation shown in Figure 6-20. The semantic rules for this relation are the following:

1. Each student may major in several subjects.
2. For each major, a given student has only one advisor.
3. Each major has several advisors.
4. Each advisor advises only one major.
5. Each advisor advises several students in one major.

From this information, we may diagram the dependencies in this relation:

Student-ID $\twoheadrightarrow$ Major
Student-ID, Major $\rightarrow$ Advisor
Major $\twoheadrightarrow$ Advisor
Advisor $\rightarrow$ Major
Advisor $\twoheadrightarrow$ Student-ID

In this relation, no single attribute is a candidate key (that is, no single attribute is a determinant for the remaining two attributes). There are two candidate keys that are composite keys:

Student-ID, Major $\rightarrow$ Advisor
Student-ID, Advisor $\rightarrow$ Major

In Figure 6-20, we have arbitrarily selected (Student-ID, Major) as the key for the relation ST-MAJ-ADV. (Student-ID, Advisor) could equally well have been chosen.

The relation is clearly in 3NF, since there are no partial functional dependencies and no transitive dependencies, but nevertheless, there are still anomalies in the relation. For example, suppose that student #456 changes her major from Biol to Math. When the tuple for this student is

ST-MAJ-ADV

Student-ID	Major	Advisor
123	Physics	Einstein
123	Music	Mozart
456	Biol	Darwin
789	Physics	Bohr
999	Physics	Einstein

Figure 6-20
ST-MJ-ADV relation

updated, we lose the fact that Darwin advises in Biol (update anomaly). Also, suppose we want to insert a tuple with the information that Babbage advises in Compsci. This, of course, cannot be done until at least one student majoring in Compsci is assigned Babbage as an advisor (insertion anomaly). Finally, if student 456 withdraws from school we lose the information that Darwin advises in Biol (deletion anomaly).

The type of anomalies that exists in this relation can only occur when there are two (or more) overlapping candidate keys. For example, as we have noted, there are two candidate keys in ST-MAJ-ADV: (Student-ID, Advisor) and (Student-ID, Major). These candidate keys overlap (since they share Student-ID). This situation is relatively rare but nevertheless can occur, as shown in this relation.

R. F. Boyce and E. F. Codd identified this deficiency and proposed a stronger definition of 3NF that remedies the problem. Their definition relies on the concept of a determinant (defined earlier). We say a relation is in Boyce-Codd normal form if and only if every determinant is a candidate key. Applying this rule to ST-MAJ-ADV, we see that this relation is not in BCNF (even though it is in 3NF). The reason is that although advisor is a determinant, it is not a candidate key (since each advisor advises several students).

The ST-MAJ-ADV relation can be converted into BCNF by dividing it into two relations. The attribute that is a determinant but not a candidate key (in this case, Advisor) must be placed in a separate relation and it must be the key of that relation. There are two ways to divide the relation ST-MAJ-ADV so that the resulting relations are in BCNF:

1. ST-ADV (Student-ID, Advisor); ADV-MAJ (Advisor, Major)

2. ST-MAJ (Student-ID, Major); ADV-MAJ (Advisor, Major)

The result of using the first of these two approaches is shown in Figure 6-21. You can check that these relations are in BCNF by applying the basic definition.

Fourth Normal Form   When a relation is in BCNF, there are no longer any anomalies that result from functional dependencies. However, there may still be anomalies that result from multivalued dependencies (defined below). For example, consider the unnormalized relation called OFFERING in Fig-

Figure 6-21
Two relations in
BCNF

ST-ADV

Student-ID	Advisor
123	Einstein
123	Mozart
456	Darwin
789	Bohr
999	Einstein

ADV-MAJ

Advisor	Major
Einstein	Physics
Mozart	Music
Darwin	Biol
Bohr	Physics
Einstein	Physics

OFFERING

COURSE	INSTRUCTOR	TEXTBOOK
Management	White Green Black	Drucker Peters
Finance	Gray	Weston Gilford

(a)   Unnormalized Relation

OFFERING

COURSE	INSTRUCTOR	TEXTBOOK
Management	White	Drucker
Management	Green	Drucker
Management	Black	Drucker
Management	White	Peters
Management	Green	Peters
Management	Black	Peters
Finance	Gray	Weston
Finance	Gray	Gilford

(b)   Normalized Relation

Figure 6-22
Relation with multivalued dependency

ure 6-22a. This user view shows for each course the instructors who teach that course and the textbooks that are used. In this relation the following assumptions hold:

1. Course $\longrightarrow\!\!\!\rightarrow$ Instructor (each course may have several instructors).

2. Course $\longrightarrow\!\!\!\rightarrow$ Textbook (each course uses several textbooks).

3. Instructor $\longleftrightarrow\!\!\!/$ Textbook (the text that is used for a given course is *independent* of the instructor; that is, the same set of textbooks is used *regardless* of the instructor).

In Figure 6-22b, the OFFERING relation has been normalized. Thus, for each course, all possible combinations of instructor and text appear in the resulting table. Notice that the primary key of this relation consists of all three attributes (Course, Instructor, and Textbook). Since there are no determinants (other than the primary key itself), the relation is in BCNF. However, it does contain much redundant data, which, in turn, can easily lead to update anomalies. For example, suppose that we want to add a third textbook (author: Middleton) to the Management course. This would require the addition of *three* new rows to the table in Figure 6-22b, one for each Instructor (otherwise that text would apply to only certain instructors!).

The dependencies in this example are multivalued and appear as follows:

The type of dependency shown in this example is called a **multivalued dependency,** which exists when there are at least three attributes (for example, A, B, and C) in a relation, and for each value of A there is a well-defined set of values of B and a well-defined set of values of C. However, the set of values of B is independent of set C, and vice versa.

To remove the multivalued dependency from a relation, we divide the relation into two independent attributes. Figure 6-23 shows the result of this division for the OFFERING relation of Figure 6-22b. Notice that the relation called TEACHER contains the Instructor attribute, while TEXT contains the Textbook attribute (these two attributes are independent of each other in Figure 6-22b). A relation is in **fourth normal form** (4NF) if it is in BCNF and contains no multivalued dependencies. You can easily verify that the two relations in Figure 6-23 are 4NF, and the original relation (OFFERING) can easily be reconstructed by joining these two relations.

Fifth Normal Form (5NF)　This normal form is designed to cope with a type of dependency known as a **join dependency.** When a relation has a join dependency, it cannot be divided into two (or more) relations and then the resulting tables recombined to form the original table. For example, throughout the discussion of normalization in this chapter, we have repeatedly used the technique of dividing a relation that has two (or more) smaller relations, in order to eliminate anomalies. In each of the examples, since there were no join dependencies present, it was possible to recreate the original tables. However, it is possible to create examples of relations with join dependencies where the original table cannot be recreated without spurious results.

Fifth normal form (5NF) provides a definition for removing join dependencies if they exist and can be described. However, according to Date (1981, p. 263), "It is tempting to suggest that such relations are pathological cases and are likely to be rare in practice." For this reason we do not provide an example of 5NF.

Domain–Key Normal Form (DK/NF)　Fagin (1981) has proposed a conceptually simple normal form called **domain-key normal form** (DK/NF). According to this definition, a relation is in DK/NF if and only if every constraint on the relation is a logical consequence of key constraints and domain constraints. Fagin shows that any relation that is in DK/NF is automatically in 5NF, 4NF, and so on.

Fagin's definition is an important contribution, since it provides an all-encompassing definition of the various normal forms. Unfortunately, however, it does not provide a methodology for converting a given relation to DN/NF. Thus, we do not pursue the definition of DK/NF in this text.

INTEGRATING THE RELATIONS

View Integration

View integration is the process of merging individual user views into an integrated data structure called the *conceptual data model* or *conceptual schema.* In the database design process we have described in Chapter 5 and in this

TEACHER

COURSE	INSTRUCTOR
Management	White
Management	Green
Management	Black
Finance	Gray

TEXT

COURSE	TEXTBOOK
Management	Drucker
Management	Peters
Finance	Weston
Finance	Gilford

Figure 6-23
Relations in fourth normal form

chapter, view integration occurs when the E-R diagrams for individual user views are combined to form a consolidated E-R diagram. For example, E-R diagrams for four user views at Mountain View Community Hospital are shown in Figures 5-19, 5-21, 5-22, and 5-23. These individual views will be merged to form a conceptual data model later in this chapter (see Figure 6-25).

As part of database design, E-R diagrams are often transformed into relations. For example, relations derived from the conceptual data model for Mountain View Community Hospital are shown in Figure 6-26. If the resulting relations refer to the same entity, it may be necessary to merge these relations. For example, suppose that modeling a user view results in the following 3NF relation:

   EMPLOYEE1 (<u>Employee#</u>, Name, Address, Phone)

Modeling a second user view might result in the following relation:

   EMPLOYEE2 (<u>Employee#</u>, Name, Address, Jobcode, #Years)

Since these two relations have the same primary key (<u>Employee#</u>), they describe the same entity and may be merged into one relation. The result of merging the relations is the following relation:

   EMPLOYEE (<u>Employee#</u>, Name, Address, Phone, Jobcode, #Years)

Notice that an attribute that appears in both relations (such as Name in this example) appears only once in the merged relation.

View Integration Problems

When integrating views either at the E-R diagram or normalized relation level, the database analyst must understand the data and must be prepared to resolve any problems that may arise in that process. In this section we describe and briefly illustrate four problems in view integration: *synonyms, homonyms, transitive dependencies,* and *class/subclass relations.* To simplify the discussion, we will use relations to illustrate each situation.

Synonyms   In some situations, two attributes may have different names but the same meaning, as when they describe the same characteristic of an entity. Such attributes are called **synonyms.** For example, Employee-ID and Employee-Number may be synonyms.

When merging the relations that contain synonyms, the analyst should obtain agreement from users on a single, standardized name for the attribute and elimination of the other synonym. (Another alternative is to standardize the use of one name, but retain the other as a synonym or alias.) For example, consider the following relations:

STUDENT1 (<u>Student-ID</u>, Name)
STUDENT2 (<u>Matriculation#</u>, Name, Address)

In this case, the analyst recognizes that both the Student-ID and Matriculation# refer to a person's social security number, and are identical attributes. One possible resolution would be to standardize on one of the two attribute names, such as Student-ID. Another option is to use a new attribute name, such as SSN, to replace both synonyms. Assuming the latter approach, merging the two relations would produce the following result:

STUDENT (<u>SSN</u>, Name, Address)

Homonyms   In other situations, a single attribute, called a **homonym,** may have more than one meaning or describe more than one characteristic. For example, the term "account" might refer to a bank's checking account, savings account, loan account, or other type of account.

A database analyst must be alerted to homonyms during view integration. Consider the following relations:

STUDENT1 (<u>Student-ID</u>, Name, Address)
STUDENT2 (<u>Student-ID</u>, Name, Phone-Number, Address)

In discussions with users, the analyst may discover that the attribute Address in STUDENT1 refers to a student's campus address, while in STUDENT2 the same attribute refers to a student's permanent (or home) address. To resolve this conflict, it would probably be necessary to create new attribute names, so that the merged relation would become:

STUDENT (<u>Student-ID</u>, Name, Phone-Number, Campus-Address, Permanent-Address)

Transitive Dependencies   When two 3NF relations are merged to form a single relation, *transitive dependencies* (described earlier in this chapter) may result. For example, consider the following two relations:

STUDENT1 (<u>Student-ID</u>, Major)
STUDENT2 (<u>Student-ID</u>, Advisor)

Since STUDENT1 and STUDENT2 have the same primary key, the two relations may be merged:

STUDENT (<u>Student-ID</u>, Major, Advisor)

However, suppose that each major has exactly one advisor. In this case, Advisor is functionally dependent on Major:

Major → Advisor

If this is the case, then STUDENT is 2NF but not 3NF, since it contains a transitive dependency. The analyst can create 3NF relations by removing the transitive dependency:

    STUDENT (<u>Student-ID</u>, Major)
    MAJOR-ADVISOR (<u>Major</u>, Advisor)

Class-Subclass (ISA)   These relationships may be hidden in user views or relations. Suppose that we have following two hospital relations:

    PATIENT1 (<u>Patient#</u>, Name, Address)
    PATIENT2 (<u>Patient#</u>, Room-Number)

Initially, it appears that these two relations can be merged into a single PATIENT relation. However, the analyst correctly suspects that there are two different types of patients—inpatients and outpatients. PATIENT1 actually contains attributes common to *all* patients. PATIENT2 contains an attribute (Room-Number) that is a characteristic only of inpatients. In this situation, the analyst should create *class-subclass (ISA)* relationships for these entities. Following our discussion earlier in this chapter, these relations might result:

    PATIENT (<u>Patient#</u>, Name, Address, Subclass-Type)
    INPATIENT (<u>Patient#</u>, Room-Number)
    OUTPATIENT (<u>Patient#</u>, Date-Treated)

For an extended discussion of view integration in database design, see Navathe (1986).

DEVELOPING ACTION DIAGRAMS

The last step in conceptual database design is to develop action diagrams (see Figure 6-1). **Action diagrams** are logical representations of database operations. These database operations are required to update the database to keep it current and to produce user views such as reports and displays. Typical database operations add and delete records, modify records, and produce reports and displays.

Action Diagram Symbols

The basic building block of an action diagram is a bracket, which is used to enclose a simple sequence of actions. Following is an example:

    READ SALES AMOUNT
    CREDIT SALES
    DEBIT ACCOUNTS RECEIVABLE
    . . .

Execution begins with the first statement and proceeds from top to bottom. The statements within the bracket may be high-level English statements (as in the above example), or they may be computer programming language statements. Since we are interested in logical design, we confine our examples to high-level statements.

The brackets in an action diagram may be modified to represent the various logical structures in program design. Figure 6-24 shows the action diagram representation for the three most common structured programming constructs: sequence, selection, and repetition.

Selection is used when the statements in a bracket are executed only when a certain condition is satisfied. For example:

```
┌──── IF QUANTITY_ORDERED>QUANTITY_ON_HAND
│     CREATE BACKORDER
│     NOTIFY CUSTOMER
│     PLACE ORDER FOR ITEM
└────
```

If the condition at the top of the bracket is satisfied, all three statements are processed; otherwise, none of the statements are processed.

In Figure 6-24, the selection structure has two parts, one indicating what happens if the condition is satisfied, the other what happens if the condition is not satisfied. Following is an example:

```
┌──── IF QUANTITY_ORDERED>QUANTITY_ON_HAND
│     CREATE BACKORDER
│     NOTIFY CUSTOMER
├──── PLACE ORDER FOR ITEM
│     ELSE
│     SHIP ORDER
│     REDUCE QUANTITY_ON_HAND
│
└────
```

The **repetition** structure is used when a sequence of actions must be repeated. As shown in Figure 6-24, a double line is used at the top of a repetition bracket. Some condition must be used to control execution of the statements in the structure. The following is an example of the use of this structure:

```
╒════ DO WHILE MORE DISHES
│     SELECT DISH
│     WASH DISH
│     DRY DISH
└──── PLACE IN CUPBOARD
```

This example illustrates a "DO WHILE" construct, which works as follows: First, the condition at the top of the bracket is tested. If the condition

SEQUENCE

> action 1
> action 2
> action 3
> • • •

SELECTION

> IF CONDITION A
>   action 1
>   action 2
> ELSE
>   action 3
>   action 4

REPETITION

> DO WHILE (CONDITION)
>   action 1
>   action 2
>   action 3
>   • • •

Figure 6-24
Basic structures in an
action diagram

is false, the statements inside the bracket are skipped. If the condition is true, the set of statements is executed. The condition is tested again, and the statements are repeatedly executed until the condition is false.

An alternative form is the "DO UNTIL" construct, which appears as follows:

> DO
> SELECT DISH
> WASH DISH
> DRY DISH
> PLACE IN CUPBOARD
> UNTIL NO MORE DISHES

With this construct, the statements inside the bracket are executed sequentially. Then the UNTIL condition is tested. If the condition is true, execution of these statements is terminated. If the condition is false, execution of the statements is repeated until the condition is true. Notice that with the DO UNTIL construct, the statements inside the bracket are *always* executed at least one time.

The logic of most programs can be easily portrayed using combinations of the above structures. See Martin and McClure (1985) for additional action diagram structures to deal with more complex situations.

Database Actions

Since the action diagrams we develop will be related to databases, we need additional symbols to represent database actions. A **simple database action** is an operation applied to *one row of a relation* (or to *one instance of a record* *type*). There are four types of simple database actions: create, read, update, and delete. We use a rectangle (a box) to indicate one of these actions. The name of the action is written to the left of the rectangle, while the name of the relation (or record type) is written inside the box. Following are examples:

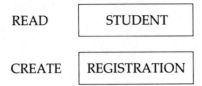

A **compound database action** is a statement that processes multiple rows in a table (or multiple rows in two or more tables). For example, a SQL SELECT statement will select all qualified rows from a table. We use a double rectangular box to represent a compound database action:

Notice that the qualifier for the SELECT statement (GPA > 3.0) is written to the right of the box.

A SELECT statement may retrieve data from two (or more) tables, a procedure called a "join" operation. We indicate a join by linking the rectangles, as in the following example:

The qualifier for the join is written to the right of the rectangle.

We provide an example of an action diagram for Mountain View Community Hospital in the next section.

Case Example: Mountain View Community Hospital

The project team at Mountain View Community Hospital reviewed the results of requirements definition and prepared for conceptual database design. The team had successfully used a CASE tool to support requirements definition and planned to continue to use this tool during conceptual database design.

Conceptual Data Modeling

The first step was to consolidate the individual E-R diagrams form requirements definition into an integrated data model. In Chapter 5, we illustrated E-R diagrams for four user views: Patient Bill (Figure 5-19), Room Utilization Report (Figure 5-21), Patient Display (Figure 5-22), and Physician Report

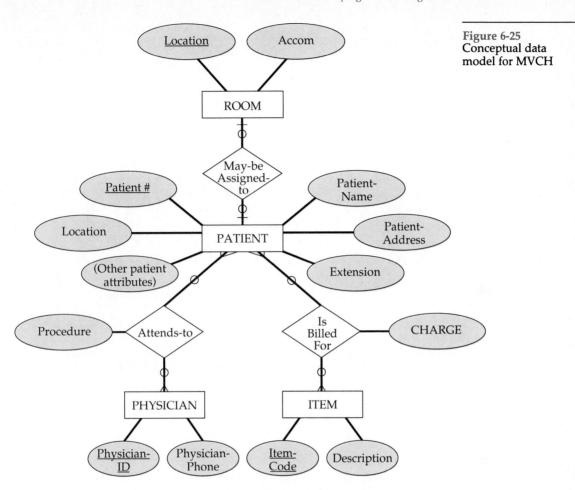

Figure 6-25
Conceptual data model for MVCH

(Figure 5-23). When these diagrams are consolidated, the result is the conceptual data model shown in Figure 6-25.

There are four entities in this data model: Room, Patient, Physician, and Item. Of course, more entities will be added to the model when other user views are included. There are two *M:N* relationships: Attends-To (linking Patient and Physician), and Is-Billed-For (linking Patient and Item). Also, there is a 1:1 conditional relationship (linking Room and Patient).

Transforming E-R Diagram to Relations

The project team next addressed the question of whether the data in the conceptual data model (Figure 6-25) was properly normalized. They realized that they could use the definition of functional dependency to normalize the attributes within the E-R diagram. However, since they planned to implement the database using the relational database model, they decided to transform the E-R diagram to relations before attempting normalization.

ROOM   (3NF)

Location	Accom
100-1	PR
101-1	PR
102-1	SP
• • •	• • •

PHYSICIAN   (3NF)

Physician-ID	Physician-Phone
Wilcox	329-1848
Nusca	516-3947
• • •	• • •

ITEM   (3NF)

Item-Code	Description
200	Room semi-pr
205	Television
307	X-ray
413	Lab tests
• • •	• • •

PATIENT   (2NF)

Patient #	Patient-Name	Location	Extension	• • •
3249	Baker, Mary	137-2	248	
6213	Rose, David	100-1	137	
1379	Cribbs, John	101-1	142	
• • •	• • •	• • •	• • •	

CHARGES   (3NF)

Patient #	Item-Code	Charge
3249	200	150.00
3249	205	10.00
3249	307	25.00
6213	205	15.00
• • •	• • •	• • •

TREATMENT   (3NF)

Patient #	Physician-ID	Procedure
3249	Wilcox	X-ray
1379	Gomez	Tonsillectomy
• • •	• • •	• • •

Figure 6-26
Relations derived from conceptual data model

The project team used the rules described earlier in this chapter to derive the relations shown in Figure 6-26. Following is a brief description of transforming the E-R diagram to relations:

1. The four entities in the E-R diagram were transformed to relations: ROOM, PHYSICIAN, ITEM, and PATIENT. (The primary keys for these relations are the same as for the corresponding entities.)

2. The *M:N* relationship Attends-To (between Patient and Physician) was converted to a relation (TREATMENT) with the composite key (Patient#, Physician-ID). The attribute Procedure is functionally dependent on this key.

3. Similarly, the *M:N* relationship Is-Billed-For was converted to the relation CHARGES (see Figure 6-26).

4. The case of a 1:1 relationship was not discussed earlier in this chapter; this may be viewed, however, as a special case of a 1:*N* relationship. The relationship May-Be-Assigned-To was represented by including the foreign key Location in the PATIENT relation (Location is the primary key of ROOM).

Normalizing the Relations

In this step, the project team examined each of the relations created from the conceptual data model to check for third normal form. As shown in Figure 6-26, all of the relations except PATIENT are in 3NF (verify this statement by examining the functional dependencies in each 3NF relation). By using a systematic procedure in documenting the entities, attributes, and relationships during requirements definition, the project team had intuitively normalized much of the data.

The PATIENT relation (Figure 6-26) is in second (but not third) normal form. There is a transitive dependency, which may be illustrated as follows:

Patient# → Patient-Name, Location, Extension
Location → Extension

In other words, each bed location in the hospital has its own telephone extension. To convert the PATIENT relation to 3NF, we move the Location attribute to the ROOM relation. Following is a summary of the 3NF relations for Mountain View Community Hospital:

ROOM (<u>Location</u>, Accom, Extension)
PHYSICIAN (<u>Physician-ID</u>, Physician-Phone)
ITEM (<u>Item-Code</u>, Description)
PATIENT (<u>Patient#</u>, Patient-Name, Patient-Address, City-State-Zip, Date-Admitted, Date-Discharged, Third-Party, <u>Location</u>)
CHARGES (<u>Patient#, Item-Code</u>, Charge)
TREATMENT (<u>Patient#, Physician-ID</u>, Procedure)

Developing Hospital Action Diagram

The project team created action diagrams for several of the more complex updating and reporting functions at Mountain View Community Hospital. Figure 6-27 shows an action diagram to create a patient bill (the patient bill is shown in Figure 5-13).

The first step in the action diagram is to read patient data from the PATIENT table. A bill is not created for a patient unless that patient has been discharged, so a selection structure is used to test this condition. If the condition is satisfied, the header information for the bill (Patient-Code, Patient-Name, Address, Date-Admitted, and other data) is printed. (If the patient has not been discharged, this fact is displayed.) The Balance-Due field is initialized by setting its value to zero. The inner repetition structure is then executed for each item charged to the patient. A row is read from the CHARGE table, and a detail line is printed for each charge (including Item-Code, Date, Description, and Amount). For each item, the balance due from the customer is incremented by the amount of the item. When all patient charges have been printed, the balance due is printed to complete preparing the patient bill.

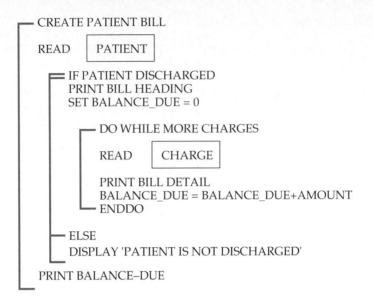

SUMMARY

Conceptual database design is the process of constructing a detailed architecture for a database that is independent of implementation details, including the DBMS that is to be used. Conceptual design (which is also called logical design) is the second phase of the database design process. The objectives of conceptual database design are structural validity, nonredundancy, simplicity, shareability, extensibility, and integrity.

In this chapter, we described a five-step process for conceptual database design. The five steps in this process are the following:

1. Develop conceptual data model
2. Transform data structures to relations
3. Normalize the relations
4. Integrate the views
5. Develop action diagrams

The conceptual data model is developed by consolidating the E-R diagrams that were developed from individual user views during requirements definition. The resulting E-R diagram is both complete and nonredundant (by complete we mean that each of the E-R diagrams is a subset of this integrated model). CASE tools are often used to support this analysis.

In the next step, the conceptual data model (E-R diagram) is transformed to relations. Each entity in the E-R diagram is transformed to a relation that has the same primary key as the entity. A one-to-many relationship is represented by placing a foreign key in the relation that represents the entity on the many-side of the relationship (this foreign key is the primary key of the entity of the one-side of the relationship). A many-to-many relationship is represented by creating a new relation. The primary key of this relation is a composite key, consisting of the primary key of each of the entities that participate in the relationship.

The relational model does not directly support class-subclass (or ISA) relationships. However, these relationships can be modeled by creating a separate table (or relation) for the class and for each subclass. A subclass identifier attribute must be created in the class relation.

The purpose of normalization is to derive well-structured relations that are free of anomalies (inconsistencies or errors) that would otherwise result when the relations are updated or modified. Normalization is generally accomplished in several stages. Relations in first normal form (1NF) contain no multivalued attributes or repeating groups. Relations in 2NF contain no partial dependencies, while relations in 3NF contain no transitive dependencies. Boyce-Codd normal form which guarantees that a relation is free of anomalies that result from functional dependencies, is a stronger definition than 3NF. Fourth normal form (4NF) defines relations that have no multivalued dependencies. Domain–key normal form (DK/NF) is a generalized definition that subsumes all of the other normal forms but does not provide a practical mechanism for implementation. Care must be taken when combining relations to deal with problems such as synonyms, homonyms, transitive dependencies, and class-subclass relationships.

The last step in our approach to conceptual database design is to develop action diagrams that define the logical database operations that are required to access and maintain the database. Action diagrams are best prepared through the use of CASE tools, which also may be used to translate the action diagram to application code.

Chapter Review

REVIEW QUESTIONS

1. Define each of the following terms concisely:
   - a. functional dependency
   - b. transitive dependency
   - c. partial dependency
   - d. determinant
   - e. key
   - f. composite key
   - g. unnormalized relation
   - h. candidate key

2. Contrast the following terms:
   - a. unnormalized relation; normalized relation
   - b. full dependency; partial dependency
   - c. transitive dependency; multivalued dependency
   - d. insertion anomaly; deletion anomaly
   - e. key; foreign key
   - f. E-R diagrams; action diagram

3. Fill in the blanks in each of the following statements:
   a. A relation that has no partial functional dependencies is in _____ normal form.
   b. A relation that has no multivalued dependencies is in _____ normal form.
   c. A relation that has no repeating group is in _____ normal form.
   d. A relation that has no transitive dependencies is in _____ normal form.
   e. A relation that has no anomalies due to functional dependencies is in _____ normal form.

4. Briefly describe five steps in conceptual database design.

5. What is a well-structured relation? Why are well-structured relations important in logical database design?

6. What are action diagrams?

7. Briefly describe two problems that may result from normalization. How may these problems be minimized?

8. If every determinant in a relation is a candidate key, the relation is said to be in _____ normal form.

9. Describe six criteria (or objectives) for conceptual database design.

10. Describe how each of the following components of an E-R diagram is transformed to relations:
    a. entity
    b. relationship (1:*N*)
    c. relationship (*M:N*)
    d. relationship (class-subclass)

PROBLEMS AND EXERCISES

1. Match the following terms to the appropriate definitions:

_____ well-structured relation	**a)** relationship between two attributes
_____ anomaly	**b)** multivalued dependencies eliminated
_____ functional dependency	
_____ determinant	**c)** determinant that can be used as a key
_____ key	
_____ candidate key	**d)** repeating groups have been removed
_____ 1NF	
_____ 2NF	**e)** inconsistency or error
_____ 3NF	**f)** transitive dependencies eliminated
_____ 4NF	**g)** contains a minimum of redundancy
_____ DK/NF	
_____ unnormalized relation	**h)** uniquely identifies each nonkey attribute
_____ composite key	

      i) partial functional dependencies eliminated

      j) all normal forms are satisfied

      k) contains repeating groups

      l) attribute on left-hand side of a functional dependency

      m) contains two (or more) attributes

2. Examine the COURSE relation (Figure 6-9) and answer the questions.
   a. Diagram the functional dependencies.
   b. What are the determinants?
   c. What is (are) the candidate key (or keys)?
   d. In what normal form is the relation? Why?

3. Examine the relations EMPLOYEE-COURSE and COURSE-FEE (Figure 6-10).
   a. Diagram the functional dependencies in each relation.
   b. What is the key of each relation?
   c. In what normal form is each relation? Why?

4. Examine the EMPLOYEE-SCHEDULE relation (Figure 6-11).
   a. Are there any functional dependencies in this relation? If so, diagram them.
   b. Diagram all other dependencies in this relation.
   c. Does this relation contain any unwanted dependencies? If so, what kind?
   d. In what normal form is this relation? Why?

5. Following are several 3NF relations:

STUDENT	(ST#, Stname, Phone#)
COURSE	(CRS#, Crsname)
MAJOR	(ST#, Major)
ENROLL	(ST#, CRS#, Section#)
UNITS	(CRS#, Crsname, Units)
TEXT	(CRS#, Section#, Textname)
LOCATION	(CRS#, Section#, Room#)

   a. Merge these relations to produce a set of 3NF relations.
   b. Draw an E-R diagram based on the relations obtained in part (a).

6. The following table records information about students and their activities this semester.

Student-ID	Major	Course#	Lab#	Package
268300458	IS	350	D325	Ingres
268300458	Acctg	201	L301	Lotus 1-2-3
317496824	FIN	201	L301	Lotus 1-2-3
804210637	IS	465	D325	Excelerator
804210637	Mktg	300	L200	SPSS

   Based on the sample data in the table, answer the following questions:
   a. What are the determinants in this relation?
   b. What is (are) the candidate key (or keys) for this relation?
   c. In what normal form is this relation?

d. Give an example of each of the following:
   (1) Insertion anomaly
   (2) Deletion anomaly
   (3) Update anomaly
e. Convert this relation to:
   (1) a set of 3NF relations
   (2) a set of BCNF relations
   (3) a set of 4NF relations

7. Consider the following relation:

   EMPLOYEE

EMP#	Courses	Interest
123	COMM. I	Bowling
123	COMM. II	Bowling
456	Q.C.	Skiing
456	Q.C.	Bowling

   Assume that there is no relationship between the courses an employee takes and his or her interests.
   a. In what normal form is this relation?
   b. Give an example of an insertion and deletion anomaly, if any exists.
   c. Further normalize the relation, if needed, to eliminate anomalies.

8. Consider the following relation:

   FOOTBALL

Player	Position	Coach
Earl	FB	Joe
John	G	Ed
Tony	FB	Pete
Carl	T	Jim
Mack	FB	Joe

   Assuming that each coach coaches only one position, answer the following questions:
   a. In what normal form is this relation?
   b. Give an example of an insertion and deletion anomaly, if any exist.
   c. Further normalize the relation, if needed, to eliminate anomalies.

9. Staff physicians at Mountain View Community Hospital have decided to modify the Physician's Report. Under the proposed format, there will be two changes:
   a. A given patient may receive the same treatment (or procedure) from a physician more than once on the same day.
   b. The charge (or dollar amount) for each treatment will be shown on the report.

   Following is a sketch of the proposed format for the new report.

Mountain View Community Hospital
Physician Report

Date: 10-17-9X   Specialty: Internal Medicine
Physician: A Campbell
Phone: 329-1848

Patient-Code	Patient-Name	Procedure	Charge
32968	Baker, Mary S.	Examination	35.00
392718	Redford, Ronald	Chemotherapy	50.00
419871	Emery, Margaret	Examination	25.00
32968	Baker, Mary S.	X-Ray	75.00
32968	Baker, Mary S.	Therapy	50.00
32968	Baker, Mary S.	Examination	30.00

---

(1) Draw an E-R diagram for this view.

(2) Derive a set of 3NF relations for this view.

10. A conceptual data model for Vacation Property Rentals is shown in figure 5-8.
    a. Transform this E-R diagram to a set of relations.
    b. Normalize the relations (3NF).

11. The conceptual data model for Pine Valley Furniture Company is shown in Figure 6-4.
    a. Transform this diagram to a set of relations.
    b. Normalize the relations (3NF).

REFERENCES

Chouinard, P. 1989. "Supertypes, Subtypes, and DB2." *Database Programming and Design* 2 (10) (Oct.), 50–57.

Date, C. J. 1981. *Introduction to Database Systems.* 3rd ed. Reading, MA: Addison-Wesley.

Fagin, R. 1981. "A Normal Form for Database That is Based on Domains and Keys." *ACM Transactions on Database Systems* 6 (Sept.), 387–415.

Fleming, C. C., and B. von Halle, 1990. "An Overview of Logical Data Modeling." *Data Resource Management* 1 (1) (Winter), 5–15.

Kent, W. 1983. "A Simple Guide to Five Normal Forms in Relational Database Theory." *Communications of the ACM* 26 (Feb.), 120–125.

Martin, J., and C. McClure. 1989. *Action Diagrams.* 2nd ed. Englewood Cliffs, NJ: Prentice-Hall.

Navathe, S., R. Elmasri, and J. Larson, 1986. "Integrating User Views in Database Design." *Computer* (Jan.), 50–62.

Teory, T. J., and J. P. Fry. 1982. *Design of Database Structures.* Englewood Cliffs, NJ: Prentice Hall.

PART III

Physical Design and Data Administration

DATABASE CONCURRENCY CONTROL

Apple Computer, Inc.

Database design and administration encompasses many topical areas. Among these is the subject of concurrency control. Concurrency refers to the simultaneous access of database files by many different system users. Failure to control concurrency can lead to data inaccuracies. To the extent that a database is distributed across multiple locations and computers, concurrency control can be a more difficult problem.

Apple Computer, Inc., headquartered in Cupertino, California provides an excellent example of concurrency control in a distributed database environment. Apple operates computer assembly plants in Cork, Ireland and Singapore, Malaysia. Control of the assembly process is achieved through a three-layer, computer-based architecture.

The first layer consists of compact style Macintosh computers which are used as workstations on the shop floor. These work-stations enable the capture of data which reflects up-to-the-minute assembly and work-flow activities. The workstations enable such tasks as optically scanning UPC labels on component parts in order to identify the components by part number. Other tasks include collecting and passing information about the status of quality control testing during the production process.

Data are passed to and from the second layer which consists of Macintosh II computers serving as communication servers. These servers continually poll the first layer workstations in a round-robin fashion. Standardized information requests are passed as SQL commands to the server. This enables the maintenance of a database which stores the status of jobs in process as well as job routing information.

The servers also pass data to and from the third layer of this architecture. This upper layer is a Digital Equipment Corporation VAX host computer. While the number varies, there are an average of eight workstations to each Macintosh II server and 18 servers. The number of servers is scheduled to triple in the future.

The INGRES database management system is used to maintain the job and routing database files. These database files are stored on both the VAX host and the Macintosh II communication servers, thus it is necessary to maintain the consistency of the data across these platforms. As the factory receives update information affecting the manufacture of products to fill customer orders, the host computer database is updated in real time. As a result, manufacturing shop floor control is also in real time. This provides optimal flexibility in terms of meeting customer demands.

By redundantly storing the databases at two levels in this architecture, manufacturing can continue to be supported whenever the host computer is unavailable. In such a situation, the redundant databases on the Macintosh II servers provide necessary job control and routing information assembly operations in a manufacture-for-stock production environment. This system enables Apple to maximize use of the production assembly facilities.

CHAPTER 7

Data Structures and Storage Techniques

INTRODUCTION

This chapter provides the background on the storage and accessing of data in secondary computer memory that you will need to understand the issues presented in Chapter 8 on the implementation and physical design of databases. You may believe that this material is important only if you are building an operating system or database management system. However, it is also necessary for many tasks you will perform as a designer and builder of database applications, including:

- Understanding the meaning of and appropriately responding to error messages from data management technologies
- Identifying and suggesting solutions for possible causes of poor database processing performance
- Designing and writing some types of queries and programs to access databases

This material is essential for the development of high-performance databases. Database designers and programmers should therefore be sensitive to the concepts, techniques, and issues raised in this chapter.

Consider the situation of the New Jersey Division of Motor Vehicles (DMV) database built during 1983–1985 (see Kull, 1986, for an excellent survey of this "disaster"). The poor choice of a high-level programming language and database management system, which severely restricted their ability to use the proper *physical* database structures, caused thousands of motorists to drive with invalid registrations or licenses. Overtime of staff cost the state hundreds of thousands of dollars. The DMV had to support more than 1,000 terminals and tens of thousands of transactions per day against a database of 7 million drivers, 6 million vehicles, and 20 million title documents. Although obviously this case involved a very large database with very high performance requirements, it highlights the point that an understanding of physical database design is essential for the proper design of database applications.

This chapter concerns the physical database, or lowest level in the ANSI/SPARC model introduced in Chapter 3 (see Figure 7-1, where this model is repeated for our purposes here). This is the *only* level at which an organization's database exists in physical form (if we can regard a series of magnetized spots as a physical form!). All the remaining levels in the ANSI/SPARC model are abstract views of the physical database. Thus, although the higher levels are very important for ensuring that we are "doing the right things" in a database, this physical level concerns "doing the right things right." That is, issues related to the physical level concern making trade-offs in alternative data structures and file organizations for efficiency in maintenance and retrieval of data.

Figure 7-1
Levels of views of
data (ANSI/SPARC
model)

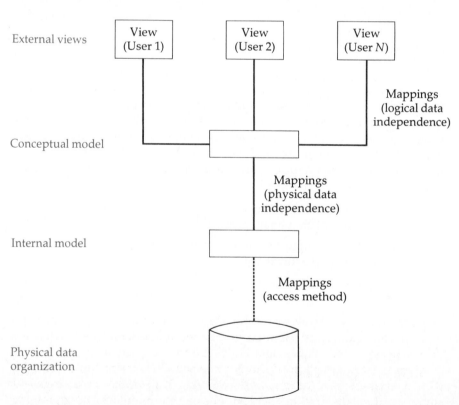

At the physical level, a database may be viewed as a collection of stored records and files. Here are the typical operations we may want to perform on a file:

- Fetch an arbitrary record from the file based upon primary key value.
- Insert a record into the file.
- Update a record in the file.
- Read the entire file.
- Read the next record in the file.
- Read the records in a file that have a common field value (what we have called a secondary key).
- Delete a record from the file.
- Reorganize the file.

In this chapter, we examine the basic techniques for storing and accessing data in files on secondary storage devices. These techniques are called **data structures,** which are the basic building blocks used to develop access methods and file organizations in computer operating systems and database management systems. Data structures represent the associations between data elements and records outlined in Chapter 3. They connect one element of data with another related element—for example, data structures can link a Product# to its Description and can connect a Customer record to its associated Order records.

Data structures are the brick, mortar, and glue that hold databases together. Data management technologies utilize data structures, but the detailed processing of data structures is often hidden from programmers and end users during systems development and programming. The logic of some database programming, however, depending on the type of DBMS, can change according to the data structures that exist. Thus, understanding the basics of data structures and how to "navigate" or "traverse" them is essential for the database processing and programming to be discussed in Chapters 10-14 of this book.

The efficiency of a database application depends on the use of well-chosen data structures. There is no one best data structure for all data processing needs, so we will introduce a variety of structures useful in different circumstances. Several of the most important concepts to be introduced in this chapter and to appear repeatedly in later chapters are:

- Various types of address pointers
- Primary key record retrieval by hashing functions
- Design and selection of indexes (including the frequently used B-tree method)
- List (or chain) data structures (the understanding of which is essential for writing programs for network database technology)

In selecting a physical data organization, the system designer must consider many important factors, including:

- The physical characteristics of the secondary storage devices
- Available operating system and file management software (or access methods)
- A set of parameters that reflect user needs for storing and accessing data (for example, frequency of different processing requirements, volume of data in different logical files, number of distinct values for certain data elements, and user response time demands)

The capture and modeling of this information will be addressed in Chapter 8.

The criteria that are normally important in selecting physical data organizations include:

- Fast access for retrieval
- High throughput for processing transactions
- Efficient use of storage space
- Protection from failures or data loss
- Minimizing need for reorganization
- Accommodating growth
- Security from unauthorized use

Often these objectives are conflicting, and the designer must select a physical data organization that provides a reasonable balance among the criteria within the resources available.

We assume here that the reader is already familiar with such computer and operating system concepts as:

- The physical characteristics of secondary storage devices, including the steps of seek time and rotational delay in the process of accessing data
- The concepts of data blocks, paged memory, and record blocking as schemes for reducing disk access overhead
- The functions of an operating system, virtual memory and other memory paging schemes (like buffering), and queueing of input/output requests
- The computer hardware needed to access secondary storage, including channels, controllers, and local area networks

We also assume some familiarity with file processing programming languages, like COBOL or PL/I, and the relative capabilities for data processing found in basic sequential and random access file organizations used in such third-generation programming languages. Those who need a basic coverage of these topics or a review of this material are referred to O'Leary & Williams (1989).

BASIC ELEMENTS AND CONCEPTS OF DATA STRUCTURES

All data structures assume that data are to be organized so one element of data follows another, and so on. Thus, terms like *prior/next* or *predecessor/successor* are frequently used when talking about placing and accessing data—that is, finding or storing data is relative to having already found some other piece of data. Data are also usually assumed to have a natural, logical sequence or sorting rule (such as ascending on part number). Furthermore, it is not uncommon for a given element of data (such as a Customer record) to be a part of multiple data structures (for example, to be sequenced by Customer Number, to be related to Customer Order data, and so forth).

Types of Pointers

Basic to many data structures is the use of extra data (that is, data without a business use) to connect elements of data. Most often these extra data are called pointers. A **pointer** is a field associated with one piece of data that is used to identify the location of another piece of data: That is, a pointer contains some type of address that can be used to locate associated data. In this section, we introduce the three types of pointers—physical, relative, and logical—and discuss their relative capabilities. Then in the later sections we will show how pointers and other constructs are used to build data structures, file organizations, and database structures.

Figure 7-2 illustrates the basic differences among the three different types of pointers. A **physical (address) pointer** resolves absolutely where the associated data reside, since it includes the disk cylinder, track, and block numbers of the data to which we are pointing.

A physical pointer is the fastest type of pointer, since it does not need to be further manipulated to specify data location. It is, however, the most restrictive. If the associated data change location in any way (for example, because of reorganization of a file), then the pointer must be changed. The pointer value has no alphanumeric relationship to meaningful database contents, so once a pointer is destroyed, it can be difficult to reconstruct. Physical pointers are of fixed size (the length of disk addresses) and usually rather short (for example, four to eight bytes).

A **relative (address) pointer** contains the relative position (or "offset") of the associated data from the beginning of the data structure in which the associated data are located. This could specify a certain byte position within a record, a certain relative record number within a file, or a certain relative block within a file. The reference can be from one file to another. For example, a pointer in a Customer record could connect that record to an associated Order record in the Orders file.

Relative pointers require marginally more computer time (several microseconds) to access the associated data. This is because the relative address must be translated into a physical address either by data management soft-

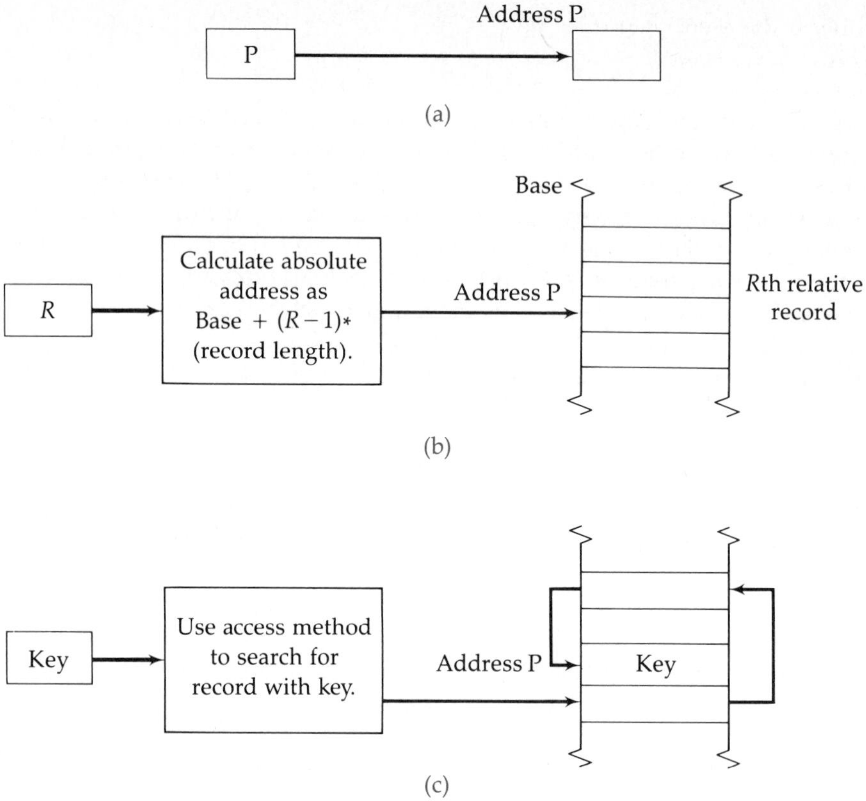

Figure 7-2
Types of pointers:
(a) physical address pointer
(b) relative address pointer for Rth record in file
(c) logical key pointer for record with key

ware or by the operating system access method (disk controllers understand only absolute, physical addresses). This translation process has to "look up" such values as record length and blocking factor to perform this calculation.

The primary advantage of relative pointers is that when the *whole* data structure changes location and all relative data placement within the structure is preserved, relative pointer values in that structure need not change. For the preceding example, the Orders file can be moved from one disk device to another to better distribute disk activity, and the relative pointers in the Customer file need not be changed. Relative pointers are difficult to reconstruct, since they have no alphanumeric relationship to meaningful data. The length of a relative pointer varies between applications and is less than the length of a physical pointer, since a relative address must be no larger than the largest physical address. The length depends on the range of possible relative positions in the data structure. For instance, given a 10,000-record Order file, a relative pointer in the Customer file to link a customer to an associated order would have to be at least 14 bits long (or, more likely, a whole 2 bytes).

A **logical (key) pointer** contains meaningful data (that is, contents of the database) about the associated element of data. Logical pointers are useful only if the associated data have some additional structure (like a primary key index or a hashing function, to be discussed later in this chapter) that supports key access on pointer values. Logical pointers are used when very rapid, direct access is not required and meaningful data exist anyhow. For example, an Order file record is likely to contain the Customer# found on the order sales form. This field is included directly in Order file records so it is readily available to print on shop orders, invoices, status reports, and the like. Occasionally, other customer data (name, address, and so on) are also required. To access these additional data, the Customer# is used to locate the Customer file record via its primary key index or hashing function on Customer#.

Logical pointers require the most computer time to retrieve the associated record because a purely hardware-independent value is used. This value must be transformed into a relative or physical pointer via table lookup, index searching, or a mathematical calculation. In any case, this translation time may include several physical file accesses to retrieve key synonyms or several index blocks. However, use of this hardware-independent value means that data can be moved, even relative placement within a structure can be changed, and logical pointers need not change. The cost to accomplish this location independence includes both time and space to maintain the key access method.

Logical pointers often are the longest type of pointer. Most data keys are relatively long compared to the length of a relative pointer (which must be capable of holding the value of the number of records in a file) or compared to the length of a disk address (for physical pointers). For example, assume that the Pine Valley Furniture Product file has only ten active records with logical pointers (keys) that are, say, four bytes long. In this case, a physical pointer might be eight bytes (depending on the computer addressing scheme), but only a single-byte relative pointer is required. A distinct advantage of logical pointers is that they do have real-world meaning. If destroyed on computer media, they can be readily reconstructed from business documents and other computerized data. Finally, logical pointers are data that are in common between two nodes (for example, records). This common data perspective is inherent (even required) in the relational data model developed in Chapter 3.

Table 7-1 summarizes this comparison of types of pointers. The remainder of this chapter and later chapters will frequently rely on a clear understanding of the different types of pointers and their applications in data management.

Data Structure Building Blocks

All data structures are built from several alternative basic building blocks for connecting and locating data. Connecting methods allow movement between related elements of data. Locating methods allow data within a structure to first be placed or stored and then found.

Table 7-1 Comparison of Types of Pointers

	Type of Pointer		
Characteristic	**Physical**	**Relative**	**Logical**
Form	Actual secondary memory (disk) address	Offset from reference point (beginning of file)	Meaningful business data
Speed of access	Fastest	Medium	Slowest
Sensitivity to data movement	Most	Only sensitive to relative position changes	Least
Sensitivity to destruction	Very	Very	Often can be easily reconstructed
Space requirement	Fixed, usually short	Varies, usually shortest	Varies, usually longest

There are only two basic methods for *connecting* elements of data, as outlined by Severance (1974):

1. An **address sequential (AS) connection,** in which a successor element is placed and located in the physical memory space immediately following the current element (see Figures 7-3a and c).

2. A **pointer sequential (PS) connection,** in which some additional data (called a pointer) are explicitly stored in the current element to identify the location of the successor element (see Figures 7-3b and d).

Also, there are only two basic methods for *placement* of data relative to the connection mechanism:

1. **Data direct (DD) placement,** in which the connection mechanism links an item of data directly with its successor (and/or predecessor) item (see Figures 7-3a and b)

2. **Data indirect (DI) placement,** in which the connection mechanism, not the data themselves, links pointers to the data (see Figures 7-3c and d)

Any data structure or file organization is simply a combination of these basic methods.

Address Sequential Connection Address sequential data direct (ASDD, or simply sequential) is what is typically called the sequential access method. It is simple, easy to understand and process, uses no extra storage space above that required for data, and supports efficient sequential access. Now

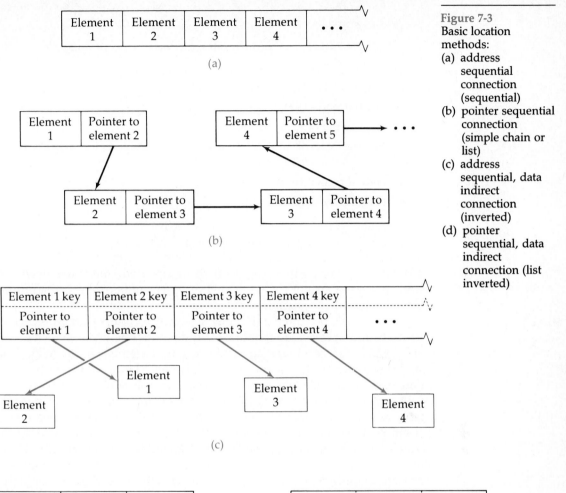

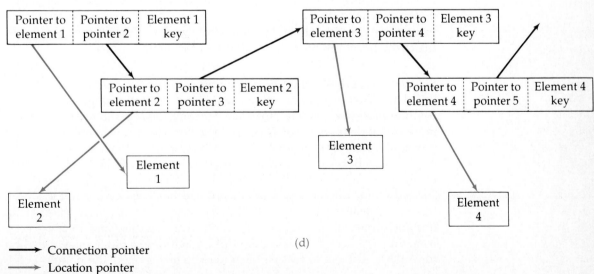

Connection pointer
Location pointer

Figure 7-3
Basic location
methods:
(a) address
    sequential
    connection
    (sequential)
(b) pointer sequential
    connection
    (simple chain or
    list)
(c) address
    sequential, data
    indirect
    connection
    (inverted)
(d) pointer
    sequential, data
    indirect
    connection (list
    inverted)

let's take another look at the list of typical database operations for record processing introduced at the beginning of this chapter:

- Fetch an arbitrary record from the file based upon primary key value.
- Insert a record into the file.
- Update a record in the file.
- Read the entire file.
- Read the next record in the file.
- Read the records in a file that have a common field value (what we have called a secondary key).
- Delete a record from the file.
- Reorganize the file.

Sequential performs rather well for the fourth and fifth operations (reading an entire file or the physically next record). It can be economical for the third operation (updating a record) if the media supports update-in-place, if roughly 10% or more of the file is being updated, and if the amount of storage space does not change. However, it is cumbersome, if not impractical, for the other operations.

With ASDD, arbitrary (randomly selected) records or multiple records with a common key value cannot be found without possibly extensive scanning of the data structure. Insertion of a new element in an ASDD data structure requires that all subsequent elements be moved, which can be time consuming. Update is easy if we can simply write the new element values over the old; however, sequential data storage media, like magnetic tape, require the whole set of data to be rewritten. Element deletion itself is simple if we only mark the deleted element as purged and do not immediately recover this now unused space. Depending on the amount of deletion activity, this practice of only marking deletions can lead to excessive wasted space and frequent data reorganizations (called "garbage collection"). However, this practice does eliminate costly dynamic space reclamation that can slow down an on-line application. Reorganization requires the costly act of rewriting the whole set of elements.

Pointer Sequential Connection   Pointer sequential data direct (PSDD, or list) data structures greatly decrease the cost of performing insertion and deletion of new elements. However, fetching random elements is usually more costly than with ASDD (since logically adjacent data are not usually physically adjacent). Figures 7-4a and b, respectively, illustrate how new product numbers can be added to and deleted from a PSDD data structure for the Pine Valley Furniture Product Master File. For insertion of product# 200, space for this new product record can be *anywhere* in the file where there is an available record slot. The first step in the insertion process is to find the proper insertion position in the structure (this may involve a scan from the beginning to the proper position, which can be a longer scan than for ASDD). Then only two pointers need to be changed: the pointer in the

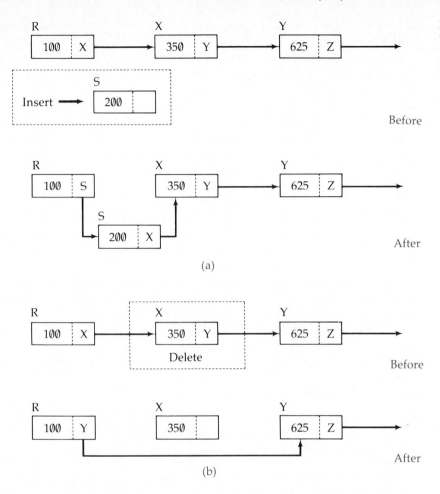

Figure 7-4
Maintaining a pointer
sequential data
structure:
(a) insertion
(b) deletion

predecessor record of product# 200 (100 at location R) and the pointer in the product# 200 record itself (set to location of the successor of 100 before the insertion). The remainder of the data structure is independent of this change. This can be viewed as adding a new link to a chain.

Deletion of an element from a PSDD data structure is even simpler and can be viewed as welding two links of a chain together. In Figure 7-4b, product# 350 at location X is to be deleted. The successor of the element being deleted (product# 625 at location Y) is to become the new direct successor of the predecessor element to the one being deleted (100 at location R). Only the one pointer value has to be changed—the pointer associated with product# 350 does not have to be changed. Special provisions are often necessary when deleting from (or inserting into) an empty pointer sequential data structure.

One negative factor is that pointer sequential connection requires "overhead" space beyond meaningful data. This overhead space may seem small, but practice has shown that in total, for all uses of pointers in a database (in key indexes, record chains, synonym chains, and so on), 100% overhead is not uncommon!

Retrieval of a random record in a pure PSDD data structure is very likely more time consuming than in an ASDD structure. The same arbitrary record will be in the same relative sequential position in each set. The greater time for PSDD is because each movement from a node (for example, record to next record in sequence) will be at least as far physically as the equivalent step for ASDD. With ASDD, this move is to an adjacent physical location of often blocked data (so a physical access is not needed for each record); with PSDD, the move could require the disk head to move to access each record.

Finding the records with a common secondary key value may be rapid in PSDD. This will be true if a separate list is created that points to one of the records with a common value, and then pointers are used to connect this one to the next one with the same value, and so on.

In summary, PSDD performs very well for record insertion, record update, and record deletion if the time to reach the desired position in the list is reasonable (certainly true for short lists). PSDD can also be acceptable for operations of next record access and file reorganization, but PSDD is worse than sequential for reading the entire file. PSDD, like ASDD, does not fetch an arbitrary record very well on average.

Indirect Data Placement

Besides connection methods (AS and PS), data structures are also characterized by the relative placement of data and the connection mechanism. Either indirect or direct placement and access to the actual data can be employed.

Indirect placement (see Figures 7-3c and d) usually makes scanning a data structure more efficient than with data direct, since the connection nodes are often smaller than the actual data being managed. Hence, the nodes can be scanned more quickly and possibly kept in main computer memory for long periods. Because the pointers are so compact compared to the actual data records, many of these pointers can be kept in computer main memory while the file is being used. This means that frequently a physical read of secondary memory to retrieve pointers will not have to be made. Finally, because all the connections are stored in these compact blocks, insertions and deletions are more efficient than with the data direct (DD) counterparts in Figure 7-3.

PSDI (list inverted) provides the greatest flexibility of reorganization. The pointer connections in the index permit record insertions and deletions to occur with minimal movement of index data, which is desirable for very large indexes (themselves called *files*).

The four alternatives of ASDD (sequential), PSDD (chain), ASDI (inverted), and PSDI (list inverted) are all extreme points and "pure" situations, but hybrids, or combinations, frequently occur in one structure. The next section will show how pointer sequential connections can be used to advantage in organizing records within and between files. Later sections will then address basic data structures for organizing groups of related records, so called file organizations.

Processing Chain Data Structures

We present in this section a more detailed account of procedures for processing chain data structures. An understanding of how to process a data structure is important because we often use procedural language programs written in COBOL with some database management systems (especially hierarchical and network systems, described in Chapters 10 and 11, respectively). These programs initiate some of the detailed movement from one data record to another. In addition, the more you as a programmer or database designer know about how a DBMS works (for example, how it inserts new records into a database), the better prepared you will be for selecting data management technologies appropriate for the application at hand, handling errors during program execution, and tuning the database structures for satisfactory operational efficiency of database processing.

Three basic chain data structures are presented here—stacks, queues, and sorted lists/files—with emphasis on the sorted lists since these are the most commonly found in database systems. Each can be developed using address sequential or pointer sequential connections. When pointer sequential connections are used, these structures are collectively called linked lists, or more descriptively, chains. Chained, or pointer sequential, versions of these structures will be used for all the illustrations.

Stacks   A **stack** has the property that all insertions (addition of new records) and deletions (removal of no-longer-needed records) are made at the same end of the data structure. Stacks exhibit a last-in-first-out (LIFO) property. A common example of a stack is a vertical column of plates in a cafeteria line that are in a push-down, pop-up rack. In business data processing, stack-like structures are useful in maintaining a set of unprioritized or unsorted records. For example, we might use a chained stack structure to link together all the ORDER-LINE records that are related to a common ORDER record for Pine Valley Furniture. The advantageous property of a stack is that insertions and deletions are quite efficient, since no scanning of the stack has to occur. A frequent use for stacks in database processing is to keep track of unused storage space. In this case, for example, the address of a deleted record slot is added to a stack, and the next time a record is to be inserted, the just-deleted record slot is used. By the way, many operating systems do the same with deleted space, which is why you may not be able to recover a deleted file after you write any new data to the diskette.

Queues   A **queue** has the property that all insertions occur at one end and all deletions occur at the other end. A queue exhibits a first-in-first-out

(FIFO) property. A common example of a queue is a check-out line at a grocery store. In business data processing, queue-like structures are often used to maintain lists of records in chronological order of insertion. For example, Figure 7-5 illustrates a pointer sequential, or chained, queue of ORDER-LINE records kept in order of arrival (and, hence, filling sequence) for a common PRODUCT record in Pine Valley Furniture.

In this example, the PRODUCT record acts as the head-of-chain or start node of the data structure. The value of the OLDEST-ORDER-LINE field is a pointer to the oldest (that is, chronologically first entered) ORDER-LINE record. The NEXT-ORDER-LINE field in the ORDER-LINE record contains the pointers to the next record in reverse chronological sequence. The value of Ø in the ORDER-LINE record in relative position Z is called a **null pointer** and signifies the end of the chain.

This example also introduces the concept of a bidirectional chain (to make queue maintenance easier). A **bidirectional chain** has both "forward" and "backward" pointers emanating from each record. There is real benefit in having both forward and backward (NEXT/PRIOR) pointers. When processing a bidirectional chain in one direction (forward), you do not have to remember or find the immediate predecessor (which often must be updated during insertions and deletions), since it is known directly from the pointer (backward). The NEWEST-ORDER-LINE field serves as the head-of-chain pointer for entering new orders (insertions), since new orders have the lowest priority to be filled. The PRIOR-ORDER-LINE field in the ORDER-LINE record maintains the newest-to-oldest record sequence. It is assumed that records are inserted as orders are received, so order receipt sequence is the same as the insertion sequence.

Figure 7-5
Example of a queue with bidirectional pointers

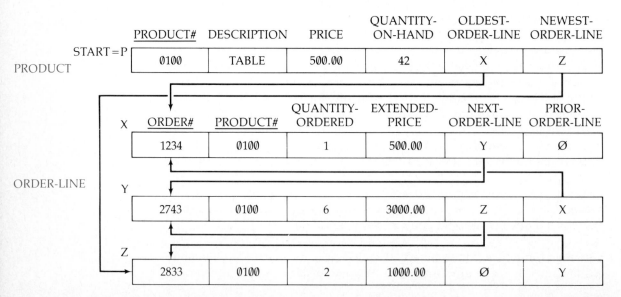

New ORDER-LINE

Sorted Lists   A **sorted list** has the property that insertions and deletions may occur anywhere within the list; elements of data are maintained in logical order based on a key field value, and elements are inserted or deleted by specifying the key value involved. A common example of a sorted list is a telephone directory. In business data processing, sorted lists occur frequently, since updating or reporting data is most natural in a specified order. For example, Figure 7-6 illustrates a pointer sequential, or chained, sorted list of ORDER records related to a CUSTOMER record. The ORDER records are maintained in a single, unidirectional sorted order by DELIV-ERY-DATE, with the oldest ORDER on the "top" of the list. Sorted lists are maintained to avoid resorting a set of data (records) each time the oldest, newest, or all in sequence is desired.

In this example, the FIRST-ORDER field serves as the head-of-chain pointer, and it points to the ORDER record for the given CUSTOMER that has the earliest DELIVERY-DATE. The process of inserting the new record for ORDER# 3318, which we will outline below, is much more complex than that in stack or queue chained data structures. The greater complexity (and, hence, more required processing time) is due to the need to scan the chain to find the proper position in which to place the new record. Chain scanning can take considerable time if there is no control over the relative physical placement of records. Further, special logic is required if the logical position for a new record happens to be on either end of the chain or is in an empty chain. To guarantee that insertion (and later deletion) will always be in the interior of the chain, "dummy" first and last records are often included in the chain. This is shown in Figure 7-6b. Although these dummy records require additional space and must be skipped in scanning, the savings in insertion and deletion speed and ease are usually considered to be greater. Since the use of these dummy records will simplify our discussion here, we will assume this convenience.

Figure 7-6c shows the result of inserting the record with ORDER# 3318 into the sorted list of Figure 7-6b. The list is scanned starting from the relative record number in FIRST-ORDER. If duplicate key values are not permitted, then the process must check at each "visit" of an ORDER record that the key there does not match the key for the new ORDER. This type of check is not required in the situation in Figure 7-6, since duplicate key values are allowed (the key is a secondary key).

Since duplicate keys are allowed, we must also decide where to insert a new duplicate: before existing records with the same key value, after these duplicate records, or somewhere else. The position that requires the least scanning and, hence, the least time, is before all existing duplicates. If there are no business reasons to do otherwise, the correct position of the record with ORDER# 3318 is found when the first DELIVERY-DATE greater than or equal to 031083 is located (this is called the **stopping rule**); it occurs when the scan reaches the record with ORDER# 3217. This ORDER now becomes the successor of the record with ORDER# 3318, so the NEXT-ORDER pointer of the record with ORDER# 3318 is set to value Z. The tricky part is to remember the predecessor (without the aid of backward pointers).

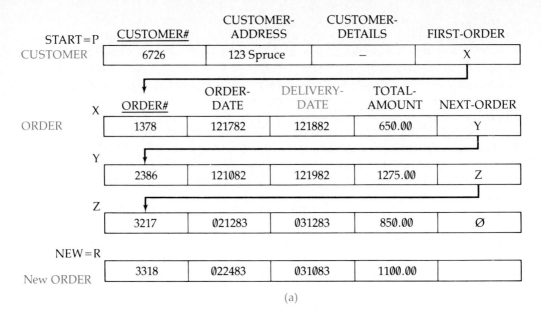

(a)

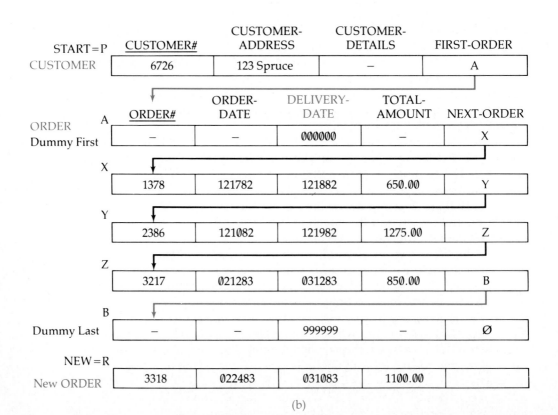

(b)

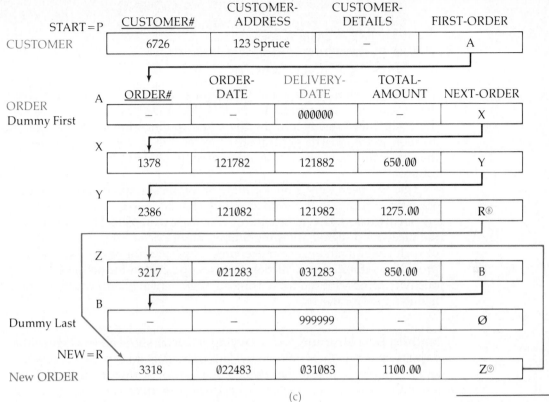

START=P CUSTOMER	CUSTOMER#	CUSTOMER- ADDRESS	CUSTOMER- DETAILS	FIRST-ORDER
	6726	123 Spruce	–	A

A ORDER Dummy First	ORDER#	ORDER- DATE	DELIVERY- DATE	TOTAL- AMOUNT	NEXT-ORDER
	–	–	000000	–	X
X	1378	121782	121882	650.00	Y
Y	2386	121082	121982	1275.00	R⑧
Z	3217	021283	031283	850.00	B
B Dummy Last	–	–	999999	–	Ø
NEW=R New ORDER	3318	022483	031083	1100.00	Z⑨

(c)

Figure 7-6
Example of a sorted list:
(a) before new ORDER insertion and without dummy first and dummy last ORDERS
(b) before new ORDER insertion and with dummy first and dummy last ORDERS
(c) after new ORDER insertion (Circled numbers next to pointers indicate the step number in the associated maintenance procedure that changes that pointer value.)

To provide a perspective on the typical steps in updating a chain, we present the following sketch of a chained sorted list insertion procedure. In this outline, position variables PRE and AFT are used to hold the values of the predecessor and successor, respectively, of the new ORDER record. Step 7 is included in brackets to show where a check for duplicate keys would appear if required. The symbol '←' means replace the value of the variable on the left with the value of the variable on the right. Steps 8 and 9, which change pointer values, are noted in Figure 7-6 to show exactly which pointers would change for the example of this figure. The insertion procedure is:

```
/* Establish position variables beginning values */
1 PRE ← FIRST-ORDER(START)
2 AFT ← NEXT-ORDER(PRE)
/* Skip/scan through chain until proper position is found */
3 DO WHILE DELIVERY-DATE(AFT) < DELIVERY-DATE(NEW)
4   PRE ← AFT
5   AFT ← NEXT-ORDER(AFT)
6 ENDO
```

7 [If DELIVERY-DATE(AFT) = DELIVERY-DATE(NEW)
    then indicate a Duplicate Error and terminate procedure]
/* Weld in new chain element */
8 NEXT-ORDER(PRE) ← NEW
9 NEXT-ORDER(NEW) ← AFT

Step 3 says that if we have not yet found a DELIVERY-DATE in the chain that is greater than or equal to the DELIVERY-DATE of the new ORDER, then skip ahead one link in the chain and continue to test for the desired position to insert. The general structure of this procedure is outlined by the three comment lines. These three sections are common to most insertion routines.

This has been only a brief outline of a typical chain insertion routine. Many special conditions (such as empty chains, broken chains, and so on) are not discussed. Given the nature of database management systems today, the database designer and programmer do not need extensive knowledge of such chain maintenance procedures. However, the review here should provide a sufficient introduction to and appreciation for the possible productivity gains achieved from using a DBMS, which handles such database maintenance for us.

Multilist Data Structure   An annoying characteristic of address sequential data structures is their inflexibility. Not only must related data follow one another in physical sequence (which causes a lot of work to maintain), but also only *one* sequence (sorted order or association) can be supported with these structures. A chained list data structure, like the sorted list presented in the prior section, avoids the problem of maintaining physical sequential placement. However, these basic structures are still limited to representing a *single* logical ordering.

Often in business data processing, and certainly in a database environment, the same data will be associated in several groups, or several sorted sequences will be desired to support processing of shared data. Consider, for example, the same set of Customer Orders that need to be (1) connected to their associated Customer record, (2) maintained in order date sequence for auditing purposes, and (3) grouped together by delivery date for producing reports for the shipping dock. It would be desirable to be able to maintain all these associations without having to duplicate or triplicate the many Order records (a goal of data management). The multilist data structure, among others to be presented later, is a means to achieve this goal.

A **multilist data structure** (better, but not usually, called multichain) is one for which more than one NEXT element of data may emanate from a given element. Thus, multiple pointers (multiple chains) are employed, one each for the different "paths" through the data. Each path links records with a common characteristic or in a different sequence. With multilist, it is possible to be "walking" through one association and in the middle decide to follow another. For example, while accessing the Order records for a given Customer (one chain), we could find all the Orders to be delivered on the same day of one of those Orders (another chain). This would allow us to anticipate, for instance, possible shipping delays due to a bottleneck (excess work load) on the shipping dock. A multilist data structure for this situation is depicted in Figure 7-7a.

Multilist is a basic building block for implementation of the CODASYL network data model presented in Chapter 11. As a preview of what we will see in that chapter, consider the data structure depicted in Figure 7-7b. In this example, ORDER-LINE records for the same ORDER are linked via one list in PRODUCT# sequence (FIRST-ORDER-LINE and NEXT-ORDER-LINE pointers), and ORDER-LINE records for the same PRODUCT are linked via another list in DUE-DATE sequence (FIRST-LINE-ITEM and NEXT-LINE-ITEM pointers). Thus, the same ORDER-LINE data can be shared by both product management and order processing applications.

Hazards of Chain Structures   The disadvantage of any list (chain) structure arises with long chains. Scanning a long chain can take an enormous amount of time, since each movement from, say, record to record, may require a disk cylinder change. With single lists, it is often possible to cluster the associated data together into the same cylinder, but with multiple lists it is very difficult to place each element of data relatively near to each of its associated data.

Long chains also cause a problem when we try to find one or a few records that fall into some group or range of key values. For example, we may want to know which orders to be shipped today were entered one week ago. This could be a concern because data entry errors have been discovered in other orders entered that same day and we wish to take precautions to ship the right orders. Answering this question could require scanning a long list of orders (in order-date or delivery-date sequence) and then checking the other qualification on each record accessed. The indexed or inverted list for file organization, to be discussed later in this chapter, is designed to handle this so-called multiple-key query more efficiently than multilist.

Also, list data structures are vulnerable to being broken. If an abnormal operating system event occurs in the middle of a list maintenance routine, the list can be partially updated and all links may not be completed. The use of bidirectional pointers, storing logical pointers in addition to physical ones, and utilities for finding and repairing broken chains can be used to deal with these hazards.

FILE ORGANIZATION

A **file organization** is a technique for physically arranging the records of a file on a secondary storage device (we will continue to assume the use of magnetic disks). A file organization contains a systematic combination of the kinds of data structures outlined in the previous section.

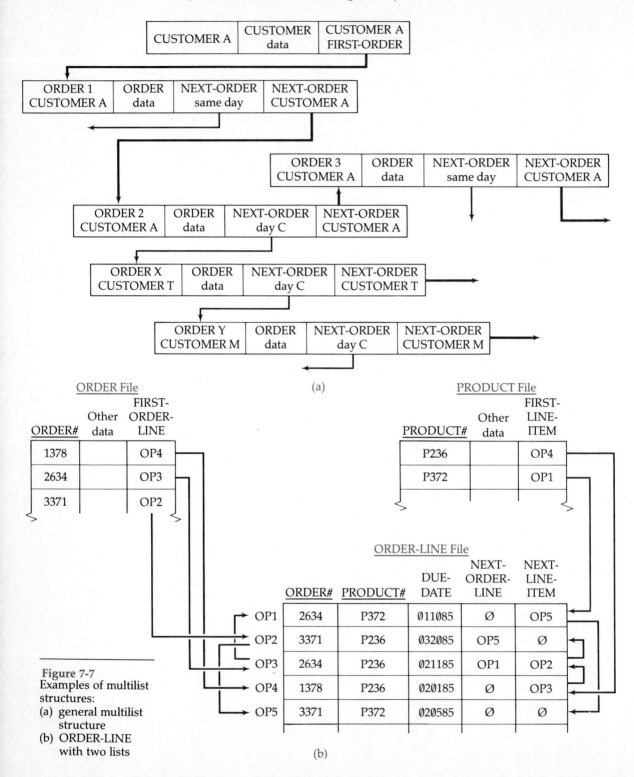

Figure 7-7
Examples of multilist
structures:
(a) general multilist
    structure
(b) ORDER-LINE
    with two lists

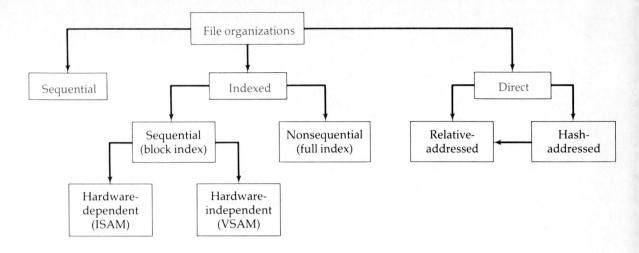

Figure 7-8
Overview of basic file
organizations

An overview of the basic file organizations appears in Figure 7-8. Three file organizations are shown: sequential, indexed, and direct. Sequential is the ASDD data structure for records that was outlined above. In an indexed organization, the records may be stored sequentially by key value (in which case a block index is used), or stored nonsequentially (in which case a full index identifying each record by key value is required). This latter category is frequently called an inverted index.

In a direct file organization, two addressing schemes are frequently used: relative addressing and hash addressing. When hash addressing is used, the addressing algorithm usually generates a relative address (this is shown by an arrow from Hash-addressed to Relative-addressed in Figure 7-8).

Comparison of Basic File Organizations

In a **sequential file organization** (Figure 7-9a), the physical order of records in the file is the same as that in which the records were written to the file. Normally, this is in ascending sequence of the primary key (as shown in the example). A given record can be accessed only by first accessing all records that physically precede it.

In an **indexed sequential organization** (Figure 7-9b), the records are also stored in physical sequence (at least within blocks) according to the primary key. The file management system, or access method, builds an index, separate from the data records, that contains key values together with pointers to the data records themselves. This index permits individual records to be accessed at random without accessing other records. The entire file can also be accessed sequentially in an indexed sequential organization.

We will use the term *relative organization* to refer to a direct file organization in which relative addressing is used. In a relative organization (Figure 7-9c), each record can be retrieved by specifying its relative record number.

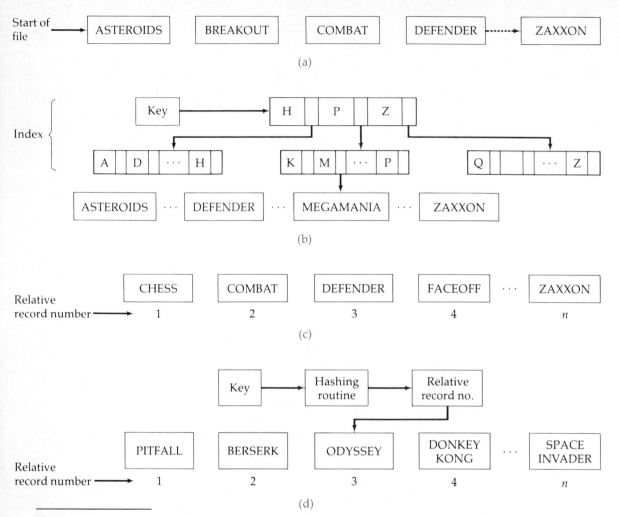

Figure 7-9
Comparison of file
organizations:
(a) sequential
(b) indexed
    sequential
(c) relative
(d) hashed

The **relative record number** is a number from 0 to n that gives the position of the record from the beginning of the file. For example, a program can issue a command such as "read the fourth record in the file." The programmer (or application program) must correctly specify the relative location of a desired record. Records in a relative file are often loaded in primary key sequence (as shown in Figure 7-9c) so the file may be processed sequentially. However, the records may also be in random sequence, which occurs when the relative file organization is used with hash addressing.

The term *hashed organization* refers to a direct file organization in which hash addressing is used. In a **hashed organization** (Figure 7-9d), the primary key value for a record is converted by an algorithm (called a **hashing routine**) into a relative record number. The record is then located by its relative record number, as for a relative organization. The hashing algorithm

Table 7-2 File Organizations and Record Access Modes

File Organization	Record Access Mode	
	Sequential	**Random**
Sequential	Yes	No (impractical)
Indexed sequential	Yes	Yes
Direct-relative	Yes	Yes
Direct-hashed	No (impractical)	Yes

scatters the records throughout the file, and they are normally not in primary key sequence.

Table 7-2 shows the combinations of file organizations and record access modes that are permitted in most systems. As shown in the table, all the file organizations except sequential permit random access; also, all the organizations except hashed permit sequential access. (Although physical sequential access to a hashed file is technically possible, it is not usually useful, since the records are not in logical sequential order.) Two of the file organizations—indexed sequential and relative—permit access in both the sequential and random modes.

Since sequential is a relatively straightforward file organization, we will not discuss it directly any further. In the following sections, we will describe the indexed sequential and hashed organizations in greater detail. To illustrate each organization, we will use a portion of the Product file for Pine Valley Furniture (see Table 7-3). To simplify the presentation, only four data items are shown: PRODUCT# (the primary key), DESCRIPTION, FINISH, and ROOM.

Notice there are gaps in the product number values in Table 7-3. Because of these gaps, it would not be practical to use a relative organization for this file, with product number as the relative record number, since there would be massive gaps in the storage file. (For example, the record for product 100 would be followed by 24 empty record slots, then the record for product 125.) This is a typical problem with primary key values, and it suggests why "primary key equals relative address" is not often an acceptable addressing technique for direct files.

INDEXES OR INVERTED LISTS

A student preparing a term paper for an economics course needs some additional information. She knows that economist Milton Friedman has written on the topic for which she needs information and that she has

Table 7-3   Product File (Pine Valley Furniture Company)

PRODUCT#	DESCRIPTION	FINISH	ROOM	(Other data)
100	Stereo cabinet	Maple	LR	
125	Coffee table	Walnut	LR	
153	Hutch	Maple	DR	
207	Wall unit	Oak	LR	
221	Stereo cabinet	Pine	FR	
252	Dining table	Maple	DR	
286	Desk	Birch	O	
314	Chair	Pine	FR	
363	Room divider	Walnut	LR	
394	Dining table	Oak	K	
418	Hutch	Birch	DR	
434	Bookcase	Pine	FR	
488	Lamp table	Cherry	LR	
500	Computer desk	Pine	O	
515	Bookcase	Maple	LR	

already found many relevant Friedman publications. From some recent reading, she knows that she needs additional publications related to certain terms that describe (identify, classify, or are associated with) the kind of information now needed.

The student goes to the university library, where she finds two indexes of periodical literature. One index identifies publications by author name and the second identifies key word topical groupings. Each index identifies (or addresses) a publication by common pieces of data: the periodical name, the publication date, and the page numbers. (If you find this analogy helpful, you will see the similarity of these data to a disk address.) The student quickly scans each index and writes down two lists of "addresses": those from the first index for Milton Friedman and those from the second index for the relevant topical key words. She then compares the two lists and finds that only four papers meet both search criteria. Finally, she walks (physically) through the library to retrieve the few relevant publications, having avoided very time-consuming browsing of many publications through the library stacks.

The student in this example has used indexes or inverted lists to speed up significantly a multiple-key search of the library. An **inverted list** is a table, list, index, or directory of data addresses that indicates all the data (records) that have a common property. The address sequential data indirect data structure covered earlier in this chapter is a convenient way to view this table.

Figure 7-10 views a possible inverted list structure for the PRODUCT file of Pine Valley Furniture. Indexes are created to speed processing, usually for qualified access questions that use primary or secondary keys. Recall

Figure 7-10
Inverted list structure (Pine Valley Furniture)

PRODUCT# index
(primary key)

PRODUCT#	Address
0100	1
0350	2
0625	3
0975	4
1000	5
1250	6
1425	7
1600	8
1775	9
2000	10

DESCRIPTION
Index
(secondary key)

DESCRIPTION	Addresses
BOOKCASE	7
CHAIR	3, 6
DRESSER	5, 9
STAND	8
TABLE	1, 2
WALL UNIT	4, 10

ROOM index
(secondary key)

ROOM	Addresses
BR	5, 8, 9
DR	1, 2, 3
FR	4
LR	6, 7, 10

PRODUCT
data file

Address	PRODUCT#	DESCRIPTION	FINISH	ROOM	PRICE
1	0100	TABLE	OAK	DR	500
2	0350	TABLE	MAPLE	DR	625
3	0625	CHAIR	OAK	DR	100
4	0975	WALL UNIT	PINE	FR	750
5	1000	DRESSER	CHERRY	BR	800
6	1250	CHAIR	MAPLE	LR	400
7	1425	BOOKCASE	PINE	LR	250
8	1600	STAND	BIRCH	BR	200
9	1775	DRESSER	PINE	BR	500
10	2000	WALL UNIT	OAK	LR	1200

that secondary keys were defined in Chapter 3 to be data items that normally do not uniquely identify a record but identify many records that share the same property.

Although DESCRIPTION, FINISH, and ROOM are all potentially secondary keys, indexes on only DESCRIPTION and ROOM were created in Figure 7-10. This is because the cost to maintain a FINISH index (when records are added or deleted, or when FINISH values change) was assumed to be more than the retrieval savings from use of a FINISH index. This is in comparison to the alternative of physically *scanning all* PRODUCT records to find those with the specified FINISH. Also, it was observed (hypothetically for our discussion here) that questions involving FINISH were not very discriminating; that is, *many* records satisfied queries on FINISH. A rough rule of thumb is that if more than 10% of the records in a file satisfy a key qualification, an index on that key is not very helpful—a complete file scan is equally or more efficient. In Chapter 8, we will present a more complete discussion of the selection of inverted indexes, which is a major implementation design issue in relational database systems.

Indexes are more compact than the data records they reference. Often, indexes can be kept in computer main memory for extended periods so secondary memory access costs to retrieve indexes can be reduced. However, indexes for files with many records can also be very large. An index, then, can be viewed as a file itself on which an index can be created. Later in this section we will review several popular schemes used as file organizations for an index file.

Not all secondary keys need to be indexed, as noted earlier. Before a database designer can decide which indexes to create, however, all secondary keys must be identified. When all data processing is known in advance, computer program specifications provide an excellent source to identify secondary keys. Before these program specifications are developed or when significant ad hoc database queries are expected, some general guidelines are required to help in identifying secondary (and even alternative primary) keys. Guidelines for identifying secondary (and primary) keys appear in Table 7-4, which summarizes this taxonomy and includes examples from the Pine Valley Furniture database for each key type.

Trees

The typical data structure used to organize an index file is a tree. Many types of tree have been developed, but we will outline only a few that are most prevalent in database processing. Three particular "species" will be reviewed later in this section: ISAM, VSAM, and B-tree. The B-tree variety is now the most frequently used in relational database systems (although some systems give the database designer a choice).

It was stated in the preceding section that an index with many entries can itself present an interesting index data structuring problem. If an index is helpful in storing and searching through data records, could an index

Table 7-4 Primary and Secondary Key Taxonomy

Key type	Description and motivation	Example from Pine Valley Furniture
Simple primary key	This is one data item whose values are unique to each record in a file; frequently required in on-line applications	PRODUCT# for PRODUCT records
Partial value key	A data item with long values may be cumbersome to index. The first *n* characters may be very discriminating, but not unique	PRODUCT-DESCRIPTION for PRODUCT records
Concatenated primary key	Records that contain data about (the relationship between) two entities are identified by a combination of the related entity primary keys	ORDER# and PRODUCT# for ORDER-LINE records
Concatenated retrieval key	Although lists of addresses from two separate indexes can be intersected to answer queries with AND conditions, a combined key index can avoid this cost	FINISH and ROOM for PRODUCT records
Simple category key	Frequently, records are sought that have a common characteristic (single, nonunique value or range of values)	FINISH for PRODUCT records
Complex category key	Often, queries arise that simply ask which records exist with specified interdata item characteristics	QUANTITY-ON-HAND less than REORDER-POINT for PRODUCT records
Existence/ count key	Some queries ask only if any record exists or how many exist with specified properties; these can be answered from just an index	DELIVERY-DATE of today for ORDER records
Intrafile concatenated key	Complex relationships can exist between records within the same file, such as Bill-of-Materials; a key that is a concatenation of these related record keys can speed access	Parent PRODUCT# and component PRODUCT# for Bill-of-Materials in PRODUCT file

Table 7–4   continued

Missing value key	This is a special case of the simple category key in which the characteristic sought is the null value	PRICE for PRODUCT records
Interfile key	This is an inverted list equivalent to a chain structure. Here records are identified by a common characteristic that is also the primary key of another file	PRODUCT# for ORDER-LINE records
Audit/change key	Frequently, data processing audit and control procedures need to know which records have been modified, added, or deleted during the most recent period	PRODUCT# for PRODUCT records (e.g., to tag records with price changes)
Sort key	An index can be used to maintain a sorted order to avoid sorting records before every batch reporting	CUSTOMER-ZIPCODE for CUSTOMER records

also help to organize another index? This type of hierarchy of data and pointers to data is generalized by the tree data structure. Trees can be used to organize data directly or to organize indexes into data.

A **tree data structure** has the property that each element of the structure (except the root) has only one path coming in (that is, there is only one pointer that points to any given element), but there may be zero or many paths coming out (that is, there can be several pointers in any given element pointing to other elements). This set of pointers may be address sequential or pointer sequential connected. A **binary tree** permits at most two paths coming out of an element.

There is specialized terminology associated with trees, some of which has already been introduced. Figure 7-11 graphically depicts many of the terms. We may view trees genealogically. The **root** is the element (node) with no parents. All the direct offspring of a common parent are collectively called a **filial set;** each member (node) of a filial set is a **sibling.** All the offspring (both direct descendants and all future generations) form a **sub-tree.** All terminal elements that have no offspring are called **leaves. Level** refers to the distance from the root, defined as the number of branches to backtrack to return to the root. In addition, the term **degree** signifies the maximum number of offspring from an element. A binary tree is a tree of degree (or order) 2.

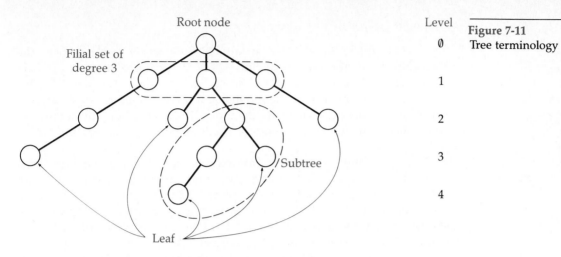

Figure 7-11
Tree terminology

Properties of Trees   In this section we introduce several important properties of trees, which suggest the possible applications of different tree structures as well as desirable properties for all trees. The properties to be discussed are uniform accessibility, insertion dependence, branching factor, and depth.

In certain types of trees, some records are closer to the root than others. This means that a different number of comparisons and branches will be required to access different records. If frequently accessed records could be placed close to the root, then overall database performance could be improved. Most types of trees build **uniform accessibility** by placing *all* records in leaves and requiring that all leaves be an equal distance from the root. The structure of a tree may also be dependent on the order in which records were inserted. The worst case usually is when the records are loaded in ascending or descending primary key order. Many trees that store data records only in leaves do not exhibit this **insertion dependence** property. However, if the type of tree being used can become pathological in shape with certain insertion sequences, care should be taken in loading records. In general, bushy trees provide the best performance.

The **branching factor** (or degree) of a tree is the maximum number of children allowed per parent. Large branching factors, in general, create broader, more shallow trees. Since access time in a tree depends more often on depth than on breadth, and since movement between levels means a disk access, it is usually advantageous to have bushy, shallow trees.

Depth is the number of levels between the root and a leaf in the tree. Depth may be the same from the root to each node, producing a tree called a **balanced tree,** or it may vary across different paths. Balanced trees are democratic in that all leaves have about the same access costs—however, balancing can be costly to maintain as the tree contents are updated. B-trees, to be introduced in a later part of this section, overcome the costly update problems of other types of balanced trees.

Indexed Sequential Organization

For several years, the indexed sequential file organization has been the "workhorse" organization for primary key index files that are stored on direct access storage devices. The reason is that this organization allows access to records in both the sequential and random modes. Most vendors supply access methods that support indexed sequential organizations and automatically maintain the indexes used to randomly access individual records.

The type of index used in an indexed sequential organization is referred to as a **block index**, in which each index entry refers to a block of records (rather than a single record). This simplified index structure is possible since the records within each block are in primary key sequence. To locate a specific record, the index is searched to locate a block of records, then the block is scanned until the desired record is found.

There are two basic implementations of the indexed sequential organization: hardware-dependent and hardware-independent. In IBM systems, the access methods that support these organizations are called, respectively, indexed sequential access method (ISAM) and virtual sequential access method (VSAM). Most other vendors provide similar access methods or file management systems. The hardware-independent version, or VSAM, is newer and more powerful and has replaced ISAM in many applications. VSAM is based on a tree variety called B-tree, which will be reviewed after we introduce ISAM and VSAM.

Hardware-Dependent Implementation (ISAM)

ISAM is called a hardware-dependent method since where data is located and how the data are reorganized when records are added or deleted depend on the physical characteristics of the disk drive used for file storage. ISAM uses three (conceptual) levels of indexes: a **master index,** which shows which disk volume to access (for files that span multiple volumes), a **cylinder index,** which shows which cylinder to access on the given volume, and a **track index,** which shows which track to scan (see Figure 7-12).

Indexed sequential files are normally composed of three areas:

1. The **prime area,** which contains the data records and the track index. (An index to the tracks of each cylinder is stored at the beginning of each cylinder.)

2. An **overflow area,** used for records that are added to the file but will not fit in the prime area.

3. An **index,** which contains the master index and cylinder indexes.

The use of the multilevel index is illustrated in Figure 7-12. Each arrow in this diagram represents a pointer from one index to a lower-level index. Suppose we wish to locate the record for product 500. Referring first to the

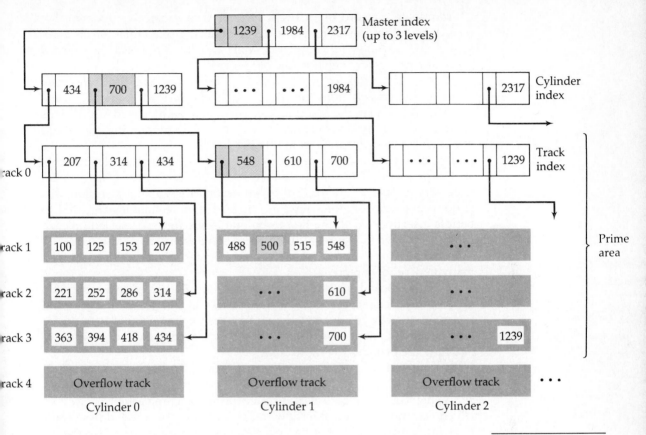

Figure 7-12
ISAM architecture

master index, we are directed to the first cylinder index. Searching that index, we see that record 500 will be contained on cylinder 1 (if it is in the file). At this point, the disk access mechanism is moved to cylinder 1 (if necessary) and the track index for that cylinder is read into main memory (we assume that the track index is contained on track 0). Searching the track index, we find that the desired record will be on track 1 of that cylinder if it exists. The target record can then be sought by scanning track 1 in the prime area. In this case, the product record would be found.

Processing ISAM Files When records are first loaded onto an ISAM file, the access method creates the indexes such as those shown in Figure 7-12. During subsequent processing of the file, searching and maintenance of this index are also carried out by the access method and are completely transparent to the program that accesses the file. For example, a program can request a particular record by specifying its primary key value (as discussed in the previous paragraph). The access method (not the program) searches the indexes and delivers the requested record to the program data area.

To update a record in an ISAM file, the data subblock containing the record is read into main memory using either the sequential- or random-access mode. The record is updated, then written on top of the old record (thus, the new record replaces the old record).

Records to be deleted from an ISAM file are normally not physically removed (or erased) from the file immediately. Instead, a special delete character is placed in the first character position of each deleted record. This character is then used in later accesses to inform a program that the record has been logically dropped from the file.

Inserting new records into an ISAM file (or any sequential file) presents special problems. To maintain the records in key sequence, it might seem necessary to push all the records down beyond the point of insertion; this is not a practical solution, however. Instead, two techniques are used to handle insertions. With the first technique, some free space is left on each track (not shown in Figure 7-12). This free space will allow occasional insertions but cannot accommodate insertions of clusters of records (for example, many new product records).

With the second method, overflow areas (as illustrated in Figure 7-12) are reserved for records that overflow tracks in the prime area. Several tracks are usually reserved at the end of each cylinder for this purpose. Also, an independent overflow area may be reserved to receive records that overflow the cylinder overflow areas.

The method of handling overflows in ISAM is illustrated in Figure 7-13. First, record 176 was inserted into the file shown in Figure 7-12. To maintain key sequence, this record was inserted on track 1, replacing record 207, which was moved to the overflow track. A pointer was created from track 1, giving the address of the first overflow record for that track. (In reality, the pointer is placed in the track index, but we will not consider this technical detail.) Next, records numbered 254 and 270 were inserted into the file on track 2. The records they replaced (286 and 314) were moved to the

Figure 7-13
Managing overflows in ISAM

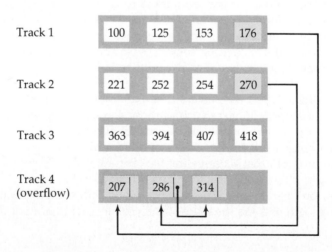

overflow track. These records are chained together, as shown by the arrow from record 286 to record 314. Thus, the records in the prime area are maintained in logical sequence by physical position, while the records in the overflow area are maintained in logical sequence by pointers.

Over time, the number of records in the overflow areas of an ISAM file will increase. As this occurs, the performance will decline, since more accesses are required on the average to retrieve each record. Thus, an ISAM file needs to be reorganized periodically. In reorganization, the entire file is reloaded and records in the overflow areas are moved to their proper location in the prime area. Also, the indexes are updated as necessary at this time.

ISAM Performance.   A major advantage of indexed sequential files is that they permit rapid sequential access, the mode used for sequential retrieval or updating. Since the records are in primary key sequence (or chained in an overflow area), an entire cylinder may be read without moving the access arm. The average access time for sequential processing is therefore equal to the average rotational delay, usually under 10 msec.

In comparison, the average time for random access to an ISAM file is relatively slow. Although the master index to a file is often moved to main memory when the file is opened, the lower levels of a large index normally reside on disk. Thus, two or three disk accesses are required to search the index for random retrieval of a record; this might be roughly 70-80 msec. Also, when the target track is searched, it may turn out that the search must continue to an overflow area.

Advantages and Disadvantages of ISAM   The major advantages of an ISAM organization are that the file can be processed in both sequential and random modes, records can be inserted in the middle of the file and processed either randomly or sequentially, and most vendors provide an access method that supports an indexed sequential organization.

The disadvantages of this file organization are that the file must be reorganized periodically to "clean up" overflow records and deleted records, random access to individual records is relatively slow, and the indexes are organized by hardware boundaries (tracks and cylinders). Because of this last item, when a file is transferred to a new disk volume (say with greater track capacity), the indexes must be completely reorganized.

Hardware-Independent Implementation (VSAM)

Virtual sequential access method (VSAM) is a more powerful and flexible access method than ISAM. It supports an indexed sequential organization with multilevel indexes that is similar in concept to ISAM. However, where ISAM organizes records (and therefore indexes) around tracks and cylinders, VSAM is free of these hardware boundaries.

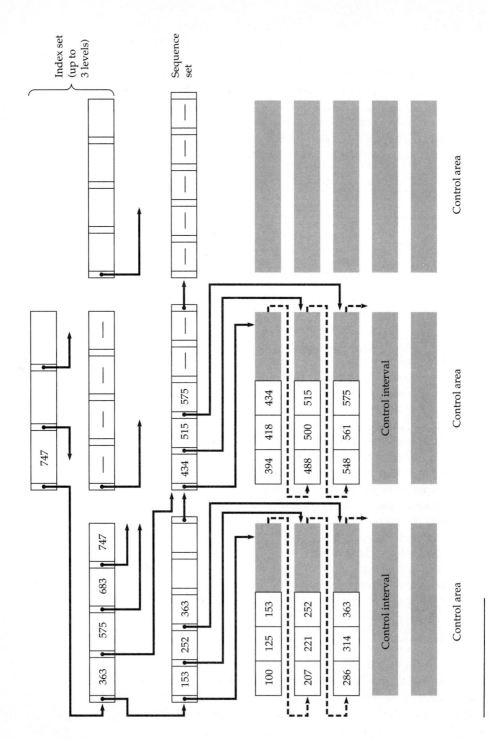

Figure 7-14
VSAM architecture

VSAM Architecture   The basic architecture of VSAM appears in Figure 7-14. In an ISAM file, the basic indexed group of records is the collection of records on a track. In a VSAM file, the basic indexed group is called a **control interval** (which is a virtual track). The size of a control interval is chosen by the file designer and may be less than, equal to, or greater than the length of a track. As tracks on a disk are grouped into cylinders, control intervals in VSAM are grouped into **control areas** (or virtual cylinders).

Figure 7-14 shows some of the product records loaded on a VSAM file. As with an ISAM file, the records are loaded in primary key sequence in the control intervals. Notice that space for insertion of new records is reserved automatically at the end of each control interval. This is called **distributed free space.** Also, some control intervals in each control area are left empty. The amount of empty space in each control interval and the number of empty control intervals in a control area are specified by the file designer.

The index structure in VSAM is similar to that in ISAM. As shown in Figure 7-14, the index is divided into two sections: the index set (up to three levels) and the sequence set. As with ISAM, locating a random record proceeds by starting with the highest level in the index set and progressively searching the index until the target control interval is identified. The control interval is then scanned to locate the desired record.

Record Insertions   The method of handling record insertions in VSAM is more refined (and efficient) than that in ISAM. When a new record is inserted, if the appropriate control interval is not full, the existing records are moved to the right by the access method and the new record is inserted in key sequence. This is illustrated in Figure 7-15a, where record 350 has been inserted into control interval 02. To make room for this new record, record 363 is moved back in the control interval.

Figure 7-15 also illustrates how insertions are managed when a control interval is full. Suppose we wish to insert record 240 into the file. This record should be placed in control interval 01, between records 221 and 252—however, control interval 01 is already full. Therefore, the access method (VSAM) performs a **control interval split.** About half the records in control interval 01 are placed into an empty control interval. In Figure 7-15b, records 252 and 263 are placed in control interval 03, while records 207, 221, and 240 remain in control interval 01. A new entry is also placed in the sequence set so this new control interval can be accessed. The dashed line pointers linking control intervals support rapid sequential processing of the records by avoiding the need to return to indexes once the control interval with the smallest key value is located.

Following many record insertions, a sequence set may become full; when this happens, it is no longer possible to perform another control interval split for further insertions. In this case, VSAM performs a **sequence set split,** allocating a new control area to the file. About half the records in the control area that has become full are moved to the new control area. The

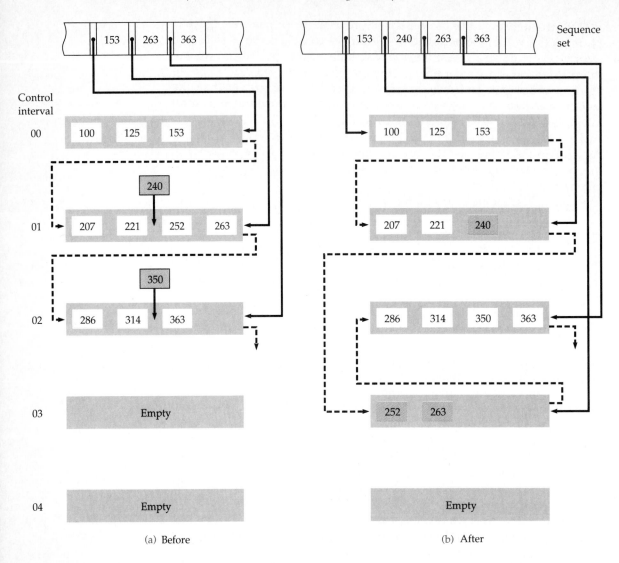

(a) Before   (b) After

Figure 7-15
Managing record
insertions in VSAM:
(a) before
(b) after

splitting of control intervals and sequence sets in an expanding VSAM file resembles the division of cells in a biological organism. No periodic reorganization of the file is required (unlike ISAM), since in essence the file is reorganized incrementally as splits occur. Deletion of records from a VSAM file may cause similar combining of control intervals and sequence sets. The rules that govern when a control interval overflows or underflows relate to the properties of B-trees (the basic data structure behind VSAM), which will be discussed in a section below.

Advantages of VSAM   VSAM offers three major advantages over ISAM. First, periodic file reorganization is not required since the file can grow indefinitely by the splitting process. Second, the file organization is independent of hardware characteristics. (Thus, a file can be moved to a different volume without restructuring the indexes.) And finally, some versions of VSAM support secondary keys and variable-length records.

B-Trees

The VSAM file organization is based on a tree data structure called a B-tree. The B, many people believe, stands for "balanced," meaning that all leaves are the same distance from the root. (For VSAM, *leaves* means the control intervals where the data records are located.) B-trees guarantee a predictable efficiency that many other types of trees do not. For example (according to Knuth, 1973, p. 476), with a B-tree of degree 199, any record in a file as large as 1,999,998 records can be retrieved in three accesses! Although hashing, to be discussed in the next section, may yield fewer accesses for random record retrieval, hashing does not support sequential retrieval and B-trees do. In addition to VSAM, many database management systems now use B-trees as the principal method for primary and secondary key access.

There are several varieties of B-trees, with the standard B-tree and the B+-tree being the most common. Since most B-tree implementations are of the B+-tree, it is this variety that we will define. See Comer, 1979, and Korth and Silberschatz, 1986, for detailed discussion and examples of issues of maintaining B-trees.

A **B+-tree of degree** *m* has the following properties:

1. Every node has between *m*/2 and *m* children (*m* is an integer greater than or equal to 3 and usually odd) except the root, which is not bound by the lower limit.

2. All leaves are at the same level (same depth from root).

3. A nonleaf node that has *n* children will contain $n - 1$ keys.

Figure 7-16 illustrates the general structure of nonleaf and leaf nodes in a B+-tree, and Figure 7-17 illustrates a B+-tree of degree 3 (which is very small, for illustrative purposes only) for the Product Master File of Pine Valley Furniture. As with any index, access for each retrieval or maintenance request begins at the root and works through the tree, taking branches associated with a comparison of the desired key with index entries. In a nonleaf node (these would be a sequence set or higher-level index node in VSAM; see Figure 7-16a), each pointer entry addresses the root of a subtree. The $n - 1$ keys in a nonleaf node divide the keys found in that subtree into *n* subsets or further subtrees. A search starts at the root and continues through one node at each level. If the desired key to retrieve, delete, or insert is greater than or equal to K_i and less than $K_{i + 1}$, then the search continues by accessing the root of the subtree pointed to by $P_{i + 1}$.

The processing at a leaf node (equivalent to a control interval in VSAM; see Figure 7-16b) is somewhat different. First, the pointers address record

Figure 7-16
B + tree node
structure:
(a) non-leaf node
(b) leaf node

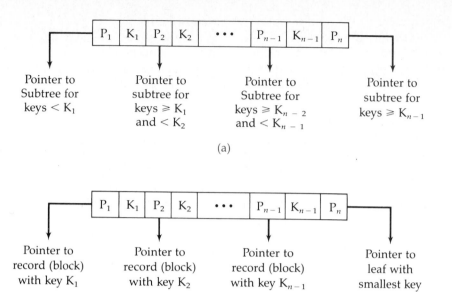

blocks (usually the case in a primary key index) or may reference individual records (usually the case in a secondary key index). Thus, pointers here are to real data, not index nodes. Note that, because of this fact, each key in nonleaf nodes is repeated in some leaf (see Figure 7-17). Second, the pointer P_n is an exception, in that it addresses the leaf with keys that follow directly in sequence. This permits rapid sequential processing without having to backtrack to nonleaf nodes. In fact, for sequential processing the accessing method could keep track of not only the root but also the address of the leaf with the lowest key, and sequential processing could start directly in the leaves. Since real data are referenced indirectly (that is, outside the index itself), then multiple B + -tree indexes can be maintained on the same data as long as index leaves reference individual data records. As with any index structure, the data records can be stored in any sequence (physical location) since the index maintains the desired sequence. Further, data may be stored without any (or with very few) empty record slots.

The reader may refer to Comer (1979) for an excellent discussion of the various special circumstances that occur when maintaining B + -trees. A discussion of these is not necessary here since the splitting and combining of leaves (control intervals) and nonleaves (sequence sets) will be performed *automatically* by either the operating system access method or the database management system. You, as a designer of a database, will choose on what attributes to create a B + -tree index, and you may have some control over the degree (bushiness) of the tree index. Obviously, you want to choose attributes for indexing that, in balance, save more time in rapid random and sequential retrieval than they cost in storage space and maintenance

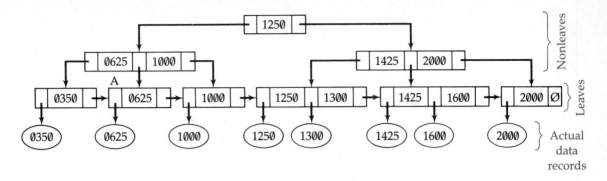

Figure 7-17
Example of a
B+-tree

expense. Higher-degree B+-trees are usually preferred, but the amount of buffer space in main memory available to an application program will limit the maximum size of a control interval and hence limit the tree's degree.

Review of Indexes and Trees

The preceding discussion of various index and tree data structures and file organizations has illustrated that they can permit rapid retrieval of data for both random and sequential processing. The examples shown here have all dealt with access to records within one file based on primary keys. The structures illustrated can easily be changed, however, to work with secondary keys. When tree structures are used to connect records in different files, another name is used—the hierarchical data model, which is introduced in Chapter 8.

HASHED FILES

In many on-line systems, the dominant mode of file access is random; that is, individual or a few records are sought based upon a primary or secondary key value. Typical of these are reservation systems (for example, airline, hotel, and car rental) and information retrieval systems (for example, library and stock market quotation). In these systems, both updating and retrieval are accomplished in the random mode, and there is rarely a need for sequential access to the data records.

In such applications, a **hashed file organization** is often preferred, an organization that provides rapid access to individual records, since no extra structures, such as indexes, are searched. The major disadvantage of this organization is that sequential processing is not convenient because the records are not stored in primary key sequence, nor are there any pointers to link records sequentially. However, this is not an important consideration for many on-line applications.

Figure 7-18
Major components of
hashed files
(Source: Severance
and Duhne 1976)

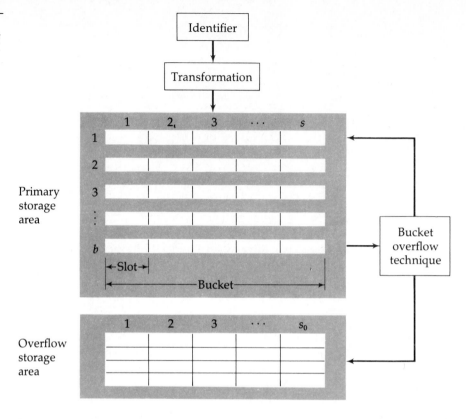

Hashed File Principles

The major features of hashed files are shown in Figure 7-18. The primary storage area is divided into many addressable locations, called **buckets.** Each bucket consists of one or more **slots** where records may be stored. An addressing algorithm transforms each record identifier into a relative address (or bucket number), and the record is stored in that bucket if there is an empty slot. If all slots in the bucket are full, then the record is stored in a bucket in an overflow area.

Hashing Routines   Records are assigned to buckets by a **hashing routine** or transformation, an algorithm that converts each primary key value into a relative disk address. Ideally, the hashing routine that is chosen should distribute the records as uniformly as possible over the address space to be used. This provides two important benefits. First, collisions are reduced (a **collision** is the assignment of two or more records to the same bucket), and second, file space is utilized as efficiently as possible.

Of the many hashing algorithms that have been proposed (see Martin, 1977, for a summary), the one that consistently performs best under most

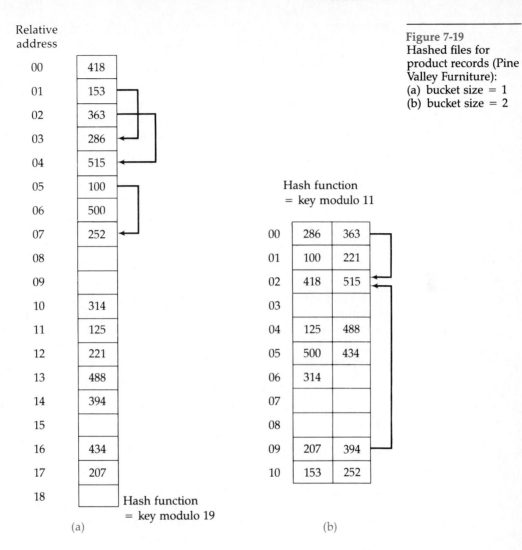

Figure 7-19
Hashed files for product records (Pine Valley Furniture):
(a) bucket size = 1
(b) bucket size = 2

conditions is the **division/remainder method.** The steps used in this procedure are as follows:

1. Determine the number of buckets to be allocated to the file.
2. Select a prime number that is approximately equal to this number.
3. Divide each primary key value by the prime number.
4. Use the remainder as the relative bucket address.

Figure 7-19 shows the results of applying this hashing routine to the product file of Table 7-3. In part (a) of this figure, a bucket size of 1 is used, while in part (b) the bucket size (or record-blocking factor) is 2. To simplify the illustration, only the primary key values (rather than the complete records) are shown in each bucket.

Since there are 15 product records (that is, no more than 15 exist at any one time), with a bucket size of 1 at least 15 buckets will be required. In designing a hashed file, it is best to allow some free space. In this example, 19 buckets (numbered 00 to 18) are allocated, which results in a file-load factor of 15/19, or about 80%. The hashing routine consists of dividing each product number by 19 (a prime number) to generate the address. Note that with this procedure the range of addresses possible is zero up to the divisor minus 1.

The first product number (100) is divided by 19, with the following result:

$$
\begin{array}{r}
5 \\
19\overline{)100} \\
95 \\
\hline
5
\end{array}
$$

Since the remainder is 5, this record is stored in bucket 05. Next, this procedure places record 125 in bucket 11 and record 153 in bucket 01 and continues until we reach 252. When 252 is divided by 19, the remainder is 5. Since bucket 05 is already full, we have our first collision. A common procedure is to place a record that will not fit in its "home" address into the next available empty bucket (this is called **open** or **sequential overflow**). In this case, record 252 could be placed in bucket 06. However, this might displace another record (yet to be loaded) whose hashed address is 06. To avoid this, record 252 is set aside until all other records have been loaded into their home address.

The result of loading this file is shown in Figure 7-19a. The records were loaded in two passes. In the first pass, all records that fit in their home addresses were stored. In the second pass, the records that created collisions in the first pass were stored in the first available address following their home address. Although the hashing routine distributed the records fairly uniformly throughout the file, there were three collisions: records 252, 286, and 515. For each of these displaced records, a pointer is placed in the home bucket to indicate its overflow location—a technique called **chained overflow.**

In Figure 7-19b, a hashed file with a bucket capacity of 2 is shown for the same product records. In this case, 11 buckets (numbered 00 to 10) were used. Each product number was hashed by dividing by the prime number 11 and saving the remainder. As in the previous example, the records were loaded in two passes. Two collisions resulted: for records 418 and 515. Since the home address for record 515 is bucket 09, the search for an available space for this record resulted in the record being placed in bucket 02 (in this case, the search "spilled over" to the beginning of the file).

To retrieve a record in a hashed file, the hashing algorithm is applied to the primary key value to calculate the relative bucket address. If the record is located at its home address, only one disk access is required; if it is in an overflow area, two (or more) accesses are required. Referring to Figure 7-19a, 12 of the records will require one disk access, while the other 3 records will require two accesses. Assuming that the frequency of accesses to these records is equal, the **average search length** (or number of accesses per record) is 1.2, computed as follows:

$$\text{Average search length} = \frac{(12 \times 1) + (3 \times 2)}{15} = 1.2$$

This might represent about 30 msec for the typical hard disk drive.

Hashed File Design

Managing overflows is the most complex part of the hashed file organization. Fortunately, as with the management of most popular data structure, the operating system hashing access method or database management system hashing routine manages this for our application programs. We as programmers simply need to know that collisions can occur, so retrieval time can be slowed as the file develops a high load factor. One control that may exist for some applications is the sequence in which records are loaded into the hash file. As discussed above, it is best to load the initial set of records in two passes. In the first pass, all the records that can fit into their home addresses are loaded. Then in the second pass, the synonyms are placed by the overflow technique to minimize the number of additional accesses. A discussion of various "tricks" to minimize the overflow handling effort is beyond our needs in this text.

In designing hashed files, use of any of the following three processes (which may be under the control of the database developer) will reduce collisions and minimize the average search length:

1. Use a hashing routine that distributes the records as evenly as possible over the available address space (the division/remainder method should normally be used).

2. Select a low load factor (assign more disk capacity than is required for the file).

3. Use a larger bucket capacity (blocking factor).

Load Factor   The **load factor** is the percentage of space allocated to the file that is taken up by records in the file. For example, the load factor in the file shown in Figure 7-19b is 15/22, or about 68%.

A low load factor reduces the number of records that overflow their home addresses, which, in turn, reduces the average search length. In practice, load factors between 50% and 80% should normally be used. If the file is expected to grow, then a lower load factor should be used initially, since it will increase as insertions occur.

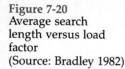

Figure 7-20
Average search
length versus load
factor
(Source: Bradley 1982)

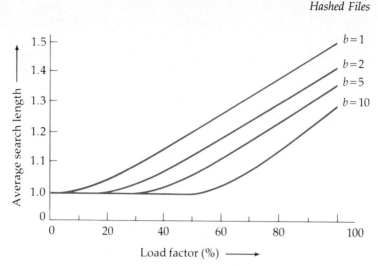

Hashed Files

Bucket Capacity   Increasing the bucket capacity will also reduce the number of overflows and hence the average search length. This is true because with a bucket capacity greater than 1, some collisions can occur before overflow becomes necessary. Unfortunately, the bucket capacity, as was the control interval size for VSAM, is limited by the available buffer space in main memory to hold the contents of a block.

Given the load factor and bucket capacity, we can use formulas or curves to estimate the average search length. The curves shown in Figure 7-20 show the average search length versus load factor for bucket sizes of 1, 2, 5, and 10 (chained overflow is assumed). For a load factor of 100% and a bucket capacity of 1, the average search length is about 1.5. Notice that for a given load factor (say 80%), we can reduce the average search length by increasing the bucket capacity.

Advantages and Disadvantages of Hashed Files

Hashed files offer two major advantages over indexed sequential organizations: Random access is faster (nearly three times as fast as ISAM), and insertions and deletions are more easily handled.

However, hashed files have four disadvantages: Sequential access is impractical; disk space is not as efficiently utilized (because of lower load factors); periodic reorganization is required; and the programming task may be more complex (not true when a DBMS is used).

SUMMARY

This chapter presented a review of the basic principles and methods of data structures and file organizations. The purpose was to provide the groundwork for understanding physical database structures in later chapters, beginning with Chapter 8.

Throughout the chapter, we have assumed the use of magnetic disk storage devices. Vendor-supplied access methods insulate the user from many of these hardware details. They allow us to visualize a file as a series of storage locations, each of which can hold one or more records and can be addressed by specifying its location from the beginning of the file. The access method or file organization translates this relative address to the necessary hardware address and manages other hardware-dependent details.

Three basic file organizations are frequently used: sequential, indexed sequential, and direct (hashed). Indexed sequential organizations (the most common) are used when both sequential and random access to a file are required. Sequential file organizations are used primarily in making backup copies of databases. Direct files with hashed addressing are frequently employed in on-line database applications when fast random access to records is required for updating and retrieval.

We showed that each data structure and file organization exhibits its own performance. Some structures manage small sets of data better than large; other structures provide very rapid data retrieval but are costly to maintain. A database designer must carefully match the characteristics of the data processing to be performed (sequential processing, random record retrieval, quantity of record insertions and deletions, and so on) with an appropriate, efficient data structure. Most of the time this matching is done by selecting operating system access methods and database management systems that best satisfy the data processing requirement.

The next chapter utilizes these data structures to discuss different implementation and physical database design choices.

Chapter Review

REVIEW QUESTIONS

1. Give concise definitions for each of the following terms:
   a. null pointer
   b. division hashing
   c. buffer
   d. multiprogramming
   e. virtual storage
   f. hashing routine
   g. control interval
   h. bucket
   i. collision
   j. load factor
   k. data structure
   l. pointer

m. data indirect access
n. relative pointer
o. home address
p. queue
q. bidirectional chain

r. multilist data structure
s. inverted list
t. tree
u. root
v. B+-tree

2. Contrast the following terms:
   a. physical address; relative address
   b. ISAM; VSAM

3. Prepare a table showing the major advantages of each of the following:
   a. sequential file organization
   b. indexed sequential file organization
   c. hashed file organization

4. Give two examples (other than those presented in the text) of everyday occurrences of indexed sequential files.

5. List and explain at least three criteria that could be used to measure the efficiency of data structures.

6. Summarize the relative advantages and disadvantages of the three types of pointers.

7. Discuss the relative advantages and disadvantages of multilist and inverted list structures for managing multiple associations and answering multiple-qualification questions.

8. Give at least one example of each type of secondary key from a situation of your choice (other than Pine Valley Furniture).

9. Explain why a B+-tree is such an appealing data structure.

10. Discuss how bidirectional pointers can make chain maintenance simpler.

11. What is the purpose of "dummy" nodes at the front and end of a list data structure?

12. What factors should be considered when selecting a file organization for a particular database processing application?

13. Outline the advantages of blocked records compared to unblocked records.

14. List the hazards of chain data structures.

15. Compare the capabilities and performance of VSAM to those of hashed file organization.

16. What can the designer of a hashed file organization do to improve the performance if accesses are taking too long?

PROBLEMS AND EXERCISES

1. Match the following terms with the most appropriate definition:

_____ B+-tree

_____ stack

_____ sorted list

a. file management subprogram

b. field used to reference a piece of data

_____ pointer
_____ branching factor
_____ depth
_____ data indirect
_____ chain
_____ inverted index
_____ prime area
_____ overflow
_____ access method
_____ collision

c. two records hash to the same bucket

d. series of pointer sequential connections

e. data stored outside of home address

f. insertions may occur anywhere in the list

g. data structure to access data by content, not location

h. maximum number of children per parent

i. LIFO data structure

j. number of levels between root and leaf

k. data structure used in VSAM

l. placement of data separate from mechanism to connect data

m. contains data records and track index

2. Redraw Figure 3-11 to show the use of single directional pointers (chains) to manage the associations in this figure. Show the additional "data about data" (pointers) required in each record type.

3. Consider the following questions processed using the Pine Valley Furniture database depicted in Figure 3-11:
   a. List all customers with an order due for delivery today.
   b. Count the number of times PRODUCT# 1425 has been ordered in the past year.
   c. List the price of each of the products with a DESCRIPTION of TABLE (Pine Valley makes more varieties of tables than all other types of products combined!). Identify the secondary keys used in these queries and for each, explain whether an inverted index would be advantageous.

4. Obtain a copy of Solomon and Bickel (1986) and review the self-assessment questions on file processing as a way to combine your understanding of material in Chapter 7.

5. Redraw the VSAM file in Figure 7-15b to show the effect of inserting the following records:
   a. primary key value 248
   b. primary key value 337

6. Redraw the ISAM file in Figure 7-13 to show the effect of inserting the following records (create an additional overflow track if necessary):
   a. primary key value 215
   b. primary key value 328

7. The prime number 997 will be used as a divisor in a hashing routine. What addresses will be generated for records with the following key values: 762, 20439, 618472?

8. Redraw the hashed file in Figure 7-19a to show the effect of inserting the following records:
   a. primary key value 170
   b. primary key value 695
   c. primary key value 40

9. Refer to the ISAM file shown in Figure 7-12. On what cylinder and track are each of the following records located?
   a. product 573
   b. product 685

REFERENCES

Bradley, J. 1982. *File and Data Base Techniques*. New York: Holt, Rinehart & Winston.

Comer, D. 1979. "The Ubiquitous B-tree." *ACM Computing Surveys* 11 (June), 121-137.

Knuth, D. 1973. *The Art of Computer Programming*. Vol. 3: *Sorting and Searching*. Reading, Mass.: Addison-Wesley.

Korth, H. F., and A. Silberschatz. 1986. *Database System Concepts*. New York: McGraw-Hill.

Kull, D. 1986. "Anatomy of a 4GL Disaster." *Computer Decisions* (February 11), 58–65.

Martin, J. 1977. *Computer Data Base Organization*. 2nd ed. Englewood Cliffs, N.J.: Prentice-Hall.

O'Leary, T. J., and B. K. Williams. 1985. *Computers and Information Processing with Business Applications*. Menlo Park, Calif.: Benjamin/Cummings.

Severance, D. G. 1974. "Identifier Search Mechanisms: A Survey and Generalized Model." *ACM Computing Surveys* 6 (Sept.), 175-194.

Severance, D., and R. Duhne. 1976. "A Practitioner's Guide to Addressing Algorithms." *Communications of the ACM* 19 (June), 314-326.

Solomon, M. K., and R. W. Bickel. 1986. "Self-Assessment Procedure XV." *Communications of the ACM* 29 (Aug.), 745-750.

CHAPTER 8

Implementation and Physical Design

INTRODUCTION

The logical data model described in Chapter 6 is a model of the organization and its data, completely independent of any database management system or any other software or hardware considerations. This model must be refined so that it can be implemented on the DBMS used by the organization.

The refinement of the logical data model often occurs in two stages: implementation design and physical design. **Implementation design** is concerned with mapping the conceptual data model from Chapter 6 into logical database structures such as hierarchical, network, or relational data models. **Physical design** is concerned with selecting file organizations and access methods, deciding on the use of indexes, and related factors.

Implementation design and physical design are the last steps in the database design process (see Figure 5-2). They must be performed carefully, since they affect performance, integrity, security, and a number of other factors that have a direct impact on users. Generally, these steps are performed by different persons than those who performed previous design tasks, and the objectives are different. Requirements definition and conceptual database design are performed by database analysts and data administrators who understand user needs and the data modeling process.

Implementation and physical design are performed by technical persons who understand the details of the DBMS and the organization's computing environment. While the major objective of conceptual design is to accurately model an organization's data, the major objective of implementation and physical design is to ensure adequate performance and security of that data.

IMPLEMENTATION DESIGN

As shown in Figure 8-1, there are three major inputs to implementation design:

1. **The conceptual data model.** This model, which was described in Chapter 6, is normally expressed in the form of an E-R diagram or as a set of normalized relations (a number of other representations such as semantic data models or object-oriented representation can also be used).
2. **Database management system (DBMS) characteristics.** These will be used for the DBMS, to implement the conceptual data model.
3. **User processing requirements.** These include usage patterns, response time requirements, and backup and security parameters.

The output from implementation design is a set of **logical database structures** for a target DBMS.

HIERARCHICAL AND NETWORK MODELS

In performing implementation design, we map the conceptual (or logical) data model to a data model that can be processed by a contemporary DBMS.

Figure 8-1
Implementation
design process

This is usually a hierarchical, network, or relational data model (although other models such as the object-oriented data model are also becoming more important). Because of its importance, we described the relational

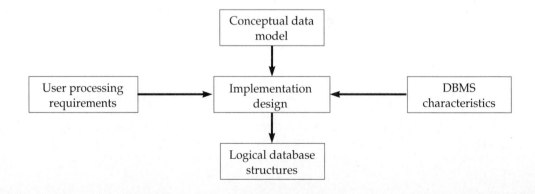

data model throughout the beginning chapters of this text (a formal definition is provided in Chapter 3). Also, we described how to transform an E-R diagram to relations in Chapter 6. In this section we introduce the hierarchical and network data models and in the next section describe how to map (or transform) an E-R diagram to each of these models. Complete descriptions of the hierarchical and network data models are provided in Chapters 10 and 11, respectively.

Hierarchical Data Model

A hierarchy is a familiar structure. Organizations are usually viewed as a hierarchy of positions and authority; computer programs can be viewed as a hierarchy of control and operating modules; and various taxonomies of animal and plant life view elements in a hierarchical set of relationships. Today, the hierarchical data model is used exclusively with hierarchical database management systems; since such systems are, in general, being phased out, we will review this model only briefly.

The **hierarchical data model** represents data as a set of nested one-to-many relationships (one-to-one relationships are also permitted). For example, Figure 8-2 shows a hierarchical database structure for Pine Valley Furniture Company. The record type CUSTOMER "owns" the record type ORDER. CUSTOMER is referred to as the **parent** in this relationship, while ORDER is the **child**. In turn, ORDER is the parent of two record types: ORDERLINE and SHIPMENT. The single-headed arrow in this diagram denotes a one-to-many relationship (there is no need to use a more complicated notation, since each relationship in a hierarchy is presumed to be 1:M).

Following are the rules that govern a hierarchical data structure:

1. A parent record type may "own" an arbitrary number of child record types (for example, in Figure 8-2 ORDER owns both ORDERLINE and SHIPMENT).

2. No single occurrence of a record type may have more than one parent record type (or occurrence) in the hierarchy.

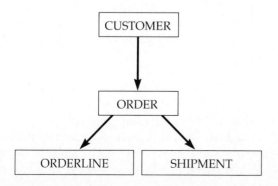

Figure 8-2
Example of hierarchical data model

Figure 8-3
Resolving multiple
parentage

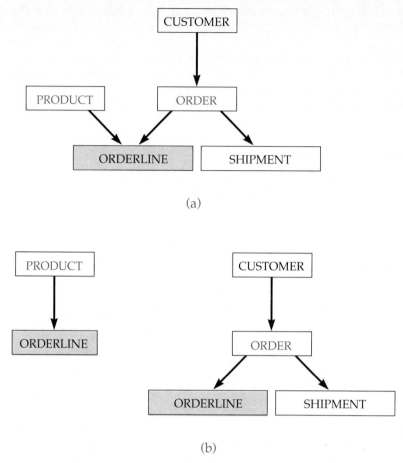

(a)

(b)

The second rule is an obvious limitation of hierarchical data structures. For example, as shown in Figure 8-3a, ORDERLINE has two "natural" parents: PRODUCT and ORDER. This violates the single-parent rule of hierarchical structures.

As shown in Figure 8-3b, we can resolve the problem of multiple parentage by splitting the relation in Figure 8-3a into two hierarchical data structures. This solution produces redundancy since ORDERLINE is now repeated under PRODUCT and ORDER. Some hierarchical implementations (such as the one described in Chapter 10) allow the designer to implement the structure shown in Figure 8-3a without redundancy (although some processing overhead is required).

Network Data Model

It was stated in the previous section that the single-parent rule of the hierarchical data model forces redundant and excessive data and structure. When this rule may be violated, we can create a network data model and further eliminate redundancy. The network model permits as much or as little structure as is desired. We can even create a hierarchy (a special case of a network) if that is what is needed. As with the hierarchical data model, if a certain relationship is not *explicitly* included in the database definition, then it cannot be used by a DBMS in processing a database.

An example of a network data model was shown earlier in Figure 8-3a, in which the ORDERLINE record type has two parent record types: PRODUCT and ORDER. In general, a record type may have an arbitrary number of parents in the network data model.

The **simple network data model** supports 1:N (but not M:N) relationships (all the relationships in Figure 8-3a are 1:N). This is the most common implementation of the network data model (we discuss this model in Chapter 11). The **complex network data model** supports M:N (as well as 1:N) relationships. A few DBMS products support the complex network data model.

In the following sections, we illustrate mapping the conceptual data model first to a hierarchical, then network data model. We use the conceptual data model for Mountain View Community Hospital (Figure 8-4) to illustrate this process. This mapping is relatively straightforward since the E-R diagram shown in the figure already resembles a network data model. However, this model does contain two M:N relationships (Attends-To and Is-Billed-For) that must be transformed to 1:N relationships. If this transformation results in multiple parents for a given record type, the multiple parentage must be resolved in the hierarchical data model.

Mapping to a Network Model

The most common implementation of the network model is the CODASYL model (described in Chapter 11). Assuming that this model is to be used, the following steps are usually required:

1. Define record types and associations
2. Define sets (owner-member relationships)
3. Eliminate redundant keys (if unneeded)
4. Define record access strategies

Figure 8-5 shows the result of transforming the conceptual data model (Figure 8-4) to a network data model. Following is a brief description of each of the above steps.

Defining Record Types   Each entity in the conceptual data model becomes a CODASYL record type. The primary keys for each record type are underlined (nonkey data are omitted for simplicity). Also, each many-to-many relationship is transformed to a record type. In Figure 8-5 there are two such record types: TREATMENT (which is derived from the Attends-To relationship) and CHARGES (which is derived from the Is-Billed-For relationship). This transformation is similar to that for the relational model described in Chapter 6.

Figure 8-4
Conceptual data
model

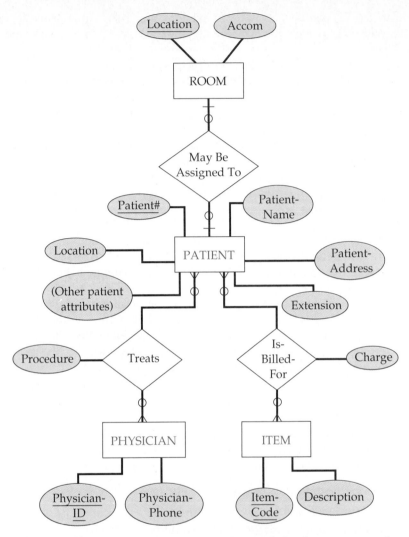

In the CODASYL model, a one-to-many association between record types is usually represented by an arrow with a single head. We use this convention in Figure 8-5: for example, there is a 1:M association from PATIENT to TREATMENT.

There is no provision in the CODASYL model to enforce the optional and mandatory characteristics of associations, which appear in the conceptual (or logical) data model. Instead, these constraints must be enforced through the application programs that access the database.

Defining Sets   The set is the basic building block in the CODASYL model. A **set** is a one-to-many association between two record types, where the first record type is called the **owner** and the second record type is called the **member**. Each set type is given a unique name.

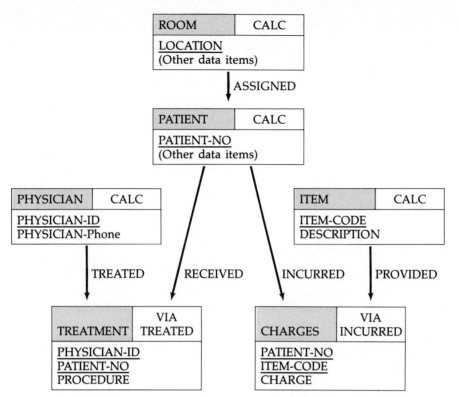

Figure 8-5
Network data model

In mapping to a network data model, we define a set for each 1:M association in the logical data model. For example, in Figure 8-5 the 1:M association between PHYSICIAN and TREATMENT is defined as a CODA-SYL set with the name TREATED. PHYSICIAN is the owner record type for this association, while TREATMENT is the member record type. For each occurrence of a PHYSICIAN record type, there may be zero, one, or more than one occurrence of a TREATMENT record type.

In the logical data model (Figure 8-4), the association from ROOM to PATIENT is optional. This means that each bed location is either assigned to a patient or is unassigned. In the CODASYL model, there is no provision for directly enforcing only one patient per location; this will have to be handled by the application program for room assignment.

Eliminating Redundant Keys In the logical data model, composite primary keys and foreign keys are normally redundant. For example, in Figure 8-5 the composite key for CHARGES is (Patient-No, Item-Code). The Patient-No data item is contained in the parent PATIENT record type, while Item-Code is contained in the parent ITEM record type. When mapping to a CODASYL data model, these duplicate keys are candidates for elimination because the associations they imply are represented by the CODASYL sets.

For example, the composite key (Patient-No, Item-Code) can be eliminated from the CHARGES record type.

Whether keys should in fact be eliminated (to avoid redundancy) is a design decision. In general, they should *not* be eliminated if either of the following two conditions holds:

1. The key in question is required for direct access to a record (for example, the composite key (Patient-No, Item-Code) could be used for direct access to CHARGES records if this is a requirement).

2. The key in question is normally required for reference purposes and if removed will often necessitate referencing the owner record occurrence.

To illustrate the second situation, suppose that in examining an occurrence of the CHARGES record, we normally need to identify the Patient-No. If Patient-No were removed from the CHARGES record type, we would have to reference a PATIENT record occurrence (owner record) to determine this information.

In summary, deciding whether or not to eliminate keys requires a trade-off between redundancy and performance. The designers must consider the anticipated usage patterns to evaluate each individual case. In Figure 8-5, we have retained the redundant data items so that they can be used for reference purposes.

Defining Record Access Strategies   The last major step in mapping to a network model is to define the basic techniques to be used to access occurrences to each record type in the model. Although there are many variations, there are two basic record access strategies in the CODASYL model:

1. **CALC.** We access records directly by supplying a primary key value.

2. **VIA.** We access records through a set relationship; that is, we first access an owner record occurrence (often using CALC), and then we access each set member occurrence for that owner. VIA results in a *physical* clustering of records by the owner.

The access strategies to be used depend on the way data will be accessed by various users and their applications. In Figure 8-5, notice that four of the record types are accessed directly in CALC mode: ROOM, PATIENT, PHYSICIAN, and ITEM. That is, an instance of each of these records can be accessed by supplying a primary key value. The other two record types (CHARGES and TREATMENT) are accessed VIA set relationships. TREATMENT is normally accessed by means of the TREATED relationship, while CHARGES is accessed primarily by means of the INCURRED relationship.

The VIA clause defines the primary access path to records, but records can also be accessed through secondary access paths. For example, CHARGES records can be accessed using the PROVIDED as well as the INCURRED set relationship. However, secondary access paths are nearly always slower and less efficient. We describe the details of various CODASYL access strategies in much more detail in Chapter 11.

Ideally, record access strategies would not be defined during implementation design but during physical design. By defining these strategies during implementation design, we lose some data independence. Thus, if we later decide to change the access strategy for a particular record type (say, from VIA to CALC), we will have to alter the data model. What is worse, changing the data model often requires that application programs be modified, since application logic often varies with the access strategies that are used.

In essence, the CODASYL approach to database implementation provides efficient, rapid access, provided that predefined access paths are used. However, the CODASYL approach is somewhat less flexible and therefore more resistant to change than some other models (especially the relational model).

Mapping to a Hierarchical Model

In discussing the hierarchical and network models earlier in this chapter, we noted that the models are similar, except that the hierarchical model does not permit multiple parentage. Therefore, mapping to a hierarchical model may be performed in two stages:

1. Map the conceptual model to a network model (as described above).

2. Map the network model to a hierarchical model by introducing redundancy as needed to resolve multiple parentage and to provide ease of access to the data.

An initial transformation of the network data model, resulting in three hierarchical structures (with some redundancy), is shown in Figure 8-6a. These are true hierarchical models, since there is no multiple parentage. However, with the hierarchical data model it is necessary to access all data by starting at the "root node" or top of the hierarchy (specific implementations often permit more flexible access). Thus, in the model in Figure 8-6a, to access Patient, Treatment, or Charges data it would be necessary to start with a Room reference, which would undoubtedly be quite awkward. To eliminate this restriction, it may be necessary to decompose the hierarchy into the four structures shown in Figure 8-6b. Notice that this solution introduces further redundancy (since the PATIENT record type appears two times). In using the hierarchical data model, designers must make numerous trade-offs such as this to arrive at an acceptable solution. We describe an implementation of the hierarchical data model in detail in Chapter 10.

PHYSICAL DATABASE DESIGN

Physical design is the last stage of the database design process (see Figure 5-1). **Physical database design** is the process of mapping the logical database structures developed in previous stages into an internal model (or set of physical database structures). The major objective of physical database design is to implement the database design as a set of stored records and

Figure 8-6
Hierarchical data structure

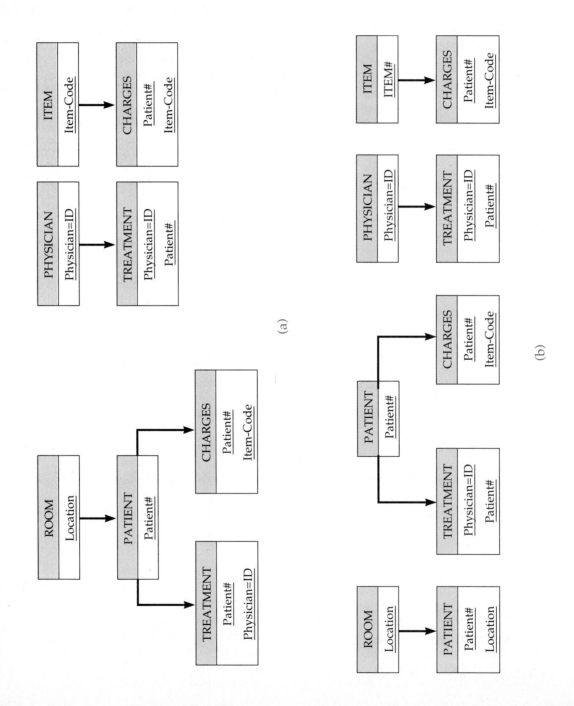

files that will provide adequate performance and ensure database integrity, security, and recoverability.

There are three major inputs to physical database design:

1. Logical database structures that were developed during logical design and implementation design, normally expressed as hierarchical, network, and/or relational data models.

2. User processing requirements that were identified during requirements definition, including size and frequency of use of the database and requirements for each of the following: response times, security, backup, recovery, and retention of data.

3. Characteristics of the database management system (DBMS) and other components of the computer operating environment.

The steps that are required for physical database design depend on a number of factors: the nature of the target DBMS, characteristics of the organization's computing environment, extent of usage of distributed processing and data communications, types of organizational applications, and so on. In the following sections we describe the typical components of physical database design:

1. Data volume and usage analysis
2. Data distribution strategy
3. Stored record design
4. Record clustering
5. Index selection

Physical database design must be performed carefully, since the decisions made during this stage have a major impact on data accessibility, response times, security, user friendliness, and similar factors.

Data Volume and Usage Analysis

The first step in physical database design is to estimate the size (or volume) and the usage patterns of the database. Estimates of database size are used to select physical storage devices and estimate the costs of storage. Estimates of usage paths or patterns are used to select file organizations and access methods, to plan for the use of indexes, and to plan a strategy for data distribution.

Data Volume Analysis for Mountain View Community Hospital   A simplified picture of the logical data model for Mountain View Community Hospital is shown in Figure 8-7. Each entity is represented by a rectangle, but the attributes have been omitted. Inside each rectangle is a number representing the estimated average volume for that entity. For example, it is estimated that an average of 1,000 Patient entities must be accommodated in the database at any one time. The numbers adjacent to the arrowheads are estimates of the average number of a given entity type associated with

Figure 8-7
Logical data model
with volumes and
ratios

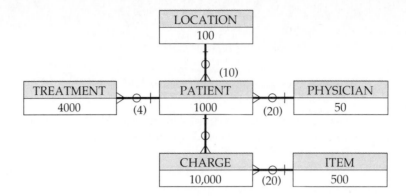

a related entity type. For example, Figure 8-7 indicates that there is an average of ten Charges associated with each Patient at any given time.

The database design team at Mountain View Community Hospital made the estimates in consultation with users. Since there are 100 beds at the hospital, the maximum number of admitted patients at any one time is limited to 100. However, the accounting staff indicated that the records for an average patient would probably be kept active for about 30 days. Since the average length of stay for a patient is 3 days, the total number of active patient records is expected to be 100 × 30/3, or 1,000. After an average period of 30 days, a PATIENT record would be archived.

Further discussions with the hospital accounting staff revealed that each patient incurs an average of Ten Charges during a hospitalization. Thus, the number of Charge entities is expected to be 10 × 1,000, or 10,000. Also, there are 500 separate Items that may appear on a patient's bill. Thus, the average number of Charges outstanding for a given Item is 10,000/500, or 20, as shown in Figure 8-7.

The design team also conferred with the medical staff and discovered that each patient receives an average of 4 treatments. Thus, the average number of Treatment entities in the database is 4 x 1,000, or 4,000.

Data Usage Analysis for Mountain View Community Hospital   In data usage analysis, the analyst identifies the major transactions and processes required against the database. Each is then analyzed to determine the access paths used and the estimated frequency of use. When all transactions have been analyzed, the composite load map is prepared, showing the total usage of access paths on the conceptual model.

At Mountain View Community Hospital, a systems analyst (Mr. Thomas) was assigned to work with the design team in analyzing user transactions. The data administrator felt that there were three advantages in having an applications specialist assist the design team during this phase of the study. First, the systems analyst could assist the team in identifying access paths for each transaction. Second, the information developed during this phase

Figure 8-8
Analysis of the
transaction create
patient bill

TRANSACTION ANALYSIS FORM

TRANSACTION# __MVCH-4_____ DATE __4/12/9X____
TRANSACTION NAME __CREATE PATIENT BILL_____
TRANSACTION VOLUME:
AVERAGE ____2/HR._____ PEAK ___10/HR.____

TRANSACTION MAP:

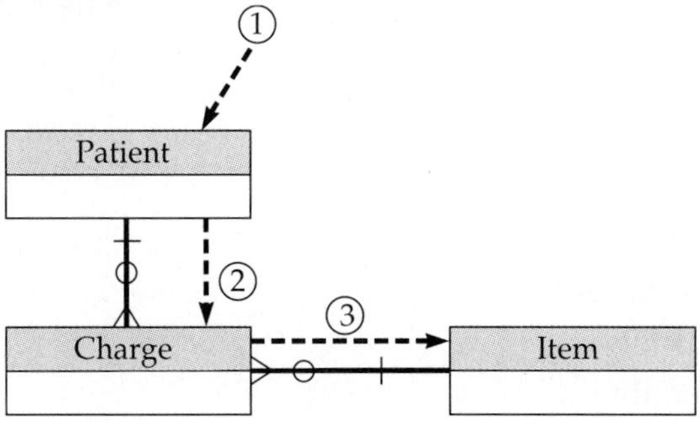

#	NAME	TYPE OF ACCESS	NO. OF REFERENCES	
			PER TRAN.	PER PERIOD
1	ENTRY-PATIENT	R	1	10
2	PATIENT-CHARGE	R	10	100
3	CHARGE-ITEM	R	10	100
	TOTAL REFERENCES		21	210

would be a starting point for designing transaction processing programs. And finally, having a systems analyst work with the design team would foster cooperation between the database group and the rest of the information systems organization.

The database design team used a form for analyzing each transaction at the hospital. Figure 8-8 shows how this form is used to analyze the transaction Create Patient Bill, which causes a PATIENT record to be read, along with the detail of patient charges, and also causes a patient bill to be printed. After talking with persons in accounting, the analysts estimated an average transaction volume of two per hour and a peak volume of ten per hour.

The number of logical references per transaction and per period are recorded on the form. Create Patient Bill requires only one Patient reference per transaction, which, at peak volume, translates to ten references per hour. Each Patient has an average of ten Charges. Therefore, the average number of times the Patient-Charge path is used per transaction is ten; this translates to a peak volume of 10 × 10, or 100 per hour. Since the Charge-Item path is traversed once for each Charge, this also results in a peak usage of 100 per hour. The analysts chose to use peak volumes to estimate references per period, since this would measure the maximum load on the database.

Transaction Map   In the middle of Figure 8-8 is a transaction map that shows the sequence of logical database accesses that is required for Create Patient Bill. The dashed line on this map shows the access path for this transaction: The entry point is at the Patient entity; then the path goes to the entity Charge; then it proceeds from each Charge to Item to pick up the description for that Charge.

A detailed analysis of each step in the access path is entered at the bottom of the form. The type of access to each entity is recorded using the following codes:

R: read an entity

I: insert a new entity

U: update an entity

D: delete an entity

For the Create Patient Bill transaction, each access is coded with an R, since this transaction requires read only.

Composite Usage Map   There are many other transactions for the database in addition to Create Patient Bill—for example, Record New Treatment, Record New Patient Charge, and Display Patient Data. When all these transactions have been analyzed, the analysts can combine the data and display them in the form of a composite usage map. A sample composite usage map for Mountain View Community Hospital is shown in Figure 8-9. The number in each rectangle shows the estimated number of entities of that type (for example, 1,000 patients). The number at the head of each dashed arrow is an estimate of the total number of references on a given access path at a peak volume. For example, the number of references to the entity Treatment from the entity Patient is estimated at 75 per hour. Also, the number of references to Patient from outside the model is estimated at 50 per hour.

The composite usage map is a concise reference to the estimated volume and usage of data in the database. It provides a basis for the remaining steps of physical database design, during which the analysts must design storage structures and access strategies to optimize performance.

We have described data volume and usage analysis as a component of physical database design, since it is most closely related to that design phase. However, when a hierarchical or network data model is to be used, at least a preliminary data volume and usage analysis should be performed *before* implementation design, since the products of data volume and usage

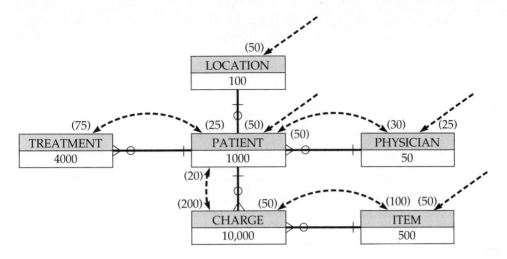

Figure 8-9
Composite usage
map

analysis (especially the composite usage map of Figure 8-9) can help the analysts make better implementation decisions.

Data Distribution Strategy

Many organizations today have distributed computing networks. For these organizations, a significant problem in physical database design is deciding at which nodes (or sites) in the network to physically locate the data. There are four basic data distribution strategies:

1. **Centralized.** All data are located at a single site. Although this simplifies the implementation, there are at least three disadvantages: (a) Data are not readily accessible to users at remote sites, (b) data communication costs may be high, and (c) the database system fails totally when the central system fails.

2. **Partitioned.** With this approach, the database is divided into disjoint (nonoverlapping) partitions. Each partition (also called a **fragment**) is assigned to a particular site. The major advantage of this approach is that data is moved closer to local users and so is more accessible.

3. **Replicated.** With this approach, a full copy of the database is assigned to more than one site in the network. This maximizes local access to data but creates update problems, since each database change must be reliably processed at all of the sites.

4. **Hybrid.** With this strategy, the database is partitioned into critical and noncritical fragments. Noncritical fragments are stored at only one site, while critical fragments are stored at multiple sites.

When all of the possible variations are considered, the problem of distributing data in a network is quite complex. In this chapter we discuss a relatively simple case of data distribution. An extended description of distributed database management is presented in Chapter 15.

An Example of Data Distribution   Hy-Tek Corporation manufactures a line of electronic products that are distributed through nationwide marketing channels. The company has five principal manufacturing locations, which are linked by a distributed processing network, a schematic of which is shown in Figure 8-10. Each of the five sites (labeled S1, S2, and so on) has a computer that is linked to the remaining nodes in the network (this example is adapted from Teorey, Chaar, Olukotun, and Umor (1989), pp. 34-42).

As shown in Table 8-1, Hy-Tek has three major relations that are to be located in the distributed processing network. The first relation (R1) is a CUSTOMER relation that contains information about Hy-Tek's customers. The second relation (R2) is a PRODUCT relation, while the third relation (R3) is a SHIPMENT relation. The table shows the size of each relation and the average time (milliseconds) to query and update each relation from both a local site and a remote site. For example, the average time to query R1 is 100 milliseconds from a local site and 500 milliseconds from a remote site (the additional time represents the communications overhead). The average time to update R1 is 150 milliseconds from a local site and 600 milliseconds from a remote site.

Table 8-2 shows the major transactions that access and update the three relations in the database. (The location for each of these transactions is shown in Figure 8-10.) Transaction T1 originates at sites S1, S4, and S5; it is executed with an average frequency of one time per second at *each* of these sites. This transaction accesses relation R1 an average of four times each time it is executed; three of these accesses are reads (R) and one is a write (W), which updates the relation. Similarly, transaction T2 originates at sites S2 and S4 an average of two times per second at each site. Transaction T2 accesses relation R1 (two reads) and R2 (three reads, one write). Finally,

Figure 8-10
Distributed computing network (Copyright C Database Programming and Design, April 1989. Reprinted by Permission of Miller Freeman Publications)

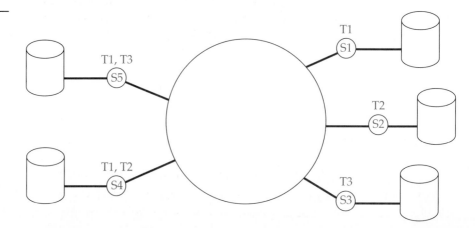

Table 8-1 Three Relations to Be Located in Distributed System

Relation	Size	Ave. Local Time (ms)		Ave. Remote Time (ms)	
		Query	Update	Query	Update
R1	300KB	100	150	500	600
R2	500KB	150	200	650	700
R3	1.0MB	200	250	1000	1100

Source: Copyright C Database Programming and Design, April 1989, Vol. 2, No. 4.
Reprinted by permission of Miller Freeman Publications

Table 8-2 Transactions That Access the Relations

Transaction	Originating Site	Frequency (Each Site)	Relation Access (R = Read, W = Write)
T1	S1, S4, S5	1 per sec.	R1: 3R, 1W
			R2: 2R
T2	S2, S4	2 per sec.	R1: 2R
			R3: 3R, 1W
T3	S3, S5	3 per sec.	R2: 3R, 1W
			R2: 3R, 1W
			R3: 2R

Source: Copyright C Database Programming and Design, April 1989, Vol. 2, No. 4.
Reprinted by permission of Miller Freeman Publications

transaction T3 originates at sites S3 and S5 and has a frequency of three per second at each site. It accesses relation R2 (three reads, one write) and R3 (two reads).

The data distribution problem for Hy-Tek can now be stated as follows: Given the network with five sites shown in Figure 8-10, the relations shown in Table 8-1, and the transactions shown in Table 8-2, at which of the sites should the relations be located? We will make two assumptions to simplify the solution to this problem:

1. The major objective in placing the data is to maximize the number of *local* references to the data (this will also minimize the number of remote references).

2. None of the relations will be partitioned, so that each relation will be located in its entirety at one (or more) sites.

The method we will use for allocating relations to sites is called the "all beneficial sites" method, which selects all sites for a relation where the benefit is greater than the cost for locating a relation at that site. The cal-

Table 8-3 Cost and Benefit for Each Relation Located at Five Possible
Sites

Relation	Site	Remote Update Trans.	Remote Update Trans. *Freq.*Time =	Cost
R1	S1	T1 from S4 and S5	2*1*600 ms	1200 ms
	S2	T1 from S1, S4, S5	3*1*600 ms	1800 ms
	S3	T1 from S1, S4, S5	3*1*600 ms	1800 ms
	S4	T1 from S1 and S5	2*1*600 ms	1200 ms
	S5	T1 from S1 and S4	2*1*600 ms	1200 ms
R2	S1	T3 from S3 and S5	2*3*700 ms	4200 ms
	S2	T3 from S3 and S5	2*3*700 ms	4200 ms
	S3	T3 from S5	1*3*700 ms	2100 ms
	S4	T3 from S3 and S5	2*3*700 ms	4200 ms
	S5	T3 from S3	1*3*700 ms	2100 ms
R3	S1	T2 from S2 and S4	2*2*100 ms	4400 ms
	S2	T2 from S4	1*2*1100 ms	2200 ms
	S3	T2 from S2 and S4	2*2*1100 ms	4400 ms
	S4	T2 from S2	1*2*1100 ms	2200 ms
	S5	T2 from S2 and S4	2*2*1100 ms	4400 ms

Relation	Site	Query (Read) Sources	No. of Reads* freq* (Remote-Local-Time) =	Benefit
R1	S1	T1 at S1	3*1* (500 − 100)	1200 ms
	S2	T2 at S2	2*2*(500 − 100)	1600 ms
	S3	None	0	0
	S4	T1 and T2 at S4	(3*1 + 2*2)* (500 − 100)	2800 ms
	S5	T1 at S2	3*1*(500 − 100)	1200 ms
R2	S1	T1 at S1	2*1*(650 − 150)	1000 ms
	S2	None	0	0
	S3	T3 at S3	3*3*(650 − 150)	4500 ms
	S4	T1 at S4	2*1*(650 − 150)	1000 ms
	S5	T1 and T3 at S5	(2*1 + 3*3)* (650 − 150)	5500 ms
R3	S1	None	0	0
	S2	T2 at S2	3*2*(1000 − 200)	4800 ms
	S3	T3 at S3	2*3*(1000 − 200)	4800 ms
	S4	T2 at S4	3*2*(1000 − 200)	4800 ms
	S5	T3 at S5	2*3*(1000 − 200)	4800 ms

Source: Copyright C Database Programming and Design, April 1989, Vol. 2, No. 4.
Reprinted by permission of Miller Freeman Publications.

culations for the relations at Hy-Tek are shown in Table 8-3; the top of Table 8-3 shows the costs, while the bottom of the table shows the benefits.

The *cost* at each site is the additional remote updates from other sites for the given relation at that site. The *benefit* at each site is measured by the difference in cost to do a remote read (when no copy is located at the site) versus a local read (when a copy is located at the site).

First, consider whether relation R1 should be located at S1. From Table 8-2, we see that the additional cost will be that of updating R1 with transaction T1, from the remote locations S4 and S5. Thus, there are transactions from two sites that originate at a rate of one per second and require 600ms (milliseconds) each. The total cost (which is shown in the first line of Table 8-3) is:

2 sites * 1 transaction/second * 600ms = 1200ms

Now consider locating R1 at site S2. Transaction T1 must now update R1 at S2 from three remote locations: S1, S4, and S5. The total cost is:

3 sites * 1 transaction/second * 600ms = 1800ms

The calculations for R1 at the remaining sites (S3, S4, and S5) are shown in Table 8-3. Perform each of these calculations to make sure you understand the process that is being used.

Now consider relation R2 at site S1. The additional cost will be due to remote updates by transaction T3 originating at sites S3 and S5 (transaction T3 is the only one that *updates* R2). The additional cost will be:

2 transactions * 3 transactions/second * 700ms = 4200ms

The remaining calculations for the costs for relations R2 and R3 are shown in Table 8-3. Again, verify each of the calculations.

Now consider the *benefit* of assigning each relation to each site (shown in the bottom half of Table 8-3). First, suppose that relation R1 is assigned to site S1. Notice that transaction T1 originates at S1 (frequency of one per second) and reads R1 (three times per transaction). With a copy of R1 at S1, each of these reads is a local reference (rather than a remote reference). Thus, the benefit is computed as follows:

3 reads * 1/second * (500 − 100) = 1200ms

If R2 is assigned to S2, then the benefit arises from local references for transaction T2. As shown in Table 8-3, the calculation is the following:

2 reads * 2/second * (500 − 100) = 1600ms

The remaining benefit calculations for R1, and for R2 and R3, are shown in Table 8-3. Verify that each of these calculations is correct and that you understand the benefit calculations.

Once the calculations in Table 8-3 have been completed, we assign a relation to a site whenever the benefit of this assignment exceeds the cost. This rule leads to the following assignments (see Figure 8-9):

- Assign relation R1 to site S4 only.
- Assign relation R2 to sites S3 and S5.
- Assign relation R3 to sites S2, S3, S4, and S5.

When the costs and benefits for an assignment are equal (as for R1 at S1), the organization is indifferent as to whether the relation is assigned to that site. In Figure 8-11 we did not assign a relation to a site when the costs and benefits were equal. However, the organization may choose to make such assignments for other reasons, such as when greater availability of data is important.

Stored Record Design

At the physical level, a database is viewed as a collection of stored records. A **stored record** is a collection of related data items that corresponds to one or more logical records. In addition to data items, a stored record includes any necessary pointers and other overhead data, such as record length indicators. Thus, a stored record format represents data as they are actually stored on physical devices.

Designing stored record formats essentially consists of deciding how to map the logical records to stored records. The stored records may closely resemble the corresponding logical records. On the other hand, several options exist for modifying stored records to improve performance, including data item storage techniques, data compression, and record partitioning. The specific options available in a given application will depend on the DBMS being used.

Figure 8-11
Final allocation of data for Hy-Tek (Copyright C Database Programming and Design, April 1989. Reprinted by permission of Miller Freeman Publications)

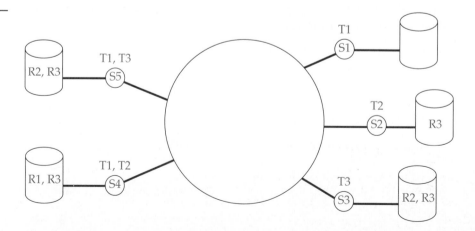

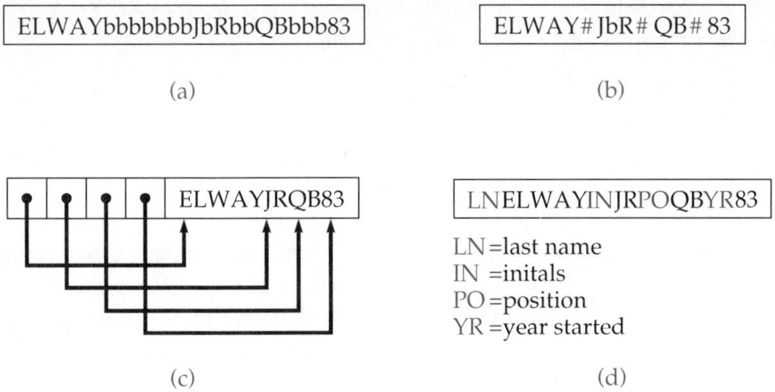

ELWAYbbbbbbbJbRbbQBbbb83

(a)

ELWAY#JbR#QB#83

(b)

ELWAYJRQB83

(c)

LNELWAYINJRPOQBYR83

LN =last name
IN =initals
PO =position
YR =year started

(d)

Figure 8-12
Data item
representation
techniques

Data Item Storage Techniques Four basic techniques are available for representing data in stored records: positional, relational, indexed, and labeled (see Figure 8-12). The positional technique is a fixed-length record representation; the remaining three techniques support variable-length records.

With the **positional technique**, fixed-length fields are used for each data item. Thus, each field must be sufficiently large to accommodate the longest anticipated data item value. When data item values are stored, they are right- or left-justified, and blanks are used to pad unused space. (In Figure 8-12a, the values are left-justified and the symbol b is used to represent blank space.) The positional technique is the most widely used technique for storing data items since it simplifies programming and data management tasks. However, it tends to waste storage space, which can be costly, especially for very large databases.

With the **relational technique**, a special character (not valid in the stored data) is used to delimit data item values. In Figure 8-12b, the symbol # is used for this purpose. The special symbol eliminates strings of blanks and therefore conserves space.

The **indexed approach** (Figure 8-12c) uses pointers to specify the beginning of each data item value in the record. The pointers normally specify the relative displacement of each value within the record. As with relational technique, the use of pointers supports variable-length records and eliminates wasted space.

With the **labeled technique** (Figure 8-12d), each data item value is preceded by a label indicating the data item type. This approach allows only certain data items to be included within each record; unwanted data items are simply omitted. The labeled approach is efficient for unstructured data or when a record has many defaulted data item values.

The physical designer may or may not be able to choose the data item storage technique, depending on the DBMS being used. When a choice exists, one of the variable-length record techniques (relational, indexed, or labeled) can be used to conserve storage space if this is an important consideration. Variable-length records, however, usually complicate the programming task and slow down input/output operations.

Data Compression   Data compression is the process of reducing the length of data item values in stored records. Several techniques are used, the three most popular being null suppression, pattern substitution, and indexing (see Figure 8-13).

Null suppression techniques suppress blanks and zeros. One common technique that is used for zero suppression is a simple extension of the relational technique already described. A special character is used to indicate the beginning of a sequence of blanks or zeros (in Figure 8-13a, the symbol # represents the beginning of a sequence of blanks, the symbol @ the beginning of a sequence of zeros). The special character is followed by a digit that represents the length of the sequence. Thus, in Figure 8-13a, the symbol @4 is the compressed version for a sequence of four zeros. Null suppression is an effective technique for compressing "sparse" data that are dominated by zeros or blanks.

Pattern substitution is a technique in which sequences of characters that occur repeatedly in the data are recognized and then represented by shorter codes. An example of this technique is shown in Figure 8-13b. In this example, two character strings (TRS80 and 000) were identified as patterns in the same data. These values were stored in a pattern table and coded with the characters @ and #, respectively. The compressed data then appear

Figure 8-13
Data compression
techniques

Original data: ATARIbbbbbbb120000
Compressed data: ATARI#712@4

(a)

Original data	Compressed data
TRS8093000X	@93#X
TRS8091000Y	@91#Y
TRS8094000Z	@94#Z

Pattern Table

TRS80	@
000	#

(b)

Original data

CUSTOMER#	CITY
0123	TUCSON
1467	MINNEAPOLIS
3247	DENVER
5914	MINNEAPOLIS
6789	DENVER

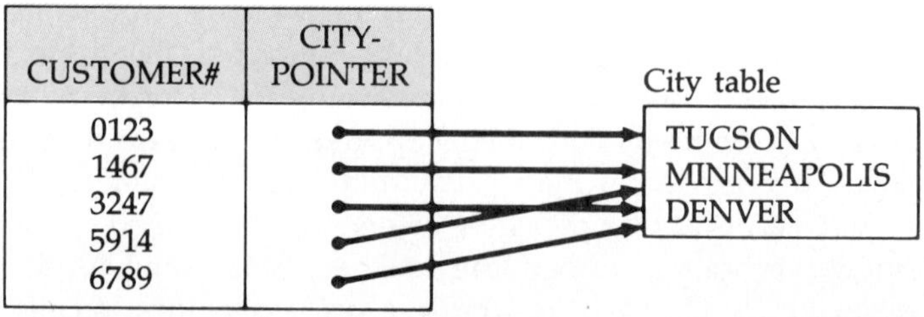

CUSTOMER#	CITY-POINTER
0123	
1467	
3247	
5914	
6789	

City table

TUCSON
MINNEAPOLIS
DENVER

(c)

with these codes replacing the character strings. Notice that this type of data compression requires additional accesses to the pattern table to store and retrieve data. However, pattern substitution is an effective means of data compression when frequent patterns exist in the data.

Indexing is a variation of pattern substitution, but instead of using a code to replace patterns, a pointer is used for each data item value. For example, in Figure 8-13c there is considerable redundancy in the CITY data item values, since the names of two cities are repeated (if there were 10,000 records, each city name would appear many times). To compress the data, a separate CITY table is created. City names are then replaced by pointers that point to the appropriate names in the table (the pointer values must be shorter than the city names for compression to occur).

Some database management systems automatically compress stored data. For example, ADABAS (DBMS from Software AG) has a compression algorithm that automatically suppresses trailing spaces on alphanumeric fields and leading zeros on numeric fields, packs numeric data, and compresses null value fields to a single character. The net result is that an ADABAS file typically requires only about 50% to 65% of the space required for the raw data.

Record Partitioning   The last aspect of stored record design that we will consider is record partitioning. **Record partitioning** (or segmentation) is the process of splitting stored records into separate segments and then allocating those segments to separate physical devices or separate extents on the same device. The reason for partitioning records is that some data items are accessed far more frequently than others. In fact, the so-called 80–20 rule often applies: approximately 20% of the data items often account for about 80% of the input/output activity. We can improve performance by locating the active data items on fast devices (such as fixed-head disks) or in readily accessible locations (such as the middle cylinders on a disk pack).

The simplest form of record partitioning divides a stored record into two segments: the **primary segment** (with the most active data items) and the **secondary segment** (with the least active data items). An example of this segmentation for the Patient record at Mountain View Community Hospital is shown in Figure 8-14. The three most active data items (which account for about 80% of all requests) are located in the primary segment: Patient#, Patient-Name, and Location. The remaining Patient data items are located in the secondary segment. The primary segment can be stored for fast access, while the secondary segment is stored on a slower device. In reality, the Patient records would probably not be segmented at all, since the database for this hospital is relatively small. Record partitioning may be an effective means of improving performance for large databases, however.

Notice that the primary and secondary segments are connected by a pointer so that they can be retrieved together when necessary. All user requests for data first generate an access to the primary segment, if the data are not found, then another access to the secondary segment is made.

Figure 8-14
Example of record
partitioning

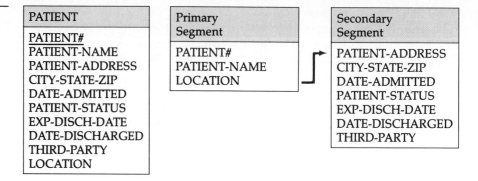

Record partitioning occurs at the physical level and is not visible to database users.

Record Clustering

A physical database consists of a collection of stored records of different types. **Record clustering** is the process of physically grouping these records according to the dominant access paths, thereby minimizing access times. For example, all stored records of a given type may be grouped together in a physical extent. However, it is often more efficient to group occurrences of different record types together when they are frequently accessed together. Optimum record clustering is a complex problem for large, integrated databases.

Clustering in Hierarchical Databases   In a hierarchical database, record clustering is the process of grouping segment occurrences into physical blocks or extents. See Figure 8-15, for example. Figure 8-15a shows a physical database record that consists of the four segment types A, B, C, and D (A is the root segment). Figure 8-15b shows one clustering option, where occurrences of each segment type are grouped together. This grouping is not likely to be efficient, since segments in a hierarchy are often retrieved in top-down, left-to-right sequence.

Another approach to grouping the segments is shown in Figure 8-15c. In this case, occurrences of segments A and B are grouped together (occurrences of segment B are grouped immediately following their parent segment occurrences). This grouping will probably be efficient if root segment (type A) occurrences are normally accessed sequentially with their child (type B) occurrences and if segments C and D are normally accessed sequentially. Certainly, many other groupings are possible even in this simple example.

Hierarchical structures for Mountain View Community Hospital are shown in Figure 8-6. If TREATMENT segments are accessed by means of PATIENT

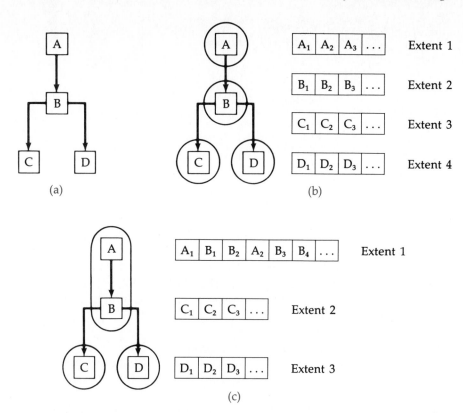

Figure 8-15
Record clustering in a
hierarchical database

root segments, then TREATMENT segment occurrences will be clustered with their PATIENT parent occurrences. For the same reason, CHARGES segment occurrences will be clustered with PATIENT parent segment occurrences.

Clustering in Network Databases   In a CODASYL (network) database, the physical database structure is specified in the Data Storage Description Language (DSDL). The DSDL is used to define the format of each stored record, the number and size of areas, and the placement of records in areas.

Record placement (or clustering) in a CODASYL database is controlled by a PLACEMENT clause in the DSDL. For each CODASYL record type, one of three placement modes may be chosen:

1. **CALC.** A data item value (record key) is hashed to produce a storage address. This results in record occurrences being dispersed randomly throughout a storage area (or extent).

2. **CLUSTERED VIA SET.** Member record occurrences in a set are clustered with their owner record occurrence.

3. **SEQUENTIAL.** Occurrences of a given record type are stored in sequential order according to their primary key.

Figure 8-16
Record clustering in a
network database

PHYSICIAN RECORD# 1	TREATMENT RECORD A	TREATMENT RECORD B
TREATMENT RECORD C		
PHYSICIAN RECORD# 2	TREATMENT RECORD D	TREATMENT RECORD E
PHYSICIAN RECORD# 3	TREATMENT RECORD F	

Referring to the network data model for Mountain View Community Hospital (Figure 8-5), there are two instances where the CLUSTERED VIA SET option will be used. CLUSTERED VIA SET TREATED will be specified for the TREATMENT record type. This clause will cause occurrences of TREATMENT records to be clustered with their PHYSICIAN owner record occurrences (see Figure 8-16). Also, a CLUSTERED VIA SET INCURRED will cause CHARGE record occurrences to be clustered with their PATIENT owner record occurrences.

Clustering in Relational Databases   Relations are logical structures that are viewed by users as completely independent of physical considerations such as files and access methods. Physically, these relations (or tables) must of course be mapped to storage media. Typically, relations are stored as sequential files with indexes that provide rapid access to individual rows within a table. Figure 8-17 shows the logical and physical representation of a table. In the physical representation, table rows are stored sequentially within pages (pages are physical subdivisions of storage media).

Rows of two (or more) relations may be clustered within pages to provide rapid multitable retrievals. For example, in Figure 8-18 there are two relations: PATIENT and CHARGE. Since we frequently need to retrieve both Patient and Charge data (e.g., to create a patient bill), rows for these tables could be clustered in pages as shown, which would allow fast access to the data. Unfortunately, clustering data in this manner also reduces flexibility. For example, Patient data must be retrieved with Treatment data in preparing the physician report. The clustering in Figure 8-18 is not designed to support this requirement, so preparing the physician report is likely to be much slower than preparing the patient bill.

Index Selection

The next topic we describe in physical database design is that of index selection. In this discussion, we limit our attention to relational databases, in which index selection is a major implementation issue. Indexes for relational databases generally follow a B-tree structure (this structure was intro-

PATIENT (TABLE P)

PATIENT-ID	PATIENT-NAME	...
123	Janet Price	
789	Thomas Hearn	
...		

(a)

Page 1	Page 2
Table P Row 1	Table P Row 20
Table P Row 2	Table P Row 21
Table P Row 3	Table P Row 22
...	...
Page 3	Page 4
Table P Row 50	
Table P Row 51	
...	

(b)

Figure 8-17
Logical and physical representation of a relation

duced in Chapter 7). For example, Figure 8-19 shows a B-tree index structure for the PATIENT relation shown in Figure 8-17. The rows for this relation are stored in the data page shown at the bottom of the diagram. The three-level B-tree index above the data page provides direct access to any row in the table. Also, the rows can be retrieved sequentially by following the lowest level (leaf nodes) of the index.

In most relational systems, an index can be specified for any attribute in a given table. If an index is specified for a primary key attribute, then it is unique (the index in Figure 8-19 is unique). If an index is specified for a nonkey attribute, then it is nonunique. An index may be composed of one or more columns. For example, an index for the primary key of the CHARGE

Figure 8-18
Clustering relations in physical storage

PATIENT (TABLE P)

PATIENT-ID	PATIENT-NAME
123	Janet Price
789	Thomas Hearn
...	

Page 1	Page 2
Table P Row 1	Table C Row 20
Table C Row 1	Table P Row 15
Table C Row 2	...
Table P Row 2	
Table C Row 3	
...	

(b)

CHARGE (TABLE C)

PATIENT-ID	ITEM-CODE	DATE
123	A219	11/13
123	B367	11/13
789	A328	12/1
...		

(a)

Figure 8-19
B-tree index structure (Copyright C Database Programming and Design, April 1989. Reprinted by permission of Miller Freeman Publications.)

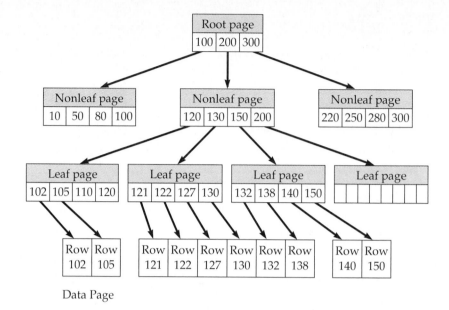

Data Page

relation (Figure 8-18) would be composed of three columns (or attributes): Patient-ID, Item-Code, and Date.

In specifying indexes, there is a trade-off between improved performance for retrievals and degraded performance for inserting, deleting, and updating the rows in a table. Indexes can dramatically improve performance for retrievals, since individual rows in a table can be retrieved directly without scanning the table (as was pointed out in Chapter 7 concerning inverted indexes). Because of the overhead associated with maintaining the indexes, however, performance is degraded for any application that inserts, deletes, or updates indexed rows or attributes. Also, indexes increase the cost of table reorganization, backup, and recovery (Pace 1989). As a result, indexes need to be specified judiciously in relational databases to balance these performance trade-offs.

The various reasons for using indexes were outlined in Table 7-4. On a practical level, attributes for which indexes should possibly be created can be identified by analyzing the known queries and reports that use a table. For example, consider the following SQL query:

SELECT Patient-Code, Item-Code, Sum (Charge)
FROM CHARGES
WHERE Date > 12/15/9×
GROUP BY Patient-Code, Item-Code

Possible indexes for this query are Date, Patient-Code, and Item-Code since these attributes are used in qualifications and sorting/grouping clauses. Also, attributes that are primary or foreign keys are candidates for indexing since they must be rapidly matched for joining tables.

SUMMARY

Implementation and physical design are the last two stages in the database design process. Implementation design is concerned with mapping the conceptual data model (which may be expressed as objects, E-R diagrams, 3NF relations, and so on) into logical database structures (hierarchical, network, or relational data models). Physical database design is concerned with mapping the logical database structures into an internal model consisting of stored records, files, and other physical structures. The objective of implementation design is to develop logical database structures that accurately reflect user needs for information and that can grow and evolve as information needs change. The objective of physical design is to implement the database to meet user needs in terms of performance, security, integrity, and related factors.

Implementation design is required especially when the target DBMS supports a hierarchical or network data model. In this case, the logical data model must be mapped to either hierarchical or network structures. Mapping to a hierarchical data model involves identifying the root node types, identifying dependent node types, and resolving multiple parentage. Mapping to a network data model includes defining record types, defining sets, eliminating redundant keys (if desired), and defining record access strategies. Although implementation design is relatively straightforward, it must be done carefully since the resulting data models must accurately represent information requirements and provide a stable basis for future growth.

Many of the decisions in physical database design depend on estimates of the size and probable usage patterns of the data. Data volume analysis is the process of estimating database size by estimating the number and size of each database entity or record type. Data usage analysis identifies the major database transactions and the access paths required for each transaction. A composite usage map provides a concise reference to the estimated volume and usage of data in the database.

One of the most interesting problems in physical database design is deciding on the distribution of data among the nodes of a network. There are three basic data distribution strategies: centralized, partitioned, and replicated. With the partitioned approach, the central database is partitioned into disjoint (nonoverlapping) partitions, called fragments. Each partition is assigned to a particular site. With a replicated approach, a full copy of the database (or at least some subset of the database) is assigned to *each* site in the network. A hybrid approach combines the elements of both the partitioned and replicated approaches. The data distribution decision can be analyzed using information describing data usage and the characteristics of the network.

There are often a number of options in designing stored records for the DBMS internal model. For example, data items may be stored in records using both fixed- and variable-length record techniques. Data may also be compressed in stored records using several different data compression techniques. Records may be clustered according to dominant access paths, to minimize access times. The options that are available for stored record design depend on the DBMS that is being used for database implementation.

In most relational databases, an index can be specified for any attribute in a given table. Although indexes improve performance for data retrievals, they do tend to degrade performance for inserting, deleting, and updating the rows of a table. Also, indexes increase the cost of table reorganization, backup, and recovery. As a result, indexes need to be chosen carefully to balance performance trade-offs.

REFERENCES

Ceri, S., and G. Pelagitti. 1984. *Distributed Databases: Principles and Systems.* New York, NY: McGraw-Hill.

Hogan, R. 1988. "Usage Path Analysis." *Database Programming and Design* 1(9) (Sept.), 37–43.

Martin, J. 1983. *Managing the Data-Base Environment.* Englewood Cliffs, N.J.: Prentice-Hall.

Pace, P. 1989. "DB2 Dataset Internals." *Database Programming and Design* 2(8) (Aug.), 46–53.

Schkolnick, M. 1977. "A Clustering Algorithm for Hierarchical Structures." *ACM Transactions on Database Systems* (Mar.), pp. 27–44.

Teorey, T. J., J. Chaar, K. Olukotun, and A. Umar. 1989. "Allocation Methods for Distributed Database." *Database Programming and Design* 2(4) (Apr.), 34–42.

Chapter Review

REVIEW QUESTIONS

1. Concisely define each of the following terms:
   a. logical data model
   b. set
   c. composite usage map
   d. root node
   e. record clustering
   f. stored record
   g. data compression
   h. fragment

2. Contrast the following terms:
   a. implementation design; physical design
   b. owner; member
   c. CALC; VIA

    d. positional technique; relational technique
    e. null suppression; pattern substitution
    f. partitioning; replication
    g. record partitioning; record clustering

3. What are the major inputs and the major outputs for each of the following?
    a. implementation design
    b. physical design

4. What are the major objectives for each of the following?
    a. implementation design
    b. physical design

5. List four steps in converting a logical model to a CODASYL model.

6. Briefly describe four techniques for representing data in stored records.

7. Describe three techniques for data compression.

8. What is the purpose of data volume and usage analysis?

9. List three disadvantages of a centralized data strategy.

10. Briefly describe each of the following data distribution strategies:
    a. partitioned
    b. replicated
    c. hybrid

11. What is meant by the "all beneficial sites" method of data distribution?

12. Briefly describe the trade-offs in selecting indexes in relational databases.

13. What is the purpose of each of the following?
    a. data compression
    b. record clustering
    c. record partitioning

PROBLEMS AND EXERCISES

1. Match the following terms to the appropriate definitions.

_____ physical design	**a)** 1:M association between two record types (CODASYL)
_____ set	**b)** partition of a database
_____ root node	**c)** grouping records according to access paths
_____ data compression	**d)** includes selecting file organization, access methods, and indexes
_____ pattern substitution	**e)** copy of a database assigned to each site
_____ replication	**f)** reducing the length of data item values
_____ record clustering	**g)** collection of related data items
_____ fragment	**h)** database is divided into subsets
_____ partitioning	**i)** entry point to a hierarchical database
_____ stored record	
_____ hybrid	

j) combines partitioning and replication
k) representing a sequence of characters

Problems 2 to 4 are based on a logical data model (abbreviated version) for Pine Valley Furniture Company. This data model is shown below:

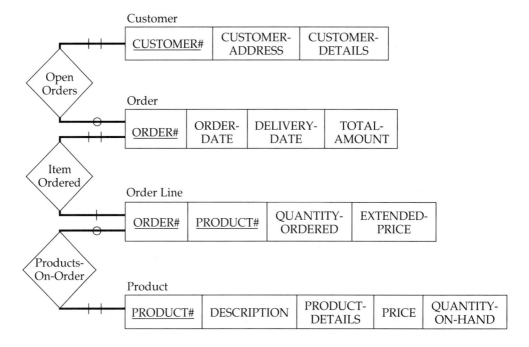

Customer

| CUSTOMER# | CUSTOMER-ADDRESS | CUSTOMER-DETAILS |

Open Orders

Order

| ORDER# | ORDER-DATE | DELIVERY-DATE | TOTAL-AMOUNT |

Item Ordered

Order Line

| ORDER# | PRODUCT# | QUANTITY-ORDERED | EXTENDED-PRICE |

Products-On-Order

Product

| PRODUCT# | DESCRIPTION | PRODUCT-DETAILS | PRICE | QUANTITY-ON-HAND |

In answering the following questions, assume that the dominant access patterns for the record types are as follows:

i.   Customer: direct retrieval
ii. Order: direct retrieval
iii. Order-Line: first retrieve an Order occurrence, then retrieve Order-Line occurrences for that Order (must also be able to retrieve Order-Line occurrences for a given Product occurrence)
iv. Product: direct retrieval

2. Map the model to a relational data model (show sample data).

3. Map the model to a network (CODASYL) data model.

4. Map the model to a hierarchical data model.

5. Consider the following data:
   APPLEbbbbbVISICALC60000
   APPLEbbbbbVISICLONE70000
   a. Show this data with null suppression (use the same symbols as in Figure 8-13).
   b. Show this data with pattern substitution. Use the following symbols, as necessary: @, #, *.

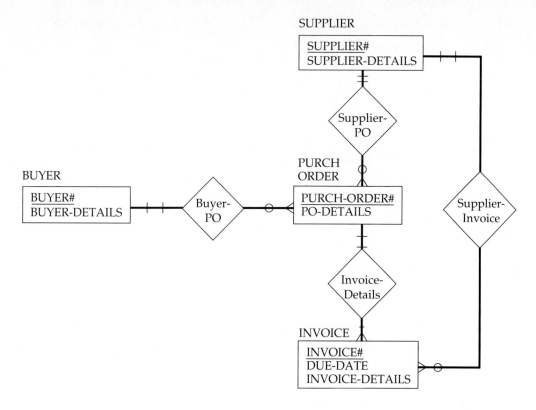

6. Show how the following data could be represented as a stored record using each of the four data item representation techniques shown in Figure 8-12:
   Lotusbbb1-2-3bbbVER3.0bbb1988

7. A logical data model for a simple purchasing database is shown in Figure 8-20. Map this logical model to a CODASYL logical model. Assume the following access patterns:
   a. SUPPLIER, BUYER and PURCH-ORDER require direct access.
   b. INVOICE occurrences are retrieved by first retrieving a PURCH-ORDER occurrence, then retrieving all related INVOICE occurrences.

8. Map the logical data model shown in Figure 8-20 to a hierarchical model (see assumption in Problem 7).

9. Based on the assumption in Problem 7, how are the records shown in Figure 8-20 likely to be clustered in a network (CODASYL) database?

10. A fourth relation (R4) is to be added to the database for Hy-Tek Corporation (see Tables 8-1 and 8-2). Relation R4 (which will be 1.0MB in size) has the following average query and update times (in milliseconds):

	Query	Update
Local	50	100
Remote	300	500

All three of the transactions shown in Table 8-2 will access relation R4 as follows:

Transaction	Accesses to R4
T1	2R, 1W
T2	4R, 1W
T3	1R, 1W

Your assignment is to decide where to locate R4 for Hy-Tek Corporation using the "all beneficial sites" method.

11. A new transaction (T4) is to be added to the distributed data processing system for Hy-Tek Corporation. Transaction T4 has the following characteristics (see Table 8-2):

Originating sites:	S1, S3, S4
Frequency (each site):	1 per second
Relation accesses:	R1: 2R, 1W
	R2: 4R, 1W
	R3: 1R, 1W

Your assignment is to recalculate and (if necessary) redistribute the three relations R1, R2, and R3 for Hy-Tek Corporation. (*Note:* This problem is *independent* of Problem 10.)

12. Hy-Tek Corporation is considering changes to its distributed processing system that would reduce the times required for remote query and updates as follows (see Table 8-1):

Relation	Size	Ave. Local Time (ms)		Ave. Remote Time (ms)	
		Query	Update	Query	Update
R1	300KB	100	150	300	400
R2	500KB	150	200	200	400
R3	1.0MB	200	250	500	700

Your assignment is to recalculate and (if necessary) redistribute the data for Hy-Tek Corporation based on these revised access times. (*Note*: This problem is *independent* of Problems 10 and 11.)

CHAPTER 9

Data Administration

INTRODUCTION

Organizations are increasingly recognizing that data and information are resources that are too valuable to be managed casually. According to a study conducted by the Center for the Study of Data Processing of Washington University (Herbert and Hartog, 1986), data utilization (that is, "assuring that data are made available to the right person in a timely manner") is the second most important issue in MIS management (the first is aligning MIS with business goals). Further, this issue moved from ninth place (1984) to fourth place (1985) and then to its current second-place position.

There are many causes of poor data utilization:

- Multiple definitions of the same data entity and inconsistent representations of the same data elements in separate databases, which makes linking data across different databases hazardous
- Missing key data elements, which makes existing data useless
- Low levels of data quality due to inappropriate sources of data or timing of data transfers from one system to another
- Not knowing what data exist, where to find them, and what they really mean

One organizational response to the data utilization issue is to create a new function called data administration. The person who heads this function is called the manager of data administration or, more popularly, the data administrator. Actual experience with computer databases has established a fundamental principle: The data administration function is *essential* to the success of managing the data resource. Establishing this function is an indication of top management's commitment to data resource management. When the data administration function is not established, or when it is weakly established, the chances of success of the database approach are significantly diminished.

The database is a shared resource, belonging to the entire enterprise—it is not the property of a single function or individual within the organization. The data administrator is "custodian" of the organization's data, in much the same sense that the controller is custodian of the financial resources. Like the controller, the data administrator must develop procedures to protect and control the resource. Also, the data administrator must resolve disputes that may arise when data are centralized and shared among users and must play a significant role in deciding where data will be stored and managed.

Data administration is responsible for a wide range of functions, including database planning, design, implementation, maintenance, and protection. Also, the data administrator is responsible for improving database performance and for providing education, training, and consulting support to users. The data administrator must interact with top management, users, and computer applications specialists.

Selecting the data administrator and organizing the function are extremely important. The data administrator must possess a high level of managerial skills and must be capable of resolving differences that normally arise when significant change is introduced into an organization. The data administrator should be a respected, senior-level middle manager selected from within the organization, rather than a technical computer expert or a new individual hired for the position.

Several concepts, methods, and tools are available to help a data administrator manage the data resources to achieve high utilization (as defined above). A database (already covered) and a DBMS are fundamental components of a data administrator's portfolio. Fourth-generation languages and system prototyping (Boar, 1984) can be used by a data administrator and others to help users better understand their data processing requirements, but an almost complete and fully defined database must be in place for 4GLs and prototyping to be of much assistance. Finally, but certainly very important, a repository or data dictionary/directory is needed so that all database users know exactly what the word *data* means, what data are available where, who controls access to the data, how data are stored, when they are maintained, and where they are used. The use of a repository is covered in considerable detail later in this chapter.

DATA ADMINISTRATION VERSUS DATABASE ADMINISTRATION

The manager of the data administration function requires a high order of both managerial and technical skills. On the one hand, this person must be capable of enlisting cooperation from users, who may at first be hostile to the idea of "giving up" their "private" data to a shared database. Also, these users must be convinced of the benefits of adhering to a set of standard definitions and procedures for accessing the database. On the other hand, the data administrator must be capable of managing a technical staff and dealing with technical issues such as query optimization and concurrency control.

To resolve the managerial versus technical complexity of data administration, numerous organizations today are creating both data administration and database administration functions. **Data administration** is a high-level management function that is responsible for developing an enterprise data model and for maintaining corporate-wide data definitions and standards. **Database administration** is a technical function that is responsible for physical database design and for dealing with technical issues such as security enforcement, database performance, and backup and recovery. We provide a more detailed discussion of the functions of data administration and database administration and their organizational placement in the next section.

Recently the concept of a data steward has emerged in the data resource management field. A **data steward** manages a specific logical data resource or entity (for example, customer, product, or facility) for all business functions and data processing systems that originate or use data about the assigned entity. A data steward is the focal point for coordinating all data definitions, quality controls and improvement programs, access authorization, and planning for the data entity for which he or she is responsible. Data stewards may be coordinated by the data administrator or may collectively satisfy the responsibilities of data administration.

Usually a data steward is a user-manager from a business management department that originates data about a data entity or has primary interest in that entity. The intent of data stewardship is to distribute (not decentralize) data administration to those most knowledgeable of and dependent on high-quality data for key data entities.

An enterprise information model (such as the one shown in Figure 4-11) would be used to identify the key data entities to be assigned to data stewards. A data steward manages an enterprise data entity not just for the good of his or her own area of the organization but also to promote organizational data sharing and access. When the organization distinguishes local data from organizational data, a particular unit may appoint data stewards for entities local to that unit.

Figure 9-1
Stages in a database
system life cycle

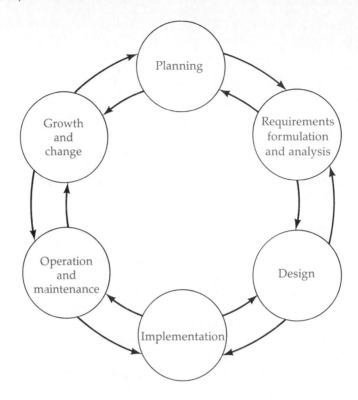

Functions of Data and Database Administration

In this section we delineate the functions of data administration and database administration in greater detail. We use the concept of a database system life cycle to provide a framework for this discussion. As shown in Figure 9-1, there are six stages in the life cycle of a typical database system:

1. Planning
2. Requirements definition
3. Design
4. Implementation
5. Operation and maintenance
6. Growth and change

Although these functions are performed more or less in the order given above, there is considerable interaction among the various stages, as shown in Figure 9-1. Also, the manner in which these functions are performed varies from one organization to the next and is influenced by the use of specific methodologies and CASE tools (we discuss CASE tools later in this chapter).

Following is a brief discussion of the major stages in the database system life cycle shown in Figure 9-1.

Planning   The purpose of database planning is to develop a strategic plan for database development that supports the overall organizational business plan. Although the responsibility for developing this plan rests with top management, data administration provides major inputs to the planning process. Database planning was described in Chapter 4.

Requirements Definition   The process of requirements definition is concerned with identifying data entities currently used by the organization, precisely defining these entities and their relationships, and documenting the results in a form that is convenient to the design effort that is to follow. In addition to identifying current data, requirements definition attempts to identify new data elements (or changes to existing data elements) that will be required in the future. Requirements definition was described in Chapter 5.

Design   The purpose of database design is to develop a logical database architecture that will meet the information needs of the organization, now and in the future. As we described in Chapter 6, there are three stages in database design: logical design, implementation design, and physical design. Although data administration has primary responsibility for database design, they must work closely with users and system specialists in performing these design activities. Database design was described in Chapters 6 and 8.

Implementation   Once the database design is completed, the implementation process begins. The first step in implementation is the creation (or initial load) of the database. The database is simply an empty superstructure until it has been "populated" with actual data values. Data administration manages the loading process and resolves any inconsistencies that arise during this process.

Operation and Maintenance   Database operation and maintenance is the ongoing process of updating the database to keep it current. Examples of updating include adding a new employee record, changing a student address, and deleting an invoice. Maintenance includes activities such as adding a new field, changing the size of an existing field, and so on.

Updating the database is not the responsibility of data administration. Rather, users are responsible for database maintenance. However, data administration is responsible for developing procedures that ensure that the database is kept current and that it is protected during update operations. Specifically, data administration must perform the following functions:

1. Assign responsibility for data collection, editing, and verification
2. Establish appropriate update schedules

3. Establish an active and aggressive quality assurance program, including procedures for protecting, restoring, and auditing the database

Growth and Change   The database is a model of the organization. As a result, it is not static but reflects the dynamic changes in the organization and its environment. Data administration must plan for change, such as adding new record types, accommodating growth, and so on. They must also monitor the performance of the database (both efficiency as well as user satisfaction), and take whatever corrective actions are required to maintain a high level of system performance and success.

A breakdown of the major functions within each of the life cycle phases is shown in Figure 9-2. Also, this figure shows which of the functions are normally performed by data administration and which are typically performed by database administration. Notice that data administration is normally responsible for the following functions: database planning, requirements definition, and logical database design. Database administration is typically responsible for physical database design and much of the database implementation, operation, and maintenance. Several functions, such as specifying database access policies, conducting user training, and managing growth and change, may be the responsibility of both groups.

The actual allocation of responsibilities between data administration and database administration varies from one organization to the next. No doubt the definition of each of these functions will continue to evolve as organizations gain experience with information resource management.

Interfaces of Data Administration

Data administration can be a highly political function that requires superb interpersonal skills. A data administrator lives between various groups that can, and frequently do, have conflicting views and expectations. A data administrator must be able to retain credibility with each of these groups and be able to deal with a variety of issues from diverse interests. Additional insight into the functions of data administration can be gained by studying the interfaces with other major groups in the enterprise. As shown in Figure 9-3, data administration interfaces with four major groups: management, users, applications development, and operations.

Communications with Management   Data administration has a number of important communications with top management. If the data resource management concept is in practice, the data administrator may well be a top manager, or at least will report to a top manager.

Management communicates to the data administration function a continuing commitment to the data resource management concept. This includes, it is hoped, the necessary budgetary support. Also, management communicates its business plans, goals, priorities, and constraints, which are

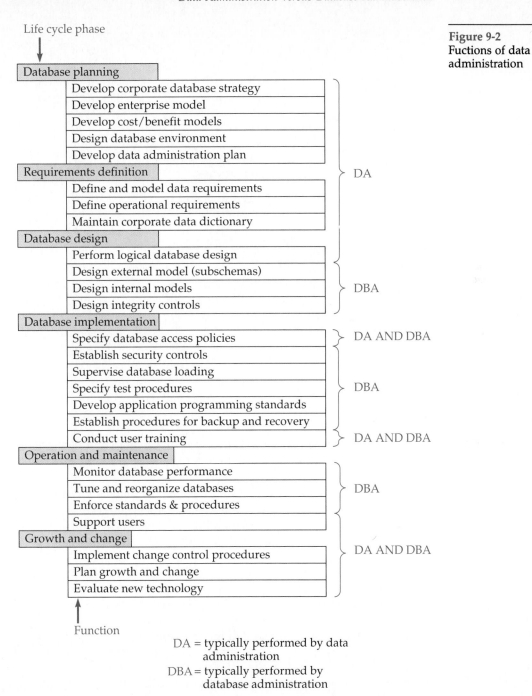

Figure 9-2
**Fuctions of data
administration**

Life cycle phase

Database planning
- Develop corporate database strategy
- Develop enterprise model
- Develop cost/benefit models
- Design database environment
- Develop data administration plan

Requirements definition
- Define and model data requirements
- Define operational requirements
- Maintain corporate data dictionary

} DA

Database design
- Perform logical database design
- Design external model (subschemas)
- Design internal models
- Design integrity controls

} DBA

Database implementation
- Specify database access policies   } DA AND DBA
- Establish security controls
- Supervise database loading
- Specify test procedures
- Develop application programming standards
- Establish procedures for backup and recovery

} DBA

- Conduct user training   } DA AND DBA

Operation and maintenance
- Monitor database performance
- Tune and reorganize databases
- Enforce standards & procedures
- Support users

} DBA

Growth and change
- Implement change control procedures
- Plan growth and change
- Evaluate new technology

} DA AND DBA

Function

DA = typically performed by data
administration
DBA = typically performed by
database administration

Figure 9-3
Major interfaces of
data administration

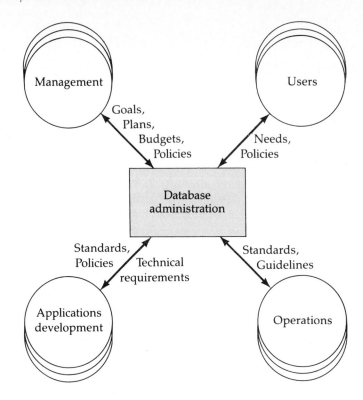

the basis for database planning. If there are any major contingencies, such as a reorganization or acquisition, these must also be communicated to data administration.

Data administration, in turn, communicates to management its budget requirements and database plans and schedules. Data administration should provide frequent status reports concerning database projects. Often, data administration is responsible for performing cost/benefit analyses of specific proposals.

One way for data administration to sustain top management support is to show these managers how they can use the database system to improve their own decision making. Data administration should make recommendations to management concerning the use of high-level query languages, graphic displays, simulation modeling, and other areas of decision support. Data administration and management also have joint responsibility for developing and maintaining the enterprise information model (see Chapter 4) and for developing plans for database evolution and technology acquisition. The database plan is typically part of a total MIS plan, so data administration works closely with both general and MIS senior management. Today, strategic systems planning methods include strategic data planning components. Many organizations establish data administration because long-range systems planning clearly indicates the need for a data management function to handle data and information in the same way the other organizational resources are administered. Thus, data administration has much to learn from general management, in order to acquire, plan, account for, secure, dispose, inventory, and so on the data resource as efficiently as other resource managers undertake their responsibilities.

Communications with Users The term *users* is a generic term, referring to any person in the organization who uses databases. Thus, users may be managers (at any level), clerical personnel, shop workers, or computer personnel. Data administration provides users with the information they require to maintain and protect the database and to develop new applications. This information includes data definitions, data relationships, and other information stored in the repository or data dictionary. However, data administration does not provide users with a hard-copy listing of the complete data dictionary—only that portion for which there is a "need to know."

One of the many advantages of the repository is the ability to perform impact studies—the ability to show the impact that a database change will have on programs and data processing (for example, the change by the postal service from a five-digit to a nine-digit zip code). Data administration also consults with users regarding education and training needs, new applications, and methods for improving performance.

During the requirements definition stage, users provide data administration with their data requirements—data element descriptions, user views, priorities, access limitations, frequency of updating, and so on. Users must also keep data administration informed of possible future database applications and changes in business practices and policies that necessitate changes in entity relationships.

Communications with Applications Development The applications development group includes the analysts and programmers who are responsible for developing user application programs. Data administration must develop and enforce standards for programs that interface with database, including programming techniques, program documentation, and quality assurance. For example, a portion of the standards should address what data manipulation language commands must be used (or are recommended) to access and manipulate the database. These standards are necessary both to protect the database and for performance reasons.

For each new application program, data administration provides the application designer with the controls required by the user. At the same time, it keeps users informed about the database itself, as well as providing documentation concerning the DBMS as needed.

Applications development provides data administration with the required application view of data for each new program. Applications development also keeps data administration informed of priorities and schedules, as well as the status of projects.

It is important that each new application program be carefully tested with test data before an attempt is made to interface it with the "live" database. The application specialist must communicate the test plan to data administration, and the two groups must work together to ensure that an adequate plan is developed.

Communications with Operations   Computer operations is concerned with the physical aspects of data processing—hardware operations, shift scheduling, security, tape and disk library, and so on. Operations is also concerned with the operating system and is often assigned technical support (systems programmers) to maintain this software.

Database administration must provide operations with schedules and standard operating procedures for routine operations, such as updating, backup, and archiving. Database administration also provides operations with standard procedures for protecting the database and for recovering from errors or abnormal conditions. It should be noted that these are not one-way communications between data administration and operations; many of the issues must be worked on and resolved jointly, although database administration is responsible for the final results.

Operations provides database administration with standard reports concerning database usage, system performance, and any errors or problems encountered. Also, operations should provide periodic verification that the standard procedures are being implemented.

Organizing the Data Administration Function

This section addresses three key management issues that arise in organizing the data administration function. The means by which top management resolves these issues is a good indication of their acceptance of information resource management. The three issues are (1) initiating the data administration function, (2) selecting the data administrator, and (3) placing the data administration function into the organization (including decentralized and other types of structures).

Initiating the Data Administration Function   Data administration and its primary tool, the repository (or data dictionary), are often viewed as extraneous and unessential to data management, yet nothing could be further from the truth. Data administration produces valuable results, but often, to those anxious to have access to data, its role seems to bottleneck or be an extra step in that process. Data administration is developed over several years and usually evolves from a systems planning or project management function.

Wherever data administration obtains its start, several steps are essential to ensure its success from the beginning:

1. Obtain management support for and commitment to the reason for the existence of the function and its role in database development.

This may require conducting a survey of other organizations to identify practical justification for data administration. Also essential here is determining the relationship of data administration and any data systems planning group(s).

2. Determine the requirements for a repository, and acquire financial support to buy or develop a repository appropriate for the database environment.

3. Train the data administration staff in database planning, database trends, data security and recovery, and other areas in which the staff will be involved.

4. Develop standards of operation (for example, data naming conventions) and measures of performance (for example, meeting project deadlines) for data administration staff so they recognize that their job has professional practices and that their good performance can be identified and rewarded.

Many organizations acquire a DBMS before a data administration function is (formally) established, yet logic would indicate that this puts the cart before the horse (or the resource before the manager). In such an organization, the DBMS is used to implement a series of unrelated applications not using shared data. Thus, expectations for database management may not be high, and user experience may not be conducive to change. The practical consequence of a situation like this is that the data administration function does not usually start with a clean slate. Database design practices, data ownership, multiple databases, multiple or no data dictionaries, and an essentially active but unorganized data management function are very likely to already be in place when the data administration function is started. The first chore then is to convince those with vested interests that methods must be changed. Thus, above all, data administration is an agent of change that must be sensitive to organizational history, politics, existing technology and systems, and attitudes.

Because of the inertia based on past practices, data administration often begins with a new, major application of system planning, and then slowly integrates other data and systems under its management. A phased introduction is almost always the wisest way to start the data administration function.

Selecting the Data Administrator A review of the functions of the data administrator (see Figure 9-2) indicates that this person must possess an unusual collection of managerial, analytical, and technical skills. However, in reviewing the full range of responsibilities, it is apparent that the job is more managerial than technical. The data administrator must perform the following typical managerial functions:

1. **Planning:** developing a comprehensive plan for the organization's data resource

2. **Organizing:** organizing and staffing the data administration function

3. **Supervising:** supervising the data administration staff

4. **Communicating:** communicating with managers, users, and computer specialists

5. **Controlling:** developing procedural controls for maintaining and protecting the data resources

Thus, the organization should define the data administrator position as a management position. The ideal candidate is a person with at least middle-management experience (line or staff), a broad knowledge and a "sense" of the enterprise (including its politics), and stature as a manager. Such a person requires some familiarity with computer-based information systems but does not have to be a computer or database expert.

Other candidates for the data administrator position might include business analysts, user-oriented systems analysts, or a data administrator with relevant experience in another, similar organization. However, a manager with experience in the enterprise is usually preferred.

Highly technical computer specialists such as system programmers are not usually good candidates for data administrator. Selecting such persons normally results from an overly narrow, technical definition of the data administration function. Most of these individuals do not have the managerial experience, aptitude, or desire to be a data administrator; however, they might be assigned to the data administrator staff.

Placing the Data Administration Function   In most organizations today, the data administration function is placed somewhere within the information systems organization. Where that function is placed within the IS organization varies from one enterprise to another, depending on the role and tasks assigned to data administration. In some organizations, data administration is viewed as a narrow technical function and is assigned to support services or even to computer operations (this indicates that regardless of its title, the role is really that of database administration). In other organizations, data administration is viewed as a high-level managerial function that reports directly to the chief information officer.

If an organization wishes to manage information as a resource, it must place data administration at a high level within the IS organization. Figure 9-4 shows one such organization structure where data administration reports directly to the CIO. In this example of organization, the functions shown within data administration are data analysis, database design, and database administration.

Data Administration in a Decentralized Organization

An advantage of establishing data administration is that numerous data management functions become centralized; such tasks as database planning, design, operation, and control (which were previously fragmented).

This, however, may lead to conflict in organizations where data processing is decentralized. Fortunately, several organizational arrangements can be used to resolve (or at least minimize) this conflict. Three typical methods of organizing data administration in a decentralized environment are shown in Figure 9-5 [for an extended discussion see Weldon (1981)].

Centralized Data Administration   With this approach, data administration is centralized within corporate systems (Figure 9-5a). The centralized data administration acts in a support, advisory, or managerial role to decentralized system development groups.

Decentralized Data Administration   In organizations where all hardware and system development activities are decentralized, decentralized data administration groups may be formed as needed within each organization (see Figure 9-5b). If there is a corporate system group, a data administration liaison may be established to coordinate activities among the several data administration groups. This approach promotes the move toward organization-wide standards and knowledge sharing. Lack of such coordination will likely result in incompatible systems and much "reinventing the wheel."

One technique for improving compatibility and avoiding excessive duplication of effort is to designate one of the sites as a pilot project. As the database development projects at the pilot site are completed, relevant portions may be transferred to the remaining sites. Also, data administration personnel at the pilot site may act as consultants to the other decentralized data administration groups.

Partially Decentralized Data Administration   With this approach, the central staff is partitioned and assigned, as needed, to local organizations. Typically, technical staff (such as DBMS support) remain at the central location. Data-base designers are separated and report to local operations managers, with a dotted-line responsibility to the data administrator (see Figure 9-5c). This alternative is a compromise between the preceding approaches and provides a good balance between flexibility and control.

DATA ADMINISTRATION TOOLS

Data administration uses a variety of computer software tools to support its various activities. In this section we describe three related software products that are used by data administrators: repositories, CASE tools, and database management systems. The relationship among these various components of the database environment was introduced in Chapter 1 (see Figure 1-9).

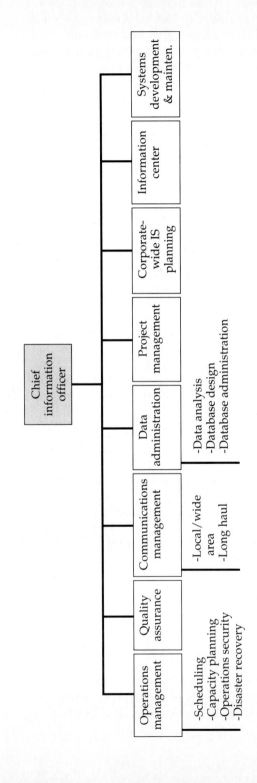

Figure 9-4
**Placement of data
administration**

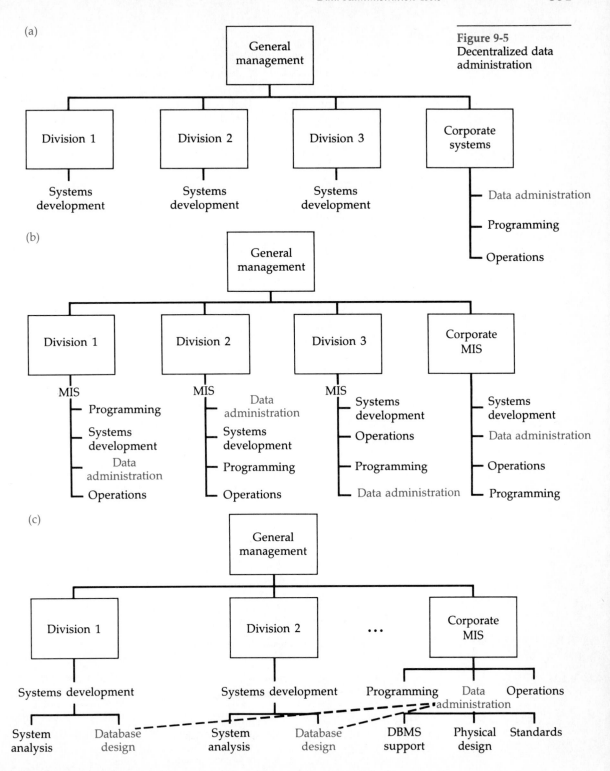

Figure 9-5
Decentralized data administration

Repositories

Data administrators are responsible for managing one of the most important databases in the enterprise—the information repository, or metadata that describes an organization's data and data processing resources. Information repositories are replacing data dictionaries in many organizations. While data dictionaries are simple data element documentation tools, information repositories are used by data administrators and other information specialists to manage the total information processing environment.

Repository Environment   The role of an information repository is shown in Figure 9-6. This diagram shows the components of a repository and the environment in which a repository is used. The application development environment is one in which people (either information specialists or end users) use CASE tools, high-level languages, and other tools to develop new applications. The production environment is one in which people use applications to build databases, keep the data current, and extract data from databases.

An **information repository** combines information about an organization's business information and its application portfolio (Bruce, Fuller, and Moriarty, 1989). Business information is the data stored in the corporate databases, while the application portfolio consists of the application programs that are used to manage business information. The information repository describes business information and applications in terms of components called **objects** (we described objects in Chapter 3).

An **Information Repository Dictionary System (IRDS)** is a computer software tool that is used to manage and control access to the information repository. It provides facilities for recording, storing, and processing descriptions of an organization's significant data and data processing resources (Lefkovitz, 1985). The term *repository* is used by some vendors to refer to the combination of the information repository and the IRDS.

Using a Repository   The repository is an essential tool for data administration and is used by both data administration and database administration throughout the entire database system life cycle. An information repository serves as a source of information for each of the following:

1. Users who must understand data definitions, business rules, and relationships among data objects
2. Automated CASE tools that are used to specify and develop information systems
3. Applications that access and manipulate data (or business information) in the corporate databases

An organization may use a repository in one of three modes, depending on the nature of the repository and the objectives of the organization.

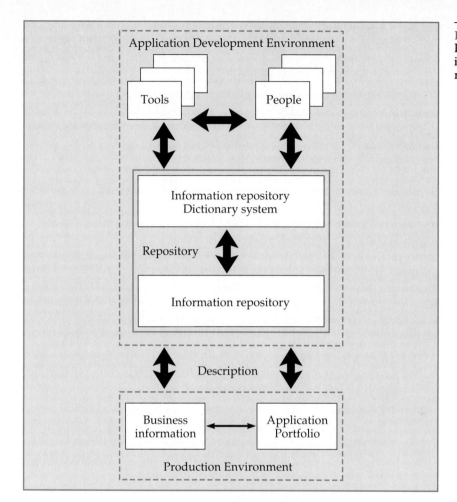

Figure 9-6
Role of an
information
repository

1. **Passive mode.** The repository is primarily a documentation tool used by people, not used by automated tools or applications.
2. **Active in development.** The repository is used by people as a documentation tool and by automated development tools (such as CASE tools) during application development. That is, automated tools make use of the repository to generate data structures, documentation, databases, models, and other components of the application environment. As an illustration, when a database analyst develops an entity-relationship diagram using a CASE tool, the E-R diagram is stored in the repository. However, the repository is not used to actively support application programs in the production environment.
3. **Active in production.** In this mode, the repository is more than a documentation and development tool. It is the mechanism through

which application programs obtain metadata in the production environment. All data integrity, data validation, and security access rules are enforced through the information repository, and changes to these rules are made in the repository.

Many organizations use a repository initially in the passive mode, then progress to the active in development mode, and finally go on to the active in production mode. The active in production mode is preferred, since all components of the information systems environment have a single, centralized source of organizational metadata.

Selecting a Repository   Selecting an appropriate repository product is a key decision for the organization. Data administration should take the lead in evaluating repositories, with substantial input from other groups such as application developers, database administrators, and key end users. At the present time there are relatively few repository products available (for example, IBM released the first version of its repository in 1989). However, as more repository products become available it is essential that organizations develop a list of criteria for evaluating them. Bruce, Fuller, and Moriarty (1989) have developed such a checklist or set of criteria. This list is shown in Figure 9-7, and each item in the list is explained briefly below.

1. **Usage Modes.** What mode (or modes) does the repository support: passive, active in development, active in production? If the repository is active, to what degree is it active?

2. **IRDS Standards.** To what standard does a proposed repository conform? (Several IRDS standards have been evolving for some time from organizations such as the American National Standards Institute (ANSI), the International Standards Organization (ISO), and IBM).

3. **Data Object Model.** Does the repository support a data object model such as the entity-relationship model? Can you add or delete new data objects, relationships, and facts to the data model that is provided?

4. **Data, Structure Integrity.** Does the repository support enough data types to identify your objects and their relationships? Does the repository enforce the defined rules for data validation, integrity, security, and other factors? Is the repository based on an industry-proven DBMS (preferably relational)?

5. **Naming Standards.** Does the repository ensure that each data object instance has one unique name? Does the repository provide support for alias names?

6. **Change Management.** Does the repository provide a mechanism to place data object instances under change control? Does it maintain an audit of changes to data object instances? Does the repository provide facilities for impact analysis?

1. Usage modes
2. IRDS standards
3. Data object model
4. Data, structure integrity
5. Naming standards
6. Change management
7. Data protection
8. Data security
9. Version control
10. Access, Reporting and Analysis
11. Multiuser environment
12. Performance
13. Screen management
14. Application development tools
15. Vendor support

Figure 9-7
Factors for evaluating
a repository

7. **Data Protection.** Does the repository provide adequate facilities for logging, backup, and recovery? If the information repository is damaged or destroyed, does the IRDS provide for automatic recovery without the need to reenter transactions that have occurred since the last backup?

8. **Data Security.** Does the repository provide the ability to restrict access to only authorized individuals? Does it distinguish between read, update, and delete access authority? Does it provide a means of logging and analyzing unauthorized access attempts?

9. **Version Control.** Does the information repository support multiple versions of data objects in the repository? Can the data object model change without affecting automated tools and applications developed under the prior model?

10. **Access, Reporting, and Analysis.** Does the repository support a standard retrieval language such as SQL? Can the user extract reports using simple nonprocedural, English-like statements?

11. **Multiuser Environment.** Can the repository support multiple concurrent users? Can it run on all the computer architectures in your organization, and can it be distributed across these computers?

12. **Performance.** Does the repository provide adequate response times and throughput for your organization?

13. **Screen Management.** Does the repository provide an on-line, user-friendly access facility? Does the screen facility allow easy definition and use of help screens?

14. **Application Development Tools.** Does the repository support the

various CASE tools, source code library managers, and other software products used by your organization?

15. **Vendor Support.** Is the vendor financially stable? Is a service and
maintenance contract available? Are on-site training and consultation
available? Is the vendor willing to provide a list of current customers
who use the repository?

CASE Tools

If you review the functions of data administration (Figure 9-2), you will
notice that data administrators (and database administrators) are responsible for numerous tasks that involve data modeling and design. Fortunately, CASE tools are now available to automate or at least assist in the
performance of many of these tasks.

Computer-aided software engineering (CASE) is technology for auto-
mating software and database development and maintenance tasks (McClure,
1989). CASE tools are designed to support (or automate) the various stages
of the systems development life cycle (SDLC—see Figure 9-8). As this figure
shows, CASE tools may be divided into two broad categories: upper-CASE
tools and lower-CASE tools. **Upper-CASE** tools are designed to support

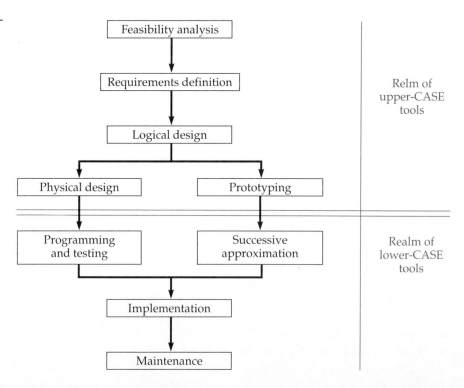

Figure 9-8
System development
life cycle

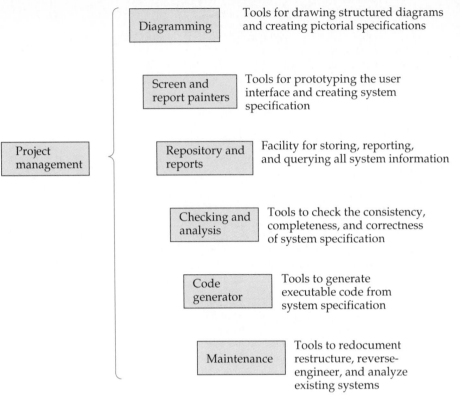

Figure 9-9
Tasks performed by
CASE tools

the "front end" task of the SDLC, including requirements definition, analysis, and design. **Lower-CASE** tools are those that automate functions later in the SDLC, such as code generation, testing, and maintenance. Both upper-CASE and lower-CASE tools are used extensively by contemporary data administrators.

A list of the tasks typically performed by CASE tools is shown in Figure 9-9. These tasks range from diagramming to screen and report generation, checking and analysis, code generation, maintenance, and project management. CASE tools must either provide or interface with an information repository (described in the previous section).

A sample problem to be addressed using the diagramming facilities of CASE tools is shown in Figure 9-10. This problem involves a simple video store that rents videos to customers on a cash basis. The analyst is to develop a data flow diagram and entity-relationship diagram based on this description.

Two such diagrams are shown in Figure 9-11. Figure 9-11a shows a level 1 (or high-level) data flow diagram. In this diagram, sources and destinations of data (such as Customer) are represented by squares. Processes such as "Rent Tape to Customer" are represented by rounded rectangles, and data flows are represented by arrows. Finally, databases (such as Rental

Figure 9-10
Sample problem for
CASE tool
diagramming

Our sample problem concerns a local video rental store (we named it Captain Video, although it has nothing to do with the real store). The following is a brief description of the business. No decision has yet been made on which parts of the business will require computer support, or what type of technology will be used.

EVENTS LIST
    1. Customer rents tape(s) and makes rental payment.
    2. Customer returns tape and may pay late charge of $1 per day.
    3. Time to notify overdue borrowers.
    4. Time to report rentals.
    5. Captain Video submits new tape.
    6. Captain Video submits rate change on some movie titles.
    7. Customer changes address.
    8. Customer requests particular movie title.

OTHER DETAILS
The standard time period for a rental is two days after the borrowed tape is rented. If the customer fails to return the tape in time, then it is time to send a tape overdue notice to the customer address with the title and copy number and past due return date. A tape is a cassette of video tape with a prerecorded movie that can be rented. Each tape has a movie title and a copy number. All copies of a movie have the same rental rate. Not all movies have the same rental rate. A rental is the lending of a tape to a person (previous or new customer) in exchange for cash. A rental has a check-out date, a return date, and a rental charge. If a tape is late, there is a standard $1 per day late charge upon return (no drop box). A customer can rent more than one tape at a time. A tape can be rented, on the shelf waiting to be rented or overdue. This video store has no membership plan and they don't take American Express. All transactions are in cash on-the-spot; no deposits are accepted.

Database) are represented by an open-ended rectangle. Compare this diagram to the narrative description (Figure 9-10) to see how this diagram portrays the data flows for the video store (the diagrams in Figure 9-11 were drawn using Excelerator, a CASE tool product of Index Technology Corporation).

An entity-relationship diagram for the video store is shown in Figure 9-11b. This diagram shows four entities: CUSTOMER, TITLES, TAPES, and RENTAL (the primary key for each entity is also shown). Each instance of TAPES represents a copy of the TITLES entity.

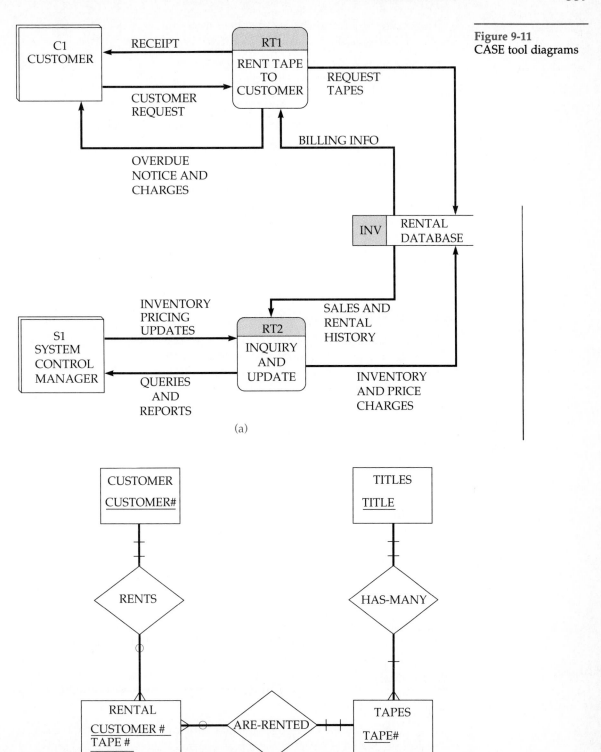

Figure 9-11
CASE tool diagrams

There are numerous benefits to data administrators and software developers from using CASE tools. Some of these benefits are:

1. Improved productivity in development
2. Improved quality through automated checking
3. Automatic preparation and updating of documentation
4. Encouragement of prototyping and incremental development
5. Automatic preparation of program code from requirements definitions
6. Reduced maintenance efforts

Unfortunately, few CASE tools at the present time are sufficiently integrated to support all of the tasks shown in Figure 9-9 or to provide all of the above benefits. For example, some are predominantly upper-CASE tools while others are predominantly lower-CASE tools. Integrated tools are beginning to emerge, however, and will undoubtedly be used as standard development environments during the 1990s.

Database Management Systems

A database management system (DBMS) is a software application system that is used to create, maintain, and provide controlled access to user databases. Database management systems range in complexity from a PC-DBMS (such as Ashton-Tate's dBase IV) costing a few hundred dollars to a mainframe DBMS product (such as IBM's DB2) costing several hundred thousand dollars.

The components of a full-function DBMS are shown in Figure 9-12. Following is a brief description of each of these components.

DBMS Engine   The engine is the central component of a DBMS. This module provides access to the repository and the database and coordinates all of the other functional elements of the DBMS. The DBMS engine receives logical requests for data (and metadata) from human users and from applications, determines the secondary storage location of those data, and issues physical input/output requests to the computer operating system. The engine provides services such as memory and buffer management, maintaining indexes and lists, and secondary storage or disk management.

Interface Subsystem   This system provides facilities for users and applications to access the various components of the DBMS. Most DBMS products provide a range of languages and other interfaces, since the system will be used both by programmers (or other technical persons) and by users with little or no programming experience. Some of the typical interfaces to a DBMS are the following:

1. A data definition language (or data sublanguage), which is used to define database structures such as records, tables, files, and views

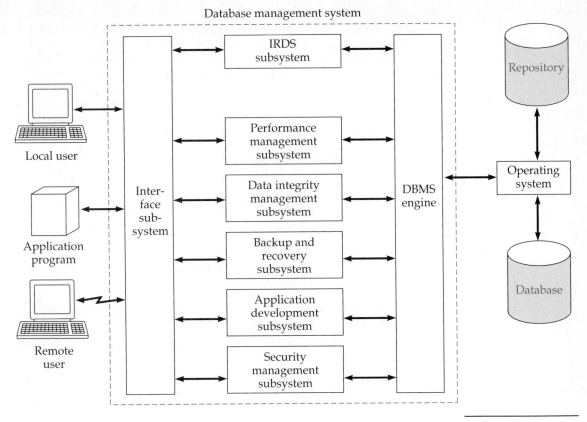

Database management system

Figure 9-12
Components of a DBMS

2. An interactive query language (such as SQL), which is used to display data extracted from the database and to perform simple updates

3. A graphic interface (such as Query-by-Example) in which the system displays a skeleton table (or tables), and users pose requests by suitable entries in the table

4. A forms interface in which a screen-oriented form is presented to the user, who responds by filling in blanks in the form

5. A DBMS programming language (such as the dBase IV, which is a procedural language that allows programmers to develop sophisticated applications)

6. An interface to standard third-generation programming languages such as BASIC and COBOL

7. A natural language interface that allows users to present requests in free-form English statements

We present examples of many of these types of interfaces in following chapters.

Information Repository Dictionary System (IRDS)   This subsystem is used to manage and control access to the repository (the IRDS was described in a previous section; see Figure 9-6). In Figure 9-12 we choose to show the IRDS as a component that is integrated within the DBMS. Notice that the IRDS uses the facilities of the database engine to manage the repository.

Performance Management Subsystem   This subsystem provides facilities to optimize (or at least improve) DBMS performance. Two of its important functions are:

1. **Query optimization:** structuring SQL queries (or other forms of user queries) to minimize response times
2. **DBMS reorganization:** maintaining statistics on database usage and taking (or recommending) actions such as database reorganization, creating indexes, and so on to improve DBMS performance

Data Integrity Management Subsystem   This subsystem provides facilities for managing the integrity of data in the database and the integrity of metadata in the repository. There are three important functions:

1. **Intrarecord integrity:** enforcing constraints on data item values and types within each record in the database
2. **Referential integrity:** enforcing the validity of references between records in the database (discussed in a later section)
3. **Concurrency control:** assuring the validity of database updates when multiple users access the database (discussed in a later section)

Backup and Recovery Subsystem   This subsystem provides facilities for logging transactions and database changes, periodically making backup copies of the database and recovering the database in the event of some type of failure (we discuss backup and recovery in greater detail in a later section).

Application Development Subsystem   This subsystem provides facilities by which end users and/or programmers may develop complete database applications. It includes CASE tools (described in a previous section) as well as facilities such as screen generators and report generators (we illustrated some of these features for dBASE IV in Chapter 2).

Security Management Subsystem   This subsystem provides facilities to protect and control access to the database and repository (we discuss security management in a later section).

DATA RESOURCE MANAGEMENT ISSUES

Earlier in this chapter we noted that data administration is responsible for ensuring database integrity and security. In this section we describe several key issues in data resource management related to integrity and security.

The issues that are discussed here are the following: referential integrity, concurrency control, backup and recovery, database security, and handling missing data. It is the responsibility of data administration to ensure that policies and procedures are in place to guarantee adequate management of these issues. In managing database security and integrity, data administration uses the tools described in the previous section.

Referential Integrity

A referential integrity constraint is concerned with the validity of references by one object in a database to some other object (or objects) in the database (Brown, 1988). For example, often a row in one relation refers to one (or more) rows in another relation. Referential integrity constraints exist because of the rules of the business or organization. They should be identified during requirements definition (see Chapter 5). Enforcement of referential integrity constraints is essential to an effective shared information asset.

The problem of referential integrity can be illustrated by a simple example (see Figure 9-13). The PART table contains a list of parts, while the VENDOR table contains a list of vendors. In this example, each part has exactly one vendor. Vendor# is a foreign key in the PART relation, and each row in the PART relation references the vendor who supplies the part in the VENDOR relation.

A referential integrity constraint requires that for each row of one table—the "referencing table"—the value in the foreign key column must be the same as the value of the corresponding primary key column in some row of the referenced table or else must be null. In Figure 9-13, the PART table is the referencing table, while the VENDOR table is the referenced table. Notice that at the present time, all referential integrity constraints are satisfied. Thus for part number 100, the vendor number (10) matches the primary key for the first vendor in the VENDOR table. Similarly, there is a match on vendor number for each # of the other parts.

Referential integrity considerations arise primarily in the context of insertions and deletions, and we limit our discussion to these operations.

Insertion Rule A row should not be inserted in the referencing table, unless there already exists a matching entry in the referenced table. In

PART

Part#	Part-Name	Vendor#
100	gizmo	10
200	widget	40
300	thumzer	30
400	whatsit	10

VENDOR

Vendor#	Vendor-Name
10	Artcraft
20	Bakeright
30	Choicetops
40	Deskmate

Figure 9-13
Two associated relations

Figure 9-13, suppose an attempt is made to enter the following row for a new part:

500 Kluge 50

This insertion request should be disallowed, since there is no entry for vendor number 50 in the VENDOR table.

In some circumstances, the organization may wish to allow the insertion of part information, even though a vendor has not yet been determined for that part. This can be accomplished without violating referential integrity constraints by leaving the vendor number null in the referencing table. Thus, the following insertion request would be allowed (the symbol "—" designates a null or missing value):

500 Kluge—

The result of inserting this row in the PART table is shown in Figure 9-14. Referential integrity is not violated, since the vendor number is not yet determined.

Deletion Rule   A row should not be deleted from the referenced table, if there is a matching row (or rows) in the referencing table. In Figure 9-13, none of the rows in VENDOR can be deleted since there are matching rows in PART.

Consider the following SQL request:

DELETE
FROM VENDOR
WHERE Vendor# = 10

This request should be disallowed since there are matching rows in PART for vendor number 10. However, considering the possible use of nulls there are three delete rules that might be used:

1. **Restrict**. Disallow the delete request.

2. **Nullify**. Reset to null any vendor number 10 in the PART relation, then delete vendor number 10 from VENDOR (see Figure 9-14a).

3. **Cascade**. Delete any part in the PART table for vendor number 10, then delete vendor number 10 from VENDOR (see Figure 9-14b).

Figure 9-14
Foreign key with nulls allowed

PART

Part#	Part-Name	Vendor#
100	gizmo	10
200	widget	40
300	thumzer	30
400	whatsit	10
500	kluge	—

PART

Part#	Part-Name	Vendor#
100	gizmo	——
200	widget	40
300	thumzer	30
400	whatsit	——

VENDOR

Vendor#	Vendor-Name
20	Bakeright
30	Choicetops
40	Deskmate

(a)

Figure 9-15
Two delete rules

PART

Part#	Part-Name	Vendor#
200	widget	40
300	thumzer	30

VENDOR

Vendor#	Vendor-Name
20	Bakeright
30	Choicetops
40	Deskmate

(b)

The choice of delete rule in a given case depends on the nature of the business situation. For example, the restrict rule is appropriate if the intent is to remove only vendors with whom no business is being done. The nullify rule (Figure 9-15a) is appropriate if the intent is to remove any vendor and all traces (that is, part references) to that vendor. The cascade rule (Figure 9-15b) is appropriate if the intent is to stop using any part supplied by a deleted vendor (Brown, 1988).

Enforcing Referential Integrity   Referential integrity constraints can be enforced through two possible mechanisms:

1. Each application program must independently enforce integrity constraints.
2. The DBMS must include facilities for enforcing integrity constraints.

The first of these approaches is not reliable, since individual application programs may or may not have included the necessary logic to enforce referential integrity. Also, it is possible that application programs that do contain referential integrity rules may conflict with each other. Thus the second approach (DBMS enforces referential integrity) is preferred since it provides consistent enforcement or rules. Unfortunately, not all DBMS products today enforce referential integrity; newer releases of some DBMS products do, however, and this feature will probably become standard for most products in the future.

Concurrency Control

Concurrency in a database environment means that more than one user can access and manipulate data at the same time. With concurrent processing involving updates, a database without concurrency control will be com-

Figure 9-16
Effect of concurrent update without locking

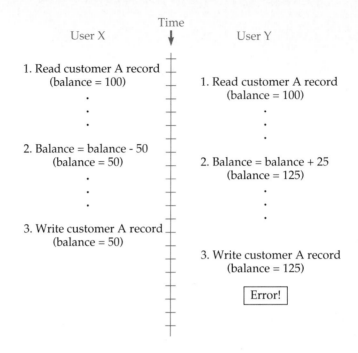

Time

User X

1. Read customer A record
   (balance = 100)

2. Balance = balance - 50
   (balance = 50)

3. Write customer A record
   (balance = 50)

User Y

1. Read customer A record
   (balance = 100)

2. Balance = balance + 25
   (balance = 125)

3. Write customer A record
   (balance = 125)

Error!

promised due to interference between users. An example of such erroneous updating is shown in Figure 9-16. Two users are in the process of updating the same database record, which contains information about the savings account for bank customer A. At the present time, customer A has a balance of $100 in her account. User X (through an application program) reads the record for customer A, intending to post a withdrawal of $50. At about the same time, user Y (through an application program) reads the same record, intending to post a customer deposit of $25. The sequence of events is shown on a time scale. User X returns his copy of the record (now showing a balance of $50) to the database first. User Y then returns his copy of the record (now showing a balance of $125) to the database, copying it on top of the version stored by user A. Thus, the record for customer A erroneously shows a balance of $125. Customer A will probably be pleased with this turn of events—but what if user Y had stored the record before user X?

Locking Mechanisms   Controlling concurrent access while making each user appear to be the only one accessing the database is the challenge faced by concurrency control mechanisms. Most commercial DBMS products use a locking mechanism to prevent erroneous updates. That is, any data that is retrieved by a user for updating must be "locked" or denied to other users until the update is completed (or aborted). Locking data is much like checking a book out of the library—it is unavailable to others until it is returned by the borrower.

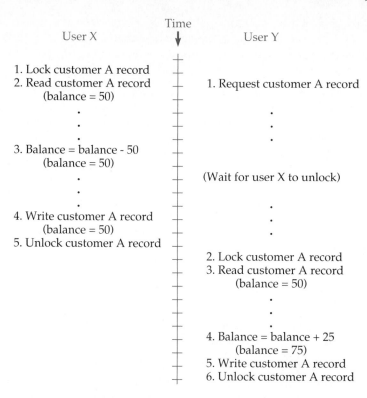

Figure 9-17
Concurrent update
with locking

The use of record locks to maintain data integrity is shown in Figure 9-17. At the time user X requests the record for Customer A, it is unlocked. Since user X intends to update the record, the application program locks this record *before* reading it into main memory. User X then proceeds to update his copy of the record. Meanwhile user Y has requested the record but must wait until user X has returned the updated record to the database and unlocked the record. The locking mechanism thus enforces a sequential updating process that prevents erroneous updates.

An important consideration in implementing concurrency control is choosing the locking level. Most commercial products implement locks at one of the following levels:

1. **Database.** The entire database is locked and becomes unavailable to other users. This level has limited application, such as during a backup of the entire database (Rodgers, 1989).

2. **Table.** The table containing a requested record is locked. This level is appropriate mainly for bulk updates that will update the entire table, such as giving all employees a 5% raise.

3. **Block or page.** The storage block (or page) containing a requested record is locked. This level is generally not desirable since a page may contain records of more than one type.

4. **Record level.** Only the requested record is locked. This is the most commonly implemented locking level since then all other records are available to other users. It does impose some overhead at run time when several records are involved in an update.

5. **Field level.** Only the particular field (or fields) in a requested record are locked. This level may be appropriate when most updates affect only one or two fields in a record. For example, in inventory control applications the quantity-on-hand field changes frequently, but other fields (such as description and bin location) are rarely updated. Field-level locks require considerable overhead and are infrequently used.

Types of Locks   So far, we have discussed only locks that prevent all access to locked items. However, it may be desirable to provide shared access to records even when some user is updating those records. Thus, DBMS products may have two types of locks:

1. **Shared locks.** When a user locks a record (or other resource), other users may read that record but may not update the record until it is unlocked.

2. **Exclusive locks.** When a record is locked, no other users may read that record until it is unlocked.

The effect of using these two types of locks is summarized in Figure 9-18. In this figure there are two users. The figure shows the result (for user B) for various requests, depending on the type of lock held by user A at the time of the request. Suppose user A has a shared lock on a record. User B cannot read that record with intention to update while it is locked, but user B can request read-only access to that record. If user B does not attempt to lock that record (either shared or exclusive), the read request is permitted. However, the data read by user B may be in the process of change, due to updates by user A. This type of read is called a "dirty read"—that is, changes may be occurring to a file as you read it.

For a "clean read," user B should use a shared lock with the read request. For example, suppose user B plans to read an entire file to produce a report. By placing a shared lock on that file, user B can ensure that no other user can update records in that file until the lock is released.

Deadlock   Locking (say at the record level) solves the problem of erroneous updates but may lead to another problem, called deadlock. **Deadlock**

Figure 9-18
Using two types of locks

User A has:	User B requests:	Result (for user B):
No lock	——	No restriction
Shared lock	No lock	Dirty read
Shared lock	Shared lock	Clean read
Exclusive lock	——	Access denied

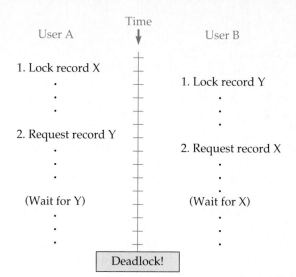

Figure 9-19
Example of deadlock

(or the "deadly embrace") is an impasse that results when two users each lock a record (or other resource), then request resources locked by the other user. An example of deadlock is shown in Figure 9-19. User A is waiting for record Y (exclusive lock by user B), and user B is waiting for record X (exclusive lock by user A). Unless the DBMS intervenes, both users will wait indefinitely.

There are two basic ways to resolve deadlock: deadlock prevention and deadlock resolution. When deadlock prevention is employed, user programs must lock all records they will require at the beginning of a transaction (rather than one at a time). In Figure 9-19, user A would have to lock both records X and Y before processing the transaction (if either record is already locked, the program must wait until it is released).

Locking records in advance prevents deadlock. Unfortunately, it is often difficult to predict in advance what records will be required to process a transaction. A typical program has many processing parts and may call other programs. As a result, deadlock prevention is not often practical.

Deadlock Resolution The second (and more common) approach is to allow deadlocks to occur, but to build mechanisms into the DBMS for detecting and breaking the deadlocks. Essentially, this is how these mechanisms work. The DBMS maintains a matrix of resource usage, which, at a given instant, indicates what subjects (users) are using what objects (resources). By scanning this matrix, the computer can detect deadlocks as they occur. The DBMS then resolves the deadlocks by "backing out" one of the deadlocked transactions. Any changes made by that transaction up to the time of deadlock are removed, and the transaction is restarted when the required resources become available. We will describe the procedure for backing out shortly.

Database Security

Today, corporations and government agencies are putting more and more sensitive data on computers. As the number and sophistication of user access paths to the database increase, those data become vulnerable to unwanted access or corruption. A recent survey of computer security professionals estimates the annual losses from computer abuse at over $500,000,000 nationally. Among the survey respondents, the average installation experienced losses of over $100,000 and 365 person-hours per year (Bloombecker, 1989).

Computer security begins with a well-designed set of controls over the computer center and its operations (see Figure 9-20). The security controls shown in this figure are a prerequisite for the controls over database access that will be described in the following sections.

Database security is defined as protection of the database against accidental or intentional loss, destruction, or misuse. As we noted earlier in the chapter, data administration is responsible for developing overall policies and procedures to protect databases. Data administration uses several facilities provided by data management software in carrying out these functions. The most important security features of data management software are:

1. Views or subschemas, which restrict user views of the database

2. Authorization rules, which identify users and restrict the actions they may take against the database

3. User-defined procedures, which define additional constraints or limitations in using the database

4. Encryption procedures, which encode data in an unrecognizable form

5. Authentication schemes, which positively identify a person attempting to gain access to a database

Views   A **view** (also called a subschema) is a subset of the database that is presented to one or more users. To illustrate, the PART and VENDOR relations shown in Figure 9-13 are base tables that are part of a larger database. Suppose that a particular user requires a view that associates part name with vendor name. We can provide this list by defining the following view:

    CREATE VIEW PART_VENDOR
            AS SELECT Part_Name, Vendor_Name
            FROM PART, VENDOR
            WHERE PART.VENDOR# = VENDOR.VENDOR#

If the user enters this query:

    SELECT*
    FROM PART_VENDOR
    ORDER BY Part_Name

1. Physical security—limit access, prohibit smoking and eating in computer room, etc.
2. Operations security—install disaster recovery procedures, divide responsibilities for sensitive computer operations, etc.
3. Computer systems—validate input data, use data encryption, log all transactions, etc.
4. Computer terminal access—use terminal identifiers, establish log in protocols, etc.
5. Data integrity—control document distribution, destroy discarded documents, etc .
6. Program development and maintenance—establish access control for program libraries, use walkthroughs and quality assurance procedures, etc.
7. Management controls—establish a computer security management committee, conduct security audits etc.

Figure 9-20
Computer center
security controls

the following result will appear:

Part_Name	Vendor_Name
gizmo	Artcraft
thumzer	Choicetops
whatsit	Artcraft
widget	Deskmate

Although views promote security by restricting user access to limited data, they are not adequate security measures, as unauthorized persons may gain knowledge of or access to a particular view. Also, several persons may share a particular view; all may have authority to read the data but only a restricted few may be authorized to update the data. Finally, with high-level query languages, an unauthorized person may gain access to data through simple experimentation. As a result, more sophisticated security measures are normally required.

Authorization Rules   **Authorization rules** are controls incorporated in the data management system that restrict access to data and also restrict the actions that people may take when data are accessed. For example, a person who can supply a particular password may be authorized to read any record in a database but cannot necessarily modify any of those records.

Fernandez, Summers, and Wood (1981) have developed a conceptual model of database security. Their model expresses authorization rules in the form of a table (or matrix) that includes subjects, objects, actions, and constraints. Each row of the table indicates that a particular subject is authorized to take a certain action on an object in the database, perhaps subject to some constraint. An example of such an authorization matrix is shown in Figure 9-21. This table contains several entries pertaining to records in an accounting database. For example, the first row in the table indicates that anyone in the Sales Department is authorized to insert a new Customer record in the database, provided that the customer's credit limit does not exceed $5,000. The last row indicates that the program AR4 is

Figure 9-21
Authorization matrix

Subject	Object	Action	Constraint
Sales Dept.	Customer Record	Insert	Credit limit LE $5000
Order trans.	Customer record	Read	None
Terminal 12	Customer record	Modify	Balance due only
Acctg Dept.	Order record	Delete	None
Luke Skywalker	Order record	Insert	Order amt LT $2000
Program AR4	Order record	Modify	None

authorized to modify Order records without restriction. Data administration is responsible for determining authorization rules.

Implementing Authorization Rules   Most contemporary database management systems do not implement an authorization matrix such as the one shown in Figure 9-21. Instead, simplified versions are normally used. There are two principal types: authorization tables for subjects and authorization tables for objects. An example of each type is shown in Figure 9-22. In Figure 9-22a, for example, we see that salespersons (who are probably identified by passwords) are allowed to modify Customer records but not delete these records. In Figure 9-22b, we see that Order records can be modified by persons in Order Entry or Accounting but not by salespersons. A given DBMS product may provide either one or both of these types of facilities.

Authorization tables such as those shown in Figure 9-22 are attributes of an organization's data and their environment and therefore are properly viewed as metadata. Thus, the tables should be stored and maintained in the repository. Since authorization tables contain highly sensitive data, they themselves should be protected by stringent security rules. Normally, only selected persons in data administration have authority to access and modify these tables.

User-Defined Procedures   Some DBMS products provide user exists (or interfaces) that allow system designers or users to define their own security procedures, in addition to the authorization rules we have just described. For example, a user procedure might be designed to provide positive user identification. In attempting to log on to the computer, the user might be required to supply a procedure name in addition to a simple password. If a valid password and procedure name are supplied, the system then calls the procedure, which asks the user a series of questions whose answers should be known only to that password holder (such as mother's maiden name).

Encryption Procedures   For highly sensitive data (such as company financial data), data encryption can be used. **Encryption** is the coding (or scram-

	Customer records	Order records
Read	Y	Y
Insert	Y	N
Modify	Y	N
Delete	N	N

(a)

	Salespersons (password BATMAN)	Order entry (password JOKER)	Accounting (password TRACY)
Read	Y	Y	Y
Insert	N	Y	N
Modify	N	Y	Y
Delete	N	N	Y

(b)

Figure 9-22
Implementing
authorization rules

bling) of data so that they cannot be read by humans. Some DBMS products include encryption routines that automatically encode sensitive data when they are stored or transmitted over communications channels. For example, encryption is commonly used in electronic funds transfer (EFT) systems. Other DBMS products provide exists that allow users to code their own encryption routines.

Any system that provides encryption facilities must also provide complementary routines for decoding the data. These decoding routines must of course be protected by adequate security, or else the advantages of encryption are lost, and they also require significant computing resources.

Authentication Schemes   A long-standing problem in computer circles is how to positively identify persons who are trying to gain access to a computer or its resources. Passwords cannot, of themselves, ensure the security of a computer and its databases because they give no indication of who is trying to gain access. To circumvent this problem, the industry is developing devices and techniques to positively identify any prospective user. The most promising of these appear to be **biometric devices,** which measure or detect personal characteristics such as fingerprints, voice prints, retina prints, or signature dynamics. To implement this approach, several companies have developed a **smart card**—a thin plastic card the size of a credit card, with an embedded microprocessor. An individual's unique biometric data (such as fingerprints) are stored permanently on the card. To access a computer, the user inserts the card into a reader device (a biometric device) that reads the person's fingerprint (or other characteristic).

The actual biometric data are then compared with the stored data, and the two must match to gain computer access. A lost or stolen card would be useless to another person, since the biometric data would not match.

Database Recovery

Database recovery is data administration's response to Murphy's law. Inevitably, databases are damaged or lost because of some system failure, caused by human error, hardware failure, incorrect or invalid data, program errors, computer viruses, and natural catastrophes. Since the organization depends so heavily on its database, the database management system must provide mechanisms for restoring a database quickly and accurately after loss or damage.

Basic Recovery Facilities   A database management system should provide four basic facilities for backup and recovery of a database:

1. Backup facilities, which provide periodic backup copies of the entire database

2. Journalizing facilities, which maintain an audit trail of transactions and database changes

3. A checkpoint facility, by which the DBMS periodically suspends all processing and synchronizes its files and journals

4. A recovery manager, which allows the DBMS to restore the database to a correct condition and restart processing transactions

Backup Facilities   The DBMS should provide an automatic dump facility that produces a backup copy (or "save") of the entire database. Typically, a backup copy is produced at least once per day. The copy should be stored in a secured location where it is protected from loss or damage. The backup copy is used to restore the database in the event of catastrophic loss or damage.

Journalizing Facilities   A DBMS must provide an audit trail of transactions and database changes. As shown in Figure 9-23, there are two basic journals or logs. First, there is the **transaction log**, which contains a record of the essential data for each transaction that is processed against the database. Data that are typically recorded for each transaction include the transaction code or identification, time of the transaction, terminal number or user ID, input data values, records accessed, and records modified.

The second kind of log is the **database change log,** which contains before and after images of records that have been modified by transactions. A **before image** is simply a copy of a record before it has been modified, while an **after image** is a copy of the same record after it has been modified.

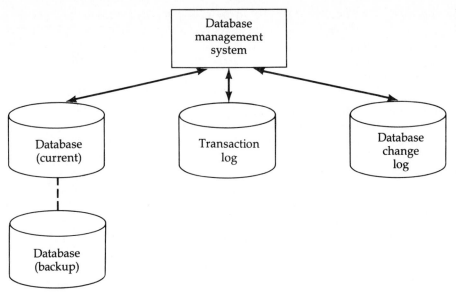

Figure 9-23
Database audit trail

Checkpoint Facility A **checkpoint** is a facility by which the DBMS periodically refuses to accept any new transactions. All transactions in progress are completed and the journal files are brought up to date. At this point, the system is in a "quiet state" and the database and transaction logs are synchronized. The DBMS writes a special record (called a checkpoint record) to the log file. The checkpoint record contains information necessary to restart the system.

A DBMS may perform checkpoints automatically (which is preferred) or in response to commands in user application programs. Checkpoints should be taken frequently (say, several times an hour). When failures do occur, it is often possible to resume processing from the most recent checkpoint. Thus, only a few minutes of processing work has to be repeated, compared with several hours for a complete restart of the day's processing.

Recovery Manager The recovery manager is a module of the DBMS that restores the database to a correct condition when a failure occurs and resumes processing user requests. The type of restart used depends on the nature of the failure. The recovery manager uses the journal files shown in Figure 9-23 (as well as the backup copy, if necessary) to restore the database.

Recovery and Restart Procedures The type of recovery procedure that is used in a given situation depends on the nature of the failure, the sophistication of the DBMS recovery facilities, and operational policies and procedures. Following is a discussion of the techniques that are most frequently used.

Restore/Rerun   Restore/rerun involves reprocessing the day's transactions (up to the point of failure) against the backup copy of the database. The most recent copy of the database (say, from the previous day) is mounted, and all transactions that have occurred since that copy (which are stored on the transaction log) are rerun.

The advantage of restore/rerun is its simplicity. The DBMS does not need to create a database change journal, and no special restart procedures are required. However, there are two major disadvantages. First, the time to reprocess transactions may be prohibitive. Depending on the frequency of making backup copies, several hours of reprocessing may be required. Processing new transactions will have to be deferred until recovery is completed, and if the system is heavily loaded, it may be impossible to catch up. The second disadvantage is that the sequencing of transactions will often be different from when they were originally processed, which may lead to quite different results. For example, in the original run, a customer deposit may be posted before a withdrawal. In the rerun, the withdrawal transaction may be attempted first and may lead to sending a "not sufficient funds" notice to the customer. For these reasons, restore/rerun is not a sufficient recovery procedure and is generally used only as a last resort in database processing.

Transaction Integrity   A database is updated by processing transactions that result in changes to one or more database records. If an error occurs during the processing of a transaction, the database may be compromised and some form of database recovery is required. Thus to understand database recovery, we must first understand the concept of transaction integrity.

A **transaction** is a sequence of steps that constitute some well-defined business activity. Examples of transactions are "Admit Patient" (in a hospital) and "Enter Customer Order" (in a manufacturing company). Normally, a transaction requires several actions against the database. For example, consider the transaction "Enter Customer Order." When a new customer order is entered, the following steps may be performed by an application program:

1. Input order data (keyed by user).
2. Read CUSTOMER record (or insert record if a new customer).
3. Accept or reject the order (if Balance-Due plus Order-Amount does not exceed Credit-Limit, accept the order; otherwise, reject it).
4. If the order is accepted:
    a. Increase Balance-Due by Order-Amount.
    b. Store the updated CUSTOMER record.
    c. Insert the accepted ORDER record in the database.

In processing a transaction, we want the changes to the database to be made only if the transaction is processed successfully, in its entirety. In this case, we say that the changes are *committed*. If the transaction fails at any

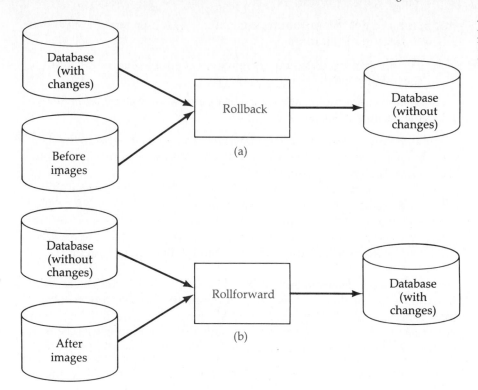

Figure 9-24
Basic recovery
techniques

point, we say that it has *aborted*, and we do not want any of the changes to be made. For example, suppose that the program accepts a new customer order, increases Balance-Due, and stores the updated CUSTOMER record. However, suppose that the new ORDER record is not inserted successfully (perhaps there is a duplicate Order# key, or perhaps there is insufficient file space). In this case, we want the transaction to abort and the changes not to be committed.

To maintain transaction integrity, the DBMS must provide facilities for the user or application programmer to define **transaction boundaries**—that is, the logical beginning and end of transactions. The DBMS should then commit changes for successful transactions and reject changes for aborted transactions.

Backward Recovery **Backward recovery** (also called "rollback") is used to back out or undo unwanted changes to the database. As shown in Figure 9-24a, before images of the records that have been changed are applied to the database. As a result, the database is returned to an earlier state (the unwanted changes are eliminated).

Backward recovery is used to reverse the changes made by transactions that have aborted, or terminated abnormally. To illustrate the need for backward recovery (or UNDO), suppose that a banking transaction will transfer

$100 in funds from the account for customer A to the account for customer B. These steps are performed:

1. The program reads the record for customer A and subtracts $100 from the account balance.

2. The program then reads the record for customer B and adds $100 to the account balance.

Now the program writes the updated record for customer A to the database. However, in attempting to write the record for customer B, the program encounters an error condition (such as a disk fault) and cannot write the record. Now the database is inconsistent—record A has been updated but record B has not—and the transaction must be aborted. An UNDO command will cause the recovery manager to apply the befe image for record A to restore the account balance to its original value (the recovery manager may then restart the transaction and make another attempt).

Forward Recovery   **Forward recovery** (also called "rollforward") starts with an earlier copy of the database. By applying after images (the results of good transactions), the database is quickly moved forward to a later state (see Figure 9-24b). Forward recovery is much faster and more accurate than restore/rerun, for the following reasons:

• The time-consuming logic of reprocessing each transaction does not have to be repeated.

• Only the most recent after images need to be applied. A database record may have a series of after images (as a result of a sequence of updates), but only the most recent "good" after image is required for rollforward.

• The problem of different sequencing of transactions is avoided, since the results of applying the transactions (rather than the transactions themselves) are used.

Types of Database Failure

A wide variety of failures can occur in processing a database, ranging from the input of an incorrect data value to complete loss or destruction of the database. Four of the most common types of errors are aborted transactions, incorrect data, system failure, and database loss or destruction. Each of these types of errors is described in the following sections, and the most common recovery procedure is indicated (see Figure 9-25).

Aborted Transactions   As we noted earlier, a transaction frequently requires a sequence of processing steps to be performed. Often, a transaction that is in progress will abort, or terminate abnormally. Some reasons for this type of failure are human error, input of invalid data, hardware failure, and

Type of failure	Recovery technique
Aborted transaction	Rollback
Incorrect data	(1) Backward recovery (or)(2) Compensating transactions (or)(3) Restart from checkpoint
System failure (Database intact)	(1) Rollback (or)(2) Restart fom checkpoint
Database destruction	Rollforward

Figure 9-25
Responses to data base failure

deadlock. A common type of hardware failure is the loss of transmission in a communications link when a transaction is in progress.

When a transaction aborts, we want to "back out" the transaction and remove any changes that have been made (but not committed) to the database. The recovery manager accomplishes this by backward recovery (applying before images for the transaction in question). This function should be accomplished automatically by the DBMS, which then notifies the user to correct and resubmit the transaction.

Incorrect Data A more complex situation arises when the database has been updated with incorrect, but valid, data. For example, an incorrect grade may be recorded for a student, or an incorrect amount input for a customer payment.

Incorrect data are difficult to detect and often lead to complications. To begin with, some time may elapse before an error is detected and the database record (or records) corrected. By this time, numerous other users may have used the erroneous data, and a chain reaction of errors may have occurred as various applications made use of the incorrect data. In addition, transaction outputs (such as documents and messages) based on the incorrect data may be transmitted to persons. An incorrect grade report, for example, may be sent to a student, or an incorrect statement sent to a customer.

When incorrect data have been introduced, the database may be recovered in one of the following ways:

1. If the error is discovered soon enough, backward recovery may be used. (However, care must be taken to ensure that all subsequent errors have been reversed.)

2. If only a few errors have occurred, a series of compensating transactions may be introduced through human intervention to correct the errors.

3. If the first two measures are not feasible, it may be necessary to restart fr the mt recent checkpoint before the error occurred.

Any erroneous messages or documents that have been produced by the erroneous transaction will have to be corrected by appropriate human intervention (letters of explanation, telephone calls, and so on).

System Failure   With a system failure, some component of the system fails but the database is not damaged. Some causes of system failure are power loss, operator error, loss of communications transmission, and system software failure.

When the system crashes, some transactions may be in progress. The first step in recovery is to back out those transactions using before images (backward recovery). However, it may not be possible to restart from this point after a system crash, since status information in main memory will likely be lost or damaged. The safest approach is to restart from the most recent checkpoint before the system failure. The database is rolled forward by applying after images for all transactions that were processed after that checkpoint.

Database Destruction   In the case of database destruction, the database itself is lost or destroyed or cannot be read. A typical cause of database destruction is a disk drive failure (or head crash).

A backup copy of the database is required for recovery in this situation. Forward recovery is used to restore the database to its state immediately before the loss occurred. Any transactions that may have been in progress when the database was lost are restarted.

Handling Missing or Ambiguous Data

It is not uncommon in database management to encounter situations where data are missing, lost, or incomplete. When data are not normalized or when data are duplicated for high operational performance, different data values for the same data item may disagree, causing ambiguity or uncertainty as to the real data value (which may have to be handled as missing the real value). Examples of data with null values are shown in Figures 9-13 and 9-14.

As we will see in later chapters, many DBMSs now support a NULL VALUE that can be used to represent missing data, but, although missing data can be represented, reporting involving missing values may be cumbersome. For example, if the gender of some employees is missing and the age of some other employees is missing, any comparison or relationship between age and gender is questionable since it would not be based on the same employees.

According to Babad and Hoffer (1984), there are six possible methods for dealing with missing data:

1. **Initialization of data fields.** Initialization ensures that all data elements are set to some value and that computations can always be

performed. But the lack of data is masked and computations may be biased.

2. **Automatic defaults.** Common default values are zero, the smallest or largest possible value for numerical fields, or a blank space for nonnumeric fields. NULL VALUE also fits into this category. Although similar to initialization methods, defaults can be applied at any time data are found to be missing.

3. **Deducing values.** The DBMS can compensate for missing data by inferring values. The most common derived value would be to use the mean of some set of values—either all values from all record instances, some appropriate or categorized subset, or simply the range of possible values. More sophisticated methods could estimate the missing value from audit trails or from characteristics of similar records. It might even be possible to represent the missing value by a confidence interval or range (set in the case of discrete data) of likely values.

4. **Track missing data.** No matter how values may be stored in the place of missing data, it is equally important to tag or identify data as missing. Use of NULL VALUE or some special code does this, but no value is actually stored. It may even be desirable to know for how long the value has been unknown or what attempts have been made to find the correct value. A tag with the "missing value" can indicate that the value stored was entered by some user, estimated in some way, reconstructed from an audit trail, or reviewed for reasonableness on the same day, among many possible annotations.

5. **Determine impact of missing data.** How we handle missing data may depend on how the data will impact those who use it. If data are listed in a report merely for descriptive purposes, then simply showing a null value may be sufficient. If the value would be crucial in putting a core summary statistic over an important threshold (for example, cause a reorder of an expensive inventory item), then the missing value should cause a message to either find the missing value or interpret the results with caution. Vassiliov (1981) discusses this situation in detail.

6. **Prevent missing data.** Even if complete prevention of missing data is not possible, the incidence of missing data can be greatly reduced by certain procedures. In batch processing, preedit programs can scan for missing data and validate all data elements (a major source of missing data is an invalid field value that has been eliminated by an edit check at data load time). Reports of missing and invalid data elements can lead to an immediate search for actual values before the data have to be entered into the database. Grouping transactions into logical sets and forcing the whole set to be valid before any single transaction takes effect is another procedure that can be used to prevent missing data (for example, make sure that a patient discharge,

which affects patient, bed, and charges data, can be processed as a whole). To avoid erroneous handling by application programs, programmers can write special utilities to scan for missing data, especially unrelated records.

No data model explicitly recognizes the possibility of missing data, yet it is an everyday fact of life for a living database. If not dealt with during database design, a database can evolve into a low integrity state and cause interrupted or erroneous data processing. A database designer must therefore design the database and database utilities to deal with the inevitable situation of missing or ambiguous data.

Case Example: Mountain View Community Hospital

At Mountain View Community Hospital, Mr. Helms was appointed data administrator following the initial planning study (described in Chapter 4). Mr. Helms is a systems analyst who is a new employee at Mountain View Community, but he has previous experience in database design. Mr. Helms reports to Mr. Heller, who is manager of information systems (an organization chart for Mountain View Community is shown in Figure 4-8). A data analyst (Mrs. Green) reports to Mr. Helms. Mrs. Green will be responsible for several database administration functions, including data integrity and security.

Mr. Helms formed a committee consisting of himself, Mr. Heller, and three department heads to select a relational DBMS product that would best meet the needs of the hospital. The team created a list of evaluation criteria and then identified five candidate products to be evaluated. After collecting additional information and talking with the respective vendors, the team narrowed the list to two contenders. The team then asked each vendor for references to customers who were using those products. Two customers for each product were contacted (only one vendor had a hospital among its customers). After further discussion, the team selected the RDBMS product that they believed best suited to Mountain View Community Hospital's needs. This product has the following features:

- SQL language interface
- Active repository/data dictionary
- CASE tools to support E-R diagrams and project management
- Interactive application development tools
- On-line backup and recovery facilities
- Resource locking at database, table, record, and field levels
- Multilevel security controls
- Basic referential integrity

The vendor of this RDBMS recommended some upgrading of the minicomputer used at the hospital to support this new environment. Mr. Helms and other members of the IS department began making detailed plans for installing the new hardware and software and for implementing the initial applications under this new system (Priorities for systems and applications at Mountain View Community Hospital are described in Chapter 4.)

SUMMARY

In this chapter we define the functions of data administration, the major tools that are used by data administrators, and several key data management issues.

Data administration is a high-level management function that is responsible for developing an enterprise data model and for maintaining corporate-wide data standards. Database administration is a technical function that is responsible for physical database design and for dealing with technical issues such as security, performance, and backup and recovery. Recently, the concept of a data steward has emerged. A data steward manages a specific logical data resource for all business functions.

There is a database system life cycle that includes the following stages: planning, requirements definition, design, implementation, operation and maintenance, and growth and change. Data administration is normally responsible for database planning, requirements definition, and logical database design. Database administration is typically responsible for physical database design and much of database implementation, operation, and maintenance. Some functions, such as specifying database access policies, conducting user training, and managing growth and change, may be the responsibility of both groups.

To be successful, data administration must have top-management support and commitment. The head of data administration (or the data administrator) must process a high level of management skills, as well as technical skills. Data administration should normally report directly to the chief information officer (or head of information systems) within the organization. In a decentralized organization, data administration may be decentralized along with other information system functions, but it is often desirable to have a corporate data administration group to coordinate the efforts of decentralized data administrators.

Data administration uses a variety of computer software tools to support its various activities. Information repositories are knowledge bases that describe an organization's data and applications. Repositories may be passive or active, depending on their role in managing the IS environment. An information repository should be carefully selected to ensure a good fit with an organization's needs.

CASE (or computer-aided software engineering) tools are used to automate software and database development and maintenance tasks. Upper-CASE tools support the earlier stages of the system development life cycle, including requirements definition, analysis, and design. Lower-CASE tools are those that automate functions later in the SDLC, such as code generation, testing, and maintenance. Both types of tools are used extensively by data administrators.

A database management system (or DBMS) is a software application system that is used to create, maintain, and provide controlled access to user databases. The central component of a DBMS is the engine, which provides access to both the repository and the database. A typical DBMS also provides an interface subsystem, and facilities for data integrity, backup and recovery, security management, and applications development.

Two major concerns in data integrity are referential integrity and concurrency control. Referential integrity is concerned with the validity of references by one object in a database to other objects in the database. Concurrency control is concerned with preventing loss of data integrity due to interference between users in a multiuser environment. The DBMS should provide facilities for both referential integrity and concurrency control.

Database security is concerned with protecting a database against accidental or intentional loss, destruction, or misuse. DBMS software provides security control through facilities such as user views, authorization rules, encryption, and authentication schemes. However, adequate security also requires physical security of the data center and its environment.

Database recovery procedures are required to restore a database quickly after loss or damage. A DBMS may provide four types of facilities for backup and recovery: backup copies of the database, journalizing facilities, checkpoint facility, and a recovery manager. Depending on the situation, three types of recovery may be used: restore/rerun (after complete failure), backward recovery (after a data error or failed transaction), and forward recovery (after a system failure).

A common problem in database management results when data are missing, lost, or incomplete. Although missing data (or null values) can be represented in many systems, using these data can lead to erroneous or ambiguous results. There are several possible ways to handle missing data, and data administrators must establish policies for dealing with these and other issues described earlier.

REFERENCES

Babad, Y. M., and J. A. Hoffer. 1984. "Even No Data Has a Value." *Communications of the ACM* 27 (Aug.), 748–756.

Bloombecker, J. J. 1989. "Short-Circuiting Computer Crime." *Datamation* 55 (19) (Oct. 1), 71–72.

Boar, B. H. 1984. *Application Prototyping*. New York: Wiley.

Brown, R. 1988. "Data Integrity and SQL." *Database Programming and Design*, 1 (3) (Mar.), 36–45.

Bruce, T., J. Fuller, and T. Moriarty. 1989. "So You Want a Repository." *Database Programming and Design*, 2 (5) (May), 60–69.

Fernandez, E. B., R. C. Summers, and C. Wood. 1981. *Database Security and Integrity*. Reading, Mass: Addison-Wesley.

Herbert, M., and C. Hartog. 1986. "MIS Rates the Issues." *Datamation* (November 15), 79–86.

Jaqua, D. J. 1988. "SQL Database Security." *Database Programming and Design* 1 (7) (July), 25–35.

Lefkovitz, H. C. 1985. *Proposed American National Standards Information Resource Dictionary System*. Wellesley, Mass.: QED Information Sciences.

Lyon, L. 1989. "CASE and the Database." *Database Programming and Design* 2 (5) (May), 28–33.

McClure, C. 1989. *CASE Is Software Automation*. Englewood Cliffs, N.J.: Prentice-Hall.

Rodgers, U. 1989. "Multiuser DBMS under UNIX." *Database Programming and Design* 2 (10) (Oct.), 30–37.

Vassiliov, Y. 1981. "Functional Dependencies and Incomplete Information." *Proceedings of the 6th International Conference on Very Large Data Bases*. Montreal, Canada, 260–269.

Weldon, J. 1981. *Data Base Administration*. New York, NY: Plenum Press.

Wertz, C. J. 1986. *The Data Dictionary: Concepts and Uses*. Wellesley, Mass.: QED Information Sciences.

Winkler-Parentz, H. B. 1989. "Can You Trust Your DBMS?" *Database Programming and Design* 2 (7) (July), 50–59.

Chapter Review

REVIEW QUESTIONS

1. Give a concise definition for each of the following terms:
   a. database management system
   b. information repository
   c. data administration
   d. database administration
   e. information repository dictionary system
   f. computer-assisted software engineering
   g. referential integrity
   h. concurrency control
   i. deadlock
   j. authorization rules

2. Contrast the following terms:
   a. data administration; database administration
   b. information repository; information repository dictionary system
   c. deadlock prevention; deadlock resolution
   d. backward recovery; forward recovery
   e. active in development; active in production
   f. upper-CASE tools; lower-CASE tools
   g. DBMS; DBMS engine
   h. restrict deletion rule; nullify deletion rule

3. What is the function of a data steward?

4. Briefly describe six stages in the life cycle of a typical database system.

5. Briefly describe four interfaces of data administration.

6. Briefly describe four steps that are required to ensure the success of data administration.

7. Briefly describe three alternative methods for organizing data administration in a decentralized organization.

8. Briefly describe three modes for using an information repository.

9. List and briefly describe 15 criteria that should be considered in selecting an information repository.

10. List and briefly describe seven tasks that are typically performed by CASE tools.

11. List six benefits that are often achieved through the use of CASE tools.

12. What is referential integrity? Why is it important?

13. Briefly describe three alternative delete rules that are used to preserve referential integrity.

14. Describe five lock levels that are commonly used to implement concurrency control.

15. What is the difference between shared locks and exclusive locks?

16. What is the difference between deadlock prevention and deadlock resolution?

17. Briefly describe five security features commonly used in data management software.

18. What are authentication schemes? How are biometric devices used for this purpose?

19. Briefly describe four DBMS facilities that are required for database backup and recovery.

20. What is transaction integrity? Why is it important?

21. List and briefly describe four common types of database failure.

22. List and briefly describe six techniques for dealing with missing data.

PROBLEMS AND EXERCISES

1. Match the following terms to the appropriate definitions.

_____ data administration   a) can draw E-R diagrams

_____ database management system   b) necessary for multiuser systems

_____ referential integrity   c) coding data for security

_____ information repository

_____ insertion/deletion rules

_____ database administration

_____ CASE tools

_____ concurrency control

_____ deadlock

_____ encryption

_____ transaction

_____ recovery manager

d) validity of references among objects

e) high-level management functions

f) users waiting for resources

g) sequence of steps for an activity

h) restores a database

i) primarily a technical function

j) support referential integrity

k) software application system

l) stores metadata

2. Fill in the two authorization tables for Mountain View Community Hospital below, based on the following assumptions (enter Y for yes or N for no):
   I. Nurses, physicians, and administrators may read Patient records but may not perform any other operations on these records.
   II. Persons in admissions may read and/or update (insert, modify, delete) Patient records.
   III. Nurses may read Patient records but may not insert, modify, or delete these records. Nurses may not access Physician or Employee records.

a.

	Patient records	Patient charges	Physician records	Employee records
Read				
Insert				
Modify				
Delete				

Authorizations for Nurses

b.

	Nurses	Physicians	Admissions	Administrator
Read				
Insert				
Modify				
Delete				

Authorizations for Patient Records

3. For each of the situations listed below, decide which of the following recovery techniques is most appropriate:
   I. backward recovery
   II. forward recovery (from latest checkpoint)
   III. forward recovery (using backup copy)
   IV. compensating transactions
   a. A phone disconnection occurs while a user is entering a transaction.

b. A disk module is dropped and is damaged so that it cannot be used.

_____

c. A lightning storm causes a power failure. _____
d. An incorrect amount is entered and posted for a student tuition payment. The error is not discovered for several weeks. _____

4. For the concurrent update situation shown in Figure 9-16, what balance would be shown if the transaction for user X was processed and the results stored before the transaction for user Y?

5. HallMart Department Stores runs a multiuser DBMS on a local area network file server. Unfortunately, at the present time the DBMS does not enforce concurrency control. One HallMart customer had a balance of $250.00 when the following three transactions were processed at about the same time:
   I. payment of $250.00
   II. purchase on credit of $100.00
   III. merchandise return (credit) of $50.00

   Each of the three transactions read the customer record when the balance was $250.00 (that is, before the other transactions were completed). The updated customer record was returned to the database in the order shown above.
   a. What was the *actual* balance for the customer after the last transaction was completed?
   b. What balance *should* have resulted from processing these three transactions?

6. Following is a portion of the STUDENT, ENROLLMENT, and COURSE tables at Lakewood College.

STUDENT		ENROLLMENT		COURSE	
Student#	Name	Student#	Course#	Course#	Cname
100	Arnold	100	A200	A200	Art
200	Betty	200	B100	B100	Biology
300	Clarence	100	B100	B300	Baking
400	Doreen	400	C300	C300	Chemistry
500	Edward	400	A200		

a. Suppose that Clarence requests enrollment in course D400. If this request is granted, will referential integrity be violated? Why or why not? (Base your answer on the data shown in the tables.)
b. Suppose that Doreen requests a "drop" in C300. If this request is granted, will referential integrity be violated? Why or why not?
c. Suppose that Arnold decides to withdraw from college. Show how the ENROLLMENT table would look if this request is granted and the "nullify" rule is in effect. Is this rule appropriate in this situation? Why or why not?
d. Suppose that Arnold decides to withdraw, and the "cascade" rule is in effect. Show how the ENROLLMENT table will look after this transaction is processed. Which rule is more appropriate in this situation: nullify or cascade? Why?

7. Fill in the following authorization tables for Pine Valley Furniture Company (Y or N) based on the following assumptions:
   I. Salesperson may read, insert, or modify (but not delete) Customer records. They may not access Employee records.
   II. Employees of the personnel department may read and/or update Employee records.

III. Quality inspectors may read Employee records (although sensitive fields such as Salary are hidden). They may not update these records.

IV. Salespersons may read Product records but may not update these records.

V. Persons other than quality inspectors and the personnel department may not access Employee records.

a.

	Customer records	Employee records	Product records
Read			
Insert			
Modify			
Delete			

Authorizations for Salespersons

b.

	Accountants	Quality inspectors	Personnel Department	President
Read				
Insert				
Modify				
Delete				

Authorizations for Employee Records

8. For each of the situations described below, indicate which of the following security measures is most appropriate:

   I. authorization rules

   II. encryption

   III. authentication schemes

   a. A national brokerage firm uses an electronic funds transfer system (EFTS) to transmit sensitive financial data between locations. _____

   b. A manufacturing firm uses a simple password system to protect its database but finds it needs a more comprehensive system to grant different privileges (such as read versus create or update) to different users. _____

   c. A university has experienced considerable difficulty with unauthorized users who access files and databases by "appropriating" passwords from legitimate users. _____

9. Customcraft, Inc. is a mail-order firm specializing in the manufacture of stationery and other paper products. Annual sales of Customcraft are $25 million and are growing at a rate of 15% per year. After several years' experience with conventional data processing systems, Customcraft has decided to organize a data administration function. At present, they have four major candidates for the data administrator position:

   • John Bach, a senior systems analyst with three years' experience at Customcraft who has attended recent seminars in structured systems design and database design.

- Margaret Smith, who has been production control manager for the past two years after a year's experience as programmer/analyst at Customcraft.
- William Rogers, a systems programmer with extensive experience with DB2 and Oracle, the two database management systems under consideration at Customcraft.
- Ellen Reddy, who is currently database administrator with a medium-size electronics firm in the same city as Customcraft.

Based on this limited information, rank the four candidates for the data administrator position, and state your reasons.

10. Referring to Problem 10, rank the four candidates for the position of database administrator at Customcraft. State your reasons.

11. Visit an organization that has implemented a database approach. Evaluate each of the following:
    a. The organizational placement of the data administration function.
    b. The functions performed by data administration and database administration.
    c. The background of the person chosen as head of data administration.
    d. The status and usage of an information repository (passive, active in design, active in production).
    e. The procedures that are used for security, concurrency control, and backup and recovery.

12. A major electronics firm has its corporate headquarters on the East Coast and manufacturing plants located throughout the country. Each plant has its own computer and data processing organization. Describe three alternative ways for organizing the data administration function in this company.

13. Find a recent article describing an incident of computer crime. Was there evidence of inadequate security in this incident? What security measures described in the chapter might have been instrumental in preventing this incident?

PART IV

Classical Systems

MANUFACTURING SUPPORT WITH IMS

McDonnell Douglas Corporation

Classical database management system technologies have been used in industry for over two decades. One of the most widely adopted is IBM's Information Management System (IMS). IMS is a hierarchical DBMS that supports high volume processing applications where speed in data retrieval and data processing performance is critical. As an example, consider the use of IMS within the McDonnell Aircraft Company (MCAIR) component of the McDonnell Douglas Corporation. MCAIR manufactures major fighter aircraft products in the defense contracting industry including the Air Force F-15, Navy F-18, and Marine Corps AV-8B.

The aircraft manufacturing process is supported by an on-line Bill of Materials and Automated Planning Application running under IBM's IMS. This manufacturing application system was first developed in the mid-1970's and has since undergone significant

enhancement. The foundation of the system is three Hierarchical Indexed Direct Access Method (HIDAM, see Chapter 10) databases which are logically related to one another. These databases are organized with numerous secondary indexes for alternative data retrieval.

One type of data stored in these databases is the "bill of materials" description of all materials used to manufacture and assemble major end-item components of the various aircraft under production. The databases also store engineering data about materials used to build aircraft parts, such as raw material size, tensile strength, raw material type, and data describing the geometric properties of aircraft parts. Special manufacturing application programs can access the databases in order to store and retrieve routing plans that describe the actual production sequence to be followed during the assembly process. This enables the firm to schedule and balance resource requirements during the assembly process.

As you might imagine, these HIDAM databases are quite large. Data for over 1.5 million aircraft parts are stored in the databases. This requires about 8,000 cylinders of storage capacity on IBM 3380 direct access storage devices. This equates approximately to 4 *billion bytes* (gigabytes) of storage capacity!

Two types of Information System organizations support this and other IMS manufacturing and business applications at MCAIR. One organizational unit is responsible for maintaining data integrity. This group includes 10 to 12 database professionals. Additionally, each computer-based system like the Bill of Materials and Automated Planning Application is supported by a team of application programmers and analysts. This particular system is maintained by about 20 programmers and analysts.

This system provides information support to a very large base of concurrent users. Peak demand can result in 800 or more concurrent users in an on-line environment! IMS is able to provide the high level of data retrieval performance necessary to enable this heavy usage workload. The system is available on-line 24 hours a day, 6½ days a week and provides MCAIR management with up-to-the-minute information about the status of the aircraft manufacturing process.

CHAPTER 10

Hierarchical Database Systems

INTRODUCTION

The earliest database management systems were based on the hierarchical data model. As database requirements have become better understood, these systems have had to evolve to handle a broader range of data structures. However, many organizations today continue to use hierarchical database management systems because of the investment they have in these products and in the related application programs.

The leading hierarchical DBMS still in use today is IBM's Information Management System (IMS). IMS was developed during the mid-1960s in response to the data processing needs of the aerospace industry. This development was undertaken as a joint project of IBM and North American Aviation. Since its introduction in the late 1960s, IMS has evolved through several versions. The current version is IMS/VS (Information Management System/Virtual Storage). IMS is widely used among installations with IBM mainframe computers.

The IMS development team chose the hierarchical structure because they agreed with the philosopher who observed that all views of life are hierarchical in nature. They began by developing a physical hierarchical view, which unfortunately does not always mirror life. Finally, through logical relationships and other improvements, IMS was able to model life by becoming a logical hierarchical system.

IMS PHYSICAL DATABASES

The physical database record is a basic building block in IMS. A **physical database record** (PDBR) consists of a hierarchical arrangement of segments. A **segment,** in turn, consists of a set of related fields. The top segment (or entry point) in a PDBR is called the **root** segment. A PDBR, then, consists of a root segment plus a hierarchical arrangement of subordinate segments called **child** segments.

A typical IMS physical database record is shown in Figure 10-1. This PDBR contains information about departments, about equipment that is assigned to each department, and about employees assigned to each department. DEPARTMT is the name of the root segment type for this PDBR, and EQPMENT and EMPLOYEE are child segment types. The EMPLOYEE segment, in turn, has two child segments, DEPENDNT and SKILL. These segments contain information about each employee's dependents and skills, respectively.

PDBR Occurrences

The physical database record shown in Figure 10-1 is a PDBR *type.* An occurrence of this PDBR type is shown in Figure 10-2. This occurrence represents data for one department (ACCTG) and contains two EQPMENT segments and two EMPLOYEE segments. The first employee (Evans) has three dependents and two skills. The second employee (Thomas) has one skill and no dependents.

Figure 10-1
IMS physical
database record

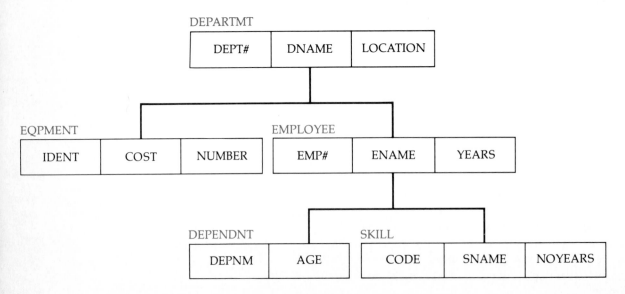

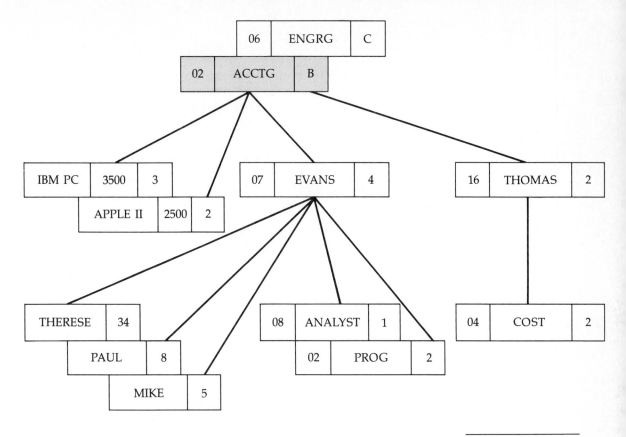

Figure 10-2
An occurrence of the PDBR

Each occurrence of a root segment represents one PDBR occurrence. Thus, all the segments constitute one such PDBR occurrence (the ENGRG root segment shown would constitute a second occurrence of this record type).

Database Description

Each IMS physical database record type is defined by a **database description** (DBD). The DBD appears as a set of macro statements that define the segments and fields within a PDBR. These macro statements are coded by a programmer or database analyst and then assembled into object form and stored in a library by the IMS control program.

A skeleton DBD for the department database is shown in Figure 10-3. The statements have been numbered for reference in the following discussion; normally, these statement numbers are omitted.

Statement 1 assigns the name DEPTDB to the database shown in Figure 10-1. Statement 2 then defines the root segment. This segment type is assigned

Figure 10-3
Database description
(DEPTDB)

```
 1   DBD    NAME=DEPTDB
 2   SEGM   NAME=DEPARTMT, BYTES=27, PARENT=0
 3   FIELD  NAME=(DEPT#, SEQ), BYTES=3, START=1
 4   FIELD  NAME=DNAME, BYTES=20, START=4
 5   FIELD  NAME=LOCATION, BYTES=4, START=24
 6   SEGM   NAME=EQPMENT, PARENT=DEPARTMT, BYTES=27
 7   FIELD  NAME=(IDENT, SEQ), BYTES=15, START=1
 8   FIELD  NAME=COST, BYTES=10, START=16
 9   FIELD  NAME=NUMBER, BYTES=4, START=26
10   SEGM   NAME=EMPLOYEE, PARENT=DEPARTMT, BYTES=42
11   FIELD  NAME=(EMP#, SEQ), BYTES=10, START=1
12   FIELD  NAME=ENAME, BYTES=30, START=11
13   FIELD  NAME=YEARS, BYTES=2, START=41
14   SEGM   NAME=DEPENDNT, PARENT=EMPLOYEE, BYTES=32
15   FIELD  NAME=(DEPNM, SEQ), BYTES=30, START=1
16   FIELD  NAME=AGE, BYTES=2, START=31
17   SEGM   NAME=SKILL, PARENT=EMPLOYEE, BYTES=28
18   FIELD  NAME=(CODE, SEQ), BYTES=6, START=1
19   FIELD  NAME=SNAME, BYTES=20, START=7
20   FIELD  NAME=NOYEARS, BYTES=2, START=27
```

the name DEPARTMT and is defined as 27 bytes in length. All names in IMS are limited to a maximum length of eight characters.

Statements 3 to 5 define the three field types that are included in DEPARTMT. Each FIELD definition statement defines the name, length, and starting position within the segment. Statement 3 contains the clause NAME=(DEPT#,SEQ). This clause defines DEPT# to be the sequence field for the DEPARTMT root segment type. As a result, physical database record occurrences within the DEPTDB database are sequenced in ascending department number sequence.

Statement 6 defines the EQPMENT segment type. The clause PARENT=DEPARTMT in this statement defines EQPMENT as a child segment of DEPARTMT. The segment is 29 bytes in length.

Statement 7 defines the IDENT field type within the EQPMENT segment type. The clause NAME=(IDENT,SEQ) means that for each occurrence of a parent DEPARTMT segment type, occurrences of the child EQPMENT segment type are stored in ascending sequence according to the IDENT field. Thus, for example, in Figure 10-2, the segment for APPLE II occurs before the segment for IBM PC. All occurrences of child segments of a particular parent occurrence are referred to as **twins**.

Statements 8 to 20 define the remaining segment types and field types in the department database. Multiple physical databases will often be needed to represent a given conceptual database model effectively and efficiently.

IMS LOGICAL DATABASES

External views of individual users in IMS are reflected in logical database records (LDBRs). A **logical database** (LDB) consists of all occurrences of a logical database record (LDBR) type. Each LDBR type is a subset of a corresponding PDBR type (or more than one PDBR type). An LDBR may differ from the corresponding PDBR in the following ways:

1. Any segment type (except the root segment) of a PDBR may be omitted from an LDBR. If any segment type in the PDBR is omitted, then all of its dependents are also omitted.

2. Any field types that occur in a PDBR may be omitted in the corresponding LDBR. Also, the fields in a PDBR may be rearranged within the LDBR segment type.

Example LDBRs

Two examples of logical database records derived from the department physical database are shown in Figure 10-4. Figure 10-4a is an "equipment" LDBR that contains the DEPARTMT and EQPMENT segment types. Figure 10-4b is a "personnel" LDBR that contains the DEPARTMT, EMPLOYEE, and SKILL segment types. Each of these LDBR types represents the view of a different user. Notice that each LDBR type contains DEPARTMT as its root segment, as required.

Although not shown in Figure 10-4, any of the fields in a PDBR segment may be omitted in the corresponding LDBR segment. For example, the YEARS field in the EMPLOYEE segment could be omitted in the LDBR

Figure 10-4
Examples of logical database records:
(a) equipment LDBR
(b) personnel LDBR

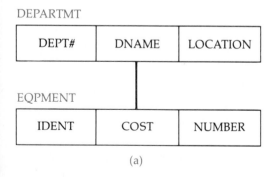

(a)

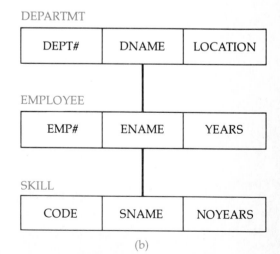

(b)

shown in Figure 10-4b. Also, the order of the fields EMP# and EMPNAME could be reversed if desired.

Program Communication Block

Each LDBR type is defined by a series of statements called a **program communication block** (PCB). The PCB for the personnel LDBR is shown in Figure 10-5.

Statement 1 defines the program communication block. The clause TYPE = DB is required for each PCB that defines a database (as opposed to an on-line transaction). The clause DBNAME = DEPTDB specifies that the DBD for the underlying database is DEPTDB (as defined in Figure 10-3).

The clause KEYLEN = 19 defines the maximum length of the concatenated key for the hierarchical path in this LDBR. In the LDBR shown in Figure 10-4b, the hierarchical path consists of the DEPARTMT, EMPLOYEE, and SKILL segment types. The fields on which these segments are sequenced, and the field lengths, are the following: DEPT#, 3 bytes; EMP#, 10 bytes; and CODE, 6 bytes. Thus, KEYLEN = 3 + 10 + 6, or 19 bytes. The KEYLEN clause is used by IMS to reserve space for concatenated keys in retrieving segments.

Statements 2 to 4 define the segments from the PDBR that are to be included in this LDBR. The term SENSEG means "sensitive segment." Segments from the PDBR that are included in an LDBR are said to be "sensitive" (the term can also be applied to fields that are to be included). In this PCB, the sensitive segments are, of course, DEPARTMT, EMPLOYEE, and SKILL.

The term PROCOPT in Figure 10-5 stands for "processing options." The PROCOPT clause specifies the operations that a user of this LDBR can perform against each segment. In Figure 10-5, the clause PROCOPT = G specifies that a user can only "get" (G) or retrieve each segment occurrence. Other options that can be specified are I ("insert"), R ("replace"), and D ("delete"). Also, any combination of these options may be specified.

Caution must be used in specifying and using the delete (D) option in IMS. When an occurrence of a sensitive segment is deleted, all children of that segment are also deleted, whether they are sensitive or not. For example, the LDBR in Figure 10-4b is sensitive to the EMPLOYEE and SKILL segment types, but not to the DEPENDNT segment type. Suppose that a user deletes an EMPLOYEE segment occurrence. All DEPENDNT segment occurrences for that employee are also deleted, even though the user may not be aware of their existence.

The sensitive segment feature of IMS offers two significant advantages:

1. Data independence: a new type of segment can be added to the database without affecting existing users. The LDBR for the existing user is not sensitive to this new segment type.

2. Data security: a user cannot access particular segment types if the user view (LDBR) is not sensitive to those segment types.

1	PCB	TYPE=DB, DBDNAME=DEPTDB, KEYLEN=19
2	SENSEG	NAME=DEPARTMT, PROCOPT=G
3	SENSEG	NAME=EMPLOYEE, PROCOPT=G
4	SENSEG	NAME=SKILL, PROCOPT=G

Figure 10-5
Program
communication block
for personnel LDBR

Program Specification Block

Each user may have one or more program communication blocks. The set of all PCBs for a given user is called a **program specification block** (PSB). The PSB for each user is assembled and stored in a system library by the IMS control program. The control program extracts the PSB from the library when a user program is executed.

IMS INTERNAL MODELS

IMS offers the user a wide variety of physical data organizations and access methods. Choosing the best internal model for each application requires a detailed knowledge of both IMS and the pattern of data usage defined during physical design. In this section, we provide only a brief overview of the IMS data structures.

Overview of IMS Internal Model

An overview of the IMS data structures and access methods that constitute the internal model is shown in Figure 10-6. As shown in this illustration, IMS supports four types of databases:

- Hierarchical sequential access method (HSAM)
- Hierarchical indexed sequential access method (HISAM)
- Hierarchical direct access method (HDAM)
- Hierarchical indexed direct access method (HIDAM)

The IMS control program contains routines to process each of these four data structures. Also, each of these routines "calls" (or uses) one of several standard access methods. The access methods used by IMS (and shown in Figure 10-6) are the following:

- Sequential access method (SAM)
- Indexed sequential access method (ISAM)
- Virtual storage access method (VSAM)
- Overflow sequential access method (OSAM)

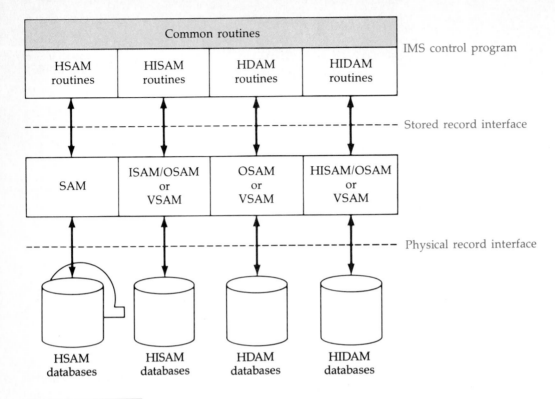

Figure 10-6
Overview of IMS
internal models
(*Source:* Date 1981,
312)

The function of each of these access methods is to retrieve a physical record (possibly containing several stored records) and to present a stored record to the IMS control program.

HSAM

The simplest IMS data structure is the hierarchical sequential access method (HSAM). With this organization, the segments that make up a physical database record are stored in physical sequence within one or more stored records. The root segment is stored first, followed by its dependent segments. The segments are stored in **hierarchical sequence,** which is a top-to-bottom, left-to-right ordering within the PDBR. Thus, the hierarchical sequence is represented by physical adjacency in HSAM.

An HSAM organization for the department data base (DEPTDB) is shown in Figure 10-7. The segment occurrences in this figure are taken from the PDBR occurrence shown in Figure 10-2. The segment occurrences are stored in two fixed-length stored records. First, the root segment (DEPARTMT 02) is stored, followed by the two EQPMENT segments in sequential order. The remaining segments are stored in hierarchical sequence as they appear within the PDBR. When the first stored record is filled, the remaining seg-

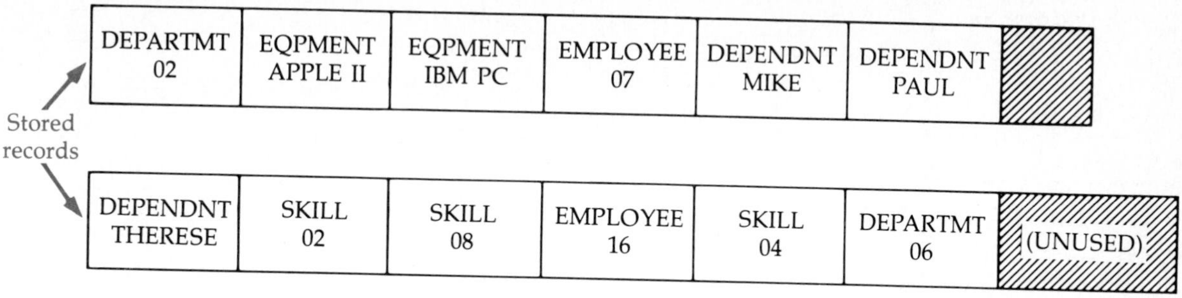

DEPARTMT 02	EQPMENT APPLE II	EQPMENT IBM PC	EMPLOYEE 07	DEPENDNT MIKE	DEPENDNT PAUL	////////

Stored records

DEPENDNT THERESE	SKILL 02	SKILL 08	EMPLOYEE 16	SKILL 04	DEPARTMT 06	(UNUSED)

Figure 10-7
HSAM organization for DEPTDB

ments continue in the next stored record. Since fixed-length stored records are used, some unused space often results.

Although simple, HSAM has the same disadvantages as any physical sequential organization of records. Locating a particular segment requires an extensive sequential scan (each stored segment has a code that identifies the segment type for retrieval). Also, insertions and deletions are difficult to manage. As a result, HSAM has very limited use in most IMS installations. Normally, this method is used for historical or archival files.

HISAM

The hierarchical indexed sequential access method (HISAM) provides an indexed sequential organization for segments. As a result, the segments of a physical database record can be retrieved either sequentially or by direct access. HISAM uses either ISAM or VSAM as its underlying access method (ISAM and VSAM are described in Chapter 4). ISAM is used with a special IMS access method called OSAM (overflow sequential access method).

A HISAM organization for the department database is shown in Figure 10-8. In this example, two data sets (or physical storage files) are used, an ISAM data set and an OSAM data set. Each of these data sets is divided into fixed-length stored records. When an IMS database is first loaded, each root segment that is stored causes a new ISAM stored record to be created. This root segment is stored at the front of the record (in Figure 10-8, DEPARTMT 02 is the first root segment). The remainder of that record is then filled with additional dependent segments in hierarchical sequence (in Figure 10-8, the first EQPMENT segment for department 02 is placed in the ISAM record).

If all dependent segments for a particular root segment fit into one ISAM record, then no OSAM record is required. However, if the dependent segments overflow this record (as in Figure 10-8), then they are stored in hierarchical sequence in an OSAM record. A pointer containing the relative address of that OSAM record is placed in the last ISAM segment. If the first OSAM record is filled, a second record is created, and so on. As shown in

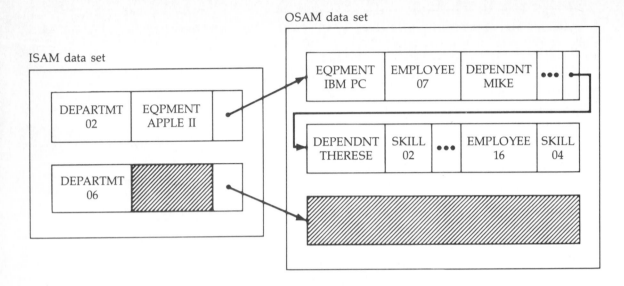

OSAM data set

ISAM data set

Figure 10-8
HISAM organization
for DEPTDB

the figure, one ISAM record and two OSAM records were required for all the segments for department 02.

The segments in a physical database record may be processed sequentially by following the pointers such as those shown in Figure 10-8. Also, each root segment can be located by direct access using the ISAM index. Thus, HISAM provides the advantages of both sequential and direct access.

When VSAM is used, the ISAM data set is replaced by a VSAM key-sequenced data set. Also, the OSAM data set is replaced by a VSAM entry-sequenced data set. Thus, the segments are stored within VSAM control intervals and managed by the VSAM indexes.

HISAM is not often used in most IMS installations. It should be used only when no logical relationships exist and adds and deletes are minimal (that is, the database is not volatile).

HDAM and HIDAM

HDAM and HIDAM are both direct access methods. Both permit direct access to the root segment of a PDBR occurrence and therefore are frequently used. The dependent segments of that occurrence can then be accessed directly by following pointer chains. The main difference between HDAM and HIDAM is in the technique for addressing root segments, as we will now explain.

Pointer Structures HDAM and HIDAM both use pointers to represent the hierarchical sequence of segments within a PDBR occurrence. As shown in Figure 10-9, the hierarchical sequence may be represented either by hierarchical pointers or by child/twin pointers.

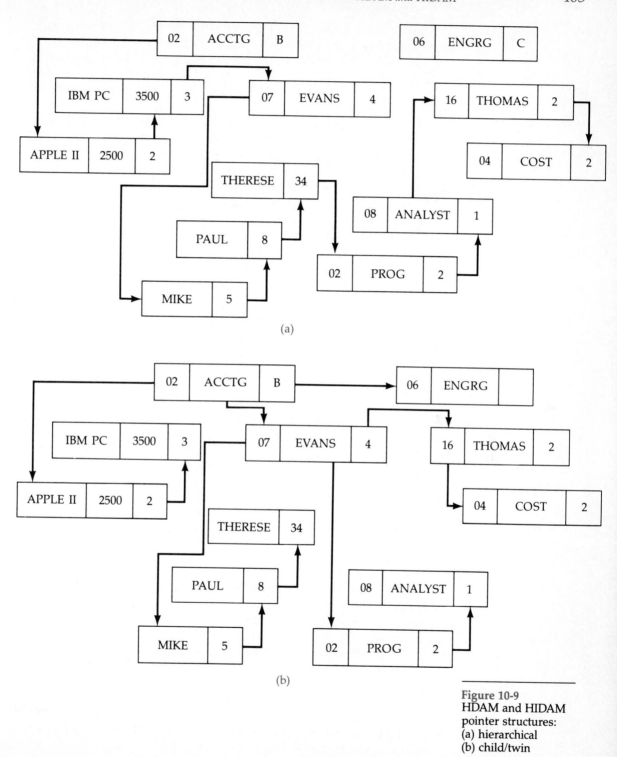

(a)

(b)

Figure 10-9
HDAM and HIDAM
pointer structures:
(a) hierarchical
(b) child/twin

The use of hierarchical pointers is shown in Figure 10-9a. These pointers are simply "threaded" through the segments in hierarchical sequence. The last segment in the PDBR occurrence (in this case, 04 COST 2) does not contain a pointer to the next root segment. Hierarchical pointers are most efficient when the segments within a PDBR are normally processed in hierarchical sequence.

The use of child/twin pointers is shown in Figure 10-9b. Each parent segment contains a pointer to its first child segment occurrence. Each child segment occurrence then contains a pointer to the next twin segment (if one exists). Also, each parent may optionally contain a pointer to the last (as well as first) child occurrence. Child/twin pointers are most efficient when only certain parent/child occurrences within a PDBR are normally processed each time (rather than the entire sequence).

Although not shown in Figure 10-9, both hierarchical and child/twin pointers may be bidirectional. That is, between any two segments, backward as well as forward pointers may be used.

HDAM Hierarchical direct access method (HDAM) provides direct access to root segments by means of a hashing algorithm. Segments are stored in fixed-length stored records. The hashing algorithm generates a relative record address that provides the location of a root segment occurrence. The dependent segments may then be accessed by following the segment pointers (hierarchical or child/twin).

When an HDAM database is initially loaded, the root segments may be loaded in any order (key sequence is not necessary). However, all dependent segments for each root segment must be loaded in hierarchical sequence after the root segment. Dependent segments are stored as closely as possible to the root segment (recall our discussion of clustering in Chapter 8).

When two root segments collide (hash to the same relative address), the second root segment is placed in the next available stored record that contains sufficient space. A pointer to the second root segment is then placed in the first root segment (several colliding root segments may be linked by such a pointer chain).

HIDAM Hierarchical indexed direct access method (HIDAM) also provides direct access to root segments. However, instead of using a hashing algorithm, HIDAM uses a dense index to locate root segment occurrences. Root segments are linked to dependent segments by pointers, as with HDAM.

The main advantage of HDAM (compared with HIDAM) is the speed of access where direct access is required. HDAM should be used where random access is required almost exclusively. Sequential processing with HDAM is difficult or inefficient.

On the other hand, the main advantage of HIDAM is that both random and sequential access are handled effectively. Thus, HIDAM is probably the most frequently used of all access methods in IMS.

Specifying the Internal Model

In IMS, the mapping of a physical database into storage is defined by adding additional statements to the database description (such as the one in Figure 10-3). For example, if HISAM is to be used, the following statement would be added to DBD:

ACCESS = HISAM

Additional entries are required to define the access method (such as VSAM versus ISAM) and the type of pointers to be used (hierarchical versus child/twin). Full specification of the internal model is often quite complex and is beyond the scope of this text.

IMS DATA MANIPULATION

The IMS data manipulation language is called Data Language I (DL/I). DL/I consists of a set of commands that are used with a host language (COBOL, PL/I, or assembler language). The application program invokes (or uses) these commands by means of subroutine calls.

An overview of the DL/I commands is shown in Table 10-1. We describe and illustrate each of these commands below. The syntax is simplified in the following examples for ease of presentation. The examples are based on the department database (Figure 10-2).

GET UNIQUE (GU)

The GET UNIQUE (GU) command is used to retrieve a specific segment occurrence. The segment may be a root segment or a dependent segment.

Table 10-1 Summary of DL/I Operations

Operations	Explanation
GET UNIQUE (GU)	Direct retrieval of a segment
GET NEXT (GN)	Sequential retrieval
GET NEXT WITHIN PARENT (GNP)	Sequential retrieval under current parent
GET HOLD (GHU, GHN, GHNP)	As above, but allow subsequent DLET/ REPL
REPLACE (REPL)	Replace existing segment
DELETE (DLET)	Delete existing segment
INSERT (ISRT)	Add new segment

Source: Date 1981, 297

The segment desired is specified in parentheses by a qualifying condition, called a segment search argument (SSA). For example, suppose that we want to retrieve the segment for department 06 (a root segment). The following command would be used:

GU DEPARTMT (DEPT# = '06')

In this example, the SSA is DEPT# = '06'. The GU command will retrieve the *first* segment that satisfies the SSA (presumably there is only one occurrence for each department).

Now suppose that we want to retrieve the segment for EVANS (EMP# = 07) in ACCTG (DEPT# = 02). The following commands would be used:

GU DEPARTMT (DEPT# = '02')
    EMPLOYEE (EMP# = '07')

In this example, a hierarchical path is specified. The GU command will retrieve only the segment at the *bottom* of this path. Thus, the employee segment for EVANS (but not the parent department segment) will be retrieved.

The SSA may be omitted from a DL/I command. For example, consider the following commands:

GU DEPARTMT
    EQPMENT (IDENT = 'APPLE II')

With this command, DL/I will retrieve the *first* occurrence of an EQPMENT segment that satisfies the indicated SSA. It will scan DEPARTMT segments sequentially until this first dependent segment is located.

GET NEXT (GN)

GET NEXT (GN) is used for sequential retrieval of occurrences of a particular segment type. For example, suppose that we use the following commands:

GU DEPARTMT (DEPT# = '02')
    EQPMENT
GN EQPMENT

The GU command will cause the first EQPMENT segment (APPLE II) for DEPARTMT 02 to be retrieved. The GN command will then cause the next EQPMENT segment (IBM PC) to be retrieved.

The GN command cannot be executed until a "current position" has been established in the database. In the preceding example, the GU command establishes the starting position by retrieving the first EQPMENT segment.

Now suppose that we add another GN command to the above example:

```
GU DEPARTMT (DEPT# = '02')
    EQPMENT
GN EQPMENT
GN EQPMENT
```

These commands will attempt to retrieve a third EQPMENT segment. However, referring to Figure 10-2, we see that there are only two such segments under DEPARTMT 02. Will this result in an error condition? The answer is that it will not. Instead, DL/I will retrieve the next EQPMENT segment in the database under a new root segment. In fact, we can retrieve *all* EQPMENT segments in the database with the following commands:

```
     GU DEPARTMT
        EQPMENT
MORE GN EQPMENT
        GO TO MORE
```

GET NEXT WITHIN PARENT (GNP)

Like GET NEXT, GET NEXT WITHIN PARENT (GNP) causes sequential retrieval of segment occurrences. However, unlike GN, only occurrences under the current parent segment are retrieved. For example, suppose that we wish to retrieve all DEPENDNT segments for EVANS in ACCTG. The following commands would be used:

```
     GU DEPARTMT (DEPT# = '02')
        EMPLOYEE (EMP# = '07')
        DEPENDNT
NEXT GNP DEPENDNT
        GO TO NEXT
```

In this example, the GU command retrieves the first DEPENDNT segment for this employee. The GNP then sequentially retrieves the remaining segments for the same employee (EVANS has three dependents). When the last segment is retrieved, DL/I will return a status message indicating that there are no more subordinate DEPENDNT segments for this employee.

The GNP command can be used to retrieve *all* subordinate segment occurrences under a current parent. For example, suppose that we wish to retrieve all segment occurrences for DEPARTMT 02:

```
     GU DEPARTMT (DEPT# = '02')
NEXT GNP
        GO TO NEXT
```

Since no segment type is specified for GNP, the loop will cause all subordinate segments to be retrieved in hierarchical sequence. DEPARTMT 02 has ten subordinate segments (see Figure 10-2).

GET HOLD

There are three GET HOLD commands: GET HOLD UNIQUE (GHU), GET HOLD NEXT (GHN), and GET HOLD NEXT WITHIN PARENT (GHNP). These commands function in exactly the same manner as GU, GN, and GNP, respectively. However, the GET HOLD versions must be used to retrieve segments that are going to be replaced (REPL) or deleted (DLET).

Replacement (REPL)

The replace (REPL) command is used to replace a segment occurrence with an updated version of the same segment. First, the segment must be retrieved by using one of the GET HOLD commands. The segment is then modified, and the REPL command writes the updated segment.

Look again at Figure 10-2. Suppose that we wish to change the age of the DEPENDNT PAUL from 8 to 9. The following commands could be used:

```
GHU DEPARTMT (DEPT# = '02')
    EMPLOYEE (EMP# = '07')
    DEPENDNT (DEPNM = 'PAUL')
    MOVE '9' TO AGE
    REPL
```

Deletion (DLET)

A segment to be deleted must first be retrieved by using one of the GET HOLD commands. For example, suppose that we wish to delete the skill PROG for EVANS in ACCTG. The following commands would be used:

```
        GHU DEPARTMT (DEPT# = '02')
            EMPLOYEE (EMP# = '07')
            SKILL (CODE = '02')
    DLET
```

A DLET command deletes not only a particular segment, but all of its subordinate children (there are some exceptions to this rule, but they are beyond the scope of this text). For example, the following command will delete the root segment for DEPARTMT 02 plus all ten of its subordinate segments:

```
GHU DEPARTMT (DEPT# = '02')
DLET
```

As a result, caution must be exercised in using this command. In general, the processing options (PROCOPT) specification in the PCB should limit the delete operation to only a few qualified users.

Insertion (ISRT)

ISRT allows the user to insert a new segment into the database. To insert a new subordinate segment, the parent segment must already exist in the database. For example, suppose that we wish to insert a new DEPENDNT occurrence for EVANS in ACCTG. The following commands could be used:

```
MOVE 'CHRIS' TO DEPNM
MOVE '0' TO AGE
ISRT DEPARTMT (DEPT# = '02')
     EMPLOYEE (EMP# = '07')
     DEPENDNT
```

First, the new segment to be inserted is built in the application program output area (indicated by the first two statements above). Next, the ISRT statement defines the hierarchical path to the segment to be inserted. The new segment occurrence is inserted in sequence among the existing child occurrences for the specified parent.

ADVANCED IMS FEATURES

So far, we have described the basic features of IMS. All these features are based on a purely hierarchical data model. In this section, we describe two additional features that extend IMS beyond this hierarchical model. These two features are logical databases and secondary indexing.

Logical Databases

Earlier in this chapter, we defined a logical datbase record (LDBR) as a subset of an IMS physical database record (PDBR). More generally, an LDBR may be defined as a subset of one or more PDBRs. In this section, we describe how an LDBR can be defined as a subset of two PDBRs.

Suppose that the department database (DEPTDB) illustrated in Figure 10-1 already exists. Now suppose that the organization wants to create a project database (PROJDB). The structure of this proposed database is shown in Figure 10-10a. The root segment type is PROJECT, and the dependent segment is EMPLOYEE.

One possible approach is to create a new PDBR type with the structure shown in Figure 10-10a. However, the new EMPLOYEE segment occurrences will contain the same data that already exist in the EMPLOYEE segments within the department database. A better approach (which avoids this redundancy) is to link the new PROJECT segment with the existing EMPLOYEE segment by means of a logical pointer segment (see Figure 10-10b). There are two PDBR types in this figure: DEPTDB and PROJDB. The

Figure 10-10

Logical databases:
(a) proposed project
    database
(b) two linked PDBRs
(c) one LDBR based
    on the first two
    PDBRs
    (PROJEMP)

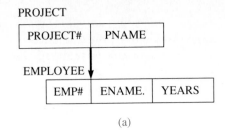

(a)

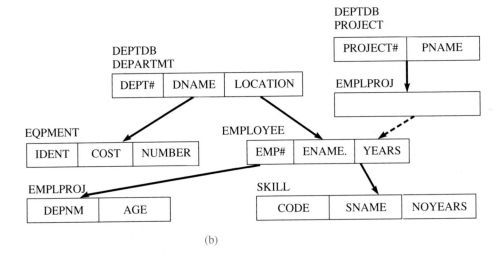

(b)

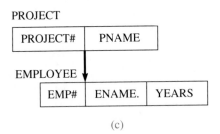

(c)

logical pointer segment (called EMPLPROJ) links the two databases. EMPLPROJ is the *physical* child of PROJECT and the *logical* child of EMPLOYEE.

As shown in Figure 10-10c, the new PROJECT database may now be represented as a logical database. The LDBR type in this figure is a subset of the two PDBR types shown in Figure 10-10b. The logical database shown in Figure 10-10c does not actually exist. However, a user application program may process the data as if it existed in this form.

```
1    DBD        NAME = PROJDB
2    SEGM       NAME = PROJECT, BYTES = 27, PARENT = 0
3    FIELD      NAME = (PROJECT#, SEQ), BYTES = 7, START = 1
4    FIELD      NAME = PNAME, BYTES = 20, START = 8
5    SEGM       NAME = EMPLPROJ, PARENT = ((PROJECT), (EMPLOYEE, P, DEPTDB))
```

(a)

```
10   SEGM       NAME = EMPLOYEE, PARENT = DEPARTMT, BYTES = 42
11   LCHILD     NAME = (EMPLPROJ, PROJDB)
```

(b)

```
1    DBD        NAME = PROJEMP, ACCESS = LOGICAL
2    DATASET LOGICAL
3    SEGM       NAME = PROJECT, SOURCE = (PROJECT, DATA, PROJDB)
4    SEGM       NAME = EMPLOYEE, PARENT = PROJECT,
                SOURCE = ((EMPLPROJ, DATA, PROJDB), (EMPLOYEE, DATA, DEPTDB))
```

(c)

Figure 10-11
Bulding the logical
database:
(a) physical DBD
(b) change to
EMPLOYEE
segment of
DEPTDB database
(c) logical DBD for
PROJEMP logical
database

Database Description   Building a logical database is a three-step process. The first step is defining a physical database description of the project database. In Figure 10-11a, statements 1 to 4 are similar to those in Figure 10-3 and the project segment is defined with two fields. Statement 5 is the description of the EMPLPROJ pointer segment. This statement identifies PROJECT as the physical parent, and EMPLOYEE (in DEPTDB) as the logical parent. The "P" in this entry denotes that the pointer in EMPLPROJ is a logical pointer. If there are data related to the combination of a project and an employee (called intersection data), these data can be stored in the EMPLPROJ segment.

The second step is to amend the Department physical database description (Figure 10-3) by adding an LCHILD (logical child) statement, as shown in Figure 10-11b. Statement number 11 in this figure indicates that EMPLOYEE has a logical child called EMPLPROJ in the PROJDB database. This statement is then followed by the FIELD statements for EMPLOYEE.

The third step in building our logical database is to define the logical database itself. As seen in Figure 10-11c, this process is rather straightforward. In statements 1 and 2, the database is named and is defined as logical. In statement 3, the PROJECT segment is defined and the source of the data to be used is shown to be the PROJDB. In statement 4, the EMPLOYEE is defined and the source of its data is the EMPLOYEE segment in the DEPTDB database and the EMPLPROJ segment in the PROJDB database.

There are two important restrictions in defining logical databases:

1. The root of a logical database must also be the root of a physical database. In Figure 10-10, PROJECT is the root of the PROJEMP (logical database) and PROJDB (physical database).

2. A logical child segment must have one physical parent and one logical parent. In Figure 10-10, EMPLPROJ is the physical child of PROJECT and the logical child of EMPLOYEE.

In this section, we have presented a simplified description of IMS logical databases. In reality, additional entries would be required. For a complete discussion of this topic, see IBM Corp. (1986).

Processing a Logical Database A logical database is accessed in exactly the same way as a physical database. The programmer does not have to know whether the database is physical or logical.

Loading a logical database is another matter. Again, it is a three-step process, assuming the logical database has been correctly defined. First, the data must be loaded onto the first physical database (DEPTDB in our example). Second, the data must be loaded onto the other physical database (PROJDB). Finally, an IMS utility is run that causes the two databases to be logically connected.

Once the logical database has been loaded, a user can process it exactly as if it were a physical database. That is, DL/I commands can be used to retrieve and manipulate the logical database. For example, suppose that we wish to retrieve all EMPLOYEE segments for employees who are assigned to PROJECT ABCD. The following DL/I commands would be used:

```
      GU PROJECT (PROJECT# = 'ABCD')
         EMPLOYEE
NEXT GNP EMPLOYEE
         GO TO NEXT
```

Notice that in filling this request, the program will retrieve segments from two physical databases.

Secondary Indexing

One of the important features of IMS is the ability to access databases using multiple keys. As an example, we normally access the DEPTDB by department number. If we now need to access the DEPTDB by location, we could use a logical database, but a better approach would be to use a secondary index. Like HIDAM databases, secondary indexes are implemented by means of a physical index database. To implement a secondary index, the DBD of the database to be indexed (DEPTDB in our example) needs to be changed.

The following two statements would need to be added to the DBD (Figure 10-3) immediately after the LOCATION field statement:

LCHILD NAME=(LOCINDX, LOCDB), POINTER=INDX
XDFIELD NAME=XLOCN, SRCH=LOCATION

The first (or LCHILD) statement specifies that this database (DEPTDB) is indexed by a segment called LOCINDX (location index). That index is defined in a database called LOCDB. The POINTER=INDX entry specifies that LOCINDX is indeed an index (not a data record). The second (or XDFIELD) statement identifies the field that is indexed; in this example, it is LOCATION, as specified by the SRCH=LOCATION entry. The NAME=XLOCN entry specifies that the variable name XLOCN will be used in referring to the indexed field.

Defining a Secondary Index   The secondary index database is described as shown in Figure 10-12. Statement 1 is a regular DBD statement and assigns the name LOCDB to this database. Statement 2 assigns the name LOCINDEX to the segment in an index, and statement 3 defines the field (LOCATION) on which the secondary index is defined. This is the only field in the LOCINDEX segment. Statement 4 is the LCHILD that connects the index database to the LOCATION field in the DEPTDB. A secondary index database such as this one is loaded using IMS utilities.

Using a Secondary Index   When an IMS database is loaded, any secondary indexes that have been defined by the user are automatically constructed by IMS. Also, IMS automatically maintains the secondary indexes as the database is modified.

To use a secondary index, the user specifies DL/I commands that invoke the variable names for the indexed field. To return to our original example, suppose that we wish to retrieve the segment for the department whose location is B100. The following statement will be used:

GU DEPARTMT (XLOCN='B100')

This statement causes IMS to retrieve the B100 index segment within LOCDB. That segment contains a pointer to the B100 data segment within DEPARTMT, which is the target segment.

In this example, we assume that values of the indexed field are unique (e.g., there is only one B100 segment). However, an IMS secondary index

1	DBD	NAME=LOCDB, ACCESS=INDEX
2	SEGM	NAME=LOCINDEX, BYTES=4,
3	FIELD	NAME=LOCATION, BYTES=4, START=1
4	LCHILD	NAME=(DEPARTMT, DEPTDB), INDEX=XLOCN

Figure 10-12
DBD for secondary index

may also be defined for fields that do not have unique values. For example, there may be more than one department at a given location. Therefore, a secondary index for LOCATION must accommodate nonunique values. Minor modifications are required in the secondary index definition for this case [for details, see IBM Corp. (1986)].

Case Example

In this section, we illustrate the use of IMS to implement a database for Mountain View Community Hospital. A structure of a database for this hospital is shown in Figure 6-11 and again in Figure 10-13 for ease of reference.

Database Definition

Figure 10-13
IMS database structures (Mountain View Community Hospital)

Three distinct physical databases are shown in Figure 10-13. These databases are linked together by logical pointers for reasons already described. A DBD for the PHYSICIAN database is shown in Figure 10-14 (we will ask you to develop DBDs for the remaining databases in the chapter problems).

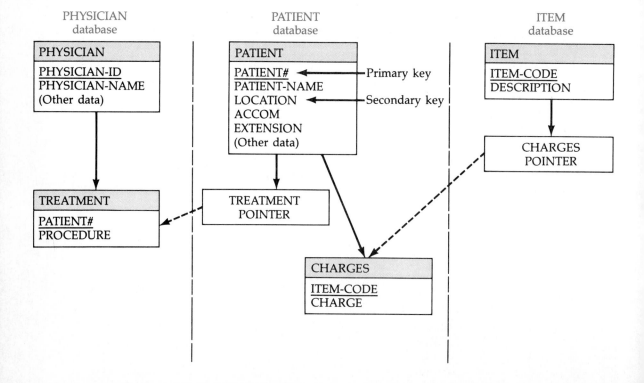

```
1   DBD      NAME=PHYSDB
2   SEGM     NAME=PHYSICN, BYTES=17, PARENT=0
3   FIELD    NAME=(PHYSID, SEQ), BYTES=10, START=1
4   FIELD    NAME=PHYPHONE, BYTES=7, START=11
5   SEGM     NAME=TREATMT, PARENT=PHYSICN, BYTES=19
6   FIELD    NAME=(PATIENT#, SEQ), BYTES=4, START=1
7   FIELD    NAME=PROCEDUR, BYTES=15, START=5
8   LCHILD   NAME=(TREATPTR, PATNTDB)
```

Figure 10-14
DBD for PHYSICIAN database (Mountain View Community Hospital)

Two segment types are defined in the PHYSICIAN database: PHYSICN (for physician) and TREATMT (for treatment). Notice that in statement 8, a logical child is defined for the TREATMT segment. This logical child is the treatment pointer (TREATPTR) in the PATIENT database (PATNTDB). This pointer links the PATIENT and PHYSICIAN databases.

Database Manipulation

To illustrate database manipulation, we use DL/I statements to retrieve data from the hospital databases. All the statements are based on the database structures shown in Figure 10-13.

Simple Retrieval   To retrieve patient data for patient number 1234, we use the following command:

    GU PATIENT (PATIENT# = '1234')

Indexed Retrieval   To retrieve patient data for the patient in location 4321, we use the following command:

    GU PATIENT (XLOCN = '4321')

This command assumes that there is a secondary index for the LOCATION field. Also, we assume that XLOCN is the variable name for the indexed field LOCATION.

Retrieval of Child Segments   To calculate total charges for patient number 1234, we use the following commands:

```
        MOVE 0 TO TOTAL
           GU PATIENT (PATIENT# = '1234')
              CHARGES
              ADD CHARGE TO TOTAL
  MORE GNP CHARGES
              ADD CHARGE TO TOTAL
              GO TO MORE
```

The GET UNIQUE (GU) statement retrieves the first CHARGES segment for this patient (if one exists). The amount of the CHARGE is added to the running total (TOTAL). The GNP statement is then executed repeatedly to retrieve additional charges, and TOTAL is updated until there are no more charges for that patient.

Retrieval Using Logical Records   To retrieve all TREATMT segments for patient number 1234, we use the following commands:

> GU PATIENT (PATIENT# = 1234)
>
> TREATMT
>
> MORE GNP TREATMT
>
> GO TO MORE

In this retrieval, the PATIENT and TREATMT segments exist in separate databases. However, use of the treatment pointer (TREATPTR) allows the user to manipulate the TREATMT segment as a child of PATIENT.

SUMMARY

In this chapter, we have presented an introduction to IMS, a database management system based on the hierarchical data model. In IMS, data are viewed as hierarchical arrangements of segments. A data manipulation language called Data Language I (DL/I) allows the user to retrieve data by traversing the tree structure.

Although the design of IMS dates from the late 1960s, a stream of enhancements has been added to provide new features. Thus, through the use of logical databases, the user can model limited networks. Also, secondary indexing permits access on fields other than primary keys. However, because these features are quite complex, IMS tends to be used only in relatively sophisticated data processing shops where considerable technical expertise is available.

Many other hierarchical DBMS products (not described in this chapter) are also available. Although it represents older technology, the hierarchical model remains a viable alternative for some DBMS implementations. However, it should be evaluated against the more recent network and relational systems.

Chapter Review

REVIEW QUESTIONS

1. Give a concise definition for each of the following terms:
   a. segment
   b. root segment
   c. logical database record
   d. physical database record
   e. database description
   f. program communication block

2. Contrast the following terms:
   a. physical database record; logical database record
   b. program communication block; program specification block
   c. root segment; child segment
   d. hierarchical pointers; child/twin pointers

3. Define each of the following acronyms:
   a. IMS   e. PSB
   b. PDBR   f. GNP
   c. LDBR   g. LCHILD
   d. PCB   h. SENSEG

4. Describe each of the following access methods briefly, and indicate the conditions favoring its use:
   a. HSAM   c. HDAM
   b. HISAM   d. HIDAM

5. Describe two ways in which an LDBR may differ from a PDBR.

6. Describe two advantages of the "sensitive segment" feature in IMS.

7. Why must caution be used in deleting a root segment with the DL/I DLET command?

8. Describe two restrictions in defining logical databases.

PROBLEMS AND EXERCISES

Problems 1 to 4 are based on the following hierarchical database structure for Pine Valley Furniture Company:

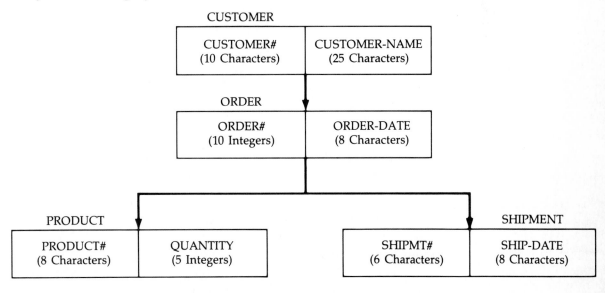

1. Write an IMS database description (DBD) for the database shown.

2. Based on the DBD in Problem 1, write a program communication block (PCB) for a logical database record that contains the CUSTOMER, ORDER, and PRODUCT segments (but omits the SHIPMENT segment).

3. Write DL/I statements for each of the following retrievals:
   a. CUSTOMER segment for customer number ABCD
   b. ORDER segment for order number 1234, customer number ABCD
   c. All ORDER segments for customer number ABCD
   d. All PRODUCT segments for customer number ABCD, order number 1234

4. Write DL/I statements for the following updates:
   a. Change the QUANTITY for product number 10 in order number 1234 for customer number ABCD from 3 to 2.
   b. Delete shipment number WXYZ for order number 6789 from customer number ABCD.
   c. Add shipment number CDEF to order number 6789 from customer number ABCD (shipment date is 6/18/8X).

5. Write an IMS database description for the ITEM database in Figure 10-13. Assume the following data item characteristics:
   ITEM CODE   10 Characters
   DESCRIPN   25 Characters

6. Write an IMS database description for the PATIENT database (Figure 10-13). Include the logical pointers. Assume the following data item characteristics:
   PATIENT#   10 Characters
   PATNAME   25 Characters
   LOCATION   5 Characters
   ACCOM   6 Characters
   EXTENSN   4 Integers
   ITEMCODE   10 Characters
   CHARGE   Decimal XXXX.XX

7. In Figure 10-13, LOCATION is identified as a secondary key in the PATIENT segment. Write an IMS secondary index DBD for this field.

8. One logical database record derived from the hospital database (Figure 10-13) appears as follows:

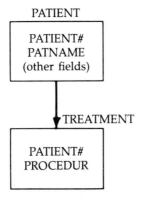

Write an IMS DBD for this logical record.

9. Write DL/I statements for the following retrievals in the hospital database (Figure 10-13):
   a. CHARGE segment for item number 1234, patient number ABCD
   b. All CHARGE segments for patient number ABCD
   c. All TREATMENT segments for patient number ABCD performed by physician number P10

10. Referring to Figure 10-2, what segment(s) will be retrieved for each of the following statements?
    a. GU DEPARTMT (DEPT# = '02')
          EQPMENT (IDENT = 'APPLE II')
    b. GU DEPARTMT (DEPT# = '02')
          EMPLOYEE (EMP# = '07')
          SKILL (CODE = '02')
    c.   GU DEPARTMT (DEPT# = '02')
             EMPLOYEE (EMP# = '07')
             DEPENDNT (DEPNM = 'THERESE')
      NEXT GNP DEPENDNT
          GO TO NEXT

REFERENCES

Atre, S. 1983. *Data Base Management Systems for the Eighties.* Wellesley, Mass.: QED Information Sciences.

Date, C. J. 1981. *An Introduction to Database Systems.* 3d ed. Reading, Mass.: Addison-Wesley.

IBM Corp. 1986. *Information Management System/Virtual Storage General Information Manual.* IBM form no. GH20-1260.

Tsichritzis, D. C., and F. H. Lochovsky. 1977. *Data Base Management Systems.* New York: Academic Press.

CHAPTER 11

Network and CODASYL Implementations

INTRODUCTION

The purpose of this chapter is to review the implementation of the network data model in industry standards and in commercial database management systems. You may want to review "The Network Data Model" section in Chapter 8 before proceeding. Remember, the network data model can be used for modeling a conceptual database (as presented in Chapter 8) or as the basis for a particular DBMS, as covered in this chapter.

The implementation of the network data model is an interesting example of the influence of industry standards and of individual vendors. The Conference on Data Systems Languages (CODASYL) through its Data Base Task Group (DBTG) is a standards organization that has developed and issued descriptions of languages for defining and processing data. The initial report describing a network database implementation was issued in 1971 (CODASYL 1971). Subsequent reports and updates describing most network DBMSs were issued in 1978 and 1981 (see references at end of this chapter).

Although represented on the original DBTG, IBM Corporation did not sign or endorse these standards and to this day has not implemented a network DBMS. But many other hardware vendors and numerous software firms have chosen to develop systems following the CODASYL guidelines (even for IBM computers). At the same time, IBM has installed IMS, its hierarchical DBMS, in many of its customers' data centers. Again, these events indicate that variety is the hallmark of database.

The CODASYL Committee is a voluntary group of individuals who represent hardware and software vendors, universities, and major developers and users of data processing systems. Their original charge had been to discuss changes to the COBOL programming language and to write position papers in this area. Member organizations were in no way bound to implement these positions in their program products. It had become clear that COBOL needed radical extension to support multiple-file (database) data processing, and the DBTG was formed.

In 1963, General Electric (later Honeywell Information Systems) began to market Integrated Data System (IDS), the forerunner of network DBMSs. The generally accepted leader of the development of IDS was Charles Bachman. Although Bachman was not on the DBTG itself, several individuals from Honeywell were represented, along with Richard Schubert of B.F. Goodrich Chemical Company, a primary user of IDS. Through these individuals and because IDS was the most fully developed DBMS by this time, the structure of IDS (and the ideas of Charles Bachman) greatly influenced the deliberations of the DBTG. Even today, many organizations draw "Bachman diagrams" to represent network databases.

Although pleased with the capabilities of IDS, B.F. Goodrich worked on expanding these functions to meet more of the DBTG guidelines. Interest grew in the computing community in bringing a DBTG network DBMS to the marketplace. John Cullinane approached B.F. Goodrich and purchased the rights to further develop and market their initial DBTG implementation along with the existing CULPRIT reportwriter product. He named his new product Integrated Database Management System (IDMS), which is still, today, the leading DBTG DBMS on IBM (and other) computers.

Many network DBMSs exist today. Most of these are DBTG implementations, but several significant exceptions have appeared. Table 11-1 lists several of these network DBMSs and pertinent information about them. Since DBTG network DBMSs dominate, most of this chapter reviews the definition and processing of data using these DBMSs. Also addressed are recent extensions to network DBMSs that provide nonnetwork views of a database managed by a network DBMS. This topic is an important development that creates a great deal of confusion in distinguishing between DBMSs.

There are actually three official versions of the DBTG guidelines (1971, 1978, and 1981 reports); we have chosen to emphasize the 1978 report because most DBTG DBMSs today come closest to following these guidelines. Some exceptions will be noted when appropriate. Because of its prominence among IBM computer installations, we will draw heavily on IDMS as an example of a DBTG implementation. For greater depth on the DBTG model, Olle (1980) provides an excellent coverage of these guidelines through several minor modifications published in 1973.

Table 11-1 Summary of Some Networks DBMSs

Package	Vendor	Equipment	Comments
CODASYL DBMSs			
IDMS	Cullinet Software (Division of Computer Associates)	IBM 360/370, 30xx, 43xx, variety of operating systems, DEC VAX under VMS operating system, several minis and a few other mainframes	Various related packages, including: Integrated Data Dictionary, CULPRIT report-writer, OnLine English natural language, distributed database facility, and Application Development System (ADS/O)
PR1ME DBMS	PR1ME Computer	Various PR1ME mini and super-mini computers under PR1MOS operating system	
DMS-170	CDC	Variety of hardware under NOS operating system	
DBMS 11	DEC	DEC VAX under VMS operating system	
IDS II	Honeywell Information Systems	Variety of HIS computers	Extension of first network DBMS; works with many host languages
DMS-1100	Univac (UNISYS)	Exec 8 and more recent operating systems for Univac 1100 computer family	Popular nonprocedural language MAPPER

INTRODUCTION TO CODASYL DBTG GUIDELINES

To begin to understand the DBTG guidelines and implementations of this data model, we must start by analyzing the concept of a DBMS that underlies the work of the DBTG. Figure 11-1 shows the conceptual database management system envisioned by the DBTG. This diagram indicates that a DBMS is conceived as software that works in conjunction with an operating system to service multiple, concurrently executing, user programs.

DBMS Operation

To comprehend the nature of a DBTG DBMS, it is important to understand the operational sequence of events that occurs when such a DBMS is used. This sequence is depicted with numbered arrows in Figure 11-1 and can be summarized as follows:

1. A user program "calls" the DBMS with a request for service (retrieval, maintenance, and so on), which has been written using special data manipulation language (DML) statements. These statements are included in a host language (e.g., COBOL) user program.

2. The DBMS analyzes the request for service by matching the parameters of the request with a stored version of a definition of the database (called a schema) and a definition of the part of the database applicable to this program (called a subschema). These two data definitions have been predefined via data description languages (DDLs) and are maintained and stored separate from user programs in a library of data definitions.

3. As long as the request for service contains no inadmissible components (e.g., improper security passwords or references to data outside the invoked subschema), the DBMS composes a series of I/O commands for the access methods of the operating system.

4. The operating system interacts with secondary storage devices to initiate database access.

5. The operating system performs the appropriate retrieval or modification of database contents, using data buffers managed by the DBMS. These buffers contain blocks of data transferred between main and secondary memory in which data are formatted as defined by the schema.

6. In the case of data retrieval, data are then moved from the system buffers to a user work area or data section of the calling user's program (steps 5 and 6 are reversed for maintenance). This transfer also often includes the reformatting of data and the elimination of data in blocks not included in the subschema.

Figure 11-1
CODASYL con-
ceptual database
management system
(*Source:* CODASYL
1971)

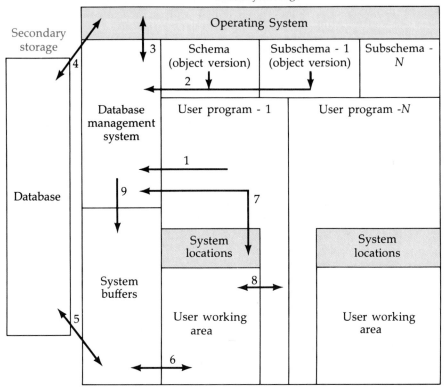

7. The DBMS then sets status-variable values in the user program with messages and error codes to indicate the nature of any problems, if any, that arose during database interaction.

8. The user program is then free to further manipulate the data it has received from the database or to compose new records for database maintenance.

9. While each user program is executing, the DBMS manages the system buffers so that, for example, if a request for data is made that asks for data already in a system buffer, the DBMS can bypass steps 3 to 5 and provide the data immediately to the calling program.

Although the outline of this interaction could be interpreted in several ways, the resulting guidelines specified an implementation in which user calls occur at the record level; that is, the user program includes DML statements to retrieve or write *each* record required for processing, one at a time from each database file.

DBTG Languages

The DBTG guidelines also specified or implied various new languages. Figure 11-2 illustrates the relationships between these languages and the roles of each in defining and using a network database. First is a **schema data description language** (schema DDL), used to define the global database. As previously mentioned, this is a combination of implementation-independent and -dependent statements. Since the schema DDL does not, however, cover all internal/physical declarations, a **device media control language** (DMCL) was proposed to specify assignment of data to particular devices, data block contents and format, database update audit trail options, and so on.

Also proposed were standards for a **subschema data description language** (subschema DDL) for specifying database structure to program compilers. Several user programs are allowed to share the same subschema. Originally, only a COBOL subschema DDL was proposed, but today a FORTRAN subschema DDL also exists. Each language requires its own subschema DDL since the idea was to define the external database in a syntax that can be easily translated into the data definitions of a programming language.

Finally, standards for a **data manipulation language** (DML), also host-language-specific, were proposed. Initially, only a COBOL version was outlined, but today a FORTRAN version also exists. The DBTG assumed a host language environment in which there would be extensions to an already existing language (as opposed to defining a new self-contained language for database manipulation). These extensions would be handled either by vendors creating new language compilers to translate the expanded vocabulary or by preprocessors (as illustrated in Figure 11-2) that would translate only the new language statements within a program into standard language sentences (usually CALL statements with parameters derived from the raw DML statement). The output from the DML preprocessor would then be given to a standard language compiler.

The DBTG proposals also called for extensive capabilities to define security controls in the schema DDL. Many initial implementations of the DBTG model chose not to include these capabilities since it was felt that given computing power in the early 1970s, database processing performance would be seriously deterred by such overhead. Today, inclusion of security controls is a standard feature of DBTG implementations. Also standard today are nonprocedural (non-record-at-a-time) query languages for DBTG implementations that permit retrieval (but often *not* update) to be accomplished in fewer statements and less programming time than in conventional procedural languages like COBOL or FORTRAN.

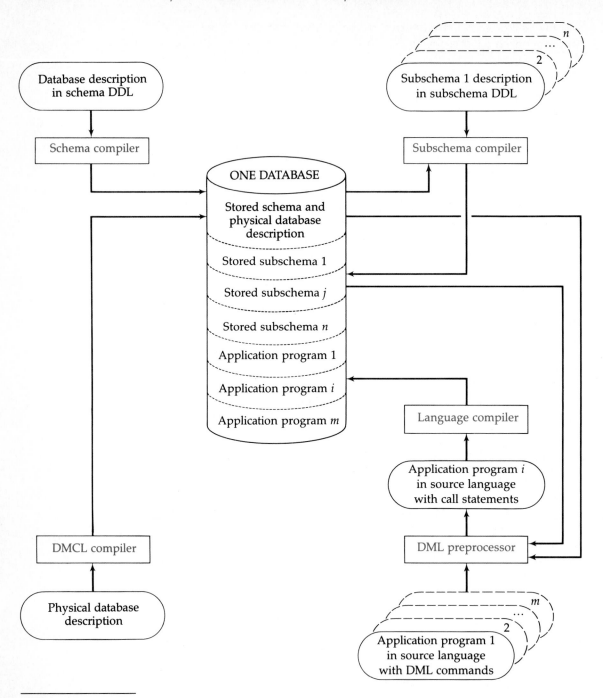

Figure 11-2
DBTG languages and
compilation cycles

This, then, is an overview of the DBTG DBMS environment. The following sections address the DBTG model and its languages in greater detail.

DBTG SCHEMA DDL: THE CONCEPTUAL/INTERNAL DATABASE

The DBTG schema DDL uses some familiar terminology but has certainly done its part to create new terms. On occasion, this terminology has been disturbing enough to cause CODASYL to change terms to clarify usage of the data model. The schema DDL has many clauses and various options in most of the clause parameters. It is beyond our purpose here to cover all features of the schema DDL, so only the most salient and frequently used features and parameters will be shown. The general structure of a DBTG schema definition is shown in Figure 11-3a. The structure illustrated here generally obeys the 1978 DBTG guidelines; exceptions are indicated with footnotes. Figure 11-3b illustrates via a network diagram the parts of a network data model that correspond to the various sections of the schema DDL.

A **schema** (definition) is a named collection of record types and pairwise associations (sets) between owner and member record types, which are located in specified, named regions of secondary memory (areas or realms).

The structure shown in Figure 11-3a can be broken into three general segments. The first segment defines contiguous physical storage regions, called areas, into which all data values will be located. Because this deals with the physical or metaphysical database, the 1981 guidelines have dropped this segment (and related clauses) to make the schema more independent of implementation.

The second segment describes all the record types or files and the data item contents that compose the database. The third segment defines the database representation, called sets, of all pairwise record type relationships designed in the conceptual database. The data model is a simple network, and link and intersection record types (called junction records by IDMS) may exist, as well as sets between them (ORDER-LINE is an example of an intersection record in Figure 11-3b). Thus, the complete network of relationships is represented by several pairwise sets; in each set some (one) record type is owner (at the tail of the network arrow) and one or more record types are members (at the head of the relationship arrow). Usually, a set defines a 1:M relationship, although 1:1 is permitted.

Two types of clauses that can appear at various points in a schema will not be addressed in detail here; these are the ON ERROR and PRIVACY clauses. ON ERROR can be used to indicate that certain user-defined procedures are to be invoked in case of specified errors in data or commands. PRIVACY LOCKs specify passwords or procedures that are to be used to

Figure 11-3
General structure of
DBTG schema
definition:
(a) schema DDL
(b) schema diagram

```
SCHEMA NAME IS _____
    [ON ERROR...]
    [PRIVACY LOCK...]
{AREA NAME IS _____
    [ON ERROR...]
    [PRIVACY LOCK...]}*
{RECORD NAME IS _____
    LOCATION MODE...
    [KEY IS...]**
    {WITHIN...}*
    [ON ERROR...]
    [PRIVACY LOCK...]
    [level-no data-base-data-name
     |(((|PICTURE...| or |TYPE...|)
          |OCCURS...|) or
          (| SOURCE...|)|
          |RESULT...|
          |CHECK...|
          | FOR (ENCODING or DECODING)...|
          [ON ERROR...]
          [PRIVACY...]|}
[SET NAME IS _____
    OWNER IS...
    |SET IS DYNAMIC or PRIOR|
    ORDER IS...
    [ON ERROR...]
    [PRIVACY LOCK...]
    {MEMBER IS _____
     INSERTION IS _____
     RETENTION IS _____
    [KEY IS...]
    |SEARCH KEY IS...|
    |CHECK IS...|
    |SET SELECTION...|
    [ON ERROR...]
    [PRIVACY LOCK...]}]
END SCHEMA


  *Deleted in 1981 CODASYL revision, but still a part of most DBMSs
 **Added in 1981 version, but not yet present in most DBMSs
    [...]—0, 1 or many occurrences of clause
    {...}—1 or many occurrences of clause
    |...|—0 or 1 occurrence of clause
```

(a)

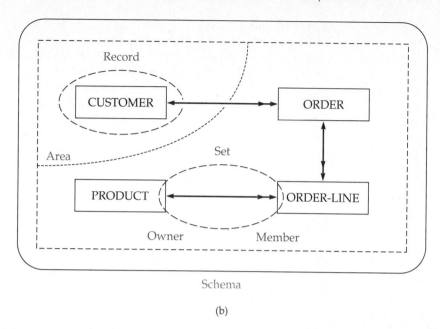

Figure 11-3
(continued)

Schema

(b)

verify that certain database manipulations are authorized for users of the database.

Before we explain the schema DDL, it is worth mentioning that you may have the most trouble understanding three components of the DDL: LOCATION MODE, SET SELECTION, and set membership clauses. Carefully study examples and discussions that involve these most frequently misunderstood parts of a DBTG database definition.

Areas or Realms

Consider the Pine Valley Furniture database of Figure 3-11. If this database were large enough to require many disk cylinders or disk packs, processing could become very expensive. If it were realized that a significant amount of data processing were related to customer geographical regions (e.g., sales reports produced by region or new orders batched by region), then it might be advantageous to cluster CUSTOMER and ORDER records (at least) from a common geographical region close together in the physical database for more rapid access between these records. Similarly, suppose that marketing applications concentrate record usage to CUSTOMER and ORDER records and that production applications primarily use PRODUCT and ORDER-LINE record types. In this case, it is advantageous to cluster CUSTOMER and ORDER records close together, but separate from a cluster of PRODUCT and ORDER-LINE records, in order to provide rapid access between records that are used together in data processing.

An **area** (or **realm** in recent CODASYL terminology) is a named, contiguous portion of secondary memory. Operationally, this is equivalent to a range of adjacent pages of some physical disk file. The purpose of the area designation is to control physical proximity of records, as illustrated in the Pine Valley Furniture cases of geographical regions and segregated data processing. The database of a schema will reside in one or more areas. Each area is named in the schema, and the definition of each record specifies which area or areas will hold records of that type (the WITHIN clause).

A skeleton of a schema for this Pine Valley Furniture situation would be:

AREA NAME IS SOUTH

. . .

RECORD NAME IS CUSTOMER

. . .

  WITHIN SOUTH, EAST, WEST AREA-ID IS CUST-REGION

. . .

  1 CUST-REGION ; TYPE IS CHARACTER 10

. . .

RECORD NAME IS ORDER

. . .

  LOCATION MODE IS VIA ORDERS-FOR-CUSTOMER SET
  WITHIN AREA OF OWNER

. . .

SET NAME IS ORDERS-FOR-CUSTOMER
  OWNER IS CUSTOMER

. . .

  MEMBER IS ORDER

. . .

In this example, it is assumed that three areas were desirable: SOUTH, EAST, and WEST (area definitions for EAST and WEST are similar to the one for SOUTH). CUSTOMER records are automatically placed in the proper area by the DBMS when a new record is stored. The customer's region (and area) name, loaded into the CUST-REGION field of a CUSTOMER record instance by a data entry program, is used to specify proper placement. ORDER records are placed in the same region as their associated CUSTOMER record (that is, their owner is the ORDERS-FOR-CUSTOMER set). Thus, if data processing requirements frequently require ORDER records associated with a given CUSTOMER record, then these records will be able to be accessed more rapidly than if placement is not controlled. For this reason, a set is said to define an access path to "walk" through a database from owner record to members (or vice versa). This placement of ORDER records near their related CUSTOMER record is controlled by the WITHIN clause of the ORDER record (makes all ORDERs closer to all CUSTOMERs than to other records) and the LOCATION MODE clause of the ORDER record (places a specific ORDER close to its particular CUSTOMER record instance).

Records

The second major data construct in the DBTG model is that of a record. A **record** is a named entity, instances of which describe individual occurrences of the entity. We define a record by specifying how the physical location of a record instance is determined (LOCATION MODE clause) and by a list of data element (or data-base-data-name) definitions.

LOCATION MODE of a Record LOCATION MODE is a physical construct that has been removed in recent guidelines but which is still present in most commercial implementations. **LOCATION MODE** specifies the method that will be employed to determine the precise disk address of an instance of a record when it is stored. Two methods are popular: CALC and VIA. Table 11-2 briefly summarizes the use of each of these methods.

Data processing frequently requires referring to records by logical key value. For example, a data entry operator may input a product number from a sales form and expect to see associated data in order to complete the entry of a customer order. The CALC LOCATION MODE would be appropriate to support this need.

The CALC LOCATION MODE can be illustrated with the following partial record definitions:

RECORD NAME IS PRODUCT
LOCATION MODE CALC USING PRODUCT# DUPLICATES NOT
   ALLOWED
. . .
  1 PRODUCT# ; PICTURE 9999.
. . .
RECORD NAME IS ORDER-LINE
LOCATION MODE CALC USING PRODUCT#, ORDER#
   DUPLICATES NOT ALLOWED
. . .
  1 PRODUCT# ; PICTURE 9999.
  1 ORDER# ; PICTURE 9999.
. . .

CALC was designed to specify that record instances will be stored and found by hashing on key values. For the preceding PRODUCT record, PRODUCT# is a primary key (since DUPLICATES NOT ALLOWED); for the ORDER-LINE record given here, the concatenated key is PRODUCT# plus ORDER#, which is also unique. If duplicates are allowed, then the DBMS will permit two or more records to have the same hash key value. Otherwise, when not allowed, the DBMS will enforce, during storing and modification, the primary key property by returning error codes for data manipulation commands that would cause a violation of the duplicates clause. The CALC key must be defined as fields within the record being CALCed, even if part of the key can be found in a related record (in this case, PRODUCT# of ORDER-LINE is also in the related PRODUCT record).

Table 11-2   DBTG Record Placement Control Using LOCATION MODE

LOCATION MODE	Explanation	Examples

CALC	Indicates that a record instance will be placed and may be accessed in secondary memory based on a value for a primary or secondary key. Usually, this is implemented by key value hashing, but index methods are possible. That is, database can be entered directly at a given record if a CALC key value is known.	RECORD NAME IS PRODUCT
		  LOCATION MODE IS CALC
		  USING PRODUCT#
		  DUPLICATES NOT ALLOWED
		–defines a single, primary key
		
		RECORD NAME IS CUSTOMER
		  LOCATION MODE IS CALC
		  USING CUST-ZIP
		  DUPLICATES ARE FIRST
		–defines a single, secondary key

VIA	Indicates that a record instance will be placed in secondary memory close to its parent record instance for *one* specified set. This helps to improve performance when used with frequently referenced set. VIA and CALC may not both be used on same record; use of VIA prevents access to record on a key value.	RECORD NAME IS ORDER-LINE
		  LOCATION MODE IS VIA
		  ITEMS-ON-ORDER SET
		. . .
		SET NAME IS
		  ITEMS-ON-ORDER
		OWNER IS ORDER
		. . .
		MEMBER IS ORDER-LINE
		  –specifies that an ORDER-LINE
		  instance should be stored close
		  to its ORDER owner instance

Some DBTG systems permit only one LOCATION MODE clause; others permit several LOCATION MODE or the more recent KEY IS clauses. Some DBTG systems even permit a database designer to use other than hashing methods for implementing CALC mode (e.g., indexes). In general, the CALC mode must be interpreted as any keyed access method (entry point into a database) using primary or secondary keys, as allowed by the DBMS. Use of CALC does not preclude accessing a record by its association with other records; it simply says that records will be *physically placed* (and can be found) based on key values.

On other occasions, users of an information system do not know primary key values for desired records, but instead know the key for some associated record. For example, we might know a PRODUCT# but not know the CUSTOMER#s of customers who have open orders for this product.

The second LOCATION MODE alternative, designed to provide efficient record access by association, is VIA. VIA means that a record will be placed as close to its associated owner record instance as the DBMS can find *for the specified set*. Use of VIA in the DBTG model prevents a user from accessing a record directly by a key value. LOCATION VIA should be used for a given record when much data processing of this record involves first accessing an associated owner record before instances of this type are required (that is, access via relationships between records, since records to be retrieved are known only by their association with other records).

Consider again the ORDER-LINE record type. Although each of these record instances could be identified by a concatenated key of ORDER# plus PRODUCT#, careful review of data processing might indicate that ORDER-LINE records are retrieved or stored only after first retrieving associated PRODUCT or ORDER records. After additional review, it is determined that ORDER-LINE records are more often processed along with ORDER records than with PRODUCT records. The following LOCATION MODE clause could then be used in the definition of the ORDER-LINE record:

```
RECORD NAME IS ORDER-LINE
LOCATION MODE IS VIA ITEMS-ON-ORDER SET
. . .
SET NAME IS ITEMS-ON-ORDER
OWNER IS ORDER
. . .
MEMBER IS ORDER-LINE
. . .
```

Figure 11-4 illustrates the effect these schema commands might have on the database of Figure 3-11 (Pine Valley Furniture).

A record can be located VIA only one set in the DBTG model, so ORDER-LINEs cannot also be specified to be placed close to PRODUCT. It should be emphasized here that VIA does not establish which owner record instance is, in fact, the owner of a given member instance, but only that a member instance will be *placed* close to its owner instance. The SET SELECTION clause in the SET definition controls the method of determining ownership; we will discuss this clause later. As illustrated in Figure 11-4, a record type located VIA one set may participate as owner or members in other sets and may be accessed through these other sets; the most efficient access for the record will be through the set on which it is VIA. If a set member record

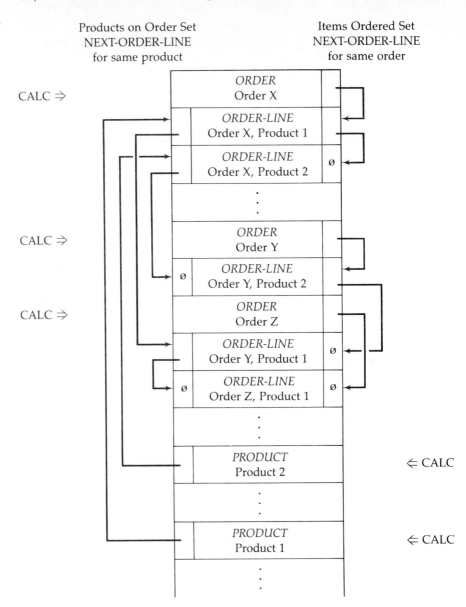

instance located VIA its owner changes ownership (by a RECONNECT or similar command), its location will not change to be close to its new owner. Thus, after the ownership change, the member will not necessarily exhibit rapid access from its owner VIA the designated set.

In the most recent CODASYL guidelines, LOCATION MODE has been eliminated in favor of a more general and logical clause called KEY IS. Under the latest guideline, not yet implemented in all commercial systems, each record type may have one or more single or concatenated primary or secondary keys with either ascending or descending logical orderings maintained. For the primary key of CUSTOMER# in the CUSTOMER record of Figure 3-11, we could include (in place of the LOCATION MODE clause)

KEY CUSTOMER# IS ASCENDING CUSTOMER#
DUPLICATES ARE NOT ALLOWED

and for the secondary key of PRODUCT# in the ORDER-LINE record, we could include

KEY PRODUCT# IS ASCENDING PRODUCT#
DUPLICATES ARE FIRST

DUPLICATES ARE NOT ALLOWED specifies a primary key. The use of FIRST or LAST indicates how to sequence records for storage and retrieval with duplicate secondary key values. FIRST means that a new record with a duplicate value will be stored as the first record (first on a chain) among any with the same value for PRODUCT#; use of LAST would tell the DBMS to store the new record last (in this key sequence) after all existing records (on a chain) with this same PRODUCT# value. A KEY IS clause will cause some type of key access method, like hashing or indexing, to be employed, depending on the implementation.

Although not part of the most current CODASYL guidelines, LOCATION MODE has been presented here because most DBTG systems use some form of this clause, even if the KEY IS clause is also supported.

Data Elements in a Record Definition   A record type may have no data elements, which is the case of a link record. Link records are possible because the DBTG data model can be classified as a simple network model. In most cases, a record type will have one or more data elements, or data-base-datanames, as part of its definition. A record type must contain data elements for each component of each key and for each data element used for sorting members of a set.

The schema not only defines what data elements are to be in each record, but also their format of representation in the database (which may be different from that for corresponding fields in user working storage). Thus, each data element must have exactly one of the following as part of its definition:

- PICTURE clause
- TYPE clause
- SOURCE clause
- OCCURS clause (not allowed in some systems)
- OCCURS and PICTURE clauses
- OCCURS and TYPE clauses

and any of the other clauses shown in Figure 11-3a, with a few limitations.

The PICTURE format is similar to that used in COBOL. Both character and numeric formats are supported. A PICTURE is used to define a display format for data elements. Consequently, data are stored using the computer's typical coding scheme (e.g., EBCDIC or ASCII). TYPE is used to cause more efficient storage formats to be used. TYPE can specify base (BINARY or DECIMAL), scale (FIXED or FLOAT), and mode (REAL or COMPLEX); length specifications for arithmetic data, or BIT or CHARACTER strings; or DATA-BASE-KEY. For example, the PRODUCT file of Figure 1-7 (Pine Valley Furniture) could be defined as a DBTG record type as follows:

RECORD IS PRODUCT
LOCATION MODE CALC USING PRODUCT#

. . .
   1 PRODUCT# ; PIC 9999.
   1 DESCRIPTION ; PIC X(20).
   1 FINISH ; PIC X(8).
   1 ROOM ; PIC X(2).
   1 PRICE ; TYPE DECIMAL 6,2.

Here most data elements are to be used for display purposes. PRICE will be stored in the computer system's DECIMAL format, with four integer digits and two decimal places (some DBTG systems have a DOLLAR TYPE in which TYPE DOLLAR 4 would be identical to this specification).

An OCCURS clause may be used with PICTURE or TYPE to indicate a repeating group of elementary data items. In addition, an OCCURS clause may appear by itself to specify a repeating data aggregate. For example, we could expand the definition of PRODUCT in Figure 3-11 to include a set of PRICEs, depending on quantity purchased. Part of the record definition might then look like this:

RECORD IS PRODUCT

. . .
   1 PRICE-SCHEDULE ; OCCURS 3 TIMES.
     2 QTY-UPPER ; PICTURE 99999.
     2 QTY-PRICE ; DECIMAL 6,2.

In this example, a three-tiered price schedule capability has been designed for each Product. If different Products have a different number of quantity-price breaks, then

RECORD IS PRODUCT

. . .
   1 NO-BREAKS ; TYPE IS DECIMAL 2.
   1 PRICE-SCHEDULE ; OCCURS NO-BREAKS TIMES.
     2 QTY-UPPER ; PICTURE 99999.
     2 QTY-PRICE ; DECIMAL 6,2.

would allow for 0 to 99 different quantity-price breaks for each PRODUCT.

Other Data Element Clauses   Any data element can be further defined in a schema by CHECK and coding clauses. A CHECK clause specifies validation criteria to be checked each time the associated data element changes value or a new value is added. Implementations vary, but most permit specification of a list of legitimate values or ranges of values or the execution of a more general user procedure.

Coding clauses inform the DBMS what to do to ENCODE or DECODE a data element value. Again, implementations vary, but the effect of such clauses is to define code tables so that long, standard character strings that are input can be converted to more compact codes to save storage space (and vice-versa for reporting). For example, coding could be used for the DESCRIPTION of the PRODUCT record. Such coding could equate TABLE with a stored value of TA, WALL UNIT with a stored value of WU, and so on, to reduce space and eliminate wasted characters (if variable-length records are not supported). Entry of WALL UNIT for DESCRIPTION would result in only WU being stored; display of a TA stored value would result in TABLE actually being reported.

Relationship Definitions: Sets

A **set** is the definition of a directed relationship from an owner record type to one or more member record types. A set usually defines a 1:*M* relationship, say, an ORDERS-FOR-CUSTOMER set from CUSTOMER as owner to ORDER as member. A set may also define a 1:1 relationship, but this is unusual. A set may not define an *M:N* relationship, since the DBTG model prescribes a simple network data model. One can generally assume that a set is implemented as a ring data structure with the owner at the head of the chain and with the last member pointing to the owner. Other structures (bidirectional chains, pointer arrays, owner pointers, and so forth) can be defined in clauses not being considered here.

Figure 11-5 illustrates a segment of the database for Pine Valley Furniture. The figure also includes a skeleton of the schema DDL necessary to define this part of the database. The figure includes a complete definition for the PRODUCT-VENDOR-LINK record. Assuming that this is only a link record, no data elements are defined, although some "data about data" (e.g., pointers to maintain sets) may be allocated from the compilation of the schema DDL.

The inclusion of a set, say, from PRODUCT to ORDER-LINE, in a schema for Figure 11-5 informs the schema DDL compiler to establish some type of data structure to permit rapid access from an instance of a PRODUCT record to instances of associated set ORDER-LINE members (and possibly vice-versa). Whenever records are inserted, deleted, or modified in either of these files, the DBMS will perform much of the maintenance of the overhead data to continue correct record association. This schema in Figure 11-5 illustrates that a record type may be an owner of several sets and also

Figure 11-5
Skeleton of the
schema for part of
Pine Valley Furniture
database:
(a) network diagram
(b) schema definition

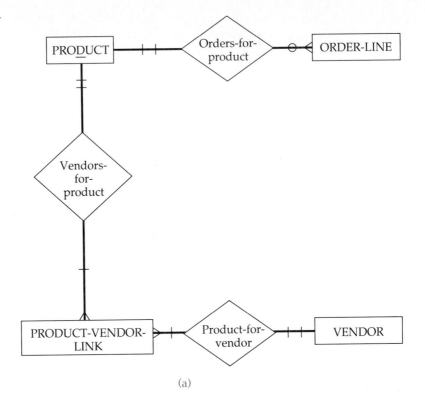

(a)

a member of several sets; some DBTG systems even permit the same record type to be both owner and member of the same set!

However, a set is not the only means of relating records in the DBTG model. Consider the same PRODUCT to ORDER-LINE relationship just discussed. If both record types contain PRODUCT# and if this data element is used in a KEY IS clause in each record definition, then associated records may also be rapidly retrieved by accessing records by this logical key. Nevertheless, a set is the usual means employed in a DBTG database to represent a relationship since this is the only way the DBMS will know about the relationship! If sets are not used to represent relationships, then the implementation is not any richer in structure and capabilities than multiple random access files.

Member Insertion Sequence   When a member instance is inserted into a set, the DBMS must know what basis is to be used to determine where in the chain of existing members the new record should be placed. The typical choices available are:

FIRST: at the beginning of the chain
LAST: at the end of the chain (FIRST and LAST support chronological order of members by date/time of entry)

```
SCHEMA NAME IS PINE
...
RECORD NAME IS PRODUCT
    LOCATION MODE IS CALC USING PRODUCT#
...
1 PRODUCT# ; PIC 9999.
...
RECORD NAME IS ORDER-LINE
    LOCATION MODE IS VIA ORDERS-FOR-PRODUCT SET
...
RECORD NAME IS VENDOR
    LOCATION MODE IS CALC USING VENDOR#
...
1 VENDOR# ; PIC 9999.
...
RECORD NAME IS PRODUCT-VENDOR-LINK
    LOCATION MODE IS VIA VENDORS-FOR-PRODUCT SET
SET IS ORDERS-FOR-PRODUCT
    OWNER IS PRODUCT
    ...
    MEMBER IS ORDER-LINE
    ...
SET IS VENDORS-FOR-PRODUCT
    OWNER IS PRODUCT
    ...
    MEMBER IS PRODUCT-VENDOR-LINK
    ...
SET IS PRODUCTS-FOR-VENDOR
    OWNER IS VENDOR
    ...
    MEMBER IS PRODUCT-VENDOR-LINK
    ...
```

(b)

SORTED: based on the value of some field in the member record

NEXT: immediately after the most recently accessed member of the set

PRIOR: immediately before the most recently accessed member of the set

We will discuss later in this chapter the difficult decision of choosing whether to sort members of a set. Very simply, the trade-off is between saving sorting time when data are reported versus storage space for the key field (this may be part of the record anyhow) and extra member insertion time to scan for the right place in the member chain. Long chains can, of course, be costly to scan, and frequent maintenance and infrequent reporting in sequence may negate the benefit of a sorted set.

Loop Relationship   Several types of 1:*M* relationships need special illustration if we are to explain their representation in schema DDL. The first is a loop relationship. Figure 11-6 shows such a relationship and indicates a skeleton of the schema parts required to represent this relationship between customers within the same parent organization under several different implementations in the DBTG model. This loop relationship would help to ascertain the total purchasing behavior of a client for which several purchasing agents or divisions are individual buyers.

Figure 11-6a illustrates the basic loop relationship and the most direct way, if permitted, to represent this type of relationship. This representation requires that the DBMS support use of the same record type as both owner and member of the same set. In this case, both the parent organization as well as the individual buying groups are represented as CUSTOMERs (which, of course, they likely are).

The approach of Figure 11-6b is to define an additional ORGANIZATION record type, instances of which own a set of CUSTOMER member instances for that parent organization. Data manipulation statements can be used to move from one member to another in a given set instance or from a member instance to the associated owner instance. The approach of Figure 11-6c is, if permitted by the particular DBMS, to define a secondary key on the PARENT-ORG data element of the CUSTOMER record type; data manipulation statements can then be used to access all CUSTOMER records with a common value for this secondary key. In all of these cases, it is still possible to define a primary key of CUSTOMER# for the CUSTOMER record.

Singular Sets   Singular or system relationships (called one-of-a-kind in IDMS) are easy to represent in a DBTG schema. The purpose of a singular relationship is to arrange all the instances of some record type into sorted sequence under a common owner, the "system."

Suppose we wanted to arrange all CUSTOMER records into ascending order by CUST-ZIPCODE to avoid the cost of sorting all CUSTOMER records for each mailing. Figure 11-7 illustrates the skeleton of the definition of a singular set that accomplishes this desired sequencing. CUSTOMER records can all be retrieved as members under one common parent (the singular system) in the zip code order because of the use of the ORDER IS SORTED clause and the KEY IS clause of the member specification for the set. Thus, now we would have two access points into CUSTOMER: (1) The primary key of CUSTOMER# is CALCed to provide direct addressing, and (2) the CUST-ZIPCODE set is used to access CUSTOMERs in zip code order.

Singular sets can also be used to logically group together records with a common characteristic (e.g., all customers who have exceeded their credit limit); that is, not all record instances from the set member record type *must* be included in the set. In IDMS, this type of set must be designed using an artificial record type (one-of-a-kind) as the owner, rather than the implicit "system" owner.

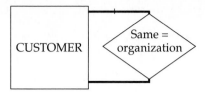

. . .

SET IS SAME-ORGANIZATION
    OWNER IS CUSTOMER
. . .
    MEMBER IS CUSTOMER
. . .

(a)

. . .

SET IS SAME-ORGANIZATION
    OWNER IS ORGANIZATION
. . .
    MEMBER IS CUSTOMER
. . .

(b)

. . .

RECORD IS CUSTOMER
LOCATION MODE IS CALC USING CUSTOMER#
KEY IS PARENT-ORG DUPLICATES ARE FIRST
. . .
1 CUSTOMER# ; PIC 9999.
1 PARENT-ORG ; 9999.
. . .

(c)

Figure 11-6
**Alternative repre-
sentations of a loop
relationship in the
CODASYL model:**
(a) loop relationship
    with the same
    owner and
    member
(b) loop relationship
    using two record
    types
(c) loop relationship
    using secondary
    key

It is very important to understand the distinct difference between singular sets and sets with an actual owner record. Singular sets create *one* set instance; other sets create one set instance *for each owner.* Thus, whereas sorted member records in a singular set provides a logical ordering for *all* the records of the member record type, sorted members in regular sets

Figure 11-7
Example of a schema
DDL for a singular
set

```
...
RECORD IS CUSTOMER
    LOCATION MODE IS CALC USING CUSTOMER#
...
1 CUSTOMER# ; PIC 9999.
1 CUST-ZIPCODE ; PIC 99999.
...
SET IS CUST-SORT
    OWNER IS SYSTEM
    ORDER IS SORTED BY DEFINED KEYS
    ...
    MEMBER IS CUSTOMER
    ...
    KEY IS ASCENDING CUST-ZIPCODE
        DUPLICATES ARE LAST
    ...
```

create logical orderings of a *subset* of member records, those with a common parent/owner.

Sets with Multiple Member Types   Any set definition contains reference to only one owner record type but may include several member record type clauses. This capability permits the representation of class relationships or any relationship in which a single owner record instance can be associated with many member instances, each of different types. Some DBTG systems permit all members to be sorted by such options as record name (all members of the same type sorted together under a common parent), database key (that is, physical address sequence, which is convenient for efficiently traversing a member chain), or key values in each member record type.

Figure 11-8 illustrates a typical situation where CUSTOMER records are related to both OPEN- and CLOSED-ORDERs. The CUSTOMER-ORDERS set definition places into a common set instance all OPEN- and CLOSED-ORDERs, in ORDER# sequence, for each CUSTOMER owner. The sorting option is used here simply to facilitate reporting of order data. A hazard of such a set with multiple members is that long member chains can be created; if individual sets are not established from owner to each member type (e.g., CUSTOMER to only OPEN-ORDER), processing for only one of the member type records can be degraded by having to access unwanted set members.

Multiple Relationships Between Records   Any number of sets may be defined between the same pair of record types. For example, if Pine Valley Furniture writes both blanket and special orders ("blanket" means an order for a series of deliveries over some extended time period, and "special" means a one-time, stand-alone order), then we might want to define two sets between CUSTOMER and ORDER: Blanket-for-Customer and Special-for-Customer. In this way, users interested in only one type of customer

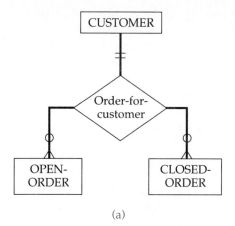

(a)

Figure 11-8
DBTG schema for a
set with two member
record types:
(a) example of a class
   relationship
(b) schema DDL for
   class relationship

RECORD IS CUSTOMER
. . .
RECORD IS OPEN-ORDER
. . .
1 O-ORDER# ; PIC 9999.
. . .
RECORD IS CLOSED-ORDER
. . .
1 C-ORDER# ; PIC 9999.
. . .
SET IS ORDERS-FOR-CUSTOMER
OWNER IS CUSTOMER
ORDER IS SORTED BY DEFINED KEYS
    DUPLICATES NOT ALLOWED
. . .
MEMBER IS OPEN-ORDER
. . .
    KEY IS ASCENDING O-ORDER#
        DUPLICATES ARE NOT ALLOWED
. . .
MEMBER IS CLOSED-ORDER
. . .
    KEY IS ASCENDING O-ORDER#
        DUPLICATES ARE NOT ALLOWED
. . .

(b)

order could use the specialized set to find only orders of the desired type
without wasted accesses to unwanted types. Multiple sets between the
same pair of record types can also be used to handle different sorting
sequences (e.g., orders by sale date, or orders by due date).

Many-to-Many Relationships   Because the CODASYL network standard is a simple network architecture, many-to-many relationships have to be implemented using link records. Figure 11-9 illustrates, by way of an instance diagram, the result of representing an *M:N* relationship between PRODUCT and VENDOR. In this case, an intersection record containing the Vendor's PRICE for that Product is used to link a PRODUCT to a VENDOR when that Vendor supplies that Product. We assume here that meaningful data, PRICE, need to be retained on each PRODUCT-VENDOR relationship instance. If no such meaningful data exist, then the structure remains the same as in Figure 11-9, except there would be only pointers in the PROD-UCT-VENDOR-LINK record. Since meaningful data exist most of the time there is a *M:N* relationship, the creation of the extra link record is almost always needed. In fact, it is recommended so that even if meaningful data are not recognized until after the database is implemented, the structure of the database will stay the same (thus minimizing reprogramming). Note that each VENDOR and PRODUCT record is stored only once, but a PROD-UCT-VENDOR-LINK record instance appears each time a Vendor can supply some Product. As will be seen later, the three record types and two sets of this figure can be used to find both the Vendors of a given Product and the Products of a given Vendor. That is, sets may be processed from either owner to member or member to owner.

Set Qualifications   A set may optionally be defined to be DYNAMIC or PRIOR. DYNAMIC means that this set has no specific member record type, but an instance of any record other than of the owner type may become associated in this set to a given owner instance. Use of DYNAMIC is rare. PRIOR, on the other hand, can be an important feature. Specification of SET IS PRIOR causes the DBMS to implement for the associated set a method that allows the set to be processed as efficiently in the backward (prior) direction as in the forward (next) direction. The effect is to create a bidirectional chain capability, although the guidelines do not specify that a bidirectional chain is *the* way PRIOR must be implemented.

Set Member Definition   The set membership clauses are an important part of a schema. Not only do they provide a necessary companion to the OWNER IS clause, but they are instrumental in set integrity control and, hence, relationships in a database. In addition, it is important to study this section of a schema carefully because three of its clauses—INSERTION, RETENTION, and SET SELECTION—typically are difficult to understand for people getting their first exposure to database management. Further, you should be aware that INSERTION is called CONNECTION and RETENTION is called DISCONNECTION by some DBTG systems.

Any set may have one or more MEMBER IS and associated clauses, one each for each record type related to the set owner in the relationship represented by the set. In explaining these clauses, we will use sets with only *one* member record type.

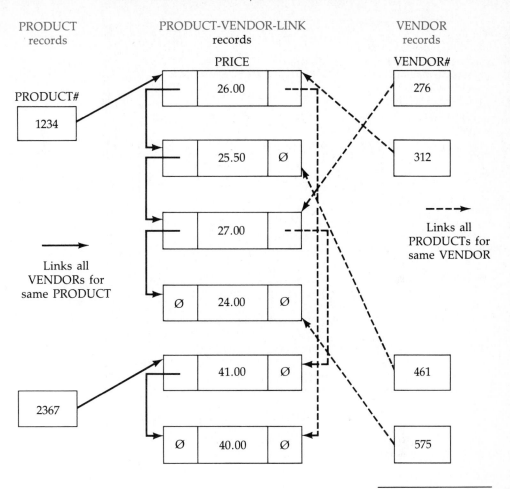

PRODUCT
records

PRODUCT-VENDOR-LINK
records

VENDOR
records

PRODUCT#

PRICE

VENDOR#

Links all
VENDORs for
same PRODUCT

Links all
PRODUCTs for
same VENDOR

Figure 11-9
Example of records
and sets imple-
mentations for a
many-to-many
relationship

For the purpose of explaining set membership clauses, consider the database shown in Figure 11-10a and a possible schema definition for this database shown in Figure 11-10b. The situation depicted here is an inventory accounting database for unique, serial-numbered, limited-life products stored at various warehouses. For this situation, we will assume that the organization permits transshipment of products between warehouses. This example would be typical of certain chemical or pharmaceutical products. This situation is another example of an *M:N* relationship and illustrates how such a relationship would be defined in the DDL.

The STORAGE set relates a generic product to particular serial-numbered instances of that product stored in warehouses. An analysis of reporting requirements involving records of this set indicates that no special set ordering of INVENTORY members for the associated PRODUCT owner is necessary, so ORDER IS FIRST is chosen to speed member record creation (since a new record would be inserted in a chained set at the beginning of

Figure 11-10
Illustration of set
membership clauses:
(a) sample inventory
    database
(b) schema DDL for
    inventory
    database

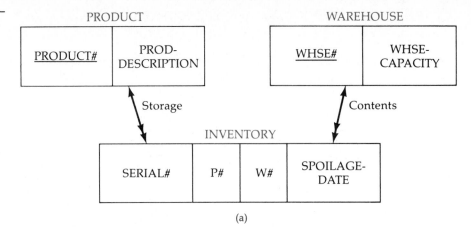

(a)

```
SCHEMA IS INVENTORY
AREA NAME IS STOCK
RECORD NAME IS PRODUCT
    LOCATION MODE IS CALC USING PRODUCT#
    1 PRODUCT# ; PIC 9999.
    1 PROD-DESCRIPTION ; PIC X(20).
RECORD NAME IS WAREHOUSE
    LOCATION MODE IS CALC USING WHSE#
    1 WHSE# ; PIC 99.
    1 WHSE-CAPACITY ; PIC 999999.
RECORD NAME IS INVENTORY
    LOCATION MODE IS VIA STORAGE SET
    1 SERIAL# ; PIC 99999.
    1 P# ; PIC 9999.
    1 W# ; PIC 99.
    1 SPOILAGE-DATE ; PIC 999999.
SET NAME IS STORAGE
    OWNER IS PRODUCT
    ORDER IS FIRST
    MEMBER IS INVENTORY
        INSERTION IS AUTOMATIC
        RETENTION IS FIXED
        CHECK IS PRODUCT# IN PRODUCT=P#
        SET SELECTION IS BY VALUE OF PRODUCT#
SET NAME IS CONTENTS
    OWNER IS WAREHOUSE
    ORDER IS SORTED BY DEFINED KEYS
    MEMBER IS INVENTORY
        INSERTION IS AUTOMATIC
        RETENTION IS MANDATORY
        KEY IS ASCENDING P# DUPLICATES ARE FIRST
        CHECK IS WHSE# IN WAREHOUSE=W#
        SET SELECTION IS STRUCTURAL WHSE#=W#
END SCHEMA
```

(b)

the chain, which we have seen is the easiest point to insert in a single-directional chain).

Controlling Member Insertion   Since an INVENTORY record may not logically exist unless it is for an already existing PRODUCT, INSERTION IS AUTOMATIC is used. This means that the DBMS will automatically link a new INVENTORY record to its associated PRODUCT owner when we store a new INVENTORY record in the database.

The other choice for INSERTION IS is MANUAL, which means that we would have to explicitly and separately program when to connect a new INVENTORY record in a data entry program. AUTOMATIC saves a minimal amount of program coding. MANUAL would be appropriate if a member record might not have an owner record in a set when initially stored in a database. For example, a set from department to employee might have INSERTION IS MANUAL, since many employees when hired are not immediately assigned to a department.

The CONTENTS set also uses INSERTION IS AUTOMATIC since it is assumed that a particular serial-numbered part must reside in some warehouse. The INSERTION IS clause is an effective mechanism for enforcing certain semantic data requirements (that is, existence dependencies upon original entry of a record). The appropriate value of AUTOMATIC or MANUAL for any given set can be established only after a careful analysis of the meaning of data and relationships involved in a set.

Controlling Member Retention   Similar to the INSERTION IS clause is the RETENTION IS clause. In the STORAGE set, RETENTION IS FIXED is used. This means that once a serial number is associated to a generic PRODUCT record, it must be *permanently* associated with the same PRODUCT. The only way to change the association to another PRODUCT would be to delete the INVENTORY record and reenter it under a new owner PRODUCT.

On the other hand, since individual parts may be transshipped from one warehouse to another, RETENTION IS MANDATORY is used in the CONTENTS set. MANDATORY says that the member record, in order to exist, must always have some WAREHOUSE owner (the part has to be somewhere!), but that the particular owner may change. In terms of the data manipulation language to be introduced later, MANDATORY allows us to RECONNECT INVENTORY records as required to indicate current location of a part.

A third option for RETENTION IS, not illustrated here, is OPTIONAL. This choice means that we may actually DISCONNECT a member record from any owner and leave the member unowned for as long as is appropriate. For example, a part is not really in any warehouse during transshipment. To permit an INVENTORY record to have no WAREHOUSE owner during this period, we would use RETENTION IS OPTIONAL. OPTIONAL also permits the deletion of an owner record without having to delete members. For example, if a warehouse is closed, the associated part records will still exist until the parts are moved to a new location.

RECONNECTing records can have a subtle effect on database performance. If, for example, INVENTORY records are located VIA the CON-
TENTS set instead of the STORAGE set, an INVENTORY record that changed
its association to other than its original WAREHOUSE would *not* be physically moved to now be near its current WAREHOUSE owner record in the
physical database.

The RETENTION IS clause also provides a method to include semantic
controls, after original loading of data, on proper database record associations and data manipulation. Table 11-3 summarizes the impact of various
combinations of INSERTION and RETENTION options. But be aware that
the terms FIXED, MANDATORY, and OPTIONAL have not had the same
meanings in all versions of the DBTG guidelines. Until 1978, FIXED did not
exist and MANDATORY meant FIXED. If you are using a DBTG DBMS,
read the reference manuals carefully to determine what is implemented by
that vendor.

Cross-Reference Key Control   The CHECK IS clauses provide yet another
level of semantic control on record associations. Each of these clauses in
the example of Figure 11-10 requires that key values in both member and
owner of a set instance must be identical. These clauses provide an extra
protection that the correct semantic connection occurs when records are
originally inserted into the database or CONNECTed to an owner. To fully
appreciate the usefulness of the CHECK IS clause, the function of the SET
SELECTION clause must be understood.

Determining a Member's Owner Instance   Whereas the INSERTION and
RETENTION clauses control *when* and *whether* a record type must have an
owner, the SET SELECTION clause determines *which instance* of the owner
record type of a set should become the "proud parent."

For the STORAGE set in Figure 11-10, SET SELECTION IS BY VALUE
OF PRODUCT# means that when a new INVENTORY record is stored in
the database (if INSERTION IS AUTOMATIC) or CONNECTed to a PROD-
UCT owner, the DBMS will use the current value in PRODUCT# from user
working storage as a key to find the appropriate owner. Thus, PRODUCT
must have a keyed access (e.g., LOCATION MODE IS CALC or a KEY IS
clause, whichever the DBMS uses) on the data element referenced (in this
case, PRODUCT#). This type of SET SELECTION clause forces the DBMS
to find the owner record automatically and forces the DBMS user to make
sure that the correct PRODUCT# is in memory. As long as P# is correctly
recorded, the CHECK IS clause on this set is a validity check that set selection was done properly. This form of the SET SELECTION clause is more
often used when the member record type does *not* contain the key of the
owner record.

The SET SELECTION clause of the CONTENTS set is the one that is
more appropriate when a member record contains the key of the associated
owner record instance. SET SELECTION IS STRUCTURAL means that the
DBMS is to find the associated owner record for a new member when it is

Table 11-3 Summary of DBTG Semantic Controls in Set Membership Clauses

	AUTOMATIC	**MANUAL**
FIXED	Member record *must* have an owner when it is stored and will continue to have *same* owner until member is deleted. DBMS will automatically CONNECT member to owner, based on SET SELECTION clause, when member is stored.	Member record is permitted to *not* have an owner when it is stored, but once CONNECTed to an owner, it *must* keep same owner until member is deleted. DBMS will *not* CONNECT member to owner until told to do so by user program.
MANDATORY	Member record *must* have an owner when it is stored, but member can be RECONNECTed to other owners as required. DBMS will automatically CONNECT member to owner, based on SET SELECTION clause, when member is stored.	Member record is permitted to *not* have an owner when it is stored, and once CONNECTed may be RECONNECTed to other owners as required. DBMS will *not* CONNECT member to owner until told to do so by user program.
OPTIONAL	Member record *must* have an owner when it is stored, but member can be RECONNECTed to other owners or DISCONNECTed from any owner as required. DBMS will automatically CONNECT member to owner, based on SET SELECTION clause, when member is stored.	Member record is permitted to *not* have an owner when it is stored; once CONNECTed, if ever, it may be RECONNECTed or DISCONNECTed as required. DBMS will *not* CONNECT member to owner until told to do so by user program.

stored (if INSERTION IS AUTOMATIC) or CONNECTed by using the value of a data element in the member (e.g., W#) as the key value of the owner (e.g., WAREHOUSE#). In this case, the CHECK IS clause is of no operational value, since the SET SELECTION clause guarantees that the check will not be violated.

Proper use of INSERTION, RETENTION, CHECK, and SET SELECTION clauses requires practice. Although use of these clauses forces a database designer to deal with many details, these clauses provide valuable tools for semantic controls of the database maintenance and processing. A database programmer also needs to be aware of these clauses in order to interpret error messages that indicate breaches of these integrity constraints.

Many DBTG DBMSs also permit a SET SELECTION THRU CURRENT OF SET option. This version is difficult to understand until one understands the DBTG data manipulation language and a construct used there called currency indicators. Basically, this form differs from the others in that the DBMS does not have to find the owner record, but rather uses the last owner record instance retrieved. This is, in fact, often the most efficient choice for SET SELECTION, especially in interactive programs. For example, if when entering a new INVENTORY record the program first finds the record for the WAREHOUSE indicated for the part, why make the DBMS find it again in order to store the INVENTORY record? The proper WAREHOUSE owner is "current"ly in working storage and does not need to be refound.

A SET SELECTION clause is not found in certain DBTG systems. In these (in particular, IDMS), the owner for a new member record being inserted into the database is essentially the most recently retrieved record of each set, which must be an instance of the proper owner record type for each set.

Sorting Members   Finally, the ORDER IS SORTED clause for the CONTENTS set needs to be explained. An analysis of reporting requirements from this database indicated that warehouse contents frequently were desired in PRODUCT# (P#) sequence for easy reading. The ORDER IS SORTED and KEY IS clauses cause the database to automatically maintain member INVENTORY records in this sequence (usually via a sorted list), thus avoiding sorting of records or report lines for each report.

Other Set Member Clauses   Not illustrated in Figure 11-10 but appearing in Figure 11-3 is the SEARCH KEY IS clause of the member section of a set definition. The set itself establishes a method (usually a chain) to access all member instances, possibly in a sorted sequence, under a common owner record instance. The SEARCH KEY IS clause defines direct access from an owner instance to a member with a specific key value. That is, SEARCH KEY IS establishes functionally a key index in each owner record that points to each member record. For example, in the database of Figure 11-10a, we might want to create a way to identify/access for each WAREHOUSE the INVENTORY that will spoil each day. To do so, we would include in the member clause of the CONTENTS set the clause

SEARCH KEY IS SPOILAGE-DATE DUPLICATES ALLOWED.

The design of efficient network databases depends on careful study of database usage maps, such as in Figure 8-9. These figures help a database designer to

- identify frequent entry points into the database (need for CALC keys)
- identify high activity access paths (possible use of VIA LOCATION MODE)

- identify entry into database to a subset of records or a group of records of same type in sorted sequence (possible use of system or singular set)

- search through members of a set in a sorted sequence (possible use of ORDER IS SORTED to sort member records)

As a summary of this section on DBTG schema definition, Figure 11-11 contains the IDMS schema DDL for the Mountain View Community Hospital database of Figure 8-5. Numbered lines are explained in the footnotes to the figure.

DBTG SUBSCHEMA DDL: EXTERNAL DATABASES

Each user of a database usually wants to use only a portion of a global, conceptual database. This portion may strictly be a subset but may also redefine, into more local terminology and different structures, selected components (records, data elements, sets) of the database. Further, as a means to secure the database against accidental damage by naive users or to ensure legislated, organizational, or personal privacy, a particular user may be limited in what components of the database he or she may use and what data manipulations may be performed on the visible data.

The CODASYL Data Base Task Group provided for these capabilities by specifying subschemas. A **subschema** is a defined subset of an associated database that gives a program invoking the subschema a customized view of the database. The view of the database as seen from a subschema may differ from the database definition in that selected data elements, records, sets, and areas may be omitted; data elements, records, sets, and areas may be renamed using terms more understandable to a class of users; and data element formats (PICTURE, TYPE, length) may be changed to suit specialized data processing needs. Subschema capabilities in some DBTG systems even permit the subschema to define logical records that are combinations of data elements from several related schema records; this capability is similar to the "view" concept in relational databases and can be considered the result of an implicit combination of record joins.

Subschemas provide a mechanism for data independence, since they yield a consistent view of the database to a group of programs; if the schema changes but the local view is unaffected, then programs (which use a subschema, not the schema) are also unaffected.

Since subschemas are the definition of the view of a database assumed by an application program, the subschema DDL is dependent on the programming language used in the application program. Over the years, subschema DDLs have been developed for COBOL, FORTRAN, PL/I, and assembler languages. A subschema is defined separately from any application program that uses it; a subschema is stored in a subschema library, managed by the DBMS, and can be invoked or included in an application

```
**********************************************************
        SCHEMA DESCRIPTION.
**********************************************************
        SCHEMA NAME IS MVCH.
 (1) FILE DESCRIPTION.
        FILE NAME IS MVCHFILE                    ASSIGN TO MVCHDS
                                                 DEVICE TYPE IS 3380.
        FILE NAME IS JOURNAL                     ASSIGN TO SYSJRNL.
**********************************************************
        AREA DESCRIPTION.
**********************************************************
 (2) AREA NAME IS MVCH-CHG                       RANGE IS 770351 THRU 770420
                                                 WITHIN FILE MVCHFILE
                                                   FROM 1 THRU 70.
        AREA NAME IS MVCH-PHY                     RANGE IS 770421 THRU 770586
                                                 WITHIN FILE MVCHFILE
                                                   FROM 71 THRU 160.

**********************************************************
        RECORD DESCRIPTION.
**********************************************************
        RECORD NAME IS ROOM.
 (3) RECORD ID IS 100.
        LOCATION MODE IS CALC                    USING LOCATION
                                                 DUPLICATES NOT ALLOWED.

        WITHIN MVCH-PHY AREA.
            02 LOCATION                           PIC 9999.
            (other data items)
        ★ ★ ★ ★ ★ ★ ★ ★ ★ ★ ★ ★
        RECORD NAME IS PATIENT.
        RECORD ID IS 101.
        LOCATION MODE IS CALC                    USING PATIENT-NO
                                                 DUPLICATES NOT ALLOWED.

        WITHIN MVCH-CHG AREA.
            02 PATIENT-NO                         PIC 9999.
            (other data items)
        ★ ★ ★ ★ ★ ★ ★ ★ ★ ★ ★ ★
        RECORD NAME IS PHYSICIAN.
        RECORD ID IS 102.
        LOCATION MODE IS CALC                    USING PHYSICIAN-ID
                                                 DUPLICATES NOT ALLOWED.

        WITHIN MVCH-PHY AREA.
            02 PHYSICIAN-ID                       PIC X(10).
            02 PHYSICIAN-PHONE                    PIC 9(7).
        ★ ★ ★ ★ ★ ★ ★ ★ ★ ★ ★ ★
        RECORD NAME IS ITEM.
        RECORD ID IS 103.
        LOCATION MODE IS CALC                    USING ITEM-CODE
                                                 DUPLICATES NOT ALLOWED.

        WITHIN MVCH-CHG AREA.
            02 ITEM-CODE                          PIC 999.
            02 DESCRIPTION                        PIC X(15).
        ★ ★ ★ ★ ★ ★ ★ ★ ★ ★ ★ ★
```

Figure 11-11
IDMS schema for
Mountain View
Community Hospital

```
        RECORD NAME IS TREATMENT.
        RECORD ID IS 104.
(4) LOCATION MODE IS VIA           TREATED SET.
        WITHIN MVCH-PHY AREA.
            02 PHYSICIAN-ID            PIC X(10).
            02 PATIENT-NO             PIC 9999.
            02 PROCEDURE             PIC X(15).
********************************
        RECORD NAME IS CHARGES.
        RECORD ID IS 105.
(5) LOCATION MODE IS VIA           INCURRED SET.
        WITHIN MVCH-CHG AREA.
            02 PATIENT-NO             PIC 9999.
            02 ITEM-CODE             PIC 999.
            02 CHARGE                PIC 9999V99 COMP-3.
********************************************************************
        SET DESCRIPTION.
********************************************************************
        SET IS ASSIGNED.
        ORDER IS FIRST.
(6) MODE IS CHAIN.
(7) OWNER IS ROOM                  NEXT DBKEY POSITION IS 1.
(8) MEMBER IS PATIENT              NEXT DBKEY POSITION IS 4
                                   LINKED TO OWNER
                                      OWNER DBKEY POSITION IS 5
(9)                                OPTIONAL AUTOMATIC.
********************************
        SET IS RECEIVED.
(10) ORDER IS LAST.
(11) MODE IS CHAIN                 LINKED TO PRIOR.
        OWNER IS PATIENT           NEXT DBKEY POSITION IS 1
                                   PRIOR DBKEY POSITION IS 2.

        MEMBER IS TREATMENT        NEXT DBKEY POSITION IS 1
                                   PRIOR DBKEY POSITION IS 2
                                   LINKED TO OWNER
                                      OWNER DBKEY POSITION IS 5
(12)                               FIXED MANUAL.
********************************
        SET IS TREATED.
(13) ORDER IS SORTED.
        MODE IS CHAIN             LINKED TO PRIOR.
        OWNER IS PHYSICIAN        NEXT DBKEY POSITION IS 1
                                  PRIOR DBKEY POSITION IS 2.

        MEMBER IS TREATMENT       NEXT DBKEY POSITION IS 3
                                  PRIOR DBKEY POSITION IS 4
                                  LINKED TO OWNER
                                     OWNER DBKEY POSITION IS 6
                                  FIXED AUTOMATIC
                                  ASCENDING KEY IS PATIENT-NO
                                     DUPLICATES ARE FIRST.

********************************
```

Figure 11-11
(continued)

(Continues)

```
SET IS INCURRED.
ORDER IS SORTED.
MODE IS CHAIN.
OWNER IS PATIENT              NEXT DBKEY POSITION IS 3.
MEMBER IS CHARGES            NEXT DBKEY POSITION IS 1
                             FIXED MANUAL
                             ASCENDING KEY IS ITEM-CODE
                                 DUPLICATES ARE LAST.


*********************************
SET IS PROVIDED.
ORDER IS LAST.
MODE IS CHAIN.
OWNER IS ITEM                 NEXT DBKEY POSITION IS 1.
MEMBER IS CHARGES            NEXT DBKEY POSITION IS 2
                             LINKED TO OWNER
                                 OWNER DBKEY POSITION IS 3
                             FIXED AUTOMATIC.
```

(1) Logical file names used in schema are matched with physical data set names and devices.
(2) Areas are assigned to page ranges in logical files. In this schema, we have chosen to have two areas: MVCH-CHG, which contains those record types related to a patient bill, and MVCH-PHY, which contains all other record types.
(3) RECORD ID simply assigns a number to identify each record type uniquely in the data dictionary.
(4) VIA is chosen here to group TREATMENT records close to PHYSICIAN records, since it is assumed that these related records are frequently used together in programs.
(5) Similar assumption as in (4), but this time for PATIENT and CHARGES records.
(6) This is a mandatory clause that simply says to create a chain from owner through members.
(7) The NEXT DBKEY POSITION clause specifies which relative pointer in the record associated with this clause (in this case, ROOM) is to be used for the next in chain pointer for this set.
(8) Again, the NEXT DBKEY POSITION clause specifies the pointer position (in this case in PATIENT); the LINKED TO OWNER indicates that each member record is to have a pointer (the pointer in the position specified) to its owner record to support rapid access to owner.
(9) OPTIONAL AUTOMATIC is used to allow PATIENTs to exist without being assigned a hospital location, but originally a PATIENT record can only be entered if the patient is admitted and placed in some location. The reader should note that IDMS does not have a SET SELECTION clause, as noted in the text.
(10) ORDER IS LAST is used to keep TREATMENT records in approximately ascending order by treatment date.
(11) LINKED TO PRIOR establishes backward chaining as well as forward chaining. The PRIOR clauses in the OWNER and MEMBER definitions indicate where in these records to find the PRIOR pointers.
(12) FIXED MANUAL is used here and in the INCURRED set to handle emergency treatment situations in which treatment is performed (and charges incurred) before the patient is admitted.
(13) ORDER IS SORTED is used to keep TREATMENT records grouped together by PATIENT (see ASCENDING KEY clause in member definition); DUPLICATES ARE FIRST is used in the member clause to keep TREATMENT records in reverse chronological order under each PATIENT.

Figure 11-11
(continued)

```
ADD SUBSCHEMA PATIENT-BILL
    OF SCHEMA MVCH.
ADD AREA ...
ADD RECORD PATIENT
    ELEMENT PATIENT-NO.
ADD RECORD ITEM
    ELEMENTS ARE ALL.
ADD RECORD CHARGES
    ELEMENTS ARE ALL.
ADD SET INCURRED.
ADD SET PROVIDED.
```

Figure 11-12
IDMS subschema for Patient Bill (Mountain View Community Hospital)

program when that program is compiled, link edited, or loaded, depending on the DBMS.

Figure 11-12 illustrates the IDMS subschema DDL via the Patient Bill user view for the Mountain View Community Hospital schema definition in Figure 11-11. Each subschema is named and is matched to a particular schema.

Areas, records, data elements, and sets to be included in the subschema are defined, along with restrictions on the use of data manipulation commands on these structural components. Also, depending on the features of the DBMS, this division may include privacy specifications and explanations of derivation of logical records as combinations of base records from the subschema. Some DBTG systems permit data names to be redefined into localized terms.

IDMS is one such DBTG DBMS that has a facility to define logical records and the process of deriving them (called a logical path). Figure 11-13 illustrates how the logical record concept could be used to define a DETAILED-BILL logical record for an identified patient.

In this case, the DBMS would automatically and transparently construct a DETAILED-BILL record for each CHARGES instance of each PATIENT record instance (that is, DETAILED-BILL represents the complete printed line item on the patient bill). We derive a DETAILED-BILL logical record by first using the current value of PATIENT-NO to FIND (that is, locate but not load any PATIENT data in working storage) a uniquely identified PATIENT; the application programmer must make sure that the proper PATIENT-NO is in working storage before requesting a DETAILED-BILL record. Then the DBMS would OBTAIN (that is, transfer data element values into working storage) a CHARGES record for this PATIENT and conclude by OBTAINing the ITEM owner of this CHARGES in the PROVIDED set.

The operational benefit of a logical record, as will be seen later, is to reduce the application programmer's burden by creating virtual data that do not have to be constructed step by step in the application program. The

ADD LOGICAL RECORD IS DETAILED-BILL
ELEMENTS ARE PATIENT, CHARGES, ITEM

ADD LOGICAL PATH OBTAIN DETAILED-BILL
SELECT FOR FIELDNAME EQ PATIENT-NO
FIND PATIENT WHERE CALCKEY IS
PATIENT-NO OF REQUEST
OBTAIN EACH CHARGES WITHIN INCURRED
OBTAIN OWNER WITHIN PROVIDED

result is less program coding (hence, faster development), less chance of erroneous data processing (since common, complicated data accesses can be coded into the subschema by a senior database programmer), and often a more understandable data model presented to the programmer (since excessive details have been masked from the programmer).

COBOL DML: RETRIEVING AND MAINTAINING DATA

We choose to illustrate here the data processing capabilities in the COBOL programming language for accessing and manipulating a DBTG database. As mentioned before, this is not the only procedural language possible, but it is the one most likely encountered in business data processing. As will be seen in the next section, nonprocedural language access is also possible with many DBTG systems.

Procedural, step-by-step (record-by-record) processing of a database requires frequent reference to some relative position in the database from which to move. That is, we must know some current position in order to find the next record on a chain or in order to identify a position for record insertion or deletion. This logic is an integral part of processing a DBTG database.

Currency Indicators

The term used in the DBTG data manipulation language (DML) for relative position is *currency indicator*. In fact, the DBMS is constantly keeping track of numerous currency indicators. A **currency indicator** is a variable that holds the physical address (database key) of the record instance most recently accessed or manipulated in a specified category of records. These categories result in the following currency indicators important in various DML statements:

1. Current of run-unit: the most recent instance of any database record referenced (that is, retrieved or maintained by some DML command, such as FIND, OBTAIN, CONNECT, or STORE)

2. Current of record type: for each record type in the subschema, the most recent record instance referenced

3. Current of set: for each set in the subschema, the most recent set record instance (owner or member) referenced

4. Current of area: for each area in the subschema, the most recent record occurrence referenced

Currency indicators are updated each time a record instance is accessed. Currency indicator updating may be suppressed, under application program control, to maintain a desired reference point. An application programmer must be well aware of the effect that each DML command has on currency indicator status.

Figure 11-14 shows the logical access map (LAM) and action diagram (AD) for a situation we will use to illustrate the maintenance of currency indicators. The situation illustrated here depicts part of the data processing

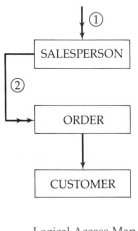

Logical Access Map
(LAM)

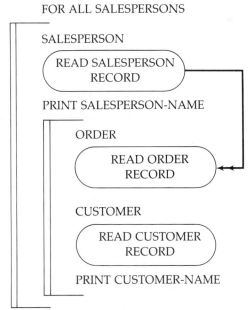

Action Diagram
(AD)

Figure 11-14
LAM and AD for all customers by salesperson

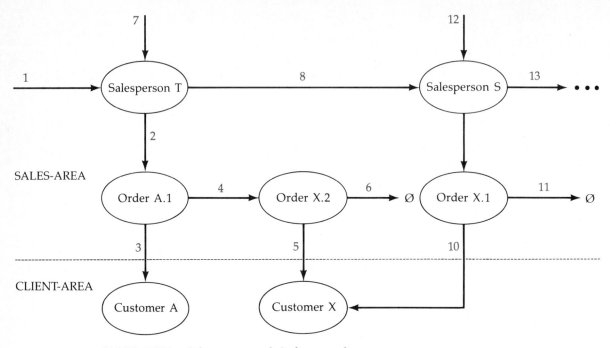

SALES-AREA: Salesperson and Order records
CLIENT-AREA: Customer records
SOLD-SET: Owner-Salesperson ; Member-Order
BOUGHT-SET: Owner-Customer ; Member-Order

(a)

Figure 11-15
Example of currency
indicator main-
tenance in a DBTG
DBMS:
(a) sample database
(b) currency
     indicators

necessary to produce a summary of the customers handled by each salesperson at Pine Valley Furniture. Figure 11-15 contains a network instance
diagram and an accompanying table that illustrates the detailed maintenance of currency indicators. There is no need to sort the data in any way,
so the process begins by accessing the first salesperson on file. To understand Figure 11-15, it is important to remember that user working storage
contains only one instance of each record type at a time. Each time we
OBTAIN (read) another ORDER record, for example, the prior ORDER record in main memory is overwritten.

In Figure 11-15b, a currency indicator is highlighted each time it is updated.
A circle indicates that the currency indicator actually changes value; a box
signifies that it was updated but no value change occurred. Logical values
for currency indicators are used for clarity; currency indicators, in practice,
are physical or relative disk addresses. Numbers on the arrows in the diagram (Figure 11-15a) correspond to the movement through the database
caused by execution of the DML statements in the table.

Several events shown in Figure 11-15 require explanation. The first step
in the table can occur without any currency indicator values established

		Records			Sets		Areas	
DML command	CURRENT OF RUN-UNIT	CURRENT OF SALESPERSON	CURRENT OF ORDER	CURRENT OF CUSTOMER	CURRENT OF SOLD-SET	CURRENT OF BOUGHT-SET	CURRENT OF SALES-AREA	CURRENT OF CLIENT-AREA
1 OBTAIN FIRST SALESPERSON WITHIN SALES-AREA	(T)	(T)			(T)		(T)	
2 OBTAIN NEXT ORDER WITHIN SOLD-SET	(A.1)	T	(A.1)		(A.1)	(A.1)	(A.1)	
3 OBTAIN OWNER WITHIN BOUGHT-SET	(A)	T	A.1	(A)	A.1	(A)	A.1	(A)
4 OBTAIN NEXT ORDER WITHIN SOLD-SET	(X.2)	T	(X.2)	A	(X.2)	(X.2)	(X.2)	A
5 OBTAIN OWNER WITHIN BOUGHT-SET	(X)	T	X.2	(X)	X.2	(X)	X.2	(X)
6 OBTAIN NEXT ORDER WITHIN SOLD-SET	[X]	T	[X.2]	X	[X.2]	[X]	[X.2]	X
7 OBTAIN CURRENT SALESPERSON	(T)	[T]	X.2	X	(T)	X	(T)	X
8 OBTAIN NEXT SALESPERSON WITHIN SALES-AREA	(S)	(S)	X.2	X	(S)	X	(S)	X
9 OBTAIN NEXT ORDER WITHIN SOLD-SET	(X.1)	S	(X.1)	X	(X.1)	(X.1)	(X.1)	X
10 OBTAIN OWNER WITHIN BOUGHT-SET	(X)	S	X.1	[X]	X.1	(X)	X.1	[X]
11 OBTAIN NEXT ORDER WITHIN SOLD-SET	[X]	S	[X.1]	X	[X.1]	[X]	[X.1]	X
12 OBTAIN CURRENT SALESPERSON	(S)	[S]	X.1	X	(S)	X	(S)	X
13 OBTAIN NEXT SALESPERSON WITHIN SALES-AREA	–	–	–	–	–	–	–	–

(b)

Figure 11-15
(continued)

since it accesses an absolute, not relative, record (the first SALESPERSON record found in the SALES-AREA). All the OBTAIN NEXT ORDER commands require that there be an established value for CURRENT OF SOLD-SET. Since there is no NEXT ORDER after orders X.2 and X.1, the DBMS would return an error message to the calling program and leave currency indicators unchanged after execution of these commands. The OBTAIN CURRENT SALESPERSON is necessary in step 7 to establish the proper value for CURRENT OF RUN-UNIT so that step 8 will work as desired (if CURRENT OF RUN-UNIT remained X.2, step 8 would actually access Salesperson T again).

Overview of DML Commands In addition to currency indicators, special data elements defined automatically in the user working area by the sub-schema compiler can be used for application program control. These data elements include the following:

- DB-STATUS: a code that is set after each DML command and that contains a value indicating the type of error, if any, that occurred;

although implementation-dependent, this code is usually composed of an indicator for the type of command on which the error occurred (e.g., FIND) and several other characters symbolizing the specific error encountered (e.g., no next record found in set).

• DB-RECORD-NAME, DB-SET-NAME, DB-AREA-NAME, and DB-DATA-NAME: codes in which the DBMS places the subschema names for the record, set, area, and data element (where applicable) for the error that has just occurred (e.g., step 6 in Figure 11-15 would result in DB-RECORD-NAME equaling ORDER, DB-SET-NAME equaling SOLD-SET, DB-AREA-NAME equaling SALES-AREA); DB-DATA-NAME is applicable only on operations involving data elements (usually for violations of CHECK clauses on data values).

The DBTG COBOL DML commands can be divided into three categories: retrieval statements, modification statements, and control statements. Table 11-4 lists the various DML commands included in each of these categories.

Data Retrieval

In record-at-a-time processing, records can be retrieved on the basis of:

• Unique key or address value (entry into database)
• Next with same or duplicate key value (secondary key)
• Next or prior in set or area possibly in a specified order (related records navigation)
• Owner of a member record in a set (usually used to change from processing along one set to processing along another)

Further, since retrieval is the basis for navigating/moving through a database, we might want to (1) locate only the position of a record in order to verify its existence or as a reference point for subsequent movement (FIND); (2) once located (that is, current of run-unit), put the record's data into working storage for processing (GET); or (3) combine the first two steps into one for both data manipulation and subsequent movement (OBTAIN). In addition, we may want to retain exclusive access to data while retrieving in order to prohibit other programs from updating data. (The need to do this depends on the concurrency control of the DBMS; see Chapter 9.)

To understand some of these data retrieval capabilities, consider again the subschema in Figure 11-12 for the Mountain View Community Hospital Patient Bill user view; Figure 11-16a is a logical access map (LAM) for a variety of processing using this subschema. Recall that the DBTG COBOL DML contains statements that extend the standard COBOL examples; all the following examples represent parts of a COBOL program necessary to perform the data retrieval function specified (the IDMS COBOL DML is used as an example DML; IDMS uses the variable ERROR-STATUS instead of DB-STATUS).

Table 11-4 Typical COBOL DML Commands

Retrieval

FIND	Locates record in database
GET	Transfers record to working storage
OBTAIN	Combines FIND and GET

With each command, we can retrieve
- unique record
- duplicate record
- next or prior record in set or area
- owner of a member record

Modification

STORE	Puts a new record into database and links it to all sets in which it is an automatic member
MODIFY	Changes data values in an existing record
CONNECT	Links an existing member record into a set occurrence
DISCONNECT	Removes (unlinks) an existing member record from its current set occurrence
RECONNECT	A combination of DISCONNECT and CONNECT to unlink a record from its current set and link it to a new set occurrence of the type
ERASE	Deletes record from database, DISCONNECTs it from all set occurrences in which it participates, and deletes other records for which this is an owner in set

Control

COMMIT	Makes permanent all database updates made since last COMMIT command executed
ROLLBACK	Aborts all updates since last COMMIT and restores database to status at time of last COMMIT
KEEP	Places concurrent access controls on database records

Suppose we simply wanted to retrieve data for a specified patient (PATIENT-NO 1234). To do so, we need to store the desired key value (1234) in the PATIENT-NO field of the PATIENT record in working storage and then issue the proper DML OBTAIN command in order to enter the database along the path labeled (1) in Figure 11-16a. This would be accomplished by

```
MOVE '1234' TO PATIENT-NO IN PATIENT.
OBTAIN CALC PATIENT.
IF ERROR-STATUS = 0 THEN NEXT SENTENCE
    ELSE . . . error routine . . .
```

Figure 11-16
Mountain View
Community Hospital
subschema:
(a) logical access map
 (LAM)
(b) AD for a patient's
 total charges
(c) AD for description
 of all items for
 which a patient is
 charged

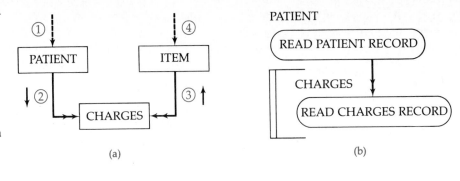

(a)

(b)

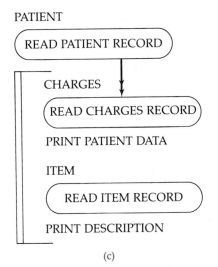

(c)

The preceding OBTAIN command would make the PATIENT record for PATIENT-NO 1234 current of run-unit, current of PATIENT record type, and current of INCURRED set. If we then wished to calculate this patient's total charges, we would continue accessing along path (2) in Figure 11-16 with the following code (see Figure 11-16b for an AD of the procedure):

```
        MOVE 0 TO TOT-CHARGE.
LOOP.
        OBTAIN NEXT CHARGES WITHIN INCURRED.
        IF ERROR-STATUS = error code for no next record
            THEN GO TO B.
        IF ERROR-STATUS = some other error code
            THEN GO TO error routine.
        ADD CHARGE IN CHARGES TO TOT-CHARGE.
        GO TO LOOP.
    B.

        . . .
```

In this example, CHARGES record instances related to the current of INCURRED set are (logically) sequentially retrieved and processed as required. At the first iteration, the set PATIENT owner (PATIENT-NO 1234) is current of set. The looping terminates when ERROR-STATUS indicates that there are no more CHARGES records within this set instance; any other error code in ERROR-STATUS indicates an unexpected error in the database, which may require user intervention or even termination of the program. It is highly advisable to fully use the error-monitoring capabilities of the DBMS after every DML statement (some implementations have ON ERROR clauses as part of each DML command).

As a final example of retrieval statements, consider a reporting requirement to display the description of all the items charged to a specified patient (again, PATIENT-NO 1234). In this case, all three subschema records have to be accessed, but no data from the CHARGES record for this patient are desired. Figure 11-16c illustrates an AD for this retrieval, which is frequently referred to as a "V" retrieval since a path resembling a V is formed by accessing records in steps (1), (2), and then (3) in Figure 11-16a. The following DML statements could be used to retrieve the necessary data:

```
        MOVE '1234' TO PATIENT-NO IN PATIENT.
        OBTAIN CALC PATIENT.
        IF ERROR-STATUS = 0 THEN NEXT SENTENCE
            ELSE. . .error routine. . .
        Display or print desired PATIENT data.
LOOP.
        FIND NEXT CHARGES WITHIN INCURRED.
        IF ERROR-STATUS = error code for no next record in set
            THEN terminate this procedure.
        IF ERROR-STATUS = some other error code
            THEN. . .error routine. . .
        OBTAIN OWNER WITHIN PROVIDED.
        IF ERROR-STATUS = any error code
            THEN. . .error routine. . .
        Display or print DESCRIPTION in ITEM.
        GO TO LOOP.
```

In this example, note that current of INCURRED set was not affected by accessing a CHARGES owner in the PROVIDED set. CHARGES records act in the same way as link records in this example; since link records have no meaningful contents, only FIND needs to be used to retrieve them.

Data Maintenance and Control

Data maintenance within the DBTG model, although limited to only six commands (see Table 11-4), requires careful development because of the various semantic controls that may be specified in a DBTG schema (refer to Table 11-3 for a summary of these controls). Further, to ensure the integrity of a database against concurrent record update and abnormal program termination in the middle of a set of update statements, data maintenance routines require careful design.

When a database (or database area) is opened by a program, most DBTG DMLs require a specification of the mode of processing to be performed by the program (retrieval or update). If the mode is retrieval, then the DBMS will prohibit use of any data modification command in the program. If the mode is update, then two options are often permitted. The first, PROTECTED, means that concurrent update is prevented but that concurrent retrieval is allowed. The second, EXCLUSIVE, prevents any concurrent use of the database (or area).

In addition, many DBTG DMLs permit record-level controls, called locks, to maintain a finer level of concurrent update management. In IDMS, for example, a program can place a SHARED lock on a record to prevent other run-units from updating a record temporarily while permitting retrieval. An EXCLUSIVE lock prohibits any other activity on a record until the lock is released. Exclusive locks are implicitly placed on a record that is altered by a STORE, MODIFY, or ERASE DML command.

Further control can be imposed to protect the integrity of a database from abnormal termination of a program during the middle of a series of related maintenance statements. Consider the situation of entering a new customer order into the Pine Valley Furniture database. Roughly, the procedure to enter this information into the database is as follows:

1. Accept order header data and enter a new ORDER record.

2. Accept PRODUCT#, QUANTITY-ORDERED, and so on, for a LINE-ITEM and store the Line Item.

3. If there are more LINE-ITEMs, then repeat step 2.

Suppose that after accepting and storing the ORDER data and several LINE-ITEM records, an on-line order entry operator realizes that she has been reading data from several order forms. She then decides to abort this "logical transaction" and wants to delete all the previously entered data for this order. Using the ORDER# in working storage and the set between ORDER and LINE-ITEM, the program could ERASE these records. But a simpler approach in which the DBMS automatically performs these deletions is frequently available. The beginning of the logical transaction is indicated by some special DML control statement (a START TRANSACTION, COMMIT, or some other command). If during the logical transaction a user wishes to abort processing or if a fatal database error occurs, the transaction can be aborted and the database will be restored automatically to its state at the time the transaction began (the command ROLLBACK is used in IDMS).

Storing a New Record   The data modification statements will be illustrated using the Mountain View Community Hospital subschema of Figures 11-12 and 11-16a and some variations. Consider the situation of storing the charge for an additional item charged to a patient. Since (from the schema in Figure 11-11) CHARGES is an AUTOMATIC member of the PROVIDED set and a MANUAL member of the INCURRED set, we will have to use a CONNECT command to insert the CHARGE into the proper INCURRED set instance. Further, since the SET SELECTION of the INCURRED set is implicitly THRU CURRENT OF SET, we will have to first make the proper PATIENT record current. A CHARGES record instance is automatically linked to the correct ITEM owner in the PROVIDED set by common key values. The logical access path for this storage is step (1), then step (2) in Figure 11-16a. The DML for this update for PATIENT# 1234 would be as follows:

```
/* Verify patient record exists and make it current */
MOVE '1234' TO PATIENT-NO IN PATIENT.
FIND CALC PATIENT.
IF ERROR-STATUS = 0 THEN NEXT SENTENCE
    ELSE . . . error routine . . .
/* Build new CHARGES record in working storage */
MOVE 150 TO CHARGE IN CHARGES.
MOVE '1234' TO PATIENT-NO IN CHARGES.
MOVE 307 TO ITEM-CODE IN CHARGES.
STORE CHARGES.
IF ERROR-STATUS = 0 THEN NEXT SENTENCE
    ELSE . . . error routine . . .
/* Connect manual set member */
CONNECT CHARGES TO INCURRED.
IF ERROR-STATUS = 0 THEN NEXT SENTENCE
    ELSE . . . error routine . . .
    . . .
```

Deleting an Existing Record The schema for this database (see Figure 11-11) indicates that CHARGES is a FIXED member of both sets (INCURRED and PROVIDED). We may simply delete a CHARGES for PATIENT# 1234 and ITEM-CODE 307 in the case of misbilling by first FINDing the desired PATIENT (based on its CALC key), then searching for CHARGES for ITEM-CODE 307 among the members of the INCURRED set instance for PATIENT# 1234, and then ERASEing the proper CHARGES record. This is the same logical access path as in Figure 11-16b, but in this case searching can stop once the desired CHARGES record for deletion is found. Thus, we would

```
/* Find desired PATIENT record */
MOVE '1234' TO PATIENT-NO IN PATIENT.
FIND CALC PATIENT.
IF ERROR-STATUS = 0 THEN NEXT SENTENCE
    ELSE . . . error routine . . .
/* Search for desired CHARGES record within INCURRED set */
LOOP.
```

> OBTAIN NEXT CHARGES WITHIN INCURRED.
> IF ERROR-STATUS = error code for no next record in set
>   THEN indicate error and terminate.
> IF ERROR-STATUS = some other error code
>   THEN . . . error routine . . .
> IF ITEM-CODE IN CHARGES NOT = 307
>   THEN GO TO LOOP.
> ERASE CHARGES.
> IF ERROR-STATUS = 0 THEN NEXT SENTENCE
>   ELSE . . . error routine . . .
>   . . .

Changing a Member Record's Owner   RETENTION IS FIXED prevents us from moving a CHARGES to a different owner record, which is a natural semantic for this database. If, however, we had indicated RETENTION IS MANDATORY for CHARGES in the PROVIDED set, we could then RECONNECT (but not DISCONNECT) CHARGES records in this set. Suppose we want to change the CHARGES stored earlier to the 413 ITEM-CODE. To do so, we must first find the record for PATIENT# 1234 [access (1) in Figure 11-16a], then verify that the new ITEM record owner exists [access (4) in Figure 11-16a], then search through the CHARGES records under the desired patient looking for the CHARGES record to be reconnected [access (2) in Figure 11-16a]. Thus, assuming that we had used MANDATORY, not FIXED, for the PROVIDED set, we would

> /* Find the desired PATIENT record */
>
> MOVE '1234' TO PATIENT-NO IN PATIENT.
> FIND CALC PATIENT.
> IF ERROR-STATUS = 0 THEN NEXT SENTENCE
>   ELSE . . . error routine . . .
>
> /* Find the ITEM to which CHARGES is to be connected */
>
> MOVE 413 TO ITEM-CODE IN ITEM.
> FIND CALC ITEM.
> IF ERROR-STATUS = 0 THEN NEXT SENTENCE
>   ELSE . . . error routine . . .
>
> /* Search in INCURRED set for CHARGES to be reconnected */
>
> LOOP.
>   OBTAIN KEEP EXCLUSIVE NEXT CHARGES WITHIN
>   INCURRED.
>   IF ERROR-STATUS = error code for no next record in set
>   THEN indicate error and terminate.
>   IF ERROR-STATUS = some other error code
>   THEN . . . error routine . . .
>   IF ITEM-CODE IN CHARGES = 307 THEN NEXT SENTENCE
>   ELSE GO TO LOOP.

/* Change CHARGES record and reconnect to new owner */

MOVE 413 TO ITEM-CODE IN CHARGES.
RECONNECT CHARGES TO PROVIDED.
IF ERROR-STATUS = 0 THEN NEXT SENTENCE
    ELSE . . . error routine . . .
COMMIT.

The KEEP EXCLUSIVE clause on the OBTAIN command prevents any other run-unit from retrieving or modifying this CHARGES record while this run-unit is updating it. The COMMIT command releases this concurrency lock and makes the updates permanent (that is, the updates may not be aborted and undone after this point). KEEP EXCLUSIVE and COMMIT are vocabulary particular to IDMS but are representative of the data maintenance controls available in DBTG COBOL DMLs.

To illustrate DISCONNECT, suppose that miscellaneous charges (ITEM-CODE 999) do not have an ITEM record and that to support storage of such charges, we had made CHARGES an OPTIONAL member of the PROVIDED set. The logical access path for this situation is the same as in the previous example, except that the operation will be to DISCONNECT the record rather than to RECONNECT it. We could then change the charge for ITEM-CODE 413 to ITEM-CODE 999 for PATIENT# 1234 by

/* Find the desired PATIENT record */

MOVE '1234' TO PATIENT-NO IN PATIENT.
FIND CALC PATIENT.
IF ERROR-STATUS = 0 THEN NEXT SENTENCE
    ELSE . . . error routine . . .

/* Find the ITEM from which CHARGES is to be disconnected */

MOVE 413 TO ITEM-CODE IN ITEM.
FIND CALC ITEM.
IF ERROR-STATUS = 0 THEN NEXT SENTENCE
    ELSE . . . error routine . . .

/* Search in INCURRED set for CHARGES to be disconnected */

LOOP.
OBTAIN KEEP EXCLUSIVE NEXT CHARGES WITHIN
    INCURRED.
IF ERROR-STATUS = error code for no next record in set
    THEN indicate error and terminate.
IF ERROR-STATUS = some other error code
    THEN . . . error routine . . .
IF ITEM-CODE IN CHARGES = 307 THEN NEXT SENTENCE
    ELSE GO TO LOOP.

/* Disconnect CHARGES record and change contents */

DISCONNECT CHARGES FROM PROVIDED.

```
IF ERROR-STATUS = 0 THEN NEXT SENTENCE
    ELSE . . . error routine . . .
MOVE 999 TO ITEM-CODE IN CHARGES.
MODIFY CHARGES.
IF ERROR-STATUS = 0 THEN NEXT SENTENCE
    ELSE . . . error routine . . .
COMMIT.
```

Note that in this and the prior example, we had to OBTAIN, not just FIND, CHARGES in order to MODIFY its contents. It is also worth emphasizing again that it is wise not to execute the COMMIT until after all aspects of the logical transaction are complete. If we were to COMMIT after each DML modification command (e.g., after the DISCONNECT above), then, if for some reason the user program aborts before the MODIFY command, the database would be left in a low integrity state, with only part of the total update done.

Special Maintenance Considerations   In addition to deleting a record instance, the ERASE command can have a much broader effect on database contents. Assuming the original schema and subschema from Figures 11-11 and 11-12, respectively, consider deletion of an ITEM record occurrence. Since CHARGES are FIXED members of the PROVIDED set (the same would be true of MANDATORY), they cannot exist without an ITEM owner. If we ERASE an ITEM record in this case, the CHARGES records associated with this ITEM would also automatically be erased by the DBMS.

If CHARGES were an OPTIONAL member of the PROVIDED set, then we would have a choice on what to do with CHARGES members (and members of any other set owned by ITEM) when deleting an ITEM owner. If we were to use

ERASE ITEM PERMANENT MEMBER.

then any MANDATORY or FIXED member for a set owned by ITEM would also be ERASEd, but OPTIONAL members (such as CHARGES under the preceding assumption) would only be automatically DISCONNECTed. If we

ERASE ITEM SELECTIVE MEMBER.

then all MANDATORY or FIXED members would be ERASEd, but OPTIONAL members would also be ERASEd *if* they do not currently have a member in any other set (e.g., INCURRED) occurrence. In the case of CHARGES records, since each must be a member of some INCURRED set, none would be ERASEd. This would apply only to members that are OPTIONAL members of other sets. All members can be ERASEd irrespective of other set membership by using ERASE ITEM ALL.

Logical Record Processing in IDMS

In Figure 11-13, we introduced the IDMS logical record construct that can be defined in a subschema. The purpose of a logical record is to define a simple view of the database that consolidates several database records into one virtual record. Logical records can be used to simplify OBTAIN, STORE, MODIFY, and ERASE processing by permitting *one* such DML statement to implicitly retrieve and appropriately process a group of related records.

Figure 11-13 contains a definition for a DETAILED-BILL logical record. We can use this logical record to produce a listing of all charges for a given PATIENT (say, PATIENT# 1234) by

```
PRINT-LIST.
    OBTAIN NEXT DETAILED-BILL WHERE PATIENT-NO = '1234'
        ON LR-NOT-FOUND GO TO AFTER-LIST.
    Display or print data from CHARGES and ITEM records
        (but not PATIENT, since logical record definition uses FIND for
        PATIENT record)
    . . .
    GO TO PRINT-LIST.
AFTER-LIST.
    . . .
```

The ON error clause also represents a logical/symbolic way to check database error codes instead of using detailed IF statements involving ERROR-STATUS and other variables.

NETWORK DATABASE DESIGN ISSUES AND ADVANCED TOPICS

The network data model presents a database designer with many options to customize a database for efficient processing. Many of the design decisions have been ignored or covered very briefly in the previous sections. This section elaborates on the topics of prior sections and introduces more subtle points and advanced options, as well as focuses on particular network implementation design decisions.

Because network systems frequently are used for high-volume, transaction processing applications, efficiency of database design is important. Further, most of the topics addressed here deal with basic structural choices for a database, which do not exhibit data independence. Thus, redesign to incorporate or change these design elements would typically require application program maintenance; for this reason, it is important to design the database in the best way possible the first time.

Record Placement Control

Two internal network model constructs control the physical absolute and relative placement of records: areas and LOCATION MODE. Areas are physically contiguous disk tracks that are opened and closed together. In designing a database, one would more likely choose to create an area and to place selected records in that area if:

- we wanted a single level of security control (that is, by area) on all the designated records
- database navigation time would be noticeably improved by restricting placement of the related records to relatively nearby disk tracks (that is, to minimize disk head movement)

LOCATION MODE is determined by how records will be accessed. CALC is used when some application program will *know* (from user entry or other database records) the key of a record (or records in the case of a secondary key) to be accessed. That is, the application needs direct entry into the database on that record type. Such entry points would be apparent from a composite usage map like that in Figure 8-9. Choice of CALC requires the key to be a field (or fields, for a concatenated key) in the record being CALCed (so storage space is necessary to support CALC). The ability to CALC a record is unaffected by changes in set membership for that record. The existence of a primary key for a record type that is itself meaningful business data (e.g., ORDER# for an order, LADING# for a shipment) usually means that the record should be CALCed, whereas records with artificial primary keys or concatenated keys are less likely for CALC. One easy way to decide whether a record should be CALCed is to determine if it is a member of any set—if it is not a member of any set, it should be CALCed.

A database designer will usually begin by CALCing the obvious entry points; other record types are then considered for VIA. Since many of the record types not CALCed may be members of several sets, the issue is really: VIA *which* set? A composite usage map (see, for example, Figure 8-9) is very useful. The set chosen for VIA would be the one associated with the path into the record that has the largest frequency of access. One caution with VIA: Since record placement is related to the owner of a member record when the member is first stored, MANDATORY and OPTIONAL sets (in which ownership may change) are not attractive as VIA sets.

Record Data Elements

Three particular database design issues arise when determining the data elements of a record. First is the issue of whether to include the key of the associated owner record (and any of the other nonkey owner data) in the member record of a set. For example, consider the ORDER-LINE record in Figure 11-3b. Since pointers will be maintained by the DBMS for the two sets in which ORDER-LINE participates, PRODUCT# and ORDER# are not necessary in order to access the owner PRODUCT or ORDER for a particular ORDER-LINE. However, if we want to sort ORDER-LINE records in the ORDER to ORDER-LINE set by PRODUCT#, then we must include PRODUCT# in ORDER-LINE. In addition, we could include PRODUCT# in ORDER-LINE simply as insurance, to be able to relink an ORDER-LINE with the right PRODUCT if the physical pointers are damaged.

Owner nonkey data can be stored in a member to make accessing the owner in order to retrieve the data unnecessary, but this causes redundancy from unnormalizing the data. Thus, such storage would typically only be done when real-time processing requirements necessitate squeezing every extra record access out of a program.

The second design issue for data elements deals with the creation of repeating groups or definition of a separate record type. Use of a repeating group is not really feasible when repeating data are or could be related to multiple base records. That is, repeating data are very similar to the members of a set, and if the repeating data are members of only one set, then they can be embedded within the owner as a repeating group. For example, consider Figure 11-17, which depicts EMPLOYEE and DEPENDENT data, as well as other personnel data entities. Since the collection of DEPENDENT data for a particular EMPLOYEE is related only to the EMPLOYEE, this could easily be designated as repeating group data in the EMPLOYEE record type. On the other hand, ASSIGNMENT data are not a characteristic of just EMPLOYEE, but also JOB. Although we could make ASSIGNMENT a repeating group within EMPLOYEE (thus, denormalizing the database), we would then have to either duplicate it as a repeating group within JOB or create a *M:N* relationship between JOB and EMPLOYEE, which is not allowed in many network systems.

The third data element design issue is whether to store derived or calculated data for an entity in the associated record (and recalculate them as the parameters change) or to recalculate them in an application program as they are needed each time. For example, some users of a database may want to manipulate the price and quantity ordered of products; other users, in accounting, perhaps, may only want to see the derived product amount due. But can we be sure that all accounting user programs will calculate amount due correctly?

The DBTG guidelines introduced the concept of virtual data, or data that appear to exist in a record but that do not physically reside in an instance of that record. Two clauses, the SOURCE and the RESULT clauses, deal with the distinction between ACTUAL and VIRTUAL data elements. These

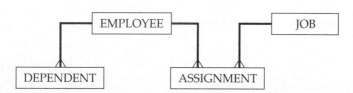

Figure 11-17
Repeating group data
in a network

clauses and options together allow the database to appear to contain data that, at least in the form or location perceived, do not actually exist.

If the SOURCE clause is associated with a given data element definition, it signifies that a value for that data element is to be the same as a specified data element from its owner in a designated set. For example, ORDER# in an instance of an ORDER-LINE record from Figure 7-5 (Pine Valley Furniture Company) must have the same value as the ORDER# in its associated ORDER record. SOURCE provides a form of integrity control of the database. Use of SOURCE prohibits use of PICTURE or TYPE on the same data element since these are implied from the "source" data element. An appropriate SOURCE clause for this example would be

RECORD IS ORDER-LINE

. . .

1 ORD# ; ACTUAL SOURCE IS ORDER# OF OWNER
    ITEMS-ON-ORDER SET.

In this case, ACTUAL specifies that ORD# is to be redundantly stored again in the ORDER-LINE record. Use of VIRTUAL instead of ACTUAL would tell the DBMS to allow use of ORD# as if it were a data element of the ORDER-LINE record, but retrieve it from the associated ORDER record instead (and save the redundant space).

The RESULT clause also utilizes the ACTUAL and VIRTUAL designations. The RESULT clause says that the data element to which it applies is to be calculated or derived from a procedure involving other data elements from the same record; from all members for this record, in which the owner is some set (e.g., to calculate a total across all members, the equivalent of a class attribute in the semantic data model); or from some more general calculation. If ACTUAL RESULT is specified, then the derived value is constantly maintained by the DBMS and stored in the record. If VIRTUAL RESULT is specified, then the derived value is calculated by the DBMS each time a record instance is retrieved and appears to be included in the physical record but actually only exists in the user's working storage area (or subschema).

Sets

Since it is a set that provides navigation through a network database, the choice as to which sets to include directly affects database processing performance. A database designer will certainly choose to build a set for each relationship between record types in the conceptual data model of the database. The issue is whether to build extra, redundant sets. Such redundant sets serve two purposes:

1. **To maintain different member sorting sequences for the same relationship** (e.g., one set between CUSTOMER and ORDER for ORDERs in promised delivery date sequence and another set in salesperson

sequence). Recall, each time we choose to sort the members of a set, the sorting variable must be included in the member records (e.g., salesperson id might have to be included in the ORDER record only if we were to sort ORDERs on this in some set). A database designer, to be able to decide on this type of sorted set, needs to understand not only access paths in the composite usage map but also desirable member access sequence. A sorted set saves scanning members until the desired one or group is found in a random sequence and saves a post-database access sort to rearrange the data.

2. **To "short cut" access along several component links.** For example, consider the network database of Figure 11-18a. To determine the products ordered by a given customer, we must enter the database on customer and navigate to ORDER, then to ORDER-LINE. In Figure 11-18b the redundant, transitive link from CUSTOMER to ORDER-LINE can be used to navigate directly to ORDER-LINE from CUSTOMER. Such shortcuts can only be made along a set of (nested) 1:1 or 1:*M* relationships. A shortcut 1:*M* link from CUSTOMER to PRODUCT, which is along a *M*:*N* transitive relationship, is infeasible since the same PRODUCT record can have only one owner for the set, yet it must be able to have several in the actual relationship.

The additional set design issues of choice of singular sets, and insertion and retention controls have been covered adequately in prior sections.

DEVICE MEDIA CONTROL LANGUAGE

Although the schema DDL specifies some internal database characteristics, the schema still has a great deal of data independence from the internal database. The device media control language (DMCL) is used to complete the database definition.

Because the DMCL is used to prescribe physical database characteristics, use of the DMCL should be limited to the database administrator. PR1ME Computer, in fact, has made this implicit by calling their version of the DMCL for their DBTG DBMS the Database Administrator Control Program

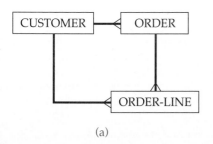

(a)

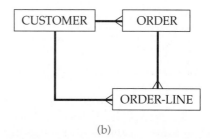

(b)

Figure 11-18
Redundant set for processing efficiency:
(a) typical database design
(b) design with "shortcut" set

(DBACP) and by requiring that a user have special computer system privileges in order to perform most of the DBACP functions.

In IDMS, the DMCL is used to:

- Specify the number of secondary memory pages to keep in a main memory buffer area (this would specify the size of the system buffers block in Figure 11-1)

- Specify the characteristics of each area, such as the number of characters per page in the area, amount of space for expansion of variable-length records, and alias names for the area

- Define the physical characteristics of journal files used to store record and transaction images useful in database recovery

Similar functions are performed by most DMCLs or equivalent utilities. In general, these functions allocate physical space for the database, specify which options to use (if any) for representing sets, name all the various physical operating system files and/or data sets used to construct the database, and indicate whether and how to create audit trails and data modification journals.

NONPROCEDURAL ACCESS: QUERY AND NATURAL LANGUAGES

Most vendors of DBTG systems provide nonprocedural query languages for ad hoc, interactive retrieval of data and/or report writer programs for nonprocedural production of customized reports. For example, PR1ME provides DBMS/Query (or DISCOVER) with its DBTG DBMS. Cullinet provides OnLine Query (OLQ) as a query language, IDMS/CULPRIT as a report writer, and OnLine English (OLE) as a natural language processor. (OnLine English is marketed by Cullinet, but is one version of Intellect, a product of Artificial Intelligence Corp.) Further, Cullinet now has a new version of IDMS, IDMS/R, which includes a relational-like query language. Their claim is that this marriage of network data storage with relational access provides both high performance and ease of access.

Query Languages

Query languages permit an interactive programmer, often a non–data processing professional, to write record retrievals using expressions that specify which records are desired, and not have to go through the process of record-by-record retrieval. Often such query languages resemble relational calculus; thus, it is possible to give an end user a relational-like view of a network database.

As an example of a query language for a network database, we will present a few sample queries using Cullinet's OnLine Query (OLQ). For this illustration, consider the inventory database of Figure 11-10. We could retrieve the first sequential PRODUCT record in the database by

(1) GET FIRST SEQUENTIAL PRODUCT RECORD

and OLQ would immediately display the contents of this record on the terminal. We could then retrieve the first INVENTORY for this PRODUCT by

(2) GET FIRST INVENTORY BELONGING TO THIS PRODUCT

and could continue to retrieve other INVENTORY records one by one using

(3) REPEAT WITH LAST

Otherwise, if we wanted to see all the INVENTORY records for this PRODUCT, we could issue the following command immediately after (1):

(4) GET ALL INVENTORY BELONGING TO THIS PRODUCT

Such query languages are helpful in that they can rapidly produce the result of a simple end user question, check on the contents of a database after a series of COBOL data maintenance program executions, or provide a user with a prototype of the type of report that could be produced in a fancier format by a batch report writer or COBOL report program. These languages do, however, have a precise grammar and syntax that must be learned by anyone who wishes to write a query. Release 10.0 of OLQ from Cullinet has a menu-driven front end for end users.

Natural Languages

Natural language processors eliminate the need to learn a specific grammar, vocabulary, and syntax. Cullinet explains their package OnLine English (OLE) in this way:

> OnLine English (OLE) is an English-language query system that enables users to obtain computer-stored information by means of simple request. OLE accepts and interprets a freely worded request, retrieves the appropriate data, and performs all processing necessary to display the results in a meaningful format. The capacity to accept everyday English phrases is a powerful feature of OnLine English that distinguishes it from traditional query systems. (Cullinet 1982b)

Consider again the inventory database of Figure 11-10. After signing on and being greeted by OLE, Figure 11-19 illustrates some possible dialogue between OLE and the user. In this figure, OLE prompts and responses are shown in capital letters and user questions in lowercase. Prior to processing each English question, OLE displays a structured query version of its interpretation of the original question. The user can abort the processing at this point in order to restate the query if OLE has misinterpreted the question. If the user uses key words such as *average, minimum,* or *bar graph,* OLE will generate the appropriate result.

Figure 11-19
Example of IDMS
OnLine English
dialogue

PLEASE ENTER YOUR FIRST REQUEST

What are the fields in the inventory file?

FIELDS IN THE INVENTORY FILE

S#   P#   W#

NEXT REQUEST

What is the S# and P# of all inventory in 04 warehouse?

PRINT THE S# AND P# OF ALL INVENTORY WITH W#=04
THE NUMBER OF RECORDS TO RETRIEVE IS 3

S#	P#
12345	1234
72843	5436
92371	3476

NEXT REQUEST

Where is part 1234 stored?

PRINT THE W# OF ALL INVENTORY WITH P#=1234
THE NUMBER OF RECORDS TO RETRIEVE IS 2

W#

04

12

NEXT REQUEST

How many warehouses are there?

COUNT THE WAREHOUSE
ANSWER: 16

NEXT REQUEST

...

Given that such nonprocedural languages exist for access to a network database, why should we ever program in COBOL? First, most of these facilities are limited to only data retrieval and reporting; data update is usually not supported. Second, the computer time required to dynamically translate query or English statements into the record-level commands adds significant overhead to computer processing. A prewritten procedural language routine would execute the same type of retrieval much faster (but, of course, would take significantly more time to code). The trade-off, basically, is between machine efficiency and programmer efficiency. When rapidly developed, ad hoc, frequently modified, or one-time reports are desired, nonprocedural languages are suitable; if high-volume transaction processing or repeated rapid response queries characterize the computing work load, then procedural languages will be more appropriate for processing the network database.

SUMMARY

This chapter has reviewed the major network data model implementation, the CODASYL DBTG model (and IDMS, a leading commercial product). Although the discussion has been dominated by an examination of record-level access to data, we have also shown example query languages for access data in network databases. Such query and natural languages can provide a relationlike front-end view of a network database.

The network data model has been much maligned since the introduction of the relational model. Criticisms have primarily focused on issues of ease-of-use and processing complex queries, which generally favor the relational model. However, in practice, the network data model DBMSs have continued to be popular data management technologies, usually because of the better performance possible by the explicit record-level processing. Today, because of relational-like query language front ends, we can "have our performance and ease of use, too."

Chapter Review

REVIEW QUESTIONS

1. Define each of the following terms:
   a. CODASYL DBTG
   b. IDS
   c. DDL
   d. DML
   e. DMCL
   f. schema
   g. subschema
   h. area
   i. host language
   j. location mode
   k. manual insertion
   l. automatic insertion
   m. fixed retention
   n. mandatory retention
   o. optional retention
   p. CALC location mode
   q. virtual data
   r. currency indicator
   s. search key
   t. IDMS logical record
   u. natural language

2. Contrast the functions of the three DBTG retrieval commands FIND, GET, and OBTAIN.

3. Discuss the advantages of using a network DBMS with a relational-like query language.

4. Describe the use of the system buffers shown in Figure 11-1. When are data moved in and out of these buffers? What effect would paging in a virtual memory operating system have on buffer contents?

5. Describe the role of a computer operating system in database access under the DBTG guidelines.

6. Explain why there are different subschema DDLs, one for each host programming language.

7. Explain why a record may not have a CALC key and also be located VIA some set.

8. Explain the factors to consider for selecting among FIRST, LAST, and SORTED for the ORDER IS clause of a set definition.

9. Explain the benefit of the IDMS logical record construct.

10. Explain the purpose of the IDMS COMMIT command and discuss where in a program this command can be usefully placed.

11. Under what circumstances (database schema characteristics) is the DML command RECONNECT permitted?

PROBLEMS AND EXERCISES

1. Match each term with the appropriate definition:

_____ DBTG

_____ schema

_____ subschema

_____ status variable

_____ DDL

_____ DML

_____ VIA location mode

_____ virtual data element

_____ singular set

_____ RECONNECT

_____ current of set

_____ logical access map

_____ COMMIT

_____ Intellect

a. language used to state data retrieval and modification operations

b. diagram indicating navigation path or steps through a database

c. task force that developed the CODASYL network standard

d. most recent record accessed

e. a natural language processor

f. contains error codes and other data about command execution

g. command that makes recent database changes a part of the actual database

h. data that are not actually stored in the database but appear as if they are

i. a database description for a DBMS

j. command that changes a set member's owner

k. view of a database used by an application program

l. placement of a member instance close to its owner instance

m. language used to define a database

n. used to sort all records of some type into sequence

2. Consider the entities of Agent, Policy, Client, Beneficiary, and Insurance Company in an independent insurance agency. Design a DBTG network diagram (similar to Figure 11-5a) for this situation.

3. For the database designed in Problem 2, suggest several data processing requirements for which use of more than one area would be beneficial in the schema.

4. Specify the LOCATION MODE clause for each record type in Problem 2 and justify your choice of mode and duplicates specification.

5. For each of the sets in your answer to Problem 2, specify and justify INSERTION and RETENTION clauses. Write complete set definitions for this problem.

6. Consider the entities of Project, General Task, and Employee in a project management or job shop organization. Design a DBTG network diagram (similar to Figure 11-5a) for this situation.

7. For the situation in Problem 6, assume there is a need to report the employees working on a project in order by their job classification. Write the schema DDL necessary to support this requirement through the database structure.

8. Consider the situation of an automobile dealership and entities Owner, Vehicle, Sale, and Salesperson. Assume all the usual relationships between these entities plus the association of a sale to vehicles traded in on that sale. Design a DBTG network diagram (similar to Figure 11-5a) for this situation and write the schema DDL, using data items of your choice.

9. In the situation in Problem 8, assume that the dealership's general manager frequently sends promotional mailings to owners of vehicles on file. To minimize mailing costs, she wishes this to be printed in customer zip code order. Add to your schema and network diagram for Problem 8 the constructs necessary to support this data processing.

10. Review the alternatives of representing a loop relationship presented in Figure 11-6. Evaluate each of these and suggest situations in which each would be a desirable approach.

11. For the database schema of Problem 8, draw a logical access map and then write the COBOL and DML commands necessary to change ownership of a vehicle. Assume any data elements you believe are essential; include skeletons of database error checks.

12. For the database of Problem 2, write the COBOL and DML commands required to enter a new policy into the database. Assume any data elements you believe are essential; include skeletons of database error checks.

13. Consider again the database of Problem 2. Draw a logical access map and action diagram and then write the COBOL and DML commands required (skeleton of the code is all that is necessary) to produce a report of the policy numbers and anniversary dates for each policy of each client. The policy numbers and dates are to be grouped by client; the clients are not to be printed in any particular logical order.

14. In the preceding database design problems, you were not given much information about the data processing requirements of the situation, but instead were asked to design the database in more general terms. Specifically, what clauses of a DBTG schema are affected by knowledge of particular data processing requirements? How is each affected?

15. Consider again the data processing required in Problem 13. Design some sample data for this problem and develop an illustration of currency indicator maintenance, as in Figure 11-15, for your sample data and the program fragment you wrote for Problem 13.

REFERENCES

ANSI X3H2. 1981. *Proposed American National Standard for a Data Definition Language for Network Structured Databases*. American National Standards Institute.

CODASYL. 1971. *Data Base Task Group April 71 Report*. New York: Association for Computing Machinery.

CODASYL COBOL Committee. 1978. *COBOL Journal of Development*. Available from Federal Department of Supply and Services, Hull, Quebec, Canada.

CODASYL Data Description Language Committee. 1978. *DDL Journal of Development*. Available from Federal Department of Supply and Services, Hull, Quebec, Canada.

Cullinet. 1986. *IDMS/R COBOL Programmer's Reference Manual*. Westwood, Mass.: Cullinet.

Cullinet. 1986. *IDMS/R Logical Record Facility*. Westwood, Mass.: Cullinet.

Cullinet. 1986. *IDMS/R Systems Overview*. Westwood, Mass.: Cullinet.

Olle, T. W. 1980. *The CODASYL Approach to Data Base Management*. Chichester, England: Wiley.

Tsichritzis, D., and F. Lochovsky. 1982. *Data Models*. Englewood Cliffs, N.J.: Prentice-Hall.

PART V

Relational and Distributed Systems

IMAGE STORAGE AND RETRIEVAL IN A DISTRIBUTED RELATIONAL ENVIRONMENT

A T & T

As Confucius said, "One picture is worth 10,000 words." Image now takes its place in the data model as an integral piece of information available to the user. Databases are more than words and numbers. Databases can now capture the essence of the visual world as well.

This fifth part of your text focuses on relational and distributed systems. The AT&T Consumer Communications Services Marketing organization provides a state of the art example of the use of database technology in a distributed environment where mainframe-to-micro linkages exist. AT&T has developed a database system which stores advertising promotional images as digital data. This enables designers to visually review promotion pieces, such as direct mail advertisements during the promotion planning process.

The importance of integrating data, text and images became apparent in the strategic analysis of information requirements for AT&T. Joint application design sessions enabled a determination of the functional and data requirements for the promotion planning process. The use of color digitized images was identified as a system requirement.

Images have special characteristics that impact the logical and physical architecture of the system. Logically, images are represented in the data model by the entity IMAGE and related to the entity PROMOTION. Physically, however, because image files are very large, they cannot be stored in a mainframe computer and transmitted in real time to remote users. It is necessary to store the color digitized images of a promotional item locally in external files and relate the file to the promotion data in the mainframe database. A three-tiered approach provided a solution to this problem.

The relational database is stored in a mainframe and available for access by 300 users nationwide via a Wide Area Network (WAN). The image files are distributed to each location and stored locally on a file server. The user can access the mainframe via a desktop personal computer and query the database.

The results of the query are passed to the personal computer which, in turn, uses a 10 megabit StarLan Local Area Network (LAN) to access the image on the file server and display it on the desktop.

The image is brought to the desktop in a virtually seamless electronic environment meaning that the system user is unaware of the actual location of the databases and the networks over which images are processed. Images can be received from outside advertising agencies using AT&T electronic mail (E-Mail). Within each location, a single imge can be shared by all groups during the internal review process ensuring the most current version of the promotional item is available at all times.

Sometimes it is necessary to make modifications to a promotional piece. This can be completed electronically using "paint" programs to adjust the image and E-Mail to transmit the images to the outside agency as the image changes and develops.

Successful images can be reused in future promotions to visually reinforce brand identity in the marketing arena and create synergy across promotions. The final promotional image is then stored in the database for historical access and to inform other groups in the company as to what is being promoted to the public.

Image as data has now taken its place as a valuable shared corporate asset.

CHAPTER 12

SQL and Relational Implementations on Mainframes

INTRODUCTION

This chapter begins a sequence of three on relational database management systems. Many different database management systems built for the relational data model (see Chapter 3 and Codd, 1970 and 1982) exist. More than one type of relational DBMS is available; however, most products now include a particular relational language called the Structured Query Language (SQL) (introduced in Chapter 2). Thus, we will concentrate in this chapter on this standard of data creation and manipulation. Although the basics of the relational data model are present in all products mentioned, the style of relational data manipulation languages and the extent of vendor-introduced enhancements vary across products.

The primary purpose of this chapter then is to review in depth the most common approach for relational systems, SQL. The SQL style has been widely adapted into many products and has been accepted as a standard by the American National Standards Institute. It has been implemented in both mainframe and personal computer systems, so this chapter is relevant to both computing environments. In addition, we provide examples of the QUEL language, which is part of INGRES, another popular relational system that is also implemented on both mainframe and personal computer systems. We do this to show that alternatives to SQL are available and to show some capabilities not available in SQL systems. Both SQL and QUEL are called relational calculus languages.

A secondary purpose of this chapter is to outline the general capabilities of relational systems on mainframe computers. We do this by discussing issues of security and control of concurrent access to a database by multiple users and by briefly introducing the features of a few mainframe DBMSs. We give special attention to Query-By-Example, a novel relational language introduced for mainframe systems that is now a part, in some form, of many mainframe and PC systems. In Chapter 13 we will review the implementations of the relational data model in personal-computer-based products and concentrate on what are called relational algebra systems. Relational algebra was the dominant style for PC systems until SQL was introduced into these products. Then in the third relational implementation chapter, Chapter 14, we discuss and illustrate the development of complete programs and applications using relational systems, including embedding relational commands in third-generation language programs.

A list of many of the most widely used mainframe relational DBMSs appears in Table 12-1 (a similar list for personal computer products appears in Table 13-1). We list here both SQL-based and non–SQL-based products. The next section gives an overview of the general structure and characteristics of a mainframe relational DBMS.

A RELATIONAL DBMS—AN OVERVIEW

Many DBMSs are said to be relational. In fact, without even trying to generate an exhaustive list, we can safely say that more data management products claim to be relational than claim to be all other data models combined. Although for practical purposes it does not matter what it is called (what matters is that the DBMS has the features required for our data processing), an attempt to carefully distinguish relational from nonrelational systems will highlight the important features of relational implementations. Of course, a system that obeys the rules of a *truly* relational DBMS has certain desirable properties and capabilities that give it tremendous power and provide integrity of database processing.

Most people agree that a relational database is one perceived by its users as a collection of tables in which all data relationships are represented by common values, not links. A relational DBMS (or RDBMS), then, is a data management system that uses this view of data, which was outlined in Chapter 3.

We will not debate here what constitutes a truly relational system. The interested reader is referred to an article by Kim (1979) and to the appendix on "Codd's 12 Rules for a Truly Relational System" (Codd, 1985a and b, two issues of *Computerworld*) at the end of this book. These rules apply to any relational system, both mainframe and personal computer, and both SQL and non-SQL relational query languages.

Not only have relational DBMSs been implemented in the classical fashion of DBMSs as software utilities, but also numerous special-purpose DBMS machines using the relational data model have been developed in laboratories (see Banerjee, Baum, and Hsiao, 1978; Epstein, 1983; McEnany, 1985) and for commercial sale (see *Computerworld*, January 28, 1985 and *Computerworld*, June 24, 1985). Database computers will be discussed in detail in Chapter 15. In the current chapter it is important to know that an SQL relational DBMS may be implemented in either software or hardware.

Basically, such a special "back-end" computer is attached to a general-purpose computer. The database computer receives a stream of requests for database processing from the host computer's operating system (generated from application programs). These requests are queued, sequenced for efficient processing, and satisfied in parallel to the host CPU doing nondatabase tasks. The database computer is configured in ways to optimize database processing (for example, special architectures such as array or associative processors, table data distributed across different disk drives attached to the associative processors, fast channels for data transfer, and DBMS functions built into hardware or firmware). Relational DBMSs implemented in hardware are steadily emerging in commercial applications, and their progress requires attention.

Structure and Components of Relational Systems

A modern RDBMS is typically a family of products or modules, each of which manipulates data in a particular way. For example, different modules may exist for line-by-line queries, screen or forms painting, stylized reports, and graphs. The ability to include RDBMS commands in procedural (third-generation) language programs is a rather standard feature, referred to as the embedded query language capability. This embedded query language approach is commonly used for building application systems on mainframes, where there has been a tradition of using third-generation programming languages. We will cover this approach in Chapter 14. An interactive query language will still be used to supplement such embedded programming for program testing, for system prototyping, and for writing ad hoc queries.

In addition, some RDBMSs have modules or associated products that support natural language processing against the database, inclusion of database data in an electronic spreadsheet (by using a database query as a cell value), and merging database contents with text documents in specific word processing packages. Because no one software package can provide all the decision support or information processing capabilities a user may require, a RDBMS usually provides a file import/export facility for transfer of data (often in standard text file formats) between the RDBMS and other systems such as word processors, statistical packages, mathematical programming packages, and other DBMSs. Finally, a growing number of mainframe rela-

Table 12-1 Summary of Some Mainframe Relational Systems

Product	Vendor	Equipment	Comments
Database Computers			
(attached to mainframes and other computers)			
Sharebase II	Britton Lee	Attach to IBM, DEC VAX, Sun, computers and several LANs	Primarily for office or local applications on LAN; software on dedicated micro with proprietary disk drives; SQL supported
DBC/1012	Teradata	Attach to IBM, UNISYS, Honeywell, DEC VAX, and other mini and mainframes	Large data center database computer; SQL database engine, parallel processing with data redundancy
Relational Software Systems			
SQL/DS	IBM	S/370, 30xx, 43xx, VM/CMS operating system	Host language interfaces to COBOL, PL/I, and assembler, logical views supported; SQL supported
DB2	IBM	Same as SQL/DS except DOS/VSE and MVS operating system	Similar to SQL/DS
INGRES	Relational Technology	DEC VAX, VMS & UNIX operating systems; also IBM, Data General, HP, UNISYS, and others	Host language interfaces to C, Pascal, FORTRAN, BASIC, and COBOL; views and SQL supported; native language is QUEL; query-by-forms and other development aids
ORACLE	Oracle Corp.	DEC VAX (VMS, UNIX, RSX) and IBM S370, 30xx 43xx (VM/CMS & MVS), and other main-	Host language interfaces to COBOL, PL/I, FORTRAN, C, BASIC, and assembler; views supported; comprehensive SQL implementation

Table 12-1 Summary of Some Mainframe Relational Systems

Product	Vendor	Equipment	Comments
		frames & PCs	
SQL Server	Sybase Inc.	DEC VAX, Sun, Pyramid	SQL client/server architecture on LAN
Graphical/Tabular Systems			
Query-by-Example	IBM	S/370, 30xx, 43xx; VM/CMS and MVS	Unique graphical, fill-in-the-blanks query language
Relational-Like Systems			
ADABAS	Software AG	IBM S/370 and others; DOS/VSE, VM/CMS, MVS; DEC VAX/VMS	Inverted file organization with relational-like query language
CA-DATA-COM/DB	Computer Associates International	IMB S/370 and others; MVS, DOS/VSE, VM/CMS	Inverted files; relational query language; access to VSAM and IMS; 4GL with SQL support
FOCUS	Information Builders	IBM S/370 and others; VM/CMS and MVS; DEC VAX/VMS and PCs	A leading 4GL; hierarchical and relational views of data; comprehensive system building tools; SQL support
IDMS/R	Cullinet Software	IBM S/370 and others; MVS, VM/CMS, DOS/VSE	CODAYSL network system enhanced to support relational operators; application generator, natural language processor, integrated dictionary, some SQL support
NOMAD	Must Software International	IBM S/370 and others; VM/CMS and MVS	Leading 4GL; interfaces to SQL/DS, DB2, DBC/1012, IMS, and IDMS
SUPRA	Cincom Systems	IBM and DEC/VAX with a variety of operating systems	Designed for high-volume transaction processing

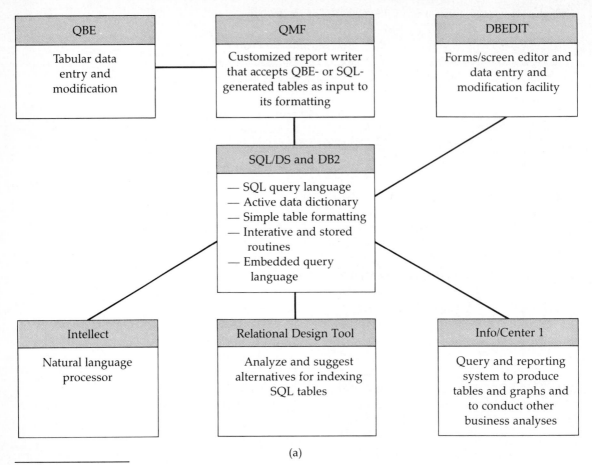

(a)

Figure 12-1
Mainframe relational
DBMS environments:
(a) SQL/DS and DB
(b) INGRES (partial
list)

tional systems have associated personal computer products that provide all or nearly the same functionality as their mainframe counterpart, plus the ability to upload and download data between a package's mainframe database and PC database or other PC package (such as an electronic spreadsheet).

Figure 12-1 illustrates the environment of two popular and typical mainframe RDBMSs: SQL/DS and INGRES (see IBM Corp., 1985, 1987; Relational Technology, Inc., 1989). For each of these systems there is a kernel or core module and a variety of optional modules available at additional cost. A general trend is for new modules to be added periodically, each using similar command structures and syntax and all sharing a common data definition and storage. In this way RDBMS products are being enhanced to be very similar to fourth-generation languages.

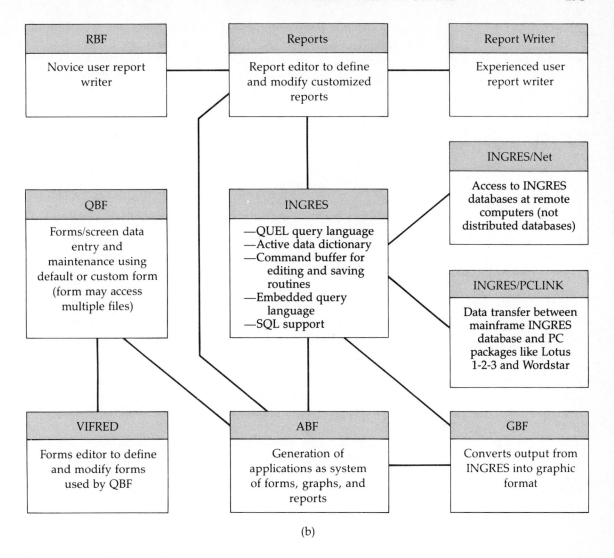

(b)

SQL: A Standard for Relational Systems

As was mentioned in Chapter 11, the development of network DBMSs has been guided by the work of the CODASYL Data Base Task Group and the published guidelines it has produced. These guidelines have had a major impact by strongly encouraging network DBMS vendors to provide a minimal set of capabilities and a general architecture for their products. The consequence is that different network implementations have very similar functional capabilities.

In order to provide some direction for the development of RDBMSs, the American National Standards Institute (ANSI) has approved a standard for the SQL relational query language (functions and syntax) proposed by the X3H2 Technical Committee on Database (Technical Committee X3H2—Database, 1986). The ANSI X3 Committee is the same group that developed the three-level data architecture presented in Figure 3-1.

The purposes of this standard are

1. To specify the syntax and semantics of SQL data definition and manipulation languages
2. To define the data structures and basic operations for designing, accessing, maintaining, controlling, and protecting an SQL database
3. To provide a vehicle for portability of database definition and application modules between conforming DBMSs
4. To specify both minimal (Level 1) and complete (Level 2) standards, to permit different degrees of adoption in products
5. To provide an initial standard, although incomplete, that will be enhanced at later times to include specifications for handling such topics as referential integrity, transaction management, user-defined functions, join operators beyond the equi-join, and national character sets (among others)

An indirect effect, which may not have been intended, is that acceptance of *an* SQL standard has been interpreted by many as acceptance of SQL as *the* approved RDBMS query language. Even before the Technical Committee began its work, several SQL-based products were on the market (for example, SQL/DS and DB2 from IBM and ORACLE from Oracle Corp.; see Table 12-1 for a list of other SQL-based RDBMSs). Since the adoption of the SQL standard, various mainframe and PC RDBMS vendors have announced that their packages will be enhanced to include an SQL language interface to their existing product. Thus, the market is accepting SQL as a necessary structured query language, although certainly not the only programming language, for relational database access. In addition, the SQL standard is being reviewed by the International Standards Organization (ISO) and may become the international standard for relational query languages.

The existence of such a relational language standard has several benefits, including

- **Reduced training costs:** Training in an organization can concentrate on one language, and a large labor pool of IS professionals trained in a common language reduces retraining when hiring new employees
- **Application portability:** Applications can be moved from machine to machine when each machine uses SQL; further, it is economical for the computer software industry to develop off-the-shelf application software when there is a standard language

- **Application longevity:** A standard language tends to remain so for a long time, so there will be little pressure to rewrite old applications; rather, applications will simply be updated as the standard language is enhanced or new versions of DBMSs are introduced

- **Reduced dependence on single vendor:** When a nonproprietary language is used, it is easier to use different vendors for the DBMS, training and educational services, application software, and consulting assistance; further, the market for such vendors will be more competitive, which may lower prices and improve service

- **Cross-system communication:** Different DBMSs and application programs can more easily communicate and cooperate in managing data and processing user programs

On the other hand, a standard can stifle creativity and innovation, one standard is never enough to meet all needs, and an industry standard can be far from ideal since it may be the offspring of compromises between many parties. A standard may be difficult to change (because so many vendors have a vested interest in it), so fixing such deficiencies may take considerable effort.

SQL is not without its critics, who claim that the *initial* SQL standard, although a good start, has definite flaws. Date (1987b) claims that important features (such as referential integrity rules and certain relational operators) are omitted and that the language is extremely redundant (that is, that there is more than one way to write the same query). These limitations will become clear in this chapter. It can be expected that, like the CODASYL DBTG network standard, the SQL standard will be modified, probably led by the capabilities of SQL-based DBMSs.

RELATIONAL DATA DEFINITION IN SQL

There is not much variety among relational data definition language (DDLs) since the relational data model is rather simple and standardized. Significant differences do occur, however, in embellishments such as the inclusion of integrity and security constraints, definition of user views (external databases), and physical implementation clauses or commands to indicate, for example, creation of a key index. The process of designing a relational database has been covered elsewhere in this text (see Chapters 3 and 6); normalization is used to derive the relations to be defined. In this section we assume that this design has occurred, and we concentrate on the translation of these relations into DDL.

To illustrate the use of typical relational DDLs, we again refer to the Mountain View Community Hospital database of Figure 6-25. Figure 12-2 contains a definition of this database using the DDL of SQL/DS.

Not shown in Figure 12-2 or subsequent SQL commands is a line continuation character. SQL is a line-oriented language; for example, in interactive mode, SQL/DS interprets each line as it is entered. Thus, if the command cannot all fit on one line, it must be continued and SQL/DS must be told to wait to process the command until all lines for that command have been entered. In SQL/DS this continuation symbol is the '-' (hyphen), which is placed at the end of a continued line. For simplicity, in this chapter we will ignore the need for this.

Data Types

Each DBMS will support various types of data for columns in a relational table. These types for an SQL system typically include

DECIMAL(m,n)	To store numbers in decimal notation, where m is the total number of digits in the number and n is the number of digits to the right of the decimal point. A part's unit weight or dimensions may be stored in this form.
INTEGER	This is for large positive or negative whole numbers. A country's population or the quantity on hand of a part may be stored in this form.
SMALLINT	This is for small positive or negative whole numbers. By specifying this data type, less storage space can be reserved for the data. For example, the maximum absolute value that can be stored in this type of data might be 32,767. Data such as age, temperature, or an airline flight number might be stored in this form.
FLOAT	This is for positive and negative, whole and fractional numbers that are represented in scientific notation. Numbers that might be very small or very large (often involved in mathematical calculations) and for which only a limited number of significant digits are needed are suitable for this form. Data such as engineering specifications might be stored in this form.
CHAR(n)	This is alphanumeric (character) data where n is the maximum length for this character string. Usually the largest value of n is 254. n character positions are allocated to each instance of a CHAR column. Data such as customer name or product description might be stored in this form.
VARCHAR(n)	This is for character data that vary significantly in length. Because of the highly variable length,

```
          CREATE TABLE ROOM
             (LOCATION           CHAR(4) NOT NULL UNIQUE,
              ACCOM              CHAR(2),
              EXTENSION          SMALLINT,
              PATIENT-NO         INTEGER)


          CREATE TABLE PATIENT
             (PATIENT-NO         INTEGER NOT NULL UNIQUE,
              DATE-DISCHARGED    CHAR(8)
           . . .Other data elements. .)


          CREATE TABLE PHYSICIAN
             (PHYSICIAN-ID       CHAR(10) NOT NULL UNIQUE,
              PHYSICIAN-PHONE    CHAR(8)


          CREATE TABLE ITEM
             (ITEM-CODE          SMALLINT NOT NULL UNIQUE,
              DESCRIPTION        CHAR(15))


          CREATE TABLE ATTENDS
             (A-PHYSICIAN-ID     CHAR(1O) NOT NULL,
              A-PATIENT-NO       INTEGER NOT NULL,
              PROCEDURE          CHAR(15))


          CREATE TABLE BILLED
             (B-PATIENT-NO       INTEGER NOT NULL,
              B-ITEM-CODE        SMALLINT NOT NULL,
              B-CHARGE           DECIMAL(6,2))
```

Figure 12-2
SQL/DS database
definition for
Mountain View
Community Hospital

this type of data will be stored in a variable-length format, so that wasted space is reduced. However, the maximum value of n may still be limited to, say, 254. Data such as a detailed product description or an address might be stored in this form.

LONG VARCHAR   This is for variable-length character data that can be longer than allowed by the VARCHAR data type. Data such as comments on a customer order or instructions on how to build a custom product might be stored in this form.

DATE   This is used to store calendar dates. A system variable can be used to set the format for the date data type (for example, month/day/year or year/month/day). Data such as order date or subscription anniversary date might be stored in this form.

The specification of these data types for the columns of a database is illustrated in Figure 12-2 above. Other data types for graphic images and voice patterns, among others, may be supported. The choice of data type should be made to allow any legal value for the column to be entered. In addition, a wise choice for data type also helps to control the integrity of data by causing invalid values to be rejected by the DBMS.

In SQL, columns are not objects separate from tables, so it is possible to use the same column name in several tables and each time to define that column to be of a different data type. Such homonyms, obviously, do not help to clarify the meaning of columns or to control data integrity. In many queries it is necessary to prefix a column name by the name of the associated table. We will see examples of this later in the chapter.

Data Definition Commands

Various data definition commands are possible in SQL systems. In SQL/DS (see IBM Corp., 1985), seven are frequently used (these are typical of many relational DBMSs):

CREATE TABLE:	Defines a new table and its columns
DROP TABLE:	Destroys a table (definition and contents as well as any views and indexes associated with it)
ALTER TABLE:	Adds a new column to a table (in some RDBMSs this would also permit deleting columns or redefining the column's data type)
CREATE INDEX:	Defines an index on one column (or a concatenation of columns) that enables rapid access of the rows of a table in a sequence or randomly by key value; a table may have many indexes and each may be specified to be UNIQUE (primary key) or not, and may be sequenced in ascending or descending order
DROP INDEX:	Destroys an index
CREATE VIEW:	Defines a logical table from one or more tables or views (views may not be indexed)
DROP VIEW:	Destroys a view definition (and any other views defined from the deleted view)

Table Definition

Tables, or more explicitly base tables, usually correspond to the normalized relations resulting from the conceptual design of the database. (For reasons of performance, nonnormalized relations may be defined.) Most relational systems allow dynamic or iterative table definition in order to support changes in the understanding of database requirements. Dynamic definition is relatively easy to permit, since there are no physical links between tables; rather, indexes are used to support retrieving associated records.

A table is defined by the set of columns associated with it, as illustrated in Figure 12-2. The various data types permitted for columns were outlined above. In addition, two other column characteristics can be added as part of a table definition: NOT NULL and UNIQUE.

NOT NULL is a semantic control that informs the DBMS to not permit the specific column of any row in the table to have a null value (for example, see the definition of the ITEM table and the ITEM-CODE column in Figure 12-2). This is enforced on all data manipulation statements. NOT NULL is usually applied to key fields (the relational data model requires key columns to be not null in order to support unique rows) but may be applied to any column as appropriate.

UNIQUE is also a semantic control that specifies that the values of this column must be unique across all rows of the table. UNIQUE indicates a single primary key or candidate key column (again, see, for example, the ITEM table in Figure 12-2). UNIQUE is used only with single columns, so unique concatenated keys (like ORDER–NO + PRODUCT–NO for an order line item record in Pine Valley Furniture) can only be handled by creating a unique index, which is illustrated below.

In Figure 12-2 we show both NOT NULL and UNIQUE as qualifications that may be added to a column specification in a table definition. However, in some SQL implementation, in particular SQL/DS and DB2, only the NOT NULL clause can be used in this way. UNIQUE can only be applied to an index definition in SQL/DS. For example, the uniqueness semantic constraint on ITEM-CODE would have to be specified by creating an index on this column (which is very likely to be desirable for processing efficiency, anyhow).

Changing Table Definitions   Table definitions may be changed in many mainframe RDBMSs by ALTERing column specifications. In SQL/DS, the ALTER TABLE command is provided to add new columns to an existing table; previously defined columns may not be dropped nor may the data type of an existing column be changed. To drop a column, one must define a view (see the following section on view definition) on the base table that omits the column no longer desired. There are relational systems that do support column dropping and data type changes. The ALTER command is invaluable for adapting the database to inevitable modifications due to changing requirements, prototyping, evolutionary development, and mistakes.

Additional Table Definition Features   SQL/DS provides several commands to assist in documentation of table definitions and flexibility of using defined data. These commands are

COMMENT:	Provides an explanatory remark for table columns (stored as part of the internal system definition tables and can be queried via SQL, thus extending the built-in data dictionary features of SQL/DS)
CREATE SYNONYM:	Specifies an alternative name for a table or view; often used to define an abbreviation or to avoid prefacing a table name with the owner name of the table
DROP SYNONYM:	Destroys a synonym declaration
LABEL:	Defines a column heading to be used in place of the column name in query results; an advantage is the uniform heading of columns across all applications

The following are examples of the use of these handy commands for the DESCRIPTION column of the ITEM table defined in Figure 12-2:

```
COMMENT ON ITEM COLUMN DESCRIPTION
   IS 'Selected from medical dictionary of terms'
CREATE SYNONYM IT FOR ITEM
DROP SYNONYM IT
LABEL ON TABLE ITEM COLUMN DESCRIPTION
   IS 'Standard Description'
```

View Definition

The major purpose of a view is to simplify query commands, as was the case with the logical record concept in IDMS (see Figure 11-13). Consider the Patient Bill of Figure 5-19. Construction of the lines of this bill requires access to three tables: PATIENT, CHARGE, and ITEM. A novice database user may not be able to formulate properly or may be unproductive in formulating queries involving so many tables. A view allows this association to be predefined into a single virtual table as part of the database, so that a user who wants only Patient Bill data does not have to reconstruct the joining of data in order to produce the report or any subset of it.

In SQL/DS a view is defined by specifying an SQL query that has the view as its result. For the Patient Bill, this would be

```
CREATE VIEW DETAILED-BILL
  AS SELECT (PATIENT-NO,ITEM-CODE,DESCRIPTION,
    B-CHARGE, PATIENT-NAME and other columns as required)
    FROM PATIENT, BILLED, ITEM
    WHERE PATIENT-NO = B-PATIENT-NO
      AND ITEM-CODE = B-ITEM-CODE
```

Not shown here is the ability to rename the columns included in the view. The SELECT clause specifies what data elements (columns) are to be included in the view table. The FROM clause lists the tables involved in the view development. The WHERE clause specifies the names of the common columns used to join BILLED to ITEM and to PATIENT. Because a view is a table, and one of the relational properties of tables is that the order of rows is immaterial, the rows in a view may not be sorted (the ORDER BY clause in SQL). However, queries that refer to this view may display their results in any desired sequence.

After this view definition is added to the database, the DETAILED-BILL table may be used as any other (base) table. For example, other views can be defined from this view. This view table is not maintained as real data; rather it is constructed automatically as needed by the DBMS. Therefore, a view is a virtual table. As the base data used to construct the view change values, so will the contents of the view table. A view always contains the most current derived values and thus is superior in terms of data currency to constructing a temporary real table from several base tables. Also in comparison to a temporary real table, it obviously consumes very little storage space. It is costly, however, since its contents must be calculated each time they are requested.

A view can be a SELECTion or a PROJECTion of a base table or may simply reorder the columns of a base table. As above, it may join multiple tables together and it may contain derived (or virtual) columns. A view may also be constructed from a combination of other views as well as base tables. For example, a user in Mountain View Community Hospital may simply want to know the total charges by patient for room and special items in the room (item codes between 200 and 300). A view for just this aggregate data can be created from the DETAILED-BILL view in SQL/DS as

```
CREATE VIEW ROOM-CHARGE (OCCUPANT, ROOM-CHARGES)
  AS SELECT (PATIENT-NAME,SUM (B-CHARGE))
    FROM DETAILED-BILL
    WHERE ITEM-CODE BETWEEN 200 AND 300
    GROUP BY PATIENT-NAME
```

Here, OCCUPANT is a renaming of PATIENT-NAME, local to only this view, and ROOM-CHARGES is the name given total charges by patient.

The power of such a view can be illustrated by the following example of a query that asks for the names of all patients with total charges greater than $500. The ROOM-CHARGE-based query is:

    SELECT OCCUPANT FROM ROOM-CHARGE
        WHERE ROOM-CHARGES > 500

which would be translated by the DBMS into a more complex, equivalent query on the DETAILED-BILL view:

    SELECT PATIENT-NAME FROM DETAILED-BILL
        WHERE ITEM-CODE BETWEEN 200 AND 300
        GROUP BY PATIENT-NAME
        HAVING SUM (B-CHARGE) > 500

Access to a view may be restricted with GRANT and REVOKE statements (security statements). For example, some users can be granted access rights to aggregated data (for example, averages) in a view and denied access to base, detailed data.

Updating data directly from a view rather than from base tables is possible under certain limitations outlined in a later section on data modification. Both SQL-based RDBMSs and INGRES permit some update operations to data in a view, as long as the update is unambiguous in terms of base table data modification.

Internal Schema Definition in RDBMSs

The internal schema of a relational database can be controlled for processing and storage efficiency. Typically a database designer can tune the operational performance of the internal data model of a relational database by one or more of the following techniques:

1. Choosing to index primary and/or secondary keys to increase the speed of row selection and table joining (and to drop indexes to increase speed of table updating); you may want to review the section in Chapter 9 on selecting indexes

2. Selecting file organizations for base tables that match the type of processing activity (for example, keep table physically sorted by a frequently used reporting sort key) on those tables

3. Selecting file organizations for indexes (which are also tables!) suitable for how they are used and allocating extra space for an index file to allow it to grow without having to be reorganized

4. Clustering data so that frequently joined tables have related rows stored close in secondary storage to minimize retrieval time

Indexes   Indexes may be created in most RDBMSs to provide rapid random and sequential access to tuples. (Although indexes are not directly referenced by a user when writing any command, SQL/DS, for example, recognizes when existing indexes would improve query performance.) The Relational Design Tool is provided with SQL/DS to help a database designer decide on beneficial indexing. Indexes can usually be created for both primary and secondary keys and often on both single and concatenated keys. For example, to create an index on the ATTENDS relation for A-PHYSI-CIAN-ID (a secondary key) in SQL/DS, we would

> CREATE INDEX A-PHYS
>   ON ATTENDS (A-PHYSICIAN-ID)

and to create a concatenated key index on the BILLED relation for B-PATIENT-NO and B-ITEM-CODE (a primary key), we would

> CREATE UNIQUE INDEX B-PAT-ITEM
>   ON BILLED (B-PATIENT-NO,B-ITEM-CODE)

Indexes may be created at any time; if data already exist in the key column(s), index population will automatically occur for the existing data. Indexes will remain up to date with subsequent data maintenance. SQL/DS also permits specification of the percentage of space in each index page to reserve for later insertions; such free space reduces the time for subsequent key data maintenance.

When tables, views, or indexes are no longer needed, the associated DROP statements may be used. For example, to delete the A-PHYS index above, we would use

> DROP INDEX A-PHYS

Several cautions should be applied when deciding on index creation. First, an index consumes extra storage space and requires maintenance time when indexed data change value. Together, these costs may noticeably retard retrieval response times and cause annoying delays for on-line users. Second, some RDBMSs do not use all indexes available for query keys or common columns for a JOIN. A system may use only one index even if several are available for keys in a complex qualification. The database designer must know exactly how indexes are used by the particular RDBMS in order to make wise choices on indexing. With SQL/DS, the Relational Design Tool understands the SQL/DS query processing algorithms and can be very helpful in picking the right combination of indexes.

File Organization   Many relational systems do not give the user control over the physical file organization used to store each table or index. INGRES is an exception: A user has control over the file organization of each file. A file can be organized as a heap (new tuples added to end of file), sorted/ sequential, hashed, B-tree, or ISAM. A file may be dynamically reorganized, but each such reorganization requires indexes to be rebuilt (since the pointers to rows need to be changed to refer to the new addresses). Each index, since it is a table, may also be organized using any of these file organizations.

Simply stated,

- **Heap** is useful when data sequencing in reporting is unimportant.
- **Sorted/sequential** is helpful for minimizing sorting costs or increasing the speed of tuple selection by continuous range key qualifications.
- **Hashing** is appropriate for tables and indexes where exact matches on unique values are used (for example, find a row by primary key or join on equality of common columns).
- **B-tree** is suitable when volatile data will be accessed both randomly and sequentially.
- **ISAM** is useful to provide a balance of the benefits of sorted/sequential and hashing (random access) when data insertion and deletion are infrequent.

Row Clustering   A feature now becoming common in RDBMSs is the ability to cluster rows of different tables into adjacent physical storage in order to minimize access between related tables. Remember, the relational data model assumes that a table is a logical construct, so a table need not correspond to a physical file of contiguous records. For example, in ORACLE we can specify that we want ATTENDS rows for a given PATIENT to be clustered with the associated PATIENT table row for that patient by using

```
CREATE CLUSTER PATIENT-DATA
    (PATIENT-NO INTEGER NOT NULL)
ALTER CLUSTER PATIENT-DATA
    ADD TABLE PATIENT
        WHERE PATIENT.PATIENT-NO = PATIENT-DATA.PATIENT-NO
ALTER CLUSTER PATIENT-DATA
    ADD TABLE ATTENDS
        WHERE ATTENDS.PATIENT-NO = PATIENT-DATA.PATIENT-NO
```

In this case, each distinct value of PATIENT-NO will be associated with a separate page of secondary storage and all PATIENT and ATTENDS data for a given PATIENT-NO will be stored together. Note that physical contiguity is used, not pointers, to tie together related rows. This is similar to the VIA SET file organization in the CODASYL guidelines for network DBMSs.

Given such capabilities as indexing, controlling file organizations, and row clustering, relational systems are now considered appropriate for on-line transaction processing, not just information retrieval. When these performance techniques are not enough for a very high transaction volume application, then dedicated relational database machines can be used to gain additional performance improvements.

Data Integrity Control

Data integrity control tries to ensure that only valid data are entered and that data are consistent across all tables of a database. A part of this is transaction integrity, or making sure that complete units of work are properly terminated and do not interfere with each other. Transaction integrity is covered in a later section.

The type of integrity discussed here is data validity. In relational systems, such validity is controlled by data type specification, valid ranges or lists of values (as in the CHECK clause in CODASYL systems), limitations on allowing null values (especially for primary key columns), and forcing values of foreign and cross-reference keys to exist in other tables.

Other than the data type specification and UNIQUE and NOT NULL qualifications on table columns that we have already illustrated, integrity assertions are not implemented in either the ANSI SQL standard or in SQL/ DS. INGRES, however, does provide some data integrity control as part of its data definition facility (see Relational Technology, Inc., 1989). Suppose we wanted to limit the amount of a charge to a patient. If we wanted to restrict the B-CHARGE column in the BILLED relation to be greater than $9.99 (charges less than this are recovered as overhead) but less than $1000.00 (requires special handling), we would include the following integrity definitions in an INGRES database description:

DEFINE INTEGRITY ON BILLED IS B-CHARGE > 9.99
DEFINE INTEGRITY ON BILLED IS B-CHARGE < 1000.00

Cross-table integrity controls (for example, to provide referential integrity) can also be specified using the Visual Forms Editor (VIFRED) or the PERMIT command of INGRES. For example, if we wanted to guarantee that a B-ITEM-CODE assumed an ITEM-CODE value of only existing ITEMs, then an appropriate PERMIT definition would be

DEFINE PERMIT ALL TO BILLED TO ALL
    WHERE BILLED.B–ITEM–CODE = ITEM.ITEM-CODE

Note that it would be necessary to first load a new ITEM into the database before any charges could be entered; this places certain constraints on the sequencing of data loading programs. The lack of referential integrity control in SQL has been one of the major criticisms of this standard. The ANSI committee has been working on a way to include this feature, and an enhancement to the SQL standard to handle this is expected soon.

Such integrity constraints may become very complex. INGRES even supports the use of data aggregation functions such as sum or average in integrity statements. For example, suppose we wanted to limit the Mountain View Community Hospital database to manage only patients with small to medium-sized bills and force high-expense patients to be handled by special procedures not included in the database applications (for example, when patient total charges exceed $100,000). INGRES could stop further data entry (either data REPLACEment or APPENDing new charges) once a patient exceeded this limit by monitoring the following integrity constraint:

DEFINE PERMIT REPLACE, APPEND TO BILLED (B-CHARGE)
    TO ALL
  WHERE SUM (BILLED.B-CHARGE BY BILLED.B–PATIENT–NO)
    < 100000

Such integrity constraints may be issued at any time; if issued after affected data have been entered into the database, INGRES will not accept the integrity definition if any existing tuple violates the restriction. Subsequently, whenever new data are appended or existing data modified, INGRES will not process any update that would result in the violation of some integrity definition. Integrity constraints, if not carefully designed and specified, can cause operational problems. For example, if a database owner accidentally revokes retrieval access to a table to all users, access may also have been revoked to the owner. Further, suppose that for some reason the hospital specified a minimum value for the sum of patient charges for each patient. Then, since the first charge entered is below the aggregate minimum, the data entry will be rejected. Fortunately, the dynamic definition of integrity constraints helps the database designer deal with such problems.

Security Controls

Tables and views may also be given security restrictions. Typically, unless otherwise specified, only the creator of a table has any rights to use that table. To allow another user to perform any particular commands, the right to use only those commands on that table must be given to that user. For example, in SQL/DS

GRANT INSERT ON ITEM TO INV-MANAGER

gives the user identified as INV-MANAGER privilege to insert rows in the ITEM relation, and

REVOKE UPDATE ON ITEM FROM STOCKROOM

denies update capability to the ITEM table for the user identified as STOCK-ROOM (this assumes that STOCKROOM was previously given this privilege).

In most cases, data element- (column-) level restrictions are possible only by creating views with different column combinations and applying GRANTs and REVOKEs to views. In this case, users are not granted access to the base tables but only to the views containing the data they are permitted to see. Complex combinations may be difficult or impossible to specify. For example, a user may be permitted to see employee names and employee salaries but not both. Such so-called statistical constraints are not yet supported in SQL.

Control can be placed on commands SELECT (retrieval), INSERT (adding new rows), DELETE (deleting rows), UPDATE (data maintenance, as this may be applied to specified columns), ALTER (table redefinition), and for some SQL-based systems INDEX (index creation). Privileges are granted on tables or views and each GRANT or REVOKE can be applied to all (PUBLIC) or selected users. Further, when a table owner grants a certain right (for example, DELETE) to a user, the owner can specify whether the grantee may pass this right on to others. For example,

> GRANT UPDATE (B-CHARGE), DELETE ON BILLED TO NURSE
>   WITH GRANT OPTION

gives the user identified as NURSE rights to update the B-CHARGE column, to delete rows from the BILLED table, and to grant these same rights to others (WITH GRANT OPTION). Other database administrator privileges may also be granted to users and to stored database routines.

INGRES has an interactive command, PERMIT, that specifics who (by user name) can do what (by DML command) under certain conditions (for example, time of day, day of week). A PERMIT is applied to a table and is checked each time that table is used. Suppose we wanted to allow only retrieval and adding new CHARGE data (APPEND command) by billing clerks in the Accounts Receivable office (terminal TTA4) only during normal business hours from Monday through Friday. The PERMIT command for this situation would be

> DEFINE PERMIT RETRIEVE, APPEND ON CHARGE
>   TO BILLING-CLERK AT TTA4 FROM 8:30 TO 17:50
>   ON MON TO FRI

Other options can be used to restrict access to certain columns and to data in specified ranges of values (for example, to permit an employee to be able to see only her own salary history).

Data Dictionary Facilities

Since RDBMSs typically store table, column, and view definitions, integrity rules, security constraints, and other data about data in tables, the RDBMS can itself be used to write queries and routines to produce data dictionary-type output. Further, understanding this definition structure, a user can extend existing tables or build other tables to enhance the built-in features (for example, to include data on who is responsible for data integrity). A user is, however, often restricted from modifying the structure or contents of these definition tables directly since the DBMS depends on them for its interpretation and parsing of queries.

SQL/DS maintains a set of tables that contain various pertinent data definitions. These include

SYSTABAUTH	Records the table privileges held by database users
SYSCOLUMNS	Describes the columns in the tables
SYSINDEXES	Defines index characteristics
SYSKEYS	Describes keys used in indexes
SYSTABLES	Describes tables and views
SYSVIEWS	Defines each view
SYSSYN	Contains synonyms for table and view names

For example, SYSTABLES contains such information on tables as the table name, owner/creator name, and number of columns. SYSCOLUMNS lists the names of all database columns, the associated table (thus, if the same column name is used in more than one table, it will appear in several rows of SYSCOLUMNS), and data types. A user can query these tables to discover which tables contain an ITEM-CODE column by

SELECT TBNAME FROM SYSTEM.SYSCOLUMNS WHERE NAME =
    'ITEM-CODE'

Rettig (1989) provides an excellent review of how to retrieve data definitions from the DB2 system catalog.

In INGRES, three specific commands are available, and the user can build other queries to access the stored data definitions. These built-in commands are

CATALOGDB:	Lists the names of databases created by the user
HELP:	Lists the names of relations in the database currently being used
HELP relation:	Lists the column names and associated data formats for the specified relation as well as general relation statistics such as number of existing tuples and file organization

Summary of Data Definition Commands

The preceding remarks describe the salient, typical data definition features of relational DBMSs, with special emphasis on SQL. As can be seen, except for some syntactical differences, similar DDL features are provided in both SQL-based and INGRES systems. Differences are due more to style than to substance.

Similarities can be more pronounced in relational data manipulation languages than in the definition languages. Relational algebra and relational calculus represent two different forms of relational data manipulation. Since SQL and most mainframe systems use relational calculus and many personal computer products use relational algebra, in this chapter we address only the capabilities of and variations on calculus-based systems and associated products. Then in Chapter 13 we address relational algebra.

DATA MANIPULATION IN SQL

Some authors (for example, see Date, 1987, Kroenke, 1983, and Ullman, 1980) distinguish among three different but related forms of relational calculus: tuple calculus, domain calculus, and transform languages. INGRES (Relational Technology, Inc., 1989) and the query language on which it is based, QUEL (Stonebraker et al., 1976) are representative of tuple calculus. A few rare implementations of domain calculus exist [see Date (1987a) for a discussion]. Most popular products today—SQL/DS and ORACLE (ORACLE Corp., 1988), for example—are based on the transform language SEQUEL (Chamberlin et al., 1976). Even INGRES now includes the capability to use either QUEL or SEQUEL! Thus, it is most important that systems builders learn the SEQUEL (SQL) language, which is what we concentrate on in this section.

General Structure of SQL Calculus

Commands in SQL (and other relational calculus systems) specify in a specific syntax which columns to manipulate, from what tables, and for what rows. For those already familiar with relational algebra-based products (like dBASE and R:BASE), there are two fundamental differences between relational algebra and relational calculus: (1) calculus combines the SELECT and PROJECT commands and the binary operators (such as SUBTRACT) into one SELECT (or similar) statement that lists the column names to appear in the result (PROJECT) and uses a WHERE clause to specify the selection criteria; and (2) calculus also uses the WHERE clause to specify the inter–table associations used for implicitly JOINing relations in the RETRIEVE command. Thus, whereas the JOIN operator of the relational algebra is a binary operator (and a table that is the combination of *n* relations must be generated in *n*-1 JOINs), one SELECT command can JOIN numerous tables (implicitly). Several examples of SQL were given in Chapter 2.

Basic SQL Retrieval Command Structure

SQL structures data retrieval statements into three distinct clauses:

SELECT: Lists the columns to be projected into the table that will be the result of the command

FROM: Identifies the tables from which output columns will be projected and that possibly will be joined

WHERE: Includes the conditions for tuple/row selection within a single table or between tables implicitly joined

For example, we can display the patient charges from the BILLED relation of Figure 12-1 for B-PATIENT-NO = 1234 by

SELECT B-CHARGE
　FROM BILLED
　　WHERE B-PATIENT# = 1234

If the user does not wish to see duplicate rows in the result, then SELECT DISTINCT may be used. All the columns of the referenced tables can be displayed by use of SELECT *, where * is shorthand for all columns. Also, some SQL implementations allow the result to be placed INTO a temporary table so that this subset of the database does not have to repeatedly be derived. Care must be taken when using an INTO, since the temporary table will not reflect any subsequent changes made to the data in the original tables (as is done by a view).

AND, OR, and NOT operators can be used to create complicated WHERE clauses, and parentheses can be used to properly group the logical operations (we will see many examples of the use of logical operators later in this chapter). One example of such a query would be a display of the patient-NO for a particular name or (since we may not spell the name correctly but do remember some of the patient's other characteristics) all the patient-nos and names for patients that do not live in 'FOXBORO' and were discharged on 03/14/90. This query would be

SELECT PATIENT-NO, NAME
　FROM PATIENT
　　WHERE PATIENT-NAME = 'the name we remember' OR
　　(NOT (PATIENT-CITY = 'FOXBORO') AND
　　DATE-DISCHARGED = '03/14/90')

In contrast to this SQL approach, INGRES combines the SELECT and FROM clauses into one RETRIEVE statement. Also, INGRES requires all data elements to be referred to with the syntax tablename.attributename. The equivalent INGRES query to the SQL/DS one above that retrieves the charges for patient# 1234 would be

RETRIEVE (BILLED.B-CHARGE)
　　WHERE BILLED.B-PATIENT# = 1234

Built-in Functions　Functions such as COUNT, MIN, MAX, SUM, and AVG of specified columns can also be used to specify that the resulting table query answer is to contain aggregated data instead of row-level data. All of these functions are found in most SQL implementations. For example, in SQL

SELECT COUNT(PROCEDURE) FROM ATTENDS
　　WHERE A-PATIENT-NO = 1234

would display the number of times a physician performed a procedure on patient with number 1234 (that is, would count the number of rows for patient 1234). This, however, is not the same as the number of distinct procedures performed on this patient when several physicians are involved in the same procedure (and, hence, there are multiple rows). To obtain the number of distinct procedures, the query would be slightly modified as

SELECT COUNT(DISTINCT PROCEDURE) FROM ATTENDS
   WHERE A-PATIENT-NO = 1234

Limitations on the use of data aggregate functions vary from system to system. In SQL/DS, data aggregates and individual row-level data may not be mixed in the same SELECT clause; that is, data aggregation is a function of groups of rows, and row and group data cannot appear together. INGRES is more lenient. For example, it is possible in INGRES to request that B-CHARGE minus AVG(B-CHARGE) be displayed as a column in the query result, in which case the query is actually requesting a display of row-level data derived from both row and group data. SQL/DS cannot handle this type of derived data specification in the SELECT clause.

Besides the commonly found functions listed above, a wide variety of arithmetic, character, date, logical, and other functions are found in different SQL systems. For example, ORACLE has functions for calculating absolute value and the square root, for capitalizing the first letter of each word in a character string, and for coding and decoding a character string. Sayles (1989) provides a review of the built-in functions in many SQL systems.

Displaying Constants and Calculated Values The column list after the SELECT verb can include not only column names but also constants and computed values. For example, the multiplication of two column values (like price times quantity) or 110% of a column value (like salary) can be displayed. Consider the following SQL query for the Mountain View Community Hospital database:

SELECT 'The total number of procedures for ', A-PATIENT-NO,
   ' is ', COUNT(PROCEDURE)
   FROM ATTEND
   WHERE A-PATIENT-NO = 1234

displays the same result for a previous example but this time in a more narrative, rather than columnar, form.

Computed values can also be used in a WHERE clause. For example, the query

SELECT PATIENT-NO
   FROM PATIENT
   WHERE (DATE-DISCHARGED - DATE-ADMITTED) > 10

would list those patients who had stayed in the hospital for more than ten days (note that in some SQL systems special functions would have to be used to allow arithmetic on dates).

Sorting and Grouping the Result   If the resulting rows are desired in a sorted sequence, an ORDER BY clause may be added to the query to achieve ascending or descending sequence with major and several minor sort keys. A GROUP BY clause can be used to have functions performed on groups of rows with common values. The following illustrates the use of ORDER BY and GROUP BY clauses. We can produce a list of the total charges per patient for major medical items (item codes in the range 500–800) for those patients with large major medical expenses (total charges over $50,000) by

```
SELECT B-PATIENT-NO, SUM(B-CHARGE)
   FROM BILLED
      WHERE B-ITEM-CODE BETWEEN 500 AND 800
      GROUP BY B-PATIENT-NO
      ORDER BY B-PATIENT-NO
      HAVING SUM(B-CHARGE) > 50000
```

Here the GROUP BY clause is used to specify subtotal control breaks. This query will display a subtotal of B-CHARGE for each patient. Since B-PATIENT-NO is the grouping variable, it may be used in the SELECT column list. In fact, every nonaggregate column in the column list must be part of the GROUP BY in SQL. The HAVING clause is necessary because of the qualification on group-level data. HAVING is like WHERE, except it involves group-level data. The ORDER BY phrase simply sorts the output into patient number sequence for easier scanning. Some relational languages require ORDER BY to accompany each GROUP BY phrase. This is used to sort tuples together with the same GROUP BY value to facilitate subtotal calculations. An optional DESCENDING clause on the SORT BY will sort the results in reverse sequence.

In contrast to SQL, functions may also be used in WHERE clauses for INGRES. If we wish to display all the patient numbers for patients who have had charges above the average charge, in INGRES we would say

```
RETRIEVE (BILLED.B-PATIENT-NO,BILLED.B-CHARGE)
   WHERE BILLED.B-CHARGE > AVG(BILLED.B-CHARGE)
```

NULL in Qualifications   In addition to being able to use AND, OR, and NOT in qualifications, other options and keywords may be possible. For example, since SQL recognizes a NULL value, qualifications can include NULL and NOT NULL. For example, WHERE DATE-DISCHARGED IS NOT NULL would limit a query to only discharged patients. Care should be taken when using NULL in compound qualifications. SQL follows what is called three-value logic: true, false, and unknown. Research has shown that some complex queries based on three-value logic can generate unexpected results. When using NULL in qualifications, you should review the users' manual to see what are called truth tables, which indicate how NULL will be interpreted in Boolean qualifications.

The IN Operator   The OR operator can be replaced by IN to simplify query writing. In addition, IN is needed in some more complex queries to be shown later in this chapter, so programmers frequently use IN instead of OR for consistency. For example, the query

SELECT A-PATIENT-NO FROM ATTENDS
 WHERE A-PHYSICIAN-ID IN ('BAKER,J.','FISCUS,A.')

would display the patient numbers of all patients treated by BAKER,J. or FISCUS,A. The logical operator NOT may precede IN to specify the complement of a list of values.

The BETWEEN Operator   As IN simplifies queries involving many OR conditions, the BETWEEN operator simplifies query writing for range qualifications. When a qualification says BETWEEN x and y, this is equivalent to $> x$ AND $< y$. For example, suppose we wanted to find all the patients who had been charged between \$200 and \$400 for item 207. The SQL query for this would be

SELECT B-PATIENT-NO
 FROM BILLED
 WHERE B-ITEM-CODE = 207 AND B-CHARGE BETWEEN 200 AND 400

The LIKE Operator   Frequently, with search conditions that involve character data, exact matches are not needed or may be problematic. Spelling errors on data entry, inconsistent use of upper- and lowercase, and various punctuation marks can result in missing desired data. Other times a user cannot be specific about what data are sought (for example, when we are not sure of the spelling of a name or when we want all values that include a particular substring). The LIKE operator is useful in these circumstances.

 LIKE uses two special character symbols: '%' and '_'. % means ignore zero or more characters and _ means ignore exactly one character where these symbols are used. For example, the clause WHERE LAST-NAME LIKE 'Mc%' would qualify all people whose names begin with 'Mc', and WHERE LOCATION LIKE '_2%' would ask for rooms on the second floor in any building (the first position of the location code is a building number).

MULTIPLE TABLE OPERATIONS IN SQL

Relational query languages are distinctive from network and most hierarchical languages in that explicit reference to access paths between related records is not necessary. Rather, data are related and related data are referenced simply by common values. How this is specified varies among different types of relational systems. The SQL SELECT command is also used for multiple table operations, as we will illustrate below. In fact, SELECT can actually include references to two, three, or more tables in the same command. Relational algebra systems (like dBASE), as you may know, can refer to only one or two tables per command.

The most frequently used relational operation, which brings together data from two (or more) related tables into one resultant table, is called *join*. SQL specifies a join implicitly by referring in a WHERE clause to the matching of common columns over which tables are joined. Two tables may be joined when there is a column in each table that has the same domain of values, a condition that is frequently referred to as having common columns. The result of a Join is a table with columns possibly from all the tables being Joined and with each row containing data from rows in the different input tables with matching values for the common columns.

There are many possible types of joins in relational database queries (although each SQL implementation may support only some of these types of joins). Three types of joins are described in this chapter: equijoin, natural join, and outer join (see Figure 12-3).

Equijoin   With an **equijoin,** the joining condition is based on *equality* between values in the common columns. For example, in Figure 12-3a there is a row in the result table (called BILL-DATA) whenever there is a match between PATIENT-NO (PATIENT table) and B-PATIENT-NO (CHARGES table). Notice that with an equijoin the common columns both appear (redundantly) in the result table (so that PATIENT-NO and B-PATIENT-NO both appear in BILL-DATA).

It is also possible to define joins basd on inequality conditions; for example, "greater than" joins, "less than" joins, "not equal" joins, and so on. However, joins with inequality conditions are used less frequently than those with equality conditions.

Natural join   A **natural join** is the same as an equijoin, except that one of the duplicate columns is eliminated. For example, Figure 12-3b shows the BILL-DATA table for a natural join. This table is the same as the one in Figure 12-3a except that the B-PATIENT-NO column has been eliminated. (Alternately, the PATIENT-NO column could have been eliminated.)

The natural join is the most commonly used form of join operations. The SQL command for the join operation in Figure 12-3b is the following:

```
SELECT PATIENT-NO, DATE-DISCHARGED, B-CHARGE
    FROM PATIENT, BILLED
    WHERE PATIENT-NO = B-PATIENT-NO
```

The SELECT clause identifies all attributes to be displayed, the FROM clause identifies the tables from which attributes are selected, and the WHERE clause specifies the joining condition for common columns.

Outer Join   Often in joining two tables, a row in one table does not have a matching row in the other table. (That is, there is no matching value in

PATIENT

PATIENT-NO	DATE-DISCH.
1234	05/20/83
0675	06/23/83
2345	02/28/83

BILLED

B-PATIENT-NO	B-CHARGE
2345	23.00
2345	65.00
1234	80.50
1234	125.00

Figure 12-3
Examples of join
commands:
(a) equijoin
(b) natural join
(c) outer join

Result of natural JOIN

BILL-DATA

PATIENT-NO	DATE-DISCH.	B-CHARGE
1234	05/20/83	80.50
1234	05/20/83	125.00
2345	02/28/83	23.00
2345	02/28/83	65.00

(a)

Result of equi-JOIN

BILL-DATA

PATIENT-NO	DATE-DISCH.	B-PATIENT-NO	B-CHARGE
1234	05/20/83	1234	80.50
1234	05/20/83	1234	125.00
2345	02/28/83	2345	23.00
2345	02/28/83	2345	65.00

(b)

Result of outer JOIN

BILL-DATA

PATIENT-NO	DATE-DISCH.	B-CHARGE
1234	05/20/83	80.50
1234	05/20/83	125.00
2345	02/28/83	23.00
2345	02/28/83	65.00
0675	06/23/83	?

where? indicates a NULL value.

(c)

the common columns.) For example, in Figure 12-3 there is an entry for patient number 0675 in the PATIENT table, but no entry for this patient in the CHARGES table. (Perhaps no charges have yet been billed to this patient.) As a result, with an equijoin or natural join, there is no entry for this patient in BILL-DATA (see Figures 12-3a and 12-3b).

The user may want a row from one of the tables to appear in the result table, even when there is no matching value in the other table. This may be accomplished by using an **outer join:** rows that do not have matching values in common columns are also included in the result table. Null values appear in columns where there is no match between tables. Notice that in Figure 12-3c, there is an entry for patient number 0675, with a null value for B-CHARGE (since there is no charge for that patient). Compare Figures 12-3a, 12-3b, and 12-3c carefully to make sure you understand each of these join operations.

Although still not found in many relational systems, the outer join (available in ORACLE) is appearing in newer versions of systems and is likely, in some form, to become a standard feature. The advantage of outer join is that information is not lost; in Figure 12-3c, patients with no charges can be handled in the same table as patients with charges. Unless otherwise stated in this section, all joins will be natural joins.

Table Name Abbreviations

When columns from several different tables are referenced in one command, the DBMS must be able to identify unambiguously which columns are found in which table. This is especially difficult when the system permits the same column name to be used in several tables (which a designer may do if the columns have the same domain of values). The way SQL and most relational systems handle clarifying which table is involved is to prefix a column name with the associated table name, as tablename.columnname. When potentially each column name must be prefixed by a reference to its associated table, commands can require many keystrokes. To minimize the length of commands, therefore, most relational systems support defining abbreviations for table names.

In SQL/DS when more than one table is being referenced, such abbreviations may be defined within the query as part of the FROM clause as, for example,

```
SELECT R.EXTENSION FROM ROOM R, ATTENDS A
    WHERE A.PROCEDURE = 'Tonsillectomy' AND
        A.A-PATIENT-NO = R.PATIENT-NO
```

which would tell us the telephone numbers of all patients who are in the hospital for a tonsillectomy. These abbreviations in SQL/DS are needed only when column names are not unique; when a table is joined with itself (a self-join), to be illustrated below; and with so called correlated subqueries, also to be illustrated below. The abbreviation applies only to the one command, so subsequent commands in an interactive session must restate any abbreviation needed there. Table name synonyms, mentioned earlier, can also be used as prefixes to column names.

INGRES takes a more global approach. In INGRES we would define shorthand names for the tables of Figure 12-2 with the RANGE command as

RANGE OF R IS ROOM
RANGE OF P IS PATIENT
RANGE OF H IS PHYSICIAN
RANGE OF A IS ATTENDS
RANGE OF I IS ITEM
RANGE OF B IS BILLED

These abbreviations can then be used during the whole interactive session or program in all commands.

Joining by Subqueries

The SQL example above illustrates one of the two basic formats in SQL/DS for joining two tables: the joining technique. SQL/DS provides two different syntaxes for formulating queries which involve multiple-related tables: (1) the joining technique uses one combination of SELECT, FROM, WHERE clauses and uses the WHERE clause in specifying the linking columns (this approach is very similar to that found in INGRES); (2) the subquery technique involves placing one query (SELECT, FROM, WHERE) within another query.

The subquery approach to joining can be used when qualifications are nested (that is, one is within another) or when qualifications are easily understood in a nested way. Nesting uses pairwise joining of *one and only one* column in an inner query with *one* in an outer query. Data from only the table(s) referenced in the outer query can be displayed. Up to 16 levels of nested queries are typically supported. Queries are processed inside out.

Suppose that as part of a hospital audit we wanted to know what patients had been charged more than twice the average rate for X-ray work (ITEM-CODE = 307). This would be specified in SQL/DS as

```
SELECT DISTINCT B-PATIENT-NO
    FROM BILLED
    WHERE B-ITEM-CODE = 307
          AND B-CHARGE >
              (SELECT 2 * AVG(B-CHARGE)
               FROM BILLED
               WHERE B-ITEM-CODE = 307)
```

This query also illustrates that a table (BILLED) can be compared with itself, even using an inequality (>) operator (an inequality JOIN). In this illustration, the inner query acts like a function that calculates a constant to be compared to a column value.

When an inner query returns a *set* of values and the matching is on equality to any of the values, then the keyword IN is used. Suppose we wanted to display the ITEM-CODE and DESCRIPTION for all work performed on Patient Number 1234 in Mountain View Community Hospital. In SQL's subquery approach, we would

```
SELECT ITEM-CODE, DESCRIPTION
  FROM ITEM
  WHERE ITEM-CODE IN
    (SELECT B-ITEM-CODE FROM BILLED
      WHERE B-PATIENT-NO = 1234)
```

Qualifiers NOT, ANY, and ALL may be used in front of IN or logical operators such as =, >, and < (see Figure 12-4 later in this section for examples).

Often a query is simpler to construct in the subquery approach than in the joining approach because the hierarchical decomposition is easier to understand. However, the subquery approach requires that the relationships over which tables are being joined be nested.

The joining technique for query construction, in contrast to the subquery approach, is useful when data from several relations are to be retrieved and displayed, and the relationships are not necessarily nested. The joining technique can be used to determine the items and associated descriptions charged to PATIENT-NO 1234, as

```
SELECT ITEM-CODE, DESCRIPTION
  FROM ITEM, BILLED
  WHERE ITEM-CODE = B-ITEM-CODE AND
    B-PATIENT-NO = 1234
```

The equivalent subquery-style query, which may be easier for some people to understand and compose, would be

```
SELECT ITEM-CODE, DESCRIPTION
  FROM ITEM
  WHERE ITEM-CODE =
    (SELECT B-ITEM-CODE
      FROM BILLED
      WHERE B-PATIENT-NO = 1234)
```

Correlated Subqueries   In the previous examples it was possible to examine the inner query before considering the outer query. For some queries, the processing of the inner query depends on data from the outer query. That is, the inner query is somewhat different for each row referenced in the outer query. In this case, the inner query must be "computed" for each outer row, whereas above the inner query was computed only once.

Suppose we wanted to know which patients had been charged more than twice the average rate for any type of work performed on them. This question can be answered with correlated subqueries in which one of the queries above is modified to have B-ITEM-CODE of the inner query refer to the B-ITEM-CODE in the outer query as each row is processed. This more general query is

```
SELECT DISTINCT C.B-PATIENT-NO, C.B-ITEM-CODE
   FROM BILLED C
   WHERE B-CHARGE >
       (SELECT 2*AVG(B-CHARGE)
           FROM BILLED
           WHERE B-ITEM-CODE = C.B-ITEM-CODE)
```

Qualified Subqueries   Several other operators are included in SQL to handle situations in which more complex conditions about the results of the subquery occur. These operators are [NOT] EXISTS, ALL, and ANY. In WHERE clauses, the logical operators EXISTS and NOT EXISTS restrict outer table row display to situations in which subqueries have and have not, respectively, any qualified rows. For example, suppose we wanted to know the patient numbers of any patient that had been charged for both treatments 307 and 807. We would write this query as follows in SQL/DS:

```
SELECT DISTINCT B-PATIENT-NO
   FROM BILLED A
   WHERE EXISTS
       (SELECT *
           FROM BILLED B
           WHERE A.B-PATIENT-NO = B.B-PATIENT-NO
           AND A.B-ITEM-CODE = 307 AND B.B.-ITEM-CODE = 807)
```

In this correlated subquery example, both the outer query and the subquery refer to the same relation, BILLED. We distinguish rows from each use of the BILLED table by an abbreviation, as explained earlier. The subquery will be true if the same patient (qualified by the first WHERE clause of the subquery) has two BILLED rows, one for item 307 and another for item 807 (qualified by the second WHERE condition of the subquery). Also note that in the case of the EXISTS operator, the inner query is evaluated simply as true or false, so SELECT *, rather than SELECT of one column is okay.

The ALL operator can be used (among other uses) as a substitute for the MAX or MIN built-in function and frequently makes for more understandable queries. Suppose we wanted to audit charging practices in Mountain View Community Hospital. To find these, one of the tests is to determine the numbers and names of all patients who had been charged more for item 125 than all patients were charged for item 126, two similar laboratory tests. An SQL/DS query for this inquiry would be

```
SELECT PATIENT-NO, PATIENT-NAME
   FROM PATIENT
   WHERE PATIENT-NO IN
```

```
(SELECT PATIENT-NO
   FROM BILLED
   WHERE B-ITEM-CODE = 125 AND
          B-CHARGE >ALL
      (SELECT B-CHARGE
       FROM BILLED
       WHERE B-ITEM-CODE = 126))
```

The ANY operator finds rows for which the column mentioned in the WHERE clause has a value less than or greater than any (some) value from another column. Suppose we wanted to know the numbers and names of all patients who had been charged more for item 125 than any patient had been charged for item 126. That is, in this audit test, we expect that all the item 125 charges should be less than all the item 126 charges. An SQL/DS query for this inquiry would be

```
SELECT PATIENT-NO, PATIENT-NAME
   FROM PATIENT
   WHERE PATIENT-NO IN
      (SELECT PATIENT-NO
       FROM BILLED
       WHERE B-ITEM-CODE = 125 AND
              B-CHARGE >ANY
          (SELECT B-CHARGE
           FROM BILLED
           WHERE B-ITEM-CODE = 126))
```

Other Multiple Table Operations

Because relational query languages like SQL are set-oriented languages (that is, commands operate on and generate sets of rows), the equivalent of various set operations may also be available.

Appending Query Results Together   The UNION command combines the result of two queries into one table as long as the two tables being combined have compatible corresponding columns (that is, the same data types). UNION can be used to simulate an outer JOIN when one is not available in the SQL implementation. A typical way in which UNION is used is to label or identify different types of similar rows. For example, the following would identify and label patients treated for tonsillectomy or charged for X-rays:

```
SELECT A-PATIENT-NO, 'Treated'
   FROM ATTENDS
   WHERE PROCEDURE = 'Tonsillectomy'
UNION
SELECT B-PATIENT-NO, 'Charged'
   FROM BILLED, ITEM
   WHERE B-ITEM-CODE = ITEM-CODE AND DESCRIPTION = 'X-Ray'
```

We could produce a list of charges for all patients, even those for whom there were no charges so far (so that we could work with patients with zero charges) by using UNION in the following query:

```
SELECT B-PATIENT-NO, PATIENT-NAME, B-CHARGE
    FROM BILLED, PATIENT
    WHERE B-PATIENT-NO = PATIENT-NO
UNION
SELECT PATIENT-NO, PATIENT-NAME, 0
    FROM PATIENT
    WHERE PATIENT-NO NOT IN
        (SELECT B-PATIENT-NO
            FROM BILLED)
```

This use of UNION could be accomplished directly by an outer-JOIN operator. The equivalent ORACLE outer-JOIN command would simply be

```
SELECT PATIENT-NO, PATIENT-NAME, B-CHARGE
    FROM PATIENT, CHARGES
    WHERE PATIENT-NO = B-PATIENT-NO (+)
```

where the (+) indicates that the outer-JOIN is to be performed.

The MINUS and INTERSECT Operators   Depending on the implementation, both set difference (MINUS) and set intersection (INTERSECT) operators may be available. Both of these can be very helpful in simplifying query writing. Suppose we wanted to know which of the patients who have been treated by Dr. Wilcox have not been charged for anything, yet. This query can be written using the MINUS operator as

```
SELECT DISTINCT A-PATIENT-NO
    FROM ATTENDS
    WHERE A-PHYSICIAN-ID = 'Wilcox'
MINUS
SELECT DISTINCT PATIENT-NO
    FROM BILLED
```

The first query finds all the patients treated by Dr. Wilcox. The second query determines which patients have been billed so far. Any patient number in the result of the first query and not in the second (the first set minus the second set) satisfies the query. Note that the sequence in which these two queries are listed is important, since A-B does not necessarily equal B-A in set mathematics.

As an example of the use of INTERSECT, suppose we wanted to know which patients had been treated by both Dr. Wilcox and Dr. Snyder. This query can be written using the INTERSECT as

```
SELECT DISTINCT A-PATIENT-NO
    FROM ATTENDS
    WHERE A-PHYSICIAN-ID = 'Wilcox'
INTERSECT
```

SQL	INGRES

What patients (displayed in PATIENT -NO order)
have been charged more than $300 for item 307?

SELECT B-PATIENT-NO	RETRIEVE (B.B-PATIENT-NO)
FROM BILLED	
WHERE B-ITEM-CODE = 307	WHERE B.B-ITEM-CODE = 307
AND B-CHARGES > 300.00	AND B.B-CHARGES > 300.00
ORDER BY B-PATIENT-NO	SORT BY B.B-PATIENT-NO

What physicians have not treated patient 1234?

SELECT PHYSICIAN-ID	RETRIEVE (H.PHYSICIAN-ID)
FROM PHYSICIAN	
WHERE PHYSICIAN-ID NOT IN	WHERE COUNT (A.A-PHYSICIAN-ID
(SELECT A-PHYSICIAN-ID	BY A.A-PHYSICIAN-ID
FROM ATTENDS	WHERE A.A-PHYSCIAN-ID =
WHERE A-PATIENT-NO = 1234	H.PHYSICIAN-ID) = 0

Create a new table containing data on the phone numbers of physicians
and what procedures they have performed on what patients.

CREATE TABLE WORK	RETRIEVE INTO
...Table definitions...	WORK(H.PHYSICIAN-ID,
INSERT INTO WORK	H.PHYSICIAN-PHONE,
SELECT A-PHYSICIAN-ID,	A.A-PATIENT#, A.PROCEDURE)
PHYSICIAN-PHONE,	
A-PATIENT-NO, PROCEDURE	
FROM PHYSICIAN,ATTENDS	WHERE H.PHYSICIAN-ID =
WHERE PHYSICIAN-ID =	A.A-PHYSICIAN-ID
A-PHYSICIAN-ID	

How many procedures have been performed on patient# 1234?

SELECT COUNT(*)	RETRIEVE (N = COUNT(A.PROCEDURE
FROM ATTENDS	WHERE A.PATIENT-NO = 1234))
WHERE A-PATIENT-NO = 1234	

Figure 12-4
SQL and INGRES
(QUEL) command
comparison

SQL | INGRES

How mant (distinct) physicians have treated patient# 1234?

SELECT COUNT(DISTINCT*)	RETRIEVE (N =
FROM ATTENDS	COUNT (A.A-PHYSICIAN-ID
WHERE A-PATIENT-NO = 1234	WHERE A.A-PATIENT-NO = 1234))

What patients have total charges greater than $1000?

SELECT B-PATIENT-NO	RETRIEVE (B.B-PATIENT-NO)
FROM BILLED	WHERE SUM(B.B-CHARGE
GROUP BY B-PATIENT-NO	BY B.B-PATIENT-NO)
HAVING SUM(B-CHARGE) > 1000	> 1000

What is the total charge of items 307 and 415 to each patient
who has had both items billed to their account?

SELECT CA.B-PATIENT-NO	RANGE OF CA IS BILLED
CA.B-CHARGES = CB.B-CHARGES	RANGE OF CB IS BILLED
FROM BILLED CA, BILLED CB	RETRIEVE (CA.B-PATIENT-NO,
WHERE CA.B-ITEM-CODE = 307 AND	TOT = (CA.B-CHARGE +
CB.B-ITEM-CODE = 415 AND	CB.B-CHARGE
CA.B-PATIENT-NO =	WHERE CA.B-PATIENT-NO =
CB.B-PATIENT-NO	CB.B-PATIENT-NO-
	AND CA.B-ITEM-CODE = 307
	AND CB.B-ITEM-CODE = 415)).

```
SELECT DISTINCT A-PATIENT-NO
    FROM ATTENDS
    WHERE A-PHYSICIAN-ID = 'Snyder'
```

Figure 12-4 illustrates some additional capabilities of relational calculus query languages and compares SQL/DS syntax with that of INGRES for the same queries.

DATA MODIFICATION IN SQL

The SQL/DS data maintenance operators, typical of relational systems, are:

INSERT: Places a new row in a table based on values supplied in the statement, or copies one or more rows computed from other database data into a table

INPUT:	Enters new rows into a table via an interactive command
UPDATE:	Changes values in one or more qualified rows of a table by replacing current values with constants or the results of calculations
DELETE:	Deletes one or more qualified rows of a table

INGRES has, in addition, a COPY command that permits rows to be transferred between database tables and external files. COPY is useful for batch loading of data, where the external file, containing new tuples, was created by a separate data entry or text editor program.

Adding Data to a Table

In SQL/DS, one new row could be added to the BILLED relation by

    INSERT INTO BILLED
        VALUES (1234,300,220.00)

In this form, the sequence in which the values are listed must correspond to the sequence in which the associated columns were defined for the table. If values were to be supplied for only some of the columns or for the columns in a different sequence, the table name can be followed by the list of column names (in parentheses) for the columns (in sequence) to receive data.

In addition, one or more rows may be copied from one table to another. Suppose there were also an OUT-PATIENT relation in the database of Figure 12-2, for patients receiving treatment without occupying a hospital sleeping room. When such a patient is admitted for overnight, we could copy (without destroying) the demographic data by

    INSERT INTO PATIENT
        SELECT PATIENT-NO, ...
            FROM OUT-PATIENT
            WHERE PATIENT-NO = 1234

Whole groups of rows can be copied when the WHERE clause involves secondary keys.

Batch Input   When entering multiple rows in batch, the INPUT command is used. For example, if we were to enter a batch of rows for the BILLED table we would say

    INPUT BILLED

and then enter the values for each of the new rows. Again, the values must be entered in the sequence the columns were defined, with one input line for each new row. The key word END is entered at the beginning of a line to tell SQL when all the data have been entered.

Deleting Database Contents

Rows can be deleted individually or in groups. Deletion must be done with care when tuples from several relations are involved. For example, if we delete a PATIENT tuple before deleting associated BILLED rows, we will have a referential integrity violation (integrity rules on BILLED to ensure that B-PATIENT-NO must contain a value from the PATIENT-NO column of the PATIENT table are checked only when B-PATIENT-NO is entered or modified). Suppose we wish to delete all treatments performed by physicians in a given department (these physicians have the same phone extension, X3422). In this case, in order to preserve database integrity, we must delete the ATTENDS rows before we can delete the PHYSICIANs. Therefore, we would

```
DELETE ATTENDS
    WHERE A-PHYSICIAN-ID IN
        (SELECT PHYSICIAN-ID
            FROM PHYSICIAN
            WHERE PHYSICIAN-PHONE = 'X3422')
DELETE PHYSICIAN
    WHERE PHYSICIAN-PHONE = 'X3422'
```

Changing Database Contents

To update data in SQL/DS we must inform the DBMS what relation, columns, and tuples are involved. Suppose an incorrect charge were entered for patient number 1234 and item number 307. The following SQL/DS UPDATE statement would institute an appropriate correction:

```
UPDATE BILLED
    SET B-CHARGE = 322.50
    WHERE B-PATIENT-NO = 1234
        AND B-ITEM-CODE = 307
```

The SET command can also change a value to NULL by SET columnname = NULL. With UPDATE as well as DELETE, the WHERE clause may contain a subquery.

Modifying Data Through a View

Views are primarily intended for ease of data retrieval, but it is possible under limited circumstances to modify (INSERT, DELETE, and UPDATE) base table data by referring to a view. In SQL/DS, view data modification is limited by the following restrictions:

1. Only views that are simple row-and-column subsets of a single base table are updatable (that is, the view cannot include such operations as join, group by, distinct, or any data aggregation function).

2. A column in a view derived from mathematical expressions on base data may not be updated.

3. A view defined from another view is not updatable.

4. A new row may not be inserted into a view table when the base table affected would have a missing value for a column defined as NOT NULL.

One feature of view definition that was not mentioned in the prior section on defining views is the WITH CHECK OPTION. If this option is included in the view definition, all INSERTs and UPDATEs against this view will be checked to ensure that the new or changed row does still fit the view definition. For example, consider the following simple view for a selected subset of items:

```
CREATE VIEW SOME-ITEMS
    AS SELECT *
        FROM ITEM
        WHERE ITEM-CODE BETWEEN 200 AND 300
        WITH CHECK OPTION
```

This view can be used to insert new rows or change existing rows in the ITEM table. However, attempts to insert an item with a code outside this range will be rejected. The check option is not, however, inherited. Thus, a view created from another view does not implicitly have the check option of the original view. Keller (1986) provides further discussion of interpreting and handling updates through a view.

Special Language Features

Relational DBMSs support both interactive entry and processing of commands as well as the ability to develop and save procedures or routines, possibly parameter-driven, for repeated execution. SQL when used in interactive mode processes one query at a time. That is, as soon as the user presses the RETURN key, SQL tries to process the command. The most recent command is held in memory until the next command is entered. Thus, if the previous command did not work as expected, due to a typing, syntax, or logical error, a CHANGE command can be used to modify the most recent command. A RECALL command is used to display the most recent command. One would likely use RECALL right after a CHANGE to ensure that only the desired modifications were performed as expected.

In contrast, INGRES provides procedure processing through buffer management. As the user enters INGRES commands, they are placed in a workspace and held until a \GO is entered. Thus, the buffer may contain one or many INGRES commands. This buffer may be edited at any time by entering \E, at which time INGRES is exited and the user is automatically put into his or her editor of choice, with the current buffer as the file being edited. When this editing is complete, the user terminates the editor in the normal way and is returned to INGRES in the place where he or she exited, but with the updated buffer. The user can then add more lines to the buffer and execute or may at any time issue a \W and provide a file name to save the buffer. Later, whenever the user wishes to run this same procedure again, a \I with the file name will include this prewritten routine into the buffer for execution, editing, or enhancement.

Stored Commands   SQL/DS provides two methods for using stored commands, so that frequently used commands do not have to be rekeyed each time. The first method is for individual commands. After a single command is entered and executed (and the user sees that it was processed as expected), the command can be saved to a file. SQL/DS uses the STORE filename command to specify the saving of a command into a named file. RECALL filename will retrieve a command file, and START tells SQL/DS to execute the retrieved command. These two steps can be combined in one via the START filename command. LIST SQL * displays a list of all the stored query file names. LIST SQL filename simply lists the contents of the stored command file named in the command. A RECALLed command may be changed and restored afterward by STORE filename REPLACE. Finally, a command file can be dropped by ERASE filename.

The second method for handling stored commands is for procedures that involve multiple commands or commands with parameters to be filled in when run. Such procedures are handled through a relational table called ROUTINE. The user may create the table and then store different routines or procedures for subsequent execution. Further, these routines may contain parameters, values for which are to be provided when executed. A user's routines are all stored in the same ROUTINE table and are identified by name in this table. Suppose we wanted to be able to display on demand the locations of a given physician's patients. The part of the ROUTINE table that would store this function would be

ROUTINE

NAME	SEQNO	COMMAND	REMARKS
PHREPORT	10	SELECT PATIENT-NO, LOCATION	
PHREPORT	20	FROM ROOM, ATTENDS	
PHREPORT	30	WHERE A-PHYSICIAN-ID IN &1	
PHREPORT	40	AND A-PATIENT-NO = PATIENT-NO	
PHREPORT	50	DISPLAY	

Remarks can be added to each line to document the routine for others who might use the routine. The &1 indicates that the user of the routine is to provide one value or a set of values for the parameter (A-PHYSICIAN-ID) of this procedure.

Customizing Output Format   Because the result of a relational operation on one or more tables is itself a table, the standard SQL output format is that of a table. When this "bare bones" approach is not sufficient, special output formatting commands can be used to spruce up the output appearance. Although different SQL implementations will vary, the following formatting options are frequently available:

- Specifying a column heading other than the column name or default expression label
- Changing a column width
- Placing blank lines between groups of rows and/or creating group subtotals
- Adding a title at the top or bottom of the page or screen
- Excluding a column from the display of the previous command
- Changing the symbol used as a column separator (for example, from two blanks to five or to a vertical bar)

Each of these functions is specified in a FORMAT command. The FORMAT command is entered after the SQL command to which it applies and, similar to STORE, is a separate command that applies to the contents of the command buffer. The effect of FORMAT commands are cumulative until another SQL command is entered.

Suppose we had entered the following SQL command that prints the contents of the BILLED table assuming a 10% increase on all charges.

SELECT B-PATIENT-NO, B-ITEM-CODE, B-CHARGE*1.1
    FROM BILLED

The three columns in the result of this query would appear with column headings as

B-PATIENT-NO   B-ITEM-CODE   EXPRESSION 1

The FORMAT commands

FORMAT COLUMN 1 NAME 'THE PATIENT'
FORMAT COLUMN 2 NAME 'THE ITEM'
FORMAT COLUMN 3 NAME 'THE NEW CHARGE'

would cause the previous query to be reexecuted with the result shown with the following column headings

THE PATIENT   THE ITEM   THE NEW CHARGE

Columns may be referenced by their position number in the display (as is done here) or by current column heading/name.

Creating an Interactive Session Log   When using a RDBMS interactively, it may be convenient for the user to create a transcript of the session in order to have a hard copy as a data entry audit trail or for other purposes. Many systems provide an automatic facility to accomplish this (SQL/DS installations vary since SQL/DS itself does not provide a logging facility). In INGRES this is called the script function and can be activated by entering

\SCRIPT and entering a file name into which the session log will be stored. Everything that appears to the user on the screen will be written to this file, which can then be printed or sent to other users. Session logging can be dynamically turned on and off by using \SCRIPT as a toggle switch. Note that this is a screen journal function, which is quite distinct from the data modification journalizing capability related to database recovery (discussed later in this chapter).

Host Language Interface Most relational DBMSs and most implementations of SQL not only have a self-contained interactive command processor but also permit access to the database from a host procedural language. In this case, SQL commands are embedded in a procedural language (like COBOL, FORTRAN, or C) program. Special language features are needed to convert the set orientation of the SQL commands for use by record-by-record commands in the third-generation language program. We will address these procedural programming capabilities of SQL and other relational systems in Chapter 14.

TRANSACTION INTEGRITY FACILITIES

Relational DBMSs are no different from other types of database managers in that one of their primary responsibilities is to ensure that database maintenance is properly and completely handled. Data maintenance is defined in units of work called transactions, which, like the network systems of Chapter 11, involve one or more data manipulation commands. What is needed are commands to define the boundaries of a transaction, to commit the work of a transaction as a permanent change to the database, and to purposely and properly abort a transaction. In addition, data recovery services are required to clean up after abnormal termination of database processing in the middle of a transaction.

In SQL/DS, the relevant transaction integrity commands are

SET AUTOCOMMIT:	Specifies whether changes to a table are made permanent after each command (ON) or only when work is explicitly made permanent (OFF) by the COMMIT WORK command
COMMIT WORK:	Specifies that all changes made to a database since the last COMMIT WORK command are to be made permanent (useful only when AUTO-COMMIT is OFF)
ROLLBACK WORK:	Informs SQL/DS to undo all changes made to the database since the last COMMIT WORK command

BACKOUT:	Informs SQL/DS to nullify all changes made since the last SAVE (sub) command during the execution of an INPUT command (only relevant if AUTOCOMMIT is ON)

In SQL/DS, the effects of any data maintenance command do not occur immediately. If changes are *not* to be automatically made by the DBMS (AUTOCOMMIT OFF), then all changes are held in a workspace until the user explicitly issues the command that defines the end of one transaction and the beginning of the next (COMMIT WORK). If, before executing this command, the user enters ROLLBACK WORK, then the workspace is cleared and the database retains the same contents present before the transaction began (and users have no idea any changes were attempted). (ROLLBACK WORK is equivalent to ABORT TRANSACTION in CODASYL network systems.)

If changes are to be automatically made (AUTOCOMMIT ON), then they still are not made until the next SQL command is given or an END command is issued; END indicates that the transaction is complete (in this case each transaction is composed of a single SQL command). Before the issue of END or the next command, a ROLLBACK WORK will undo the changes of the last modification command. Although the AUTOCOMMIT ON feature is convenient, it does force one to do work one command at a time, which may not correspond to the logical units of business transactions.

SET AUTOCOMMIT is an interactive command, so a given user session of SQL/DS can be dynamically controlled for appropriate integrity measures. Since each SQL INSERT, INPUT, UPDATE, and DELETE command typically works only on one table at a time and some data maintenance (such as deletion of all patient data for a given patient from the Mountain View Community Hospital database) requires updating of multiple tables for the work to be complete, these transaction integrity commands are very important in clearly defining whole units of database changes that must be completed in full for the database to retain integrity.

Further, some RDBMSs have concurrency controls that handle the updating of a shared database by concurrent users and journalizing database changes so that a database can be recovered after abnormal terminations in the middle of a transaction or to undo erroneous transactions. A relational database designer, to ensure the integrity of a particular database, must be sensitive to transaction integrity and recovery issues and must make sure that application programmers are appropriately informed of when these commands are to be used.

QUERY-BY-EXAMPLE

Relational DBMSs have been designed for a variety of users, not all of whom want to use a structured query language, no matter how much more productive and easy it may be compared to conventional procedural programming languages. Today the most common end-user interface into an SQL (and other) relational database is a style known as Query-By-Example, or QBE. We address this style in detail here. Since many personal computer products have also adopted this as one of the available user interfaces, this section is also important to a variety of PC SQL and non-SQL system.

Query-By-Example was originally developed by Zloof (1977) and is a program, QBE (IBM Corp., 1980), available for use with SQL/DS and DB2. Not only is it visually quite different, but several research studies (for example, Greenblatt and Waxman, 1978; Thomas and Gould, 1975) have also shown that even with relatively little training, student subjects formulated QBE queries in less time and with greater accuracy than did subjects using SQL or a relational algebra-based language.

QBE is available under the Query Management Facility (QMF) as a data manipulation language (SQL may also be accessed through QMF). QMF takes the table that results from a query formulated in QBE or SQL and produces a stylized report to the users' specifications. QMF is, therefore, a shell under which QBE can be run. Since QBE (and SQL) produce only one kind of output, simple relational tables, QMF greatly enhances the output generation capabilities for relational data management, although business graphics output is not supported.

QBE is not really meant to provide any type of data definition facility, although table definition is possible. QBE is typically used to access an existing SQL database, although under the IBM VM/CMS operating system it can also extract data from IMS databases.

A user interacts with QBE on a cathode ray tube (CRT) terminal by filling in values in different cells of a table template. QBE displays a skeleton table, and the user enters values:

TABLE NAME HERE	Column name here	Column name here
	Condition or examples in here	Condition or examples in here

The symbol P. may be entered in these cells to indicate what the user would like printed. For example, if we forget what columns there are in the PATIENT table, we can ask QBE to DRAW PATIENT or we can complete a blank table template:

PATIENT P.			

QBE would respond with

PATIENT	PATIENT-NO	PATIENT-NAME	PATIENT-ADDR

If a complete table is too wide to appear on one screen, only the left part of it is shown; function keys can then be used to scroll left and right to see other segments of the table. Other function keys can be used to scroll vertically, add a row or column, and widen columns.

If we do not know the names of any tables in the database, we simply ask to use the TABLES table and enter P. under the TBNAME column. The TABLES table is part of the SQL data catalog.

Suppose we wanted to display in ascending order by patient number those patients who had been charged for item 307. With QBE we would formulate this query by indicating the condition directly in a table. This particular query would be formulated as

BILLED	B-PATIENT-NO	B-ITEM-CODE	B-CHARGE
	P.AO.	307	

The equivalent SQL/DS query is

> SELECT B-PATIENT-NO FROM BILLED WHERE
>   B-ITEM-CODE = 307
>   ORDER BY B-PATIENT-NO

The result would be a display of a similar table, with only the B-PATIENT-NO data column, listing all the patient numbers for people who have had a charge for item 307. If we wanted patients charged for item 307 or 807, we would complete a table template with two rows (and an implied OR logical operator between these rows), as follows:

BILLED	B-PATIENT-NO	B-ITEM-CODE	B-CHARGE
	P.	307	
	P.	807	

The equivalent SQL/DS query is

> SELECT DISTINCT B-PATIENT-NO FROM BILLED
>   WHERE B-ITEM-CODE IN (307, 807)

These examples clearly illustrate one of the main advantages of QBE—that is, a significant reduction in keystrokes compared to a structured query langauge such as SQL. This ease of use through minimal keystrokes, coupled with the input/commands and output being in the same format, makes QBE easy to learn. Also, the opportunity to use a database is opened to more users—those who do not want to invest in learning a structured query language or who have a fear of such languages and keyboard usage.

We can also write queries that involve multiple conditions in QBE. To associate multiple conditions together we must use example column values (from which Query-By-Example gets its name). Consider the situation in which we want to know if anyone has been charged between $550 AND $600 for item 807. To answer this in QBE we would

BILLED	B-PATIENT-NO	B-ITEM-CODE	C-CHARGE
	P._ 2222	807	>550
	_ 2222	807	<600

The equivalent SQL/DS query is

SELECT B-PATIENT-NO FROM BILLED
    WHERE B-ITEM-CODE = 807 AND
        B-CHARGE BETWEEN 551 and 599

The second condition line in the QBE example specifies finding all CHARGES tuples with item code 807 and with a charge less than $600; the example 2222 in the second line stands for whatever patient number is stored in a qualified tuple (the _ in front of the 2222 signifies that 2222 is an *example* value, not a constant qualifier, as 807 is in the following column). The first condition line says print this patient number if the charge is also greater than $550. The example patient number is used to link these two joint conditions together.

Frequently used queries can be stored by name and recalled. Stored commands can be simply recalled (printed in their table form) and possibly modified/customized, or can be directly executed.

Data maintenance is performed in a similar fashion. For example, we indicate update with a U., instead of P., under the table name. The symbols D. and I. are used, respectively, to indicate delete and insert. To illustrate, if we wanted to increase the charge 10% for all people who have been charged for item 807, we would complete the template as follows:

BILLED	B-PATIENT-NO	B-ITEM-CODE	B-CHARGE
U.		807	_ 500*1.1

The equivalent SQL/DS update command is:

UPDATE BILLED SET B-CHARGE = CHARGE*1.1
    WHERE B-ITEM-CODE = 807

In this case, _500 is an "example" of an existing value for B-CHARGE. QBE will take whatever value actually exists and multiply it by 1.1. It is from the use of such "example" data that QBE gets its name.

Other more complex queries are possible in QBE. Suppose we know that patient with number 1234 had been charged for item 450 and we wanted to know if anyone else had been charged more for this item than had patient 1234. This would be written in QBE as

BILLED	B-PATIENT-NO	B-ITEM-CODE	B-CHARGE
	1234	450	_ 500
	P.	450	> _ 500

In this situation we do not even need to know exactly what patient 1234 was charged for item 450; we simply use an example to relate the two tuples.

The equivalent SQL/DS query is

SELECT B-PATIENT-NO FROM BILLED CA
   WHERE CA.B-ITEM-CODE = 450 AND CB.B-CHARGE >
   (SELECT B-CHARGE FROM BILLED CB
   WHERE CB.B-ITEM-CODE = 450 AND
   CB.B-PATIENT-NO = 1234)

When these conditions are too difficult to state by linking different condition rows or too long to enter in a column cell, QBE supports a Condition Box, separate from the table template, for entry of such conditional statements. Suppose we wanted to know what patients had been charged more than $500 combined for item codes 307 (X rays) and 413 (lab tests). Since the condition involves arithmetic across two rows of the BILLED table, the condition box is required. This query would be represented in QBE as

BILLED	B-PATIENT-NO	B-ITEM-CODE	B-CHARGE
	P._ 1234	307	_ Q
	_ 1234	413	_ P

CONDITIONS

_ Q + _ P > 500

Refer to Zloof (1977) for additional examples of this powerful capability.

Data aggregation functions are also permitted in QBE. For example, the total charges for patient no. 1234 would be specified as

BILLED	B-PATIENT-NO	B-ITEM-CODE	B-CHARGE
	P.1234		P.SUM.ALL._Q

for which the equivalent SQL query would be

SELECT SUM(B-CHARGE) FROM BILLED GROUPED BY
   B-PATIENT-NO HAVING B-PATIENT-NO = 1234

Other aggregation functions for counting number of rows, averaging, and finding minimum and maximum values are available.

As a final example of the capabilities of QBE we will illustrate how two tables can be linked and queries written that place conditions on the related tables. Suppose we want to know the descriptions of the items for which patient 1234 has been charged. This query involves both the BILLED and the ITEM tables. There is a way to get QBE to display two table templates. We would then fill these templates in as follows:

BILLED	B-PATIENT-NO	B-ITEM-CODE	B-CHARGE	
	1234	_333		P._D

ITEM	ITEM-CODE	DESCRIPTION
	_333	_D

Here again, the example item code of 333 is used to link tuples. Since the result of any query must be a single table, the _D is used to "pull" the description into the one table.

QBE is especially interesting when we use a color CRT. QBE is designed to highlight column names in different colors, depending on their usage (condition, example, printing, and so on).

SUMMARY

Relational DBMSs have been characterized in this chapter as viewing data in flat files or tables; manipulating data using commands that are, or are equivalent to, the relational algebra operators of PROJECT, SELECT, and JOIN; and providing an implementation-independent access to data (for example, independent of the existence or nonexistence of key indexes).

This chapter has concentrated on the SQL language for relational database definition and manipulation. This standard has been criticized for many flaws, and in reaction to these and to increase the power of the language, extensions are constantly under review by the ANSI X3H2 committee responsible for the SQL standard. In addition, other standard bodies (European Community Norms, International Standards Organization, and others) are working on updates to the original SQL standard.

Some of the flaws identified for SQL are

- Inefficient syntax in which many queries can be written in several different ways (sometimes with vastly different processing speeds)
- Permitting duplicate rows in relations
- Inadequate support of subqueries (for example, not all of the relational operators can be used in subqueries)
- Inadequate support of true, false, and unknown logical operations and handling of unknown or missing values in data aggregation functions (like MAX and AVG)

The potential extensions to SQL (which now appear in some SQL implementations and will be added to others in the future) include

- Specification of a default value clause to column definitions; options would include NULL, a specified constant for that column, or a global default value constant
- Integrity clause (similar to the INGRES integrity command) that can be included with a column definition
- Primary key and foreign key clauses to specify referential integrity restrictions
- Allowing UNION, MINUS, and INTERSECT to be used in view definitions, in a subquery, and in INSERT commands

- Allowing the range points in a BETWEEN expression to be listed either smaller-to-larger value or larger-to-smaller value

Relational systems were criticized for many years because of their relative inefficiency compared with network systems. However, with recent performance improvements, with judicious use of key indexes, or with the implementation on a database machine, a database designer is now able to construct relational databases that can be efficiently processed. Host language interfaces to relational systems can be used to provide the detailed data processing controls still necessary for customized programming. Report writers, graphics generators, screen and form painters, and a variety of other related tools make many relational DBMSs like SQL/DS, DB2, ORACLE, and INGRES very comprehensive system development environments. Increasingly, relational systems are being used to initially develop and iteratively evolve all types of information systems.

It is our suggestion that no one DBMS architecture, even relational, will be totally dominant. First, different applications require different data management capabilities. Second, different organizations have various data processing traditions and skills that will naturally make them tend to select different technologies. Third, the large installed base of database applications means that it can be very expensive to convert all organizational data and programs to one DBMS. And finally, there is no reason to doubt that a new Charles Bachman or Ted Codd is already at work on a new generation of DBMS. In fact, systems for the object-oriented data model are now appearing, and many believe these will be superior to relational systems. Some insights into the trends in the database field will be presented in Chapter 15. One of the major trends is the increasing use of stand-alone and networked personal computers for data management. Relational systems for this computing environment will be addressed in the next chapter.

Chapter Review

REVIEW QUESTIONS

1. Define each of the following terms:
   - a. view
   - b. relational algebra
   - c. relational calculus
   - d. embedded query language
   - e. Query-By-Example
   - f. integrity assertion
   - g. equi-JOIN
   - h. natural JOIN
   - i. outer JOIN
   - j. SQL/DS subquery
   - k. SQL/DS joining
   - l. INTERSECT
   - m. row clustering
   - n. null value
   - o. Boolean operator
   - p. LIKE operator
   - q. commit
   - r. rollback
   - s. correlated subquery

2. Explain the following statement regarding SQL/DS: Any query that can be written using the subquery approach can also be written using the joining approach, but not vice-versa.

3. Explain the difference between features like HELP in INGRES and the ability to query the data definition catalog in SQL with the capabilities of a data dictionary/directory.

4. Explain why JOIN is called a binary operator. How is JOIN accomplished, in general, in SQL?

5. Drawing on material covered in prior chapters, explain the factors to be considered in deciding whether to create a key index for a table.

6. Explain why it is sometimes necessary to prefix a column name with a table name in query language statements.

7. Explain the purpose of the RANGE statement in INGRES.

8. In the section on Query-By-Example two queries were illustrated: one for an implied OR logical operator between the two rows of the query template and one for an implied AND logical operator between the two rows of the query template. What construct was used to distinguish between ORing and ANDing the conditions in two rows?

9. Explain why it is necessary to limit the kinds of updates performed on data when referencing data through a view.

10. What kinds of modules are typically found in a RDBMS or in related products for the total management and presentation of data?

11. What makes a RDBMS truly relational?

12. Explain how a view can be used for data security.

13. Suppose you are a user of SQL/DS and you are unfamiliar with the tables stored on your system. What on-line facilities exist to help you learn what data is kept on your system?

14. What is the difference between COUNT and COUNT DISTINCT in SQL? When will these two commands generate the same and different results?

15. When would you use an outer JOIN instead of a natural JOIN?

16. What is the difference between a stored SQL command and an SQL routine?

17. What is the purpose of the COMMIT command in SQL? How does COMMIT relate to the notion of a business transaction (such as entry of a customer order or issuing a customer invoice)?

PROBLEMS AND EXERCISES

1. Match the following terms to the appropriate definitions.

_____ equi-JOIN

_____ natural JOIN

_____ outer JOIN

_____ relational algebra

_____ relational calculus

a) a standard relational query and definition language

b) provides rapid access to rows

c) accomplishes JOIN within WHERE clause

d) also called a virtual table

_____ SQL

_____ view

_____ index

_____ commit

_____ rollback

_____ database machine

_____ null value

_____ host language interface

e) all rows are kept in result table

f) changes to a table are made permanent

g) redundant columns are kept

h) uses SELECT, PROJECT, and JOIN commands

i) changes to a table are undone

j) redundant columns are not kept

k) allows access to a relational database from procedural langauge programs

l) hardware that performs DBMS functions

m) missing or nonexisting value

Problems 2-10 are based on the Mountain View College database from Chapter 7. The 3NF relations for that application are repeated below.

STUDENT#	STUDENT-NAME	MAJOR
38214	BRIGHT	IS
69173	SMITH	PM
. . .		

STUDENT (STUDENT#, STUDENT-NAME, MAJOR)

INSTRUCTOR-NAME	INSTRUCTOR-LOCATION
CODD	B104
KEMP	B213
LEWIS	D317
. . .	

INSTRUCTOR (INSTRUCTOR-NAME, INSTRUCTOR-LOCATION)

COURSE#	COURSE-TITLE	INSTRUCTOR NAME
IS 350	DATA BASE	CODD
IS 465	SYS ANAL	KEMP
PM 300	PROD MGT	LEWIS
QM 440	OP RES	KEMP
. . .		

COURSE (COURSE#, COURSE-TITLE, INSTRUCTOR-NAME)

STUDENT #	COURSE#	GRADE
38214	IS 350	A
38214	IS 465	C
69173	IS 465	A
69173	PM 300	B
69173	QM 440	C
. . .		

REGISTRATION (STUDENT#, COURSE#, GRADE)

2. Write a full database description using the SQL data definition language. Assume the following attribute data types:

STUDENT# (integer, primary key)
STUDENT-NAME (25 characters)
MAJOR (5 characters)

INSTRUCTOR-NAME (25 characters, primary key)
INSTRUCTOR-LOCATION (5 characters)
COURSE# (6 characters, primary key)
COURSE-TITLE (10 characters)
GRADE (1 character)

3. Write commands to document your table definitions as follows:
   a. Include the following comment for the COURSE-TITLE column of the COURSE relation: "Title must be approved by the curriculum committee."
   b. Permit the name COURSE-GRADE to be used as an alternative name for the REGISTRATION table.
   c. Permit the name OFFICE to be used instead of the column heading INSTRUCTOR-LOCATION in queries.

4. Define the following view using a SQL view definition.

STUDENT#	STUDENT-NAME	MAJOR	COURSE#		GRADE
38214	Bright	IS	IS	350	A
38214	Bright	IS	IS	465	C
69173	Smith	PM	IS	465	A
69173	Smith	PM	PM	300	B
69173	Smith	PM	QM	440	C

5. Write a SQL command to create an index called FIND-GRADE for the concatenated primary key (STUDENT# and COURSE#) in the REGISTRATION relation.

6. Write ORACLE commands that will cause rows from the REGISTRATION table to be clustered with the associated row from the STUDENT table (call the cluster STUDENT-DATA).

7. Before any row can be entered in the REGISTRATION table, it is important that the COURSE to be entered already exists in the COURSE table (referential integrity). Write a PERMIT definition (INGRES) that will enforce this constraint.

8. Write SQL retrieval commands for each of the following queries:
   a. Display the instructor location for the instructor Lewis.
   b. Display the student number and student name for all information system (IS) majors.
   c. Display the total number of students who are IS majors.

9. Write a SQL retrieval command to produce the table shown in Problem 4 above. Note the similarity between the view definition (Problem 4) and the retrieval command (Problem 8). Under what conditions would each of these commands be used?

10. Write SQL commands to perform the following operations:
    a. Add a row to the REGISTRATION table for student number 12345 who received a B in IS 200.
    b. Delete all rows for student number 56789 in the REGISTRATION table.
    c. Change the grade for student number 38214 in IS 465 from C to B.

11. Formulate the following using Query-By-Example:
    a. Queries in Problem 8
    b. Query to produce the table in Problem 4

     c. Listing of all student numbers for students who received an A or a B in IS 350

     d. Listing of all student names for students who received a B in QM 440.

12. Suggest several alternative ways for a relational DBMS, such as SQL/DS, to handle the ALTER TABLE command. Consider the possibility of both adding and deleting columns.

13. Write SQL commands to answer the following question from the Mountain View Community Hospital database of Figure 12-2: What physicians have performed a tonsillectomy?

14. Write SQL commands to answer the following question from the database of Figure 12-2: What patients (display PATIENT-NAME) have been charged for the item TELEVISION?

15. Show how you would complete QBE skeleton templates to answer the question of Problem 13.

16. Write an SQL/DS query to answer the following question about Mountain View Community Hospital: What patients (display PATIENT-NO) are being treated by Dr. Wilcox and not Dr. Franklin?

17. Write an SQL/DS query to answer the following question about Mountain View Community Hospital: What patients (display PATIENT-NO) have not been treated by Dr. Jefferson?

18. Write integrity assertions for INGRES to restrict DATE-DISCHARGED in Figure 12-2 to values greater than DATE-ADMITTED for each patient in the database.

19. Write SQL/DS commands to find those physicians that have not yet treated any patients at Mountain View Community Hospital.

20. Assume that the ITEM relation of Figure 12-2 is altered to also include STD-CHG, the standard charge for an item. Write the SQL/DS commands to display the patient numbers for those patients that have been charged above standard.

21. Suppose you are designing the application program that deletes all patient-related information at the predetermined purging date (six months after discharge). The update of what tables would have to be included in the logical transaction for this database maintenance?

22. Compare the data integrity capabilities of the CODASYL data model with the SQL data definition facilities. What types of data integrity problems (if any) can be avoided in the one and not in the other?

23. Discuss the advantages and disadvantages of creating a standard for a relational system as ANSI has done for SQL.

24. Sketch a QBE query template to answer the query: What patients are being treated by Dr. Wilcox and Dr. Franklin?

25. Consider a relational system with which you are familiar. Rate this system against Codd's "12 Rules for a Truly Relational System" that appear in the appendix.

26. Review Chapter 3 and list the types of semantic controls mentioned there. Which of these can be enforced by SQL and which cannot be enforced by SQL?

27. Write an SQL command to restrict user TANN from deleting records in the PRODUCT table.

REFERENCES

Banerjee, J., R. I. Baum, and D. K. Hsiao. 1978. "Concepts and Capabilities of a Database Computer." *ACM-TODS* 3 (December), 347–383.

Chamberlin, D. D., M. M. Astrahan, K. P. Eswaran, P. P. Griffiths, R. A. Lorie, J. W. Mehl, P. Reisner, and B. W. Wade. 1976. "SEQUEL: A Unified Approach to Data Definition, Manipulation and Control." *IBM Journal of Research and Development* 20 (Nov.), 560–574.

Codd, E. F. 1970. "A Relational Model of Data for Large Shared Data Banks." *Communications of the ACM* 13 (June), 377–387.

Codd, E. F. 1982. "Relational Database: A Practical Foundation for Productivity." *Communications of the ACM* 25 (Feb.), 109–117.

Codd, E. F. 1985a. "Does Your DBMS Run by the Rules?" *Computerworld* (Oct. 21), 49-64.

Codd, E. F. 1985b. "Is Your DBMS Really Relational?" *Computerworld* (Oct. 14), ID/1-ID/9.

Computerworld. 1985a. "Britton Lee Unwraps Trio of Data Base Machines." (Jan. 28), 5.

Computerworld. 1985b. "DBC/1012 Tool Upgraded." (June 24), 42.

Date, C. J. 1987a. *An Introduction to Database Systems,* Vol. 1. (4th ed.) Reading, Mass.: Addison-Wesley.

Date, C. J. 1987b. "Where SQL Falls Short." *Datamation* (May 1), 83, 84, 86.

Epstein, R. 1983. "Why Database Machines?" *Datamation* (July), 139, 140, 144.

Greenblatt, D., and J. Waxman. 1978. "A Study of Three Database Query Languages." In *Database: Improving Usability and Responsiveness,* ed. B. Shneiderman. New York: Academic Press.

IBM Corp. 1980. *Query-by-Example: Terminal User's Guide.* Form SH2 0-2078-1. Irving, Tex.: IBM Corp.

IBM Corp. 1985. *SQL/Data System: Concepts and Facilities for VM/System Product.* Nov. Form GH24-5065-1. Endicott, N.Y.: IBM Corp.

IBM Corp. 1987. *IBM DATABASE 2 (DB2) General Information.* May. Form GC26-4073-03. Endicott, N.Y.: IBM Corp.

Keller, A. M. 1986. "The Role of Semantics in Translating View Updates." *IEEE Computer* (Jan.), 63-73.

Kim, W. 1979. "Relational Database Systems." *ACM Computing Surveys* 11 (Sept.), 185–211.

Kroenke, D. 1983. *Database Processing.* (2d ed.) Chicago: Science Research Associates.

McEnany, M. 1985. "Data Base Machine's Appeal Rising." *Computerworld* (May 20), 63, 70.

ORACLE Corp. 1988. *ORACLE Application Tools for MS-DOS User's Guide.* Menlo Park, Calif.: ORACLE Corp.

Relational Technology, Inc. 1989. *Introducing INGRES for the UNIX and VMS Operating Systems.* (Release 6.3). Nov. Alameda, Calif.: Relational Technology.

Rettig, M. 1989. "Gourmet Guide to the DB2 Catalog." *Data Base Programming and Design* 2 (Feb.), 26-32.

Sayles, J. S. 1989. "All in a Row." *Data Based Advisor* 7 (Dec.), 36-42.

Stonebraker, M. R., E. Wong, P. Kreps, and G. Held. 1976. "The Design and Implementation of INGRES." *ACM-TODS* 1 (Sept.), 189–222.

Technical Committee X3H2—Database. 1986. *Database Language SQL.* (Jan.). American National Standards Institute.

Thomas, J. C., and J. D. Gould. 1975. "A Psychological Study of Query by Example." *Proceedings of National Computer Conference*. New York: AFIPS Press.

Ullman, J. D. 1980. *Principles of Database Systems*. Potomac, Md.: Computer Science Press.

Zloof, M. M. 1977. "Query-by-Example: A Data Base Language." *IBM Systems Journal* 16 (4), 324–343.

CHAPTER 13

Personal Computer Relational Systems

INTRODUCTION

The purpose of this chapter is to present an overview of the features of some of the most widely used personal computer relational DBMSs (or PC-RDBMSs). This chapter builds on Chapter 2, which introduced PC-RDBMS features through a sample database and the dBASE IV package.

This chapter does not present a complete, in-depth description of any particular PC-RDBMS—the goal is not to make you a skilled programmer in one package. Instead it is to prepare you to understand rapidly *any* package you might use by reviewing the salient features of PC-RDBMS products and the features of several typical kinds of products. In addition, you will be able to compare the capabilities of various packages and know what features to evaluate.

Further, this chapter concentrates on the "classical," or non-SQL, features of PC-RDBMSs. This is not to say that the SQL capabilities of PC-RDBMSs are not important—to the contrary, SQL provides a portability and migration capability not previously possible in such products. However, Chapter 12 discusses SQL within the context of mainframe systems, and the coverage there is transferable to PC products. Therefore, we will not repeat that discussion.

AN OVERVIEW OF PC-RDBMSs

It is difficult to put boundaries around the topic of DBMSs on personal computers. The power of personal computers (PCs) today, the migration of mainframe DBMS software to PCs, and the increasing sophistication of personal computer DBMSs all contribute to the difficulty in clearly distinguishing the unique characteristics of PC-DBMSs from products on mainframes. Further, PC-DBMSs today often cooperate with mainframe and local area network data management technologies. Thus, we can no longer think of PC-DBMSs as primarily stand-alone, single-user systems, or as separate technologies.

PC-RDBMSs are powerful systems building and prototyping tools. Typically, a PC-RDBMS includes or has available as add-on elements screen formatters, report writers, query languages, multiple host language interfaces, and special procedural or command languages for database processing. Not only are PC-RDBMSs used to build personal computer applications, but they are also used to prototype applications to be migrated to mainframes.

Many of the features of PC-RDBMSs are similar to the features of mainframe RDBMSs. However, this chapter has been written to stand on its own, separate from Chapter 12, which covered mainframe systems. On the other hand, we will assume familiarity with the basic relational terminology and database design presented in Chapter 3 and other earlier chapters. You may also want to read the appendix "Codd's 12 Rules for a Truly Relational System" to review the basic principles on which PC relational systems are built.

This chapter covers

- Unique features and issues in the design of personal computer databases

- The structure of relational algebra, the typical language form in current PC-RDBMSs

- User interfaces, including forms designers and report writers

- Capabilities to exchange data between different PC and mainframe file and database systems

- Multiuser environments for PC databases

Primarily, dBASE IV, R:BASE for DOS (version 2.11[1]), and some PARADOX 3.0 will be used to illustrate PC-RDBMSs (with a few references to ORACLE). These products will be used because they are among the most popular and because they are characteristic of many other products. A list of some of the most widely used PC-RDBMSs appears in Table 13-1.

---

[1] A new version of R:BASE, version 3.0, was released while this book was in production. Version 3.0 contains all of the same R:BASE capabilities discussed in this chapter, plus a more complete implementation of SQL. It includes a query-by-example query facility and an improved menu-driven user interface.

Table 13-1   Summary of Some Personal Computer Relational Systems

Package	dBASE IV	R: BASE for DOS	Paradox 3.0	DataEase 4.0	FoxBase + 2.1	PC/FOCUS 4.0	Professional ORACLE
Vendor	Ashton-Tate	Microrim	Borland International	DataEase	Fox Software	Information Builders	Oracle Corp.
SQL sublanguage	Yes	Single tables	No	No	No	Yes	Yes
Minimum memory	640K	512K	512K	640K	370K	640K	1536K
Multiuser	Yes	Yes	Yes	Yes	Yes	Yes	Yes
Maximum # open files	10	80	**	60	10	64	**
Maximum # fields per table	255	400	255	255	128	—	254
Data types*	CFL MD	ICF DT	IC FD	ICF LDT	ICF LDM	IC FL	ICF DB
QBE interface	Yes	No	Yes	Yes	Yes	Yes	Yes

* No limit   ** No limit   — Not known

* I = integer
C = character
F = float
M = memo
L = logical
D = date
T = time

Unique Features of PC-RDBMSs

Although the leading PC and mainframe DBMSs are becoming more equal in capabilities, there still are some differences. What makes a PC-RDBMS unique from its mainframe counterparts? First, some DBMS functions may be missing from PC-RDBMS products. Such functions have frequently been dropped because (at least in the past) PC databases have been used by only one user. Applications have been too simple to require the full range of DBMS power (which is why a PC implementation was chosen in the first place). However, the trend today is to include more and more features from the mainframe environment (for example, dBASE IV, R:BASE for DOS, and ORACLE have some functions to help in database backup and recovery).

The second difference between a mainframe system and a PC-RDBMS is in the operating environment of database processing. With mainframe systems, database processing occurs in a multiprogramming, multiuser environment. Concurrent access to the database must be controlled, and security protection is essential because of the shared data. In the PC arena, there are, in contrast, varying environments, which are discussed in the following sections.

Single-User Stand-Alone Approach   The single-user stand-alone approach remains a very common PC-DBMS environment. Here, a single user at a time uses a PC dedicated to that user's processing. The database is private in the sense that the user can take the diskettes away after use to prohibit other users from accessing the data. Further, the database on the PC is separate from any other database, including those on the mainframe from which some of the PC database may have been extracted. Thus, data may be duplicated, and synchronization of updating is a problem with which designers and users must deal.

Multiuser Stand-Alone Approach   In the multiuser stand-alone approach, a hard-disk-based database is shared among several concurrent users, who may all be using the same microprocessor with a multiprogramming-type operating system. More typically, they share a hard-disk file or database server from several PCs in a local area network (LAN). The LAN may also provide a gateway for access to other databases. Concurrency control and security may be limited or handled at a very coarse level (for example, file-level rather than record- or element-level lockout for update control). Here, as in the prior situation, the PC database is maintained separately from any mainframe database. This is, in fact, a major advantage, since unstructured, end-user access to the separate LAN database does not harm the performance of mainframe databases. Mainframe databases become high-volume warehouses that supply multiple-user databases (what some firms call "retail outlets").

Mainframe Link Approach The mainframe link is a relatively new but rapidly expanding class of PC-RDBMSs, in which the same or very similar DBMS products are provided at both the PC and mainframe computers. A communications link (hardware and software) is provided as part of the PC package. From the PC, a user can access a mainframe database as he or she would from a terminal. This access is done in so-called terminal emulation mode, in which the PC is made to act as a special terminal, such as an IBM 327x. The user can also have selected data from the mainframe transferred to the PC (often using the same type of retrieval command as in any data access statement but with an extra clause to specify that the destination of the result is a file, database, or table on the PC). And finally, the user can manipulate data at the PC using the same language and range of commands as on the mainframe. Thus, users familiar with the mainframe product require minimal training time to learn the PC version. The benefit is that the PC can be used to relieve a mainframe doing production database processing from also having to perform ad hoc inquiry processing. Performing both production and ad hoc processing can be expensive to support and can degrade the performance of the production database. Besides ORACLE, products such as PC/FOCUS (by Information Builders, Inc.) and PC/Nomad (by Must Software International) are examples of this category of product.

Multifunction Package Approach Multifunction packages have integrated DBMS functions along with other management support tools. For example, several spreadsheet packages (for example, Lotus 1-2-3, Quattro, Framework, and Microsoft Works) combine some simple RDBMS functions with spreadsheet and graphics capabilities. This class of PC-RDBMS should continue to expand as more general decision support system generators are created for personal computers.

Other Differences In addition to these environmental differences, a PC-RDBMS differs from its mainframe predecessors in the size of the database that it can manage. See Table 13-1 for examples of such restrictions. Newer versions of PC-RDBMS products relax such size constraints considerably. For example, R:BASE for DOS (version 2.11) from Microrim, Inc. (1988) permits as many records as the storage medium can handle, 80 tables per database, 800 data elements per table, and 4,096 characters per row. As word sizes and operating system capabilities on PCs expand, larger databases will become possible via PC-RDBMSs. A PC-RDBMS is also limited by the processing speed of a personal computer, especially the time required to access hard-disk or diskette storage. Actually, newer microprocessors (for example, the Intel 80386 or 80486) have processing speeds and main memory capacities equal to or greater than some minicomputers. Thus, the real limitation is the disk input/output rates.

Role of PC-DBMS in Data Management

A PC-DBMS has several distinct features that make it attractive as part of a general data management strategy:

1. A PC-DBMS provides *mainframelike DBMS functions* for organizations or organizational units that do not require the power of a mini- or mainframe computer.

2. A PC-DBMS allows computer users in organizations that have an existing mainframe DBMS to develop *end-user database applications that are truly independent from production, high-transaction volume databases.* Thus, the costly unstructured end-user access does not degrade production database processing and does not interfere with the performance of these production databases.

3. Newer PC-DBMS technologies essentially permit an organization to create *a type of distributed database* (decentralized with planned transfer of data between databases). This achieves greater host performance as well as reduces communication traffic in the computer network (see Chapter 15 for a discussion of distributed databases).

4. For those already using personal computers for management support, a PC-DBMS provides an additional *powerful tool to manage and present relevant data and information.*

5. A PC-DBMS and a database are *portable*, since for many of these products the DBMS and databases can be easily transported by moving diskettes. This not only benefits mobile managers but also means that the same DBMS and database can be used on mixed, yet compatible, machines (for example, several PCs running the MS-DOS operating system). This portability also impacts education—students learning a DBMS can do so at home or in a classroom or laboratory. Further, they can learn without disrupting other students (when their errors crash the DBMS or destroy a file of input transactions, it only affects their own workspace).

The principles of database management hold whether we deal with mainframe or PC databases. The major issues are shareability, integrity, consistency, security, and accessibility. PC and mainframe databases should all be managed as part of an organizational plan for the data resource. PC databases create a special burden on data administration and can be quite redundant and inconsistent, so integrity of data may be difficult to manage. Further, security of such distributed and independently managed data can be a challenge to ensure.

PC and mainframe products alike should be measured on the same features and data processing requirements. As with many mainframe products, the label *DBMS* is often given to a PC product that may only manage a single file or may only help in producing stylized reports from a single file. Thus, care should be taken to apply the same stringent requirements for PC data management products as have been introduced elsewhere in this text for DBMS products in general. PC-DBMSs exist on a different type of computer but should provide the same functionality.

PC-DBMSs and End-User Computing

End-user computing involves the development and use of computer-based applications by managers, executives, and occupational professionals, with little or no involvement by trained information system professionals. The proliferation of personal computers and the ease of use of spreadsheet, file management, word processing, business graphics, and desktop publishing software have opened new opportunities for the explosive, and potentially uncontrolled, deployment of systems in organizations.

Personal computer database applications can range from very simple data systems to databases with as complex a structure as any mainframe system. Today, personal computer DBMSs should not be treated as toy systems. They are sophisticated software packages that can either effectively solve significant data management problems or can be abused. Users of a PC-DBMS should be thoroughly trained in

- The use of the package
- Principles of good database design and documentation
- The need for proper backup and recovery practices
- The application of appropriate data security measures

In addition, the experience with end-user computing to date suggests that organization-wide support systems and policies are needed to manage the introduction of PC-DBMSs. Most organizations will standardize on one or just a few PC-DBMSs to more effectively provide training and consulting support. This control also means that the organization can write agreements with DBMS vendors that can result in significant savings from large-quantity purchases.

Equally important is the need to manage data as a corporate resource, which requires that databases on personal computers be defined and designed to be consistent with corporate methods. For example, data element naming conventions should still be applied. The need for a database on a PC should be reviewed by a data administrator or end-user consulting specialist to help the user determine if a PC-DBMS is the appropriate technology. If a PC-DBMS is appropriate, these advisors can help determine the best source of data for the PC database (for example, a mainframe database, local data entry, or possibly an external public data source). The end-user consultant can also help the user establish a local area network or PC-mainframe connection if the database is to be used by multiple employees.

Experience with PC databases and DBMSs should be shared throughout an organization. An information center or computer club is an excellent forum. A newsletter or users' group can also be effective in helping users better utilize the DBMS and in keeping issues of organization-wide data management before those using the PC-DBMS.

Structure and Components of PC Relational Systems

A PC-RDBMS is a multiple component product that frequently includes

- The **core DBMS,** which provides data definition, a relational query language, and data definition and retrieval functions (repository)

- An optional **run-time version** of the DBMS (basically the database control program—see Chapter 9) that allows only prewritten (and pre-compiled) programs to execute (that is, the user cannot enter ad hoc, interactive queries); this facility reduces the main memory requirements and allows software developers to bundle the DBMS with application software without requiring the purchaser to buy the complete DBMS

- A **programming language** that provides IF-THEN-ELSE logic, forms input and output, and presentation of menus and prompts to interactive users; programs can then be stored in command files to be used by nonprogrammers or to provide frequently used routines for inclusion in interactive sessions

- A **menu-driven front end** that uses "pop-up" or "pull-down" menus to prompt the user in completing each clause of each DBMS data definition, retrieval, modification, or other command; frequently this user-friendly aid will display the actual structured query on the screen as menu selections are made, allowing the user to verify visually the correctness of the query as interpreted, to be able to use the DBMS quickly without extensive training, and to learn the structured language by actually doing some database processing

- A **screen painter** that supports building CRT screen forms that make data entry and update easy and similar to the manual forms found in the organization and provides such features as drawing boxes, use of color and intensity, displaying cross-reference data (for example, automatically displaying on the screen the customer's name and address after the user enters the customer number in an order-entry-form), making data entry pleasant and reducing entry errors

- A **report writer** that supports extensive reporting features beyond those provided by the query or programming languages; such features as subtotals and totals, custom report layouts, control breaks, data value formatting, statistical analysis, page numbering and dating, and column labeling (often the report writer accepts only one database file as input, so a query or program must first merge data from related tables into a single file (or view), if necessary)

- A **business graphics** module that allows quick summarization of database contents in pie charts, line graphs, bar charts, and other business graphical formats

- An **applications generator** that supports building complete "turnkey" application systems from multiple stored programs and tree-structured menus to guide the user to the desired program in the application system (for example, entry of a new customer, entry of a customer order, or printing a product sales summary report)

- **File import/export utilities** that allow data to be entered into or extracted from a database and files used by other popular PC packages (for example, electronic spreadsheet and desktop publishing systems)

- A **natural language or tabular language processor** that allows a user to state a query in near English or select desired data by filling in a form or template on the screen

Usually the standard version of the PC-RDBMS is designed for single-user database access. Special versions of the DBMS are required for local area network environments or when interacting with both mainframe and PC databases.

Figure 13-1 illustrates the single-user environment of three popular and typical PC-RDBMSs: dBASE IV, R:BASE for DOS (version 2.11), and ORACLE (see Ashton-Tate, 1988; Microrim, Inc., 1987; ORACLE Corp., 1988).

The main structural difference between mainframe and PC relational systems is the style of query language. Relational calculus (typical of most mainframe products) and relational algebra (typical of the original style of many PC products) are the two major general styles. Chapter 12 deals extensively with relational calculus, especially the SQL standard. An SQL language, or some subset, is now frequently one of the query interfaces provided with PC-RDBMSs. The reader is referred to Chapter 12 to learn about this part of PC-RDBMSs, although we will discuss in this chapter some nonstandard SQL features in PC products. One additional PC-RDBMS that has significantly influenced the field is PARADOX 3.0, which uses the query-by-example programming style that was also introduced in Chapter 12.

A relational algebra language essentially has unary and binary table operators, whereas a relational calculus language allows more than two tables to be referenced in one command. Thus, relational algebra decomposes complicated retrieval statements into many statements, each of which deals with operations on one or two tables. A single relational algebra statement can be simpler to construct than a relational calculus statement. However, the full effect of database processing cannot be seen in relational algebra unless one analyzes potentially many statements.

DATA DEFINITION, REDEFINITION, AND INTEGRITY CONTROLS

Since the relational data model is relatively simple and uniformly adopted in PC-RDBMSs, there is little variation across packages in database creation

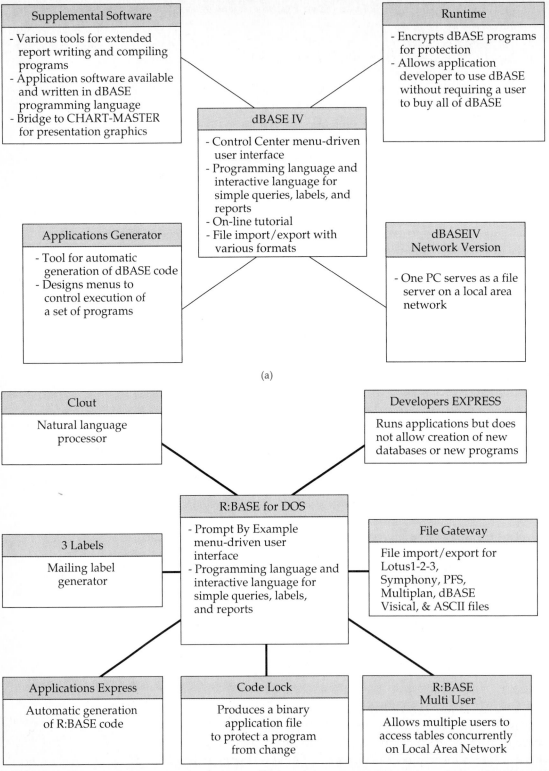

Supplemental Software

- Various tools for extended report writing and compiling programs
- Application software available and written in dBASE programming language
- Bridge to CHART-MASTER for presentation graphics

Runtime

- Encrypts dBASE programs for protection
- Allows application developer to use dBASE without requiring a user to buy all of dBASE

dBASE IV

- Control Center menu-driven user interface
- Programming language and interactive language for simple queries, labels, and reports
- On-line tutorial
- File import/export with various formats

Applications Generator

- Tool for automatic generation of dBASE code
- Designs menus to control execution of a set of programs

dBASEIV Network Version

- One PC serves as a file server on a local area network

(a)

Clout

Natural language processor

Developers EXPRESS

Runs applications but does not allow creation of new databases or new programs

R:BASE for DOS

- Prompt By Example menu-driven user interface
- Programming language and interactive language for simple queries, labels, and reports

3 Labels

Mailing label generator

File Gateway

File import/export for Lotus1-2-3, Symphony, PFS, Multiplan, dBASE Visical, & ASCII files

Applications Express

Automatic generation of R:BASE code

Code Lock

Produces a binary application file to protect a program from change

R:BASE Multi User

Allows multiple users to access tables concurrently on Local Area Network

(b)

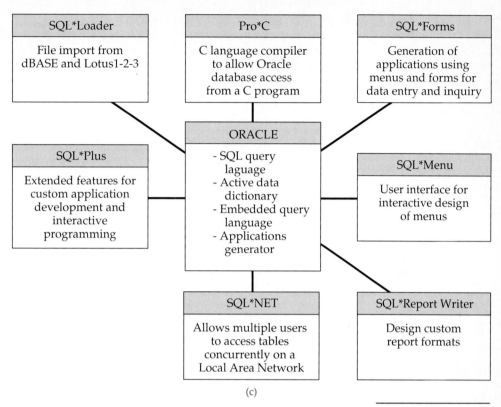

(c)

Figure 13-1
PC relational DBMS
environments:
(a) dBASE IV
(b) R:BASE for DOS
(c) ORACLE

capabilities. The most visible differences are in the user interface that guides a user through the database definition process.

Given a set of database requirements (say in entity-relationship notation) and a translation of this into relational notation (this translation process was outlined in Chapter 6), the designer of a personal computer relational database has only a few choices to make:

- Name, data type, length, and format for each column (called a field by most products)
- Rules or constraints to include in the data definitions to control database integrity (for example, do not allow missing or null values for a certain column)
- Columns or combinations of columns for which to create primary or secondary key indexes (see Chapter 7 for a discussion of indexes)

Data definition is usually done interactively by filling in blanks and choosing options on a data definition screen, which is a visual equivalent of a CREATE table command. Chapter 2 includes several illustrations of the database definition process in dBASE IV (see section "Database Definition in dBASE IV") for Pine Valley Furniture. We will not repeat the basic steps in database creation here. Although the particular data types, length of data names, and so on of data definitions may differ from product to product, the basic steps remain the same. In the remainder of this section we will highlight aspects of database creation not addressed in Chapter 2.

Data Definitions

One data type not illustrated in Chapter 2 but supported by most PC-RDBMSs is a very long, variable-length character string (called memo field by dBASE and note field by R:BASE). This type of field is helpful for recording comments, annotations, abstracts, or any other unstructured data. For example, a customer record could include a memo field that contains unstructured comments from sales staff about the sales potential of that customer. For simplicity of space management, such fields are not stored along with the other fields defined for a file but rather in a separate file. Usually, the user is unaware of this separation. In dBASE IV, a memo field can be up to 512K characters, although space for only 10 characters is initially allocated.

A table structure does not have to be specified interactively in dBASE IV, but rather the structure definition can itself be stored as data in one table and a new data table created from this definition table. This is especially useful when two tables are to have very similar structures. For example, the dBASE commands

.USE PRODUCT
.COPY TO ITEMDEF STRUCTURE EXTENDED

create a table ITEMDEF that contains the five fields that define each data element in a table (see, for example, Figure 2–12 for the PRODUCT table): field name, field type, field width, number of decimal places, and an index flag. (When we show dBASE commands directly, rather than selected from the Command Center, we show the dBASE command processor prompt, a period (.), at the beginning of a line as it would appear on the screen.) Each row in ITEMDEF is the definition of a field from the PRODUCT table. Data modification statements (to be covered later) can then be used to change the contents of the ITEMDEF table. That is, we can change field names or lengths, add new fields, delete fields, and so on, all appropriate for the new file being created. For example, this new file might specify field names that are local to a particular department. The ITEMDEF file could also be created and populated as is any other data file, rather than copied from an existing file structure. Then, the command

.CREATE ITEM FROM ITEMDEF

would define a new table, ITEM, for which field definitions would come from the contents of the ITEMDEF table. This command does not store data in ITEM but only defines the table structure. This CREATE (table) FROM (structure) command is especially useful as part of a prewritten program to perform all the necessary data definition building functions for a novice user. A similar command

.COPY STRUCTURE TO <filename> [FIELDS <field list>]

combines the above steps into one command (obviously without the ability to first change the table definitions). In the above notation, lowercase words inside <…> stand for names that someone would enter, and a clause in […] is optional. The above COPY command says: Copy the structure of the current database file to the named file, optionally including in the definition of the new file only the fields from the current file that are listed in the field list.

The R:BASE for DOS database definition approach is different from that in dBASE IV. In dBASE, columns are not objects by themselves but rather are characteristics of a file; that is, there is no recognition that two fields in two files might stand for the same domain of values. In R:BASE, each column in the database is itself a separate object. A file definition is a set of field definitions. When the same column (domain) appears in multiple tables (usually as primary, foreign, and cross-reference keys), the DBMS can then ensure that exactly the same data types, lengths, and so on are used each time the column is referenced. Columns may be defined directly as objects at the R:BASE DEFINE command level, or the definitions can be captured implicitly via the interactive screen input module Definition EXPRESS. This type of dictionary-driven database definition is very helpful in achieving database integrity.

R:BASE supports date, currency, integer, real (both single and double precision), text, and time data types for columns. A column may also be the result of an expression involving constants, global variables, and other columns from that table. We will illustrate here the process of defining columns and a table in the DEFINE mode. The following indicates the definition of just those columns for the PRODUCT table, although all database columns could be defined:

```
D> COLUMNS
D> PROD_NO TEXT 4 KEY
D> DESCRIPT TEXT 12
D> ROOM TEXT 10
D> FINISH TEXT 10
D> U_PRICE CURRENCY
D> QOH INTEGER
```

A KEYed column is frequently used for database access or sorting, just as an index field is used in dBASE. A column name cannot be longer than eight characters in R:BASE. Multiple columns may be keyed, but each creates a separate index. A separate INDEX command is needed to define a concatenated key (that is, involving multiple columns) index. A concatenated key can be defined directly as part of a table definition in PARADOX 3.0.

The PRODUCT table could then be defined in the definition processor by simply listing the table and the names of its columns:

D> TABLES
D> PRODUCT WITH PROD_NO DESCRIPT ROOM FINISH U_PRICE QOH

Changing a Database Definition

PC-RDBMSs are frequently used to prototype an application to meet changing database needs. Thus, it is very convenient to be able to redefine a database without having to unload and reload all the data. With some products, adding or deleting a field or changing a field width is done with minimal update overhead, but in most systems, files whose structure has changed must be copied into a new file. This may be done automatically, however, without the user entering any additional commands. Previously stored data are restored, but new columns are, of course, blank until data are entered.

In dBASE IV, we can completely redefine any aspect of a file; for example, a column name, data type, and length can all be changed. The easiest way to change the structure of a file is to use the Control Center to display and change the current file definition. (The structure of a table can also be changed at the dBASE Dot Prompt level using the MODIFY STRUCTURE command, but we do not show this here.) The result of this process is illustrated in Figure 13-2. The process started on the Control Center screen by first moving the cursor bar to the PRODUCT table name in the Data column and pressing the Enter key to place this file in use. Then pressing the SHFT-F2 key combination causes the current stored definition of the file in use, PRODUCT, to be displayed.

Figure 13-2
Modifying a file definition in dBASE IV

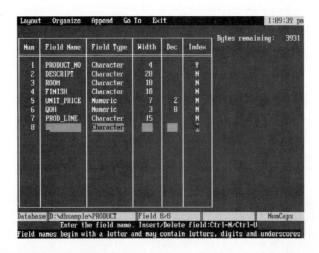

In this example, the PRODUCT file is redefined with a longer description field and a new field that holds the name of the line of products to which the product has been assigned. These changes are reflected in Figure 13-2. After all the file definition changes have been entered, dBASE asks if the changes should be saved. When this is confirmed, the PC stores the definition and builds a new file under the new format. All the old data would be moved and converted to this new file (automatic conversion between data types follows anticipated restrictions); all the previous descriptions still would be no longer than the original 12-character maximum and the product line field would be empty.

Changing the structure of a database file is, obviously, a highly sensitive process. If something goes wrong in the middle of the conversion, some of the data or a whole file of data can be lost. For example, if in Figure 13-2 we had erroneously changed the description field length to 10 instead of 20, existing data values would be truncated and significant data might be lost. dBASE automatically makes a backup copy of a file before it is changed and then destroys the backup when the conversion is successful. In case an undetected error occurs, it is always safe to make your own backup, too, which can be used for file archives. As an additional caution, recognize there may be subtle restrictions to changing definitions. For example, in dBASE, you cannot modify both a field name and its width or type at the same time. You must first change the field name, save the modifications, and then again modify the file definition to incorporate the width or type change. Thus, redefinition of a file should be done carefully and with the ability to undo any changes that might result in lost data.

Integrity and Security Controls

Chapter 3 outlined a wide range of database semantics that can be described in a logical data model. The most ideal way to enforce these semantic rules of data integrity and any security restrictions on who can see or do what with data is to include them as part of the database definition. In that way, all users who enter or change data will be forced to conform to these standards.

Integrity Controls   PC-RDBMS are, in general, still lacking in such controls. Even forbidding null values and specifying columns that must have unique values across all rows of a table are not common semantic controls available in PC-RDBMSs. R:BASE is an exception. R:BASE for DOS provides a facility called Rules that enables specification of integrity conditions to which data must comply. A rule, applied to a column of a table, is checked during all data entry and update statements. Rules can check referential integrity, prevent duplicate values, or limit data to a certain range of values.

To illustrate the R:BASE Rules feature, consider again the Mountain View Community Hospital database of Figure 6-25. R:BASE is demonstrated here using direct entry of commands. Later we will illustrate the Prompt

```
R>DEFINE D:\MVCH
 Begin R:BASE Database Definition
D>COLUMNS
D>LOCATION TEXT 4 KEY
D>ACCOM TEXT 2
D>EXTNSION INTEGER
D>PATIENTN INTEGER KEY
D>PNAME TEXT 20
D>PADDR TEXT 20
D>DATEDISH DATE
D>PHYSID TEXT 10 KEY
D>PHYSPHNE TEXT 8
D>ITEMCODE INTEGER KEY
D>DESCRIPT TEXT 15
D>PROCDURE TEXT 15
D>CHARGE CURRENCY
D>TABLES
D>ROOM WITH LOCATION ACCOM EXTNSION
D>PATIENT WITH PATIENTN PNAME PADDR DATEDISH LOCATION
D>PHYSCIAN WITH PHYSID PHYSPHNE
D>ITEM WITH ITEMCODE DESCRIPT
D>ATTENDS WITH PHYSID PATIENTN PROCDURE
D>BILLED WITH PATIENTN ITEMCODE CHARGE_
```

(a)

```
R>DEFINE
 Begin R:BASE Database Definition
D>RULES
D>"Duplicate Location" LOCATION IN ROOM NEA LOCATION IN ROOM
D>"Duplicate Patient" PATIENTN IN PATIENT NEA PATIENTN IN PATIENT
D>"Duplicate Physician" PHYSID IN PHYSCIAN NEA PHYSID IN PHYSCIAN
D>"Duplicate Item" ITEMCODE IN ITEM NEA ITEMCODE IN ITEM
D>"Charge Too Large" CHARGE IN BILLED LT 10000
D>"Charge Too Small" CHARGE IN BILLED GE 10
D>"Invalid Item-code" ITEMCODE IN ITEM GE 300 AND ITEMCODE IN ITEM LT 8000
D>"Physician Does Not Exist" PHYSID IN ATTENDS EQA PHYSID IN PHYSCIAN
D>"Patient Does Not Exist" PATIENTN IN ATTENDS EQA PATIENTN IN PATIENT
D>"Patient Does Not Exist" PATIENTN IN BILLED EQA PATIENTN IN PATIENT
D>"Item Does Not Exist" ITEMCODE IN BILLED EQA ITEMCODE IN ITEM
D>"Patient# Must Exist" PATIENTN IN PATIENT EXISTS
D>"Location Must Exist" LOCATION IN ROOM EXISTS
D>"Physician ID Must Exist" PHYSID IN PHYSCIAN EXISTS
D>"Item-code Must Exist" ITEMCODE IN ITEM EXISTS_
```

(b)

```
R>LIST RULES
(RULES    ) ON   Check data validation RULES
RULE 1          LOCATION IN ROOM NEA LOCATION IN ROOM
   Message:Duplicate Location
RULE 2          PATIENTN IN PATIENT NEA PATIENTN IN PATIENT
   Message:Duplicate Patient
RULE 3          PHYSID IN PHYSCIAN NEA PHYSID IN PHYSCIAN
   Message:Duplicate Physician
RULE 4          ITEMCODE IN ITEM NEA ITEMCODE IN ITEM
   Message:Duplicate Item
RULE 5          CHARGE IN BILLED LT 10000
   Message:Charge Too Large
RULE 6          CHARGE IN BILLED GE 10
   Message:Charge Too Small
RULE 7          ITEMCODE IN ITEM GE 300
     AND        ITEMCODE IN ITEM LT 8000
   Message:Invalid Item-code
RULE 8          PHYSID IN ATTENDS EQA PHYSID IN PHYSCIAN
   Message:Physician Does Not Exist
RULE 9          PATIENTN IN ATTENDS EQA PATIENTN IN PATIENT
   Message:Patient Does Not Exist
RULE 10         PATIENTN IN BILLED EQA PATIENTN IN PATIENT
   Message:Patient Does Not Exist
More output follows - press [ESC] to quit, any key to continue_
```

(c)

Figure 13-3
Definition of a database in R:BASE for DOS:
(a) columns and tables definition
(b) data integrity rules definition
(c) listing rules from dictionary

By Example menu-driven interface, from which these commands can also be generated. Figure 13-3a contains an R:BASE definition for this database, and several rules to help in data integrity are defined in Figure 13-3b. Figure 13-3c shows the first screen of all the rules stored. The general structure of a rule is

"error message" CONDITION

A rule begins with a message that is displayed whenever a data update statement causes the condition specified to be violated. Conditions can be compound with logical operators AND, OR, and NOT. Rules fall into two categories:

Value Checking

- Compare the value of a column with a specified constant [for example, CHARGE greater than or equal to (GE) 10].

- Check that a value exists for a specified column (equivalent to NOT NULL clause in some languages; for example, PATIENTN EXISTS).

Table Checking

- Compare values in two columns of the same row.
- Compare values in two columns from different tables [this can be used to check referential integrity; for example, to store a PHYSID in ATTENDS, the value must equal a (EQA) PHYSID in PHYSCIAN].
- Compare the value of a column with values for that column in other rows of the table [for example, LOCATION not equal to a (NEA) value of an existing value of LOCATION; this implements a primary key restriction on the table].

R:BASE performs some data editing automatically, for example, checking that a legitimate date is entered. However, if a legitimate date must have some relationship to another date, then an explicit rule would have to be written (this would be an example of the first kind of table-checking rule above). "Discharge date greater than or equal to admit date" is an example of this type of rule.

Rules are applied to the database. The LIST RULES command can be entered at any R> prompt to display the rules for the currently open database (see Figure 13-3c). It is common practice in relational systems to store all database definitions in the database as tables. This allows any part of the database description to be retrieved using commands similar to those used to retrieve real data. Rules, therefore, are stored as part of the database in a table called RULES; specific rules may be dropped from the RULES table by use of the REMOVE RULES command, with a specification of exactly which rules (rows) are to be cut. One restriction to the RULES capability is that rules cannot be used to check concatenated key duplication (for example, to check that an ITEMCODE + PATIENTN pair is unique for each BILLED row).

Rules do not always have to be checked. The SET RULES OFF/ON command allows for rule checking to be dynamically turned off and on. R:BASE has a limit of 20 rules per table. There is one caveat with R:BASE rules: When a rule is entered, it only applies to tables that have already been defined. If, for example, we had a rule

"Location must exist everywhere" LOCATION EXISTS

this would enforce a not nulls condition on LOCATION only in *all* currently defined tables. If we then defined a new table that included LOCATION, we would have to DROP this rule and reenter it for it to still apply to all tables.

Security Controls   R:BASE also can assign passwords to a database to provide security against unauthorized use of data. Passwords can be applied to the whole database or to individual tables. A database password is called an "owner password" and restricts use of commands to define, dump, and restore a database. A table password restricts access to tables by limiting use of update and/or retrieval commands. For example, to specify a modification password of "move" on the LOCATION table of Figure 13-3a, a database developer would specify in define mode

> D> PASSWORDS
> D> MPW FOR LOCATION IS move

The database creator may change or remove passwords. As multiple-user PC databases become more prevalent, security features will be necessary in a database package.

Physical Database Definition

PC products allow the database designer some control over the physical storage of database tables (although this is not usually as extensive as is available with mainframe RDBMSs). These controls are implemented through the creation of key indexes and, in some systems, the ability to cluster related rows from different rows close together in secondary memory. Another physical control, use of a variety of file organizations tuned to the type of database processing to be encountered, is usually not available on PCs. This is because PC operating systems typically have only sequential and relative record random accessing. In this section we will review indexing, since it is the one physical design tool available in almost every system.

Chapter 2 illustrated the basic capabilities of key indexing in dBASE IV, typical of most PC products. On the data definition screen (see, for example, Figure 2–12) or in data definition commands, individual fields can be designated for creation of an index. Figure 2–13 illustrated various options available for customizing an index.

In dBASE, index entries are maintained in an index file separate from the data file. Index entries are kept in alphabetical, chronological, or numerical order (depending on the data type). Optionally, an index may be defined in descending order, and an index with only unique values can be specified. The placement of actual data records is unaffected by indexing. Logical and long text (memo) data type fields may not be indexed (this is typical of most products). Indexing is sensitive to upper- and lowercase and, unless so stated, searches of an index must match exactly the desired value.

This sensitivity to case and requirement of exact matches can cause sticky problems for text data search strings (the key value we are seeking) and keys. Several options are available in dBASE to deal with this. First, the SET EXACT OFF command says that if the characters in the search string match the corresponding characters in the index key entry, consider the row found even if the entire length of both strings does not match. This solves the problem of trailing blanks. A second option is to index a character field by applying the UPPER or LOWER string function to change all characters to the same case, if case is, in fact, immaterial. In this situation, the key is, for example, UPPER(*fieldname*), not just *fieldname*. Then, each search string must be similarly converted to find the matching key values. This and other indexing problems [numeric data left justified in text fields, ignoring leading articles ("a", "and", "the"), and so on] are discussed in Nebel (1989).

A dBASE index can be assigned to its own index file (with an .NDX extension) or can be placed as one (called a tag) of up to 47 in a multiple-index file (with an .MDX extension). dBASE actually allows several different multiple indexes to be created per file, but we will not address such subtleties here. The advantage of a multiple-index file is that it (and all of its indexes) are automatically activated when the data file associated with it is opened (USEd). To activate an .NDX index file, the USE command must explicitly open that index. To access rows in a multiple-index file, dBASE has to be told which index (tag) to use by declaring one index as the master (at that point). This can be done via the Control Center or by the dBASE SET ORDER command. The master index controls the sequence in which rows will be retrieved (until a SET ORDER is again entered to change which index is master).

Concatenated key indexes may be created by forming one key expression involving string operators to append the different fields together. For example, to form a concatenated (primary) key index on PATIENT_NO and ITEM_CODE in the CHARGES table of the Mountain View Community Hospital database, a dBASE command would be

.INDEX ON STR(PATIENT_NO) + STR(ITEM_CODE)
   TO CHGINDEX UNIQUE

The STR() function converts the numeric PATIENT_NO and ITEM_CODE into character strings to form the index value. The INDEX command causes the current contents of the table to be indexed. The UNIQUE keyword restricts index entries to one entry per key value (a primary key).

Indexes are opened when the associated table is put into use by dBASE. To use a particular table in dBASE, one must enter a USE command or select the equivalent from the Control Center. For example, to use the CHARGES table and open with it the CHGINDEX index table, one would enter the following command:

. USE CHARGES IN 1 INDEX CHGINDEX

If CHGINDEX is a multiple index, an optional ORDER clause can be added to specify which index tag to choose as the master index. Each table is put in use in a particular buffer area (in this case buffer 1). Until the CHARGES table is closed, the CHGINDEX can provide rapid access to rows of the CHARGES table by qualifications on values for the concatenated key index. When a file is opened via the Control Center, the user is prompted for which indexes to open along with it.

As long as an index is open (all the tags in the current master index and any single index files mentioned when the file is put into use are open), it will be updated whenever the associated base table is changed. If one forgets or decides not to open a single index (an .NDX index file), a REINDEX command will update all single and multiple indexes without creating new indexes. Updating a file with all indexes open can significantly delay update times, so a user may elect not to open all single indexes during file updating. Updates to the index are then in a sense batch processed via the REINDEX command. Reindexing is important, else indexes and tables will not agree.

The purpose of an index is, of course, to provide rapid access to data based upon key value. However, as pointed out in Chapter 7, indexes carry overhead that can cost valuable storage space and maintenance time. Litwin (1989b) reports a test that shows some hazards in the unjudicious use of indexes. Litwin developed a 10,000 row table with and without an index on a unique key field, called ID1. He used R:BASE for DOS version 2.11 running on an IBM PS/2 Model 80. In this test, the record with ID1 value 7140 was the last record in the table and other keys were stored randomly throughout the table. He ran a variety of queries and obtained timings for each. The following table summarizes his results:

Qualification	# of Records Satisfying Qualification	Processing Time	
		No Index	With Index
ID1 = 7140	1	0:11	0:04
9001 <= ID1 <= 9010	10	0:13	0:04
9001 <= ID1 <= 9100	100	0:14	0:14
1001 <= ID1 <= 2000	1000	0:28	3:07

Some general observations from this test are

1. Indexing makes most sense for unique or almost unique qualifications. This test would suggest a rule of thumb of creating an index if you expect qualifications to request typically 1% or less of the table rows.

2. Sometimes a file should be updated without changing any indexes, then the indexes can be rebuilt after all the updates are done. Much less total time is required to change the indexes this way.

3. If possible, use commands that do not make use of existing indexes when you expect more than 1% of the table records to satisfy the query.

4. Experiment and monitor query processing times during the development of a new application and in early operational stages of a new application. Be prepared to add and delete indexes and to make necessary programming changes as you do so.

View Definition

As illustrated in Chapter 2, a view is a virtual table (that is, it does not actually exist) composed of columns from one or more related base (or permanent) tables. Various views of the same data allow different users to see these data in different ways. A view is also a way to give the user the impression of manipulating data from just one table, which makes data manipulation easier. Views are sometimes necessary since some database processing commands must work on only one base table or one view table, not on several tables in combination. Views also help in database security since we can restrict a user's access to the database by permitting the user to use only certain views, ones that contain only the data he or she is authorized to see. Views are now common features of PC-RDBMSs.

As illustrated in Figure 2-29, dBASE IV uses a visual programming style called query-by-example for specifying a view. A file skeleton or template of each base table from which columns are to be selected is called up on the screen, and the user then indicates which columns to include in the new view. dBASE allows use of up to eight base tables to build a view (views may not be used to define other views).

Qualifications (what dBASE calls filters) can be specified to restrict which rows from the base tables to include in a view. For a view, qualifications may be entered directly in the file skeleton cells (for example, a qualification such as '<100' could be entered under ORDER_QTY in Figure 2-29). Alternately, a qualification may be entered in a separate condition box (the use of a condition box for restricting the ORDER_DATE is shown in Figure 2–29). Such qualifications restrict which rows the user can see and manipulate (remember, views can be used just like tables, so the contents can be compared, summed, and so on). In the dBASE command language, the equivalent of the conditions in a view is the SET FILTER TO conditions command. Here the conditions are as above or the condition entry is the name of a file in which the conditions are stored. A view can be used in the Control Center or initiated in the command language by the SET VIEW TO <filename> command, where the named file contains the view definition (possibly created from the Control Center).

Data in the view table can be sorted, and virtual fields can be defined as calculations of selected columns. The view can also be defined to include the summary of base data. For example, a view could include the sum or average sales grouped by PRODUCT_NO. Any indexes on a base table of a view are automatically included in the view (data are still stored in the base tables, and the view table data are virtually built into single table form whenever the view table is referenced).

Figure 13-4 illustrates a view of the dining room furniture shipments for Pine Valley Furniture Company. The dBASE IV view definition appears in Figure 13-4a (shown in two screens), the data in the two base tables appear in Figure 13-4b (shown in four screens), and the view table data, composed of data combined from the Shipment and Product tables, appear in Figure 13-4c (shown in two screens).

In Figure 13-4a, the view itself has so many fields that they cannot all be displayed on one screen; the first screen shows the first four fields and the second screen shows the rest. The example field value 'PR' is used to link the two base tables into the one view table. Only dining room furniture records are requested by placing the qualifying value "DINING" in the

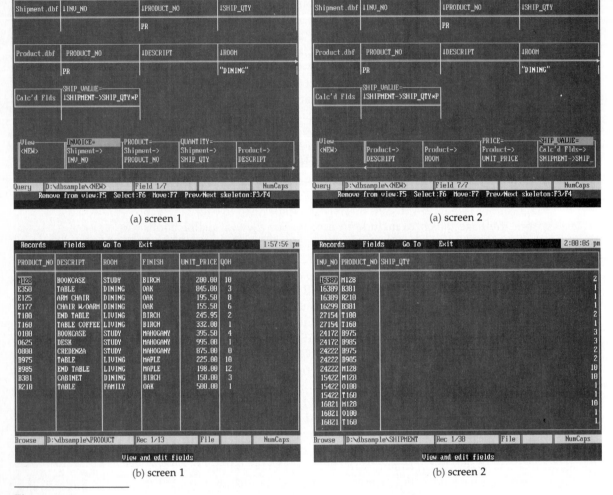

(a) screen 1

(a) screen 2

(b) screen 1

(b) screen 2

Figure 13-4
Dining room
furniture shipment
view:
(a) view definition
(b) base tables data
(c) view table data

Room column. To make the dollar value of each shipment explicit, a calculated field is defined as the shipment quantity times the unit price. Due to limited space in the calculated field box, only part of the equation is shown; the whole formula is

$$\text{SHIPMENT->SHIP\_QTY*PRODUCT->UNIT\_PRICE.}$$

This notation says "the SHIP_QTY field of the SHIPMENT file times the UNIT PRICE field of the PRODUCT file." The view definition also illustrates the capability to rename fields in the view. For example, the INV_NO field included in the view has been locally renamed to INVOICE for this view. This is a convenient feature since those who use a view may have special terms for certain data which are different from the standard names used in the database.

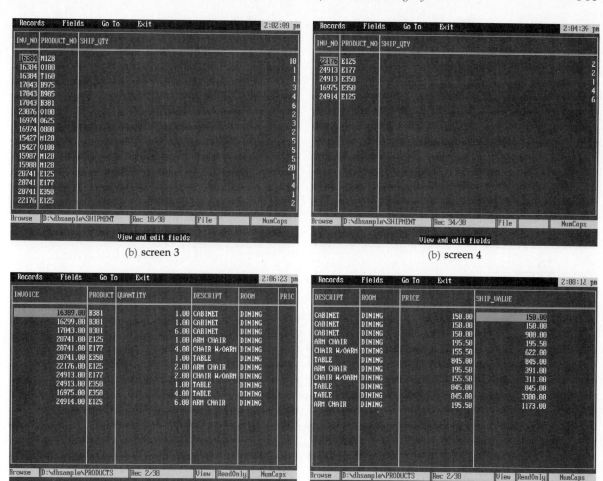

(b) **screen 3**

(b) **screen 4**

(c) **screen 1**

(c) **screen 2**

Figure 13-4b shows the contents of the two base tables, PRODUCT and SHIPMENT. All the fields and records of both tables are included. The SHIPMENT file requires three screens to show all 38 records.

The PRODUCTS view data appear in Figure 13-4c. Two screens are needed to display the full width of this table. Note that INVOICE and QUANTITY fields are not in the most convenient format: Integers in the base tables, they now have two (useless) decimal places. The reason for this is that a certain default dBASE condition, which we did not change, controls the format of such fields. The shipment value has been properly extended and appears to be actual data. Forms and reports (see Figure 2-31 for an example of the use of a view in a report) can now be defined that use the PRODUCTS view as if it were a table. dBASE commands can query against this view table as well.

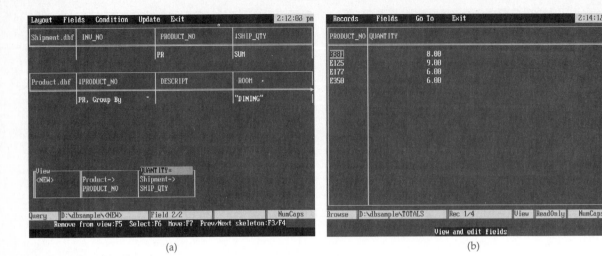

(a)   (b)

Figure 13-5
Total dining room
shipments view:
(a) view definition
(b) view table data

For managerial decision making and other activities, database contents are usually summarized by calculating simple statistics like counts, sums, and averages. Views can also be used to perform such summarizations. In Figure 13-5 we define a view showing the total quantity shipped of dining room furniture grouped by product number. Thus, the quantity shipped from multiple shipment records will be summed and displayed with the associated product. This was accomplished by using the key word SUM under the field to be summarized and the key word Group By under the field on which the aggregation is made. Again, the view definition in Figure 13-5a renames the sum of the SHIP_QTY fields as QUANTITY. The results in Figure 13-5b agree with the shipment data displayed in Figure 13-4b.

So far, the above two views have demonstrated a common use of views: the combining (or joining) of matching rows from two (or more) separate tables. Our final example of a view demonstrates the ability to create a view that combines two rows from the *same* table—called a *self-join*, since a table is joined with itself. The need for a self-join is not rare. For the Pine Valley Furniture database, consider the need to audit invoices. Although many possible consistency checks could be applied, one indicator of a potential problem could arise when there are multiple invoices for the same order (which was allowed when we defined this database). We would expect a customer to sequentially pay invoices; that is, if an invoice for an order is marked paid, so should all prior invoices for that order. Any such prior invoice not paid should be investigated, since we may have lost or not recorded the payment. Obviously, someone could scan the whole INVOICE file looking for this condition.

The current contents of the INVOICE file are shown in the two screens included in Figure 13-6. An inspection of this figure shows that no such condition exists. If, however, the second record in the file had a value of

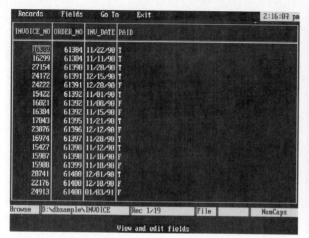
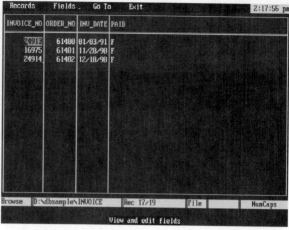

Figure 13-6
Example INVOICE
FILE contents

False for the PAID field, this invoice would meet our special condition. Manual scanning to do this check is tedious; fortunately, we can define a view to do this for us.

The view for the payment consistency check is defined in Figure 13-7a, and the resultant view table contents (assuming the above change to the second record in the INVOICE file) appear in Figure 13-7b. As expected, both file skeletons are for the INVOICE table. The two rows from this table have to match on ORDER_NO, shown by the example value of 'LINK1'. Further, for the invoice record that is marked paid (the second skeleton), the invoice date must be greater than the invoice date of the other invoice for the same order that is marked not paid (the first skeleton). The date relationship between the two records is specified in a condition box. The view contains the invoice number, order number, and invoice date from the unpaid invoice, and the invoice number and date of the newer paid invoice for the same order.

One final note about views is that frequently there are restrictions on updating the database via views. In dBASE IV, for example, only views that have simple data (that is, no aggregation) from one base table can be used to update the database. Otherwise, the updating might be ambiguous. For example, QUANTITY in Figure 13-5b cannot be changed since it is unclear what base data row used to form the sum would change. Some systems do not allow some types of updating from views.

Data Repository Access

The data repository (or dictionary) is an important part of database management systems. The repository of most relational systems is active and integrated, meaning it contains the actual database description used by the

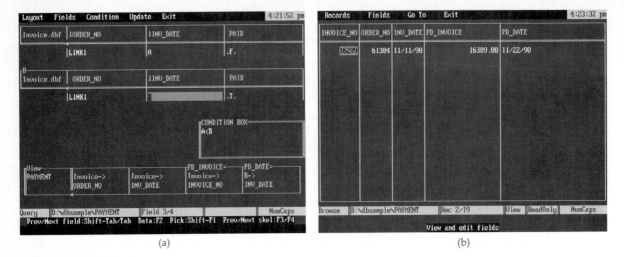

(a)   (b)

Figure 13-7
Payment consistency
check view:
(a) view definition
(b) view table data

DBMS. Most database users use so many databases, and use only a small portion of one database regularly, that most data are unfamiliar to most users. Thus, when a somewhat different query arises or an unfamiliar report is seen, a user may not know which data to use or how to interpret the data reported. The data repository is the source of which data is stored where, how it is formatted, who created it, and a host of other "data about data."

Most PC-RDBMSs store data definitions in special tables that are defined along with a database when it is created. Thus, an R:BASE user may not, for example, have a real data table called RULES since a table with this name is automatically created to store rule definitions. The data repository can be accessed via either special commands or standard relational query commands. Users can inquire about column names, file names, data types or whatever they need to understand database contents and to formulate queries.

dBASE has a feature called a catalog that allows tables and associated screen forms, labels, reports, and other definitions in the repository to be logically grouped, usually because of their common use in applications. Thus, an organization may have an accounting catalog, an engineering catalog, and a marketing catalog. This helps to isolate not only data manipulation but also definition access to only relevant portions of all the data maintained. This is very helpful when multiple databases are stored on the same medium. The SET CATALOG TO command informs dBASE which catalog to use. The active catalog may be changed during an interactive session or within a program.

Table 13-2 lists and defines the various data definition access and manipulation commands built into dBASE IV and R:BASE for DOS. In addition, with dBASE, its SQL module uses predefined relational tables to contain the data repository. Table 13-3 lists and defines these data repository tables found in the dBASE IV SQL module, and which are typically found in any

Table 13-2 Selected dBASE and R:BASE Data Definition Access
Commands

Explanation	dBASE IV	R:BASE for DOS
Show complete definition of a table	DISPLAY STRUCTURE	LIST TABLE tablname
Show complete definition of all tables	N/A	LIST ALL
Show names of all tables in database	N/A	LIST TABLES
Show names of all columns in database	N/A	LIST COLUMNS
Show names of all databases	N/A	LIST DATABASES
Show information about active/open database	DISPLAY STATUS	N/A
Show all rules applied to current database	N/A	LIST RULES
Change table definition	MODIFY STRUCTURE	
— rename a column		RENAME COLUMN colname TO newname IN tablename
— change column definition		REDEFINE colname to newcolspec in tablename
— add new column		EXPAND tablename WITH colname newspec
Change table name	RENAME oldname newname	RENAME TABLE oldname TO newname
Delete table from database	ERASE tablename	REMOVE TABLE tablename
Duplicate structure of a table	COPY STRUCTURE TO newtablename	N/A
Store table definition in another table	COPY TO tabledefname STRUCTURE EXTENDED	N/A
Define new table from stored table definition	CREATE newtablename FROM tabledefname	N/A

Table 13-3 dBASE SQL Data Repository Tables

Table Name	Description
SYSTABLS	Characteristics of each table in the database, including table name, type (base versus view), number of columns, date created, and size
SYSCOLS	Description of all the columns in all the tables in the database, including column name, table name, data type, length, and whether nulls are allowed
SYSVIEWS	Definition of views, including name, whether view is read only, and the SQL command text used to define the view
SYSVDEPS	List of tables referenced in each view
SYSIDXS	Description of each index file in the database, including table being indexed, whether index should enforce unique values, and an outline of the tree structure for the index
SYSKEYS	Definition of keys, including name of index for the key, column name being indexed, and whether index is ascending or descending
SYSSYNS	List of table name synonyms
SYSAUTH	Description of grants (security clearances) given on database tables, including table name, userid for user being granted rights, and a list of commands user is permitted to use
SYSCOLAU	Description of grants on columns
SYSTIMES	Times and dates the systems tables were last updated

SQL system. Because the data repository tables are relational tables, they can be accessed using the same SQL commands used to access other "real data" tables. For example, the SQL command

SELECT * FROM SYSCOLS;

lists the names of all the columns in all the tables of the database, and the command

SELECT * FROM SYSCOLS WHERE TBNAME = 'CUSTOMER';

lists the names of columns in only the CUSTOMER table.

DATA MANIPULATION IN RELATIONAL ALGEBRA

Relational algebra-based data manipulation languages were, historically, the first type of "programming language" developed for the relational data model (see Codd, 1970). Relational algebra uses certain primitive operators (SELECT, PROJECT, JOIN, UNION, PRODUCT, and others) that take tables as input and produce tables as output. Each operator performs its data manipulation on one or two tables at a time (that is, all operators are unary or binary). Thus, queries that involve more than two tables have to be broken into a series of binary (or unary) algebra commands.

Relational algebra languages are special-purpose languages. That is, they are self-contained languages that are by themselves sufficient for a wide variety of data retrieval and maintenance operations. These languages are relation-at-a-time (or set) languages in which all tuples, possibly from several relations, are manipulated in one language statement without explicit looping. Single query statements can be entered interactively and processed, or stored programs can be built. We will illustrate in this chapter the kinds of algebra commands available; Chapter 14 illustrates the development of whole programs in relational algebra and relational calculus languages and the ability to embed database query commands in third-generation programming languages.

The basic relational algebra commands were introduced in the first major paper published by Codd (1970) on the relational model and are common, in some form, to all relational algebra systems. SELECT (originally called restriction), PROJECT, and JOIN are most frequently used. Other relational algebra operators are union, difference, intersection, and product. Table 13-4 lists the most frequently used relational operators found in dBASE IV and R:BASE for DOS (remember, ORACLE is an SQL relational calculus language).

Single-Table Algebra Commands

Single-table operators display in table form all or some row or column subsets of a specified database table. As an option, some systems allow the result to be stored as a new database table. The ability to store the result as a table means that a series of related statements can provide the desired final result, without building one complex query, which can yield significant operational time savings. However, storing the result of an operation in a table creates redundant data, so this intermediate table should be treated as transient and destroyed as soon as possible after it is no longer useful. This is necessary since there is no guarantee that the intermediate table will remain consistent with the table(s) from which it was created.

Although it is a set-oriented language, some relational algebra implementations still follow the concept of record-by-record processing. Consistent with this, dBASE keeps track of the "current" row of each table. Some commands reference the current row. For example, in its basic form, the DISPLAY command shows on the screen the contents of only the current row. Other commands—FIND, SEEK, and LOCATE—search a table for a row that meets a specified condition and make that row current. Subsequent commands may be relative to this place in the table (for example, the next query may ignore rows before the current row!). The programmer should understand this nuance of any PC-RDBMS to avoid making programming errors.

Table 13-4   Summary of Relational Retrieval Operators in dBASE IV and R:BASE for DOS

Explanation	dBASE IV	R:BASE for DOS
Single-table operators		
Compute the mean of a domain or an expression of domains for specified rows	AVERAGE	COMPUTE . . . AVERAGE
Display the number of rows in a table (with specified qualification)	COUNT	COMPUTE . . . COUNT
Display the row with the minimum (maximum) column value	N/A	COMPUTE . . . MINIMUM (COMPUTE . . . MAXIMUM)
Display sum of a column or an expression of domains for specified rows	SUM	COMPUTE . . . SUM
Display distribution of values for a specified column	N/A	TALLY
Calculate sum or count of pairs of values of two columns	N/A	CROSSTAB
Display selected columns of a table for qualified rows	DISPLAY or LIST	SELECT PROJECT (to store result in a table) (both commands can involve sorting)
Position row pointer of table to first row with specified value	FIND (indexed col.) LOCATE (unindexed)	N/A
Position row pointer of table on specific relative row in table	GO TO	N/A
Cause current row pointer to advance or back up a specified number of rows	SKIP	NEXT
Create a row-ordered copy of a table	SORT TO	(sorting part of SELECT command)
Create a summary table with subtotals by key value	TOTAL TO	(requires report definition)

Table 13-4   (continued)

Explanation	dBASE IV	R:BASE for DOS
Copy a table into another table	COPY TO	COPY
Two-table operators		
Join of two tables into a third table	JOIN (only = comparison)	JOIN (permits none-quality comparison)
Intersection of two tables into a third table	N/A	INTERSECT
Difference of two tables into a third table	N/A	SUBTRACT
Union of two tables into a third table	N/A	UNION

Figure 13-8 contains several examples of single-table relational algebra commands for dBASE IV and R:BASE for DOS. The Mountain View Community Hospital database defined in Figure 13-3 for R:BASE is used in these examples (some of the definitions are slightly different for this database in dBASE due to the permitted length of data names and a few other minor aspects). The major difference between dBASE and R:BASE syntax is that some results that can be produced in one R:BASE command must be produced by more than one dBASE command. This is primarily, but not exclusively, due to the dBASE USE filename command—the table name is not embedded within other commands, as is done in R:BASE.

Group Qualifications   In all the examples shown in Figure 13-8, the FOR (or WHERE) clauses restrict data retrieval to table rows that satisfy a row qualification (for example, Patient-No = 1234). When group statistics are desired, occasionally qualifications need to be specified at the group level. For example, suppose we wanted to see a list of Patient-Nos for patients who had accumulated charges above $20,000. Although in almost all PC-RDBMSs it is easy to calculate the total charges grouped by patient (similar to the third query of Figure 13-8, but for all patients), not all systems permit selection of groups based upon group characteristics. The SQL language includes a HAVING clause, equivalent to WHERE, but used for group-level qualifications.

One PC-RDBMS in which it is especially easy to specify group qualifications is PARADOX 3.0, a query-by-example style system. For example, the following illustrates how the total charges query for patients with more than $20,000 of charges would be formulated in PARADOX (this is not an exact PARADOX screen):

```
BILLED──┬─Patient-no──┬─Itemcode──┬─Charge────┐
        │ √           │           │ sum>20000 │
```

Figure 13-8
dBASE IV and
R:BASE for DOS
single table command
examples

Display the identifiers of physicians who have
treated patient with patient number 1234

```
.USE ATTENDS                    R>SELECT PHYSID FROM ATTENDS
.LIST PHYSID                        WHERE PATIENTN= 1234
  FOR PATIENTNO= 1234
```

dBASE IV | R:BASE for DOS

Display the number of procedures that have been performed
on patient with the patient number1234
(See Figure 12-4 for calculus versions of this query.)

```
.USE ATTENDS                    R>COMPUTE COUNT PATIENTN
.COUNT FOR PATIENTNO =1234         FROM ATTENDS
                                   WHERE PATIENTN = 1234
```

Display the total charges for patient
with the patient number 1234.

```
.USE BILLED                     R>COMPUTE SUM CHARGE
.SUM CHARGE                        FROM BILLED
  FOR PATIENTNO = 1234             WHERE PATIENTN = 1234
```

Display by procedure the patient number (in numerical order)
for those patients given that procedure.

```
.USE ATTENDS                    R>SELECT PROCEDURE,PATIENTN
.SORT TO TSORT ON PROCEDURE,       FROM ATTENDS
  PATIENTNO                        SORTED BY PROCEDURE,
.USE TSORT                         PATIENTN
.LIST PROCEDURE, PATIENTNO
```

Display the patient numbers in order for those patients
that have been charged more than $300 for item 307.
(See Figure 12-4 for calculus versions of this query.)

```
.USE BILLED                     R>SELECT PATIENTN FROM BILLED
.SORT TO SCHG ON PATIENTNO         SORTED BY PATIENTN
.USE SCHG                          WHERE ITEMCODE = 307 AND
.LIST PATIENTNO FOR                CHARGE > 300.00
  ITEM_CODE = 307 .AND.
  CHARGE > 300.00
```

This is a very straightforward and easy-to-understand method for specifying a query that cannot be formulated in some systems. PARADOX also has a unique group operator, 'ONLY'. For example, suppose that we wanted to know who had been charged *only* for item 307. This query would involve several steps in relational algebra. First, a file (A) would be created of all the Patient-Nos in the BILLED table for rows involving Itemcode = 307. Then, a second file (B) would be created of all the Patient-Nos in the BILLED table for rows that do not involve Itemcode = 307. Finally, the Patient-Nos in file B would be set subtracted (using the SUBTRACT or DIFFERENCE command to be defined later in this chapter) from those in file A to answer the query. In PARADOX, however, this query is simply

BILLED—⊤—Patient-no—⊤—Itemcode—⊤—Charge—┐
        | √ | only 307 |

JOIN—the Heart of Relational Algebra

The **JOIN** operator requires special attention for three reasons. First, it is the most powerful of the algebra operators frequently implemented in relational DBMSs. Second, although only two types of JOINs, the equi-JOIN and the natural JOIN, appear in most relational algebra implementations (and are implied in many relational calculus implementations), other more general JOIN operators have been defined (for example, the outer and inequi-JOINs). Third, JOIN is one of the most computer-time-consuming relational commands, so its proper usage must be understood.

With the equi- and natural JOINs, tuples from the two relations being joined (JOIN is a binary operator) are concatenated only if they have common values in matching columns (matching columns must have the same domains). This is the type of JOIN that we illustrated in Chapter 2 and previous sections of this chapter. With the natural JOIN the matching fields must have the same name; with the equi-JOIN, the names may be different as long as the domains are the same. PROJECTion can be combined into this concatenation by restricting the resultant table to only certain columns. Some systems will, in this case, automatically DROP duplicate tuples; others, such as R:BASE, leave to the discretion of the user the decision whether to use the DELETE DUPLICATES command.

Figure 13-9 contains some examples of JOINs in both dBASE and R:BASE. Both dBASE and R:BASE permit the columns over which joining is to occur to have different names in the two tables (the equi-JOIN). The "B-> column name" notation in the dBASE examples indicates that the column name is from the table in buffer 2, or the B buffer. Both R:BASE and dBASE allow inequi-joining (we will illustrate this below). dBASE allows the user to specify that only selected columns are to be included in the resultant table, whereas R:BASE automatically includes all columns from both tables (the common column appears only once); a subsequent PROJECT command is necessary in R:BASE to accomplish the same effect. dBASE, but not R:BASE, supports

Figure 13-9
Examples of relational
algebra JOINs in
dBASE IV and
R:BASE for DOS

dBASEIV	R:BASE for DOS

Create a new table containing data on the phone numbers of
physicians and what procedures they have performed on what patients.
(See Figure 12-4 for calculus versions of this query.)

dBASEIV	R:BASE for DOS
.SELECT 2 .USE PHYSCIAN .SELECT 1 .USE ATTENDS .JOIN WITH PHYSCIAN TO PHONETBL FOR PHYSID = B - >PHYSID FIELDS PHYSID, B - > PHYSPHNE, PATIENTNO, PROCEDURE	R>JOIN PHYSCIAN USING PHYSID WITH ATTENDS USING PHYSID FORMING PHTBL R>PROJECT PHONETBL FROM PHTBL USING PHYSID, PHYSPHNE, PATIENTN, PROCDURE

Create a new table containing location and patient number
for each patient that has been charged for item 307.

dBASEIV	R:BASE for DOS
.SELECT 2 .USE BILLED .SELECT 1 .USE ROOM .JOIN WITH BILLED TO PLACE FOR PATIENTNO = B ->PATIENTNO .AND. B - >ITEM_CODE = 307 FIELDS PATIENTNO, LOCATION	R>JOIN BILLED USING PATIENTN WITH ROOM USING PATIENTN FORMING PL R>PROJECT PLACE FROM PL USING PATIENTN, LOCATION WHERE ITEMCODE = 307

Create a new table containing physician identification,
physician phone, patient identification, and date discharged
for all treatments on all patients.

dBASEIV	R:BASE for DOS
.SELECT 2 .USE PATIENT .SELECT 1 .USE ATTENDS .JOIN WITH PATIENT TO PT FOR PATIENTNO = B - >PATIENTNO FIELDS PATIENTNO, PHYSID, B - >DATE_DISH .SELECT 2 .USE PHYSCIAN .SELECT 1 .USE PT .JOIN WITH PHYSCIAN TO RESULT FOR PHYSID = B - > PHYSID FIELDS PATIENTNO, DATE_DISH, PHYSID, B - > PHYSPHNE	R>JOIN PATIENT USING PATIENTN WITH ATTENDS USING PATIENTN FORMING PL R>JOIN PHYSCIAN USING PHYSID WITH PL USING PHYSID FORMING PL2 R>PROJECT RESULT FROM PL2 USING PATIENTN, DATEDISH, PHYSID, PHYSPHNE

row qualifications in either table, which allows only qualified rows to be joined (for example, to join only CHARGES and ITEM tables for selected patients). dBASE supports joining on multiple columns (that is, joining on a concatenated key), but R:BASE does not. Finally, the last example in Figure 13-9 indicates what has to be done in relational algebra to join data from more than two tables.

One feature similar to a JOIN is found in dBASE. Two tables can be linked when they have a common named column that is indexed in both tables. The two tables can have a many-to-one or a one-to-one relationship. With the table (called the parent table) on the many-side (either side for a 1:1 relationship) active, the command

.SET RELATION TO key field INTO filename

links the active table to the one mentioned in the INTO clause (called the child table). Once the tables are linked, when the current row of the parent table changes, the current row of the child table changes to the matching row. With this feature, related data from the two tables are always available without having to execute a JOIN command.

Outer JOIN

The natural JOIN and equi-JOIN operators restrict the result to rows from the two tables that have matching values on a common column (or columns). Thus, rows from each table that do not have a match in the other table do not appear. For example, the result of the first query in Figure 13-9 would not include data on physicians who had not yet attended any patients. It is as though these entities do not exist. The outer JOIN overcomes this limitation. Besides joining together matching rows, the result also includes "orphan" rows from each table being joined, with null values inserted for columns in the "other" table. PARADOX 3.0 supports the outer JOIN operator. An outer JOIN for the first query in Figure 13-9 using PARADOX would be

```
PHYSICIAN──┬─PHYSID──┬─PHYSPHNE──┐
           │√  P!    │√          │

ATTENDS──┬─PHYSID──┬─PATIENTNO──┬─PROCEDURE──┐
         │√        │√           │√           │
```

The special symbol, '!', specifies that an outer, not natural JOIN, is expected. The resultant table from this outer JOIN would include rows with null values for PATIENTNO and PROCEDURE, for the physicians who had not attended any patients.

Inequality JOIN

Although the need for joining on other than equality is rare, the requirement may arise. Consider the following two relations:

CURRENT-SALES		PAST-SALES	
PRODUCT#	SALES-YTD	YEAR	AVG-TOTAL-SALES
1234	10000	1980	9000
3256	8000	1981	11000
5426	12000	1982	10500
6788	9500		
7392	6600		

If we wanted to know what products, to date, have exceeded prior average total product sales, in R:BASE we could

JOIN CURRENT-SALES USING SALES-YTD
    WITH PAST-SALES USING AVG-TOTAL-SALES
    FORMING WINNERS WHERE GT

and the resulting table would be

WINNERS			
PRODUCT#	SALES-YTD	YEAR	AVG-TOTAL-SALES
1234	10000	1980	9000
5426	12000	1980	9000
5426	12000	1981	11000
5426	12000	1982	10500
6788	9500	1980	9000

In this R:BASE command, the GT qualifier at the end of the last line specifies the inequality condition. The GT operator specifies a relationship between the two columns used for joining. More specifically, two rows will be joined when a row from the CURRENT-SALES table and a row from the PAST-SALES table have the following relationship:

SALES-YTD > AVG-TOTAL-SALES

In other words, if the year-to-date sales of a product are greater than the average total sales in any year, then join the rows together.

There are other types of JOINs, but these are not commonly implemented in commercial packages, so we do not mention them here. Refer to Codd (1970), Date (1981), Gardarin and Valduriez (1989), and Ullman (1980) for a discussion of some other types. In addition, these references define other relational algebra operators that are also not typically implemented.

Cost of JOINs

The cost to perform a JOIN suggests that it should be done only when needed. Some database implementors will purposely violate third normal form to combine data into one table to avoid this cost. The cost of a JOIN can be significantly reduced when the common columns from the two tables being joined are indexed. In some systems, the processing cost varies depending on which table is first and which is second. It may be advisable to formulate a JOIN from the many- to the one-side of a one-to-many relationship. This would be helpful if the DBMS knows to stop scanning the second table when a match is found. Considerable table scanning may be saved with this approach.

Without indexes, a JOIN is performed by scanning all the rows of the second table for each row of the first. Thus if there are n rows in the first table and m rows in the second, $n + nm$ rows must be accessed for a JOIN. In the situation outlined in the previous paragraph (that is, stop scanning the second table when a match is found), this procedure can be reduced to $n + nm/2$ on average. This scanning time can be slightly reduced if the smaller table (fewest rows) is the first, but this is usually not true when joining from the many- to the one-side of a 1:M relationship.

Other Multiple-Table Operations

Although not present in many relational algebra systems, there are several other multiple-table (two-table) operators present in some PC-RDBMSs [introduced by Codd (1970)]. R:BASE for DOS has several of these operators, as previously indicated in Table 13-4, which we will illustrate.

UNION   In general, with UNION, two tables that have corresponding columns with the same domains can be merged into one table with duplicate tuples removed. Two tables that have the same number of columns and corresponding columns with the same domains are called **union compatible**. The order in which tables are unioned is immaterial. The dBASE IV command closest to the general UNION operator is APPEND FROM. This command copies rows from one table to the end of the active table. Duplicate rows are not removed. With this command, only field names found in both tables are used, so the same column names must be used in both tables when the columns have the same meaning. Other columns that do not match may exist, and the columns with the matching names may be in different sequences in the two tables. The result follows the data type of the active database, so if a corresponding column is longer in the FROM table, its value will be truncated. APPEND FROM can also be used to import data from non-dBASE files, which will be discussed in a later section of this chapter.

In the R:BASE UNION command, two tables are unioned into a third table. The two original tables need have only one column in common, although more than one is permitted. The resultant table contains a union of the columns from the two original tables. When the two rows, one from each table, have the same values for the common columns, the two rows are simply attached to one another. Null values are filled in for missing column values for rows from each table that do not have a matching row in the other table. Thus, UNION is actually the outer JOIN operator discussed earlier! The R:BASE command for union is APPEND. This observation highlights the nonstandard nature of the relational system and the need to carefully select the right command for the data processing need.

Difference   The DIFFERENCE of two tables, A and B, is a third table, C, which contains the tuples that are in A but not in B. We can only perform difference if the two tables are union compatible. Obviously, A – B does not equal B – A. dBASE does not have a DIFFERENCE operator. R:BASE for DOS has such an operator, called SUBTRACT. With R:BASE, the difference can be restricted to selected columns, in which case only the relations defined by projection on these selected columns need to be union compatible.

Difference (SUBTRACT) is often useful to compare two tables that are the result of other data manipulation statements. For example, in the Mountain View Community Hospital database, we might first derive table A, a list of those patients treated by physician WILCOX, and then derive a similar table, B, for physician HENRY. The difference A – B would be those patients treated by WILCOX but not treated by HENRY. The particular R:BASE commands to derive tables A and B and to perform the difference would be

```
R>PROJECT A FROM ATTENDS USING PATIENTN WHERE
     PHYSID = 'WILCOX'
R>PROJECT B FROM ATTENDS USING PATIENTN WHERE
     PHYSID = 'HENRY'
R>SUBTRACT B FROM A FORMING C USING PHYSID
R>SELECT ALL FROM C
```

This particular query could not be handled by the PARADOX 'only' operator, discussed earlier in the chapter, since we are not interested in those patients who have been treated *only* by WILCOX.

INTERSECTION   The INTERSECTION of two tables is a third table that contains those tuples that are common to both original tables. Again, the tables must be union compatible. dBASE does not have an INTERSECTION operator. R:BASE provides a rather general form of INTERSECTion, in which selected columns may be used to define common tuples. For example, assume the following two instances of relations:

EMPLOYEE			SALARY		
NAME	DEPT	JOB	DEPT	JOB	PAY
Smith	A	Writer	A	Writer	1000
Jones	C	Prgmr	B	Writer	700
Smith	B	Writer	C	Writer	600
Franks	C	Writer			

Then

> R>INTERSECT EMPLOYEE WITH SALARY FORMING CLASSIFIED
>   USING DEPT NAME JOB

would produce the following table:

CLASSIFIED		
DEPT	NAME	JOB
A	Smith	Writer
B	Smith	Writer
C	Franks	Writer

The CLASSIFIED table contains three columns, those named in the USING clause. Matches are made on the common columns, DEPT and JOB, to determine which rows to include in CLASSIFIED. When all the columns of the intersected tables are not used, duplicate rows can result; in this case, R:BASE provides the DELETE DUPLICATES command to eliminate duplicate tuples.

SQL in dBASE IV and R:BASE for DOS

Most PC-RDBMSs have chosen to implement a subset of or implement in some special way the ANSI standard SQL language. ORACLE has a complete SQL version that is quite portable across its mainframe, mini, and PC product version. PARADOX 3.0 does not provide an SQL sublanguage. dBASE IV and R:BASE for DOS, however, have implemented their own versions of SQL (the latest version of R:BASE, version 3.0, has a rather complete SQL implementation).

In dBASE, a database is not automatically made available for SQL access. Instead, if a database is first created and populated in the dSE IV language, a special utility, DBDEFINE, must be run to create the SQL data repository entries for this database. SQL commands are not available from the Control Center menu system but must be run in an SQL mode, in which the user must type in the complete SQL command. While in SQL mode, some dBASE commands can be run, to run others, the user must dynamically switch between SQL and dBASE command modes.

dBASE does provide a very complete set of SQL commands, including the CURSOR command that keeps track of which row in a table is being currently manipulated. There are also commands to load data into and export data from an SQL database using Lotus 1-2-3 and other formats. More will be said about such import/export functions later in this chapter.

In R:BASE for DOS (version 2.11), many SQL commands are available from its menu system, Prompt By Example. Additional SQL commands are available when using the R:BASE command language directly. In contrast to dBASE, any database can be queried by either normal R:BASE commands or SQL statements without any conversion or additional effort. However, from Prompt By Example, only single tables can be referenced in SQL commands. To perform an SQL join in the SELECT statement, one must use the command language.

Newer versions of PC-RDBMSs almost always add or improve upon their SQL capabilities. Products retain an ability to access data from their traditional language so that previous users have an easy transition to new product versions.

RELATIONAL ALGEBRA MODIFICATION STATEMENTS

Database modification commands in relational algebra vary in name among DBMSs. In dBASE, the modification commands include the following (equivalent R:BASE for DOS commands are listed in parentheses):

APPEND:	Enters additional rows onto end of a table or INSERT may be used to insert row into specified row position (LOAD)
APPEND FROM:	Copies selected rows from one table into another table (APPEND)
APPEND:	Adds rows to a table using a predefined form for data entry (ENTER)
REPLACE:	Replaces existing values in rows with specified new values for rows that satisfy a selection clause (CHANGE)
UPDATE:	Replaces existing values in rows based on batched changes specified in another database table (no equivalent in R:BASE)
BROWSE:	Displays the table on the screen and permits user to browse through the rows and columns of a table to change values or delete rows (EDIT)
DELETE:	Deletes selected rows from a table; DELETE only marks rows for deletion; then PACK is used to actually delete the marked rows; ZAP removes all the table records without first marking them (DELETE ROWS both marks and deletes in R:BASE)

Other maintenance commands may exist to drop or rebuild indexes, change table definitions, rename files, and change stored programs.

Although most of these commands perform with very natural results, several require elaboration. As indicated, the dBASE IV DELETE command for removing rows from a database file simply marks the rows and the rows are actually removed in a second step by the PACK command. The RECALL command or special keystrokes in the BROWSE and EDIT commands can unmark rows. The greatest benefit of this two-step process is that it prevents accidental deletion. Marked records appear in displays of the file contents, but they are shown as marked for deletion. Data in marked records can be used in numerical and alphabetic operations, just as if they were still active (a dBASE SET DELETED ON command specifies that deleted rows are to be used).

An important observation about relational algebra data modification commands is that they are all *single*-table commands. That is, rows cannot be directly changed or deleted based on relationships with data in other tables. Except in the case where the contents of one table can be loaded into another table, a user must determine pertinent data relationships from one set of commands, record these manually, and then provide the necessary commands to complete the data update.

For example, suppose we wanted to delete the BILLED records from the Mountain View Community Hospital database (see Figure 13-3 for an R:BASE definition of the database) for all discharged patients. This could be done in one command in relational calculus by performing an implied JOIN in the WHERE clause of the deletion command. In SQL this would be

DELETE FROM BILLED
    WHERE BILLED.C-PATIENT# = PATIENT.PATIENT# AND
        PATIENT.DATE_DISCHARGED < = "today's date"

where today's date would be filled in. But in R:BASE, several multiple-step approaches would be possible:

1. Discharged patients could be determined from inquiry on the PATIENT table, and then the list could be used to compose individual DELETE ROWS commands on the BILLED table for the identified PATIENTNs.

2. A table, say DISCHG, of discharged patients could be generated from a PROJECT command, and a SUBTRACT command could then construct a new table, NCHARGES, which would be BILLED – DISCHG and would have only the desired rows remaining in it.

One goal of the modification languages is to give the user several options for entering or changing data; this, the language designers believe, helps to achieve greater user friendliness (since ease of use is relative to the skills and experience of each user). For this reason, the command list shows several commands for the same basic operation, and also for this reason a given command often has several forms. For example, consider the R:BASE

LOAD command for adding rows to a table. The full syntax of this command is

$$\text{LOAD tablename} \quad \begin{bmatrix} \text{WITH PROMPTS} \\ \text{FROM filename} \\ \text{FROM filename AS ASCII} \end{bmatrix} \quad \text{[USING columnlist]}$$

where none or one of the items in each set of brackets may appear. As an option via the USING clause, a user can choose to load values for selected columns or to rearrange the order of column data entry into any convenient sequence—not just the order used in the table definition. In the basic LOAD tablename form, the user has to enter both the column names and values in the order columns were defined (useful when different rows have different missing columns). The WITH PROMPTS option causes R:BASE to display the column names to remind the user of what data are to be entered. The two FROM options allow batch data entry from external data files. The ENTER and APPEND commands provide additional options for data entry.

Also common in most data modification languages is the ability to conduct a full-screen browsing of a database table and to replace in-place selected values. The R:BASE EDIT command (for display of existing data in typical table row and column format) and EDIT USING command (for browsing via a predefined custom table format) support such full-screen operations. For example, with the EDIT command R:BASE displays a tabular window on the table for the specified rows and columns to be browsed. The user may scroll up, down, left, or right. When more rows or columns than can fit on the screen are to be browsed, scrolling will rewrite the screen to move a new row or column onto the screen and move another off. Page up and down keys move through the file in complete window segments. Values can be written over or dropped, new characters in current values can be inserted, or selected current characters can be deleted. Whole rows can be deleted in one keystroke. Full-screen editing of a file is convenient for reviewing the contents of a file and selectively making changes as errors are found. It is not practical for large files, and it is not efficient if the desired changes can be easily and explicitly specified in CHANGE or DELETE commands.

Transaction and Recovery Control

As PC-RDBMSs support larger databases and multiuser access, they include more constructs to help in recovering corrupt databases and to roll back transactions. Users of a PC-DBMS should periodically back up or copy critical database components; a convenient way to do this is to code such backup directly into stored routines so users do not have to remember to do this.

dBASE IV includes commands to ensure the integrity of the database if transactions fail before completion, due to program errors, data entry mistakes, or the user simply wanting to abort the transaction. A transaction is any set of dBASE commands contained between BEGIN TRANSACTION and END TRANSACTION commands. A transaction is a complete business unit of work, for example, entry of a new customer order, which might involve entering one order record and many line-item records. We may not want any of this permanently recorded in the database unless all the records in the order are entered satisfactorily. After a BEGIN TRANSACTION command is processed and before the next END TRANSACTION command is executed, a ROLLBACK command will restore the database to the contents it had just before the BEGIN TRANSACTION command. In between, database changes are stored temporarily in a transaction log, which ROLLBACK uses to undo the changes. Such features have been in mainframe systems for many years and are now typically in PC products as well.

R:BASE has three commands that help provide backup protection:

COPY: Works like an operating system copy command to duplicate the contents of one (or several if wild-card characters are used) file(s) into another file (or set of files)

UNLOAD: Converts data and/or data definitions for a complete database or selected parts for later recovery or transfer to another system

RELOAD: Copies the contents of the active database into another database (this is *not* the opposite of UNLOAD)

Both R:BASE and dBASE have the capability to log terminal activity into a text file to produce an audit trail of database transactions; however, this audit trail cannot be automatically reapplied if it becomes necessary to restore a database. This feature is, nonetheless, handy for producing documentation or class assignments. In R:BASE, the command is

OUTPUT filename WITH TERMINAL

This command can be entered at any time during a session. Once executed, R:BASE will begin to log all command line operations into this file, overwriting any prior contents. Only line-oriented commands and output are logged; interactive or screen-oriented functions cannot be recorded. The equivalent dBASE command is SET ALTERNATE TO filename; logging can be dynamically turned on and off with the SET ALTERNATE ON/OFF command.

USER INTERFACES

One way in which the personal computer industry has led the information systems field is in providing computer system interfaces for the casual and non-data processing professional user. We have, of course, already extensively illustrated the dBASE IV menu interface, the Control Center. An

Figure 13-10
dBASE IV Control
Center main menu

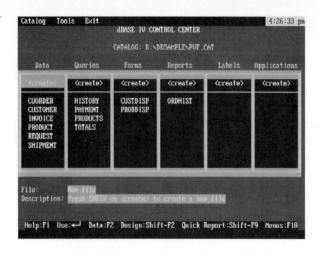

example main menu of the Control Center for the Pine Valley Furniture database catalog appears in Figure 13-10. From this screen, a user can make menu and submenu selections to enter dBASE subsystems to

- Create and change table definitions
- Create, change, and use queries (views) via the QBE style illustrated earlier
- Create, change, and process data via stylized screen formats
- Create, change, and produce customized reports
- Create, change, and produce mailing lists of tailored label formats
- Define and run application systems that involve prewritten database programs
- Switch to a different database catalog; execute various tools (for example, to import and export data into and out of a dBASE database and to exit dBASE)

The dBASE user interface hides the dBASE command language from a user. All commands are executed from menu selections or by filling in values on an interface form. That is, the Control Center does not reveal anything of the underlying nature of dBASE or its programming language.

The R:BASE general user interface is called Prompt By Example (see Figure 13-11 for a copy of the main menu). The R:BASE philosophy for the user interface is quite different from that in dBASE. First, R:BASE uses the relational table format whenever possible. For example, Figure 13-12 shows two screens that would appear during the definition of the PRODUCT table for Pine Valley Furniture. These screens are produced from Definition EXPRESS, the user interface used to define tables, views, and rules. Definition EXPRESS is called from choice (1) on the Prompt By Example main menu. Each PRODUCT table column is, in fact, a column on the screen. In

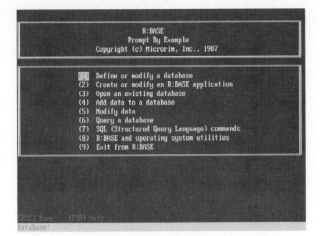

Figure 13-11
R:BASE Prompt By
Example main menu

Figure 13-12a, the current cursor position is in the cell directly under the DESCRIPT column name. At this point, the user must select the data type for this column. The primary key column, PROD_NO, has already been defined as a text (character string) with a maximum of four characters. The '*' in front of PROD_NO specifies that it is a key (the '*' was placed there automatically by a menu choice after the column was defined). Figure 13-12b shows the completed table definition, just before the ESC key is entered to stop the definition process.

The second distinguishing feature of the Prompt By Example (PBE) style is that R:BASE commands are not hidden from the user. Rather, as the user picks context-sensitive choices from PBE menus, the resultant R:BASE command is developed and shown step by step on the screen. In this way, the user can be sure that his or her choices appear to be as desired and have been interpreted properly. Further, seeing the actual R:BASE commands on the screen can be a useful method of teaching the R:BASE language. Thus, when complete programs, not just single interactive queries, must be developed, the user will be familiar with the R:BASE programming command language.

Figure 13-13 contains a series of screens that illustrate how R:BASE PBE iteratively builds up a query. The query being developed in this figure is: "What are the average unit prices for products grouped by room?" Figure 13-13a is the display generated after selecting option (6) on the main PBE menu. This PBE screen presents a brief explanation of each query choice, and the user picks the "Look at data" option. Figure 13-13b then lists and explains the various "Look at data" commands available. The "Group By SELECT" is chosen. Interestingly, JOIN is not listed on the menu of query commands. In fact, only single table commands are available via PBE. What the user must do is first to use PBE and Definition EXPRESS to define a view, and then reference that view to build the query.

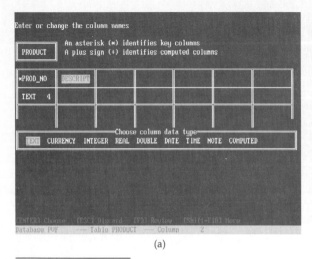

(a)

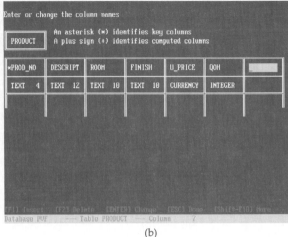

(b)

Figure 13-12
R:BASE for DOS
Definition EXPRESS
screens:
(a) screen for
    selecting column
    data type
(b) completed table
    definition screen

Figure 13-13
R:BASE Prompt By
Example query
development (pages
589, 590):
(a) initial query
    screen
(b) selecting specific
    query command
(c) selecting Product
    table for query
(d) selecting ROOM
    column to display
(e) defining the
    group level
    computed field:
    average unit price
(f) specifying a
    WHERE clause
    (none used here)
(g) specifying the
    ROOM column to
    group by
(h) the final query
    with choices for
    what to do with it

Figures 13-13c through 13-13h illustrate the iterative development of this query. After each step, the next screen shows the formation of the query so far, as well as options at that step.

As a final note to the discussion of user interfaces, business graphics are an important way to present information. Databases from several PC-DBMSs can be read by business graphics packages for the production of customized graphs. PARADOX 3.0, however, can generate a bar chart, pie chart, line graph, and many other formats directly from data in a relational table. Typically, the first column of a table provides the X-axis or other labels, and one other designated column contains the data being drawn. Graphs can be generated with a few simple key strokes, much as is done in an electronic spreadsheet package.

FORMS FOR INPUT AND OUTPUT

A **form** is simply a stylized format used to prompt data entry or to display database contents on a screen. The development and use of a form in dBASE IV was illustrated in Figures 2-19 through 2-24. One form can be shown on a screen at a time (although some systems permit multiple-page forms), and usually data from only one record in a table can be accepted or displayed in a form. Some PC-RDBMSs will allow lookup of related data in other tables. For example, if a form were displaying the contents of a customer order record, data from the associated customer record could be looked up and displayed.

A computer form, like a printed invoice or tax form,

• Can contain instructions

• Can include boxes for highlighting areas to enter data

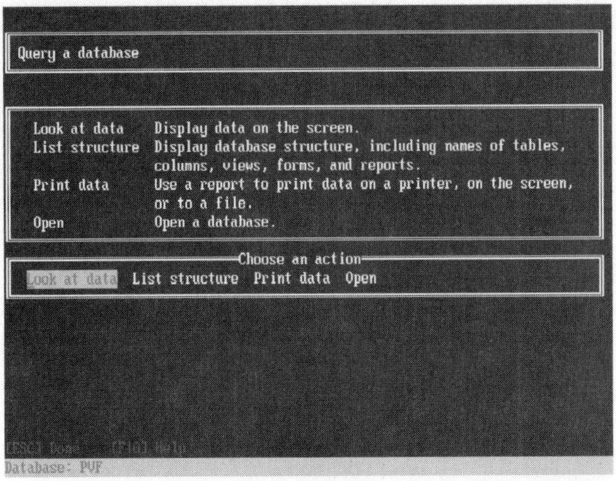
Query a database
Look at data Display data on the screen.
List structure Display database structure, including names of tables, columns, views, forms, and reports.
Print data Use a report to print data on a printer, on the screen, or to a file.
Open Open a database.
Choose an action
Look at data List structure Print data Open
[ESC] Done [F10] Help
Database: PVF

(a)

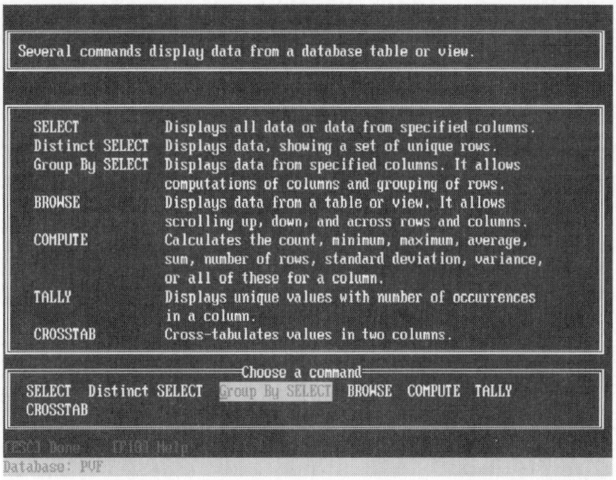
Several commands display data from a database table or view.
SELECT Displays all data or data from specified columns.
Distinct SELECT Displays data, showing a set of unique rows.
Group By SELECT Displays data from specified columns. It allows computations of columns and grouping of rows.
BROWSE Displays data from a table or view. It allows scrolling up, down, and across rows and columns.
COMPUTE Calculates the count, minimum, maximum, average, sum, number of rows, standard deviation, variance, or all of these for a column.
TALLY Displays unique values with number of occurrences in a column.
CROSSTAB Cross-tabulates values in two columns.
Choose a command
SELECT Distinct SELECT Group By SELECT BROWSE COMPUTE TALLY CROSSTAB
[ESC] Done [F10] Help
Database: PVF

(b)

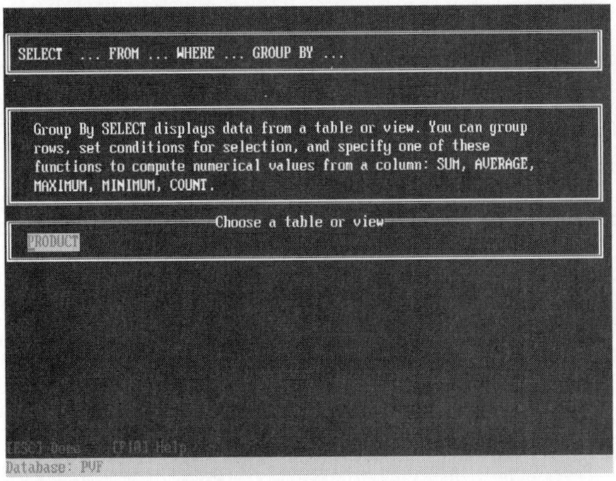
SELECT ... FROM ... WHERE ... GROUP BY ...
Group By SELECT displays data from a table or view. You can group rows, set conditions for selection, and specify one of these functions to compute numerical values from a column: SUM, AVERAGE, MAXIMUM, MINIMUM, COUNT.
Choose a table or view
PRODUCT
[ESC] Done [F10] Help
Database: PVF

(c)

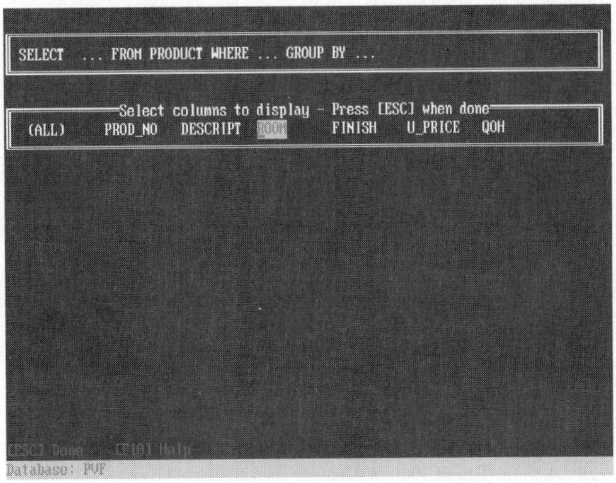
SELECT ... FROM PRODUCT WHERE ... GROUP BY ...
Select columns to display - Press [ESC] when done
(ALL) PROD_NO DESCRIPT ROOM FINISH U_PRICE QOH
[ESC] Done [F10] Help
Database: PVF

(d)

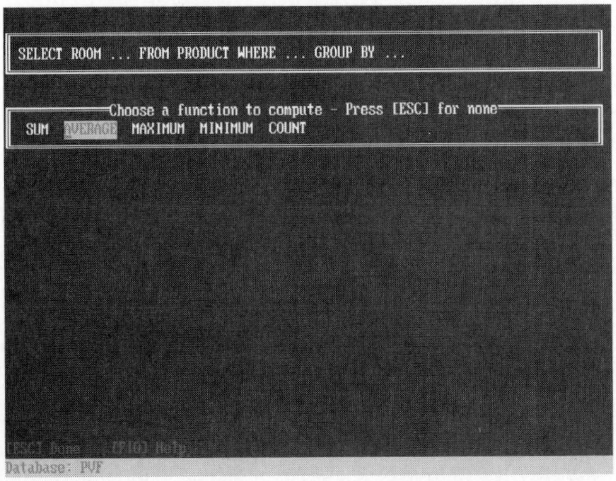
SELECT ROOM ... FROM PRODUCT WHERE ... GROUP BY ...
Choose a function to compute - Press [ESC] for none
SUM AVERAGE MAXIMUM MINIMUM COUNT
[ESC] Done [F10] Help
Database: PVF

(e)

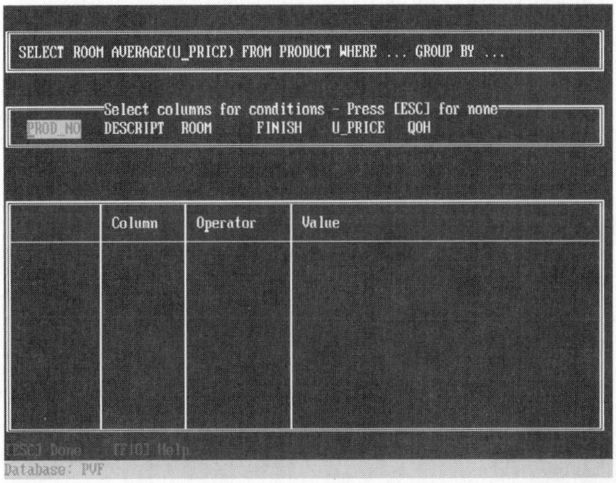
SELECT ROOM AVERAGE(U_PRICE) FROM PRODUCT WHERE ... GROUP BY ...
Select columns for conditions - Press [ESC] for none
PROD_NO DESCRIPT ROOM FINISH U_PRICE QOH
Column Operator Value
[ESC] Done [F10] Help
Database: PVF

(f)

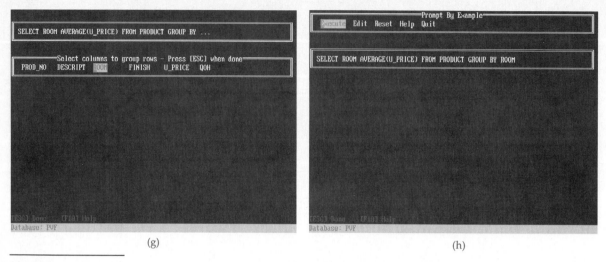

(g)   (h)

Figure 13-13
(continued)

- Can have shaded or colored areas for special use (for example, display only)
- Might show derived values not actually entered (for example, total price as the result of multiplying price times quantity)

More sophisticated forms management systems support blinking, reverse video, colored, underline, or high-intensity field displays, as well as multiple-page forms. Some systems even provide data entry validation and can be programmed to display error messages or other prompts depending on the data values entered or displayed. Several different forms might be used to display the contents of the same database file. In this situation, each format may be appropriate for a different user or users or when the record has so many fields that not all fields can appear on the screen at the same time. Some of these features for custom form design were illustrated in Chapter 2; we will not elaborate on them here. The interested reader is referred to Rubel (1989a and b) for a discussion of many of the features available in dBASE IV.

Most form subsystems permit the user to move from field to field on the screen at will to enter or change data. Special keys can be used to move to the next or prior field, to move between the next or prior character within a field, to insert or delete characters within a field, or to inform the system when to move to the next or prior record in the file for display or entry. In dBASE, the SET CARRY ON/OFF command controls whether data entered onto one screen are carried forward as default values for the next screen. If this flag is ON, the user will see the values from the last record entered displayed on a new screen. SET CARRY can also be applied to individual fields so this can be controlled also at the field, not only the record, level. The carry forward feature is very convenient if data are entered in a sorted sequence where only a few values change from record to record.

```
*****************************************************
*-- Name....: PRODDISP.FMT
*-- Date....: 8-24-89
*-- Version.: dBASE IV, Format 1.0
*-- Notes...: Format files use "" as delimiters!
*****************************************************
*-- Format file initialization code
-----------------------------------------------------
IF SET("TALK")="ON"
   SET TALK OFF
   lc_talk="ON"
ELSE
   lc_talk="OFF"
ENDIF
*-- This form was created in COLOR mode
SET DISPLAY TO COLOR
lc_status=SET("STATUS")
*-- SET STATUS was ON when you went into the Forms Designer.
IF lc_status = "OFF"
   SET STATUS ON
ENDIF
*-- @ SAY GETS Processing. *-- Format Page: 1
** Actual form code displays 80 columns per line for all 20
** lines. Most blank lines and trailing blanks have been
** eliminated in this listing for brevity of presentation.
@ 1,0 SAY "                                  PRODUCT DISPLAY"
@ 4,0 SAY "                        PRODUCT NO        "
@ 4,40 GET product_no PICTURE "A999"
@ 5,0 SAY "                        DESCRIPTION          "
```

```
@ 5,40 GET descript PICTURE "XXXXXXXXXXXX"
@ 5,52 SAY "|                          "
@ 6,0 SAY "                          ROOM              "
@ 6,40 GET room PICTURE "XXXXXXXXX"
@ 6,50 SAY "|                          "
@ 7,0 SAY "                          FINISH            "
@ 7,40 GET finish PICTURE "XXXXXXXXX"
@ 7,50 SAY "|                          "
@ 8,0 SAY "                          UNIT PRICE        $"
@ 8,41 GET unit_price PICTURE "9999.99" ;
   RANGE 0 ;
   MESSAGE "Price per unit of product"
@ 9,0 SAY "                          QUANTITY ON HAND  "
@ 9,40 GET qoh PICTURE "999" ;
   RANGE 0 ;
   DEFAULT 0
*-- Format file exit code
-----------------------------------------------------
*-- SET STATUS was ON when you went into the Forms Designer.
IF lc_status = "OFF"  && Entered form with status off
   SET STATUS OFF      && Turn STATUS "OFF" on the way out
ENDIF
IF lc_talk="ON"
   SET TALK ON
ENDIF
RELEASE lc_talk,lc_fields,lc_status
*-- EOP: PRODDISP.FMT
```

A form is defined in a special language that specifies on which row and starting at which column of the screen certain text or field values should be placed. However, the form designer or painter can use the Control Center Forms module in dBASE or the Forms EXPRESS module in R:BASE to develop or paint the form on the screen. Then the system will generate the actual form definition code from the visual layout. These commands are stored in a file. The dBASE screen format file for the screen form used in Figure 2-24 appears in Figure 13-14. Such screen control commands will be further illustrated in Chapter 14 when we cover database programming.

Figure 13-14
Sample dBASE IV form definition code

Figure 13-14 contains the actual in-line documentation generated by dBASE (the lines that begin with an '*'). This file is, of course, editable, so the dBASE Control Center can be used to prototype a form, and then the file can be changed for even more screen control. The first section of this forms definition sets the environment for showing the form. TALK is a global or environment variable in dBASE that when ON tells the system to display each command on the screen as it is executed. For clear forms processing, this should be turned OFF. The form was developed in IBM CGA color format. Finally, the status bar is the line near the bottom of the form that shows the current record, row and column position of the cursor, and other general status information. This should be ON for clear forms processing.

The second section of the forms definition lays out each line on the screen. Nineteen lines are available after space for border and status lines are allotted. Within each line where data will be entered, a PICTURE clause specifies the proper field format. For unit_price and qoh fields, a RANGE statement forces positive values. A MESSAGE statement for unit_price displays a custom prompt on a status line when the cursor is on that field. A DEFAULT statement sets qoh to 0 if no value is entered.

The final section of the forms definition restores STATUS and TALK environment conditions to their values before the form was used, and local variables are released from memory.

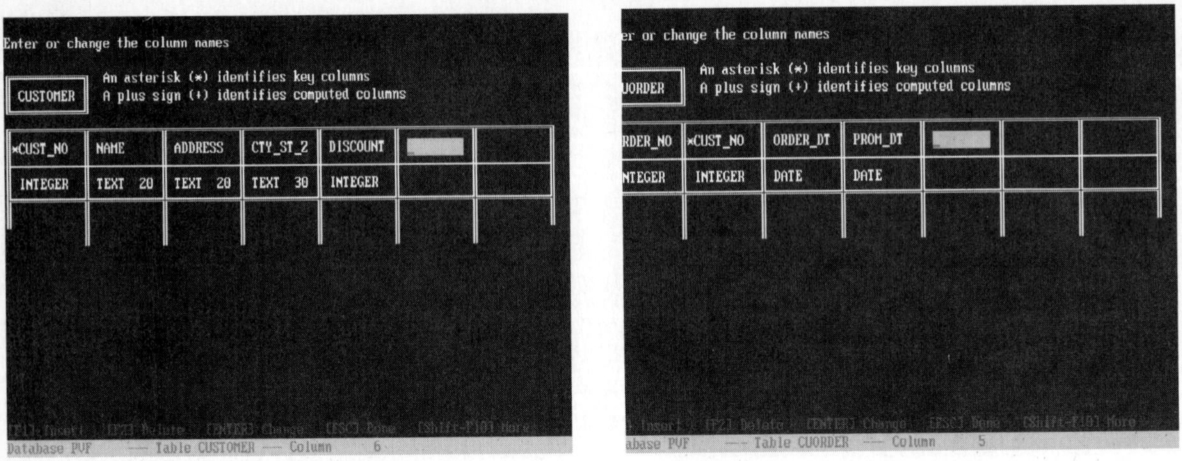

(a)

(b)

Figure 13-15
R:BASE Customer
and Order table
definitions:
(a) Customer table
definition
(b) Order table
definition

Multiple-Table Forms

The forms illustrated so far have all handled fields from one table. In contrast, consider the need for a form to enter or display customer order data. Since each order for the same customer will reuse the customer name and address, these data do not need to be entered for each order but rather can be looked up in the customer table. Thus, an order entry form involves data from two tables: Order and Customer. Figure 13-15 shows table definitions in R:BASE for DOS for these two tables. The fields correspond to the data elements outlined in Chapter 2 for the Pine Valley Furniture database. The CUST_NO field in the CUORDER table is used to link an order with its associated customer data.

We base the design of the order form on the Order Entry screen shown in Figure 2-4a. For illustrative purposes, we will limit our attention to the top half of this form (that is, we drop the product-related data) that includes order-specific data (order#, customer#, order date, and promised delivery date) and customer data (customer#, name, address, and city-state-zip). The development of the order entry and display form appears in Figures 13-16 and 13-17. With R:BASE Forms EXPRESS, each form and field on a form may have customized characteristics pertinent to the use of that form. Figure 13-16 contains the Forms EXPRESS screens that specify these characteristics for this form and for the ORDER_NO and CUST_NO fields on it. Most of the options are self-explanatory. The R:BASE ENTER command is what we will illustrate for data entry, and the EDIT USING command can be used for changing record contents. For both the ORDER_NO and CUST_NO fields, we have chosen to use as a default field value the corresponding values from the most recently entered record/row. This is equivalent to the SET CARRY ON in dBASE.

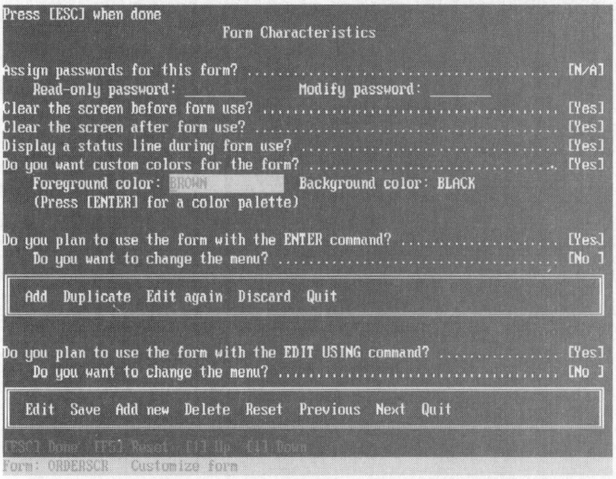

Press [ESC] when done
Form Characteristics

Assign passwords for this form? .... [N/A]
   Read-only password: _____ Modify password: _____
Clear the screen before form use? .... [Yes]
Clear the screen after form use? .... [Yes]
Display a status line during form use? .... [Yes]
Do you want custom colors for the form? .... [Yes]
   Foreground color: BROWN   Background color: BLACK
   (Press [ENTER] for a color palette)

Do you plan to use the form with the ENTER command? .... [Yes]
   Do you want to change the menu? .... [No]

  Add Duplicate Edit again Discard Quit

Do you plan to use the form with the EDIT USING command? .... [Yes]
   Do you want to change the menu? .... [No]

  Edit Save Add new Delete Reset Previous Next Quit

[ESC] Done [F5] Reset [↑] Up [↓] Down
Form: ORDERSCR Customize form

(a)

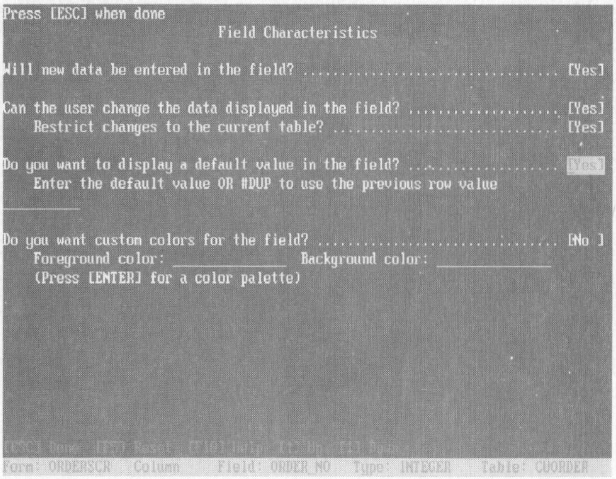

Press [ESC] when done
Field Characteristics

Will new data be entered in the field? .... [Yes]

Can the user change the data displayed in the field? .... [Yes]
   Restrict changes to the current table? .... [Yes]

Do you want to display a default value in the field? .... [Yes]
   Enter the default value OR #DUP to use the previous row value

Do you want custom colors for the field? .... [No]
   Foreground color: _____   Background color: _____
   (Press [ENTER] for a color palette)

[ESC] Done [F5] Reset [F10] Help [↑] Up [↓] Down
Form: ORDERSCR Column Field: ORDER_NO Type: INTEGER Table: CUORDER

(b)

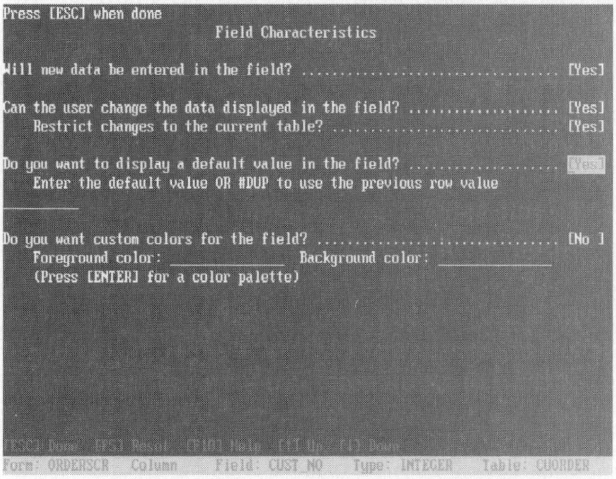

Press [ESC] when done
Field Characteristics

Will new data be entered in the field? .... [Yes]

Can the user change the data displayed in the field? .... [Yes]
   Restrict changes to the current table? .... [Yes]

Do you want to display a default value in the field? .... [Yes]
   Enter the default value OR #DUP to use the previous row value

Do you want custom colors for the field? .... [No]
   Foreground color: _____   Background color: _____
   (Press [ENTER] for a color palette)

[ESC] Done [F5] Reset [F10] Help [↑] Up [↓] Down
Form: ORDERSCR Column Field: CUST_NO Type: INTEGER Table: CUORDER

(c)

Figure 13-16
Order form custom characteristics:
(a) form characteristics
(b) ORDER_NO field characteristics
(c) CUST_NO field characteristics

Figure 13-17 shows the key steps in the development of the simple customer order entry and display form. This form is used to enter data into the CUORDER table, so customer name, address, and city-state-zip do not need to be entered. Once the CUST_NO is entered, R:BASE can look up the associated customer fields and automatically display them on the form.

The first key step is the specification of how to find the customer name; the address and city-state-zip fields would be specified similarly but are not shown. Figure 13-17a shows the form layout up to the point of locating the customer name field on the form. The 'S' and 'E' symbols mark the beginning and ending of a field position.

The customer name field, CUNAME, is defined as an expression. A label for the name field has been placed on the second content line of the screen. The expression, which appears on the top status line of the form

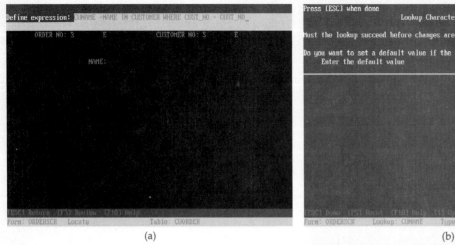

(a)

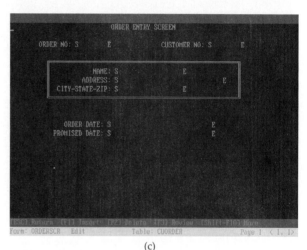

(b)

Figure 13-17
Order form layout
(a) lookup field
    definition
(b) lookup field
    characteristics
(c) final form layout

(c)

work surface, says that the CUNAME is the NAME field from the CUS-
TOMER table where the CUST_NO just entered on this form matches a
CUST_NO in the CUSTOMER table. This is the method R:BASE uses for
so-called table lookup. In Figure 13-17b this lookup is customized to ensure
that data entry cannot continue unless a name for the matching CUST_NOs
is found. This and an R:BASE rule for referential integrity of CUST_NO in
the CUORDER table are useful for ensuring quality data entry and maintenance. Figure 13-17c shows the final order entry screen format.

Figure 13-18 demonstrates the use of this form, called ORDERSCR, for
the entry of one new customer order. The R:BASE PBE menu system is used
to generate the proper R:BASE commands. Figure 13-18a is the form that
appears after selecting the 'Add data to a database' choice on the PBE main
menu. The appropriate command for our purpose is ENTER. This choice
is made and Figure 13-18b shows the next PBE screen, which asks the user
to select one of the available forms. The form is selected, and Figure 13-18c

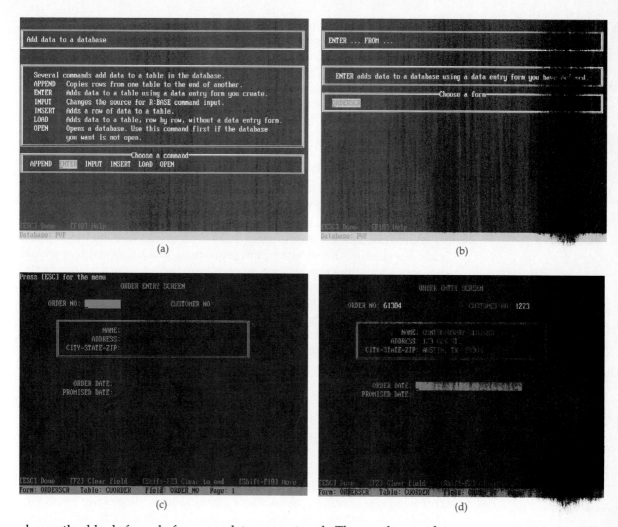

(a)

(b)

(c)

(d)

Figure 13-18
Customer order entry:
(a) selection of ENTER command
(b) selection of ORDERSCR form
(c) blank form
(d) screen after table lookup

shows the blank form before any data are entered. Then order number 61384 and customer number 1273 are entered. Figure 13-18d shows the screen just after the customer number was entered. As soon as the user presses the RETURN key for the customer number, R:BASE automatically looks up that customer record in the CUSTOMER table and fills in the name, address, and city-state-zip on this form. The form is now ready for entry of the remaining two pieces of order data, the two dates. This display of data from two database tables helps the user to verify that the correct customer number was entered. A referential integrity rule on the CUST_NO of the CUORDER table makes sure that a customer record exists for that CUST_NO. This screen goes one step further to provide visual confirmation that the correct customer was referenced.

Even more complex multiple-table forms are possible with R:BASE and PARADOX 3.0. For example, a region of the screen can be defined to hold multiple table rows. With this feature the complete order entry screen from

Figure 2-4a could be developed. In PARADOX, the order data would be contained in a master form and the details of the items being ordered in a detail form. The user can scroll through detail form rows. Only order line items for the order data in the master form can be displayed. That is, there must be a 1:*M* relationship from master to detail forms. The multiple-table form and other advanced R:BASE form features are described in Litwin (1989a).

Guidelines for Forms Design

Most systems analysis textbooks provide guidelines for screen and form displays. Fields should be clearly labeled in a similar fashion within and across screens. To reduce misentry, the sequence of fields should resemble the source documents. Forms should not be cluttered or contain too many fields. For ease of human search, titles, prompts, and help messages should appear in about the same location on each form for the same system. Finally, it is advisable that each screen be uniquely identified with some code and that each be marked to show whether it is one of several used for the total data entry task (for example, three of five).

When these guidelines are followed and easily readable forms are created, forms data entry and display can contribute to building a user-friendly database application system.

Windows

Forms are certainly handy for customized data entry and display. One additional feature, often used with a form, is windows. A **window** is a rectangular area that overlays a screen—that is, a window covers, but does not erase, an underlying screen. A window is especially helpful for displaying error messages, calling special attention to options, displaying important messages, displaying and editing long character string fields, and displaying help messages. In a sense, a window becomes a mini display screen, in which data may be displayed and entered.

Up to 27 windows can be displayed in dBASE; only one window, the last one activated, is active at a time. The basic window command defines the portion of the screen allocated to the window and various options for window display. The basic form of this command in dBASE is

    DEFINE WINDOW windowname
        FROM row1,col1   TO row2,col2

The FROM and TO clauses define the northwest and southeast corners, respectively, of the window rectangle. Additional optional clauses define window border characteristics and window foreground and background colors. A border may be a single line, double line, inverse video lines, any ASCII character, or blank. The DEFINE WINDOW command only defines

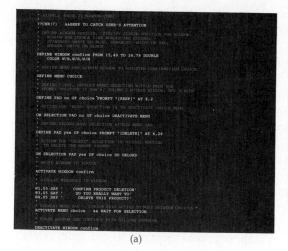

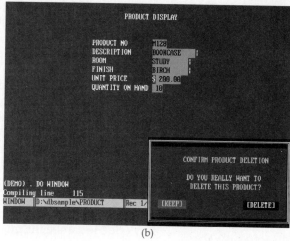

(a)

(b)

Figure 13-19
Example dBASE
window:
(a) example dBASE
    windowing code
(b) example
    confirmation
    window on
    product screen

the window; a separate ACTIVATE command is needed to display the window on the screen. A DEACTIVATE command removes a window from the screen. These and other window commands are not usually run interactively but rather are stored in program files.

The interested reader is referred to Prague (1989) for an excellent tutorial on the dBASE IV windows capability. One example adapted from Prague illustrates a typical use for and capabilities included in a window. Consider a situation in which a product record in Pine Valley Furniture has been dropped, and its associated record must be deleted. It is often advisable to confirm such actions, to give the user a chance to abort the transaction in case of an error. Thus, a window can be designed to overlay a screen to ask the user for such confirmation.

In this example, one additional feature often used with windows will be illustrated: a menu bar. A menu bar is composed of pads for each of the options or selections in the menu. The code in Figure 13-19a, adapted from Prague (1989), would be used within a larger program for this example situation. Each command in Figure 13-19a is explained by in-line comments. Figure 13-19b shows this window as it might be used, positioned on top of the product entry and display screen of Figure 2–24.

REPORT GENERATORS

Many PC-RDBMSs also include a subsystem for specifying customized printed reports. A form generator builds a screen format that contains data from one record or several related records. A report generator (or report writer) builds a printed report format that contains data from usually multiple records. Each record is displayed in one or several printed rows and in the same format. Most report generators are limited to the use of one database file or view, but some permit data from multiple, related files to be included in a report line.

The basic features of the dBASE report writer module were illustrated in Figures 2-31 through 2-34. We have seen that a report generator can support including header and footer titles, page numbers, and date and time of printing the report; substitution of field names with more meaningful column headings; calculation of column totals, control break subtotals, and averages and counts; and possibly production of multiple-line-per-record layouts. As an alternative, a report generator or similar subsystem will produce mailing labels or form letters instead of reports. Even more complex and data-dependent formats can be built using a procedural programming language, but this requires special programming skills.

A limitation of the dBASE report generation capability is that data from only one file can be included in a report. When data from multiple, related files must appear in the same report line, the user must use a view table or perform a JOIN or other multiple-table operation first to merge all desired data into one file. The R:BASE for DOS Reports EXPRESS module can retrieve data from multiple, related records on the same report using the same table lookup feature we demonstrated earlier for its form design module.

We will not take the space here to elaborate on the report writer capabilities of PC-RDBMSs. Such capabilities are extensive, and the illustration in Chapter 2 should provide a basic understanding. The interested reader is referred to Rubel (1989c, d, and e) for a comprehensive tutorial on dBASE IV's report generator module.

FILE IMPORT AND EXPORT

Since most personal computer users do not use just a PC-DBMS, it can be very convenient to be able to transfer data between different personal computer file formats. A typical personal computer user will use, in addition to one or more PC-DBMSs, word processors, electronic spreadsheets, simple filing systems, and operating system files. The ability to convert files among these various file formats eliminates the need to reenter data and keeps data more consistent across multiple application systems.

Table 13-5 summarizes the file import and export capabilities of dBASE IV and R:BASE for DOS. File conversion is not necessarily a straightforward process. Different data types between the systems for conversion mean that the data after conversion may not be in the most desirable and understandable format. For example, if one system does not have a date data type, then a date will be stored as a character string after conversion.

Conversion between a spreadsheet and a database presents special considerations. A spreadsheet must not have any summary rows or else each row of the database table will not be about the same type of entity. Further,

Table 13-5 Summary of File Import and Export Formats in dBASE IV and R:BASE for DOS

dBASE IV	R:BASE for DOS
IMPORT and APPEND FROM	*FileGate Way and LOAD*
PFS:FILE	PFS:FILE
— Data file	— Data file
— Screen format	
ASCII	ASCII
— Delimited with any character	— Delimited with any character
— Fixed field	— Fixed field
DIF (Visicalc)	DIF
SYLK (Multiplan)	SYLK
Lotus 1-2-3 1A and 2.X	Lotus 1-2-3 2.0
dBASE III	dBASE II, III, III Plus
FW2 (Framework II)	
RPD (Rapidfile)	
Export	*Export*
PFS:FILE	PFS:FILE
— Data file	— Data file
— Screen format	
ASCII	ASCII
— Delimited with any character	— Delimited with any character
— Fixed field	— Fixed field
DIF	DIF
SYLK	SYLK
WKS	Lotus 1-2-3 2.0
dBASE III	
FW2	
RPD	

database field names and spreadsheet column labels are not equivalent, but the fields are named upon conversion by applying the column labels. For these and other reasons, R:BASE provides an exception reporting and handling scheme to deal with those data that cannot be directly converted.

Of growing importance is the ability to upload and download data between personal computer files and mainframe computer files. This is even more difficult than between different PC systems, since PCs and mainframes

- Often have different word sizes and very different data types
- Use different character and number coding or representation schemes
- Require data communication software to support file transfer between technologies that use vastly different transmission speeds

Mainframe vendors are developing personal computer versions of their DBMS products, and these will usually include the software to transfer data between mainframe and PC databases of that type, but likely not the whole range of file types. Special upload/download software products are necessary to expand PC-mainframe file transfer capabilities to a more complete set of file types. Personal computer vendors, recognizing that many organizations that acquire their PC-RDBMSs also have considerable mainframe data, are increasingly announcing special arrangements with mainframe software vendors to provide specific file upload/download facilities.

MULTIPLE USER DATABASE CONSIDERATIONS

Organizations have discovered that if data are valuable to one employee, those data are probably also valuable to many other employees in the same work group. PC-RDBMS vendors, recognizing this need for multiple-user access to data, have introduced local area network (LAN) and other multiuser versions for many of the most popular packages.

A **LAN** is cabling, network controller cards for PCs, and data communications software. A LAN supports a network of personal computers, each with its own storage, that are also able to share common devices (such as a hard disk) and software (such as a DBMS) attached to the LAN. Each PC and workstation on a LAN is typically within 100 feet of the others, with a total network cable length of under 1 mile. At least one PC is designated as a file server, where the shared database is stored. The LAN modules of a DBMS add concurrent access controls, possibly extra security features, and query or transaction queuing management to support concurrent access from multiple users of a shared database. However, in a basic LAN environment, sometimes called a client-based system, all data manipulation occurs at the workstations where data are requested. Thus, considerable data movement is generated across the network. Further, each workstation must devote memory to a full version of the DBMS. And possibly most important, the DBMS copy in each workstation must manage the shared database integrity.

Client/Server Architecture for LANs

A recent improvement in LAN-based PC-RDBMSs is the **client/server architecture,** which splits the DBMS functions between the database server and user workstations so data are processed more distributively. The client workstation is responsible for managing the user interface, including presenting data, and the server is responsible for storage and access.

In the client/server architecture, all database recovery, security, and concurrent access management is centralized at the server, whereas this is the

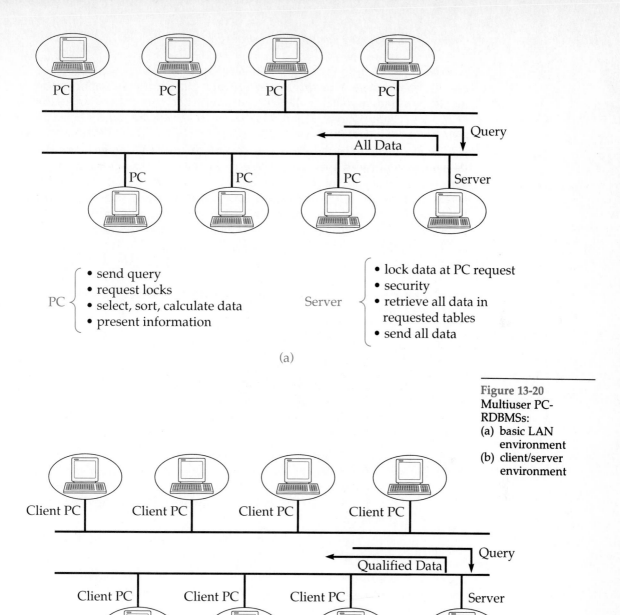

PC ⎰ • send query
    ⎱ • request locks
    ⎱ • select, sort, calculate data
    ⎱ • present information

Server ⎰ • lock data at PC request
       ⎱ • security
       ⎱ • retrieve all data in
       ⎱   requested tables
       ⎱ • send all data

(a)

Figure 13-20
Multiuser PC-RDBMSs:
(a) basic LAN environment
(b) client/server environment

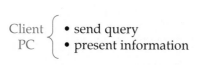

Client ⎰ • send query
PC   ⎱ • present information

Server ⎰ • lock and recover data
       ⎱ • security
       ⎱ • retrieve, select, sort,
       ⎱   calculate data
       ⎱ • send only needed data
       ⎱ • gateway to mainframe

(b)

responsibility of each user workstation in a simple LAN. Further, in the client/server architecture the server executes all data qualification statements, so data that match only the requested criteria are passed across the network to client stations. Figure 13-20 illustrates these differences between a simple LAN-based PC-DBMS and a client/server-based PC-DBMS.

The client/server architecture has several distinct advantages over the traditional client-based approach. First, each workstation requires less memory since a complete copy of the DBMS is only required at the server. Second, less network traffic is generated since only qualified data is passed through the network. The network traffic can be further reduced by storing highly used and nonvolatile data at the individual workstations. Less network traffic also means less overhead work for the workstations. Third, security, integrity, and recovery are consistently managed by the server, which means that the database is less prone to contamination (for example, in the client-based approach, even a power failure at a workstation can cause database contamination).

LAN DBMS Components

We will illustrate the typical (that is, not client/server) basic network version of a PC RDBMS by discussing dBASE IV. A tutorial introduction to the dBASE/SQL client/server version appears in Chan and Wong (1990). The network version of dBASE consists of three primary software components:

1. A multiuser version of dBASE for each workstation that provides all the same functionality and commands we have seen so far for a single-user environment, plus additional capabilities to communicate with the database server and to coordinate multiuser access to the shared database

2. Adduser4, which helps a network administrator in adding and removing database users

3. PROTECT, a security command that adds multiuser log-in security protection, data encryption, and file- and field-level access control to a database

PROTECT creates a user profile and arranges users into groups (thus, the same person may be a different user in different groups, with different privileges in each group).

Locking Concepts

Because files are shared with other network users, careful coordination is needed when several users are concurrently updating the same files. A common way to manage such concurrent use of data is to temporarily restrict access to data by locking those data for the exclusive use of only one program. Locking, in theory, can occur at any level of data. DBMSs typically provide file-level and record-level locking, and field-level locks are also possible.

Important trade-offs are made in locking at these different levels. For example, locking data at the file level results in fewer locks to be managed and, hence, less DBMS overhead. On the other hand, such coarse locking can block useful work by other programs since only one application program can use a locked file at a time. Record-level locking creates significant overhead since the DBMS would have to check for a lock on each record access. However, different users could more easily share use of the same file, only restricting access to records when they are individually being updated.

Multiuser dBASE controls concurrent access by special commands in application programs. Note that it is the individual user application programs that are responsible for concurrent access control. In the client/server architecture, these responsibilities are taken over by the DBMS on the server, much as is done in a mainframe DBMS environment. These commands used in an application program allow a user

- To specify exclusive or shared use of files
- To temporarily lock out other users from use of specified files or records while critical functions (such as value changing) are occurring
- To retry commands when a database access command is blocked by temporary locking or exclusive use of files and records by other users

Both exclusive and shared locks are possible. An **exclusive lock** prohibits any use of the locked file or record by any other application program. A **shared lock** permits other programs to place a shared lock on the data (that is, read the data) but they may not place an exclusive lock. Certain commands require exclusive use of a file and will not work unless the user has opened the file for exclusive use; these are INSERT (inserts a new row at a specified position), MODIFY STRUCTURE, PACK (delete marked records), REINDEX, and ZAP (deletes all the records in a file). Explicit exclusive use of a file is specified by

.SET EXCLUSIVE ON
.USE filename

After the SET EXCLUSIVE ON command, access to all opened files will not be shared among users. SET EXCLUSIVE OFF then allows shared use, but any files previously opened in EXCLUSIVE mode remain exclusive. If a user wants to open only one or selected files for exclusive use, the USE EXCLUSIVE filename command can be issued.

In addition to explicit file-locking commands that a user can place in a program, certain other commands imply automatic file locking while the command is being executed; these commands include all data update commands that affect multiple rows, plus AVERAGE, COPY, COUNT, INDEX,

JOIN, SORT, SUM, and TOTAL. A file is automatically unlocked after any of these commands completes execution. Other commands implicitly place an exclusive lock on the current record; these commands include APPEND, BROWSE, CHANGE, DELETE (current record), EDIT, and REPLACE (current record).

Explicit locking is done via two commands: FLOCK(), for locking the file currently in use, and RLOCK(), for locking the current record in the current file in use. These functions not only lock an unlocked file or record but also test for a lock and return a T or F to indicate the result. Neither dBASE or any of the other PC-RDBMSs now support locking at the field level. An UNLOCK command releases a particular lock, and UNLOCK ALL releases all locks.

If the file or record being tested is already locked, the locking function cannot be performed, the program must then go into a loop to try the locking request later. For example, DO WHILE .NOT. RLOCK() would start a loop that would cause a program to pause until the current record of the file in use were unlocked (that is, available to be locked) by another program. As an alternative, the dBASE command SET REPROCESS TO n can specify the number of times to retry a command that is blocked by a lock. For example, consider the following dBASE code module:

```
SET REPROCESS TO 250
IF .NOT. FLOCK()
    DO progress
    RETURN
ENDIF
DO blocked
```

In this example, the IF statement would be tried up to 250 times to test that the current record in the file in use is unlocked. If the record is still locked after 250 tries, the program would execute the 'blocked' routine. Otherwise, the program would execute the 'progress' routine and then return to the calling routine.

Shared Locks   dBASE includes a utility program, CONVERT, that adds file and record-locking information to a data file. This information is updated each time dBASE locks a record in that file, each time a record is updated, or the file is locked. This information helps in concurrent access control.

Suppose programs A and B are both reading and updating data in the same Product file in Pine Valley Furniture, but neither program has taken exclusive use of that file (that is, they have a shared lock on the file). Exclusive use can cause serious delays in work by blocking all use of a file, so it should be used in only the most critical circumstances. Suppose program A reads the product M128 record from the file and displays it on the screen of one of the network workstations. The quantity on hand of product M128 is below the reorder point, so the user at this workstation thinks for a while about what action to take. Before this user can input an action, program B reads this same record and increases the quantity on hand by 100 due to a receipt of new goods from the supplier. This now puts the on-hand balance above the reorder point. Unless the first program is notified that the quantity on hand has changed, an incorrect action could be taken (and the database could be improperly updated).

dBASE provides a function that allows these two application programs to recognize the above concurrent access and update situation. The CHANGE() function accesses the record-locking information stored in a file to determine whether a specific record has been updated since it was last read in that program. If the record was updated, then the new contents can be displayed and the user of program A above can reconsider an appropriate action.

Deadlock

File deadlock can occur when several programs are trying to access the same set of files for exclusive use and none can progress without the complete set of desired files. For example, suppose programs A and B each want exclusive use of the same two database files (or records) F1 and F2. Neither program can complete unless it has both files. If program A first takes exclusive use of F1 and, before it can put an exclusive lock on F2, program B locks F2, then deadlock has occurred.

A special dBASE function, LKSYS(), can help in recovery from a deadlock situation. LKSYS() returns which user has locked a particular record and the date and time it was locked. This information can be useful in determining what programs need to be aborted to stop a deadlock situation.

There are several schemes for preventing deadlock. A common approach is to open files (records) in a prescribed sequence (for example, alphabetical order by file name or ascending order by record number or primary key value). In this way if two programs both require simultaneous use of files (records) A and B, one program cannot capture B and want A when the other program has captured A and wants B. This approach can be awkward and may require programs to take exclusive use of a file (or record) well before it is needed.

Evaluating Multiuser PC-RDBMSs

Several factors are unique in evaluating multiuser PC-RDBMSs that are not relevant for assessing single-user products:

- **Speed:** Speed can vary considerably as a function of the number of workstations, so one package that is the fastest with 5 workstations may not be the fastest with 25 workstations.

- **Lock granularity:** Packages that support locks at the file and record level are generally more useful than ones that can lock only at the file level.

- **LANs supported:** Each multiuser PC-RDBMS works with a certain set of LAN software and hardware products, so the DBMS must be matched with the current LAN environment or considered jointly with the purchase of compatible LAN hardware and software.

- **Security and encryption:** The amount of security needs to be assessed and the security and data encryption requirements outlined.

- **Recovery:** The time delay required to recover a database from a crash can be important in many shared database applications.

- **SQL language:** Users who might use a PC-based multiuser DBMS may also be users of mainframe DBMSs, so portability of their skills may be a concern; thus, they must consider availability of an SQL language and its compliance to standard SQL.

- **Deadlock:** The ability to prevent, detect, and recover from a deadlock situation is also an important criteria.

SUMMARY

This chapter has summarized the salient features of personal computer relational database management systems (PC-RDBMSs). These systems are now powerful data management systems that provide an alternative to a central mainframe-based DBMS, especially in local area network environments.

For a small business, a PC-RDBMS may be sufficient as a tool to help in managing and processing organizational data. In a large organization, however, one would typically find both mainframe and personal computer DBMSs in use. A major organizational issue is how to manage data as a corporate resource when data are distributed among many different processors, some of which may be stand-alone with their own separate sources of input. This chapter, as well as Chapters 9 and 15, suggest that decentralized databases can have the same shortcomings as the department-based file systems outlined in Chapter 1. All data must be cataloged and definitions managed for consistency; data must be purposely placed on distributed machines with recognized redundancy. A well-organized and powerful data administration function is also needed when both mainframe and PC databases exist.

Data have been classified in many organizations into three tiers: corporate, departmental, and individual. Data cannot by default be classified as individual just for the expediency of the individual worker. The power of data is not linear, but it grows exponentially as it is shared. A PC-RDBMS is a valuable tool that, when used within an overall organizational scheme for providing rapid access to relevant data, can serve the needs of individual end users as well as the corporate desire for well-managed data and information.

Database management on personal computers has become rather commonplace, but only a few years ago such technology was immature and innovative. The database field is ever-changing, and now new areas have emerged as the leading edge of database management. Chapter 15 reviews one of the most important of these emerging topics: distributed databases.

Chapter Review

REVIEW QUESTIONS

1. Define each of the following terms:

a. relational algebra	i. intersect
b. single-user DBMS	j. UNION
c. mainframe link	k. DIFFERENCE
d. end-user computing	l. view
e. run-time version	m. mark and pack
f. report writer	n. form
g. JOIN	o. LAN
h. window	p. client/server
	q. deadlock

2. In what ways are PC-RDBMSs different from their mainframe counterparts?

3. What are the additional data management issues that arise in a multiuser database environment that are not present in a single-user, stand-alone environment?

4. What are the advantages of a run-time version of a PC-RDBMS?

5. Contrast the data definition philosophy in dBASE to that in R:BASE. What are the limitations or disadvantages of each approach?

6. What can the R:BASE rules capability accomplish?

7. Why is a DELETE DUPLICATES command found in some PC-RDBMSs?

8. What is the purpose of a template in a dBASE form definition?

9. Why are file import and export capabilities important for a PC-RDBMS?

10. Why would an organization that already has a mainframe relational DBMS support the use of PC-RDBMSs by occupational and managerial personnel?

11. What training should an end user have before developing her own database applications?

12. Contrast the result obtained by an equi-JOIN to that obtained by an outer JOIN.

PROBLEMS AND EXERCISES

1. Match the following terms to the appropriate definitions.

_____ mainframe link

_____ referential integrity

_____ form

_____ session log

_____ lock

_____ catalog

_____ product

a) communication between DBMS on PC and mainframe

b) every pairwise combination

c) mandatory matching of keys in two tables

d) grouping of tables, forms, and so on that are typically used together

e) transcript of PC database activity

f) stylized screen format

g) mechanism to prohibit use of a piece of data

Problems 2 through 11 are based on the Mountain View Community College database from Chapter 6 (the 3NF relations for that application are repeated here):

STUDENT#	STUDENT NAME	MAJOR
38214	BRIGHT	IS
69173	SMITH	PM
...		

STUDENT (STUDENT#, STUDENT-NAME, MAJOR)

INSTRUCTOR-NAME	INSTRUCTOR-LOCATION
CODD	B104
KEMP	B213
LEWIS	D317
...	

INSTRUCTOR (INSTRUCTOR-NAME, INSTRUCTOR-LOCATION)

COURSE#	COURSE-TITLE	INSTRUCTOR-NAME
IS 350	DATA BASE	CODD
IS 465	SYS ANAL	KEMP
PM 300	PROD MGT	LEWIS
QM 440	OP RES	KEMP
...		

COURSE (COURSE#, COURSE-TITLE, INSTRUCTOR-NAME)

STUDENT#	COURSE#	GRADE
38214	IS 350	A
38214	IS 465	C
69173	IS 465	A
69173	PM 300	B
69173	QM 440	C
...		

REGISTRATION (STUDENT#, COURSE#, GRADE)

2. Write R:BASE table commands and rules to define this database.

3. Justify your use of KEY phrases in your answer to Problem 2 and suggest other indexes that you would create to make the processing of this database efficient (assume the queries listed below are the only ones for this database).

4. Write dBASE IV and R:BASE commands for each of the following queries (refer to Figure 13-8 for sample commands):
   a. Display the instructor location for the instructor Lewis.
   b. Display the student number and student name for all information systems (IS) majors.
   c. Display the total number of students who are IS majors.

5. Write dBASE IV and R:BASE commands to produce a table with columns STU-DENT #, STUDENT-NAME, MAJOR, COURSE#, and GRADE. (*Hint:* Data are contained in multiple base tables.)

6. What dBASE IV command would be used to:
   a. Add a new row to the end of the REGISTRATION table.
   b. Delete all rows for student number 56789 in the REGISTRATION table.
   c. Change the grade for student 38214 in IS 465 from C to B.

7. Write the R:BASE command(s) necessary to display those students who have taken IS 465 but who have not taken IS 350.

8. Write the dBASE IV and R:BASE command(s) to display the names and locations of all instructors for courses taken by student with STUDENT# 69173.

9. Draw a picture of the dBASE view definition screen for the creation of a view that could be used to allow a user to answer Problem 8.

10. Write the dBASE IV command to create a primary key index on the REGISTRA-TION table.

11. Write the dBASE IV and R:BASE commands to display the STUDENT# and STUDENT-NAME of those students who have taken a course from both instruc-tor CODD and instructor KEMP.

12. Write a relational algebra query using either dBASE IV or R:BASE to answer the following question from the Mountain View Community Hospital database of this chapter: What physicians have performed a tonsillectomy?

13. Use the SUBTRACT operator of R:BASE to find those physicians that have not yet treated any patients at Mountain View Community Hospital.

14. Assume that the ITEM relation in the Mountain View Community Hospital database is altered to also include STD-CHG, the standard charge for an item. Write the R:BASE commands to display the patient numbers for those patients that have been charged above standard.

15. Given what you know about data structures from Chapter 7, explain what you would expect dBASE or R:BASE to do when columns are redefined, added, or deleted from a table definition.

REFERENCES

Ashton-Tate. 1988. *dBASE IV Language Reference.* Torrance, Calif.: Ashton-Tate.

Borland International. 1988. *Paradox 3.0 User's Guide.* Scotts Valley, Calif.: Borland.

Chan, A., and H. K. T. Wong. 1990. "Serving Up dBASE." *Data Base Programing & Design* 3 (2) (Feb.), 44–53.

Codd, E. F. 1970. "A Relational Model of Data for Large Shared Data Banks." *Communications of the ACM* 13 (June), 377–387.

Date, C. J. 1981. *An Introduction to Database Systems.* (3rd ed.) Reading, Mass.: Addison-Wesley.

Gardarin, G., and P. Valduriez. 1989. *Relational Databases and Knowledge Bases.* Reading, Mass.: Addison-Wesley.

Litwin, P. 1989a. "Faking Multi-Table Forms." *Data Based Advisor* 7 (10) (Oct.), 32–44.

Litwin, P. 1989b. "16 Ways to Rev up R:BASE, Part 1." *Data Based Advisor* 7 (11) (Nov.), 24–32.

Microrim, Inc. 1987. *R:BASE for DOS User's Manual.* Redmond, Wash.: Microrim.

Nebel, S. E. 1989. "Five Index Tricks for dBASE." *DBMS* 2 (13) (Dec.), 54–62.

Oracle Corp. 1988. *ORACLE Application Tools for MS-DOS User's Guide.* Belmont, Calif.: Oracle.

Prague, C. 1989. "Doing Windows." *DBMS* 2 (8) (July), 50–56.

Rubel, M. C. 1989a. "Keeping The Garbage Out." *Data Based Advisor* 7 (4) (April), 36–41.

Rubel, M. C. 1989b. "Entering Data into Screen Forms." *Data Based Advisor* 7 (5) (May), 43–46.

Rubel, M. C. 1989c. "Creating a Report." *Data Based Advisor* 7 (7) (July), 48–54.

Rubel, M. C. 1989d. "More on Reports." *Data Based Advisor* 7 (8) (Aug.), 44–51.

Rubel, M. C. 1989e. "Basic Reporting, Part 3." *Data Based Advisor* 7 (9) (Sept.), 38–42.

Ullman, J. D. 1980. *Principles of Database Systems.* Potomac, Md.: Computer Science Press.

CHAPTER 14

Programming With Relational Database Systems

INTRODUCTION

We have seen in the prior two chapters how powerful relational database management systems and their query languages can be. Many examples illustrated that, like any fourth-generation language (4GL), one command in a relational database query language is equivalent to 10, 25, or more 3GL (procedural language) commands. This power notwithstanding, one relational query command, or even several stored in a simple procedure, are not sufficient for building most information systems. Stored programs of commands are needed to construct a typical information system.

Most relational DBMSs support the stored program concept. These systems provide special programming languages that include the query commands we have seen so far. In addition, they include process control commands (for example, for looping), the ability to embed query commands in programs written in a 3GL, or both. Such stored programs are needed for the following reasons:

- To reuse a commonly needed set of one or more query commands in several query sessions, possibly with parameter value substitution

- To supplement the capabilities of a relational query language with commands that can support more flexible data input and output formats

- To support more sophisticated record selection logic than the Boolean logic structure of relational systems can handle (this may be because a single query command cannot provide the desired logic or because the WHERE, HAVING, and other clauses do not support the type of selection needed)

- To extend and convert existing programs written in a 3GL to access a relational database rather than nondatabase files
- To provide a menu-driven user interface for selecting among a variety of stored queries
- To build complete application systems for complex data processing needs

Most relational systems provide two choices for building stored programs. First, a program containing a sequence of special language instructions can be built. This special language contains all the query commands of the interactive relational system plus commands for sequence control (DO WHILE, IF...THEN...ELSE, and so forth), getting and putting data from and to the screen, printing format control, and accessing nondatabase data (among other capabilities). The second choice frequently available for building a stored program is to embed the type of relational commands we have seen into 3GL programs, which extends the data management capabilities of a 3GL. A precompiler translates the relational commands into call statements or their equivalent so the 3GL program can then be passed through a standard language compiler.

A third option for building a stored program available with some relational systems is an automatic code generator, or application generator. An application generator automatically produces source code programs in one of the two styles above from options selected by the programmer. Menus and the programs they link provide a comprehensive data processing and information retrieval application. A generated program can be manually changed to eliminate unnecessary code or to include features not generated.

Some of the queries we illustrated in previous chapters can be written either by systems professionals or end users. The database programming we illustrate in this chapter is usually written by professional programmers, end-user computing support staff, or similar people trained in programming principles.

The purpose of this chapter is to give an overview of these advanced capabilities for programming with relational systems. Programming in any language is a difficult task that must be approached systematically. Program and application design, building, testing, documenting, and so on must be followed with discipline. We do not discuss the programming process or guidelines for good program development. Rather, the goal is to introduce enough of the programming capabilities of relational systems for you to appreciate such facilities. You can then apply the principles of good program development learned in other courses and books to use these capabilities.

We will illustrate the programming capabilities of both personal computer and mainframe relational DBMSs, using dBASE IV and SQL/DS for this purpose. These are representative of many personal computer and mainframe RDBMSs. For dBASE IV, we will illustrate the capability for writing keyboard macros, parameter-driven functions, procedures, and whole programs. We will also illustrate the dBASE application generator, typical of such products. Several sample programs and an application system will be illustrated. Then we will discuss the use of SQL/DS commands in a 3GL, COBOL, program. We use COBOL because of its popularity for business programming, although other 3GLs (PL/I and C, in particular) lend themselves better to embedded programming. We present the concepts needed to develop such programs, including how to make SQL—a language designed to work with sets of records—work with a record-by-record oriented language. Then we discuss a sample COBOL program that illustrates embedded SQL commands.

PERSONAL COMPUTER PROGRAMMING IN dBASE IV

Personal computer RDBMSs are used in small businesses and units of larger organizations in both single-user and multiple-user applications. Several different forms of programming can add convenience and power to such applications. In this section we review three forms of programming with dBASE IV, a typical example of a PC-RDBMS:

1. Keyboard macros for coding a sequence of commands to a single keystroke
2. The dBASE IV special-purpose programming language for building a stored procedure
3. The dBASE Application Generator for developing a menu-driven interface to forms, reports, and programs

Macros

Macros are common to many languages: You may have already used keyboard macros in an electronic spreadsheet or word processor package. A **macro** is a sequence of keystrokes and commands that are assigned to particular key or key combinations, like Alt-C. A macro may also be referenced from a menu. When selected from a menu or activated from the keyboard assignment, dBASE immediately reacts to the sequence of cursor movements, function keys, menu choices, and commands stored in that macro. Very simply, a macro is a way to turn into one keystroke a sequence of commands needed to perform a commonly used operation. A dBASE user may write an original macro for a particular database or use a prewritten macro found in a purchased or user-developed macro library (one library may contain up to 35 different macros). One macro can use another macro inside it, but a macro may not refer to itself.

The dBASE Macro Menu   The Macro menu is found as a submenu of the Tools menu in the dBASE Control Center. Figures 14-1a and 14-1b illustrate

Figure 14-1
Activating the macro submenu:
(a) Tools menu
(b) Macros submenu

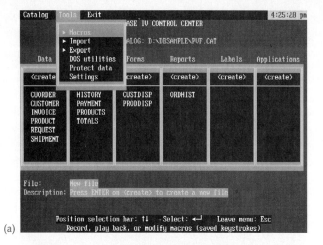

the selection of the Tools menu and then the Macros submenu. The options on this submenu are

- Begin recording a macro (that is, start creating a macro file with the keystrokes that will be entered next)
- End recording a macro
- Append new keystrokes and commands to the end of an existing macro
- Insert a break or pause in a macro to allow user input
- Modify (edit) an existing macro
- Change the name of an existing macro
- Delete a macro
- Copy a macro to another key assignment
- Play (run) a macro

- Turn on and off an echo display of macro text as it is played
- Load a library of macros
- Save the current set of macros in a library

A macro can also be executed (or played, in dBASE terminology) by pressing Alt-F10 followed by the key to which the desired macro is assigned. If a macro is assigned to a function key, Alt-function key will play the macro. In addition, a macro can be activated within a dBASE program by the PLAY MACRO command. In programs, macros are executed in a last-in first-play fashion, so if three PLAY MACRO commands are issued consecutively, they are played in the reverse order in which they were issued. Macros are played exactly as recorded. The user invoking the macro must therefore make sure the keystrokes in the macro make sense wherever it might be used in a program, in the dBASE Control Center, and in a database.

As indicated in the fourth option above, a macro may include a user-input break, in which the macro stops playing while the user enters data or performs some other database operations. The macro can then be resumed once the user is done entering whatever he or she wants or needs to enter.

Recording a Macro   A macro is recorded by selecting the first option on the Macros submenu and assigning a key to the new macro. The keystrokes for the macro are then entered one by one. As they are entered, dBASE actually performs the steps so the user can see if the macro code does what is expected. If user input is required, the macro writer presses SHIFT-F10 to specify where a user-input break is required, and then the coding of the macro continues. When the macro is completely recorded, the macro writer presses SHIFT-F10 again and selects the end recording option.

An Example of a Macro   We will illustrate the use of a macro in the Pine Valley Furniture database application used in Chapters 2 and 13. The reader should refer to the Table Definitions section of Chapter 2 for a description of this database. The purpose of the macro we illustrate is to display the number of orders received for a specific customer number (input by the user at an input break). This macro uses the CUORDER file from the Pine Valley database. This query is built by use of a view (see Chapters 2 and 13 for a discussion of a dBASE view), which counts the number of orders for a specified customer. Thus, the heart of the desired macro will be to build this view and display its results.

We assume that the macro will be invoked only from the Control Center, but the cursor may be anywhere in the Control Center when the user starts the macro. Thus, the first step in the macro is to position the cursor to build the query. The complete macro is listed in Figure 14-2. In this figure, words in {.} stand for the keyboard key with that label (for example, {Esc} means the escape key). The screen in Figure 14-2 appears from selection of the Modify option on the Macros submenu (we do not intend to modify it, but this is a quick way to display an already recorded macro). The macro had

Figure 14-2
Order count macro

been recorded and assigned to the 'C' key. Every command and key in this macro is exactly what we would use from the Control Center to build the view for this query, except for the {InpBreak} which shows where we would input the desired customer number.

This macro is explained line by line as follows:

LINE 1:   This line first causes dBASE to exit the Control Center and enter the dBASE dot prompt command system ({Esc}Y). Then, since we only need to use the CUORDER file, all other files are closed (CLOSE ALL{Enter}).

LINE 2:   The 'USE' command opens the file we need for this query (USE CUORDER{Enter}).

LINE 3:   This line returns control to the Control Center from which the view will be built (ASSIST{Enter}).

LINE 4:   Upon entering the Control Center, the cursor will be over the Data column. Thus, this line moves the cursor right to the Query column and selects the top option, <create>, there ({rightarrow} {Enter}).

LINE 5:   Query builds a default view that contains all the columns of the base table, so the first step here drops the default view ({F5}). Then the cursor is moved to the order number column in the file template and the function COUNT is entered ({Tab}COUNT). Next the cursor is moved to the customer number column where a user-input break is specified for the user to enter the desired customer number for selection ({Tab} {InpBreak}). After the user enters the customer number value, control is returned to the macro. Next the cursor is moved back (left) one column to the order number field. The Fields menu is selected from the Query work surface and the 'add column to view' option is selected ({Shift-Tab} {Alt-f} {Enter}).

LINE 6: Now the query can be executed to display the count ({F2}). A pause is inserted for the user to study the results ({InpBreak}). We are done with the query, so we exit the query work surface ({Alt-e} {Enter}).

LINE 7: We are then asked if we want to save the query. Since this is an ad hoc request, the default 'No' is chosen ({Enter}).

Since this macro was assigned to the 'C' key, the macro can be executed from the Control Center by typing Alt-F10 followed by C. Figure 14-3 shows copies of the PC screen at significant points in running the macro (called playback) to display the number of orders received for customer number 1273. Figure 14-3a shows the screen when the user-input break of line 5 occurs. Figure 14-3b shows the screen just after the customer number value is entered and just before the user presses SHIFT-F10 to resume macro playback in line 5. Figure 14-3c shows the screen with the result of this

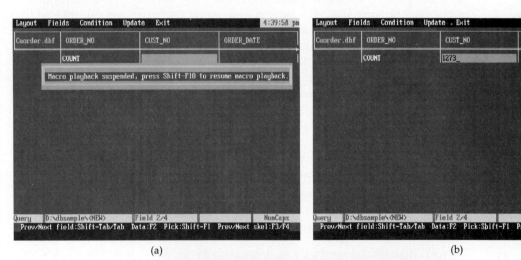

(a)

(b)

(c)

Figure 14-3
Execution of the example macro:
(a) input break before entry of customer number
(b) input break after entry of customer number
(c) macro query result

query at the point of the pause in Line 6 of the macro. For the sample database, the result for this query is 3. The display format used by dBASE is not very readable.

Macros are quite helpful for reusing common sets of operations; however, a macro is a fixed sequence of commands and keyboard strokes, so for more sophisticated requirements, other programming constructs are needed. The next section introduces those available in dBASE IV.

The dBASE Programming Language

The dBASE programming language includes the various query language commands we have already seen plus many other commands for process control (looping, branching, and conditional logic), data input from the screen and output to various devices, and setting the environment for the program. Many commands exist and a complete coverage is beyond our intent here. Our goal in this section is to show the basic capabilities and commands, including the capability to write functions (with parameters), subroutines, and whole programs. The interested reader is referred to Krumm (1990) and Senn (1990) for excellent, more detailed tutorials.

Table 14-1 lists many of the dBASE IV programming language commands, some of which we will illustrate in this section. The commands are listed in five groups:

1. Data manipulation for retrieval and maintenance
2. Input and output commands
3. Process logic for controlling the sequence of command execution
4. SET commands for specifying defaults and options for the general execution of other commands
5. Other commands not covered in the previous four groups.

We will illustrate the use of these commands as we develop various dBASE programs and program segments.

Table 14-1 dBASE Programming Language Commands

Data Manipulation

AVERAGE	Compute the arithmetic mean of an expression
BROWSE	Display a table on the screen for viewing, editing, or adding rows
CONTINUE	Search for the next row that satisfies the condition in the most recent LOCATE command
COUNT	Count number of rows of a table that meet a given condition
FIND	Search an index for first entry that matches a literal
GOTO n	Position row pointer on a particular relative row in a table (n may be a specific relative row number or TOP/BOTTOM for first/last row in table or index)
INDEX	Create a new index file for a table based on a key expression
JOIN	Create a new table by merging matching rows from two active tables
LOCATE	Search an active table for first row that matches a specified condition
REINDEX	Rebuild a specific index
REPLACE	Change the contents of specific fields in specific rows of a table
SEEK	Search an index for first entry that matches the value of a given expression
SELECT	Activate a certain buffer area
SKIP n	Move the current row pointer for a table forward or backward a specified number of rows
SORT	Create a new table that contains the rows of the active table that meet the given condition; store the rows in the new table in a specified sequence
STORE	Place the value of an expression into a memory variable (memoryvariable = expression is equivalent)
SUM	Total the value of a numeric expression of table field values for selected rows into a memory variable
TOTAL	Sum the numeric values of fields in the active database and create another table with a row that contains these sums
USE	Assign a certain table to a specified buffer area

Input and Output

?	Display value of expression
@ . . . SAY	Display value at specified row and column on screen
@ . . . CLEAR	Clear the screen starting at certain row and column
@ . . . GET	Display value at specified row and column on screen and prepare to read input (picture clause and valid range of values clause may be included)

(continued)

Input and Output (continued)

ACCEPT	Store character value entered on keyboard into a memory variable
ACTIVATE	Display a menu or window on the screen
APPEND	Add new rows to end of a table (from keyboard or from another database table)
DEACTIVATE	Erase a menu or window from the screen
DEFINE	Describe a menu, window, or box
DELETE	Mark rows of a table for deletion
DISPLAY	Show a set of rows from a table that meet a specified condition (similar to LIST command) or show contents of memory variables, table structure, file directory, or the last few commands that have been executed
INPUT	Store a complex expression in a memory variable
INSERT	Add a new row to a table before or after the current row
PACK	Remove rows that have been marked for deletion
READ	Store into memory all data entered on the screen from @ . . . GET commands since the last READ or CLEAR command was executed
RECALL	Unmark rows that have been marked for deletion

Process Logic

BEGIN TRANSAC-TION . . . END TRANSACTION	Start a transaction and keep database changes in a temporary file. END TRANSACTION commits these changes to the database. ROLLBACK clears the temporary file, effectively undoing changes.
DO	Execute (call) another dBASE procedure or program
DO CASE . . . END CASE	Select one action from a set of alternatives based on a condition that is true for one or none of the alternatives
DO WHILE . . END DO	Repeat a set of commands while a condition is true
IF . . ELSE . . ENDIF	Conditionally process two sets of commands, one for when condition is true and other for when condition is false (may be nested)
ON ERROR	Execute a specific command when a dBASE error occurs
ON ESCAPE	Execute a specific command when the ESCAPE key is pressed
ON KEY n	Execute a specific command when the specified key is pressed
ON SELECTION	Specify what command to execute when user makes any selection on a pop-up menu

Process Logic (continued)

PLAY MACRO	Execute a macro
RETRY	Allow a command that caused an error to be rerun after return from an error procedure
RETURN	Return control to the procedure that called the current procedure at the command immediately following the one that called the current procedure
SCAN . . ENDSCAN	For each row in the active table that meets the specified condition, execute the commands between SCAN and ENDSCAN
WAIT	Print a message on the screen and cause dBASE processing to pause until a key is pressed

Setting Environment

BELL	Turns bell on or off and sets frequency and duration of bell; bell sounds on errors and under other special circumstances
BORDER	Picks style of menu and window borders
CARRY	Determines if values from the last row are carried forward to next row on APPEND, BROWSE, EDIT, INSERT, and CHANGE commands
CENTURY	Turns on or off display of century in date field
CLOCK	Turns on or off display of system clock in upper right corner of the screen
COLOR	Establishes use of color and monochrome monitor, picks colors for standard, enhanced, border, and background, and for special parts of the screen (for example, highlighted characters)
CONFIRM	When on, causes cursor to move to the next field on a form when the current field is completely filled in, only when the ENTER key is pressed.
CONSOLE	Turns on or off display of output to the screen
DEFAULT	Specifies the default disk drive for data
DELETED	Establishes whether records marked for deletion are or are not used in commands
DELIMITERS	Specifies the characters to be used, if any, to designate the beginning and end of fields on displays
DEVICE	Specifies output device for @ . . SAY command
DISPLAY	Specifies type of display device (monochrome or color, CGA/VGA/EGA)
ECHO	Displays or does not display the commands to the screen or printer as they are executed
ESCAPE	Interrupts or does not interrupt program execution when the ESCAPE key is pressed

Setting Environment (continued)

EXCLUSIVE	Instructs dBASE to open all files for exclusive use (applies only to network applications)
FUNCTION	Programs the function keys
HEADING	Does or does not display field names above the fields in DISPLAY, SUM, or AVERAGE
HELP	Does or does not display pop-up help window when a command is incorrectly entered
INDEX	Opens indexes for the current table
INSTRUCT	Turns on or off the display of help messages in some dBASE full-screen commands (like BROWSE)
LOCK	Turns on or off features of automatic record locking (applies only to network applications)
MESSAGE	Displays a given user-defined message on the bottom line of the screen
PRINT	Specifies output device for commands that work with a printer (for example, which PC port, or redirect output to a file)
REPROCESS	Sets the number of times dBASE will retry a command when a record is locked (applies only to network applications)
SAFETY	Asks or does not ask for confirmation before overwriting an existing file
SCOREBOARD	Displays or does not display dBASE messages on line 1 of screen to show such status conditions as caps lock, insert or overtype mode, num lock, or current record marked for deletion
STATUS	Turns on or off the display of the dBASE status bar
STEP	Stops or does not stop program execution after each command
TALK	Determines whether dBASE's response to certain commands is or is not displayed on the screen

Other

CLOSE	Close files, indexes, and procedures
PARAMETERS	Define a list of parameters to be passed to a procedure
PRIVATE	Create memory variables local to current procedure
PROCEDURE	Identify the beginning of a procedure
PUBLIC	Define memory variables global to all active procedures
RELEASE	Delete specified memory variables and free that space in memory

User Defined Function We have already seen examples of various built-in functions in dBASE for manipulating character strings, maximum or minimum value, and mathematical calculations. Like many programming languages, dBASE also supports the specification of custom functions by the programmer. A function, similar to a macro, allows a standard procedure that calculates a specific value to be written once and reused wherever needed in a program.

A user defined function (UDF) is a set of dBASE commands that returns a single value to the command line where it is used. A UDF may accept a parameter list for input to the function. The general structure of a UDF is

```
FUNCTION function-name
PARAMETERS parameter-list
commands
RETURN(variable)
```

The PARAMETERS command assigns local names to the parameters being passed to the function. The variable after the RETURN command is a **memory variable** (that is, not part of any database table) calculated within the function. It is the value of this variable that is passed back to the command line where the function was used. A UDF does not change the value of any of the parameters passed to it. A value passed to a local parameter may actually be an expression; the commands in a function typically are arithmetic expressions. A UDF is stored in a dBASE procedure or program file for use within that procedure or program. Most database access commands are prohibited in a function—for example, APPEND, SORT, JOIN, BROWSE, and TOTAL (among many others).

The following is an example of the use of a simple UDF that might be useful in writing programs for the Pine Valley Furniture database. This function calculates the extended discounted price for a line item on a customer order (that is, a row of the Request table). The function definition is

```
FUNCTION Ex_Price
PARAMETERS E_Disc, E_Price, E_Qty
Result = (E_Price * E_Qty) * (1.0 - E_Disc)
RETURN(Result)
```

This function is used in the following dBASE program fragment, which needs the extended price value. In this fragment, it is assumed that data for a Request table row have just been retrieved and the product number, order number, and order quantity fields have been stored in memory variables R_prod, R_order, and R_qty, respectively. The following code retrieves the remaining needed data from other database files and then uses this function to display the extended price:

```
SELECT A
USE CUORDER INDEX ORDER_NO
FIND R_order
```

```
R_cust = CUST_NO
SELECT B
USE CUSTOMER INDEX CUST_NO
FIND R_cust
SELECT C
USE PRODUCT INDEX PRODUCT_NO
FIND R_prod
? Ex_Price(B->DISCOUNT,UNIT_PRICE,R_qty)
```

The first USE command opens the Order table and the order number index. The FIND command retrieves the order row for the order referenced in the Request row. Then the second USE command opens the Customer table and the index for the customer number. The following FIND retrieves the customer record associated with the order row just found. The following USE and FIND similarly retrieve the correct Product record. From these commands all three parameter values (discount from the customer table, unit price from the product table, and order quantity from the Request table) have been found. The last line displays the result returned from the function (? is a shorthand notation in dBASE that says "display the result on the screen").

Programs   As mentioned earlier, most PC-RDBMSs provide a separate programming language customized for the particular PC-RDBMS. Many of the dBASE language commands were listed in Table 14-1. This language supports looping, conditional IF-THEN-ELSE and other control logic, subroutine calls (with parameter passing), and input and output in interactive or batch mode with a variety of devices.

This is a relational-type language, but as a procedural language, only one record of each type can be stored in memory at a time. Since a user might use a programming language to calculate certain summary or statistical values for which there is no built-in function, the dBASE (and other) programming language supports a memory variable capability. A memory variable is a temporary location in computer main memory that can contain numbers, characters, dates, true/false indicators, or any other types of data the DBMS supports.

Data can be entered into a memory variable from the keyboard. Further, memory variable values can be saved to disk and restored (for example, to pass temporary variables between different program sessions). In addition, a variable may be declared only to a single program (Private) or global (Public) to all program modules. A built-in function or any other command can place its result into a memory variable. Data stored in memory variables can be displayed on the PC screen and in reports.

Figure 14-4 is an illustration of a simple program written in the dBASE IV programming language. This program uses the Mountain View Community Hospital database illustrated in Chapters 5, 6, 12, and 13. A program is stored in a program file (with a .prg extension). It can be created and changed from a text editor or the dBASE MODIFY COMMAND statement

(MODIFY COMMAND operates similarly to a word processor, and dBASE can be told to use whatever word processor the user requests for such editing). This program would be run by executing the command

DO programname

either interactively from the keyboard or by including this command in another routine (we will illustrate this latter approach below). DO will automatically compile a program if only the source file exists. dBASE can also be instructed to start a program automatically when dBASE itself is activated.

The program in Figure 14-4a receives the patient number for a user-selected patient, then calculates and displays, for each item charged to that patient, the difference between the amount charged and the average charge for all patients. The dBASE interactive query language alone cannot produce this query since dBASE does not permit the computation of the generic expression

fieldname - AVG(fieldname)

The comments in the program explain what each command does. Figure 14-4b shows the screen transcript from a sample session using this program.

Programming languages add tremendous power to PC-RDBMSs. Complex, structured programs can be written using commands that provide record-by-record (row-by-row) file processing control, as well as support intricate user-machine dialogues. Because these languages have been built along with the DBMS, they are especially tuned to database processing (as opposed to COBOL, FORTRAN, and the like, which were designed for file processing). Frequently, users do not write programs but rather contract with the data processing department to build such routines for them. This is because procedural programming training (for example, experience in detecting and handling user data entry error) is important for writing effective programs. Programs should be designed to mask the inner workings of the DBMS from the user by

- Handling errors within the program logic where possible, and passing only user-understandable error messages for user response when necessary

- Anticipating user data entry errors and providing easy mechanisms for the user to backtrack to a previous step, correct data entry mistakes, and fill in data with minimal keystrokes

- Responding to the user in meaningful terms when special circumstances (such as when no records satisfy a qualification) arise

Structured programming principles should be followed, and internal and external program documentation are essential.

Subroutine   A very common structure for a program is to have a main section that first opens files and conducts other initializing tasks, then executes calls to major task routines, and finally closes files and prints con-

```
USE BILLED INDEX PATIENT NO                          && Open the BILLED table and index
CLEAR                                                && Clear the PC screen
SET HEADING OFF                                      && Suspend display of field names
SET TALK OFF                                         && Do not allow display to screen
execute = 0                                          && Dummy variable for do while loop
DO WHILE execute = 0                                 && Program will continue to ask for patients
NOTE Next three commands display a title at top of screen
    @ 1,0 SAY ' '
    @ 2,0 SAY 'Calculate Patient Charge Deviations from Average'
    @ 3,0 SAY '                    By Item Code'
    patno = 0                                        && Variable for patient number
    patcount = 0                                     && Variable for # of charges for patient
    item = 0                                         && Variable for item code of patient
    place = 0                                        && Variable for record number of charge
    avgchg = 0                                       && Variable for avg charge for item
    @ 5,0 CLEAR                                      && Clear screen rows 5 thru bottom
NOTE Prompt and accept patient number
    @ 5,0 SAY 'Enter Patient Number: ' Get patno
    READ                                             && Read patient number from screen
NOTE Determine if there are no charges for this patient
SEEK patno
If .NOT. FOUND()                                     && If no charges, then ask for different patient
    STORE " " TO rest                               && Establish memory variable
    @ 7,0 SAY 'NO CHARGES EXIST FOR THIS PATIENT; PRESS RETURN' GET rest
    READ                                             && Pause for user to see message
    LOOP                                             && Transfer control to end of do while loop
  ENDIF
  GO TOP                                             && Reposition record at top of file
    LOCATE FOR PATIENTNO = patno                     && Find first charge for patient
    @ 7,0 SAY 'Patient  Item  Charge-Average'
    DO WHILE .NOT. EOF()                             && Repeat until end of file
      item = ITEM_CODE                               && Remember item for finding avg charge
      place = RECNO()                                && Remember which charge is processed
  NOTE Calculate the average of all charges for current item
      AVERAGE ALL CHARGE FOR ITEM_CODE = item TO avgchg
      GOTO place                                     && Return file pointer to charge record for printing
      diff = CHARGE = avgchg                         && Calculate deviation from average
NOTE Print data starting on next screen line/row
      @ ROW() +1,0 SAY PATIENTNO                     && Display patient number
      @ ROW() ,13 SAY ITEM_CODE                      && Display item code
      @ ROW() ,20 SAY CHARGE                         && Display charge
      @ ROW() ,26 SAY diff                           && Display deviation from average
      CONTINUE                                       && Find next charge for same patient
    ENDDO                                            && End of file access loop
    STORE " " TO rest
NOTE Pause for user to see data before continue to next patient
    @ ROW() +2,0 SAY 'Press Y to continue to another patient' GET rest
    READ
    IF rest = 'Y' .OR. rest = "y"
    LOOP                                             && Transfer control to end of outer do while loop
    ELSE
    EXIT                                             && Exit outer do while loop
    ENDIF
ENDO
SET TALK ON
CLEAR
RETURN
```

```
Calculate Patient Charge Deviations from Average
              By Item Code

Enter Patient Number:        1234

Patient     Item    Charge   Charge-Average

1234         200    150.00        -5

1234         200    165.00        10

1234         413     35.00        -5

Press Y to continue to another patient


AVGCHRG  A:\BILLED          Rec EOF/5     File          NumCaps
```

(b)

Figure 14-4
Sample dBASE IV
program:
(a) program code
(b) sample screen
    from program

cluding messages. Such structure may be nested several levels deep; thus, programming is frequently based on subroutines. dBASE IV supports subroutines through its structure called a procedure.

A **procedure** is a named set of commands and can thus be either a whole program or a subroutine. As illustrated above, a procedure is run by issuing the DO procedurename command anywhere in a program or at the dBASE dot prompt. A procedure can be stored within a program, in a separate procedure file, or in a separate file of several procedures. A total of 1,170 procedures may exist per program or file. Each procedure begins with the word PROCEDURE and ends with RETURN (but there is no parameter passed in the RETURN, as we saw above with a UDF). The SET PROCEDURE procedurefile command is used within a program to make a specific file of procedures active.

Parameters may be passed to a procedure (both subroutines and programs), in which case the PARAMETERS command must be the first command in a procedure. As opposed to a function, a procedure may change the value of parameters passed to it.

One particular use for a subroutine is to handle an error. dBASE errors can be trapped by use of the ON ERROR command, but this only covers actual problems encountered by dBASE, not operating system errors or other mistakes made by users while entering data. ON ERROR can appear anywhere in a program. Only the most recently executed ON ERROR command is active, so several ON ERROR commands may be used to change the handling of errors throughout a program. ON ERROR by itself cancels the most recent ON ERROR command and dBASE will handle errors in its standard fashion.

To illustrate subroutines in dBASE, consider a need to retrieve products from the Pine Valley Furniture database based on their designated room (Room is one of the fields in the Product table). We will assume that this is part of a larger program that performs many other commands before (and

Figure 14-5
Example of a
subroutine

```
* Main program
<other commands in the program>
<commands to accept room value into memory variable M_Room>
* Use subroutine Handle to manage errors
ON ERROR DO Handle WITH ERROR()
USE PRODUCT
LOCATE FOR Room=M_Room         && Retrieve a product for the room
DO Print                       && Print product data
ON ERROR                       && Revert to standard error handling
DO WHILE .NOT. EOF()           && Look for other products for
    CONTINUE                   &&      same room
    DO Print
ENDDO
<other commands in the program>
RETURN

* Print procedure
PROCEDURE Print
<commands to manipulate and print current product row>
RETURN
* End of Print procedure

* Handle procedure
PROCEDURE Handle
PARAMETERS Error
IF Error=14                          && Find not successful
    <commands to request reentry of Room value>
ELSE IF Error=3                      && File already open
    CLOSE ALL
    ELSE
        <commands to display fatal error message>
        <commands to handle fatal error>
    ENDIF
ENDIF
RETRY
RETURN
* End of Handle procedure
```

after) executing this procedure. Fragments of the main program and necessary subroutines for this example appear in Figure 14-5.

The lines in <..> are where other program code would be placed; we
will not be concerned with these lines. The first ON ERROR command in
the main program specifies that the subroutine 'Handle' will control dBASE
errors until the next ON ERROR command (which is four commands later).
Thus, this ON ERROR covers the USE and LOCATE commands that follow
it. The Handle subroutine accepts as its one parameter the dBASE error
code for the error that caused the subroutine to be called. Two specific errors
are handled in this error subroutine:

- Error 14 (no match found for the specified room in the LOCATE
  command)

- Error 3 (the PRODUCT file has already been put into use by a previous command in the main program)

Other errors (like Error 1: file does not exist) are treated as fatal errors in the last ELSE clause. After appropriate action for either Error 14 or 3, Handle issues the RETRY command, which will cause the command that encountered the error to be reexecuted upon RETURN from this subroutine.

The Print subroutine manipulates and displays the contents of the Product row just retrieved. The DO WHILE loop continues to search for additional products for the same room, until the end of the file. Since the CONTINUE command in the DO WHILE comes after the second ON ERROR, the Handle subroutine does not take charge of errors encountered with this command; rather, the standard dBASE error handling procedures that generate an error message will apply. The Print subroutine is useful since this code needs to be written only once and can be called from two places in the main program.

This program illustrated only a few of the many dBASE IV programming language commands and program structures. We will look at examples of several other programs for the Pine Valley Furniture system in the next section. With this programming language it is possible to build large programs and sets of programs—an information system. To help a programmer tie together all the screens, reports, and programs needed to build an information system, dBASE provides the Application Generator. The next and last section on dBASE addresses this helpful programming tool.

Application Generator

An **application** is one or more programs, screens, reports, views, and a database (called objects), linked together by menus to perform a set of related information processing tasks. Order entry, customer billing, sales analysis, and accounts receivable are examples of typical business applications. An application can be written as a series of dBASE procedures, linked together via a master program that presents a hierarchical set of menus for choosing which procedures to execute for a given business task. Each of the programs, including the master program, could be originally written in the dBASE programming language, and some might simply be forms, reports, or [view queries objects] previously developed from the Control Center prompts.

An **application generator** is a tool for conveniently building applications from other objects, such as prewritten procedures, databases, forms, and reports. An application can then be run and changed, or an object code (compiled) version of the application can be created for use by the dBASE RunTime module (see Chapter 13 for a discussion of this dBASE component).

The dBASE Application Generator (ApGen) is menu driven, much like the Control Center, and can be reached from either the Control Center or the dot prompt. You can instruct the ApGen to create menus as well as boxes with lists of values or procedures from which a user can make choices.

An application is designed on the ApGen work surface as it will appear to the user. The ApGen automatically creates all the dBASE code for the whole application, so once the individual forms, procedures, and so forth are defined, no more original programming is needed. This code is internally documented with many comments for readability. The application designer has considerable control over the design and operation of an application, from picking screen colors to choosing the style of menus and types of borders for objects to be displayed.

It is common to use an application generator for prototyping. Thus, frequently the code generated will be changed. Because the ApGen produces generalized code, some lines may be dropped as extraneous for the particular application being developed. Other code might be changed because the ApGen was not capable of producing exactly the right user interface. However, even in these cases, the use of the ApGen has significantly reduced the time and cost of developing the application compared to manually coding each program.

The specification of a dBASE application is relatively easy since it is menu driven, but it takes many steps to select all the options. Many ApGen screens are needed to fully specify an application. Different screens are used

- To define a sign-on banner to be displayed when the user starts the application
- To specify the type of menu style for user choices
- To set the foreground and background colors, border style, bell tone, and character highlight colors
- To change default settings for such items as carrying forward field values from the most recently entered record to the record being entered, using the ESCAPE key, and deciding whether to confirm records before they are deleted
- To select screen format file for display of database tables

and to specify many, many more options.

We will not show the process of building an application here. For such a discussion the interested reader is referred to the excellent tutorial in Senn (1990). Rather, we will illustrate here the logical design of an application in Pine Valley Furniture, the resulting programs used by and generated by the dBASE Application Generator, and a sample session from using this application.

An Example Application Session   The example application we will illustrate is a simple accounts receivable system for Pine Valley Furniture, which includes the customer order entry and invoice procedures described in Chapter 2. Example screen displays for a customer order and for an invoice appear in Figures 2-4 and 2-5, respectively, and the screens we will see in this application closely resemble these diagrams. A chart for the database built for this application is contained in Figure 14-6. Note that the column

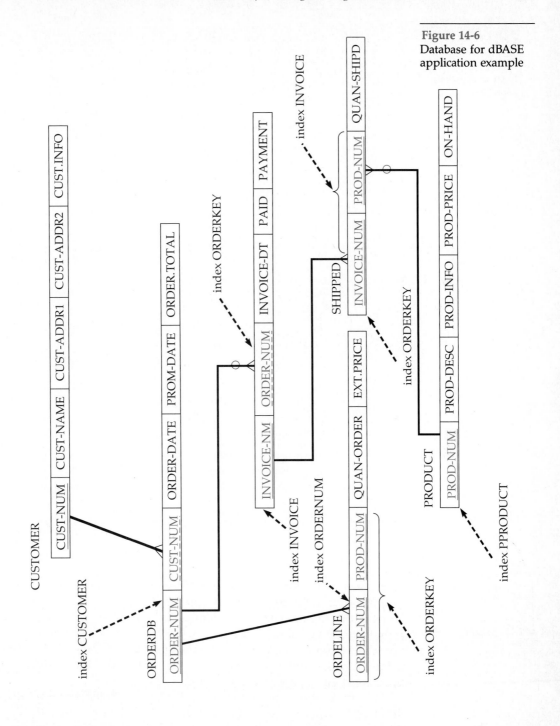

Figure 14-6
Database for dBASE application example

Figure 14-7
dBASE database
definition for
application example
(pages 632-633)

```
. use customer
. display structure
Structure for database  : B:\CUSTOMER.DBF
Number of data records:      7
Date of last update     : 02/11/90
```

Field	Field Name	Type	Width	Dec	Index
1	CUST_NUM	Character	4		N
2	CUST_NAME	Character	20		N
3	CUST_ADDR1	Character	20		N
4	CUST_ADDR2	Character	20		N
5	CUST_INFO	Character	20		N
** Total **			85		

```
. use orderdb
. display structure
Structure for database  : B:\ORDERDB.DBF
Number of data records:      0
Date of last update     : 02/15/90
```

Field	Field Name	Type	Width	Dec	Index
1	ORDER_NUM	Character	5		N
2	CUST_NUM	Character	4		N
3	ORDER_DATE	Date	8		N
4	PROM_DATE	Date	8		N
5	ORDR_TOTAL	Numeric	8	2	N
** Total **			34		

```
. use invoice
. display structure
Structure for database  : B:\INVOICE.DBF
Number of data records:      0
Date of last update     : 04/10/90
```

Field	Field Name	Type	Width	Dec	Index
1	INVOICE_NM	Character	5		N
2	ORDER_NUM	Character	5		N
3	INVOICE_DT	Date	8		N
4	PAID	Logical	1		N
5	PAYMENT	Numeric	7	2	N
** Total **			27		

names in this database are slightly different from those used in previous chapters (the differences are not important since the meaning of the columns is the same). This chart depicts the six tables in the database; the arrows show the column cross-references that are used, as needed, to join the tables together. Figure 14-7 contains a listing of the dBASE definitions for these tables and their associated indexes. Again, these dBASE definitions are slightly different from those used before.

Data have been preloaded into two database tables—CUSTOMER and PRODUCT—through the Control Center. We illustrate here the entry of one customer order and two invoices for that order, followed by an update of one of the invoices to record receipt of payment. After demonstrating

```
. use product
. display structure
Structure for database  : B:\PRODUCT.DBF
Number of data records:       13
Date of last update     : 02/15/90
Field    Field Name      Type       Width   Dec    Index
   1     PROD_NUM        Character     4              N
   2     PROD_DESCR      Character    15              N
   3     PROD_INFO       Character    20              N
   4     PROD_PRICE      Numeric       6              N
   5     ON_HAND         Numeric       3     2        N
** Total **                          49

. use ordrline
. display structure
Structure for database  : B:\ORDRLINE.DBF
Number of data records:        0
Date of last update     : 02/15/90
Field    Field Name      Type       Width   Dec    Index
   1     ORDER_NUM       Character     5              N
   2     PROD_NUM        Character     4              N
   3     QUAN_ORDRD      Numeric       2              N
   4     EXT_PRICE       Numeric       8     2        N
** Total **                          20

. use shipped
. display structure
Structure for database  : B:\SHIPPED.DBF
Number of data records:        0
Date of last update     : 02/15/90
Field    Field Name      Type       Width   Dec    Index
   1     INVOICE_NM      Character     5              N
   2     PROD_NUM        Character     4              N
   3     QUAN_SHIPD      Numeric       2              N
** Total **                          12
```

this application, we will explain the structure and coding of the application programs and procedures used in the example.

The application is started by calling the main program created by ApGen for this application, a program named MAINMENU when the application was created. This program can be selected from the Application menu on the Control Center or, at the dBASE dot prompt, we can enter

DO MAINMENU

MAINMENU calls another program, also generated from ApGen, called MENU1, to accept the user selection from the application's main menu and to initiate the desired action from the user's choice. The main menu of the

Figure 14-8
Accounts Receivable
application main
menu

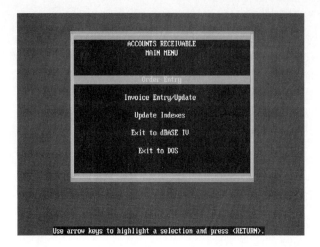

Accounts Receivable application appears in Figure 14-8. Each menu option corresponds to another program that handles that action or, for the last two options, returns to either dBASE or the DOS prompt. We will discuss the three Accounts Receivable programs later.

The Accounts Receivable main menu is a pop-up type, so the user simply moves the cursor bar to the line with the option he or she wants to select and presses return. Since there are no orders in the database yet, we will start by entering a new order. A series of screens in Figure 14-9 illustrates the operation of the ORDER program, which is called by selecting the first menu choice on the screen in Figure 14-8. The ORDER program was programmed manually without the aid of the application generator. ApGen can call any dBASE procedure, whether it was generated automatically by ApGen or written as original code. Alternatively, ApGen can call a predefined query, form, or report built from the Control Center.

Figure 14-9a shows the initial order entry screen. The cursor is positioned to accept an order number, a template that resembles Figure 2–4. A value of 00000 is displayed to show the format for this field. dBASE gets each value from the screen and writes new records to the ORDERDB and ORDRLINE tables for the header and detail data on this screen. Figure 14-9b shows the same screen just after the customer number has been entered. The ORDER program retrieves the customer name, address, and city-state-zip from the customer table. The program is now waiting for confirmation that the correct customer number was entered (the visual verification of the name and other data helps the user to determine if an input error was made). The default value of Y to this question is shown. After this confirmation, the user enters the two dates, confirms that the correct dates were entered, and then is asked to specify what products were ordered.

The first screen in the process of entering the line items on the order is shown is Figure 14-9c. Again a default value of 0000 shows the format for the product number. For our sample order, the first product is product

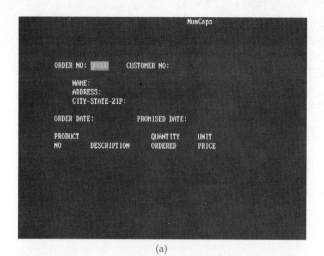

(a)

(b)

(c)

Figure 14-9
Order entry screens:
(a) initial order entry screen
(b) customer number entry
(c) start of order line entries
(d-f on page 636)

Figure 14-9
Order entry screens:
(d) product number
    entry
(e) quantity ordered
    entry
(f) order complete
    (pages 635-636)

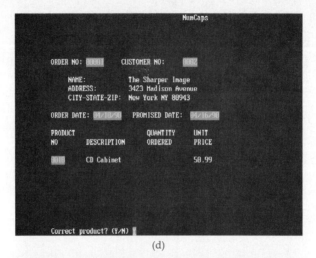

(d)

(e)

(f)

number 0010. Figure 14-9d shows the screen after entry of this product number. The ORDER program retrieves the associated product record and displays the description and unit price, and then asks for confirmation that the correct product was entered. After confirming this, the quantity ordered is entered and the screen in Figure 14-9e asks if there are more line items on this order. We will enter one more line item, for product 0007. We then respond with N to indicate no more line items, and the screen in Figure 14-9f asks if there are any more orders. We respond with N, and the program returns us to the main menu of Figure 14-8.

The process for entering an invoice is handled by the dBASE program INVOICE, which was also manually coded. This program is initiated when the user moves the selection bar to the second option on the main menu and presses the return key. Since an invoice (see Figure 2–5) has a similar layout to an order, the data entry process is almost the same as that described above. The first invoice entry screen is in Figure 14-10a. The invoice number is entered first. If this number corresponds to an existing invoice, the program assumes that the Paid field is to be updated (we will illustrate this below). Since we have not entered any invoices yet, we enter invoice number 00001 and the number of our one order, 00001 (if an incorrect order number were entered, the program would produce an error message and ask for a correction).

Figure 14-10b shows the screen after all the invoice header data are entered. As with the customer order entry, once the order number was entered, the customer number, name, and so forth were automatically displayed from already recorded rows in the ORDERDB and CUSTOMER tables. After verification that these data are correct, data for each shipment line item on the invoice are entered. The INVOICE program displays each order line item one by one, asking if any quantity has been sent for that line item on this shipment. Figure 14-10c shows this point for the first line item, for product 0010, with the cursor positioned on the quantity shipped field. The order quantity and the sum of all previous shipments (zero since this is the first invoice) of this product on this order were derived and are shown. Suppose five units of this product for this invoice were shipped. The value 5 is entered, and then the INVOICE program moves to the second line item on the order, as depicted in Figure 14-10d. Assuming two units of product 0007 are shipped on this order, the final invoice entry screen appears in Figure 14-10e. Here the totals have been calculated and the program asks if there are more invoices to enter.

For our example session, we will enter one more invoice for this order. The final screen for this invoice, number 00002, is shown in Figure 14-10f. Note that the shipment lines reflect the previous shipments from the first invoice we entered for this order. This second invoice shows shipment of the remaining order quantities of all line items.

As a final example of this order entry program, we illustrate updating an order when payment is received. For this case, we enter only the invoice number of the original invoice (00001) we entered as the one associated with

Figure 14-10

Invoice entry screens:

(a) initial invoice entry screen
(b) invoice header data entry
(c) first order line item for shipment
(d) second order line for shipment
(e) first invoice complete
(f) second invoice complete
(g) invoice for payment received
(h) invoice after PAID status changed (pages 638-640)

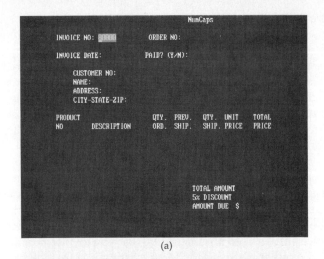

NumCaps

INVOICE NO: 00001   ORDER NO: 00001

INVOICE DATE: 04/12/98   PAID? (Y/N):

    CUSTOMER NO: 0002
    NAME: The Sharper Image
    ADDRESS: 3423 Madison Avenue
    CITY-STATE-ZIP: New York NY 80943

PRODUCT NO	DESCRIPTION	QTY. ORD.	PREV. SHIP.	QTY. SHIP.	UNIT PRICE	TOTAL PRICE
0010	CD Cabinet	10	0	5	50.99	254.95
0007	Book Stand oak	5	0	0	80.00	

                              TOTAL AMOUNT
                              5% DISCOUNT
                              AMOUNT DUE $

(d)

NumCaps

INVOICE NO: 00001   ORDER NO: 00001

INVOICE DATE: 04/12/98   PAID? (Y/N):

    CUSTOMER NO: 0002
    NAME: The Sharper Image
    ADDRESS: 3423 Madison Avenue
    CITY-STATE-ZIP: New York NY 80943

PRODUCT NO	DESCRIPTION	QTY. ORD.	PREV. SHIP.	QTY. SHIP.	UNIT PRICE	TOTAL PRICE
0010	CD Cabinet	10	0	5	50.99	254.95
0007	Book Stand oak	5	0	2	80.00	160.00

                              TOTAL AMOUNT   414.95
                              5% DISCOUNT   20.75
                              AMOUNT DUE $ 394.20

Another entry? (Y/N)

(e)

NumCaps

INVOICE NO: 00002   ORDER NO: 00001

INVOICE DATE: 01/14/98   PAID? (Y/N):

    CUSTOMER NO: 0002
    NAME: The Sharper Image
    ADDRESS: 3423 Madison Avenue
    CITY-STATE-ZIP: New York NY 80943

PRODUCT NO	DESCRIPTION	QTY. ORD.	PREV. SHIP.	QTY. SHIP.	UNIT PRICE	TOTAL PRICE
0010	CD Cabinet	10	5	5	50.99	254.95
0007	Book Stand oak	5	2	3	80.00	240.00

                              TOTAL AMOUNT   494.95
                              5% DISCOUNT   24.75
                              AMOUNT DUE $ 470.20

Another entry? (Y/N)

(f)

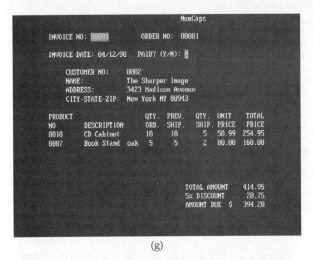

(g)

(h)

the payment just received. Figure 14-10g shows the complete status on this invoice, which has been recalled from the INVOICE, ORDERDB, and CUS-TOMER tables in the database. The current status of the invoice is not paid and the shipment line shows that, including this and all other invoices for this order, the complete order has been sent. The program accepts the status change, which is reflected in the screen in Figure 14-10h. The program then asks if we want to enter another invoice number, but we will stop at this point.

Example Application Programs   Now that you have a feel for the operation of this application, we will briefly discuss the programs that handle this data entry and maintenance. Overview structure charts (with brief descriptions of the different programs and program parts) for this application are contained in Figure 14-11. These charts show the relationships among five dBASE programs (MAINMENU.PRG, MENU1.PRG, ORDER.PRG, INVOICE.PRG, and NDXUPDAT.PRG), four other procedures (MPDEF, SET01, DBF01, and ACT01), and other program modules. MAINMENU, MENU1, and the overall structure of this application were automatically coded by ApGen from menu choices provided by its designer; the other three programs (for the first three menu functions) were manually written. Besides manually written programs, an application can use queries, forms, and reports designed from the Control Center.

A program file contains a main procedure (implicitly named as the program file name) and, potentially, other procedures. Within a program, any procedure in that program or in a program that called it can be referenced (see, for example, in Figure 14-11, that the procedure 1HELP1, defined in the MAINMENU program, is called within the SET01 procedure in the MENU1 program).

We show the MENU1 program below. The complete code for and explanation of the other four programs in this application appear in the *Instructor's Guide* for this book. We have chosen to place these programs there because of the space required to list them completely and because some instructors may not want you to explore the details of these programs. The following discussion gives a general appreciation of such programs.

The MAINMENU program is extremely long (approximately 500 lines of code plus ApGen-generated comments), which is typical of the main program of an application. Much has to be done in this program. The entire environment of the application (global variables defined, screen colors and style set up, general error routines defined, and so forth) must be included. If such a program were written manually, it could take a skilled programmer hours or, more likely, days to compose it properly. Using ApGen, this particular main program was written in under an hour!

Figure 14-12 contains the complete listing of the MENU1 program as generated by ApGen. MENU1 controls the handling of the menu in Figure 14-8. This program begins by calling the SET01 procedure. SET01 establishes that when the user presses the F1 key, the 1HELP1 procedure (the code for which is included in the MAINMENU procedure) is to be activated. We chose not to include customized help for this menu, so that procedure simply displays a "No Help Defined" message. What to do when function keys are pressed was specified in the various menus in the application generator when this application was developed.

SET01 then calls the DBF01 procedure, which closes all database files and opens the ORDERDB file and associated index, since this file is needed for all the menu actions. SET01 closes by setting the screen colors. After SET01 is done, if there was an error in opening the ORDERDB file, MENU1 returns to the program that called it (MAINMENU).

Once these opening routines are successfully complete, MENU1 activates the pop-up menu MENU1 defined in MPDEF and the procedure ACT01 reacts to the movement of the selection bar on the screen (see Figure 14-8). Within the ACT01 procedure, we can see that the appropriate action is

Figure 14-11
Structure charts for
Accounts Receivable
application
(pages 642-643)

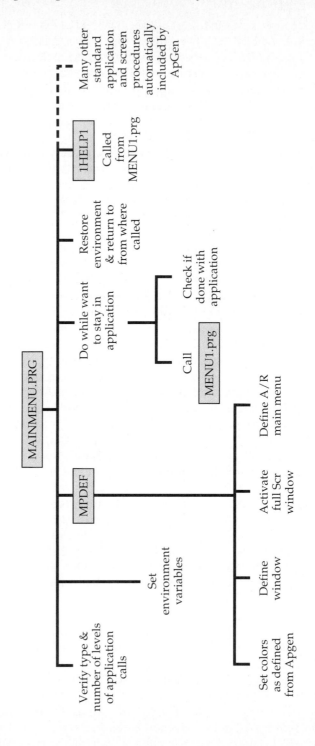

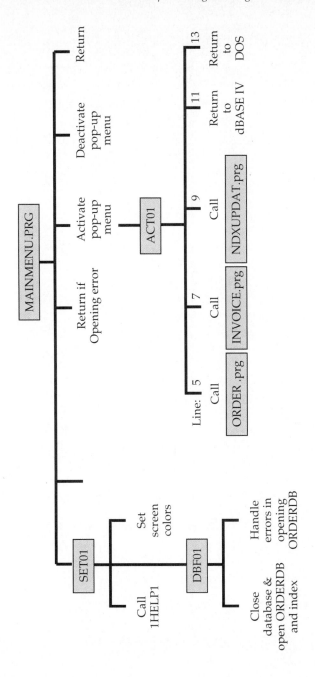

```
*****************************************************************************************
* Program . . . . . MENU1.PRG
* Author . . . . . . . :    This is an APPLICATION OBJECT
* Date . . . . . . 2-14-90
* Notice . . . . . Type information here or greetings to your users.
* dBASE Ver . . . . See Application menu to use as sign-on banner.
* Generated by . .:APGEN   version1.0
* Description . . main menu of MAINMENU    to control ORDER,INVOICE        and
NDXUPDAT

* Description.Menu actions
*****************************************************************************************
PROCEDURE   MENU1
PARAMETER   entryflg
PRIVATE   gc_prognum
gc_prognum="01"

DO SET01
IF gn_error> 0
  gn_error=0
  RETURN
ENDIF

* --Before menu code

ACTIVATE   POPUP   MENU1

* --Aftermenu
DEACTIVATE   POPUP

RETURN
* --EOP   MENU1

PROCEDURE   SET01
ON   KEY   LABEL   F1  DO   1HELP1    && This is where use of F1 as help key is set

DO DBF01                            && open menu leveldatabase
IF gn_error= 0
  If ISCOLOR()   && Ifcolormonitor
    SET COLOR   OF NORMAL   TO  W+/B
    SET COLOR   OF MESSAGES   TO  W+/N
    SET COLOR   OF TITLES   TO  W/B
    SET COLOR   OF HIGHLIGHT   TO  GR+/BG
    SET COLOR   OF BOX   TO  GR+/BG
    SET COLOR   OF INFORMATION   TO  B/W
    SET COLOR   OF FIELDS   TO  N/BG
  ENDIF
  @ 22,00
ENDIF
RETURN
```

Figure 14-12
MENU1 code generated from ApGen (pages 644-646)

```
* --Open menu levelview/database
lc_message="0"
ON ERROR  lc_message=LTRIM(STR(ERROR()))+"  "+MESSAGE()
USE ORDERDB
IF" "<> DBF()
  SET INDEX TO ORDERDB
ENDIF
ON ERROR
gn_error=VAL(lc_message)      && VAL returnnumbers at beginning of string
IF gn_error> 0               && so errornumber is extracted from message
  DO Pause WITH  ;
  "Error opening ORDERDB.DBF   or index(es)ORDERDB"
  lc_new='Y'
  RETURN
ENDIF
lc_new='Y'
RELEASE lc_message
RETURN
PROCEDURE   ACT01
* --Begin MENU1:  POPUP  Menu Actions.
* --(beforeitem,action,and afteritem)
*
PRIVATE  lc_new, lc_dbf
lc_new=' '
lc_dbf=' '
DO CASE
CASE BAR() = 5              && Order entry
  ACTIVATE  WINDOW  FullScr
  @ 24,0 CLEAR
  SET SCOREBOARD  ON
  DO ORDER

  SET SCOREBOARD  OFF
  DEACTIVATE  WINDOW  FullScr
CASE BAR() = 7              && Invoice
  ACTIVATE  WINDOW  FullScr
  @ 24,0 CLEAR

  SET SCOREBOARD  ON
  DO INVOICE

  SET SCOREBOARD  OFF
  DEACTIVATE  WINDOW  FullScr
CASE BAR() = 9              && Update indexes
  ACTIVATE  WINDOW  FullScr
  @ 24,0 CLEAR

  SET SCOREBOARD  ON
  DO NDXUPDATE

  SET SCOREBOARD  OFF
  DEACTIVATE  WINDOW  FullScr
```

```
CASE  BAR()  = 11          && Return to dBASE
  * --Return to caller
  gc_quit='Q'
  IF LEFT (entryflg,1)<>  "B"
    DEACTIVATE   POPUP      && MENU1
  ELSE
    DEACTIVATE   MENU
  ENDIF
  RETURN
CASE  BAR()  = 13          && Exit to DOS
  * --Quit dBASE
  CLOSE  DATABASES
  QUIT
ENDCASE.
SET  MESSAGE   TO          && Get ready to leave menu
IF SET ("STATUS")="ON"
  SET  STATUS   OFF
ENDIF
IF gc_quit='Q'
  DEACTIVATE   POPUP       && Menu1
ENDIF
IF lc_new='Y'
  lc_file="SET"+gc_prognum
  DO  &lc_file.
ENDIF
RETURN
```

determined by where the bar is on the screen. If the bar is on line 5 (where the option "Order Entry" is displayed), then the ORDER program is called. Similar calls to the other programs occur for the cases of lines 7 and 9. For line 11 a RETURN is executed, which returns the processing to the MAIN-MENU program. For line 13, all database files are closed and control is returned to the DOS prompt. The rest of the ACT01 procedure deactivates the menu after return to this procedure from any of the first three options. Then control is returned to MENU1, where control is returned to MAINMENU.

One operational feature of the ORDER program is of special interest. Because an application may be used by several people and the sequence of data entry steps can be rather complex, data entry errors and program malfunctions may occur. Thus, it is important in applications to protect the integrity of the database. For this reason the ORDER program includes the command

ON ERROR DO rollback_sequence

near the beginning. The main loop of the ORDER program is enclosed by BEGIN TRANSACTION ... END TRANSACTION commands. These commands control transaction integrity, a topic which was discussed in Chapter 13.

The entry of each customer order transaction is included between the BEGIN and END TRANSACTION statements. After a BEGIN TRANSACTION statement is executed, all database updates are kept in a transaction log, a type of suspense file; the actual database files are not changed. Only when the END TRANSACTION command is executed are these changes (new records in this case) written to the database files and the log file cleaned out. If any type of error occurs while a transaction is entered, the rollback_sequence routine aborts the database updates (erases the log file) since the last END TRANSACTION was executed.

The reason for this care is that unless all the actions of a business transaction (for example, order entry) are processed fully, it makes no sense to store only part of the transaction in the database. For example, assume that an ORDERDB record and two ORDRLINE records have been entered for a new customer order. Suppose that while entering a third line item, the user accidentally presses a key that causes the program to malfunction. We would not want any of the order to be stored, since an incomplete order would be an inaccurate representation of what the customer wants. The ON ERROR command would automatically call the rollback_sequence routine, which would first check that a rollback was needed. If so, the ROLLBACK command erases the transaction log, which restores the database to a high-integrity state.

Summary of dBASE Programming

This concludes our coverage of programming with PC-RDBMSs through discussing the dBASE IV procedural programming features. The dBASE language and dBASE Application Generator are powerful tools for building highly customized information systems. Packaged application software written in the dBASE language (or languages that clone this system) are available for many small business information processing needs.

Unfortunately, the dBASE language has not been standardized, like SQL has been. Thus, so called dBASE programs may work only with dBASE or a particular clone product. Further, the dBASE language is essentially controlled by vendors, not an impartial standards board, like ANSI for SQL. dBASE and its dialects are very popular programming languages today. Yet without a standard, organizations become locked-in to one product and vendor. Many of the dBASE clone languages are a superset of the dBASE language, but they also provide many other features that can not be handled by the dBASE interpreter or compiler. An organization that wants a dBASE-like programming capability should carefully evaluate the capabilities of dBASE and its clones, and consider the range of packaged application software available for each, before choosing a programming language.

SQL PROGRAMMING IN COBOL

In Chapter 12 we covered the interactive programming capabilities of SQL. This included the capability to save commands (routines) and recall these for processing. Thus, it is possible to build reasonably complete programs of only SQL commands. Frequently, however, this is not sufficient to handle information processing needs. Possibly because of wanting to preserve the use of previously written procedural programs or because SQL is not capable of handling data as desired, embedding SQL commands in a third generation language program is now common. For example, SQL has no IF...THEN...ELSE logic, so only sequential logic can be built. In fact, most SQL programming of production applications is by embedding SQL commands in a program written in COBOL, PL/I, C, FORTRAN, APL, BASIC, or other 3GL.

We will concentrate on data manipulation commands in this chapter. However, data definition commands may also be included in such a program. We also will use exclusively the COBOL language, although it is not the easiest in which to embed SQL (but it is the most widely used language for business data processing). We assume that the reader is generally familiar with COBOL and with sequential and random file processing in COBOL. Further, all the illustrations are from SQL/DS (see Chapter 12), typical of many SQL products and embedded programming capabilities of SQL.

Embedded SQL Programming

An embedded SQL COBOL program is a typical COBOL program, except COBOL file input and output statements are replaced by SQL commands that access and manipulate database contents. In fact, if there are no transaction input or output files for a program, there will be no file definitions (FDs) in the COBOL data division! Thus, the source code data division is considerably smaller than a typical COBOL program. This is because SQL/DS handles all file operations, so the COBOL program does not need to know anything about the database files. This provides considerable data independence.

An embedded SQL COBOL program must be compiled from source code into object code. A program with embedded SQL commands goes through one additional compilation step prior to execution, compared to a COBOL program without SQL commands. This step is a precompilation phase (see Figure 14-13), in which the SQL commands embedded in the source program (obviously not standard COBOL) are checked for correct SQL syntax and are translated into proper COBOL statement. Errors in the SQL commands may occur, so this phase may take several iterations for a clean precompilation. Then this modified source program (now all in proper COBOL) is given to the COBOL compiler.

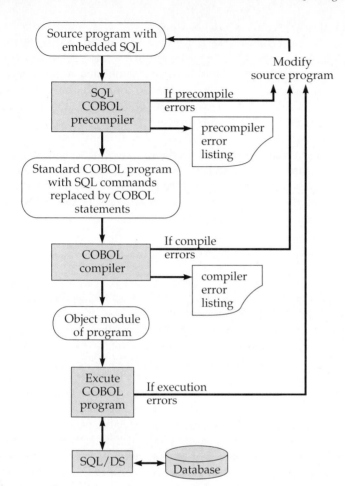

Figure 14-13
Embedded SQL
program compilation
and execution process

Some embedded SQL commands cause the precompiler to generate sections for the COBOL data division. For example, each SQL command in the procedure division requires a data structure in the data division to pass all the information the SQL/DS processing module needs to handle the command. These commands cause generation of calls to SQL/DS routines, with the appropriate passing of parameters. That is, when the COBOL program actually runs, data will be retrieved and stored by SQL/DS; various parts of SQL/DS will be called by the COBOL program, instead of traditional input/output commands for file handling. Because the program is actually a COBOL program, nondatabase files may also be accessed.

Each SQL command (for example, SELECT, DELETE, and INSERT) is preceded in the source program with EXEC SQL, to identify it as a command to be handled by the precompiler. Relative to the embedded SQL commands, a program has three main parts: a prolog, a body, and an epilog.

In the **prolog** (which is part of COBOL working storage), two functions are performed: (1) a communication area is defined to handle passing error messages and other information between the application program and the SQL modules it calls, and (2) special *host variables* are defined to hold database contents (unlike other data division variables, these will be preceded with a colon (:) when used in the program). The body and epilog are part of the procedure division. The **body** contains two parts: (1) SQL commands for accessing the database, and (2) a CONNECT statement that links the program to the desired database and checks database security clearance for the user of the program (not needed under the VM operating system). Finally, the **epilog** disconnects the program from SQL/DS and the database and may execute database transaction integrity commands to commit or roll back database changes.

Working Storage

COBOL working storage does not include file definitions for database tables, so there is considerable data independence between the program and the database. However, COBOL working storage does not obey strict data independent from the database definition. In particular, the data type of a host variable (used to hold the contents of a table column value in the memory assigned to the program) must be compatible with the data type of any database column whose value is stored in that host variable. The types do not have to be identical, but COBOL must be able to convert between the database data type and the associated COBOL host variable data type. Thus, if a database is redefined with new columns or with changed data types, every COBOL program that refers to that table may have to be changed.

Included in COBOL working storage are two primary kinds of data definitions: a communications area and host variables.

Communications Area   The communications area in working storage is defined by the

EXEC SQL INCLUDE SQLCA END-EXEC.

COBOL sentence. Precompilation will insert COBOL data definitions for the necessary communication variables into the working storage section. One particular variable, SQLCODE, returns an error code:

- 0 if no error
- A negative number if there is an error
- A positive number for a warning (for example, +100 for end of file)

after each SQL data manipulation command is executed. Similar to the ON ERROR dBASE command, the SQL data manipulation sentence

EXEC SQL WHENEVER SQLERROR command END-EXEC.

can be included anywhere in the procedure division to specify what to do in the case of an error. Different WHENEVER SQLERROR commands can be issued throughout the program when the desired error handling procedure needs to change. SQLWARNING and NOT FOUND communication variables can be similarly tested in WHENEVER statements for automatic execution of procedures under specified conditions.

Host Variables All COBOL variables used to store database column values must be defined in working storage. These COBOL variables are called host variables. They are declared as 01 or 77 level data items. For example, for the Pine Valley Furniture database illustrated earlier in this chapter, the following is a subset of what might appear for host variable definitions:

```
EXEC SQL BEGIN DECLARE SECTION END-EXEC.
77 INVOICE-NO        PIC S9(5)   COMPUTATIONAL.
77 PRODUCT-NO        PIC X(4).
77 DESCRIPTION       PIC X(12).
77 UNIT-PRICE        PIC S9(4)V9(2) COMP-3.
EXEC SQL END DECLARE SECTION END-EXEC.
```

Cursor variables, to be discussed below, are *not* defined here. The PICTURE clause is any standard COBOL picture, and the data type (for example, COMP-3) is any legal COBOL data type. OCCURS, SIGN, JUSTIFIED, and BLANK clauses may not be used, and a few other rules apply.

Host variables are referenced in SQL commands in the procedure division. For example, given the above host variables, the embedded SQL statement

```
EXEC SQL SELECT DESCRIPTION, UNITPRICE
INTO :DESCRIPTION, :UNIT-PRICE
FROM PRODUCT
WHERE PRODUCTNO = :PRODUCT-NO END-EXEC.
```

would retrieve the DESCRIPTION and UNITPRICE columns from the PRODUCT table into working storage for the product whose number was stored in host variable PRODUCT-NO.

Procedure Division

The full power of the SQL SELECT, INSERT, DELETE, and UPDATE commands is available. For example, GROUP BY and HAVING clauses on a SELECT command are allowed and expressions may appear in the select list (see Chapter 12 for a review of the SQL SELECT command). Very complex SQL commands, using many host variables, can be constructed. For example, consider the need on an invoice in the Pine Valley Furniture database to calculate the sum of the previous shipments of a product. Assume the following host variable definitions:

PREV-SHIP:	The sum we wish to calculate
ORDER-NO:	The order number for the invoice being processed
INVOICE-NO:	The invoice number for the invoice being processed
PRODUCT-NO:	The product number for the current invoice line item

The embedded SQL code for this calculated value is

```
EXEC SQL SELECT SUM(SHIP_QTY) INTO :PREV-SHIP
         FROM CUSTOMER CO, INVOICE I, SHIPMENT S
         WHERE CO.ORDER_NO = :ORDER-NO AND
         I.ORDER_NO = CO.ORDER_NO AND
         I.INVOICE_NO < :INVOICE-NO AND
         S.PRODUCT_NO = :PRODUCT_NO AND
         S.INVOICE_NO = I.INVOICE_NO END-EXEC.
  IF SQLCODE EQUALS 100 THEN
     PREV-SHIP = 0.
```

The IF statement handles the situation when this is the first shipment (invoice) for the order, so there are no previous shipment quantities. This situation stores a warning message value of +100 in SQLCODE.

Processing Queries Involving Multiple Rows

Embedded SQL data manipulation commands are of two types: those that require one or no database rows *to be stored in working storage*, and those that require potentially more than one database row to be placed into working storage. Examples of commands that require only one or none are a SELECT such as the ones above (called a single row or "singleton SELECT"), UPDATE, DELETE, and INSERT. A singleton select is one in which at most one row will be stored in working storage. UPDATE and DELETE may involve zero, one, or more database rows, but none of these rows have to be stored in COBOL working storage (they are simply manipulated in SQL/DS buffers). For example, the embedded SQL sentence

```
EXEC SQL UPDATE INVOICE
         SET PAID = :PAID
         WHERE INVOICE_DATE = :I-DATE
END-EXEC.
```

says to mark as paid all the invoice rows with the invoice date that appears in the I-DATE host variable. Although this may update many rows, none of these have to be moved into COBOL working storage to accomplish the update. INSERT, like a singleton SELECT, only applies to one row (at a time).

When potentially a set of rows will be selected (for example, when the WHERE clause involves a secondary key, like order number for invoices in Pine Valley Furniture), a cursor *must* be defined. A **cursor** is used similarly

Table 14-2 Embedded SQL Cursor Actions and Declarations

Database Action	Cursor Processing Command	Cursor Declaration Query
Retrieve next row	FETCH cursor-name INTO host-variable-list	DECLARE cursor-name CURSOR FOR select-statement [ORDER BY . . .]
Update current row	UPDATE table-name SET column-name = expression . . . WHERE CURRENT OF cursor-name	DECLARE cursor-name CURSOR FOR select-statement [ORDER BY . . .] FOR UPDATE OF column-list
Delete current row	DELETE FROM table-name WHERE CURRENT OF cursor-name	DECLARE cursor-name CURSOR FOR select-statement [ORDER BY . . .]
Insert new row	PUT cursor-name	DECLARE cursor-name CURSOR FOR INSERT INTO table-name (column-list) VALUES (host-variable-list)

to what we called a record pointer in Chapter 7. Cursors are needed since COBOL is a record-processing, not a set-processing language (SQL, as do all relational languages, processes sets of records). A cursor holds the position of the current row of those rows that satisfy the SQL statement in the cursor definition.

A cursor is associated with the SQL query statement in the cursor's definition, rather than with a database table (as the current row pointer is in dBASE). The type of query statement depends on the database action to be performed. The subset of table rows qualified by the query is called the *active set*. For the four possible database actions that use a cursor, Table 14-2 outlines the embedded SQL procedural command and its associated cursor definition. These various formats will be explained in this and following sections.

For example, suppose we wanted to retrieve all the line items on a given customer order in the Pine Valley Furniture database. Assume customer orders are stored in a table called REQUEST. The cursor for this processing would be defined by

```
EXEC SQL DECLARE X CURSOR FOR
    SELECT R.PRODUCT_NO, R.QUANTITY_ORDERED
        FROM REQUEST R
        WHERE R.ORDER_NO = :ORDER_NO END-EXEC.
```

This command defines the cursor, or pointer, and the active set of rows but does not move data into working storage. That is, this query is not fully processed when this declaration command is executed. The DECLARE also positions the cursor on the first row of the active set. This cursor definition is included in the procedure division, not the data division, of the program. Obviously, the DECLARE statement must be executed before rows in the active set can be retrieved.

As noted in Table 14-2, the select-statements themselves for retrieve, update, and delete actions may not include an ORDER BY clause. However, an important use of a cursor is to define the sequence in which rows are to be retrieved. This is accomplished by simply appending a normal SQL ORDER BY clause to the select statement associated with the cursor, as shown in this table.

Data Retrieval via a Cursor　　The FETCH command sequentially processes an active set. FETCH first moves the selected column values into the designated host variables and then advances the cursor one row. The following FETCH command for the X cursor defined above, in an appropriate loop, would retrieve each desired row one by one (in the order specified):

```
EXEC SQL FETCH X INTO
        :PRODUCT-NO, :QUANTITY-ORDERED END-EXEC.
```

Each execution of the FETCH moves the values of the two columns mentioned in the cursor's SELECT (PRODUCT_NO and QUANTITY_ORDERED) from the current row of the active set into the specified host variables (PRODUCT-NO and QUANTITY-ORDERED, respectively). Then this FETCH command moves the pointer one row ahead in an imaginary table (the active set) of all the rows that satisfy the query associated with the cursor. Cursors may not be moved backwards. An SQLCODE communications host variable of +100 is returned when a FETCH reaches the end of the active set. A cursor can be CLOSEd (deactivated) at any time and reOPENed (that is, the query reevaluated and the cursor moved to the first row in the active set).

Data Update via a Cursor　　Cursors are not used just for data retrieval. DELETE (delete a row) and UPDATE (change row contents) can also be used as we used FETCH above with a cursor associated with a SELECT query. DELETE and UPDATE commands may be issued without cursors, as mentioned above; they may be used with a cursor, however, to delete or update the current row of the active set. For example, the command

```
EXEC SQL
   DELETE FROM tablename
   WHERE CURRENT OF cursor-name
END-EXEC.
```

would delete the current row of the active set of the specified cursor.

To use the UPDATE command, an additional element must appear in the cursor definition. This clause is

FOR UPDATE OF column-list

The column-list is a list of columns for which update is permitted. The UPDATE command sets values for the columns of this list from literals or expressions, just as in the interactive SQL UPDATE command. However, one additional clause, WHERE CURRENT OF cursor-name, is appended to the UPDATE to indicate which active set is being updated.

The PUT (insert a row) command is used with a cursor associated with an SQL INSERT command, not a SELECT. For instance, suppose we wanted to add new rows to the PRODUCT table. We will use host variables PRODUCT-NO, DESCRIPTION, and UNIT-PRICE to store the data to be added for each row. The following program fragment illustrates the cursor declaration and row insertion process:

```
EXEC SQL DECLARE XX CURSOR FOR
    INSERT INTO PRODUCT (PRODUCT_NO, DESCRIPTION, UNIT_PRICE)
    VALUES (:PRODUCT-NO, :DESCRIPTION, :UNIT-PRICE) END-EXEC.
<commands needed to store values in three host variables>
EXEC SQL OPEN XX
        PUT XX
        CLOSE XX    END-EXEC.
```

The OPEN statement places the cursor at the top of the table and activates the active set. The CLOSE statement deactivates the cursor.

Transaction Integrity

The SQL commands COMMIT WORK and ROLLBACK WORK were introduced in Chapter 12. These commands are also used in embedded SQL programs to control the integrity of units of work, or transactions. An END-EXEC causes an implicit COMMIT WORK, so an explicit COMMIT WORK is needed only when several SQL commands are encased within the same EXEC SQL and END-EXEC pair. ROLLBACK WORK would normally be executed when an error has occurred in the middle of an SQL EXEC. The WHENEVER command, defined above, can be used to execute this command or to call a perform paragraph in which a ROLLBACK occurs.

Dynamic SQL

Dynamic SQL refers to facilities available with some host languages (but not COBOL) to dynamically prepare SQL statements within an application program. Frequently, the exact nature of an application is not known in advance—especially true for management and decision support applications (as opposed to transaction processing applications). For example, in a sales analysis system in Pine Valley Furniture, a user may want to see a summary of sales based upon any combination of salesperson, territory, product, and date conditions. Average or total sales may be requested. Thus, the application program cannot execute prewritten embedded SQL commands but needs to build appropriate ones based upon input received from the user. This is not to say that the user enters SQL statements—most managerial users would not have the proper training to do this. Instead, an application prompts the user for the desired specifications and dynamically builds the right SQL commands.

The two primary dynamic SQL commands are PREPARE and EXECUTE. The use of these commands is as follows. As the application prompts the user for information processing needs, the application builds an SQL command in a character host variable. The command

EXEC SQL PREPARE statement FROM :host-variable

translates the character host variable into a prepared version of the command. The command

EXEC SQL EXECUTE statement [USING arguments]

executes the prepared statement, to which arguments may be passed. For example, the prepared statement may use parameters for upper and lower bounds on a range of dates, and the arguments fill in the actual dates desired.

Only certain SQL commands can be prepared dynamically. In general, SELECT, UPDATE, DELETE, INSERT, CREATE, DROP, ALTER, GRANT, and REVOKE are typically supported.

Because dynamic SQL is not supported in COBOL, we will not elaborate on this embedded program feature.

Sample Embedded SQL Program

This section describes a sample program to illustrate the embedded SQL programming in COBOL discussed in the prior sections. SQL/DS running on an IBM 4381 computer under the VM/CMS operating system is used for this example.

Application Description   The application we illustrate here handles the Pine Valley Furniture order entry and invoicing operations described in Chapter 2. COBOL does not directly handle full-screen data entry. Thus, the application does not follow the screen formats of Figures 2–4 and 2–5, for the customer order and invoice, respectively. Line-oriented data entry is used. However, the database contents and processing are handled completely.

As illustrated earlier in this chapter for dBASE programming, this application has three transactions: entry of a new customer order, entry of a new invoice that depicts a shipment against an invoice, and receipt of payment on an invoice (marking the invoice paid).

The SQL/DS database definitions for the tables needed for this application appear in Figure 14-14. This application should be quite familiar to

Column Name	Table Name	Data Type	Lengh	NULL VALUES ALLOWED?
CUSTOM_NO	CUSTOMER	INTEGER		N
NAME	CUSTOMER	CHAR	20	Y
ADDRESS	CUSTOMER	CHAR	20	Y
CITY_STATE_ZIP	CUSTOMER	CHAR	30	Y
DISCOUNT	CUSTOMER	INTEGER		Y
ORDER_NO	CUSTORDER	INTEGER		N
ORDER_DATE	CUSTORDER	DATE		Y
PROMISED_DATE	CUSTORDER	DATE		Y
CUSTOMER_NO	CUSTORDER	INTEGER		Y
ORDER_NO	REQUEST	INTEGER		N
PRODUCT_NO	REQUEST	CHAR	4	N
QUANTITY_ORDERED	REQUEST	INTEGER		Y
PRODUCT_NO	PRODUCT	CHAR	4	N
DESCRIPTION	PRODUCT	INTEGER	12	Y
ROOM	PRODUCT	CHAR	10	Y
FINISH	PRODUCT	CHAR	10	Y
UNIT_PRICE	PRODUCT	DECIMAL	(7, 2)	Y
QUANTITY_ON_HAND	PRODUCT	INTEGER		Y
INVOICE_NO	SHIPMENT	INTEGER		N
PRODUCT_NO	SHIPMENT	CHAR	4	N
SHIP_QTY	SHIPMENT	INTEGER		Y
INVOICE_NO	INVOICE	INTEGER		N
INVOICE_DATE	INVOICE	DATE		Y
PAID	INVOICE	CHAR	1	Y
ORDER_NO	INVOICE	INTEGER		N

Figure 14-14
SQL/DS sample application database

you since it has been illustrated several other times in the book. Thus, we do not provide a transcript for it using the embedded SQL COBOL program.

Program Explanation The COBOL program with embedded SQL commands for this application is quite long. Thus, we have chosen to include the source code in the *Instructor's Guide* for this book. This source program (excluding comments) has approximately 180 lines of working storage definitions and 450 lines of procedure code. In contrast, the output from the SQL precompiler for this program has almost four times as many lines of code. Most of this expansion is in working storage. What is added are many definitions for the communications area. In addition, each procedural division SQL command requires a working storage data structure to contain all the information that is passed between the application program and the SQL routine called. As you might expect, such a program is not trivial to debug. It becomes essential to use TRACE and other facilities to check where errors occur during program testing.

If you were to inspect this COBOL program, you would find that it still has a record-by-record processing logic even with the embedded SQL. That is, as we saw in prior sections on embedded SQL, the result of each procedure division command that accesses the database must be data for *one* record (row). Although a cursor allows us to write one SQL command to "retrieve" a set of records, COBOL still requires each row in this set to be moved one by one into working storage. On the other hand, any complex SQL command can be included in the procedure division. For example, the following fragment from this COBOL program retrieves all the data needed for the top part (that is, excluding line items) for an existing invoice (the order whose number is in host variable INVOICE-NO):

```
EXEC SQL SELECT CU.CUSTOMER_NO, CU.NAME, CU.ADDRESS,
            CU.CITY_STATE_ZIP, CU.DISCOUNT, CO.ORDER_NO,
            INV.PAID
         INTO :CUSTOMER-NO, :NAME, :CU-ADDR,
              :CITY-STATE-ZIP, :DISCOUNT, :ORDER-NO
              :PAID
         FROM CUSTOMER CU, CUSTORDER CO, INVOICE INV
         WHERE INV.INVOICE_NO = :INVOICE-NO AND
              INV.ORDER_NO = CO.ORDER_NO    AND
              CO.CUSTOMER_NO = CU.CUSTOMER_NO
         END-EXEC.
```

This embedded query implicitly joins three tables. Many standard COBOL random and sequential file access commands would be required to retrieve the same results. Considerable time and effort is still required, however, to write such an embedded SQL COBOL program. With embedded SQL handling database input and output, the effort is reduced from that of a program with only COBOL statements.

We will not elaborate on this program here. However, for those who are interested in reading and understanding the program, here are some of its main features to investigate:

- A WHENEVER SQLERROR command is used to transfer control to an error routine.

- The program will create an invoice number for a new order, if told to do so, by adding one to the largest invoice number on file.

- Cursors are defined to process line items on customer orders and invoices.

- SQLCODE values are checked for important error messages after most SQL commands.

SUMMARY

The ability to write, store, and repeatedly execute complete programs greatly increases the power of relational database management systems beyond only interactive data manipulation. This chapter illustrated the database programming facilities of two major programming platforms: dBASE IV on personal computers and SQL (available for both personal and larger computer systems).

This chapter has shown such capabilities as macros, user defined functions, and procedural programs in dBASE. Looping, conditional execution of commands, transaction integrity controls, and many other programming constructs were illustrated for both dBASE and SQL. The differences between COBOL record-at-a-time processing and SQL set processing were discussed in light of the embedded SQL cursor concept. Examples of both dBASE and COBOL embedded with SQL programs were illustrated and discussed.

This chapter is meant to show that programming with relational DBMSs can be used to build very complex and useful applications. In most cases, the programming capabilities are equal or superior to those found in third-generation procedural programming languages. Considerable training is needed to take full advantage of these capabilities; therefore, most programming such as that discussed in this chapter is done by professional programmers, not end users. Although not discussed in this chapter, such programs must be carefully designed, tested, and documented.

Frequently an organization will have professional programmers write applications to handle transaction processing and reporting of business operational results. Programs must be designed to support high volumes and efficient data handling. The performance of these applications will depend on the design of the databases used, so database and application design must be coordinated. Logical access maps (see Chapter 8) and action diagrams (see Chapter 6) are very helpful in designing the database processing logic for the kinds of programs illustrated in this chapter.

This chapter concludes the coverage of relational database technologies. The next (and final) chapter looks at issues and technologies for managing a database that is distributed across several computer systems. As part of that discussion, additional features of relational systems will be introduced.

Chapter Review

REVIEW QUESTIONS

1. Define each of the following terms:

a. cursor	i. host variable
b. user defined function	j. private variable
c. subroutine	k. public variable
d. precompiler	l. application generator
e. macro	m. rollback
f. SET command	n. embedded language
g. parameter	o. communications area
h. memory variable	p. active set

2. Explain why interactive relational query languages are inadequate to develop some application systems.

3. Explain why the dBASE IV Application Generator saves time in building an application compared to writing a program directly in the dBASE programming language.

4. Explain how macros are used in an interactive query session with dBASE IV.

5. Explain why a function is not allowed to change the values of the parameters passed to it.

6. What are the differences between the FIND, LOCATE, and SEEK commands in dBASE IV?

7. What is the purpose of the ON ERROR command in dBASE?

8. What facilities exist in dBASE IV to control transaction integrity in programs?

9. What is the purpose of the WHENEVER command in embedded SQL?

10. How are host variables distinguished from database columns in embedded SQL statements?

11. What does a FETCH command in embedded SQL do?

12. Explain the purpose of the dynamic SQL facility.

PROBLEMS AND EXERCISES

1. Match the following terms to the appropriate definitions.

_____ user-input break

_____ macro playback

_____ DO WHILE

_____ application object

_____ structure chart

_____ singleton SELECT

a) an organization-chart-type diagram that shows segments of a program

b) an embedded SQL command that retrieves only one row in a table

c) execution of keystrokes that involve cursor movements, menu selections, and user input

d) a form, report, menu, or program

e) a pause in a macro to permit entry of data

f) a conditional looping structure

Problems 2 through 6 are based on the Pine Valley Furniture dBASE database from Chapter 2, which is also used in this chapter to illustrate dBASE programming.

2. Write a dBASE IV macro that calculates the average unit price for products in a specified room (for example, BEDROOM). The particular room will be entered as user input to your macro.

3. Write a dBASE user defined function that calculates the value of inventory on hand for a product. The value is computed as quantity on hand times unit price. Define memory variables as needed.

4. Write a dBASE program similar to the one in Figure 14-4 that prints the following information for every customer in the Pine Valley Furniture database:

Customer Number	Order Number	Product Number	Quantity Ordered	Total Ordered

Each row in this table is for a line item on a customer order. The line shows the customer number for the order, the order number, the product number for the line item, the quantity ordered of that product on that order, and the total amount ordered across all past orders of that product by that customer. Be sure to handle the case where an order is the first time a customer has bought that product.

5. Write a dBASE program to interactively update the product table in the Pine Valley Furniture database. This program should cover three types of transactions:
   - Entry of a new product (be sure to check for duplicate entries)
   - Deletion of an existing product
   - Changes in description, room, price, or quantity on hand

   Include transaction control statements to ensure the integrity of this program during updates.

6. Rewrite your answer to Problem 5 above using the dBASE Application Generator. Use the ApGen to create a menu-driven front end for selecting the type of transaction. Then break your program in Problem 5 into three procedures, one for each of the three types of transactions. Have the menu call the appropriate transaction procedure. Allow for ways to exit this application either to DOS or to dBASE.

Problems 7 through 11 are based on the Pine Valley Furniture SQL database used in this chapter to illustrate embedded COBOL SQL programming (see Figure 14-14 for a definition of this database).

7. Write the various working storage and procedure division COBOL sentences needed to retrieve in product number sequence all the BEDROOM furniture from the product table. Do not write COBOL commands; simply include a brief description of which COBOL commands would be needed. Include all the SQL code required for such a program. Explain any host variables you define.

8. Given the working storage definitions you wrote for Problem 7, write only the procedure division embedded SQL commands you would need to change the description of product M128 from 'BOOKCASE' to 'BOOKSHELVES'.

9. Write the embedded SQL command needed to calculate the number of line items on order 61397. Define any additional host variables you might need for this query that were not needed in the previous problems.

10. Write the embedded SQL commands needed first to retrieve the customer order with the largest discounted amount due value, and then to display this amount along with the customer's number, name, and city-state-zip. Define any additional host variables you might need for this query that were not needed in the previous problems.

11. Using a cursor, write the embedded SQL commands needed to raise the price of every product by 15%.

REFERENCES

Krumm, R. 1990. *The Student Edition of dBASE IV, Programmer's Version*. Reading, Mass.: Addison-Wesley

Senn, J. A. 1990. *The Student Edition of dBASE IV*. Reading, Mass.: Addison-Wesley.

CHAPTER 15

Distributed and Intelligent Databases

INTRODUCTION

In this last chapter we describe several related trends and new technologies in database management. The most prominent of these trends, and the one that will probably have the greatest impact on the field, is distributed database management. We describe several issues related to distributed databases, including methods for distributing data, types of remote database access, concurrency management, and extensions to SQL for remote databases. Other related topics described in this chapter are cooperative processing, database machines, and intelligent databases.

A variety of new opportunities and competitive pressures are driving the trend toward distributed databases. Corporate restructuring, such as mergers, acquisitions, and consolidations, makes it necessary to connect or (in some cases) replace existing stand-alone applications. Applications are being distributed from expensive mainframes to microcomputers and workstations that are much more user-friendly and cost-effective. New standards and technology such as Integrated Services Digital Network (ISDN) and Systems Application Architecture (SAA) are designed to support distributed applications (Schur, 1989). As distributed database management software matures, the trend to distributed databases seems likely to accelerate.

DISTRIBUTED DATABASES

When an organization is geographically dispersed, it may choose to store its databases on a central computer or to distribute them to local computers (or a combination of both). A **distributed database** is a single logical database that is spread physically across computers in multiple locations that are connected by a data communications network. The network must allow the users to share the data; thus a user (or program) at location A must be able to access (and perhaps update) data at location B. The sites of a distributed system may be distributed over a large area (such as the United States or the world), or over a small area (such as a building or campus). The computers may range from micros to large-scale computers or even supercomputers.

It is important to distinguish between distributed and decentralized databases. A **decentralized database** is also stored on computers at multiple locations; however, the computers are not interconnected by a network, so that data cannot be shared by users at the various sites. Thus a decentralized database is best regarded as a collection of independent databases, rather than having the geographical distribution of a single database.

Objectives and Trade-offs

A major objective of distributed databases is to provide ease of access to data for users at many different locations. To meet this objective, the distributed database system must provide what is called location transparency. **Location transparency** means that a user (or user program) requesting data need not know at which site these data are located. Any request to retrieve or update data at a nonlocal site is automatically forwarded by the system to that site. Thus ideally the user is unaware of the distribution of data, and all data in the network appear as a single logical database.

Compared to centralized databases, there are numerous advantages to distributed databases. The most important of these are discussed in the following sections.

Increased Reliability and Availability   When a centralized system fails, the database is unavailable to all users. A distributed system will continue to function at some reduced level, however, even when a component fails. The reliability and availability will depend (among other things) on how the data are distributed (discussed in the following sections).

Local Control   Distributing the data encourages local groups to exercise greater control over "their" data, which promotes improved data integrity and administration. At the same time, users can access nonlocal data when necessary. Hardware can be chosen for the local site to match the local, not global, data processing work.

Modular Growth   Suppose that an organization expands to a new location or adds a new work group. It is often easier and more economical to add a local computer and its associated data to the distributed network than to expand a large central computer. Also, there is less chance of disruption to existing users than is the case when a central computer system is modified or expanded.

Lower Communication Costs   With a distributed system, data can be located closer to their point of use. This can reduce communication costs, compared to a central system.

Faster Response   Depending on how data are distributed, most requests for data by users at a particular site can be satisfied by data stored at that site. This speeds up query processing since communication and central computer delays are minimized. It may also be possible to split complex queries into subqueries that can be processed in parallel at several sites, providing even faster response.

A distributed database system also faces certain costs and disadvantages.

Software Cost and Complexity   More complex software (especially DBMS) is required for a distributed database environment. We discuss this software later in the chapter.

Processing Overhead   The various sites must exchange messages and perform additional calculations to ensure proper coordination among the sites.

Data Integrity   A by-product of the increased complexity and need for coordination is the additional exposure to improper updating and other problems of data integrity.

Slow Response   If the data are not distributed properly according to their usage, or if queries are not formulated correctly, response to requests for data can be extremely slow. These issues are discussed later in the chapter.

Options for a Distributed Network

We have defined a distributed database as one that is spread across computers in multiple locations that are connected by a data communications network. As shown in Figure 15-1, there are a variety of ways to configure such a network.

A **fully connected** network is one in which each site (or computer) is physically linked to every other site. This approach provides the greatest reliability and flexibility, but it is also the most costly to install.

A **partially connected** network has links between some (but not all) of the sites. Links are generally installed between sites where the traffic density is greatest.

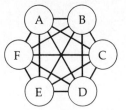

Fully connected network

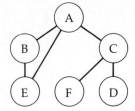

Partially connected network

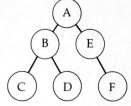

Tree-structured network

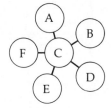

Star network

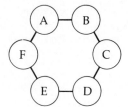

Ring network

Figure 15-1
Alternative network
configurations
(Source: Korth and
Silberschatz, 1986)

A **tree-structured** network is a hierarchical arrangement of nodes. It is often used in organizations that have a hierarchical organization structure that corresponds to the network.

A **star** network connects numerous satellite computers with a central computer (in Figure 15-1, computer C is the central computer). This approach is often used in companies with branch locations that must communicate with a central corporate computer.

A **ring** network interconnects sites in a closed loop. This approach is often used to link personal computers in a local area network.

In practice, combinations of these options are often used. For example, Figure 15-2 shows a common distributed processing approach in a manufacturing company that combines the tree-structured and ring approaches. The network contains three types of computers: a corporate mainframe, departmental computers (for engineering and manufacturing), and microcomputers or workstations. The corporate database (including personnel, marketing, and financial data) is maintained on the corporate computer. The engineering and manufacturing departmental computers each manage databases relative to their respective areas. The engineering computer is networked to several workstations (powerful microcomputers) for computer-aided design and computer-aided manufacturing (CAD/CAM).

In manufacturing, numerous personal computers are linked in a local area network (ring). These PCs are used for a variety of functions, such as controlling machines and robots, controlling materials-handling equipment, and reading manufacturing data. The local area network (LAN) has a dedicated microcomputer, called a **database server**, that manages a local database (which might contain work assignments, movements of materials, and so on). Notice that this database is centralized with respect to the local area network but in the overall scheme is just one component of the dis-

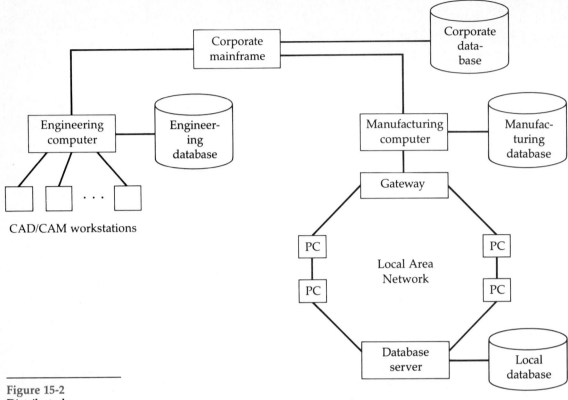

Figure 15-2
Distributed
processing system for
a manufacturing
company

tributed database. The LAN communicates with the manufacturing computer by means of a **gateway**—a microcomputer with special software to coordinate such communications.

Options for Distributing a Database

How should a database be distributed among the sites (or nodes) of a network? This important issue of physical database design was described in Chapter 8, which introduced an analytical procedure for evaluating alternative distribution strategies. In that chapter we noted that there are four basic strategies for distributing databases:

1. Data replication
2. Horizontal partitioning
3. Vertical partitioning
4. Combinations of the above

We will explain and illustrate each of these approaches using relational databases. The same concepts apply (with some variations) for other data models, such as hierarchical and network.

ACCT-NO	CUSTOMER-NAME	BRANCH-NAME	BALANCE
200	Jones	Lakeview	1000
324	Smith	Valley	250
153	Gray	Valley	38
426	Dorman	Lakeview	796
500	Green	Valley	168
683	McIntyre	Lakeview	1500
252	Elmore	Lakeview	330

Figure 15-3
Customer relation for a bank

Suppose that a bank has numerous branches located throughout a state. One of the base relations in the bank's database is the Customer relation. The format for an abbreviated version of this relation is shown in Figure 15-3. For simplicity, the sample data in the relation apply to only two of the branches (Lakeview and Valley). The primary key in this relation is account number (Acct-No). Branch-Name is the name of the branch where customers have opened their accounts (and therefore where they presumably perform most of their transactions).

Data Replication   One option for data distribution is to store a separate copy of the database at each of two or more sites. The Customer relation in Figure 15-3 could be stored at Lakeview or Valley, for example. If a copy is stored at every site, we have the case of **full replication**.

There are two advantages to data replication:

1. Reliability: If one of the sites containing the relation (or database) fails, a copy can always be found at another site.

2. Fast response: Each site that has a full copy can process queries locally, so queries can be processed rapidly.

There are also two primary disadvantages:

1. Storage requirements: Each site that has a full copy must have the same storage capacity that would be required if the data were stored centrally.

2. Complexity and cost of updating: Whenever a relation is updated, it must be updated at each of the sites that holds a copy. This requires careful coordination, as we will see later.

For these reasons, data replication is favored for data where most transactions are read-only and where updates are relatively infrequent, such as catalogs, telephone directories, train schedules, and so on. CD-ROM storage technology has promise as an economical medium for replicated databases.

Horizontal Partitioning   With horizontal partitioning, some of the rows of a table (or relation) are put into a base relation at one site, and other rows

Figure 15-4

ACCT-NO	CUSTOMER-NAME	BRANCH-NAME	BALANCE
200	Jones	Lakeview	1000
426	Dorman	Lakeview	796
683	McIntyre	Lakeview	1500
252	Elmore	Lakeview	330

(a) Lakeview Branch

ACCT-NO	CUSTOMER-NAME	BRANCH-NAME	BALANCE
324	Smith	Valley	250
153	Gray	Valley	38
500	Green	Valley	168

(b) Valley Branch

are put into a base relation at another site. More generally, the rows of a relation are distributed to many sites.

Figure 15-4 shows the result of taking horizontal partitions of the Customer relation. Each row is now located at its "home" branch. If a customer, in fact, conducts most of his or her transactions at the home branch, such transactions are processed locally and response times are minimized. When a customer initiates a transaction at another branch, the transaction must be transmitted to the home branch for processing and the response transmitted back to the initiating branch (this is the normal pattern for persons using automated teller machines, or ATMs). If a customer's usage pattern changes (perhaps because of a move), the system may be able to detect this change and dynamically move the record to another location where most transactions are being initiated.

In summary, horizontal partitions for a distributed database have three major advantages:

1. Efficiency: Data are stored close to where they are used and separate from other data used by other users or applications.

2. Local optimization: Data can be stored to optimize performance for local access.

3. Security: Data not relevant to usage at a particular site are not made available.

Thus, horizontal partitions are usually used when an organizational function is distributed, but each site is concerned with only a subset of the entity instances (frequently based on geography).

Horizontal partitions also have two primary disadvantages:

1. Inconsistent access speed: When data from several partitions are required, the access time can be significantly different from local-only data access.

PART#	NAME	COST	DRAWING#	QTY-ON-HAND
P2	Widgit	100	123-7	20
P7	Gizmo	550	621-0	100
P3	Thing	48	174-3	0
P1	Whatsit	220	416-2	16
P8	Thumzer	16	321-0	50
P9	Bobbit	75	400-1	0
P6	Nailit	125	129-4	200

Figure 15-5
Part relation

PART#	DRAWING#
P2	123-7
P7	621-0
P3	174-3
P1	416-2
P8	321-0
P9	400-1
P6	129-4

(a) Engineering

PART#	NAME	COST	QTY-ON-HAND
P2	Widgit	100	20
P7	Gizmo	550	100
P3	Thing	48	0
P1	Whatsit	220	16
P8	Thumzer	16	50
P9	Bobbit	75	0
P6	Nailit	125	200

(b) Manufacturing

Figure 15-6
Vertical partitions

2. Backup vulnerability: Since data are not replicated, when data at one site become inaccessible or damaged, usage cannot switch to another site where a copy exists; data may be lost if proper backup is not performed at each site.

Vertical Partitioning   With the vertical partitioning approach, some of the columns of a relation are projected into a base relation at one of the sites, and other columns are projected into a base relation at another site (more generally, columns may be projected to several sites). The relations at each of the sites must share a common domain so that the original table can be reconstructed.

To illustrate vertical partitioning, we use an application for the manufacturing company shown in Figure 15-2. A Part relation with Part# as the primary key is shown in Figure 15-5. Some of these data are used primarily by manufacturing, while others are used mostly by engineering. The data are distributed to the respective departmental computers using vertical partitioning, as shown in Figure 15-6.

Each of the partitions shown in Figure 15-6 is obtained by taking projections of the original relation. The original relation in turn can be obtained by taking natural joins of the resulting partitions.

In summary, the advantages and disadvantages of vertical partitions are identical to those for horizontal partitions. However, horizontal partitions support an organizational design in which functions are replicated, often on a regional basis, while vertical partitions are typically applied across organizational functions with reasonably separate data requirements.

Figure 15-7
Combination of
distribution strategies
Source: Copyright C
Database
Programming &
Design, April 1989,
Vol. 2, No. 4.
Reprinted by
permission of Miller
Freeman
Publications.

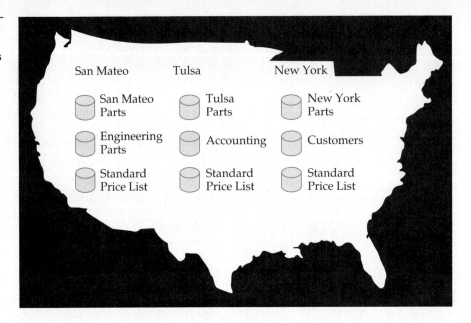

Combinations of Operations   To complicate matters further, there are almost unlimited combinations of the preceding strategies. Some data may be stored centrally, while other data are replicated at the various sites. Also, for a given relation, both horizontal and vertical partitions may be desirable for data distribution. Figure 15-7 is an example of a combination strategy; some of the data are centralized, some are replicated, and the parts data are partitioned. The overriding principle in distributed database design is that data should be stored at the sites where they will be accessed most frequently (although other considerations, such as security, data integrity, and cost, are also likely to be important). The data administrator plays a critical and central role in organizing a distributed database in order to make it distributed, not decentralized.

DISTRIBUTED DBMS

To have a distributed database, there must be a database management system that coordinates the access to data at the various nodes. We will call such a system a distributed DBMS. Although each site may have a DBMS managing the local database at that site, a distributed DBMS is also required to perform the following functions:

1. Determine the location from which to retrieve requested data

2. If necessary, translate the request at one node using a local DBMS into the proper request to another node using a different DBMS and data model

3. Provide data management functions such as security, concurrency and deadlock control, query optimization, and failure recovery

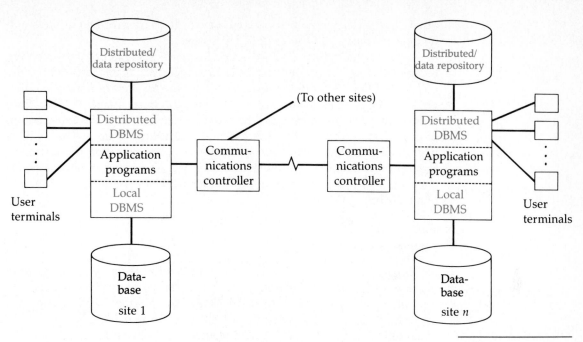

Figure 15-8
Distributed DBMS
architecture

One popular architecture of a computer system with a distributed DBMS capability is shown in Figure 15-8. Each site has a local DBMS that manages the database stored at that site. Also, each site has a copy of the distributed DBMS and the associated distributed data dictionary/directory (DD/D). The distributed DD/D contains the location of all data in the network, as well as data definitions. Requests for data by users or application programs are first processed by the distributed DBMS, which determines whether the transaction is a local or global transaction. A **local** transaction is one in which the required data are stored entirely at the local site. A **global** transaction is one that requires reference to data at one or more nonlocal sites to satisfy the request. For local transactions, the distributed DBMS passes the request to the local DBMS to be satisfied; for global transactions, the distributed DBMS routes the request to other sites as necessary. The distributed DBMSs at the participating sites exchange messages as needed to coordinate the processing of the transaction until it is completed (or aborted, if necessary). This process may be quite complex, as we will see.

The DBMS (and its data model) at one site may be different from that at another site—for example, site A may have a relational DBMS while site B has a network DBMS. In this case, the distributed DBMS must translate the request so that it can be processed by the local DBMS. The capability for handling mixed DBMSs and data models is a state-of-the-art development that is beginning to appear in some commercial DBMS products.

In our discussion of an architecture for a distributed system (Figure 15-8), we assumed that a copy of the distributed DBMS and DD/D exists at each site (thus the DD/D is itself an example of data replication). An alternative is to locate the distributed DBMS and DD/D at a central site, and other strategies are also possible. However, the centralized solution is vulnerable to failure and therefore is less desirable.

A distributed DBMS should isolate users as much as possible from the complexities of distributed database management. Stated differently, the distributed DBMS should make transparent the location of data in the network as well as other features of a distributed database. Traiger (1982) defines four objectives of a distributed DBMS that, when met, ease the construction of programs and the retrieval of data in a distributed system. These objectives, which are described below, are the following: location transparency, replication transparency, failure transparency, and concurrency transparency. We also describe query optimization, which is an important function of a distributed DBMS.

Location Transparency

Although data are geographically distributed and may move from place to place, with location transparency users (including programmers) can act as if all the data were located at a single node. To illustrate location transparency, suppose that in the distributed database shown earlier (Figure 15-7) a marketing manager in San Mateo wanted a list of customers whose total purchases exceed $100,000 (notice that data for Customers is stored in New York). From a terminal in San Mateo, the manager could enter the following request:

```
SELECT     *
FROM       CUSTOMER
WHERE      Total_Sales > 100,000
```

Notice that this SQL request does not require the user to know where the data are physically stored. The distributed DBMS at the local site (San Mateo) will consult the distributed DD/D and determine that this request must be routed to New York. When the selected data are transmitted and displayed in San Mateo, it appears to the user at that site that the data were retrieved locally (unless there is a lengthy communications delay!).

Now consider a more complex request that requires retrieval of data from more than one site. For example, in Figure 15-7 the Parts database is geographically partitioned as follows: San Mateo parts, Tulsa parts, and New York parts. Suppose that an inventory manager in Tulsa wishes to construct a list of orange-colored parts (regardless of location). This manager could use the following query to assemble this information from the three sites:

```
SELECT DISTINCT Part_number, Part_name
FROM PART
WHERE Color = 'Orange'
ORDER BY Part_Number
```

In forming this query, the user need not be aware that the parts data exist at various sites and therefore this is a global transaction.

The above examples concern "read-only" transactions. Can a local user also update data at a remote site (or sites)? With today's distributed DBMS products, a user can certainly update data stored at one remote site (such as the Customer data in this example). Thus a user in Tulsa could update Engineering Parts data stored in San Mateo. A more complex problem arises in updating data stored at multiple sites (such as the Standard Price List). We discuss this problem in the next section.

To achieve location transparency, the distributed DBMS must have access to an accurate and current data dictionary/directory that indicates the location (or locations) of all data in the network. When the directories are distributed (such as in the architecture shown in Figure 15-8), they must be synchronized so that each copy of the directory reflects the same information concerning the location of data.

Replication Transparency

Although the same data item may be replicated at several nodes in a network, with replication transparency the programmer (or other user) may treat the item as if it were a single item at a single node.

To illustrate replication transparency, see the Standard Price List (Figure 15-7). An identical copy of this list is maintained at all three nodes (full replication). First, consider the problem of reading part (or all) of this list at any node. The distributed DBMS will consult the data directory and determine that this is a local transaction (that is, it can be completed using data at the local site only). Thus the user need not be aware that the same data are stored at other sites.

Now suppose that the data are replicated at some (but not all) sites (partial replication). If a read request originates at a site that does not contain the requested data, that request will have to be routed to another site. In this case the distributed DBMS should select the remote site that will provide the fastest response. The choice of site will likely depend on current conditions in the network (such as availability of communications lines). Thus the distributed DBMS (acting in concert with other network facilities) should dynamically select an optimum route. Again, the requesting user need not be aware that this is a global (rather than local) transaction.

A more complex problem arises when one (or more) users attempts to update replicated data. For example, suppose that an accountant in New York wants to increase the price of one part in the Standard Parts List (Figure 15-7). This change must be accomplished accurately and concurrently at all three sites or the data will not be consistent. With replication transparency the New York accountant can enter the data as if this were a local transaction and be unaware that the same update is accomplished at all three sites. However, to guarantee that data integrity is maintained, the system must also provide concurrency transparency and failure transparency, which we discuss next.

Failure Transparency

Each site (or node) in a distributed system is subject to the same types of failure as in a centralized system (erroneous data, disk head crash, and so on). However, there is the additional risk of failure of a communications link (or loss of messages). For a system to be robust, it must be able to *detect* a failure, *reconfigure* the system so that computation may continue, and *recover* when a processor or link is repaired (Korth and Silberschatz, 1986).

Error detection and system reconfiguration are probably the functions of the communications controller or processor, rather than the DBMS. However, the distributed DBMS is responsible for database recovery when a failure has occurred. The distributed DBMS at each site has a component called the **transaction manager** that performs the following functions:

1. Maintains a log of transactions and before-and-after database images
2. Maintains an appropriate concurrency control scheme to ensure data integrity during parallel execution of transactions at that site

For global transactions, the transaction managers at each participating site cooperate to ensure that all update operations are synchronized. This is necessary since without such cooperation, data integrity can be lost when a failure occurs. To illustrate how this might happen, suppose (as we did earlier) that the accountant in New York wants to increase the price of a part in the Standard Parts List (Figure 15-7). This transaction is global since every copy of the record for that part (three sites) must be updated. Suppose that the parts records in New York and Tulsa are successfully updated. However, due to transmission failure the part record in San Mateo is not updated. Now the data records for this part are in disagreement, and a customer may be quoted the wrong price.

With **failure transparency,** either all the actions of a transaction are committed or none of them are committed. Once a transaction occurs, its effects survive hardware and software failures (Traiger, 1982). In the parts example, when the transaction failed at one site, the effect of that transaction was not committed at the other sites. Thus the old price remains in effect at all sites until the transaction can be successfully completed.

Commit Protocol   To ensure data integrity for update operations, the cooperating transaction managers execute a commit protocol. A **commit protocol** is a well-defined procedure (involving an exchange of messages) to ensure that a global transaction is successfully completed at each site or else that it is aborted. The most widely used protocol is called a **two-phase commit.** First, the site originating the global transaction sends a request to each of the sites that will process some portion of the transaction. Each site processes the subtransaction (if possible), but does not immediately commit (or store) the result to the local database. Instead, the result is stored in a temporary file. Each site notifies the originating site when it has completed its subtransaction. When all sites have responded, the originating site now initiates the two-phase commit protocol:

1. A message is broadcast to every participating site, asking whether that site is willing to commit its portion of the transaction at that site. Each site returns an "OK" or "not OK" message.

2. The originating site collects the messages from all sites. If all are "OK," it broadcasts a message to all sites to commit the transaction. If one or more responses are "not OK," it broadcasts a message to all sites to abort the transaction.

This description of a two-phase commit protocol is highly simplified. For a more detailed discussion of this and other protocols, see Date (1983) and Korth and Silberschatz (1986).

Concurrency Transparency

We described the problem of concurrency control for a single (centralized) database in Chapter 9. Recall that when there are multiple users accessing (and updating) a database, data integrity will be lost unless locking mechanisms are used to protect the data from the effects of concurrent updates. The problem of concurrency control is more complex in a distributed database since the multiple users are spread out among multiple sites and the data are often replicated at several sites, as well.

The objective of concurrency management is easy to define but often difficult to implement in practice. Although the distributed system runs many transactions concurrently, with **concurrency transparency,** to each transaction it appears as if it were the only activity in the system. Thus when several transactions are processed concurrently, the results must be the same as if each transaction was processed in serial order.

The transaction managers (introduced above) at each site must cooperate to provide concurrency control in a distributed database. Two basic approaches may be used: locking (introduced in Chapter 9) and timestamping.

Locking There are two locking modes: shared and exclusive. If a transaction locks a record in shared mode, it can read that record but cannot write it (other transactions can also access the record). If a transaction locks a record in exclusive mode, it can both read and write the record (but no other transaction can access the record while it is locked).

Before executing an update operation, a transaction must acquire an exclusive lock on every copy of the record to be accessed. For example, suppose that the accountant in New York wants to increase the price for part number 1234. A copy of the Standard Price List is stored at all three sites (Figure 15-7); therefore, the transaction to update the price for this part must place an exclusive lock on the record for this part at each of the three locations. The distributed DBMS at each site has a component called the **lock manager** to perform this function.

Global Deadlock Recall from Chapter 9 that a problem with using locks is the occurrence of deadlocks (or deadly embrace). This problem is mag-

Figure 15-9
Example of global
deadlock

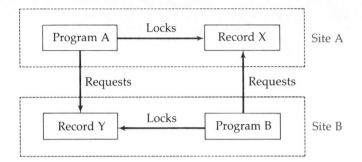

nified in a distributed environment since there may be a **global deadlock**—
a deadlock involving two or more sites (A and B). In processing a transaction, program A at site A has locked record X (we assume all locks are
exclusive). The program then requests a lock on record Y at site B (see Figure
15-9). Concurrently, program B at site B has locked record Y and has requested
a lock on record X. The system is deadlocked; no further processing can
occur without intervention.

The situation shown in Figure 15-9 is the simplest example; global deadlock may also involve three or more sites. Notice that the lock manager at
each site cannot detect the deadlock using only the information available
at that site. To detect and then resolve the deadlock, there must be a global
deadlock detection manager that assembles the information from the involved
sites. This function may be performed either in a centralized or distributed
manner [see Date (1983) for an extended discussion]. Global deadlock detection and correction incurs additional communications overhead and remains
an active area of research in distributed database management.

Timestamping   With this approach, every transaction is given a globally
unique timestamp, which generally consists of the clock time when the
transaction occurred and the site ID. Timestamping ensures that even if
two events occur simultaneously at different sites, each will have a unique
timestamp.

The purpose of timestamping is to ensure that transactions are processed
in serial order, thereby avoiding the use of locks (and the possibility of
deadlocks). Every record in the database carries the timestamp of the transaction that last updated it. If a new transaction attempts to update that
record, and if its timestamp is *earlier* than that carried in the record, the
transaction is assigned a new timestamp and it is restarted. Thus, a transaction cannot process a record until its timestamp is *later* than that carried
in the record, and therefore it cannot interfere with another transaction.

To illustrate timestamping, suppose that a database record carries the
timestamp 168. (This implies that a transaction with timestamp 168 was the
most recent transaction to successfully update that record.) A new transaction with timestamp 170 attempts to update the same record. This update
is permitted, since the transaction's timestamp is later than the record time-

stamp. (When the update is committed, the record timestamp will be reset to 170.) Now, suppose instead that a record with timestamp 165 attempts to update the record. This update will not be allowed, since the timestamp is earlier than that carried in the record. Instead, the transaction timestamp will be reset to that of the record (168), and the transaction will be restarted.

The major advantage of timestamping is that locking and deadlock detection (and the associated overhead) are avoided. The major disadvantage is that the approach is conservative in that transactions are sometimes restarted even when there is no conflict with other transactions.

Query Optimization

With distributed databases, the response to a query may require that data be assembled from several different sites (although with location transparency, the user is unaware of this need). The way in which the user formulates the query may have a drastic impact on the response time. Date (1983) provides an excellent yet simple example of this problem. Consider the following situation adapted from Date. A simplified procurement (relational) database has the three relations

SUPPLIER (SUPPLIER #, CITY)	10,000 records, stored in Detroit
PART (PART #, COLOR)	100,000 records, stored in Chicago
SHIPMENT (SUPPLIER #, PART #)	1,000,000 records, stored in Detroit

and a query is made (in SQL) to list the supplier numbers for Cleveland suppliers of red parts:

SELECT	SUPPLIER.SUPPLIER #
FROM	SUPPLIER, SHIPMENT, PART
WHERE	SUPPLIER.CITY = 'Cleveland'
AND	SUPPLIER.SUPPLIER # = SHIPMENT.SUPPLIER #
AND	SHIPMENT.PART # = PART.PART #
AND	PART.COLOR = 'Red'

Each record in each relation is 100 characters long, there are 10 red parts, a history of 100,000 shipments from Cleveland, and a negligible query computation time compared with communication time. Also, there is a communication system with a data transmission rate of 10,000 characters per second and a 1-second access delay to send a message from one node to another.

Date identifies six plausible query-processing strategies for this situation and develops the associated communication times; these strategies and times are summarized in Table 15-1. Depending on the choice of strategy, the time required to satisfy the query ranges from 1 second to 2.3 days! Although the last strategy is best, the fourth strategy is also acceptable.

Table 15-1   Query-Processing Strategies in a Distributed Database Environment (Adapted from Date 1983)

Method	Time
Move PART relation to Detroit and process whole query at Detroit computer.	16.7 minutes
Move SUPPLIER and SHIPMENT to Chicago and process whole query at Chicago computer.	28 hours
JOIN SUPPLIER and SHIPMENT at the Detroit computer, PROJECT these down to only tuples for Cleveland suppliers, and then for each of these, check at the Chicago computer to determine if associated PART is red.	2.3 days
PROJECT PART at the Chicago computer down to just the red items and for each, check at the Detroit computer to see if there is some SHIPMENT involving that PART and a Cleveland SUPPLIER.	20 seconds
JOIN SUPPLIER and SHIPMENT at the Detroit computer and PROJECT just SUPPLIER# and PART# for only Cleveland SUPPLIERs and move this qualified projection to Chicago for matching with red PARTs.	16.7 minutes
Select just red PARTs at the Chicago computer and move the result to Detroit for matching with Cleveland SUPPLIERs.	1 second

In general, this example indicates that it is often advisable to break a query in a distributed database environment into components that are isolated at different sites, then determine which site has the potential to yield the fewest number of qualified tuples/records, and then move this result to another site where additional work is performed. Obviously, more than two sites require even more complex analyses and more complicated heuristics to guide query processing. The Bernstein et al. (1981) text contains an excellent discussion of optimization of query processing in probably the most sophisticated distributed DBMS now available, SDD-1 from Computer Corporation of America. As we will see in a later section, expert systems may be employed in conjunction with a distributed DBMS for query optimization.

Evolution of Distributed DBMS

Distributed database management is a relatively new and emerging technology. Current releases of distributed DBMS products do not provide all of the features described in the previous sections. For example, some products provide location transparency for "read-only" transactions but do not yet support global updates. To illustrate the evolution of distributed DBMS products, we observe that IBM is planning a three-stage implementation of distributed database management with its mainframe DB2 product. DB2 will evolve over the next five years to a fully functional distributed DBMS (Wiorkowski, 1989). The three stages in this evolution are remote unit of work, distributed unit of work, and distributed request.

In the following discussion the term *unit of work* refers to the sequence of instructions required to process a transaction. That is, it consists of the instructions that begin with a "begin transaction" operation and end with either a "commit" or a "rollback" operation (Date, 1983).

Remote Unit of Work　The first stage allows multiple SQL statements to be originated at one location and executed as a single unit of work on a **single** remote DBMS. Both the originating and receiving computers must be running DB2. The originating computer does not consult the data directory to locate the site containing the selected tables in the remote unit of work. Instead, the originating application must "know" where the data resides and "connect" to the remote DBMS prior to each remote unit of work. Thus the remote unit of work concept does not support location transparency.

Remote unit of work allows updates at the single remote computer. All updates within a unit of work are tentative until a commit operation makes them permanent or a rollback undoes them. Thus transaction integrity is maintained for a single remote site; however, an application cannot assure transaction integrity when more than one remote location is involved (Conte, 1989). Referring to the database in Figure 15-7, an application in San Mateo could update the Standard Parts List in Tulsa and transaction integrity would be maintained. However, that application could not simultaneously update the Standard Parts List in two or more locations and still be assured of maintaining transaction integrity. Thus the remote unit of work also does not provide failure transparency.

Distributed Unit of Work　A distributed unit of work allows various statements within a unit of work to refer to **multiple** remote DBMS locations. This approach supports some location transparency since the data directory is consulted to locate the DBMS containing the selected table in each statement. However, all tables in a **single** SQL statement must be at the same location. Thus distributed unit of work would not allow the following query, designed to assemble parts information from all three sites in Figure 15-7:

```
SELECT DISTINCT    Part_Number, Part_Name
FROM               PART
WHERE              Color = 'Orange'
ORDER BY           Part_Number
```

Similarly, distributed unit of work would not allow a single SQL statement that attempts to update data at more than one location. For example, the following SQL statement is intended to update the Standard Parts List at three locations:

    UPDATE   STANDARD_PARTS_LIST
    SET   Unit_Price = 127.49
    WHERE   Part_Number = 12345

This update (if executed) would set the unit price of part number 12345 at $127.49 at Tulsa, San Mateo, and New York (Figure 15-7). The statement would not be acceptable under distributed unit of work, however, since the single SQL statement refers to data at more than one location. Distributed unit of work does support protected updates involving multiple sites, provided that each SQL statement refers to a table (or tables) at one site only. For example, suppose in Figure 15-7 we want to increase the balance of part number 12345 in Tulsa and at the same time decrease the balance of the same part in New York (perhaps to reflect an inventory adjustment). The following SQL statements could be used:

    UPDATE   TULSA_PARTS
    SET   Balance = Balance − 50
    WHERE   Part_Number = 12345

    UPDATE   NEW_YORK_PARTS
    SET   Balance = Balance + 50
    WHERE   Part_Number = 12345

Under distributed unit of work, either this update will be committed at both locations or else it will be rolled back and (perhaps) attempted again. We conclude from these examples that distributed unit of work supports some (but not all) of the transparency features described earlier in this section.

Distributed Request   This stage allows a single SQL statement to refer to tables in more than one remote DBMS, overcoming a major limitation of distributed unit of work. Distributed request supports true location transparency, since a single SQL statement can refer to tables at multiple sites. However, distributed request may or may not support replication transparency or failure transparency. It will probably be some time before a true distributed DBMS, one that supports all of the transparency features we described earlier, appears on the market.

DATABASE COMPUTERS

It is common practice to use specialized front-end communication processors to off-load computer network communication functions from a general-purpose host computer. Not only have these functions been separated into distinct machines, but these separate machines have been uniquely designed to handle the specific type of data processing in telecommunications. Simply from the viewpoint of symmetry, it seems possible that a back-end database computer can handle the specialized and high-volume activity of database processing.

It is common in large data centers today to find separate general-purpose computers performing the bulk of the database processing, especially data inquiry. Periodically, files are transferred to such separate, independent computers from others that perform transaction processing and database maintenance. Such copies of production databases frequently support information center or end-user computing tasks; some people refer to these database extracts or copies as "shadow databases." The growth in database size and processing activity creates an expensive data processing burden that one centralized computer cannot safely handle by itself.

A major problem with this use of a general-purpose computer for database processing is cost. Epstein (1983) has reported that typical mainframe computer technology costs from $100,000 to $400,000 per million of instructions per second (MIPS). However, with the use of special-purpose database computers connected to a general-purpose host, database processing costs can be reduced to as little as $10,000 or less per MIPS. Because of their special architecture to handle database searching and query processing, database computers can search as many as 30,000 records per second. This price/performance advantage means that specialized database processors will play a significant role in database processing within the next few years. In 1987, there were approximately 1000 database computers installed in organizations worldwide (including financial, manufacturing, government, telecommunications, and many other industries). Experience has shown that the use of database computers is, in general, justified when an organization exhibits a steady, high-volume stream of database transactions.

Database Computer Environment

Figure 15-10 depicts the difference between a conventional DBMS environment and a DBMS in a database computer environment. We will discuss several alternative implementations of this general picture shortly, but basically the database computer contains a customized operating system and the run-time components of the DBMS. Data dictionary, data definition, and other DBMS functions may or may not be moved to the database computer (DBC).

Operationally, with the DBC present, data manipulation commands or DBMS calls are transferred via a high-speed data channel to the DBC when encountered in an application program in the host. These commands are interpreted or queued for processing in the DBC. The database is searched for the required data and the requested data and/or DBMS messages are passed back to the host into the working storage area of the calling program. The whole process is transparent to the application program, since the DBMS call and the result appear to the user as they would in a non-DBC environment.

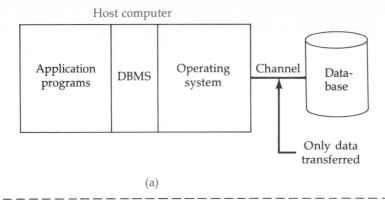

(a)

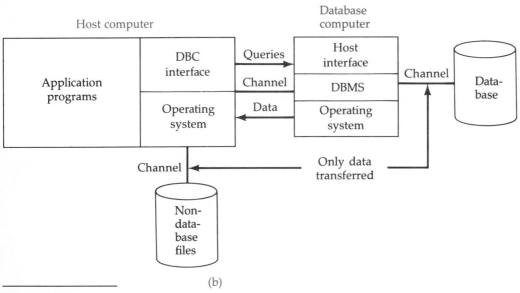

(b)

Figure 15-10
Comparison of
conventional and
DBC configurations

Objectives and Hazards of Database Computers

Database computers provide a number of important benefits which may lead to their increased usage in the future.

Portability   The DBMS, residing in its own hardware, can be connected to a wide variety of general-purpose computers. This allows an application user to use a desired DBMS (on the separate DBC) even though that DBMS was not designed to run on the host computer being used. This not only gives users greater flexibility but also opens up new markets for DBMS vendors.

Security   Data security protection can be a costly overhead expense in a database environment, since security enforcement consumes CPU cycles while other programs wait. A DBC allows extensive security controls without interfering with the productivity of nondatabase processing. Further, since a DBC can be simultaneously connected to several hosts, it can provide a centralized security service in a multiple mainframe computer environment.

Shared Database Since several mainframe host computers can all share the same DBC, an organization can achieve greater sharing of its data. Specialized department computers, laboratory computers, internal time-sharing service computers, and the like can all share the same database. The DBC handles concurrency control for all hosts, as well as providing an efficient database processing service. It is even possible for each host to be running a different DBMS, as long as there is software to translate the local host query into the language (usually SQL) of the DBC. One DBC, the IDM 500 from Britton Lee Corp., can support up to 4096 hosts, and these can be from different vendors (including IBM mainframes and PCs, DEC VAX, and UNISYS computers).

Cost Performance The most frequently mentioned advantage for a DBC is the more cost-effective manipulation of data that results. A DBC is specially designed and configured to provide rapid data searching and retrieval at an economical price. A special operating system can be utilized to concentrate on efficient secondary storage management. Some highly repetitive and stable DBMS functions can be built into the hardware or firmware of the DBC. Off-loading database processing to a DBC also makes more time available on the host(s) for doing other nondatabase processing. Various estimates of performance improvement have been reported, but a conservative figure is that a user can expect at least a 25% reduction in database processing time compared to conventional DBMS software (although as much as a 90% reduction has been reported). Higher performance gains can be achieved when single database commands require significant database processing. This is why the relational data model (set processing), not the network model (record processing), is the standard for DBCs.

These benefits of DBCs are balanced, however, by some potential hazards which have tended to limit their rate of introduction in organizations.

Vulnerability All the data in the database attached to a DBC are accessible only through the DBC. If the DBC suffers a severe failure, all database processing can cease unless appropriate backup has been performed that will allow the hosts to take over database retrieval and maintenance duties. On the other hand, most DBC technology has the capability for planned data redundancy, so that if selected disk storage devices or channels cannot operate, alternate paths to redundant data can be utilized; this means less vulnerability than with conventional database technology.

Applicability A DBC is not cost-effective in all database environments. In order for a DBC to provide significant cost/performance improvements,

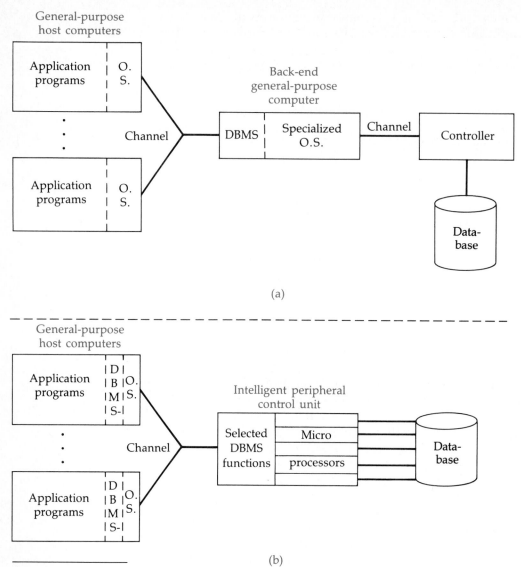

(a)

(b)

Figure 15-11
Alternative database
computer (DBC)
configurations:
(a) back-end general
    purpose processor
    DBC
(b) intelligent
    peripheral control
    unit DBC
(c) special-purpose
    processor DBC

Champine (1977) has estimated that at least 40% of the host workload should
be database accessing.

Complexity A DBC adds complexity to the database environment. Additional hardware vendors may be necessary in the data center, one for the
host computer and another for the DBC. Problems can go unresolved as
different vendors try to blame each other. The DBC, because of its possibly
different architecture, is not a widely understood technology. Special training, reliance on vendor personnel, and a small user base all contribute to
unexpected DBMS support costs.

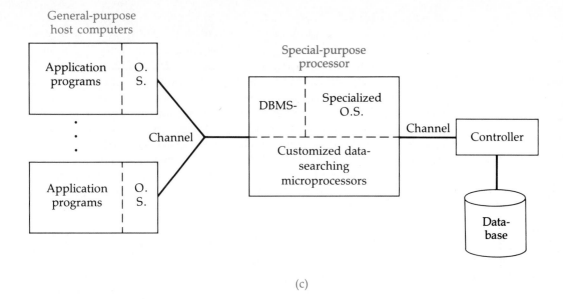

(c)

Conversion   Most organizations that have developed the need for a DBC have been using DBMS technology for many years and usually have many databases under hierarchical or network architectures. All the major DBC products work with the relational data model and the SQL processing language. Conversion can be a very time-consuming and costly effort with a large installed base of applications. Typically, therefore, a DBC is applied first to a new application, and existing database applications are converted only when major enhancements or redesigns are needed or when severe processing schedule bottlenecks have developed.

Database Computer Architectures

Various technologies are being used for database computers (see Banerjee, Baum, and Hsiao, 1978; Champine, 1977; Epstein, 1983; Hawthorn, 1981; and Maryanski, 1980). Some of the alternatives are depicted in Figure 15-11. These alternatives include the back-end general-purpose processor, the intelligent peripheral control unit, and the special-purpose processor.

Back-End General-Purpose Processor   With the back-end general-purpose processor, a master host uses a dedicated slave general-purpose computer to perform the database processing. The host may be a large mainframe and the slave may be a minicomputer, although other combinations are possible. This alternative achieves the advantage of simultaneous database and other processing but does not utilize a more cost-effective database processing technology in the dedicated slave. When several hosts share the same dedicated slave database computer, this DBC can be viewed as one node in a computer network.

Intelligent Peripheral Control Unit   With the intelligent peripheral control unit, highly repetitive and detailed functions of the DBMS are moved out of the host and placed in the logic of a mass storage unit controller device. This relieves the host from such processing steps. Such functions can include data content searching, sorting, data validation and error correction, data access scheduling, and even data recovery. Data may also be read in parallel across several surfaces of a multiple-surface secondary storage medium like a magnetic disk. This type of associative storage and parallel processing means that a whole disk cylinder can be searched for qualified data in approximately the time of one disk revolution. One version of this approach moves these database processing functions literally to the read/write heads of the secondary storage devices. Some authors refer to this approach as *logic-per-track.*

Special-Purpose Processor   The approach of the special-purpose processor is similar to the logic-per-track disk drives, except that such associative processing is done in the main memory of the special processor. Data are staged into the DBC main memory, where they can be searched rapidly in predetermined patterns that often correspond to certain relational operations such as SQL commands. Although specifically designed hardware can be most cost-effective in this case, existing array processor technology, such as the Goodyear Aerospace STARAN computer, has been used as a DBMS staging device (Maryanski, 1980). Most of the DBC products today are special-purpose processors. Frequently, a DBC is an array of microprocessors, each responsible for performing the same database operation in parallel for a segment of the database. For example, the DBC/1012 from Teradata Corp. can be configured with as many as 1024 microprocessors. A more typical 60-processor configuration offers 24 MIPS of processing power and 19 gigabytes of on-line disk storage capacity. Each database logical file is physically spread across multiple disk drives and channels so that multiple access arms and channels can work simultaneously to retrieve the desired data. A major limiting factor in DBC speed is thus the transfer rate (and associated recording density) between secondary and main memory.

Cooperative Processing

The use of database machines is one example of cooperative processing. With **cooperative processing,** the logic of a given application program is divided between two or more computers. With a database machine, for example, calculations are performed in the host machine while database searching and retrieval are performed on the database machine.

Cooperative processing is an emerging model of computing that is increasingly used in distributed systems. For example, see the distributed system for a manufacturing company described earlier (Figure 15-2). With cooperative processing, the logic for an application that schedules production might be divided between the PCs in the local area network (LAN), the database server in that LAN, and the manufacturing computer. For example, a PC would provide the graphical interface required by a user, the LAN database server might retrieve local scheduling data, and the manufacturing computer could provide the complex calculations required to develop a manufacturing schedule. By dividing the workload in this manner through cooperative processing, we are able to utilize the strengths of each processor in a processing hierarchy (Himmelstein, 1989).

INTELLIGENT DATABASE SYSTEMS

Artificial Intelligence is the use of computers to carry out tasks that, if performed by humans, would be considered intelligent. Artificial intelligence techniques are being applied to database systems on a variety of fronts and promise to have a dramatic impact in the near future. Two branches of artificial intelligence that are already being used to enhance database systems are natural language systems and expert systems. We discuss each of these developments briefly in this section.

Natural Language Systems

Natural language systems allow users to carry on a dialogue with the computer in everyday language, rather than a structured command language. For example, a user can type a query such as "WHICH SALESPEOPLE SOLD MORE THAN $100,000 IN THE LAST 6 MONTHS" rather than a structured query such as

RETRIEVE SALESID FROM SALESTABLE WHERE
TOTALSALES>100,000

The most common use of natural language today is for database query. Natural language systems facilitate database access for novice and occasional users and also often provide experienced users with a faster, more natural way to accomplish a particular task.

The components of a natural language system are shown in Figure 15-12. A program called the **parser** examines the syntax of each sentence and breaks the sentence into components (nouns, verbs, adjectives, and so on). The result of this step is a "parse tree" that resembles a sentence diagram in a high school English class. The next step is a semantic analysis of the sentence, performed by a program called the **semantic analyzer,** which refers to a dictionary that contains a list of synonyms for key English words. For example, the verb "get" may be translated as "retrieve" by the analyzer. Once the whole sentence has been analyzed, the **code generator** translates the request to an application language (such as SQL), which contains the necessary instructions to respond to the user's request.

At the present time relatively few natural language systems are mar-

Figure 15-12
Components of a
natural language
system

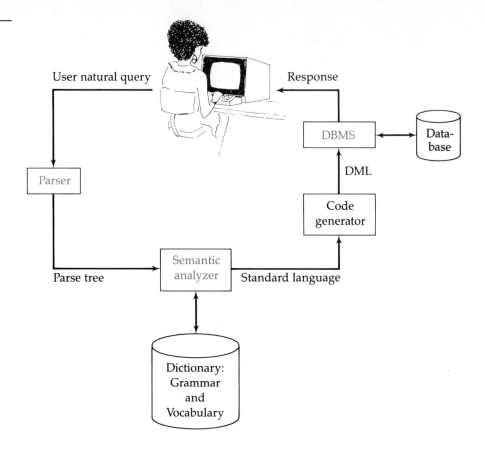

keted. A system called Intellect (Artificial Intelligence Corporation) has been available for some time as a natural language interface for mainframe database management systems such as DB2 and IDMS/R. One of the first natural languages for personal computers was Clout (Microrim), a natural language interface for R:BASE for DOS. The Intelligent Assistant (Symantec) is a natural language interface for the Q&A database system.

At the present time, natural language interfaces have two disadvantages:

1. Response time is slower than for structured languages due to the need for sentence analysis and operational query composition.

2. Current systems are limited in their ability to understand natural languages such as English. For example, at the present time, the Intelligent Assistant has a vocabulary of only a few hundred words. It is necessary for a system administrator to maintain a "lexicon" of terminology to match natural language phrases to structured language command elements, a lexicon that is time consuming and costly to construct.

A consequence of this limited and application-specific vocabulary is that user queries can be frequently rejected as nonunderstandable or, even worse, misinterpreted, which results in an erroneous response. Frequent rejection of a natural language query, especially if little help is given on why the parser has rejected it, can cause more frustration and even lower user productivity than a structured query language such as SQL. The difficulty can be overcome with more parser training, but this means a significant increase in human overhead for managing the natural language processor.

Despite these disadvantages, natural languages are easier to learn and to use than more conventional interfaces, and they save time for most users. It may also be that natural language queries promote better human retention of results since the query and response are both in a form similar to the user's conceptualization or motivation for the query. It seems likely that, in the future, most PC software (including database packages) will include a natural language interface, thus expanding the set of potential users of databases. One threat to this evolution toward natural language is icon and mouse human interfaces that may be as easy to use as natural language but not have the ambiguity.

Expert Systems

An **expert system** is a system that captures the knowledge and experience of an expert, in the form of facts and rules, in order to aid others in making decisions in a subject domain (see Sprague and McNurlin, 1986). Expert systems have been built in medicine, engineering, geology, and other fields to encode the knowledge of experts and to allow others to improve their decision making by using these systems. Expert systems are especially useful in business applications, where a combination of knowledge and judgment is required. For example, Campbell Soup Company built an expert system to help troubleshoot and maintain the large cookers used to sterilize soup.

The major components of an expert system are shown in Figure 15-13. At the center of the expert system is the knowledge base, which contains the facts, rules, and other information relative to a problem domain. Facts represent knowledge that is generally available to, and accepted by, experts in a certain field, such as accounting principles, tax regulations, labor costs, engineering standards, and so on. An example of a fact is the following: "The lead-time for Supplier A is two weeks."

Rules are the set of heuristics (or guidelines for searching for a solution) that experts typically use to reach a decision. Rules are often expressed as IF-THEN statements such as the following:

IF INVENTORY < REORDER POINT
THEN PLACE NEW ORDER

Most existing rule-based systems contain hundreds or thousands of rules such as this. The rules are captured by interviewing one or more experts for weeks or months. As shown in Figure 15-13, a special analyst called a **knowledge engineer** may be involved in interviewing or observing the

Figure 15-13
Components of an
expert system
(Source: Adapted
from Moser, 1986)

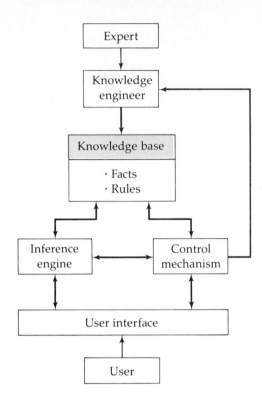

experts and encoding their knowledge (in the form of rules) into the knowl-edge base. The many rules in a knowledge base are connected together to form a network that can be traversed in solving a given problem.

Rules in the knowledge base are processed or interpreted by a program called the **inference engine**. The user engages in a dialogue through an interface, which prompts the user to answer a series of questions concern-ing the problem. The inference engine may also call outside programs to query a database for information or perform mathematical calculations. The inference engine may employ one of two principal strategies: forward chain-ing or backward chaining. With forward chaining, the program starts with the appropriate IF clauses and works forward until a desired goal-state (or solution) is found. With backward chaining, the program starts with a desired goal or result and scans the rules to find those whose consequent actions can achieve the goal. In practice, an expert system may employ both strategies.

The control mechanism in Figure 15-13 serves as a system manager. It administers all of the resources of the system and decides when to start the inference engine, when to query the user for additional information, when to stop the process, and so on.

The use of expert systems is growing rapidly, and the following are

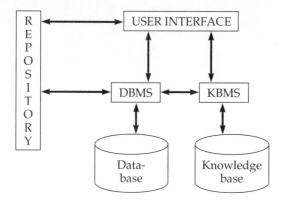

Figure 15-14
Components of an expert database system

considered prerequisites for their success [see Andriole (1985) for an elaboration]:

1. There must be at least one human expert acknowledged to perform the task well.
2. The primary source of the expert's exceptional performance must be special knowledge, judgment, and experience.
3. The expert must be able to explain the special knowledge and experience and the methods used to apply them to particular problems.
4. The task must have a well-bounded domain of application.

Expert Database Systems

Expert database systems are an active area of research today. An **expert database system** links expert systems with a DBMS and other database technology. Figure 15-14 shows a simple architecture for an expert database system. The components include a repository, user interface, DBMS and associated database, and knowledge base management system (KBMS) and its associated knowledge base.

An expert database system is especially suitable to the needs of distributed database management, which we have described throughout this chapter. As we have seen, distributed databases raise a number of complex issues, such as how to distribute data in a network and how to provide the various types of transparency that are required in a true distributed system (location, replication, failure, and concurrency transparency). As the rules for managing these complex issues are discovered, they can be incorporated into an evolving knowledge base that can then be used to support distributed database operations. For example, one set of rules can be used to detect and resolve global deadlock, while another set of rules can optimize SQL queries. Expert systems can also provide numerous functions for database users. Some of the more important of these are

1. Provide assistance to users in composing database queries—provide instructive help messages, compose queries on the user's behalf, and/or reformulate queries to minimize response times

2. Consult with users or database designers on performance evaluation and suggest ways to "tune" the database for improved performance

3. Assist users and data analysts in constructing new external schemas to meet new database requirements

4. Assist database administrators in developing improved schemes for database security and integrity

It seems likely that in the future, knowledge-based systems will have a major impact on database management, and that most DBMS products will have natural language and/or expert system "front ends."

Knowledge-Based Decision Support Systems

We introduced decision support systems in Chapter 1. In this concluding chapter we describe how an expert system can be added to a DSS to form a knowledge-based decision support system (KBDSS).

Recall that a decision support system (DSS) generally consists of a database, a model base, and a user-friendly interface. It is used by managers and others as an aid in decision making. A simple DSS may consist of a personal computer that is linked to a mainframe computer and its databases (Figure 1-11). A natural extension of the DSS is to add an expert system that helps the user use the DSS in the decision-making process. We call such a system a knowledge-based DSS, or KBDSS. A generic model of a KBDSS is shown in Figure 15-15.

Notice that the architecture of the KBDSS shown in Figure 15-15 is simply an extension of the expert database system shown in Figure 15-14. A model base and model base management system (MBMS) have been added

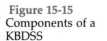

Figure 15-15
Components of a
KBDSS

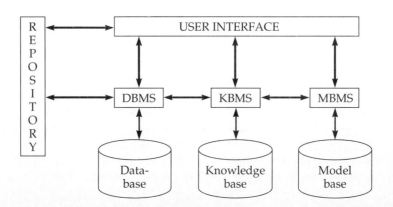

to create a KBDSS, a system that can allow users access to a database, knowledge base, and model base in solving problems. All of these components can interact with the repository, which contains definitions of databases, applications, and other organizational entities. The components shown in Figure 15-15 may be centralized or they may be distributed in a network, as described earlier in this chapter.

To our knowledge, no commercial system exists today that contains all of the components shown in Figure 15-15. However, products do exist that contain **some** of these components (for example, some products support both a database and a knolwedge base). It seems likely that architectures similar to this will evolve in distributed database management.

SUMMARY

A distributed database is a single logical database that is spread across computers in multiple locations connected by a data communications network. The network must allow the users to share the data as transparently as possible.

There are numerous advantages to distributed databases. The most important of these are the following: increased reliability and availability of data, local control by users over "their" data, modular (or incremental) growth, reduced communication costs, and faster response to requests for data. There are also several costs and disadvantages of distributed databases: Software is more costly and complex, processing overhead often increases, maintaining data integrity is often more difficult, and if data is not distributed properly, response to requests for data may be very slow. Both the advantages and disadvantages should be considered by an organization that is considering distributed database management.

There are several options for distributing data in a network: data replication, horizontal partitioning, vertical partitioning, and combinations of these approaches. With data replication, a separate copy of the database (or part of the database) is stored at each of two or more sites. Data replication can result in improved reliability and faster response; however, additional storage capacity is required, and it may be difficult to keep the data updated at each of the sites. With horizontal partitioning, some of the rows of a relation are placed at one site while other rows are placed in a relation at another site (or several sites). On the other hand, with vertical partitioning the columns of a relation are distributed among different sites. The objectives of data partitioning include improved performance and security.

To have a distributed database, there must be a distributed DBMS that coordinates the access to data at the various nodes. Requests for data by users or application programs are first processed by the distributed DBMS, which determines whether the transaction is local (can be processed at the local site) or global (requires access to data at nonlocal sites). For global transactions, the distributed DBMS consults the data directory and routes the request to nonlocal sites, as necessary.

A distributed DBMS should isolate users from the complexities of distributed database management. By location transparency, we mean that although data is geographically distributed, it appears to users as if all of the data were located at a single node. By replication transparency, we mean that although a data item may be stored at several different nodes, the user may treat the item as if it were a single item at a single node. With failure transparency, either all the actions of a transaction are completed at each site, or else none of them are committed. With concurrency transparency, although the distributed system runs many transactions concurrently, to each transaction it appears as if it were the only activity in the system. Few (if any) distributed DBMS products today provide all of these forms of transparency; however, these products are improving and it is likely that most of these features will evolve in future releases.

An important option in distributed database management is the use of database computers—computers with special architecture to manage database query and searching. Database computers can provide significant price/ performance advantages compared with general-purpose computers. However, the additional complexity and conversion effort have tended to limit their applications to date.

Intelligent database systems combine artificial intelligence with database technology. Natural language systems allow users to request data in everyday English (or another language), rather than using a specialized computer language. Although natural language systems have great potential, current systems have a limited vocabulary and often respond more slowly than conventional ones. An expert system is a system that captures the knowledge and experience of an expert, in the form of facts and rules. An expert database system links an expert system with a DBMS or other database technology and can assist users by capturing the logic and rules required to build, access, and manage databases.

Chapter Review

REVIEW QUESTIONS

1. Define each of the following terms:
   a. centralized database
   b. decentralized database
   c. distributed database
   d. partitional database
   e. replicated database
   f. database computer
   g. replication transparency
   h. failure transparency
   i. concurrency transparency
   j. location transparency
   k. expert database system

2. Explain the relative advantages of centralized, decentralized, and distributed databases.

3. What are the advantages and disadvantages of replicated databases?
4. What are the advantages and disadvantages of partitioned databases?
5. Explain how deadlock can occur in a distributed database.
6. Contrast the following terms:
   a. partitioned data; replicated data
   b. location transparency; replication transparency
   c. failure transparency; concurrency transparency
   d. locking; timestamping
   e. remote unit of work; distributed unit of work
   f. expert system; expert database system
   g. distributed DBMS; knowledge-based DSS
7. What is the purpose of the two-phase commit protocol? Briefly describe each of the two phases.
8. What are the major advantages and disadvantages of database computers?
9. Why might a natural language processor not always answer the question the user wanted to ask?
10. What can an expert system do?
11. What is the purpose of a knowledge-based DSS? What are its major components?
12. Describe how an expert database system can support users in a DBMS environment.
13. Briefly describe four types of transparency in a distributed database environment.
14. What do we mean by cooperative processing? Why is this approach becoming popular?

PROBLEMS AND EXERCISES

1. Match each of the following terms with the most appropriate definition:

   _____ star network
   _____ two-phase commit
   _____ horizontal partition
   _____ replication transparency
   _____ location transparency
   _____ inference engine
   _____ remote unit of work
   _____ distributed request
   _____ database computer
   _____ distributed database

   a) supports a single remote DBMS
   b) program that interprets rules
   c) special-purpose architecture
   d) satellite computers connected to a central computer
   e) used to preserve data integrity
   f) rows of a table are distributed to nodes
   g) user is unaware that data are distributed to several nodes
   h) one logical database allocated to several physical nodes
   i) supports true location transparency
   j) user is unaware that data are duplicated in network

2. The following statements refer to the distributed database shown in Figure 15-7. Indicate the type of transparency (location, replication, failure, concurrency) that is indicated by each statement.
   a. End users in New York and Tulsa are updating the Engineering Parts database in San Mateo at the same time. Neither user is aware that the other is accessing the data, and the system protects the data from lost updates due to interference.
   b. An end user in Tulsa deletes an item from the Standard Parts List at that site. Unknown to the user, the distributed DBMS also deletes that item from the Standard Parts List in San Mateo and New York.
   c. A user in San Mateo initiates a transaction to delete a part from San Mateo parts and simultaneously to add that part to New York parts. The transaction is completed in San Mateo but due to transmission failure is not completed in New York. The distributed DBMS automatically reverses the transaction at San Mateo and notifies the user to retry the transaction.
   d. An end user in New York requests the balance on hand for part number 33445. The user does not know where the record for this part is located. The distributed DBMS consults the directory and routes the request to San Mateo.

3. The following questions refer to the distributed database shown in Figure 15-7.
   a. Write a SQL statement that will update the Standard Parts List by increasing the Unit_Price of Part_Number 56789 by 10%.
   b. Indicate whether the statement you wrote in part (a) is acceptable under each of the following protocols:
      i)   Remote unit of work
      ii) Distributed unit of work
      iii) Distributed request

4. The following questions refer to the distributed network shown in Figure 15-7.
   a. Write one SQL statement that will increase the Balance in Part_Number 56789 in San Mateo Parts by 10%, and another SQL statement that will decrease the Balance in Part_Number 12345 in New York Parts by 10%.
   b. Indicate whether the statement you wrote in part (a) is acceptable under each of the following protocols:
      i)   Remote unit of work
      ii) Distributed unit of work
      iii) Distributed request

5. Visit an organization that has installed distributed database management. Explore the following questions:
   a. Is this truly a distributed database? If so, how are the data distributed: replication, horizontal partitioning, vertical partitioning?
   b. What commercial distributed DBMS software products are used? What are the advantages, disadvantages, and problems with this system?
   c. To what extent does this system provide each of the following: location transparency, replication transparency, concurrency transparency, failure transparency, query optimization?
   d. Does this system most closely resemble remote unit of work, distributed unit of work, or distributed request?
   e. What are the organization's plans for future evolution of this system?

REFERENCES

Andriole, S. J., ed. 1985. *Applications in Artificial Intelligence*. Princeton, N.J.: Petrocelli Books (in particular p. 48).

Banerjee, J., R. I. Baum, and D. K. Hsiao. 1978. "Concepts and Capabilities of a Database Computer." *ACM-TODS* 3 (Dec.), 347–384.

Bernstein, P. A., N. Goodman, E. Wong, C. L. Reeve, and J. B. Rothnie, Jr. 1981. "Query Processing in a System for Distributed Databases (SDD-1)." *ACM-TODS* 6 (Dec.), 602–625.

Champine, G. A. 1977. "Six Approaches to Distributed Data Bases." *Datamation* 23 (May), 69–72.

Conte, P. 1989. "In Search of Consistency." *Database Programming and Design* 2 (8) (Aug.), 42–45.

Curtice, R. M., and W. Casey. 1985. "Database: What's in Store." *Datamation* (Dec. 1), 83–88.

Date, C. J. 1983. *An Introduction to Database Systems*. Vol. 2. Reading, Mass.: Addison-Wesley.

Epstein, R. 1983. "Why Database Machines?" *Datamation* (July), 139, 140, 144.

Hawthorn, P. 1981. "The Effect of Target Applications on the Design of Database Machines." In *Proceedings ACM SIGMOD 1981*, available from Association for Computing Machinery.

Himmelstein, M. 1989. "Cooperative Database Processing." *Database Programming and Design* 2 (10) (Oct.), 66–73.

Kerschberg, L., ed. 1986. *Expert Database Systems*. Redwood City, Calif.: Benjamin/Cummings (in particular p. 7).

Korth, H. F., and A. Silberschatz. 1986. *Database System Concepts*. New York: McGraw-Hill.

Martinez-Campos, F. 1989. "Database Machines." *Database Programming and Design* 2 (11) (Nov.), 62–65.

Maryanski, F. J. 1980. "Backend Database Systems." *ACM-Computing Surveys* 12 (Mar.), 3–25.

Moser, J. G. 1986. "Integration of Artificial Intelligence and Simulation in a Comprehensive Decision Support System." *Simulation* 47 (Dec.), 223–229.

Schur, S. G. 1989. Building an Active Distributed Database. *Database Programming and Design* 2 (4) (Apr.), 46–51.

Sprague, R. H., and B. C. McNurlin. 1986. *Information Systems in Practice*. Englewood Cliffs, N.J.: Prentice-Hall.

Su, S. Y. W. 1988. *Database Computers: Principles, Architectures, & Techniques*. New York: McGraw-Hill.

Traiger, I., J. Gray, C. Galtieri, and B. Lindsay. 1982, "Transactions and Consistency in Distributed Database Systems." *ACM Transactions on Database Systems* 7 (3) (Sept.), 323–342.

Wiorkowski, G., and D. Kull. 1989. "Distributed DB2." *Database Programming and Design* 2 (4) (Apr.), 52–57.

Appendix

CODD'S 12 RULES FOR A TRULY RELATIONAL SYSTEM

So-called RDBMSs appear in many forms and with fervent marketing. How can a system that truly follows the principles of relational databases (with the associated functional capabilities) be easily distinguished from a system that does not? The founder of relational database theory, E. F. (Ted) Codd, has outlined 12 rules to test whether a product that is claimed to be "fully rational" really is. These rules are summarized at the end of this appendix.

Clearly a purist, Codd admits that "no existing DBMS product that I know of can honestly claim to be fully rational, at this time" when compared with these rules (Codd, October 14, 1985). The situation has not changed since then. Even the ANSI SQL standard comes under criticism by Codd as not complying, although he says it can be readily modified to comply.

The 12 rules and Codd's arguments are all based on a single foundation principle, which he calls Rule Zero:

> Rule Zero. For any system that is advertised as, or claimed to be, a relational database management system, that system must be able to manage databases entirely through its relational capabilities.

This is a tall order and one that, in practice, DBMSs following other data models have never had to meet in their own context in order to be considered network, hierarchical, or whatever. This and other rules are designed with users in mind; that is, they are designed to create an easy-to-use and consistent structure and user interface. Codd's orientation is that "any DBMS that advises users to revert to some nonrelational capabilities to achieve acceptable performance—for any reason other than compatibility with programs written in the past on nonrelational database systems—should be interpreted as an apology by the vendor" (Codd, October 14, 1985, ID/4).

Rather than leaving these rules and the comparison of products against them as an academic debate, Codd argues that there are practical consequences for insisting on rule compliance (Codd, October 21, 1985). Some of these are:

- Rules 1 and 4 allow a database administrator to always know exactly what kinds of data are recorded. Hence, they minimize the time needed to determine the data available while also reducing the data redundancy that would result if this information were unknowable.

- Rule 3 helps users of all types to avoid making foolish and costly mistakes (for example, miscalculating summary data when null values are coded in some uninterpretable way).

- Rule 5 supports interactive program testing, which can mean improved programmer productivity.

- Rules 8–11 contribute to lower program development and maintenance costs due to the inevitable system changes that occur in decision support and information retrieval applications systems.

People who firmly believe that RDBMSs are superior to other types of DBMSs argue that abusing the term *relational* reduces its meaning to the lowest common features of systems to which it is applied. Others—many of whom are proponents of commercial products that existed before the general popularity of relational systems—claim that user satisfaction with a tool and the ability of that tool to solve user problems should override definitions and categorization of products. Even with standards, vendors are motivated to enhance and otherwise distinguish their product from that of others. As long as this occurs, definitional debates are inevitable.

The following are Codd's 12 rules for a truly relational system.

RULE 1: Information Representation

> All information in a relational database is represented explicitly at the logical level and in exactly one way—by values in tables.

Interpretation: Even metadata (that is, table names, column names, etc.) are all stored in tables; coupled with Rule 4, data definitions are accessible via the relational manipulation sublanguage. Thus, database administrators and developers of application and system software have access to up-to-date data definitions. "All information" can be widely interpreted. A reasonable definition of "all information" is any data or metadata defined or entered into the database. This would include, for example, integrity rules and user names (since such names appear in security rules), but would reasonably exclude procedure/program documentation on references to database data. The reference to "logical level" means that physical constructs such as pointers and indexes are not represented and need not be explicitly referenced in query writing, even if they exist.

RULE 2: Guaranteed Access.

> Each and every datum (atomic value) in a relational database is guaranteed to be logically accessible by resorting to a combination of table name, primary key value, and column name.

Interpretation: This specifies a minimal accessibility in terms of content—the names of data and the one and only one primary key value. Thus, no data are to be accessible only by artificial paths, such as linked lists or physical sequential scanning. This rule is based on the fact that the relational data model deals only with data at a functional or logical level, devoid of physical constructs, and is a consequence of Rule 1.

RULE 3: Systematic Treatment of Null Values.

> Null values (distinct from the empty character string or a string of blank characters and distinct from zero or any other number) are supported for representing missing information and inapplicable information in a systematic way, independent of data type.

Interpretation: Given this rule, "nulls not allowed" can be specified to provide data integrity on primary keys or any other column for which nonexisting values are inappropriate. The systematic, uniform representation means that only one technique needs to be employed to deal with null values. Further, the treatment of null values must be persistent and be applied at any value change in order to maintain integrity.

RULE 4: Dynamic On-Line Catalog Based on Relational Model.

> The database description is represented at the logical level in the same way as ordinary data, so that authorized users can apply the same relational language to its interrogation as they apply to the regular data.

Interpretation: Thus, only one data model is used for both data and metadata and only one manipulation sublanguage needs to be learned. In addition, it would be possible to then extend the catalog of definitions to become more like a data dictionary by including any "data about data" appropriate for an application. Data definitions are stored in only one place given this rule. A subtle consequence of this rule and Rule 1 is that the distinction between data and metadata is no longer clear since both can serve as the basis for information to and inquiry by a user.

RULE 5: Comprehensive Data Sublanguage.

> A relational system may support several languages and various modes of terminal use. However, there must be at least one language whose statements can express all of the following items: (1) data definitions, (2) view definitions, (3) data manipulation (interactive and by program), (4) integrity constraints, (5) authorization, and (6) transaction boundaries (begin, commit, and rollback).

Interpretation: The key word in this rule is *comprehensive*. The six specific items indicate that Codd does expect that most of the functions of a DBMS outlined in Chapter 9 are provided within the syntax of one language. The objective of this rule is to create a comprehensive environment that does not have to be left in order to accomplish another task. For example, if in the process of manipulating data the user decides to retain a result or record some new data, he or she does not have to exit one environment and enter another in order to define the new data, and then reenter the original to populate the new tables. Although the benefits of this rule are clear in concept, the motivation for this rule may not seem obvious from an analysis of relational theory. However, it is a consequence, in part, of Rule 4 since data definitions must be accessible from the manipulation sublanguage.

RULE 6: View Updating.

> All views that are theoretically updatable are also updatable by the system.

Interpretation: A view is "theoretically updatable" if there is an update (insert, delete, or modify) procedure that, when applied at any point in time to the base tables of a view, will have the same effect as the requested modification of the view. That is, the update of the base tables necessary to effect the change in the view must be unambiguously derivable by the system. For example, increasing an extended price column value in a view (where extended price is the multiple of price from a product base table and quantity from an order base table) does not have an unambiguous meaning in terms of base table data, so the relational DBMS would not have to be able to perform this update. But, updating a product description in a view that combines product and order base data could be interpreted unambiguously as an update of product description in the product base table, and must be supported according to this rule.

RULE 7: High-Level Insert, Update, and Delete.

> The capability of handling a base relation or a derived relation (that is, view) as a single operand applies not only to the retrieval of data but also to the insertion, update, and deletion of data.

Interpretation: This basically means that all operators are set operators, not record or tuple operators. Thus, a set of table rows can be deleted in one statement or a set of rows can all be modified in a common way in one command.

RULE 8: Physical Data Independence.

> Application programs and terminal activities remain logically unimpaired whenever any changes are made in either storage rep-resentations or access methods.

Interpretation: Again, "any changes" implies a very pure view of physical data independence. One typical example of the physical data independence advocated here would be that a query or program would be written the same no matter whether an index existed or not on a column qualified in the query; programs in a network system would likely change depending on the existence of an index, hashing function, or the like. This rule also implies that constructing an optimum retrieval sequence to compose the result of a query is the responsibility of the DBMS, not the user.

RULE 9: Logical Data Independence.

> Application programs and terminal activities remain logically unimpaired when information-preserving changes of any kind that theoretically permit unimpairment are made to the base tables.

Interpretation: This and Rule 8 permit a database designer to make changes, to evolve, or to correct database definition at any point without having to completely redefine or reload the database (and take it out of service to do so). As long as information is not lost from the restructuring, no application programs or inquiry activities should have to change. To comply with this rule, it must be possible to preserve prior definitions through views, and these views must be able to be updated (Rule 6) as long as the database restructuring does not lose information. For example, the splitting of a table into two caused by recognition of new data requirements and the need to eliminate a transitive dependency (that is, a new entity is identified where only one domain of the entity was needed before the change) should not cause existing application procedures to change since the split table can be virtually reconstructed in a view.

RULE 10: Integrity Independence.

> Integrity constraints specific to a particular relational database must be definable in the relational data sublanguage and storable in the catalog, not in the application programs.

Interpretation: This rule covers the ability to define as part of the database definitions controls on the values columns may assume. Such rules may restrict values to be within a certain range, to be one of a set of permitted values, to be not null (if this column is part of a primary key, then this is called "entity integrity"), and to be a value from some other column of the database (that is, a nonnull foreign key value must match some current value from a row of the table with that as primary key, so-called referential integrity). Even user-defined constraints (such as no more than five line items per order) should be possible. These integrity rules must be able to change over time; when changed, violations must be identified and existing programs or inquiries must still be able to work.

RULE 11: Distribution Independence.

> The data manipulation sublanguage of a relational DBMS must enable application programs and inquiries to remain logically the same whether and whenever data are physically centralized or distributed.

Interpretation: A distributed database is one where data are physically dispersed across several remote computer sites and data processing requests at any one of those sites may require data stored at several of the sites. Each program treats the database as if it were all local, so distribution and redistribution do not change the logic of programs. It is important to note that this rule does not say that to be fully relational the DBMS must support a distributed database, but it does say that the data manipulation language would remain the same if and when this capability were introduced and when data are redistributed.

RULE 12: Nonsubversion.

> If a relational system has a low-level (single-record-at-a-time) language, that low level cannot be used to subvert or bypass the integrity rules and constraints expressed in the higher-level relational language (multiple-records-at-a-time).

Interpretation: This basically means that all data manipulation languages supported by the relational DBMS must rely only on the stored database definition (including integrity rules and security constraints) for control of processing. This and Rule 5 imply that it should not be possible nor is it necessary to access a relational database using any language that bypasses the data definition catalog.

Glossary of Terms

Abstraction An entity class that represents instances of entities from one or more other entity classes, for example: customer that might have specialized subclasses of Business Customer and Residential Customer. See also *Generalization and Aggregation*.

Access Method A file management subprogram provided by the operating system; used for moving data between computer main memory and peripheral devices.

Access Time The elapsed time between an instruction being given to retrieve a block of data from secondary storage, and that data being made available in primary storage.

Action A step or operation that is applied to one instance of a normalized record in a database.

Action Diagram A map or diagram that shows a sequence of actions to be performed on a database.

Active Object An object that performs operations even in the absence of an external stimulus.

Activity The lowest level unit or function on a business chart. Indicates a specific action required to carry out a business process.

Activity Ratio The proportion of records in a file that are accessed or updated during a given computer run.

Address A label or identification of a location in storage. A *physical address* is a technology-dependent and specific label; a *logical address* is some form of indirect reference to a physical address.

After Image A copy of a database record or page after it has been modified or updated.

Aggregation A collection of entities that form an entity. For example, a Work Order entity composed of Raw Material, Tool, Work Center, and Factory Worker entities.

Alternate Key A candidate key in a relation that is not selected or used as a primary key.

ANSI/SPARC The Standards Planning and Requirements Committee of the American National Standards Institute.

Application Generator A programming language that allows a database application to be built from existing programs, screen and report definitions, and from custom-built menus.

Application Program Software that supports a task or end user activity, such as a payroll program.

Area See *Realm*.

Artificial Intelligence The use of computers to carry out tasks that, if performed by humans, would be considered intelligent.

Association A relationship between two data entities in a data model. See also *Conditional Association, One-association, Many-association, and Reverse Association*.

Attribute A named characteristic or property of an entity.

Attribute Synthesis A bottom-up or detailed approach to database design.

Authorization Rules Controls incorporated into a DBMS that restrict access to data and also restrict the actions that people may take when data are accessed.

Average Search Length In hashed files, the average number of disk accesses to retrieve a specified record.

B-tree A tree data structure in which all leaves are the same distance from the root (B stands for "balanced").

B⁺-tree A B-tree in which the leaves are connected by means of a linked list.

Backward Recovery A database recovery procedure in which before images are applied to a database to back out or undo unwanted changes.

Base Table A table in the relational data model that most likely corresponds to one physical file in secondary storage.

Before Image A copy of a database record or page before it has been updated or modified.

Bidirectional Chain A list structure in which each record has both "forward" and "backward" pointers.

Binary Relationship A relationship between instances of two entity classes.

Binary Tree A tree data structure that permits at most two branches (or paths) coming out of each node or element.

Binding The process of linking an application program to its external schema or data description.

Binding Time That time at which binding occurs.

Biometric Devices Devices (used as authentication schemes) that measure personal characteristics such as fingerprints, voice prints, retina prints, or signature dynamics.

Block The smallest addressable unit of data on a disk. Also called a *physical record*.

Boolean Operator A logical operator AND, OR, or NOT.

Boyce-Codd Normal Form (BCNF) Describes a relational normal form in which every determinant is a candidate key.

Bucket A conceptual addressable storage location that may contain one or more physical records.

Buffer An area of memory that is used to receive a block of stored records from a storage device or used to transmit a block of records to that device.

Business Activities Specific actions required to carry out a business process.

Business Functions Broad groups of closely related activities and decisions that contribute to a product or service life cycle.

Business Processes Decision-related activities that occur within a business function.

Business Transaction All the data about one business event, which might cause several database transactions to add, delete, or change database records.

Candidate Key One or more attributes in a relation that uniquely identify an instance of an entity, and therefore may serve as a primary key in that relation.

Cardinality A statement of the minimum and maximum values in an association. A one-association and a many-association are statements of cardinality.

Catalog A directory of all data in a database. In a distributed database, the catalog will contain the locations of each database fragment.

Centralized A data non-distribution strategy where all data are located at a central site and accessed from remote locations.

Chain See *Linked List*.

Checkpoint A DBMS facility that allows programs to be restarted at an intermediate point, rather than at the beginning, when some abnormal condition is encountered.

Class A logical grouping of objects that share the same attributes and operations. See also *Generalization*.

Class-subclass See *Generalization*.

Client-server Model A cooperative processing environment in which the logic of an application is divided between a front-end computer (the client) and a back-end computer (the server). The client generally manages the user interface and other user-specific computations, while the server provides database management and related functions.

Clustered Database For a distributed database, each node may have unique subsets of the database as well as selected redundant copies of some files or subsets of files.

Clustering The process of dividing a logical record into distinct, noncontiguous physical parts. If the parts do not have any of the same attributes, then the process is called *partitioning*.

CODASYL Conference on Data Systems Languages. An organization of computer vendors and users that developed the specifications for the COBOL language and for the DBTG network database model.

Collision In hashed files, the situation that results when the hashing routine computes the same address for two records with unequal primary key values.

Commit Protocol An algorithm to ensure that a transaction is successfully completed, or else it is aborted.

Complex Network Data Model A network data model that supports M:N (as well as 1:N) data relationships.

Composite Key A primary key that consists of the concatenation of two or more attributes (also called a concatenated key).

Composite Usage Map A diagram that shows the data access paths and total number of references to each entity in a database. The composite usage map may show either the average or peak volume of references (or both) in the data model.

Computer-Aided Software Engineering (CASE) Automated tools used to design databases and application programs.

Concatenated Key See *Composite Key.*

Conceptual Data Model The overall logical model of an organization's database, which is independent of a particular DBMS.

Conceptual Design The process of developing a logical database design that is independent of hardware and software implementation details. The output of conceptual design is an overall information architecture (or conceptual schema) for an organization.

Concurrency Control DBMS function that prevents interference between transactions when several users are updating a database concurrently.

Concurrency Transparency A design goal for a distributed database, with the property that although a distributed system runs many transactions concurrently, to each transaction it appears that it is the only activity in the system. Thus, when several transactions are processed concurrently, the results must be the same as if each transaction was processed in serial order.

Conditional Association For a given value of data item A, there are two possibilities: either there is no associated value of data item B, or else there is one (or many, in the case of a many-association) value(s) of data item B.

Connectivity See *Cardinality.*

Control Area In VSAM, a group of control intervals.

Control Interval An indexed group of records in VSAM.

Cooperative Processing A computing environment in which the logic of application programs is divided between two or more computers or processors.

Correlated Subquery In SQL, a subquery in which processing the inner query depends on data from the outer query.

Critical Success Factors Key factors that must be done well if an organization is to succeed. For example, quality in products and services is a critical success factor for most organizations today.

Cross-reference Key A logical reference in a table (or relation) that establishes a relationship between that and another table.

Cursor In SQL, the current row of a table being manipulated by one query statement. Similar to a pointer.

Cylinder The set of tracks on a secondary storage device that can be read without moving the read/write mechanism.

Data Facts concerning entities such as people, objects, or events.

Data Aggregate A named collection of data items that are frequently referenced together (for example first name, middle initial, and last name as simply name).

Data Administrator A person who is responsible for the overall information resources of an organization.

Data Capture Applications Applications that capture and edit transaction data, populate databases, and maintain the currency of data.

Data Compression The process of reducing the length of data item values in stored records.

Data Definition Language (DDL) The language component of a DBMS that is used to describe the logical (and sometimes physical) structure of a database.

Data Dictionary/Directory (DD/D) The repository of all metadata (or data definitions) for an organization.

Data Dictionary/Directory Manager A software module that is used to manage the Data Dictionary/ Directory.

Data Distribution Applications Applications that convert data into useful information and present them to users in a readily understandable form.

Data Independence The property of being able to change the logical or physical structure of data without requiring changes to application programs that manipulate that data.

Data Integrity The control of data to insure that the data is accurate, correct for the situation, relates properly to other data, and exists when necessary.

Data Item A unit fact concerning some entity. A data item is the smallest named unit of data in an information system. Also called an *attribute* or *data element.*

Data Manipulation Language (DML) A language component of a DBMS that is used by a programmer to access and modify the contents of a database.

Data Model An abstract description (or map) of the data in an organization.

Data Semantics The meaning of data.

Data Steward A person who manages a specific data resource or entity for all business functions.

Data Structure A fundamental computer storage technique.

Data Structure Diagram   A graphic data model that uses arrows to portray the associations between entities.

Data Transfer Applications   Applications that move data from one database to another. These applications also extract, summarize, and aggregate data.

Database   A shared collection of logically related data, designed to meet the information needs of multiple users.

Database Administrator   A person who is responsible for controlling the design and use of computer databases.

Database Computer   A special-purpose computer that contains a customized operating system and the run-time components of a DBMS, used to manage the databases in a cooperative processing environment.

Database Management System (DBMS)   A software application system that is used to create, maintain, and provide controlled access to user databases.

Database Server   In a local area network, a dedicated microcomputer that manages a local database.

Database Transaction   A unit of work to a database application program that changes the contents of one database record or page. See also *Business Transaction*.

Deadlock   Impasse that may result when two users lock certain resources, then request resources locked by the other user. Also called *deadly embrace*.

Decentralized Database   A database that is stored on computers at multiple locations; however, the computers are not interconnected by a network, so that the data cannot be shared by users at the various sites.

Decision Support System   A system that supports managerial decision making by providing information and modeling tools.

Degree   The number of entities that participate in a relationship.

Delimiter   Special symbol used to indicate the end of a field or other piece of data.

Determinant   Any attribute on which some other attribute is fully functionally dependent.

Differential File   A file that is used to store only the changes that have been made to another file or database.

Direct Access   The ability to retrieve or store a record by reference to its location on a storage volume, and without having to reference previous records on the volume.

Direct Access Storage Device (DASD)   A secondary storage device (such as magnetic disk) that supports direct access.

Directory   See *Index*.

Distributed Database   A single logical database that is spread across computers in multiple locations that are connected by a data communications network.

Distributed Free Space   In VSAM, reserved space for the insertion of new records at the end of each control interval.

Division/Remainder Method   A commonly used hashing algorithm in which a primary key value is divided by a prime number, and the remainder is used as the relative bucket address.

Domain   The valid set of values for an attribute in a relation.

Domain-Key Normal Form (DK/NF)   A conceptual normal form in which every constraint on the relation is a logical consequence of key constraints and domain constraints.

Embedded Programming   The use of relational data manipulation language commands in a third-generation language program.

Encryption   The process of coding (or scrambling) data so that they cannot be read by humans.

End User Computing   An approach to data processing where users who are not computer experts provide their own computing needs through the use of high-level software and languages such as electronic spreadsheets.

Enterprise Data Model   A high-level conceptual data model for an organization.

Entity   A person, place, object, or concept about which an organization chooses to store data.

Entity Class   A collection of entities that possess similar properties or characteristics.

Entity-Relationship Data Model   A type of semantic, graphical, data model that uses special symbols to represent data entities, data elements, and associations between entities.

Equijoin   A join in which the joining condition is based on equality between values in the common columns. Common columns appear (redundantly) in the result table.

Exclusive Lock   A type of lock that denies access to other users, when granted to a particular user.

Exclusivity   A uniqueness constraint that specifies that one of several kinds of data or relationships may be present, but not all.

Existence Dependency   A semantic control that

indicates that an instance of one entity cannot exist unless an instance of a related entity also exists.

Expert Database   A database that contains or is interfaced with a knowledge base, or shared logic for assisting users in accessing and using the database.

Expert System   A system that captures the knowledge and experience of a human expert, in the form of facts and rules, so as to aid others in decision making.

Export   The process of transferring database contents to a file outside a database.

Extensibility   Feature of a data dictionary/directory that allows users to define new entities, attributes, and relationships.

External Data Model   A description of a user's or application program's view of data in a database. Also called *user view.*

Failure Transparency   A design goal for a distributed database, which guarantees that either all the actions of each transaction are committed, or else none of them are committed.

Fifth Normal Form (5NF)   A property of a relation that has no join dependency.

File   A collection of logically related records. These records are often (but not always) of the same type.

File Organization   A technique for physically arranging the records of a file in secondary storage.

First Normal Form (1NF)   A relation in which the intersection of each row and column contains only atomic (or single) values.

Flat File   A two-dimensional array of attributes or data items.

Foreign Key   A non-key attribute in one relation that appears as the primary key (or part of the primary key) in another relation.

Form   A customized screen layout.

Forward Recovery   A database recovery procedure in which after images are applied to an earlier copy of a database to move the database forward to a later state.

Fourth-Generation Language   A high-level non-procedural language (i.e., programs what is to be done, not how to do it) that allows users to write programs much faster than with COBOL or other third-generation languages.

Fourth Normal Form (4NF)   Describes a relation that is in Boyce-Codd Normal Form and contains no multivalued dependencies.

Fragment   In a distributed database, a partition of a relation (or of a database) that is assigned to a physical location.

Full Functional Dependence   Indicates that an attribute in a relation is functionally dependent on the whole of a concatenated key, but not on any subset of that key.

Functional Dependence   A relationship between two attributes in a relation. Attribute B is functionally dependent on attribute A if attribute A identifies B (that is, each value of A has exactly one value of B at any given time).

Generalization   The abstraction of entities as being special cases of other types of entities.

Gerund   A relationship that can be considered (or treated the same as) an entity.

Global Deadlock   In a distributed database, a deadlock (or deadly embrace) involving two or more sites.

Global Transaction   In a distributed database, a transaction that requires reference to data at one or more nonlocal sites to satisfy the request.

Granularity   Size or scope of an object to be protected by a system.

Hashed File Organization   A file organization that permits direct access to records through the use of a hashing routine.

Hashing Routine   An algorithm that converts a primary key value into a relative disk address.

Hierarchical Model   A data model in which data are represented as a set of nested 1:M relationships. Each record in a hierarchical model may have several offspring, but only one parent record.

Homonym   A single word that is used with different meanings in different contexts. Also, two words that are pronounced the same but have different meanings.

Horizontal Partitioning   Distributing the rows of a table into several separate tables.

Host Language   A programming language, like COBOL and PL/I, with which Data Manipulation Language commands can be combined to write a program to perform database processing.

Hybrid   In a distributed database, a data distribution strategy where the database is partitioned into critical and noncritical fragments. Noncritical fragments are stored at only one site, while critical fragments are stored at multiple sites.

ID Dependency   A semantic control or constraint that states that the primary key of one entity must include an attribute that is also the primary key of a related entity.

Identifier   An attribute in an entity that distinguishes it from other entities. Also called a *primary key*.

Implementation Design   The process of mapping a conceptual data model into implementable structures, such as network, hierarchical, and relational data models.

Import   The process of transferring data into a database from files outside the database.

Index   A table or other data structure that is used to determine the location of records in a file or database based upon a primary or secondary key.

Indexed Sequential Organization   A file organization that permits both sequential and direct access to records in a file. This organization is supported by the indexed sequential access method (ISAM).

Inference Engine   In an expert system, a program that processes and interprets the facts and rules in the knowledge base.

Information   Data that have been organized or prepared in a form that is suitable for decision making.

Information Repository Dictionary System (IRDS)   A computer software tool that is used to manage and control access to the repository.

Information Resource Management   The concept that information is an important organizational resource and must be planned, managed, and protected like other resources such as people, materials, and financial resources.

Inheritance   A property of objects by which each subclass inherits the attributes and operations of the superclass to which it belongs. For example, a Student object inherits attributes and operations of a Person object.

Instance   An occurrence of an entity or data type. For example, a personnel record is a record type; the record for Sally Jones is an instance of that record type also one member (or materialization) of an object class.

Integrity   See *Data Integrity.*

Internal Data Model   A data model that describes an entire database using a technologically-dependent style.

Internal Schema   A description of the physical structure of data, or the way data are represented on secondary storage media. Also called *internal data model.*

Interrecord Data Structures   Data structures (such as lists) that are used to connect different but related records in the same file or in separate files.

Intersection Record   A record that lies at the con-

junction of two or more record types and contains data common to those record types.

Intrarecord Data Structures   Data structures used to connect fields within a single record.

Inverted List   A table or list that is organized by secondary key values.

ISA Relationship   See *Generalization.*

Join   A relational algebra command that causes two tables with a common domain to be combined into a single table.

Join Dependency   A relation that cannot be decomposed by projection into smaller relations, and then rejoined into the original relation without spurious results.

Key   An attribute or data item that uniquely identifies a record instance or tuple in a relation. See also *Secondary Key.*

Knowledge-Based Decision Support System   An extension of a decision support system to include an expert system that assists the user in using the DSS and interpreting its results.

Knowledge Engineer   An analyst who observes and interviews experts and encodes knowledge (in the form of rules) in a knowledge base.

Leaf   In a tree data structure, a leaf is a node that has no children.

Linked List   A data structure in which the logical order of records is maintained by pointers rather than by physical sequence of the records.

Load Factor   The percentage of space allocated to a file that is actually used.

Local Transaction   In a distributed database, a transaction that requires reference only to data that are stored at the site where the transaction is originated.

Location Transparency   A design goal for a distributed database, which says that a user (or user program) requesting data need not know at which site those data are located.

Locking Mechanism (or Lock)   A procedure used by the DBMS to control concurrent access to data. When one user is updating a database, a lock denies access to other users to prevent erroneous updates.

Logical Access Map (LAM)   A chart or graph showing the sequence of accesses to the records in a data model for a particular application.

Logical Data Model   A mapping of the conceptual model into a DBMS-processible data model. Most contemporary DBMSs support either the hierarchical, network, or relational logical models.

Logical Record A collection of data items that describes an object or entity.

Macro A sequence of keystrokes assigned to a single keyboard key.

Maintenance Modifying or rewriting application programs in response to new requirements, new data formats, and so on.

Managerial Databases Databases that are used primarily by middle-level managers for planning and control, for example, summaries of sales by product and type of customer.

Many-association A many-association from data item A to data item B means that at any point in time, a given value of A has one or many values of B associated with it.

Mapping (1) An association or correspondence between data entities. (2) Rules that govern the transformation from one form or structure to another form or structure.

Metadata Data descriptors; information about an organization's data.

Multilist Organization A data structure in which there are multiple paths or linked lists connecting the records.

Multiprogramming Process by which several programs are executed concurrently in primary storage.

Multivalued Dependency A dependence that exists when there are three attributes (A, B, and C) in a relation, and for each value of A there is a well-defined set of values for B and a well-defined set of values for C. However, the set of values for B and C are independent of each other.

Natural Join The same as an equijoin except that one of the duplicated columns is eliminated in the result table.

Natural Language System An artificial intelligence-based language subsystem that allows the user to carry on a dialogue with the computer in an unstructured version of English or other language.

Network Data Model A data model consisting of records, data items, and associations between records. Each record type in the network may have 1:M associations with any other record type in that network.

Nonkey Attribute An attribute in a relation that is not part of the primary key of that relation.

Normalization The process of decomposing complex data structures into simple relations according to a set of dependency rules.

Null Pointer A pointer that is empty or contains a special character to indicate the end of a list or data structure.

Null Suppression A data compression technique that suppresses blanks and zeros in data items.

Object An inseparable package or capsule of data definitions and values and the procedures (often called methods) that act upon the data.

Object-Oriented Data Model A data model based on objects, not entities.

One-association A one-association from data item A to data item B means that at any point in time, a given value of A has one and only one value of B associated with it.

Operating System The overall supervisory and control program of a computer. The operating system allocates memory, controls the execution of tasks, and provides a variety of utility and support functions.

Operational Databases Databases that contain the business transaction history of daily business activities such as customer orders, shipments, purchases, and payments.

Outer Join A join in which rows that do not have matching values in common columns are nevertheless included in the result table.

Owner Record Type In a CODASYL database, a record type that is declared as the "owner" in a set relationship. The set may contain one or more member record types.

Partitioned Database In a distributed database, each node is allocated disjoint subsets of the organization's database.

Partitioned In a distributed database, a data distribution strategy where the database is divided into disjoint (nonoverlapping) partitions called fragments. Each fragment is assigned to a particular site.

Passive Object An object that performs a given operation only when it is asked to do so (by means of a message sent to that object).

Pattern Substitution A data compression technique in which recurring sequences of characters are replaced by shorter codes.

Physical Child In an IMS database, a child or subordinate segment.

Physical Database A representation of the form in which a database is stored on secondary storage. Generally, the physical database is represented as a collection of one or more types of stored records. See also *Internal Schema*.

Physical Design The final stage in the database design process. Physical design is concerned with selecting file organizations and access methods, deciding on the use of indexes, and related factors.

Physical Record See *Block.*

Planning Database Data collected during the database planning process that is stored in a CASE tool repository. The planning database typically includes metadata describing data, functions, users, critical success factors, projects, and information systems.

Planning Matrix Matrix that shows the relationships among planning entities. Typical planning matrices include relationships between organizations and processes, between processes and entities, etc.

Pointer A field in a record that contains data that can be used to locate another related record. A *physical pointer* contains the actual address. A *relative pointer* contains the relative position. A *logical pointer* contains the primary key of the related record.

Primary Key See *Key.*

Primary Key Attribute An attribute in a relation that is a component of the primary key for that relation.

Primary Storage Computer random access memory. Also called main memory.

QUEL A type of relational calculus language used in the INGRES relational DBMS.

Query by Example A special style of relational DBMS in which queries are written by placing example data and special codes in table templates or skeletons displayed on a CRT.

Query Languages An end user-oriented language for specifying data retrievals.

Queue A data structure in which all record insertions occur at one end and all deletions occur at the other end of the structure.

Random Access See *Direct Access.*

Realm In a CODASYL database, a named, contiguous area of secondary storage. Also called *area.*

Record A named collection of related data items that concern one entity existence.

Record Clustering The process of physically grouping records on a storage device according to dominant access paths, thereby minimizing access times.

Record Partitioning The process of splitting stored records into separate segments and then allocating those segments to separate physical devices or separate extents on the same device.

Recovery The process of restoring a database and database operations to a normal state after an error has occurred.

Recovery Manager A module of a DBMS that restores a database to a correct condition when a failure has occurred, and resumes processing user requests.

Recursive Association An association between entities in the same entity class.

Recursive Relationship See *Unary Relationship.*

Referential Integrity An integrity constraint that specifies that the value (or existence) of an attribute in one relation depends on the value (or existence) of the same attribute in another relation.

Relation A named collection of attributes. Data in a relation are represented as a flat file or two-dimensional array of data items.

Relational Algebra A data manipulation language that provides a set of operators for manipulating one or two relations. The most commonly used operators are SELECT, PROJECT, and JOIN. See also *Relational Calculus.*

Relational Calculus A data manipulation language that provides the user with a standard command structure for manipulating one, two, or more relations. JOINs are implicit by stating common columns on which to match or compare rows between columns.

Relational Model A logical data model in which all data are represented as a collection of normalized relations or tables.

Relationship See *Association.*

Relative Disk Address On a disk storage device, the address of a data block relative to the start of the file.

Replicated Database In a distributed database, each node retains a complete copy of the organization's database.

Replicated In a distributed database, a data distribution strategy where a full copy of the database is assigned to more than one site in the network.

Replication Transparency A design goal for a distributed database, which says that although a given data item may be replicated at several nodes in a network, a programmer or user may treat that data item as if it were a single item at a single node.

Report Writer A special program or module of a DBMS that supports the specification of customized printed output including subtotals, special page layouts, readable headings, and so forth.

Repository A centralized knowledge base that contains all data definitions, screen and report formats, and definitions of other organizational and system components (also called an *information repository).*

Requirements Definition   The process of identifying and describing the data that are required by users in an organization. Requirements definition is the first stage in the database design process.

Restore/rerun   A database recovery procedure that involves reprocessing a days transactions against a backup copy of a platabase. This process is generally used as a last resort when simpler methods have failed.

Retention Restriction   A restriction (or constraint) that specifies the rules under which an association between entities must be maintained.

Reverse Association   The association between two data elements in the direction opposite to that being referenced.

Ring   A closed-loop list structure in which the last element points to the first element in the structure.

Rollback   See *Backward Recovery*.

Rollforward   See *Forward Recovery*.

Root   In a tree data structure, the node at the top of the tree. The root has no parent.

Run-time Version   The portion of the DBMS needed to run an existing database application.

Schema   A representation of the logical structure of a database. A schema may be expressed in graphic form or in a data definition language.

Screen painter   A special program or module of a DBMS that supports the specifications of customized input forms and screen layouts including use of color, error controls and edit checks, automatic data lookup, and so forth.

Search Strategy   A technique used to define an access path and locate a specific stored record.

Second Normal Form   A relation that is in first normal form and in which each nonkey attribute is fully functionally dependent on the primary key.

Secondary Key   A data item that is used to identify the records in a set that share the same property (attribute value). For each value, potentially more than one record may have that value.

Secondary Storage   A storage device that is less expensive than primary storage. The primary types of secondary storage are magnetic disk and magnetic tape.

Security   Procedures for protecting a database against accidental or intentional misuse or destruction.

Segment   A named record or record component in an IMS database.

Select   A relational algebra command that extracts selected rows of a relation according to a search criterion.

Semantic Data Model   A data model that focuses on documenting the meaning of data. It is appropriate for defining a database at the external and conceptual levels.

Semantic Rules   In a data model, rules concerning the usage and meaning of data.

Sequential File Organization   A file organization in which the logical order of records is the same as the physical order. A given record in the file can ordinarily be accessed only by first accessing all records that physically precede it.

Set   In a CODASYL database, a named relationship between an owner record type and one or more member record types.

Shared Lock   A type of lock that allows various users to read (but not update) a database while it is being updated by the user placing the lock.

Siblings   In a tree data structure, the nodes with a common parent.

Simple Network Data Model   A network data model that supports 1:N (but not M:N) data relationships.

Smart Card   A thin plastic card the size of a credit card with an embedded microprocessor. An individual's unique biometric data (such as fingerprints) are stored permanently on the card.

SQL   Structured Query Language. A standard data definition and manipulation language for relational databases.

Stack   Data structure in which record insertions and deletions are both made at the same end of the list.

Stored Record   A physical record, or collection of related data items in physical storage. A stored record may consist of one or more logical records.

Strategic Databases   Databases used by senior managers to develop corporate strategy and seek competitive advantages. They often contain information on competitors and economic factors as well as corporate information.

Subject Database   A database that models important subject areas in an organization, independent of applications. Typical subject databases are for products, customers, vendors, and personnel.

Subquery   In SQL, a query which contains a nested query.

Subschema Data Model   A type of external data model that describes only the data required for a given data processing task. A subschema data model is generally defined using a particular language such as COBOL. See also *External Data Model*.

Synonyms   Two different names that refer to the same data item or attribute. In a hashed file organization, two keys that are translated into the same block address.

Teleprocessing Monitor   A software module that provides a shared interface between application programs and remote communications devices.

Ternary Relationship   A relationship among instances of three entity classes.

Third-generation Language   A procedural programming language (like COBOL, FORTRAN or PL/I) in which programs are written as a sequence of instruction that read and process one record at the same time.

Third Normal Form (3NF)   A relation that is in second normal form, and in which no nonkey attribute is functionally dependent on another nonkey attribute. Thus, there are no transitive dependencies.

Three-Schema Architecture   A database architecture that provides three levels or views of data: the conceptual level, the external level, and the internal level.

Timestamping   In distributed databases, a concurrency control mechanism that assigns a globally unique timestamp to each transaction. Timestamping is an alternative to the use of locks in distributed databases.

Transaction   A sequence of steps that constitute some well-defined business activity. A transaction may specify a query or it may result in the creation, deletion, or modification of database records. See also *Business Transaction* and *Database Transaction*.

Transaction Boundary   The logical beginning and end of a transaction.

Transaction Log   A record of the essential data for each transaction that is processed against a database.

Transaction Manager   In a distributed database, a software module that maintains a log of all transactions and maintains an appropriate concurrency control schema.

Transaction Map   A diagram that shows the sequence of logical database accesses that are required for a given transaction.

Transfer Rate   A measure of the speed with which data are moved between peripheral devices and primary storage.

Transitive Dependency   Condition where a nonkey attribute in a relation is fully dependent on another nonkey attribute.

Tree Structure   See *Hierarchical Model*.

Tuple   The collection of values that compose one row of a relation.

Two-Phase Commit Protocol   An algorithm for coordinating updates in a distributed database.

Unary Relationship   A relationship between instances of the same entity class. Also called a recursive relationship.

Unnormalized Relation   A relation that contains one or more repeating groups.

User View   See *External Data Model*.

View   A virtual table in the relational data model in which data from real (base) tables are combined so that programmers can work with just one (virtual) table instead of the several or more complete base tables.

View Integration   In conceptual database design, the process of merging the relations for each user view into a single set of relations in third normal form.

Virtual Storage   A memory management technique that permits primary storage to appear much larger to programs than it actually is, since blocks of data and/or programs are moved rapidly between primary and secondary storage.

Volume   A demountable storage unit such as a magnetic disk cartridge or magnetic tape.

VSAM   Virtual sequential access method. An updated version of the indexed sequential access method, which is device-independent.

Well-structured Relation   A relation that contains a minimum amount of redundancy and allows users to insert, delete, and modify rows of the table without errors or inconsistencies (called anomalies).

Window   A rectangular area of a CRT screen that overlays other parts of the screen.

GLOSSARY OF ACRONYMS

AD Action Diagram.

ADF Application Development Facility.

AI Artificial Intelligence.

ANSI/SPARC American National Standards Institute/Standards Planning and Requirements Committee.

ASCII American Standards Code for Information Interchange.

BCNF Boyce-Codd Normal Form.

BSP Business Systems Planning.

CAD/CAM Computer-Aided Design/Computer-Aided Manufacturing.

CASE Computer-Assisted Software Engineering.

CD-ROM Compact Disk-Read-Only Memory.

CDC Control Data Corporation.

COBOL COmmon Business Oriented Language.

CODASYL Committee On DAta SYstem Languages.

CPU Central Processing Unit.

CRT Cathode Ray Tube.

DA Data Administrator.

DASD Direct-Access Storage Device.

DB2 Data Base2 (an IBM relational DBMS).

DBA Database Administrator.

DBACP Database Administrator Control Program.

DBC Database Computer.

DBCS Database Control System.

DBD Database Description.

DBMS Database Management System.

DBSS Database Storage System.

DBTG Database Task Group (part of CODASYL).

DCB Data Control Block.

DD/D Data Dictionary/Directory.

DD/DS Data Dictionary/Directory System.

DDL Data Definition Language. *Also* Data Description Language.

DEC Digital Equipment Corporation.

DK/NF Domain Key Normal Form.

DL/I Data Language/I (part of IMS).

DMCL Device Media Control Language.

DML Data Manipulation Language.

DOS Disk Operating System.

DSDL Data Storage Description Language.

DSS Decision Support System.

E-R Entity-Relationship.

ES Expert System.

FIFO First-In-First-Out.

FORTRAN FORmula TRANslator.

GBF Graph-By-Forms.

HDA Head-Disk Assembly.

HDAM Hierarchical Data Access Method.

HIDAM Hierarchical Indexed Direct Access Method.

HISAM Hierarchical Indexed Sequential Access Method.

HSAM Hierarchical Sequential Access Method.

I/O Input/Output.

IBM International Business Machines Corporation.

IDD Integrated Data Dictionary.

IDM Intelligent Database Machine.

IDMS Integrated Database Management System.

IDMS/R Integrated Database Management System/Relational.

IDS Integrated Data System.

IMS Information Management System.

IS Information System.

ISAM Indexed Sequential Access Method.

ISN Internal Sequence Number.

ISO International Standards Organization.

KBDSS Knowledge-Based Decision Support System.

LAM Logical Access Map.

LAN Local Area Network.

LDB Logical Database.

LDBR Logical Database Record.

LIFO Last-In-First-Out.

MB Million Bytes.

MIPS Millions of Instructions Per Second.

MIS Management Information System.

N/A Not Available.

OLE OnLine English.

OLQ OnLine Query.

OSAM Overflow Sequential Access Method.

PBE Prompt By Example.

PC-DBMS Personal Computer—Database Management System.

PC-RDBMS Personal Computer—Relational Database Management System.

PC Personal Computer.

PCB Program Communication Block.

PDBR Physical Database Record.

PL/I Program Language/I.

PSB Program Specification Block.

QBE Query-By-Example.

QBF Query-By-Forms.

QLP Query Language Processor.

QMF Query Management Facility.

RDBMS Relational Database Management System.

SAM Sequential Access Method.

SDM Semantic Data Model.

SQL Structured Query Language.

SQL/DS Structured Query Language/Data System.

TODS Transactions on Database Systems.

TP TeleProcessing.

UDF User Defined Function.

VIFRED VIsual FoRms EDitor.

VSAM Virtual Sequential Access Method.

1NF First Normal Form.

2NF Second Normal Form.

3GL Third-Generation Language.

3NF Third Normal Form.

4GL Fourth-Generation Language.

4NF Fourth Normal Form.

5NF Fifth Normal Form.

INDEX

(Italicized page number indicates that term is defined on that page.)